The Masculinity Studies Reader

KEYWORKS IN CULTURAL STUDIES

As cultural studies powers ahead to new intellectual horizons, it becomes increasingly important to chart the discipline's controversial history. This is the object of an exciting new series, KeyWorks in Cultural Studies. By showcasing the best that has been thought and written on the leading themes and topics constituting the discipline, KeyWorks in Cultural Studies provides an invaluable genealogy for students striving to better understand the contested space in which cultural studies takes place and is practiced.

The Masculinity Studies Reader

Edited by

Rachel Adams and David Savran

 BLACKWELL
Publishers

First published 2002

2 4 6 8 10 9 7 5 3 1

Blackwell Publishers Inc.
350 Main Street
Malden, Massachusetts 02148
USA

Blackwell Publishers Ltd
108 Cowley Road
Oxford OX4 1JF
UK

Library of Congress Cataloging-in-Publication Data

The masculinity studies reader / edited by Rachel Adams and David Savran.
p. cm. — (Keyworks in cultural studies; 5)
Includes bibliographical references and index.
ISBN 0-631-22659-1 (alk.paper) — ISBN 0-631-22660-5 (pbk.: alk.paper)
1. Men's studies. 2. Masculinity. 3. Heterosexuality. 4. Homosexuality.
I. Adams, Rachel. II. Savran, David, 1950- III. Series.

HQ1088.M377 2001
305.31—dc21

2001043229

British Library Cataloguing in Publication Data

A CIP catalogue record for this book is available from the British Library.

Typeset in 10 on 12pt Galliard
by Kolam Information Services Pvt Ltd, Pondicherry, India
Printed in Great Britain by MPG Books Ltd, Bodmin, Cornwall

This book is printed on acid-free paper.

Contents

Acknowledgments

The editors and publishers gratefully acknowledge the following for permission to reproduce copyright material, here listed by alphabetical order of author:

Boyarin, Daniel, "What Does a Jew Want? or, The Political Meaning of the Phallus," from *The Psychoanalysis of Race*, ed. Christopher Lane (Columbia University Press, New York, 1998).

Bray, Alan, "Homosexuality and the Signs of Male Friendship in Elizabethan England," from *Queering the Renaissance*, ed. Jonathan Goldberg (Duke University Press, Durham, copyright 1994, Duke University Press. All rights reserved. Reprinted with permission).

Carrigan, Tim, Connell, Bob, and Lee, John, "Toward a New Sociology of Masculinity," from *The Making of Masculinities: The New Men's Studies*, ed. Harry Brod (Allen & Unwin, Boston, 1987, copyright 1987 from *The Making of Masculinities: The New Men's Studies*. Reproduced by permission of Routledge, Inc., part of the Taylor & Francis Group).

Cheung, King-Kok, "The Woman Warrior versus The Chinaman Pacific: Must a Chinese American Critic Choose between Feminism and Heroism?," from *Conflicts in Feminism*, ed. Marianne Hirsch and Evelyn Fox Keller (Routledge, New York and London, 1990, copyright 1990 from *Conflicts in Feminism*. Reproduced by permission of Routledge, Inc., part of The Taylor & Francis Group).

Connell, R. W., "The History of Masculinity," from *Masculinities*. Copyright © 1995 Robert Connell (University of California Press, Berkeley, 1995).

Dyer, Richard, "The White Man's Muscles," from *White* (Routledge, London and New York, 1997, reprinted by permission of Taylor & Francis Ltd.).

Fanon, Frantz, "The Fact of Blackness," from *Black Skin, White Masks*, trans. Charles Lam Markmann (Grove Press, New York, 1967, copyright © 1967 by Grove Press, Inc., used by permission of Grove/Atlantic Inc.).

Fausto-Sterling, Anne, "That Sexe Which Prevaileth," from *Sexing the Body: Gender Politics and the Construction of Sexuality*. Copyright © 2000 by Basic Books, a member of the Perseus Books Group. Reprinted by permission of Basic Books, a member of Perseus Books, L.L.C.

Freud, Sigmund, "Some Psychological Consequences of the Anatomical Distinction between the Sexes," from *Sexuality and the Psychology of Love*, trans. James Strachey (Collier Books, New York, 1925).

Geertz, Clifford, "Deep Play: Notes on the Balinese Cockfight," reprinted by permission of *Daedalus*, Journal of the American Academy of Arts and Sciences, originally from the issue entitled "Myth, Symbol, and Culture" (Winter 1972), vol. 101/1.

Halberstam, Judith, "An Introduction to Female Masculinity," from *Female Masculinity* (Duke University Press, Durham, copyright 1998, Duke University Press. All rights reserved. Reprinted with permission).

Halperin, David, "The Democratic Body: Prostitution and Citizenship in Classical Athens," *South Atlantic Quarterly* 88/1 (Winter 1989).

Kimmel, Michael, "The Birth of the Self-made Man," from *Manhood in America: A Cultural History* (The Free Press, New York, 1996).

Krishnaswamy, Revathi, "The Economy of Colonial Desire," from *Effeminism: The Economy of Colonial Desire* (University of Michigan Press, Ann Arbor, 1998).

Kulick, Don, "The Gender of Brazilian Transgendered Prostitutes," *American Anthropologist* 99/3 (1997), reprinted by permission of the American Anthropological Association and the author.

Lancaster, Roger, "Subject Honor, Object Shame," from *Life is Hard: Machismo, Danger, and the Intimacy of Power in Nicaragua*, selected pages. Copyright © 1992 The Regents of the University of California (The University of California Press, Berkeley, 1992).

Mercer, Kobena, "Skin Head Sex Thing: Racial Difference and the Homoerotic Imaginary," from *How Do I Look? Queer Film and Video* (Bay Press, Seattle, 1991).

Pateman, Carole, "The Fraternal Social Contract," from *The Disorder of Women: Democracy, Feminism and Political Theory* (Polity Press, Cambridge, 1989).

Peteet, Julie, "Male Gender and Rituals of Resistance in the Palestinian Intifada," from *Imagined Masculinities: Male Identity and Culture in the Modern Middle East*, ed. Mai Ghoussoub and Emma Sinclair-Webb (Saqi Books, London, 2000).

Sedgwick, Eve Kosofsky, "The Beast in the Closet: James and the Writing of Homosexual Panic," from *American Literature, American Culture*, ed. Gordon Hutner (Oxford University Press, New York, 1999, reprinted by permission of Oxford University Press, Inc.).

Silverman, Kaja, "Masochism and Male Subjectivity," from *Male Subjectivity at the Margins* (Routledge, London and New York, 1992, reprinted by permission of Taylor & Francis Ltd.).

Wiegman, Robyn, "Bonds of (In)Difference," from *American Anatomies: Theorizing Race and Gender* (Duke University Press, Durham, copyright 1995, Duke University Press. All rights reserved. Reprinted with permission).

Editors' Acknowledgments

Our work on *The Masculinity Studies Reader* would not have been possible without the help of many different people. At Blackwell Publishers, we have appreciated the enthusiastic support of Jayne Fargnoli and Annie Lenth, and Mary Dortch. For research assistance, thanks to Laura Braslow, Britta Feyerabend, and Milton Loayza. We are grateful to the following friends and colleagues: Jon Connolly, Julie Crawford, David Eng, Jean Howard, Greg Pfulgfelder, Sandhya Shukla, and Scott Teagarden.

Introduction

Rachel Adams and David Savran

"A man never begins by presenting himself as an individual of a certain sex; it goes without saying that he is a man," wrote Simone de Beauvoir in the introduction to *The Second Sex*. Whereas de Beauvoir's solution to the problem of man as the implicit subject of the western intellectual tradition was to concentrate on woman, *The Masculinity Studies Reader* identifies a growing body of scholarship devoted to addressing this historical imbalance by locating men and masculinity as the explicit subjects of analysis. This collection assembles some of the most significant research on masculinity produced over the last century. Bringing together work in the humanities and social sciences, it serves as an introduction and a testament to the ways in which the analysis of masculinity has revitalized questions about gender across the disciplines. The importance of many of the following essays is evident in the frequency with which they have been cited and anthologized; others promise to become equally influential. Yet having compiled them here, we remain far from certain about what they mean, or what the future of masculinity studies will be. Unlike other relatively new fields such as postcolonial criticism, gender, lesbian/gay/queer studies, or critical race theory, there are no departments, programs, or jobs created exclusively for scholars of masculinity. At the same time, the sheer quantity of recent scholarship, course offerings, and conferences devoted to this topic suggests that its impact is too great to be ignored. Without knowing exactly what direction this burst of critical activity will take, we have attempted to select a group of essays that will represent some of the most important contributions to this diverse, interdisciplinary area of inquiry, from the classic writings of Freud and Fanon to very current research. In their historical scope, these pieces extend questions about the definition of masculinity as far back as classical Greece and medieval India. The goal of *The Masculinity Studies Reader* is not to resolve these questions, but to present them in an accessible manner intended to place some very heterogeneous perspectives in productive, critical dialogue.

Masculinity studies is a product of the major reconfiguration of academic disciplines that has taken place since the 1960s. Borders have been redrawn, new methodologies have emerged, and many of the old disciplines have been rethought and reconstituted. Because many of the fields represented in this anthology have long been dominated by men and masculinist perspectives, we believe that the critical analysis of masculinity must be distinguished not only by its subject matter, but a new self-consciousness about the theoretical and methodological assumptions underlying traditional disciplinary formations. For example, Carole Pateman explores the consequences of a political theory that assumes the citizen to be middle-class and male. Eve Sedgwick's queer rereading of Henry James proposes a corrective to a literary history that has been complicit in obscuring the homosexual themes within his work. And Anne Fausto-Sterling criticizes biology for forcing intersexed people to conform to a rigid system of sexual division.

Taking its lead from feminism, masculinity studies is thus dedicated to analyzing what has often seemed to be an implicit fact, that the vast majority of societies are patriarchal and that men have historically enjoyed more than their share of power, resources, and cultural authority. Focusing critical interrogation on men, patriarchy, and formations of masculinity, scholars in many disciplines have sought to denaturalize de Beauvoir's observation that "it goes without saying that he is a man," by demonstrating that masculinities are historically constructed, mutable, and contingent, and analyzing their many and widespread effects. Yet, as Bryce Traister emphasizes, these are demanding tasks. Because "masculinity has for so long stood as the transcendental anchor and guarantor of cultural authority and 'truth,' demonstrating its materiality, its 'constructedness,' requires an especially energetic rhetorical and critical insistence" (2000: 281).

Because it is so theoretically and methodologically diverse, the scholarship on masculinity is difficult to anthologize. Our selection includes work by critics who would describe themselves as scholars of masculinity, as well as pieces that have never before been considered from this perspective, such as Clifford Geertz's "Deep Play: Notes on the Balinese Cockfight" or King-Kok Cheung's "The Woman Warrior versus The Chinaman Pacific: Must a Chinese American Critic Choose between Feminism and Heroism?" The purpose of such combinations is twofold: to represent the range of interdisciplinary scholarship about masculinity since the late 1980s, and also to contextualize those insights through the inclusion of older scholarship that is indisputably about men and masculinity, but does not frame itself explicitly in those terms. All of the essays in this book evince a certain eclecticism, even those that can most easily be pegged to a traditional field and seem most intent on using a single analytical framework. The range of essays suggests, moreover, that there is no consensus about masculinity studies' object of inquiry. Should it be a field devoted entirely to the analysis of men? Of patriarchy as an institution that affects men and women alike? Does the study of masculinity need to consider men at all? What is the role of the sexed body in the analysis of masculinity?

The organization of this volume represents our attempt to give these heterogeneous questions a thematic structure, while resisting the lure of dividing very complex work into identitarian categories such as "black masculinity," "gay masculinity," or "working-class masculinity." This choice reflects our conviction that masculinity is the product of so many complex and shifting variables that to describe them in terms of any one additive identity would inevitably be reductive. Instead, the five parts – Eroticism, Social Sciences, Representations, Empire and Modernity, and Borders – are based on what we believe to be some of the most definitive issues and approaches to the study of masculinity. These divisions are intended as helpful topical guides rather than exclusionary categories. Their organization, which includes classic essays alongside more recent scholarship, is meant to convey the fact that each of these topics has a history, one that is often rather more lengthy than might be expected. The five brief introductory essays are intended to suggest commonalities and lines of development within each category. However, reading the essays out of order or combining them under a different organizational rubric could yield equally productive results.

Whereas the topical categories we have selected are one way of making sense of the diverse field of masculinity studies, another way to approach the present state of the scholarship would be through its multiple genealogies. The plurality of approaches to studying masculinity at present are the product of the heterogeneous and sometimes conflicting social and intellectual movements that took place during the second half of the twentieth century. Examining the relationship among these movements can provide an initial understanding of the contours of the field and the primary debates taking place within it, many of which are considered in further detail in the introductions to individual sections.

Moreover, this collection of essays bridges a faultline between scholars of masculinity in the humanities and social sciences. Whereas previous anthologies have been oriented toward one disciplinary constellation or another, *The Masculinity Studies Reader* is structured to suggest lines of continuity and rupture among different approaches. In the most general terms, the social sciences contribute rigorous empirical research and greater attention to masculine rituals, organizations, and roles within different cultures; critics in the humanities add a more nuanced understanding of the importance of cultural representations to formations of gender, often placing greater emphasis on the domain of fantasy, imagination, and the unconscious. Rather than favoring one over the other, this collection proposes that each has something to contribute to ongoing critical conversations about masculinity.

Any historical account of the field's development must commence with the ascendancy of second-wave feminism during the 1960s and the consolidation of women's studies in the academy during the next decade. However, among the many coalitions involved in second-wave feminism there was no consensus about the status of men. Some groups, such as the New York Radical Women and The Feminists, called for complete segregation of the sexes, advocating either celibacy or lesbian separatism. By contrast, the liberal feminists of NOW (National Organization for Women), urged men and women to work together towards a sex/gender system that was less oppressive for all. As it entered universities in specialized programs and as a supplement to established disciplines such as literature and sociology, women's studies laid the groundwork for many of the approaches to masculinity represented in this volume. Both a form of political praxis and a mode of analysis, feminism impelled a new generation of politically engaged critics to study the social oppression of women and their impoverished representation in literature and the arts. Subsequent feminist scholarship began the project of historical recovery by bringing attention to unrecognized female authors, artists, and powerful political agents, as well as the previously invisible histories of the ordinary women who spent their lives as mothers, wives, servants, and workers. Likewise, the initial focus of women's studies on subjects who were white and middle class diversified to include poor women, women of color, and the subaltern women of colonized and postcolonial societies. In terms of its impact on the study of masculinity, perhaps the most important development of feminist criticism was the shift from "woman" to "gender" as a primary object of study. A term that applies to men and women alike, gender would enable scholars to approach masculinity as a social role that, like femininity, needed to be understood and interrogated.

The introduction of European continental philosophy into the humanities opened up the possibilities of even more dramatic reconsiderations of gender. Among the most influential of those philosophical perspectives was deconstruction, which proposed that the western intellectual tradition was founded on a structure of binary oppositions that, when subjected to close analysis, would inevitably break down as a result of their own internal contradictions. Words (or signs) have no inherent meaning; rather their connotations are derived in relation to other words, and those relationships are inevitably value-laden and hierarchical. The term *man* assumed significance through its pairing with its more degraded counterpart, *woman*. The "woman" of women's studies was suddenly open to radical interrogation, as a once relatively unified subject split into multiple and often conflicting interests. Deconstruction and related variants of poststructuralist theory questioned the stability and universality of all identity categories, positing the self as a mutable and fragmented effect of subjectivity. Influenced by poststructuralist theory, feminists came to see gender as a historically contingent construction, invariably constituted in and by its performance. Bringing together poststructuralism and psychoanalysis, the influential feminist philosopher Judith Butler argued that gender was not an essence but a performance. Describing gender as performance did not mean that it was a supplemental or voluntary aspect of identity; rather, it was a set of mandatory practices imposed from birth and repeated again and again in a doomed effort to get it right. Disengaged from the body, masculinity and femininity need not correspond to the sexed categories, man and woman. For scholars such as Butler, the transvestite who was biologically male but had learned to perform as female was the paradigmatic figure for an anti-essentialist theory of gender. Judith Halberstam, in an essay included in this collection, takes a similar approach to the analysis of female masculinity by studying biological women who perform in ways typically coded as male.

But these theoretical insights about gender have provided little pragmatic guidance for actual men. In the 1970s, the revolutionary import of the feminist insurgency in the streets, the voting booth, various professional arenas, and the academy was not lost on a generation of men who had been either actively involved with or sympathetic to the New Left. While some made it clear that they had no time for feminism, many began to hearken to the warnings and demands of their feminist comrades-in-arms. During the early 1970s, some men started to argue that sexism produces negative effects on men as well as women. Marc Feigen Fasteau, for example, wrote that because "the sexual caste system" is destructive for all, "men are beginning to seriously question the price of being thought superior." Intending his 1975 book, *The Male Machine*, as "a complement to the feminist revolution," he hoped that it would herald "the beginning of a whole new wave of both theory and activism" (pp. xiv–xv). And a significant number of men in fact did become involved in what could be described as the first wave of the men's movement, starting their own consciousness-raising groups, analyzing and trying to change their roles in patriarchal institutions, and endeavoring to forge non-sexist masculinities. Although this early men's movement was primarily a response to feminism, its political urgency was undoubtedly heightened by the emergence of the gay liberation movement at the end of the 1960s. Most of the men in the first-wave men's movement may have identified as straight, but they were deeply influenced by the diverse antihomophobic projects of gay men. In the many progressive discourses of the early 1970s that analogize the positions of women and gay men, misogyny is seen as being indissolubly linked to homophobia. By this account, patriarchal masculinities and institutions derive their power in part through the feminization of gay men and women.

During the 1970s, writings by Joseph Pleck, Marc Fasteau, and Jack Sawyer contributed to the first wave of the men's movement, which was avowedly profeminist and dedicated to personal and institutional change. In contrast, the second wave, the so-called mythopoetic men's movement that arose during the 1980s, represents, as many of its critics have argued, something of a backlash against feminism. Organized under the aegis of poet and activist Robert Bly, whose best-selling volume *Iron John* is the movement's bible, these men believed that they have been emasculated by feminism and an effeminizing culture. By retreating into the wilderness and by exercises in spiritual interrogation, they attempted to recuperate their own innate, masculine power. This movement succeeded in gaining quite a few adherents in the early 1990s and has been the subject of considerable controversy among sociologists. On the one hand, the call for a return to nature, spirituality, and male bonding compensates for pervasive feelings of emptiness and alienation among many men, sentiments that deserve serious consideration. On the other, authors such as Bly and Sam Keene replicate the discourse of early-twentieth-century wilderness movements, which advocated escape from the unwanted burdens of women, family, and social responsibilities. Michael Kimmel's book, *The Politics of Manhood*, collects many of the most important contributions to this important debate and helps frame it in terms of the history of fraternal orders, the rise of a therapeutic culture, and the changing economic position of middle-class white men since the 1970s.

At the same time that the first-wave men's movement was consolidating, scholars in a number of disciplines began to introduce the critique of patriarchal masculinities into their work. During the 1970s, essays in the social sciences by anthropologists such as Gayle Rubin, sociologists such as Joseph Pleck, and gay activist collectives such as the Third World Gay Revolution and the Gay Liberation Front, criticized patriarchal structures and analyzed oppressive masculinities from very different perspectives. While most of this scholarship was conceived within departmental boundaries (primarily anthropology, sociology, and history), it repeatedly acknowledges its debt to feminism in an attempt to politicize traditional disciplinary formations. Like the other intellectual insurgencies that arose in the wake of the 1960s (like women's or African American studies), these prototypes for what was to become masculinity studies were explicitly activist in intent. They were also the product of an identitarian politics that insisted upon the centrality and irreducibility of categories such as race, gender, and sexuality as a foundation both for activism and for the analysis of social, psychic, and cultural productions. Yet unlike the masculinity studies that emerged during the late 1980s, most of these critics implicitly or pointedly rejected psychoanalytical accounts of gender, preferring to understand sexual oppression in the context of economic and social history.

As many universities developed women's studies in the 1980s, and as feminist theory and methods permeated the disciplines, more and more men started to interrogate their own relationship to feminism. The 1987 collection of essays, *Men in Feminism*, pointedly set out to consider what men could contribute to academic feminism. And while the book reaches no consensus, it is symptomatic of the increasing concern and anxiety of many men sympathetic to feminism who were abashed by their own complicity with patriarchal institutions and somewhat envious of academic feminism's influence and prestige. The problem with men's entry into feminism, argued Tania Modleski in *Feminism without Women*, was that they threatened to reverse its accomplishments, returning the spotlight of critical attention to masculinity and male anxieties. Because the goals of feminism had not been fully realized, men needed to support the efforts of women rather than overemphasizing their own sensitivity, and highly performative renunciation of patriarchal authority. While some male scholars attempted, however problematically, to fashion themselves as feminists, others turned to the study of men as a corrective to feminism's nearly exclusive focus on women. For example, in the introduction to *Manhood in America*, Michael Kimmel praised women's studies while acknowledging that, as man, he felt alienated from its intellectual accomplishments. Because "American men have no history of themselves *as men*," he dedicated his work to the male audience that had largely been neglected by feminist discussions of gender.

Whereas Kimmel conceives of the study of men as distinct from, although often complementary to, feminism, there is a growing body of feminist scholarship that sees masculinity as a significant and necessary extension of its purview. One of the earliest and most important examples of convergence between the study of men and feminism was Eve Kosofsky Sedgwick's *Between Men: English Literature and Male Homosocial Desire* (1985). Intended as an intervention into a feminist scholarship devoted primarily to the study of women, *Between Men* shows why feminists should care about men and masculinities. It argues that in literature, relations between men have consistently been mediated by women who are treated as conduits for male homosocial desire, vehicles to ensure the heterosexual character of the erotic traffic between men. As a founding text of masculinity studies, it demonstrates that normative, heterosexual masculinities are structured by triangulating practices in which women mediate male relationships. At the same time, however, its analysis of erotic bonds between men and of the way the boundaries between the homosocial and the homosexual are policed also marks it as an inaugural text of lesbian/gay/queer studies. Ultimately, Sedgwick contends that the most important connection in the triangulated structure is not between man and woman, but between the two men who have no other way of expressing intimacies with one another.

As Sedgwick's work would suggest, much of the research on masculinity also derives from scholarship on sexuality originating within lesbian/gay/queer studies. Michel Foucault's groundbreaking 1976 volume, *The History of Sexuality*, challenged the universalizing claims of psychoanalysis and biology, arguing that the distinction between normative and dissident sexualities was culturally constructed and historically contingent. Sexual perversion was not a universal constant, but a category produced by the sciences of sexuality that arose in the nineteenth century as aspects of broader regimes of social control. In the 1980s, social historians such as Jeffrey Weeks and John D'Emilio set the agenda for an emerging field of sexuality studies by examining the changing relationship between sexual practices and sexual subjects. Looking at legal, medical, and political discourses from different periods, they linked the production of various heterosexualities and homosexualities to changing historical circumstances. Unlike heterosexual masculinity, which has long assumed its own universality and transparency, gay and other deviant forms of masculinity have more consistently been forced to interrogate their own relationship to dominant gender configurations. As Kaja Silverman argued in her 1992 study, *Male Subjectivity at the Margins*, feminists invested in dismantling what she called the "dominant fiction" of patriarchal masculinity needed to attend to masculinities that "not only acknowledge but embrace castration, alterity, and specularity" (p. 3).

Evidence for the rapid spread of masculinity studies during the last decade of the twentieth century is everywhere in the many academic conferences, topical anthologies, and courses now being offered on masculinity. As many women's studies programs move towards gender studies, masculinity may take its place alongside courses on gay/lesbian/queer topics. Yet these recent developments are by no means unproblematic and the study of masculinity continues to raise a number of important questions in an era of institutional downsizing, when academics and administrators are sensitive to the rapidly rising and falling markets of intellectual fashion. Unlike many of the fields that are its models and precursors, masculinity studies analyzes a dominant and oppressive class that has, arguably, always been the primary focus of scholarly attention. Does masculinity studies represent a beneficial extension of feminist analysis or does it represent a hijacking of feminism? In short, what is gained – and what is lost – when a field that had been defined as women's studies, understood as both a theoretical and politically activist insurgency, changes its focus to examine the construction of those subjects who historically have subjugated women? Given the limited resources in universities to support teaching and research on gender, it seems an unfortunate inevitability that masculinity studies, if it were to gain any institutional status, would enter into a competitive relationship with other related fields.

This anthology is designed less to bring definitive resolution to these problems than to give readers the materials they need to begin to formulate their own critical conversations, conversations which, we insist, must be informed by an awareness of limited resources of funding and labor as much as by the excitement of new intellectual conquest. Perhaps some might conclude, as a result of those discussions, that the most desirable goal of scholarship on masculinity would be not the formation of another interdisciplinary field but the radical transformation of its object of study.

Bibliography

Beauvoir, Simone de. 1974. *The Second Sex* [1953], trans. H. M. Parshley. New York: Vintage Books.

Bly, Robert. 1990. *Iron John: A Book About Men*. Reading, Mass: Addison-Wesley.

Butler, Judith. 1990. *Gender Trouble: Feminism and the Subversion of Identity*. New York: Routledge.

D'Emilio, John. 1983. *Sexual Politics, Sexual Communities: The Making of a Homosexual Minority in the United States, 1940–1970.* Chicago: University of Chicago Press.

Echols, Alice. 1989. *Daring to be Bad: Radical Feminism in America, 1967–1975.* Minneapolis: University of Minnesota Press.

Fasteau, Marc Feigen. 1975. *The Male Machine.* New York: Dell.

Foucault, Michel. 1980. *The History of Sexuality, Volume I: An Introduction* [1976], trans. Robert Hurley. New York: Vintage Books.

Jardine, Alice and Smith, Paul. (eds.) 1987. *Men in Feminism.* New York: Methuen.

Kimmel, Michael. 1996. *Manhood in America: A Cultural History.* New York: Free Press.

——(ed.) 1995. *The Politics of Manhood: Profeminist Men Respond to the Mythopoetic Men's Movement (And the Mythopoetic Leaders Answer).* Philadelphia: Temple University Press.

Modleski, Tania. 1991. *Feminism without Women: Culture and Criticism in a "Post-Feminist" Age.* New York: Routledge.

Pleck, Elizabeth H. and Pleck, Joseph H. (eds.) 1980. *The American Man.* Englewood Cliffs, NJ: Prentice-Hall.

Rubin, Gayle. 1975. "The Traffic in Women: Notes on the 'Political Economy' of Sex," in Rayna R. Reiter (ed.) *Toward an Anthropology of Women.* New York: Monthly Review Press, pp. 157–210.

Sedgwick, Eve Kosofsky. 1985. *Between Men: English Literature and Male Homosocial Desire.* New York: Columbia University Press.

Silverman, Kaja. 1992. *Male Subjectivity at the Margins.* New York and London: Routledge.

Third World Gay Revolution and Gay Liberation Front. 1977. "Gay Revolution and Sex Roles," in Karla Jay and Allen Young (eds.) *Out of the Closets: Voices of Gay Liberation.* New York: Harcourt Brace Jovanovich, pp. 252–9.

Traister, Bryce. 2000. "Academic Viagra: The Rise of American Masculinity Studies." *American Quarterly,* 52/2 (June) pp. 274–304.

Weeks, Jeffrey. 1985. *Sexuality and its Discontents: Meanings, Myths and Modern Sexualities,* London: Routledge.

Part I

Eroticism

There is something almost perverse about beginning *The Masculinity Studies Reader* with a section on eroticism, since it remains among the most difficult and vexed of terms. No concept appears simultaneously more transparent and more obscure. None seems more decisive yet more incidental for the construction of masculinity. None so radically undermines oppositions between gender and sexuality, between the psychic and the social. Both a mode of desire and of sexual practice, eroticism is commonly understood – like masculinity itself – in terms of the binary categories of homo- and heterosexuality. Yet, as the essays by David Halperin and Roger Lancaster demonstrate, these designations are historically contingent and severely limited in their applicability. Likewise, eroticism is commonly described as either a psychological or a social phenomenon. Yet the essays in this section implicitly or explicitly undermine the distinction between the two by proving eroticism to be the most destabilizing and unpredictable of terms.

We begin the *Reader* with psychoanalysis because it remains central to most attempts to theorize the relationship between masculinity and eroticism. The publication of Sigmund Freud's *Three Essays on the Theory of Sexuality* in 1905 revolutionized the study of gender, eroticism, and childhood sexuality. Although Freud's work is heavily indebted to nineteenth-century sexology and his own previous studies of hysteria, *Three Essays* lays out theories of sexual development and categorizes the so-called sexual aberrations in a highly systematic way, going to great lengths to challenge then-prevailing notions of congenital and essentialized sexual predispositions. Freud maintains instead that psychic structures are socially produced, principally (but by no means exclusively) by the nuclear family. And his theories of eroticism and desire are inextricably linked to the study of masculinity and male subjectivity. As a result of these arguments, *Three Essays* has had an incalculable impact on subsequent scholarship on gender, particularly work committed to analyzing the psychoanalytic dimensions of sexuality. Even those who rightly critique Freud for being masculinist or bourgeois offer alternative theories of subject formation in the shadow of *Three Essays*.

Like so much recent work on eroticism, *Three Essays* testifies to the difficulty in separating gender from sexuality, masculinity from the male anatomy. For much of the twentieth century, for example, effeminacy has been considered a privileged marker of male homosexuality. Yet history teaches us that this connection is far more tenuous than it often seems. As the product of a society in which the very concept of sexual orientation was ill-defined and in flux, Freud never completely worked out the relationship between gender and sexuality. In the first of the essays, he observes that homosexuality is not always accompanied by gender deviance, but in the third, "The Transformations of Puberty," which most explicitly attempts to theorize gender identity in relation to desire, he simply takes heterosexuality for granted. There he analyzes how children take up opposed – and heterosexualized – gendered positions by rejecting incestuous attachments to their own parents. The mechanism for this transformation is the Oedipus complex, which demands that the child identify with and imitate the parent of its own sex and desire the parent of the opposite sex (and later, a surrogate for that parent). In charting the transformations of the child's libido as it moves beyond the nuclear family, Freud shows how the normative system of gender requires that desire be decisively separated from identification. That is, once someone has identified as a man, he must, by definition, desire women.

Although the resolution of the Oedipus complex grants a primacy to heterosexual relations, Freud's theorization of homosexuality is curiously contradictory and far less condemnatory than that of the sexologists who preceded him. On the one hand, he classifies it as a pathology and sexual aberration; on the other, he insists that all human beings are innately bisexual. Not only are they "capable of making a homosexual object choice," but "have in fact made one in their unconscious" (1962: 11). Yet Freud's theory never accounts for the centrality of heterosexuality. It requires that the subject internalize the prohibition against homosexuality before the incest taboo by proposing that a child can be successfully Oedipalized only if he or she has previously forsaken desire for the parent of the same sex. But he never explains in psychic terms why homosexual object choices in most individuals are suppressed. Decades later, scholars of sexuality would return to Freud's complex and often sympathetic writings about homosexuality to develop more consistent psychoanalytic accounts of male eroticism.

When Freud turns in *Three Essays* to questions of gender identity, he is forced to admit "that the concepts of 'masculine' and 'feminine'... are among the most confused that occur in science" and he carefully distinguishes among different uses of the terms. Yet his assertion that "pure masculinity or femininity is not to be found either in a psychological or biological sense" is contradicted by his somewhat reductive, if widely influential, understanding of sexual difference and desire. Like many before and after, Freud understands sexual difference to be a result of the presence or absence of the penis. He argues that because the penis is decisive for the production of sexual identity, male and female, both sexes may be subject to what he calls the castration complex. In males, this results from a (mistaken) belief that females are castrated and males' anxiety that they could fall victim to a similar fate. In females, this complex is linked to what Freud – notoriously and controversially – calls penis envy, the desire to be male, which is sometimes accompanied by what he describes as a "masculinity complex in women" when the latter "refuse to accept the fact of being castrated" (1953: 191). Because the castration complex defines women entirely by their relation to the penis, it leads Freud to a conclusion that has long troubled feminists: "libido is invariably and necessarily of a masculine nature, whether it occurs in men or in women" (1962: 85).

Beginning in the 1930s, Freud's theories of gender, sexuality, and subject formation were revisited (and in some cases, radically revised) by the French psychoanalyst Jacques Lacan who arguably has been even more important than Freud for theorizing the relationship between men and masculinity. Although Lacan defies easy summarization, he is perhaps most important for his insistence on the primacy of language, his theorization of gender and desire as the products – and producers – of signifying systems. The linchpin to Lacan's theory is the mirror stage during which the child understands itself as an autonomous subject for the first time. Seeing its reflection, the child (mis)recognizes itself as a complete being and assumes "the armour of an alienating identity" (1977: 4). This stage marks the separation of subject from object, self from other, and signals the child's entrance into what Lacan calls the symbolic, that order of representations and linguistic signs by which meaning is produced. The mirror stage also inaugurates desire, which Lacan understands as the product of loss, the absence of the mother and the plenitude she represents. Thus for both Freud and Lacan, eroticism is always founded on a desire (for the mother) that can never be satisfied.

One aspect of the work of both Freud and Lacan that has had a tremendous impact on masculinity studies is their conceptualization of sexual difference and eroticism in visual (or specular) terms. Thus, even the essays in this anthology that analyze purely linguistic texts routinely focus on visual signs. For Freud, sexual difference is founded on the recognition of the penis – or lack of it. For Lacan, the entrance into subjectivity is the result of a specular (mis)recognition. Moreover, one of the most important contributions of Lacanian psychoanalysis to studies of eroticism is its elaboration of the difference between the visible and the invisible, the penis and the phallus. The Lacanian phallus is not an organ but a sign, a privileged symbol of patriarchal power and authority that becomes associated with the penis, but cannot *be* that with which it is associated. As Elizabeth Grosz notes, "the phallus is the valorized signifier around which both men and women define themselves" (1990: 116). The fact that the penis is phantasmatically linked to, but cannot become, the phallus, is a source of considerable anxiety. Following Freud, Lacanian psychoanalysis proposes that because no subject can actually possess the phallus, both men and women suffer the mark of castration, albeit in different ways. Men and women in a patriarchal society usually take up complementary positions of desiring subject and desired object; the one performs as if she "has" the phallus; the other as if he "is" it. Kaja Silverman's essay on male masochism demonstrates the potential for translating Freudian and Lacanian psychoanalysis into feminist terms. According to Silverman, male eroticism is always articulated in relation to castration, to the impossibility of ever really having the phallus. She focuses on masochistic – non-phallic, wounded, or vulnerable – masculinities because they make visible the lack at the center of male subjectivity, thus posing a radical threat to a phallicized masculinity and to sexual difference itself.

As the essays in this section attest, psychoanalysis does not provide the only account of masculine eroticism. Among the approaches that challenge psychoanalytical explanations of male desire and sexuality, the most influential have been provided by social scientists and, more recently, by various elaborations of Foucauldian historicism within the humanities. Both represent forms of social constructionism that differ radically from the Freudian and Lacanian paradigms. The sociological (or anthropological) models theorize subjectivity in a dialectical relationship to social formations, which both produce and are produced by the subject. Like Roger Lancaster's essay in this volume, they usually foreground the social, economic, and political construction of identity, while de-emphasizing psychic and familial structures. Lancaster's fieldwork on machismo in Nicaragua pluralizes sexual identities, demonstrating that the modern American or European understanding of heterosexual masculinity makes little sense in other parts of the world.

Michel Foucault's influential *History of Sexuality* has provided scholars in the humanities with another alternative to the psychoanalytic study of eroticism, one that has been particularly important to lesbian/gay/queer studies. Foucault shares the sociological skepticism about psychoanalysis and fascination with historical discontinuities. But particularly in his later works, he becomes distrustful of any and all totalizing systems, especially the economic determinism, invocation of science, and notion of linear historical development of certain orthodox Marxisms. At the same time, it was Foucault, more than any other theorist, who was responsible for historicizing sexuality. For example, he argued that the homosexual is not a universal type but an invention of the nineteenth century, a new "species" whose "sexuality" was believed to be "at the root of all his [*sic*] actions because it was their insidious and indefinitely active principle" (1980: 43). The more varied history of sexuality provided by Foucault is a foundation for work such as David Halperin's study of male sexual practices in classical Athens. Instead of connecting sexual acts to personal identity, Halperin argues, as is the case with the modern categories of homo- and heterosexuality, the ancient Greeks defined sex in relation to citizenship.

Despite the diversity of approaches taken by the authors of the essays in this section, all could be said to endorse modes of constructionism, which assert that eroticism is not an essential quality of self but a set of practices and desires formed (often in unpredictable ways) through the subject's interaction with family and society. And despite their divergent attitudes toward psychoanalysis, all could be said to be analyzing the positioning of the phallus, understood as both a signifier of desire and a particular kind of socially sanctioned, patriarchal – but not necessarily heterosexualized – masculinity. Even those writers who reject the vocabulary of psychoanalysis still make use of, and sometimes explicitly problematize, the binary oppositions between "having" and "being," masculinity and femininity, subject and object, activity and passivity. Their work demonstrates that eroticism remains as indefinite and historically contingent a category as masculinity itself.

Bibliography

Foucault, Michel. 1980. *The History of Sexuality, Volume I: An Introduction*, trans. Robert Hurley. New York: Vintage Books.

Freud, Sigmund. 1962. *Three Essays on the Theory of Sexuality*, trans. and ed. James Strachey. New York: Basic Books.

—— 1953. "Some Psychological Consequences of the Anatomical Distinction between the Sexes," trans. James Strachey, in *Collected Papers*, vol. 5. London: Hogarth Press, pp. 186–97.

Grosz, Elizabeth. 1990. *Jacques Lacan: A Feminist Introduction*. London: Routledge.

Lacan, Jacques. 1977. *Ecrits: A Selection*, trans. Alan Sheridan. New York: Norton.

1

Some Psychological Consequences of the Anatomical Distinction between the Sexes

Sigmund Freud

In my own writings and in those of my followers more and more stress is laid upon the necessity for carrying the analyses of neurotics back into the remotest period of their childhood, the time of the early efflorescence of sexual life. It is only by examining the first manifestations of the patient's innate instinctual constitution and the effects of his earliest experiences that we can accurately gauge the motive forces that have led to his neurosis and can be secure against the errors into which we might be tempted by the degree to which they have become remodelled and overlaid in adult life. This requirement is not only of theoretical but also of practical importance, for it distinguishes our efforts from the work of those physicians whose interests are focussed exclusively upon therapeutic results and who employ analytic methods, but only up to a certain point. An analysis of early childhood such as we are considering is tedious and laborious and makes demands both upon the physician and upon the patient which cannot always be met. Moreover it leads us into dark regions where there are as yet no sign-posts. Indeed, analysts may feel reassured, I think, that there is no risk of their work becoming mechanical, and so of losing its interest, during the next few decades.

In the following pages I bring forward some findings of analytical research which would be of great importance if they could be proved to apply universally. Why do I not postpone publication of them until further experience has given me the necessary proof, if such proof is obtainable? Because the conditions under which I work have undergone a change, with implications which I cannot disguise. Formerly, I was never one of those who are unable to hold back what seems to be a new discovery until it has been either confirmed or corrected. My *Interpretation of Dreams* [1900] and my "Fragment of an Analysis of a Case of Hysteria" [1905] (the case of Dora) were suppressed by me – if not for the nine years enjoined by Horace – at all events for four or five years before I allowed them to be published. But in those days I had unlimited time before me and material poured in upon me in such quantities that fresh experiences were hardly to be escaped. Moreover, I

Reprinted from *Sexuality and the Psychology of Love*, trans. James Strachey (New York: Collier Books, 1925), pp. 183–93.

was the only worker in a new field, so that my reticence involved no danger to myself and no risk of loss to others.

But now everything has changed. The time before me is limited. The whole of it is no longer spent in working, so that my opportunities for making fresh observations are not so numerous. If I think I see something new, I am uncertain whether I can wait for it to be confirmed. And further, everything that is to be seen upon the surface has already been exhausted; what remains has to be slowly and laboriously dragged up from the depths. Finally, I am no longer alone. An eager crowd of fellow-workers is ready to make use of what is unfinished or doubtful, and I can leave to them that part of the work which I should otherwise have done myself. On this occasion, therefore, I feel justified in publishing something which stands in urgent need of confirmation before its value or lack of value can be decided.

In examining the earliest mental shapes assumed by the sexual life of children we have been in the habit of taking as the subject of our investigations the male child, the little boy. With little girls, so we have supposed, things must be similar, though in some way or other they must nevertheless be different. The point in development at which this difference lay could not clearly be determined.

In boys the situation of the Oedipus complex is the first stage that can be recognized with certainty. It is easy to understand, because at that stage a child retains the same object which he previously cathected with his pregenital libido during the preceding period while he was being suckled and nursed. The further fact that in this situation he regards his father as a disturbing rival and would like to get rid of him and take his place is a straightforward consequence of the actual state of affairs. I have shown elsewhere ["The Passing of the Oedipus Complex"] how the Oedipus attitude in little boys belongs to the phallic phase, and how it succumbs to the fear of castration, that is, to narcissistic interest in their own genitals. The matter is made more difficult to grasp by the complicating circumstance that even in boys the Oedipus complex has a double orientation, active and passive, in accordance with their bisexual constitution; a boy also wants to take his *mother's* place as the love-object of his *father* – a fact which we describe as the feminine attitude.

As regards the prehistory of the Oedipus complex in boys we are far from complete clarity. We know that that period includes an identification of an affectionate sort with the boy's father, an identification which is still free from any sense of rivalry in regard to his mother. Another element of that stage is invariably, I believe, a masturbatory stimulation of the genitals, the masturbation of early childhood, the more or less violent suppression of which by the persons in charge of the child sets the castration complex in action. It is to be assumed that this masturbation is attached to the Oedipus complex and serves as a discharge for the sexual excitation belonging to it. It is, however, uncertain whether the masturbation has this character from the first, or whether on the contrary it makes its first appearance spontaneously as an activity of a bodily organ and is only brought into relation with the Oedipus complex at some later date; this second possibility is by far the more probable. Another doubtful question is the part played by bed-wetting and by the breaking of that habit through the intervention of training measures. We are inclined to adopt the simple generalization that continued bed-wetting is a result of masturbation and that its suppression is regarded by boys as an inhibition of their genital activity, that is, as having the meaning of a threat of castration; but whether we are always right in supposing this remains to be seen. Finally, analysis shows us in a shadowy way how the fact of a child at a very early age listening to his parents copulating may set up his first sexual excitation, and how that event may, owing to its after-effects, act as a starting-point for the child's whole sexual development. Masturbation, as well as the two attitudes in the Oedipus complex, later on become attached to this early experience, the child having subsequently interpreted its meaning. It is impossible, however, to suppose that these observations of coitus are of universal occurrence, so that at this point we are faced with the problem of "primal phantasies." Thus the prehistory of the Oedipus complex, even in boys, raises all of these questions for sifting and explanation; and there is the further problem of whether we are to suppose that the process invariably follows the same course, or whether a great variety of different preliminary stages may not converge upon the same terminal situation.

In little girls the Oedipus complex raises one problem more than in boys. In both cases the mother is the original object; and there is no cause for surprise that boys retain that object in the Oedipus complex. But how does it happen that girls abandon it and instead take their father as an object? In pursuing this question I have been able to reach some conclusions which may throw light upon the prehistory of the Oedipus relation in girls.

Every analyst has come across certain women who cling with especial intensity and tenacity to the bond with their father and to the wish in which it culminates of having a child by him. We have good reason to suppose that the same wishful phantasy was also the motive force of their infantile masturbation, and it is easy to form an impression that at this point we have been brought up against an elementary and unanalysable fact of infantile sexual life. But a thorough analysis of these very cases brings something different to light, namely, that here the Oedipus complex has a long prehistory and is in some respects a secondary formation.

The old paediatrician Lindner once remarked that a child discovers the genital zones (the penis or the clitoris) as a source of pleasure while indulging in sensual sucking (thumb-sucking)[1]: I shall leave it an open question whether it is really true that the child takes the newly found source of pleasure in exchange for the recent loss of the mother's nipple – a possibility to which later phantasies (fellatio) seem to point. Be that as it may, the genital zone is discovered at some time or other, and there seems no justification for attributing any psychical content to its first stimulations. But the first step in the phallic phase which begins in this way is not the linking-up of the masturbation with the object-cathexes of the Oedipus situation, but a momentous discovery which little girls are destined to make. They notice the penis of a brother or playmate, strikingly visible and of large proportions, at once recognize it as the superior counterpart of their own small and inconspicuous organ, and from that time forward fall a victim to envy for the penis.

There is an interesting contrast between the behaviour of the two sexes. In the analogous situation, when a little boy first catches sight of a girl's genital region, he begins by showing irresolution and lack of interest; he sees nothing or disowns what he has seen, he softens it down or looks about for expedients for bringing it into line with his expectations. It is not until later, when some threat of castration has obtained a hold upon him, that the observation becomes important to him: if he then recollects or repeats it, it arouses a terrible storm of emotion in him and forces him to believe in the reality of the threat which he has hitherto laughed at.

This combination of circumstances leads to two reactions, which may become fixed and will in that case, whether separately or together or in conjunction with other factors, permanently determine the boy's relations to women: horror of the mutilated creature or triumphant contempt for her. These developments, however, belong to the future, though not to a very remote one.

A little girl behaves differently. She makes her judgement and her decision in a flash. She has seen it and knows that she is without it and wants to have it.[2]

From this point there branches off what has been named the masculinity complex of women, which may put great difficulties in the way of their regular development towards femininity, it cannot be got over soon enough. The hope of some day obtaining a penis in spite of everything and so of becoming like a man may persist to an incredibly late age and may become a motive for the strangest and otherwise unaccountable actions. Or again, a process may set in which might be described as a "denial," a process which in the mental life of children seems neither uncommon nor very dangerous but which in an adult would mean the beginning of a psychosis. Thus a girl may refuse to accept the fact of being castrated, may harden herself in the conviction that she *does* possess a penis and may subsequently be compelled to behave as though she were a man.

The psychical consequences of penis-envy, in so far as it does not become absorbed in the reaction-formation of the masculinity complex, are various and far-reaching. After a woman has become aware of the wound to her narcissism, she develops, like a scar, a sense of inferiority. When she has passed beyond her first attempt at explaining her lack of a penis as being a punishment personal to herself and has realized that that sexual character is a universal one, she begins to share the contempt felt by men for a sex which is the lesser in so important a respect, and, at least in the holding of that opinion, insists upon being like a man.[3]

Even after penis-envy has abandoned its true object, it continues to exist: by an easy displacement it persists in the character-trait of *jealousy*. Of course, jealousy is not limited to one sex and has a wider foundation than this, but I am of opinion that it plays a far larger part in the mental life of women than of men and that that is because it is enormously reinforced from the direction of displaced penis-envy. While I was still unaware of this source of jealousy and was considering the phantasy "A Child Is Being Beaten" [1919], which occurs so commonly in girls, I constructed a first phase for it in which its meaning was that another child, a rival of whom the subject was jealous, was to be beaten. This phantasy seems to be a relic of the phallic period in girls. The peculiar rigidity which struck me so much in the monotonous formula "a child is being beaten" can probably be interpreted in a special way. The child which is being beaten (or caressed) may at bottom be nothing more nor less than the clitoris itself, so that at its very lowest level the statement will contain a confession of masturbation, which has remained attached to the content of the formula from its beginning in the phallic phase up to the present time.

A third consequence of penis-envy seems to be a loosening of the girl's relation with her mother as a love-object. The situation as a whole is not very clear, but it can be seen that in the end the girl's mother, who sent her into the world so insufficiently equipped, is almost always held responsible for her lack of a penis. The way in which this comes about historically is often that soon after the girl has discovered that her genitals are unsatisfactory she begins to show jealousy of another child on the grounds that her mother is fonder of it than of her, which serves as a reason for her giving up her affectionate relation to her mother. It will fit in with this if the child which has been preferred by her mother is made into the first object of the beating-phantasy which ends in masturbation.

There is yet another surprising effect of penis-envy, or of the discovery of the inferiority of the clitoris, which is undoubtedly the most important of all. In the past I had often formed an impression that in general women tolerate masturbation worse than men, that they more frequently fight against it and that they are unable to make use of it in circumstances in which a man would seize upon it as a way of escape without any hesitation. Experience would no doubt elicit innumerable exceptions to this statement, if we attempted to turn it into a rule. The reactions of human individuals of both sexes are of course made up of masculine and feminine traits. But it appeared to me nevertheless as though masturbation were further removed from the nature of women than of men, and the solution of the problem could be assisted by the reflection that masturbation, at all events of the clitoris, is a masculine activity and that the elimination of clitoridal sexuality is a necessary pre-condition for the development of femininity. Analyses of the remote phallic period have now taught me that in girls, soon after the first signs of penis-envy, an intense current of feeling against masturbation makes its appearance, which cannot be attributed exclusively to the educational influence of those in charge of the child. This impulse is clearly a forerunner of the wave of repression which at puberty will do away with a large amount of the girl's masculine sexuality in order to make room for the development of her femininity. It may happen that this first opposition to auto-erotic stimulation fails to attain its end. And this was in fact the case in the instances which I analyzed. The conflict continued, and both then and later the girl did everything she could to free herself from the compulsion to masturbate. Many of the later manifestations of sexual life in women remain unintelligible unless this powerful motive is recognized.

I cannot explain the opposition which is raised in this way by little girls to phallic masturbation except by supposing that there is some concurrent factor which turns her violently against that pleasurable activity. Such a factor lies close at hand in the narcissistic sense of humiliation which is bound up with penis-envy, the girl's reflection that after all this is a point on which she cannot compete with boys and that it would therefore be best for her to give up the idea of doing so. Thus the little girl's recognition of the anatomical distinction between the sexes forces her away from masculinity and masculine masturbation on to new lines which lead to the development of femininity.

So far there has been no question of the Oedipus complex, nor has it up to this point played any part. But now the girl's libido slips into a new position by means – there is no other way of putting it – of the equation "penis = child." She gives up her wish for a penis and puts in place of it a wish for a child: and *with this purpose in view* she takes her father as a love-object. Her mother becomes the object of her jealousy. The girl has turned into a little woman. If I am to credit a single exagger-ated analytic instance, this new situation can give rise to physical sensations which would have to be regarded as a premature awakening of the female genital apparatus. If the girl's attachment to her father comes to grief later on and has to be abandoned, it may give place to an identification with him and the girl may thus return to her masculinity complex and perhaps remain fixated in it.

I have now said the essence of what I had to say: I will stop, therefore, and cast an eye over our findings. We have gained some insight into the prehistory of the Oedipus complex in girls. The corresponding period in boys is more or less unknown. In girls the Oedipus complex is a secondary formation. The operations of the castration complex precede it and prepare for it. As regards the relation between the Oedipus and castration complexes there is a fundamental contrast between the two sexes. *Whereas in boys the Oedipus complex succumbs to the castration complex, in girls it is made possible and led up to by the castration complex.* This contradiction is cleared up if we reflect that the castration complex always operates in the sense dictated by its subject-matter: it inhibits and limits masculinity and encourages femininity. The difference between the sexual development of males and females at the stage we have been considering is an intelligible consequence of the anatomical distinction between their genitals and of the psychical situation involved in it; it corresponds to the difference between a castration that has been carried out and one that has merely been threatened. In their essentials, therefore, our findings are self-evident and it should have been possible to foresee them.

The Oedipus complex, however, is such an important thing that the manner in which one enters and leaves it cannot be without its effects. In boys . . . the complex is not simply repressed, it is literally smashed to pieces by the shock of threatened castration. Its libidinal cathexes are abandoned, desexualized and in part sublimated; its objects are incorporated into the ego, where they form the nucleus of the super-ego and give that new structure its characteristic qualities. In normal, or rather in ideal cases, the Oedipus complex exists no longer, even in the unconscious; the super-ego has become its heir. Since the penis (to follow Ferenczi) owes its extraordinarily high narcissistic cathexis to its organic significance for the propagation of the species, the catastrophe of the Oedipus complex (the abandonment of incest and the institution of conscience and morality) may be regarded as a victory of the race over the individual. This is an interesting point of view when one considers that neurosis is based upon a struggle of the ego against the demands of the sexual function. But to leave the standpoint of individual psychology is not likely to be of any immediate help in clarifying this complicated situation.

In girls the motive for the destruction of the Oedipus complex is lacking. Castration has already had its effect, which was to force the child into the situation of the Oedipus complex. Thus the Oedipus complex escapes the fate which it meets with in boys: it may either be slowly abandoned or got rid of by repression, or its effects may persist far into women's normal mental life. I cannot escape the notion (though I hesitate to give it expression) that for women the level of what is ethically normal is different from what it is in men. Their super-ego is never so inexorable, so impersonal, so independent of its emotional origins as we require it to be in men. Character traits which critics of every epoch have brought up against women – that they show less sense of justice than men, that they are less ready to submit to the great necessities of life, that they are more often influenced in their judgements by feelings of affection or hostility – all these would be amply accounted for by the modification in the formation of their super-ego which we have already inferred. We must not allow ourselves to be deflected from such conclusions by the denials of the feminists, who are anxious to force us to regard the two sexes as completely equal in position and worth; but we shall, of course, willingly agree that the majority of men are also far behind the masculine ideal and that all human individuals, as a result of their bisexual disposition and of cross inheritance, combine in themselves both masculine and feminine characteristics, so that pure masculinity and femininity remain theoretical constructions of uncertain content.

I am inclined to set some value on the considerations I have brought forward upon the psychological consequences of the anatomical distinction between the sexes. I am aware, however, that this opinion can only be maintained if my findings, which are based on a handful of cases, turn out to have general validity and to be typical. If not, they would remain no more than a contribution to our knowledge of the different paths along which sexual life develops.

Notes

1 Cf. *Three Essays on the Theory of Sexuality* [1905] (English translation, 1949).
2 This is an opportunity for correcting a statement which I made many years ago. I believed that the sexual interest of children, unlike that of pubescents, was aroused, not by the differences between the sexes, but by the problem of where babies come from. We now see that, at all events with girls, this is certainly not the case. With boys it may no doubt happen sometimes one way and sometimes the other; or with both sexes chance experiences may determine the event.
3 In my first critical account of the "History of the Psychoanalytic Movement," written in 1914, I recognized that this fact represents the core of truth contained in Adler's theory. That theory has no hesitation in explaining the whole world by this single point ("organ inferiority," "the masculine protest," breaking away from "the feminine line") and prides itself upon having in this way robbed sexuality of its importance and put the desire for power in its place. Thus the only organ which could claim to be called "inferior" without any ambiguity would be the clitoris. On the other hand, one hears of analysts who boast that, though they have worked for dozens of years, they have never found a sign of the existence of a castration complex. We must bow our heads in recognition of the greatness of this achievement, even though it is only a negative one, a piece of virtuosity in the art of overlooking and mistaking. The two theories form an interesting pair of opposites: in one of them not a trace of a castration complex, in the other nothing at all but its effects.

2

Masochism and Male Subjectivity

Kaja Silverman

Perversion: Turning aside from truth or right; diversion to an improper use....

(*OED*)

What is the "truth" or "right" from which perversion turns aside, and what does it improperly use? The *OED* goes some way towards answering these questions when it quotes, by way of illustration, part of a line from Francis Bacon: "Women to govern men . . . slaves freemen . . . being total violations and perversions of the laws of nature and nations." According to this grammatically "deviant" citation, perversion turns aside from both biology and the social order, and it does so through the improper deployment or negation of the binarisms upon which each regime depends – binarisms that reinforce each other in the case of gender, if not that of class. The "truth" or "right" which is thus subverted is the principle of hierarchy.

Freud's account of perversion also stresses its diversionary and decentering character. "Perversions," he writes in *Three Essays on the Theory of Sexuality*, "are sexual activities which either (a) extend, in an anatomical sense, beyond the regions of the body that are designed for sexual union, or (b) linger over the intermediate relations to the sexual object which should normally be traversed rapidly on the path towards the final sexual aim."[1] Here, in utter disregard for western metaphysics, the "true" or "right" is heterosexual penetration. All other sexual activities belong either to the category of "fore-play," in which case they are strictly subordinated to "end-pleasure," or perversion.

Coitus is "ideally" a reprise in miniature of the history of infantile sexuality, a history that begins with oral gratification and culminates with genital desire for an object of the opposite gender. Here too the subject is exhorted to keep his or her eyes on the finish line, and to move as expeditiously as possible through the preliminary stages. But in both cases perversion intrudes as the temptation to engage in a different kind of erotic narrative, one whose organization is aleatory and paratactic rather than direct and hypotactic, preferring fore-pleasures to end-pleasures, and browsing to discharge. Since every external and internal organ is

Reprinted from *Male Subjectivity at the Margins* (New York and London: Routledge, 1992), pp. 185–206, 208–10, 413–16.

capable of becoming an erotogenic zone, sexuality need not even be limited to the three stages Freud decreed for boys, or the four he ordained for girls. Infantile sexuality is polymorphously perverse, and even in the erotic activities of the most "normal" adult there are "rudiments which, if they had developed, would have led to the deviations described as 'perversions.' "[2]

I do not mean to suggest that polymorphous sexuality is more "natural" than genital sexuality. There is no form of human sexuality which does not marginalize need or substitute a fantasmatic object for the original and nutritive object. As Laplanche explains, "Sexuality is . . . a localized, autoerotic pleasure, a pleasure of the organ 'in place,' in opposition to a functional pleasure with all which that term implies of an opening towards the object . . . Thus a natural, functional rhythm (that of rutting) disappears, while elsewhere there emerges a different kind of sequence, which is incomprehensible without calling into play such categories as repression, reminiscence, work of elaboration, 'deferred action.' "[3]

The notion of a deferred action has a particular relevance within the present discussion, since infantile sexuality assumes the narrative coherence of "stages" only after the fact, from the vantage-point of the Oedipus complex. The concept of perversion is equally unthinkable apart from the Oedipus complex, since it derives all its meaning and force from its relation to that structuring moment and the premium it places upon genital sexuality. It is in fact something of a misnomer to characterize infantile sexuality as "polymorphously perverse" since sexuality only becomes perverse at the point where it constitutes either a retreat from Oedipal structuration, or a transgressive acting out of its dictates. Perversion always contains the trace of Oedipus within it – it is always organized to some degree by what it subverts.

Those writers who have engaged theoretically with the topic of perversion tend to emphasize one of these aspects at the expense of the other. For Foucault, who stands at one extreme, perversion has no subversive edge; it merely serves to extend the surface upon which power is exercised. He insists in *The History of Sexuality* that "polymorphous conducts [are] actually extracted from people's bodies and from their pleasures" by what might be called "the society of the panopticon" – that perversion is "drawn out, revealed, isolated, intensified, in-corporated, by multifarious power devices."[4] At the other extreme there is a volume like the polysexuality issue of *Semiotext(e)*,[5] which heaps perversion upon perversion with wild abandon in the vain hope of burying Oedipus al-together. Neither position is adequate to the complexities of the issues involved.

Ironically, it is a rather hateful book by Janine Chasseguet-Smirgel – a book which consistently comes down on the side of the father, "mature" sexuality, and a well-fortified ego – that seems best to intuit the challenge that perversion poses to the symbolic order. Its author cautions that "The pervert is trying to free himself from the paternal universe and the constraints of the law. He wants to create a new kind of reality and to dethrone God the Father."[6] Chasseguet-Smirgel's reading of perversion suggests that its significance extends far beyond the domain of the strictly sexual (if, indeed, such a domain ever existed) – suggests, that is, that it turns aside not only from hierarchy and genital sexuality, but from the paternal signifier, the ultimate "truth" or "right." As I will attempt to demonstrate later with respect to masochism, at certain moments perversion may pose such a radical challenge to sexual difference as to enact precisely the scenario condemned by Bacon.

The theoretical interest of perversion extends even beyond the disruptive force it brings to bear upon gender. It strips sexuality of all functionality, whether biological or social; in an even more extreme fashion than "normal" sexuality, it puts the body and the world of objects to uses that have nothing whatever to do with any kind of "immanent" design or purpose. Perversion also subverts many of the binary oppositions upon which the social order rests: it crosses the boundary separating food from excrement (coprophilia); human from animal (bestiality); life from death (necrophilia); adult from child (pederasty); and pleasure from pain (masochism).

Of course not all perversions are equally subversive, or even equally interesting. It is unfortunate but not surprising that the perversion which has commandeered most of the literary and theoretical attention – sadism – is also the one which is most compatible with conventional heterosexuality. (The first thing that Freud says about sadism in *Three Essays* is that "the sexuality of most male human beings contains an element of aggressiveness – a desire to subjugate." He adds that the "biological significance" of this combination

> seems to lie in the need for overcoming the resistance of the sexual object by means other than the process of wooing. Thus sadism would correspond to an aggressive component of the sexual instinct which has become independent and exaggerated and, by displacement, has usurped the leading position.[7]

The Ego and the Id describes sadism's combination of cruelty and eroticism as a "serviceable instinctual fusion.")[8] The work of Sade commands enormous intellectual prestige – something inconceivable with the novels of Leopold von Sacher-Masoch, rescued from oblivion by Deleuze.[9] One thinks in this respect not only of Bataille,[10] Barthes,[11] and Gallop,[12] but of the massive double issue of *Obliques* dedicated to Sade, which includes materials from Benoît, Klossowski, Blanchot, Robbe-Grillet, Sollers, Paulhan, Breton, Mandiargues, Masson, and Labisse, to name only a few of its contributors.[13]

The focus of this essay is the perversion which is most commonly linked with sadism, sometimes as its complement and at other times as its instinctual opposite. I refer of course to masochism,[14] variously described by Freud as an unusually dangerous libidinal infraction,[15] and as one of the "kindliest."[16]

Three Kinds of Masochism

In his last work to deal extensively with masochism, Freud distinguishes between three forms of that perversion: "erotogenic," "feminine," and "moral."[17] However, no sooner are these distinctions enumerated than they begin to erode. Erotogenic masochism, which Freud defines as "pleasure in pain," provides the corporeal basis both for feminine and moral masochism. The tripartite division thus gives way rather quickly to one of those dualisms of which Freud is so fond, with both feminine and moral masochism "bleeding" into each other at the point where each abuts into erotogenic masochism.

The adjective "erotogenic" is one which Freud habitually links with "zone," and with which he designates a part of the body at which sexual excitation concentrates. Implicit, then, in the notion of masochism, whether feminine or moral, would seem to be the experience of corporeal pleasure, or – to be more precise – corporeal pleasure-in-pain. This stipulation poses no real conceptual difficulties with respect to the first of those categories; erotogenic masochism would seem to be literally "at the bottom" of feminine masochism, which Freud associates with fantasies of being bound and beaten, and with the desire to be "treated like . . . a naughty child."[18] It is far less clear how moral masochism could be said to have a necessary corporeal substratum, until we recall that the ego is for Freud "first and foremost a bodily ego"[19] – or, as Strachey explains in an author-ized gloss, "derived from bodily sensations, chiefly from those springing from the surface of the body."[20] If, as "The Economic Problem of Masochism" suggests, the "true" masochist "always turns his cheek whenever he has a chance of receiv-ing a blow,"[21] the moral masochist's cheek is the ego. That is the erotogenic zone of choice, the site where he or she seeks to be beaten.

Curiously, after characterizing feminine masochism as "the one that is the most accessible to our observation," Freud announces that owing to the "material at [his] command," he will limit his discussion of that libidinal economy entirely to male patients.[22] The inference is obvious: feminine masochism is a specifically *male* pathology, so named because it positions its sufferer as a woman. Freud in fact says as much:

> if one has an opportunity of studying cases in which the masochistic phantasies have been especially richly elaborated, one quickly discovers that they place the subject in a characteristically feminine situation; they signify, that is, being castrated, or copulated with, or giving birth to a baby. For this reason I have called this form of masochism, *a potiori*, as it were . . . the feminine form, although so many of its features point to infantile life.[23]

The reader is likely to object at this point that only five years earlier Freud had clearly identified the beating fantasy primarily with women. (Of the six patients upon whom he bases " 'A Child is Being Beaten,' " four are female, and only two male.)[24] And from *Three Essays* until *New Introductory Lectures*, Freud was to maintain, albeit with certain crucial qualifications, the connection between femi-ninity and masochism.[25] Yet "The Economic Problem of Masochism" is not the only major work on masochism to focus primarily upon male patients. Richard von Krafft-Ebing, who gave masochism its name and its first definition, cites thirty-three cases of male masochism, and only four of female.[26] (He also names maso-chism after a male masochist, Sacher-Masoch.) Theodor Reik's research had similar results, leading him to conclude that "the male sex is more masochistic than the female."[27] In his study of cruelty, Deleuze not only focuses exclusively on the novels of Sacher-Masoch, but elaborates a theoretical model of masochism in which the suffering position is almost necessarily male. What is to be made of this anomaly, whereby Freud designates as "feminine" a psychic disorder whose victims are primarily men? While I would certainly dispute Reik's notion that men are more masochistic than women, it does seem to me that it is only in the case of men that feminine masochism can be seen to assume pathological proportions. Although that psychic phenomenon often provides a centrally structuring element of both male and female subjectivity, it is only in the latter that it can be safely acknowledged. It is an accepted – indeed a requisite – element of "normal" female subjectivity, providing a crucial mechanism for eroticizing lack and subordination. The male subject, on the contrary, cannot avow feminine masochism without calling into question his identification with the masculine position. All of this is another way of suggesting that what is acceptable for the female subject is pathological for the male. Freud indicates as much when he tells us that whereas the beating fantasy can be effortlessly accommodated within the little girl's *positive* Oedipus complex, it can only be contained within the little boy's *negative* Oedipus complex.[28] Feminine masochism, in other words, always implies desire for the father and identification with the mother, a state of affairs which is normative for the female subject, but "deviant" for her male counterpart.

The disruptive consequences of male masochism are also underscored by an extraordinary passage from Reik, in which he distinguishes the masochistic fantasies of women from those of men:

> Compared with the masculine masochism that of women shows a somewhat attenuated, one could almost say anemic character. It is more of a trespassing of the bourgeois border, of which one nevertheless remains aware, than an invasion into enemy terrain. The woman's masochistic phantasy very seldom reaches the pitch of savage lust, of ecstasy, as does that of the man. Even the orgy in the phantasy does not ascend in so steep a curve. There is nothing in it of the wildness of the chained Prometheus, rather something of Ganymede's submission. One does not feel anything of the cyclonelike character that is so often associated with masculine masochism, that blind unrestricted lust of self-destruction. The masochistic phantasy of woman has the character of yielding and surrender rather than that of the rush ahead, of the orgiastic cumulation, of the self-abandonment of man.[29]

Reik suggests here that even the clinically masochistic woman does not really exceed her subjective limits; she merely stretches them a bit. The male masochist, on the other hand, leaves his social identity completely behind – actually abandons his "self" – and passes over into the "enemy terrain" of femininity. I will have more to say later about the "shattering"[30] qualities of male masochism, but suffice it to note here that the sexual fantasies cited by Reik fully bear out these characterizations, as do those included by Krafft-Ebing.

Not only does it turn out that feminine masochism doesn't have very much to do with women, but that moral masochism doesn't have very much to do with virtue. Although the moral masochist seems to be under the domination of a hyperdeveloped conscience, his or her desire for punishment is so great as to pose a constant temptation to perform "sinful" actions, which must then be "expiated." Freud warns that moral masochism is in fact capable of swallowing up conscience altogether, of perverting it from within.[31] This invisible sabotage occurs through the complete reversal of the process whereby the Oedipus complex was earlier "dissolved," i.e. of the operation whereby the paternal voice and imago were internalized as the super-ego. By deriving erotic gratification from the super-ego's censorship and punishment, the morally masochistic ego not only assumes an analogous position to that adopted by his or her more flamboyantly "feminine" counterpart in fantasy or actual sexual practice, but reactivates the Oedipus complex.[32]

Significantly, what flares up with renewed intensity is that form of the Oedipus complex which is positive for the female subject, but negative for the male – the form, that is, which turns upon desire for the father and identification with the mother. Freud is quite explicit about this:

> We were able to translate the expression "unconscious sense of guilt" as meaning a need for punishment at the hands of a parental power. We know that the wish, which so frequently appears in phantasies, to be beaten by the father stands very close to the other wish, to have a passive (feminine) sexual relation to him and is only a regressive distortion of it. If we insert this explanation into the content of moral masochism, its hidden meaning becomes clear to us.[33]

Thus through moral masochism the ego is beaten/loved by the father, a situation which – once again – is "normal" for the female subject, but "abnormal" for the male.

It would consequently seem that moral and feminine masochism develop out of the same "fantasmatic," to borrow a word from Laplanche and Pontalis[34] – out of the same unconsciously structuring scenario or action. However, the moral masochist remains oblivious to the passion for self-destruction that burns ferociously within; Freud observes that whereas the sadism of the super-ego "becomes for the most part glaringly conscious," the masochism of the ego "remains as a rule concealed from the subject and has to be inferred from his behavior."[35] With the feminine masochist, on the other hand, the beating fantasy assumes a shape which is available to consciousness, albeit not necessarily to rational scrutiny.

Let us look rather more closely at these two categories of masochism, and at the forms they assume in both conscious and unconscious life.

Moral Masochism

With a frankness which is more alarming than engaging, Freud acknowledges in *The Ego and the Id* that under certain circumstances the super-ego promotes a "pure culture of the death [drive]."[36] The stronger that psychic entity – i.e. the more thoroughly the subject has been subordinated to prohibition and denial – the greater the possibility that the ego will be driven to the last extremity. In moral masochism the super-ego assumes titanic proportions, but even under much more auspicious conditions its authority and severity are so considerable as to call fundamentally into question the notion of a "healthy" subject, let alone one who might be said to be in a position of mastery or control. Since conventional subjectivity so closely adjoins moral masochism, I want to examine it briefly through the grid of Freud's late topography before turning once again to its pathological correlate.

We recall that the super-ego is the agency whereby the Oedipus complex is neutralized, but its effects indefinitely prolonged. It is formed through the fantasmatization and introjection of what cannot be possessed in reality, and must consequently be renounced – the parents. This process of introjection is a complex one, more hinted at than specified in *The Ego and the Id*, but clarified somewhat in *New Introductory Lectures on Psycho-Analysis*.[37] It develops out of two sets of relationships, one of which is synonymous with the positive Oedipus complex, and the other of which is equivalent to the negative Oedipus complex, a point to which I will return in a moment. The super-ego would also seem to involve two different kinds of introjection, one of which I will characterize as "imaginary" and the other as "symbolic." What I mean by imaginary introjection is the psychic process whereby once-loved figures are taken into the self as subjective models or exempla, i.e. with the formation of that image or cluster of images in which the ego sees itself as it would like to be seen. Symbolic introjection, on the other hand, designates the psychic process whereby the subject is subordinated to the Law and the Name-of-the-Father. Although the category of the super-ego subsumes both kinds of introjection in Freud, it more specifically designates the product of symbolic introjection. Imaginary introjection, on the other hand, results in what is strictly speaking the ego-ideal.

Because the subject usually goes through a negative as well as a positive Oedipus complex, he or she enters into two sets of identifications at the end of that complex: one with the imago of the mother, and the other with the imago of the father.[38] One of these identifications is generally much stronger, and so tends to eclipse the other. If all goes according to cultural plan, the stronger identification conforms to the positive Oedipus complex. Nevertheless, both have a part to play in the agency which they form within the ego, an agency which Freud describes as the "ego ideal or super-ego," but which is more usefully designated by the first of those appellations.

The ego-ideal, I would maintain, represents one area or function of the super-ego but not its entirety, that "face" of each parent which is loved rather than feared. It articulates the ideal identity to which the ego aspires, and by which it constantly measures itself, but in relation to which it is always found wanting. It is the mirror in which the subject would like to see itself reflected, the repository of everything it admires.

Freud argues in *The Ego and the Id* that the introjection of these parental images desexualizes them, with the positive Oedipus complex canceling out the object-choice of the negative complex, and the negative Oedipus complex canceling out the object-choice of the positive complex. Desire for the father, in other words, gives way to identification with him, and desire for the mother to identification with her:

> The father-identification will preserve the object-relation to the mother which belonged to the positive complex and will at the same time replace the object-relation to the father which belonged to the inverted complex: and the same will be true, *mutatis mutandis*, of the mother-identification.[39]

This desexualization has grave consequences for the ego, since it results in an instinctual defusion; when object-libido changes to narcissistic libido (that is, when love changes to identification), the aggression which was earlier commingled with that libido also loses its purchase, and turns around upon the subject's own self. No longer in the protective custody of eros, that aggression falls under the jurisdiction of the super-ego, which directs it against the ego.[40]

Freud says some very inconsistent things about the gender of the super-ego. At some points in *The Ego and the Id* he associates it with both parents, as we have seen, but at other points he connects it exclusively with the father. In one particularly important passage, in which he places great emphasis upon the paternal identity of the super-ego, he refers to the "double aspect" of that psychic entity, an aspect which he equates with two mutually exclusive imperatives: "You *ought to be* like this (like your father)" and "You *may not be* like this (like your father) – that is, you may not do all that he does; some things are his prerogative."[41] The first of these commands clearly issues from the ego-ideal, whose function is to promote similitude between itself and the ego, but where does the second command come from?

It comes, as Freud's reference to a "double aspect" would suggest, from another component of the super-ego, and one whose gender is much more delimited than that of the ego-ideal. This other component is formed through the introjection of the symbolic father rather than his imaginary counterpart – through the internalization of the father as Law, gaze, voice-on-high. This element of the super-ego has no necessary relation to any historical figure, but its gender is irreducibly masculine, at least within the present social order. It is, quite simply, the paternal function, and the ego is always-already guilty in relation to it – guilty by virtue of Oedipal desire.

Curiously, in light of the double parental complex, with the expectation it creates that both parents would have a part to play in the constitution of the super-ego, Freud asserts in *The Ego and the Id* that this entity is always "a substitute for a longing for the father."[42] The context in which he makes this observation indicates that he is speaking not about the ego-ideal, but about what, in the strictest sense of the word, is the super-ego. Freud adds that the psychic entity which replaces desire for the father "contains the germ from which all religions have evolved," and produces "the self-judgment which declares that the ego falls short of its ideal." This passage from *The Ego and the Id* consequently has staggering implications. It suggests that what is really at issue in the dissolution of the male Oedipus complex – what really motivates Freud to insist so strenuously upon its definitive terminus – is the male subject's *homosexual attachment to the father*. The relationship of the male ego to the super-ego would seem to grow out of, and "ideally" undo, the romance between father and son – or, to be more precise, the libidinal economy of the negative Oedipus complex, which hinges upon desire for the father and identification with the mother.[43]

The situation is even more explosive than I have so far shown it to be. There is a fundamental impossibility about the position in which the male subject is held, an impossibility which has to do with the self-canceling structure of the Oedipal imperative. The only mechanism by which the son can overcome his desire for the father is to transform object libido into narcissistic libido, and in so doing to attempt to *become* the (symbolic) father. However, this metamorphosis is precisely what the super-ego prohibits by decreeing: "You may not be like [your father] . . . you may not do all that he does; some things are his prerogative." The paternal law thus promotes the very thing that its severity is calculated to prevent, a contradiction which must function as a constant inducement to reconstitute the negative Oedipus complex.

It is hardly surprising, in view of all this, that the relationship of the ego to the super-ego should be susceptible to sexualization; eros is in fact never far away. But what form does this "sexuality" take? Freud leaves us in no doubt on this particular point. In *Civilization and its Discontents* he describes a situation where the ego comes to take pleasure in the pain inflicted upon it by the super-ego – where fear of punishment gives way to the wish for it, and where cruelty and discipline come to stand for love:

> The sense of guilt, the harshness of the super-ego is...the same thing as the severity of the conscience. It is the perception which the ego has of being watched over in this way, the assessment of the tension between its own strivings and the demands of the super-ego. The fear of this critical agency (a fear which is at the bottom of the whole relationship), the need for punishment, is an instinctual manifestation on the part of the ego, which has become masochistic under the influence of a sadistic super-ego; it is a portion...of the instinct towards internal destruction present in the ego, employed for forming an erotic attachment to the super-ego.[44]

This description conforms precisely to what Freud was somewhat later to name "moral masochism." However, the condition it describes differs from "normalcy" only in degree and erotic intent. The prototypical male subject oscillates endlessly between the mutually exclusive commands of the (male) ego-ideal and the super-ego, wanting both to love the father and to be the father, but prevented from doing either. The morally masochistic male subject has given up on the desire to be the father, and may in fact have turned away from the paternal ego-ideal to the maternal one, and from identification with the father to identification with the mother. However, he burns with an exalted ardor for the rigors of the super-ego. The feminine masochist, to whom I shall return later in this chapter, literalizes the beating fantasy, and brings this cruel drama back to the body.

Christian Masochism

Theodor Reik's exhaustive study of masochism warrants some attention at this point, both because it has been so extensively mined by Deleuze and others, and because it manifests so extreme a sensitivity to the formal features of that pathology. Although it begins with a discussion of masochism as a sexual perversion – a discussion studded with some quite compelling fantasies, to one of which we will circle back later – its chief focus is moral (or what Reik calls "social") masochism. *Masochism in Sex and Society* characterizes that psychic economy as closed and self-referential, and associates it with exhibitionism or "demonstrativeness," revolutionary fervor, and "suspense" – a surprising catalogue at first glance. As I will attempt to demonstrate, certain parts of this definition clearly pertain to that model of moral masochism which Freud associates with the ego/super-ego dynamic, but other parts point toward a rather different paradigm.

   Like Freud, Reik stresses that in moral or social masochism the subject functions both as the victim and as the victimizer, dispensing with the need for an external object. Even when punishment seems to derive from the external world, it is in fact the result of a skillful unconscious manipulation of "adverse incidents."[45] The psychic economy of moral masochism is therefore strikingly self-contained:

> social masochism springs from the intermediate phase of the development of phantasy, during which the pain-inflicting and the pain-enduring person are identical, *impersonating* simultaneously object and subject [my emphasis]. Also in the masochistic attitude toward life there is generally no object discernible that imposes the

suffering and is independent of the ego. It is certainly extant in phantasy, but it does not appear in reality and remains in the twilight where it merges into the ego. This type of masochistic character behaves almost autoerotically.[46]

However, Reik does not foreground the role of the super-ego in moral masochism; the internal agency of punishment remains curiously unspecified in his text. He also gives fantasy a more privileged position within moral masochism than does Freud; indeed, he maintains that it plays as centrally structuring a role there as it does in what he calls "perverse" masochism. Here, again, the emphasis falls exclusively on the ego; even when other figures appear in these fantasies, they are in effect stories with a single character. Finally, Reik claims that the fantasies at the heart of masochism remain strictly unconscious, and that they always express the same desire – the desire to be rewarded for good behavior. Consequently, although they invariably dramatize the sufferings and defeats of the fantasizing subject, that is "only to make the final victory appear all the more glorious and triumphant."[47] ...

The second of the qualities enumerated above – exhibitionism or "demonstrativeness" – is one which Reik claims to be an indispensable feature not only of moral or social masochism, but of all masochism:

> in no case of masochism can the fact be overlooked that the suffering, discomfort, humiliation and disgrace are being shown and so to speak put on display...
> In the practices of masochists, denudation and parading with all their psychic concomitant phenomena play such a major part that one feels induced to assume a constant connection between masochism and exhibitionism.[48]

As we will see later in this chapter, the demonstrative feature occupies a prominent place within Reik's account of feminine or "perverse" masochism. However, many of the most striking examples of exhibitionism that he cites are drawn from moral or social masochism. Once again, this places him in opposition to Freud, who claims that whereas the super-ego's desire to inflict injury is usually "glaringly" obvious in moral masochism, the ego's desire for punishment generally escapes the attention both of others and of the subject itself. What are we to make of this discrepancy?

A quick survey of Reik's examples suggests that his attention may be focused upon a different variety of moral masochism than that spotlighted by Freud – that his concern may ultimately be with Christian masochism, even when he is discussing more secular instances. Not only does he devote a whole chapter to "the paradoxes of Christ," but most of the other cases of moral masochism that he cites are drawn from the lives of saints and martyrs. As in Freud's account of moral masochism, Reik's typical subject seems ardently given over to self-mortification of one kind or another (one particularly commodious sentence functions as a kind of display-window, disclosing "Benedict rolling himself in thorn hedges, Macarius sitting naked on an ant-hill, [and] Anthony flagellating himself incessantly,"[49] but the psychic dynamics are otherwise quite different.[50] To begin with, an external audience is a structural necessity, although it may be either earthly or heavenly. Second, the body is centrally on display, whether it is being consumed by ants or roasting over a fire. Finally, behind all these "scenes" or "exhibits" is the master tableau or group fantasy – Christ nailed to the cross, head wreathed in thorns and blood dripping from his impaled sides. What is being beaten here is not so much the body as the "flesh," and beyond that sin itself, and the whole fallen world.

This last target pits the Christian masochist against the society in which he or she lives, makes of that figure a rebel, or even a revolutionary of sorts. In this particular subspecies of moral masochism there would thus seem to be a strong heterocosmic impulse – the desire to remake the world in another image altogether, to forge a different cultural order. The exemplary Christian masochist also seeks to remake him or herself according to the model of the suffering Christ, the very picture of earthly divestiture and loss. Insofar as such an identification implies the complete and utter negation of all phallic values, Christian masochism has radically emasculating implications, and is in its purest forms intrinsically incompatible with the pretensions of masculinity.[51] And since its primary exemplar is a male rather than a female subject, those implications would seem impossible to ignore. Remarkably, Christianity also redefines the paternal legacy; it is after all through the assumption of his place within the divine family that Christ comes to be installed in a suffering and castrated position.

The demonstrative feature, as I have been implicitly arguing, works very much against Reik's premise that the driving force behind moral masochism is the victory and reward of the ego. Reik suggests at one point that the moral masochist seeks to be "raised on an invisible pedestal,"[52] but the passage I quoted a moment ago thoroughly belies this formulation. In that passage, Reik not only associates all forms of masochism with exhibitionism or self-display, but he acknowledges that what is thus rendered visible is the subject's "suffering," "discomfort," "humiliation," and "disgrace" rather than its grandeur or its triumph. The demonstrative feature also runs counter to the notion that moral masochism is an entirely self-contained system, since at least within Reik's Christian examples the gaze comes dramatically into play, either in a heavenly or an earthly guise. There are also other ways in which moral masochism opens onto the world on which it ostensibly forecloses, whether it assumes the form described by Freud, or that theorized by Reik. The super-ego is produced through the introjection of the paternal function, and the ego through the subject's identification both with its own corporeal imago, and with a whole range of other external images. The interior drama is thus the refraction of a familial structure, which itself interlocks with the whole social order. Christian masochism, as we have seen, involves a similar identificatory system.[53]

The last of the qualities associated by Reik with moral masochism – suspense – would seem to be at the center of all forms of masochism, in addition to being one of the conditions out of which conventional subjectivity develops. Reik rings some complex changes on this word, which he connects with uncertainty, dilatoriness, pleasurable and unpleasurable anticipation, apparent interminability, and – above all – excitation. Masochism exploits all these themes in one way or another because it always seeks to prolong preparatory detail and ritual at the expense of climax or consummation. Since in moral masochism this implies the endless postponement of the moment at which suffering yields to reward, and victory to defeat, suspense clearly works to prioritize pain over pleasure, and so to further undermine the ego. . . .

Freud's moral masochist also lives in suspense, but without the promise of a redemptive end-pleasure. Here suspense has a double face. It signifies both the endless postponement of libidinal gratification, and the perpetual state of anxiety and apprehension which is the result of that renunciation and of the super-ego's relentless surveillance. Of course these forms of suspense are not limited to the moral masochist; they are also part of the cultural legacy of even the most conventionally structured of subjects. All that distinguishes the former from the latter is that his or her ego seeks to increase rather than decrease that tension, whether through the commission of misdeeds which will then elicit punishment, or – more classically – through the punctiliousness of its obedience. Freud warns us that the more perfectly the ego conforms to the super-ego's mandates, the more ferocious and exacting that censoring mechanism becomes.[54] It would thus seem that the ego's "goodness" can actually become a request to be beaten. The moral masochist, in short, seeks to intensify both forms of the suspense which is so (seemingly) intolerable to the "ordinary" subject. Freud is quite explicit about the challenge which this poses to the stability and robustness of the ego, remarking in "The Economic Problem of Masochism" that "In order to provoke punishment from [the super-ego], the masochist must do what is inexpedient, must act against his own interests, must ruin the prospects which open out to him in the real world and must, perhaps, destroy his own real existence."[55]

Feminine Masochism

Let us now turn to feminine masochism via " 'A Child is Being Beaten,' " which is without a doubt the most crucial text for understanding that perversion. Significantly, although Freud focuses primarily upon female patients there, he manages to articulate the masochistic desire he attributes to them only through recourse to one of his male patients, who gives voice to what they cannot – the second phase of the beating fantasy.[56] Let us effect a reverse displacement, and approach the male version of the beating fantasy through its female counterpart. Doing so will permit us to see how fully that fantasy subverts sexual difference.

The female fantasy consists of three phases, the first and third of which are available to analysis, but the second of which remains unconscious. Here is the complete sequence, after it has been "doctored" by Freud (the phrases within square brackets represent either his interpolations, or additions made by the patient at his prompting):

Phase 1: "My father is beating the child [whom I hate]."
Phase 2: "I am being beaten by my father."
Phase 3: "Some boys are being beaten. [I am probably looking on.]"

Freud says of the first phase that it is neither sexual nor sadistic, but "the stuff from which both will later come."[57] He adds that it may not even constitute part of the fantasy proper, but may simply be a memory out of which the fantasy subsequently develops. It is savored for the erotic value it retroactively assumes, a value which Freud translates with the phrase: "My father does not love this other child, *he loves only me*."

Oedipal desire and its prohibition intervene between phase 1 and 2 of the fantasy. By inserting herself into the imaginary scene in the position earlier occupied by the other child, the girl submits herself to punishment at the hands of the father, and so atones for her incestuous guilt. This new fantasy evokes intensely pleasurable feelings, however, pointing to an erotic as well as a punitive content. Phase 2 – "I am being beaten by my father" – thus functions as a mechanism for bringing about a regression to an earlier stage of sexuality; the desire which is blocked at the genitals, in other words, finds expression instead at the anus.

On account of its prohibited content, phase 2 undergoes repression. It is replaced at the level of consciousness by the third variant, which disguises the identity both of the person being beaten and of the one administering the punishment. A group of boys now replaces the little girl, and a paternal representative supplants the father. The fantasizing subject is inscribed into this scenario as an ambiguous spectator.[58] Phases 1 and 3 are ostensibly sadistic. Only phase 2 is unequivocally masochistic.

In a move equivalent in daring to Monsieur D's open concealment of the purloined letter in Poe's short story, Freud disarms his critic by acknowledging what might otherwise have been discovered about phase 2: he admits, that is, to having fabricated that sequence in the fantasy upon which he bases his entire interpretation:

> This second phase is the most important and the most momentous of all. But we may say of it in a certain sense that it has never had a real existence. It is never remembered, it has never succeeded in becoming conscious. It is a construction of analysis, but it is no less of a necessity on that account.[59]

Every time I read this passage, I find myself momentarily paralyzed both by the audacity of the confession, and by the realization that to challenge Freud's right to speak in this way *for* his female patients would be to place my rhetorical weight on the side of the "real" as against the "constructed," the "authentic" against the "inauthentic."

Yet, struggle as I inevitably do against this paralysis, I can find nothing to dispute in Freud's account of phase 2, apart from the fact that he finds what he is looking for in one of his male patient's case histories. The change from the active to the passive form of the verb "to beat" – from phase 1 to phase 3 – can only have been effected through the mediation of the instinctual vicissitude indicated in phase 2. In other words, the transition from phase 1 to phase 3 moves the subject from heteroaggression to what appears to be sadism, and hence from the dimension of simple self-preservation to that of sexuality. As Laplanche has compellingly argued, that movement necessitates not only the propping of sexuality upon aggression (i.e. upon the death drive), but the turning around of that sexualized aggression upon the fantasizing subject's own self.[60] It is only in a second movement that the now eroticized aggression can be redirected outward once again, this time in the form of sadism. I would therefore agree with Freud that what he identifies as phase 2 is behind phase 3, and that implicit in the later moment is a masochistic identification with the beaten children.

At the same time, I do not think that phases 2 and 3 can be completely collapsed, or that the wish for pleasurable pain exhausts the latter's meaning. Greater attention should be paid here to the manifest content of the conscious fantasy, and to its substitution of boys for a girl. The final phase attests to three transgressive desires, not one of which Freud remarks upon, but which clamor loudly for my attention: to the desire that it be boys rather than girls who be loved/disciplined in this way; to the desire to be a boy while being so treated by the father; and, finally, to the desire to occupy a male subject-position in some more general sense, but one under the sign of femininity rather than that of masculinity.

These three desires clearly converge around one thing: a narcissistic investment in a subject-position which it would be transgressive for a man to occupy, but which is almost unthinkable for a woman, since it implies an identification with male homosexuality. Why should this identification fall so far outside the social pale? Because even what generally passes for "deviance" is held to a recognizable and "manageable" paradigm, i.e. to one that reinforces the binary logic of sexual difference, despite inverting its logic. Thus when a woman doesn't identify with a classically female position, she is expected to identify with a classically male one, and *vice versa* in the case of a man. The female version of the beating fantasy, then, attests to the desire for imaginary variations that fall outside the scope of the psychoanalytic paradigm.

Freud comes close on two occasions to commenting upon the last of the wishes enumerated above, but both times he pulls back from what he is on the verge of discovering. At the end of Section IV he observes that

> When [girls] turn away from their incestuous love for their father, with its genital significance, they easily abandon their feminine role. They spur their "masculinity complex" . . . into activity, and from that point forward only want to be boys. For that reason the whipping-boys who represent them are boys too.[61]

Here the contradiction between having a "masculinity complex" and representing oneself as a group of "whipping-boys" goes unnoted by Freud. In a subsequent passage, however, he points out that the girl's identification with the male position does not imply an identification with activity ("[the girl] turns herself in phantasy into a man, without herself becoming active in the masculine way.")[62]

In Section VI of "'A Child is Being Beaten,'" Freud suggests that the female subject occupies not only one, but *two* unconventionally masculine positions in phase 3 of the beating fantasy. In the course of describing the various shifts that occur over the history of the beating fantasy, he explicitly states that in phase 3 the girl turns herself into the group of boys.[63] A few pages later, however, he indicates that in her capacity as onlooker of the beating scene, the girl occupies another position indicative of a masculinity under erasure. After observing that the girl "turns herself in phantasy into a man without herself becoming active in the masculine way," he adds that she is "no longer anything but a spectator of the event which takes the place of a sexual act."[64]

The first of these masculine positions – that of (passive) male homosexuality – is the position into which the male subject inserts himself in the masculine version of the beating fantasy, and there it has an emphatically maternal significance; Freud maintains that it is "derived from a feminine attitude toward his father,"[65] i.e. from the negative Oedipus complex. The male subject thus secures access to femininity through identification with the mother. By turning herself in fantasy into the "whipping-boys," the female subject is in turn given imaginary access to this "borrowed" femininity through the image of the male body. Femininity is thus both radically denatured, and posited as the privileged reference point by means of the curious relay that is set up between these two versions of the beating fantasy. But there is also an ineluctable difference at work here, since it is clearly not the same thing, socially or even psychically, for the girl to be loved/beaten by the father as it is for the boy. Through her identification with the "whipping-boys" in phase 3, the girl establishes an imaginary connection not only with a feminized masculinity, but with that difference. Is not this the beginning of a sexual relation?

It is perhaps less evident how the girl's spectatorial position in phase 3 also aligns her with an "unmanly" masculinity. Voyeurism has been heavily coded within western culture as a male activity, and associated with aggression and sadism. Here, however, masculinity, aggression, and sadism are definitively elsewhere in the scene, concentrated in the figure of the punishing father-surrogate. Like the child in the primal scene, the shadowy onlooker is more mastered than mastering. The tentativeness with which Freud's female patients insert themselves into this position ("I am probably looking on") points to the irresolute character of the position itself, which is less the site of a controlling gaze than a vantage point from which to identify with the group of boys.

Before leaving the female beating fantasy, I want to note that the pronoun "I" is conspicuously missing from those parts of it which are available to consciousness, except in the adumbrative qualification about spectatorship, and in fact figures prominently only in that phrase which is "a construction of psychoanalysis" – a detail which [a later chapter of *Male Subjectivity at the Margins*] will attribute to hetero-pathic identification. Heteropathic identification is the obverse of idiopathic identi-fication; whereas the latter conforms to an incorporative model, constituting the self at the expense of the other who is in effect "swallowed," the former subscribes to an exteriorizing logic, and locates the self at the site of the other. In heteropathic identification one lives, suffers, and experiences pleasure through the other.[66] In phase 3 of the female beating fantasy, that other is of course the male subject.

Within the male sequence, all three phases, including the conscious one, begin with the assertion of pronominal possession. The subject-position which each phase maps out, however, bends that "I" in a "feminine" direction:

Phase 1: "I am being loved by my father."
Phase 2: "I am being beaten by my father."
Phase 3: "I am being beaten by my mother."

The beating fantasies confided to Freud by his male patients have also been subjected to far less censorship and distortion than those recorded by his female patients. The only significant difference between the conscious scenario (phase 3) and the unconscious scenario (phase 2) bears upon the identity of the person administering the punishment; the conscious fantasy translates into the verbal formula "I am being beaten by my mother," whereas the unconscious one reads "I am being beaten by my father".[67] Even this disguise is lightly worn, since the beating woman manifests such aggressively masculine qualities as to unmistakably resemble the paternal figure she replaces. (Phase 1, which is presumed to lie concealed behind phase 2, is not available to consciousness.)

Finally, although some effort is made to conceal the *homosexual* content of the conscious fantasy, no corresponding attempt is made to hide its *masochistic* content; the two male patients discussed by Freud, like those cited by Krafft-Ebing, Reik, and

Deleuze, openly "flaunt" their desire for punishment and degradation both within their conscious fantasies and within their sexual practices. We clearly have an extreme instance here of what Reik calls the "demonstrative feature." In the conscious fantasies of the four female patients, on the other hand, masochism is concealed behind sadism, even though it is more compatible with their cultural position.

What is it precisely that the male masochist displays, and what are the consequences of this self-exposure? To begin with, he acts out in an insistent and exaggerated way the basic conditions of cultural subjectivity, conditions that are normally disavowed; he loudly proclaims that his meaning comes to him from the Other, prostrates himself before the gaze even as he solicits it, exhibits his castration for all to see, and revels in the sacrificial basis of the social contract. The male masochist magnifies the losses and divisions upon which cultural identity is based, refusing to be sutured or recompensed. In short, he radiates a negativity inimical to the social order....

The propensity for impersonation is even more marked in feminine masochism than it is in moral (or at least Christian) masochism, which is not surprising given that it is centrally concerned with subject-positioning and gender "roles." [An omitted portion of this chapter] looked closely at one quite flamboyant mental masquerade, a masquerade which changes its "author's" age, his historical moment, and his national identity, as well as the circumstances of his life (and death). The creator of the Moloch fantasy generates other identities for himself as well, including one where he is a Portuguese prisoner of the Aztecs who is first forced to watch a number of other men be skinned alive, and is then subjected to the same fate. Krafft-Ebing recounts numerous cases of male masochists who act out the part of a slave or a page, and others where the preferred role is that of a dog, a horse, a slaughter animal, a count, a surface (such as a floor) on which women walk, and a receptacle for urine, excrement, and menstrual blood. The "hero" of Sacher-Masoch's *Venus in Furs* assumes the disguise of a servant for much of that novel, and – near the end – that of a bull.[68]

The sexual practitioners of feminine masochism generally extend the masquerade to include the person inflicting the pain or humiliation as well, and indeed the entire "scene" of the erotic adventure, in effect remaking the world. This heterocosmic impulse is . . . strikingly evident in *Venus in Furs*, where Severin and Wanda actually leave the country in which they are living for one in which they will be better able to pass as mistress and slave. The crucial question to ask here is whether the heterocosmic impulse exhausts itself altogether in the boudoir, or whether the "play" spills over into social intercourse as well, contaminating the proprieties of gender, class, and race.[69]

Freud maintains that it is not only at the level of his sexual life, but at that of his fantasmatic and his *moi* that the male masochist occupies a female position. In " 'A Child is Being Beaten,' " he writes that femininity assumes the status of a "subjective conviction" for the male masochist,[70] he suggests, that is, that the male masochist believes himself to be a woman at the deepest level of his desire and his identity. Near the end of " 'A Child is Being Beaten,' " he also notes that the fantasy of corporal punishment manifests itself only in "unmanly boys" and "unwomanly girls," and that it is "a trait of femininity in the boy and of masculinity in the girl which must be made responsible" for the construction of the fantasy.[71] The degree to which this femininity manifests itself in the conscious existence of the male masochist depends, of course, upon the strength of the "masculine protest"[72] which he brings to bear against it – upon whether or not he fortifies himself against the "woman" within. It is, however, a significant fact that phase 3 of the male version of the beating fantasy makes no attempt to disguise the masochistic position of the fantasizing subject, although it is somewhat more reticent about the latter's homosexuality. Ironically, moreover, the transformation of the agent of punishment from the father to the mother actually functions to accentuate the male masochist's femininity, since it effects so dramatic a reversal of traditional gender roles.

Freud makes the astonishing observation in "'A Child is Being Beaten'" that there is no trace within the masochistic unconscious, whether male or female, of the wish to be loved by the father – of the taboo desire from which the entire condition of masochism ostensibly derives. In regressing back to the anal stage of sexuality, the masochist apparently manages to erase all record of that variant of Oedipal genitality which is generally held to be positive for the girl, and negative for the boy:

> Whatever is repressed from consciousness or replaced in it by something else remains intact and potentially operative in the unconscious. The effect of *regression* to an earlier stage of the sexual organization is quite another matter. As regards this we are led to believe that the state of things changes in the unconscious as well. Thus in both sexes the masochistic phantasy of being beaten by the father, though not the passive phantasy of being loved by him, lives on in the unconscious after repression has taken place.[73]

If Freud is to be believed on this point, male masochism constitutes a veritable hermeneutic scandal. The passage I have just quoted suggests that the first phase of the male beating fantasy ("I am being loved by my father") is *entirely* a construction of psychoanalysis, and in a much more extreme sense than the second stage of the female sequence can be said to be. It also suggests that the unconscious significance of the fantasy is *completely* exhausted by phase 2, which as I have already noted differs from phase 3 only with respect to the gender of the person administering the punishment. Here there is no radical divide of manifest from latent content. The door to the unconscious need not be picked; it is already slightly ajar, and ready to yield at the slightest pressure.

There are other implications as well. If no record can be found within his unconscious of the desire to be genitally loved by the father, the male masochist cannot be domesticated by substituting the penis for the whip. His (barely) repressed desire runs directly counter to any reconciliation of father and son, attesting irrefutably to the violence of the familial and cultural contract. His sexuality, moreover, must be seen to be entirely under the sway of the death drive, devoid of any possible productivity or use value. It is no wonder that Freud pulls back from promising a psychoanalytic "cure" in the case of the feminine masochist.[74]

Notes

1 Sigmund Freud, *Three Essays on the Theory of Sexuality*, in *The Standard Edition of the Complete Psychological Works*, trans. James Strachey (London: Hogarth Press, 1953), vol. 7, p. 150.
2 Freud, *Three Essays*, p. 149.

3 Jean Laplanche, *Life and Death in Psychoanalysis*, trans. Jeffrey Melhman (Baltimore: Johns Hopkins University Press, 1976), pp. 28, 30.

4 Michel Foucault, *The History of Sexuality, Volume I: An Introduction*, trans. Robert Hurley (New York: Vintage Books, 1980), pp. 47–8.

5 *Semiotext(e)*, 4/1 (1981).

6 Janine Chasseguet-Smirgel, *Creativity and Perversion* (New York: Norton, 1984), p. 12.

7 Freud, *Three Essays*, pp. 157–8.

8 Sigmund Freud, *The Ego and the Id, Standard Edition*, vol. 19, p. 41.

9 Gilles Deleuze, *Masochism: An Interpretation of Coldness and Cruelty*, trans. Jean McNeil (New York: George Braziller, 1971).

10 See George Bataille, "The Use Value of D. A. F. de Sade," in *Visions of Excess: Selected Writings, 1927–1939*, trans. Allan Stoekl (Minneapolis: University of Minnesota Press, 1985), pp. 91–102, and *Literature and Evil*, trans. Alastair Hamilton (New York: Urizen Books, 1973), pp. 83–107.

11 Roland Barthes, *Sade, Fourier, Loyola*, trans. Richard Miller (New York: Hill and Wang, 1976), pp. 15–37, and 123–71.

12 Jane Gallop, *Intersections: A Reading of Sade with Bataille, Blanchot, and Klossowski* (Lincoln: University of Nebraska Press, 1981).

13 *Obliques*, 12 & 13 (1977).

14 I have returned frequently to this topic over the past eight years, but always through a literary or cinematic intermediary. See, for instance, "*Histoire d'O*: The Story of a Disciplined and Punished Body," *Enclitic*, 7/2 (1983), pp. 63–81; "Changing the Fantasmatic Scene," *Framework*, 20 (1983), pp. 27–36; "Male Subjectivity and the Celestial Suture: *It's a Wonderful Life*," *Framework*, 14 (1981), pp. 16–21 . . . and "Masochism and Subjectivity," *Framework*, 12 (1980), pp. 2–9. This time the approach will be more insistently theoretical and speculative.

15 Sigmund Freud, "The Economic Problem of Masochism," in *Standard Edition*, vol. 19, p. 159.

16 See Freud, "Economic Problem of Masochism," p. 166, and "Dostoevsky and Parricide," *Standard Edition*, vol. 21, p. 179.

17 Freud, "Economic Problem of Masochism," p. 161.

18 Ibid., p. 162.

19 Freud, *The Ego and the Id*, p. 26.

20 Ibid., p. 26f.

21 Freud, "Economic Problem of Masochism," p. 165.

22 Ibid., p. 161.

23 Ibid., p. 162.

24 Sigmund Freud, " 'A Child is Being Beaten,' " *Standard Edition*, vol. 17, pp. 175–204.

25 The most crucial of Freud's qualifications on this point is of course central to the present discussion – the qualification that whereas "femininity" may indeed imply passivity, and in many cases masochism, there is no necessary connection between "woman" and "femininity." See *Civilization and its Discontents*, Standard Edition, vol. 21, pp. 105f. for an extremely interesting discussion of the slippage between these last two categories.

26 Richard von Krafft-Ebing, *Psychopathia Sexualis: A Medico-Forensic Study*, trans. Franklin S. Klaf (New York: Stein and Day, 1965), pp. 86–143.

27 Theodor Reik, *Masochism in Sex and Society*, trans. Margaret H. Beigel and Gertrud M. Kurth (New York: Grove Press, 1962), p. 243.

28 Freud, "A Child is Being Beaten," pp. 194–8.

29 Reik, *Masochism*, p. 216.

30 I borrow the concept of "shattering" from Leo Bersani, who develops it at length in his important book, *The Freudian Body: Psychoanalysis and Art* (New York: Columbia University Press, 1986).

31 Freud, "The Economic Problem of Masochism," p. 169.
32 Ibid.
33 Ibid.
34 In *The Language of Psycho-Analysis*, trans. Donald Nicholson-Smith (New York: Norton, 1973), Jean Laplanche and J.-B. Pontalis suggest that "the subject's life as a whole...is seen to be shaped and ordered by what might be called, in order to stress this structuring action, a 'phantasmatic.' This should not be conceived of merely as a thematic – not even as one characterized by distinctly specific traits for each subject – for it has its own dynamic, in that the phantasy structures seek to express themselves, to find a way out into consciousness and action, and they are constantly drawing in new material" (p. 317)....
35 Freud, "Economic Problem of Masochism," p. 169.
36 Freud, *The Ego and the Id*, p. 53.
37 Sigmund Freud, *New Introductory Lectures on Psycho-Analysis*, Standard Edition, vol. 22, pp. 60–8.
38 Freud, *The Ego and the Id*, pp. 31–4.
39 Ibid., p. 34.
40 Ibid., pp. 54–5.
41 Ibid., p. 34.
42 Ibid., p. 37.
43 For an extended discussion of the female version of the negative Oedipus complex, and its relation to feminism, see chapters 4 and 5 of my *The Acoustic Mirror: The Female Voice in Psychoanalysis and Cinema* (Bloomington: Indiana University Press, 1988). For a further analysis of the male version, see Bersani, *The Freudian Body*, p. 49...
44 Freud, *Civilization and its Discontents*, p. 136.
45 Reik, *Masochism*, p. 304.
46 Ibid., p. 333.
47 Ibid., pp. 314, 315.
48 Ibid., p. 72.
49 Ibid., p. 351.
50 There are striking similarities between the degradations Reik associates with Christian masochism, and those Krafft-Ebing links with the sexual perversion of masochism. See, for instance, Cases 80, 81, 82, and 83 in *Psychopathia Sexualis*.
51 Of course, Christian masochism rarely exists in the form I have described here. It is more often deployed as the vehicle for worldly or heavenly advancement, i.e. put to extrinsic uses. Observing the expedient uses to which such suffering can be put, Reik mistakenly assumes self-advancement to be an inherent part of Christian masochism.
52 Reik, *Masochism*, p. 315.
53 Here, too, there is an implied familial prototype, that provided by the relation of God to Christ. The Christian models himself on the latter, and directs against himself what is in effect a "divine" punishment.
54 Freud, *The Ego and the Id*, p. 54.
55 Freud, "Economic Problem of Masochism," pp. 169–70.
56 Freud constructs phase 2 of the girl's beating fantasy by inverting phase 3 of the boy's fantasy, a discursive action that points to the asymmetrical symmetry of the two sequences.
57 Freud, "A Child is Being Beaten," p. 187.
58 For a different account of "A Child is Being Beaten" in general, and phase 3 of the girl's fantasy in particular, see D. N. Rodowick, *The Difficulty of Difference: Psychoanalysis, Sexual Difference, and Film Theory* (New York: Routledge, 1991), pp. 1–17.
59 Freud, "A Child is Being Beaten," p. 185.

60 Laplanche, *Life and Death*, pp. 85–102.

61 Freud, "A Child is Being Beaten," p. 191.

62 Ibid., p. 199.

63 Ibid., p. 196

64 Ibid., p. 199.

65 Ibid., p. 198.

66 The concepts of idiopathic and heteropathic identification derive from Max Scheler, *The Nature of Sympathy*, trans. Peter Heath (Hamden: Conn.: Archon, 1970).

67 Freud, "A Child is Being Beaten," p. 198.

68 Leopold von Sacher-Masoch, *Venus in Furs*, in Deleuze, *Masochism*, pp. 80–130; Deleuze, *Masochism*, p. 96.

69 Mary Russo has some very thoughtful things to say about the social and political implications of masquerade in "Female Grotesques: Carnival and Theory," in *Feminist Studies/Critical Studies*, ed. Teresa de Lauretis (Bloomington: Indiana University Press, 1986), pp. 213–29.

70 Freud, "A Child is Being Beaten," p. 197.

71 Ibid., p. 202.

72 In " 'A Child is Being Beaten,' " Freud writes that "it seems to be only with the girl that the masculine protest is attended with complete success. . . . With the boy the result is not entirely satisfactory; the feminine line is not given up, and the boy is certainly not 'on top' in his conscious masochistic phantasy" (p. 203). In an essay critiquing the article from which this chapter derives, Paul Smith argues that masochism is never more than a passing moment within male subjectivity ("Action Movie Hysteria, or Eastwood Bound," *Differences*, 1/3 (1989), p. 106). While I am clearly in disagreement with this formulation, I do concur with his claim that masochism is generally narratively contained within Hollywood cinema. This, however, tells us less about the place of masochism within male subjectivity than about the normalizing operations of the dominant fiction.

73 Freud, "A Child is Being Beaten," pp. 199–200.

74 Ibid., p. 197.

3

Subject Honor, Object Shame

Roger Lancaster

Before the wide use of the word heterosexual, I suggest, women and men did not mutually lust with the same profound, sure sense of normalcy that followed the distribution of "heterosexual" as a universal sanctifier.

According to this proposal, women and men make their own sexual histories. But they do not produce their sex lives just as they please. They make their sexualities within a particular mode of organization given by the past and altered by their changing desire, their present power and activity, and their vision of a better world.

(Jonathan Ned Katz, "The Invention of Heterosexuality")

What is machismo? Why do Nicaraguan men behave as they do (as Nicaraguan women vigorously complain): beating their wives, simultaneously fathering children in multiple households, abandoning compañeras and children, gambling away hard-earned money, and drinking to excess? And why did a decade of efforts to roll back the culture of machismo achieve so few tangible results?

An easy answer would be that the strain on Nicaragua's economic resources has made social restructuring impossible for the time being. That is indeed a partial answer. For those men already engaged in the culture of machismo, what AMNLAE and the Sandinistas call "responsibility" would prove costly even under the best of circumstances. Under the current economy of scarcity, such restructuring is probably prohibitively costly. Perhaps under a recovered economy, men might be more likely to support the children they father, and perhaps under better circumstances, sex education and contraception might make alternatives to the status quo available. But amid the dislocations of war and hyperinflation, and among all the personal turmoils thus engendered, it is difficult to speak realistically of any systematic restructuring of the personal life and of personal relations. Richard Adams's survey of Nicaraguan society suggests that its "loose family structure" is in part the outcome of the same sort of social and historical dislocations that are occurring today (1956: 892; 1957: 189–95). In the earlier instance, these dislocations revolved around the rise of *latifundismo* (the concentration of land into fewer and fewer hands), the uprooting of traditional peasants, and the emergence of mobile rural labor patterns. In the present instance, the dislocations

Reprinted from *Life is Hard: Machismo, Danger, and the Intimacy of Power in Nicaragua* (Berkeley: University of California Press, 1992), pp. 235–45, 247–55, 265–73, 274–8, 313–19.

center around the destruction of Nicaragua's economy and the emergence of labor mobility on a global scale. The real extent to which war and economic collapse perpetuate the status quo in gender relations is at present an open question; the answer will await the social and economic recovery of Nicaragua.

But there is more to the matter than that, for the arrangement of interpersonal relations depends on far more than the immediate state of the economy. A certain kind of standard Marxist political economy – itself a critique and revision of classical political economy – would perhaps relegate machismo to the level of an ideological or cultural superstructure. But the question of machismo cannot be addressed adequately if it is viewed as an ideology in the classical sense of the term. Machismo is not a set of erroneous ideas that somehow got lodged in people's heads. Rather, it is an organization of social relations that generates ideas. Machismo, therefore, is more than an "effect" produced by other material relations. It has its own materiality, its own power to produce effects. The resilience of machismo as a system has nothing to do with the tendency of ideological systems to "lag" behind changes in the system of economic production, for machismo is more than a "reflection" of economic practices. It is its own economy.

As in the case of colorism, and no less than in economic production proper, machismo produces and circulates values: the value of men and women. What is ultimately produced – in all three systems – is one's social standing. Machismo is more, too, than a political conceit of the body politic. It conceives myriad politics and inscribes all bodies with power. Machismo is a real political economy of the body, a field of power entailing every bit as much force as economic production.

Nor can the question of machismo be fully addressed as a matter of relations between men and women. It is that, but it is also more. Machismo (no less than Anglo-American concepts of masculinity and appropriate sexuality) is not exclusively or even primarily a means of structuring power relations between men and women. It is a means of structuring power between and among *men*. Like drinking, gambling, risk taking, asserting one's opinion, and fighting, the conquest of women is a feat performed with two audiences in mind: first, other men, to whom one must constantly prove one's masculinity and virility; and second, oneself, to whom one must also show all the signs of masculinity. Machismo, then, is a matter of constantly asserting one's masculinity by way of practices that show the self to be "active," not "passive" (as defined in a given milieu). On the surface, it is a primarily gestural system, for it is only through the competent performance of certain stereotyped gestures that machismo may be read, both by others and by the actor himself. Every gesture, every posture, every stance, every way of acting in the world is immediately seen as "masculine" or "feminine," depending on whether it connotes activity or passivity. Every action is governed by a relational system – a code – that produces its meanings out of the subject matter of the body, its form, its engagement with other bodies. As a gestural system, machismo has a steep temporal dimension, and yesterday's victories count for little tomorrow. Every act is, effectively, part of an ongoing exchange system between men in which women figure as intermediaries. To maintain one's masculinity, one must successfully come out on top of these exchanges. To lose in this ongoing exchange system entails a loss of face and thus a loss of masculinity. The threat is a total loss of status, whereby one descends to the zero point of the game and either literally or effectively becomes a cochón.

The cochón, itself a product of machismo, thus grounds the system of machismo and holds it in its place – just as machismo grounds the cochón and holds him in his place.

The Social Construction of Sexual Practices

The *cochón*, at first glance, might be interpreted as a Nicaraguan "folk category." The noun itself appears in both masculine (*el cochón*) and feminine (*la cochón, la cochona*) genders; either case typically refers to a male. The term is loosely translated as "queer" or "faggot" by English-speaking visitors; educated Nicaraguans, if they are fluent in international terminologies, are apt to translate the term in a similar (but more polite) fashion, giving "gay" or "homosexual" as its English equivalents. It becomes clear on closer inspection, however, that the term differs markedly from its Anglo-American counterparts of whatever shade. (And therein lies the danger of treating it as a folk category, which suggests that it is simply the rural version of some larger cosmopolitan concept.) In the first place, the term is not always as derogatory as the slanderous English versions are. Of course, it can be derogatory, and it almost always is. However, it can also be neutral and descriptive. I have even heard it employed in a particular sort of praising manner by ordinary Nicaraguan men: for instance, "We must go to Carnaval this year and see the cochones. The cochones there are very, very beautiful."[1]

Second, and more important, the term marks and delimits a set of sexual practices that partially overlaps but is clearly not identical to our own notion of the homosexual. The term specifies only certain practices in certain contexts. Some acts that we would describe as homosexual bear neither stigma nor an accompanying identity of any special sort whatsoever; others clearly mark their practitioner as a cochón.

If homosexuality in the United States is most characteristically regarded as an oral phenomenon, Nicaraguan homosexual practice is understood in terms of an anal emphasis. The lexicon of male insult clearly reflects this anal emphasis in Nicaraguan culture, even as the North American lexicon generally reflects an oral orientation. *Cocksucker* is the most common sexually explicit pejorative in the United States. Although equivalents to this term are sometimes used in Nicaragua, men there are more likely to be insulted in reference to anal intercourse. The dominant assumptions of everyday discourse, too, reflect the assumption of privileged, primary, and defining routes of intercourse in each case. That is, in Anglo-American culture, orality defines the homosexual; whatever else he might or might not do, a gay man is understood as someone who engages in oral intercourse with other men. In Nicaragua, anal intercourse defines the cochón; whatever else he might or might not do, a cochón is tacitly understood as someone who engages in anal intercourse with other men. But more is involved here than a mere shifting of the dominant sites of erotic practice or a casting of stigma with reference to different body parts. With the exception of a few well-defined contexts (e.g., prisons) where the rule may be suspended, homosexual activity of any sort defines the Anglo-American homosexual. In Nicaragua, by contrast, it is the passive role in anal intercourse that defines the cochón. Oral or manual practices receive scant social attention; everyday speech does not treat them in great detail, and non-anal practices appear far less significant in the repertoire of actually practiced homosexual activities.

The term *cochón* itself appears to indicate the nature of that status and role. None of my informants was certain about the origin of the term; it is *Nica*, a word peculiar to the Nicaraguan dialect of Spanish. Moreover, one encounters different pronunciations in various neighborhoods, classes, and regions, so there can really be no agreed spelling of the word: I have heard it rendered *cuchón, culchón*, and even *colchón*.[2] The last suggests a possible origin of the word: *colchón* means "mattress." As one of my informants suggested when prompted to speculate on the origin of the word, "You get on top of him like a mattress."

In neighboring Honduras, the point is made with even greater linguistic precision. There, "passive" partners in anal intercourse are known as *culeros*, from the term *culo*, meaning "ass," with the standard ending -*ero*. A *zapatero* is a man who works with shoes (*zapatos*); a *culero* is a man whose sexual activity and identity are defined as anal. As in Nicaragua, the act of insertion carries with it no special identity, much less stigma.

"You get on top of him like a mattress" summarizes the nature of the cochón's status as well as any phrase could, but it also points to the question, *Who* gets on top of him like a mattress? The answer is, Not only other cochones. Indeed, relationships between cochones seem relatively rare and, when they occur, are generally short-term. It is typically a noncochón male who plays the active role in sexual intercourse: a machista or an *hombre-hombre*, a "manly man." Both terms designate a "masculine man" in the popular lexicon; cochones frequently use either term to designate potential sexual partners. Relationships of this type, between cochones and hombres-hombres, may be of any number of varieties: one-time-only affairs; purchased sex, with the purchase running in either direction (although most typically it is the cochón who pays); protracted relationships running weeks or months; or full-scale emotional commitments lasting years.

The last sort is preferred but carries its own type of difficulties, its own particular sadness. As one of my informants related, "I once had a lover for five continuous years. He was a sergeant in the military, an hombre-hombre. During this period of time he had at least fifteen girl friends, but I was his only male lover. He visited me and we made love almost every day. You have asked me if there is love and romance in these relations; yes, there is. He was very romantic, very tender, and very jealous. But he is married now and I rarely see him."

The actual range of sexual practices employed by cochones may be wider than the prevailing sexual ideology would suggest. My research did not involve extensive or numerous interviews with members of this sexual minority; rather, my strategy was to explore the general social conception of sexual categories and practices, primarily as maintained by my usual network of informants. Systematic investigation of the lives, beliefs, and practices of cochones might well yield very different results. It goes almost without saying that the stigmatized and oppressed resist, reinterpret, and recode the social conventions they find around them (Certeau 1984). Notwithstanding, from a sociological point of view, it would seem necessary first to understand the social conventions – the entrenched code – that situate resistance before understanding strategies and tactics of resistance proper.[3]

In spite of my research strategy, and in settings as diverse as the marketplace and the school, I did meet and interview a number of men classified as cochones.[4] In our discussions, many of them told me that they were really comfortable only in the anal-passive position. Others alternate between active and passive roles, depending on whether they are having relations with an hombre-hombre (almost always passive) or with another cochón (passive or active). Some reported practicing oral sex, though not as frequently as anal intercourse. Several of my non-cochón informants denied having any knowledge of oral techniques. Nicaraguans in general express revulsion at the idea of oral intercourse, whether heterosexual or homosexual. "Oral sexual relations? What's that?" was a common response to my queries about varied sexual positions in heterosexual intercourse. "*Me disgusta*" (That's disgusting) was the typical response to my descriptions of cunnilingus and fellatio. A series of (not necessarily sexual) aversions and prohibitions concerning the mouth seems to be involved here. The mouth is seen as the primary route of contamination, the major path whereby illness enters the body, and sex is quintessentially *sucio* (dirty). This conception is socialized into children from infancy onward. Parents are always scolding their small children for putting things in their mouths. This oral prohibition curbs the possibilities of oral intercourse.

The resultant anal emphasis suggests a significant constraint on the nature of homoerotic practices. Unlike oral intercourse, which may lend itself to reciprocal sexual practices, anal intercourse invariably produces an active partner and a passive partner. It already speaks the language of "activity" and "passivity," as it were.[5] If oral intercourse suggests the possibility of an equal sign between partners, anal intercourse in rigidly defined contexts most likely produces an unequal relationship: a "masculine" and a "feminine" partner, as seen in the context of a highly gendered ordering of the world. But this anal emphasis is not merely a negative restraint on the independent variable (homosexuality); positively, it produces a whole field of practices and relations.

The Specific Routes of Stigma

There is clearly stigma in Nicaraguan homosexual practice, but it is not a stigma of the sort that clings equally to both partners. Only the anal-passive cochón is stigmatized. His partner, the active hombre-hombre, is not stigmatized at all; moreover, no clear category exists in the popular language to classify him. For all purposes, he is just a normal Nicaraguan male. The term *heterosexual* is inappropriate here. First, neither it nor any equivalent of it appears in the popular language. Second, it is not really the issue. One is either a cochón or one is not. If one is not, it scarcely matters that one sleeps with cochones, regularly or irregularly. Indeed, a man can gain status among his peers as a vigorous machista by sleeping with cochones in much the same manner that one gains prestige by sleeping with many women. I once heard a Nicaraguan youth of nineteen boast to his younger friends: "I am very sexually experienced. I have had a lot of women, especially when I was in the army, over on the Atlantic coast. I have done everything. I have even done it with cochones." No one in the group thought this a damning confession, and all present were impressed with their friend's sexual experience and prowess. This sort of sexual boasting is not unusual in male drinking talk.

For that matter, desire is not at issue here, and it is irrelevant to what degree one is attracted sexually to members of one's own sex, as long as that attraction does not compromise one's masculinity, defined as activity. What matters is the *manner* in which one is attracted to other males. It is expected that one would naturally be aroused by the idea of anally penetrating another male. (In neighboring Honduras, it is sometimes said that to become a man, one must sleep with a culero and two women.)

This is not to say that active homosexual pursuits are encouraged or even approved in all social contexts. Like adultery and heterosexual promiscuity, the active role in homosexual intercourse is seen as an infraction. That is, from the point of view of civil-religious authority, and from the point of view of women, it is indeed a "sin" (*pecado* or *mal*). But like its equivalent forms of adultery and promiscuity, the sodomizing act is a relatively minor sin. And in male–male social relations, any number of peccadillos (heavy drinking, promiscuity, the active role in same-sex intercourse) become status markers of male honor.

Nicaraguans exhibit no true horror of homosexuality in the North American style; their responses to the cochón tend rather toward amusement or contempt. The laughter of women often follows him down the street – discreet derision, perhaps, and behind his back, but the amusement of the community is ever present for the cochón. For men, the cochón is simultaneously an object of desire and reproach – but that opprobrium knows tacit limits, community bounds. A reasonably discreet cochón – one who dresses conservatively and keeps his affairs relatively discreet – will rarely be harassed or ridiculed in public, although he may be the target of private jokes. If he is very discreet, his status may never even be publicly acknowledged in his presence, and his practices will occupy the ambiguous category of a public secret.

The stigma involved here is not at all the same as the stigma implied in the Western or North American concept of "the perverse," meaning "mis-use." It is certainly not the stigma of the fully rationalized, medicalized system of sexual meaning that elaborates a category, "the homosexual," to identify both practice and identity. Rather, it is anal passivity alone that is stigmatized, and it is anal passivity that defines the status identity in question. Moreover, the social definition of the person and his sexual stigma derive from culturally shared meanings not just of anal passivity and penile activity in particular but of passivity and activity in general. While the lexicon involved varies, its meanings are neither plural nor ambiguous. Thus, "to give" (*dar, meter, poner*) is to be masculine; "to receive" (*recibir, aceptar, tomar*) is to be feminine. At the same time, however, when the idiom of violence or coercion comes into play – as the word *verga* (cock) most frequently connotes (*hacer verga, verguiar*) – "to take by force," "to seize," or "to grab hold of" (*coger*, sometimes *tomar*) is to be masculine, whereas "to surrender," "to yield," or "to give up" (*rendirse*; sometimes *dar*), is to be feminine. In any case, the one who initiates action, dominates, or enters is masculine; whoever is acted upon, dominated, or entered is feminine. This relationship holds as the ideal in all spheres of transaction between the genders. It is symbolized by the popular interpretation of the male sexual organ as active in intercourse and the female sexual organ (or male anus) as passive.

Cochones are therefore feminine men, or, more accurately, feminized men, not fully male men. They are men who are "used" by other men. Their stigma flows from this concept of use. Used by other men, the cochón is not a complete man. His "passive" acquiescence to the active drive of other men's sexual desires both defines and stigmatizes his status. Consequently, when one "uses" a cochón, one acquires masculinity; when one is "used" as a cochón, one expends it. The nature of the homosexual transaction, then, is that the act makes one man a machista and the other a cochón. The machista's honor and the cochón's shame are opposite sides of the same coin. The line that this transaction draws is not between those who practice homosexual intercourse and those who do not (for this is not a meaningful distinction at all in Nicaragua's popular classes) but between two standardized roles in that intercourse. Machistas make cochones out of other men, and each is necessary to the definition of the other in a dynamic sense that is very different from the way North American categories of the heterosexual and homosexual define each other. Although each is defined by his exclusion from membership in some normative category, the cochón is defined by his inclusion in the sexual practices of ordinary men, albeit in a standardized and stigmatized role, and the homosexual by his exclusion from the sexual practices of ordinary men.

This inclusive aspect of sex also has implications for the cochón's status as a political concept, for that category lacks the theoretical independence attributed to Western homosexuality as a distinct category of activity and personal identity. A cochón requires ordinary men, and his activity and identity can never be quite independent of them. Defined by its passivity, the status is ever a dependent one.

The stigma of the cochón applies, in its strictest and most limited sense, to a relatively small minority of men: those who are the "passive" participants in anal intercourse. In its broadest sense, however, the stigma threatens, even taints, all men.

The circulation of stigma implies a complex economy, an ambiguous discourse, and incessant power struggles. In the words of Erving Goffman, stigma requires of us a carefully staged "presentation of self in everyday life" (1959); it entails multiple levels of public, private, and intermediate transactions. To extend the dramaturgic metaphor, it brings into play many stages, many backstages, and many choruses. Or, to employ a game analogy: everyone wishes to pass the stigma along; no one wishes to be left holding it. As cunning and artful as are those who dodge it, by that very token must the invocation of stigma be coarse, generalized, and to some degree nondiscriminating. Thus, although the system of stigma produces certain distinct categories, its operation is never entirely categorical, for stigma is necessarily "sticky."

In the culture of machismo, the cochón is narrowly defined as anal-passive, but the concept of anal passivity serves more loosely as a sort of extreme case of "passivity." The term *cochón* may thus be invoked in both a strict and a loose sense. Which aspect of the concept is emphasized – anality or passivity – will determine whether it encompasses a small minority or a potentially large majority of men. Therein lies the peculiar power of stigma to regulate conduct and generate effects: it ultimately threatens all men who fail to maintain a proper public face. In machismo, as in colorism, the ambiguity of discourse is a highly productive feature of the system.

Thus, the hombre-hombre's exemption from stigma is never entirely secure. He might find his honor tainted under certain circumstances. If an hombre-hombre's sexual engagement with a cochón comes to light, for example, and if the nature of that relationship is seen as compromising the former's strength and power – in other words, if he is seen as being emotionally vulnerable to another man – his own masculinity would be undermined, regardless of his physical role in intercourse, and he might well be enveloped within the cochón's stigma. Or if the *activo*'s attraction to men is perceived as being so great as to define a clear preference for men, and if this preference is understood to mitigate his social and sexual dominion over women, he would be seen as forgoing his masculine privileges and would undoubtedly be stigmatized. However, the Nicaraguan hombre-hombre retains the tools and strategies to ward off such stigma, both within and even *through* his sexual relationships with other men, and his arsenal is not much less than that which is available to other men who are not sleeping with cochones.

This is a crucial point. These kinds of circumstances are perhaps not exceptions at all but simply applications of the rules in their most general sense. Such rules apply not only to those men who engage in sexual intercourse with other men but also to men who have sex only with women. The sound of stigma is the clatter of a malicious gossip that targets others' vulnerabilities. Thus, if a man fails to maintain the upper hand in his relations with women, his demeanor might well be judged passive, and he may be stigmatized, by degrees, as a *cabrón* (cuckold), *maricón* (effeminate man), and cochón. Whoever fails to maintain an aggressively masculine front will be teased, ridiculed, and, ultimately, stigmatized. In this regard, accusations that one is a cochón are bandied about in an almost random manner: as a jest between friends, as an incitement between rivals, as a violent insult between enemies. Cats that fail to catch mice, dogs that fail to bark, boys who fail to fight, and men who fail in their pursuit of a woman: all are reproached with the term. And sometimes, against all this background noise, the charge is leveled as an earnest accusation.

That is the peculiar and extravagant power of the stigmatizing category: like Nietzsche's "prison-house of language" (Jameson 1972), it indeed confines those to whom it is most strictly applied; but ambiguously used, it conjures a terror that rules all men, all actions, all relationships.

Discourse, Domination, Sex

... "The Siege," a short story by Sergio Ramírez (1986: 27–35), narrates the plight of Septimio and Avelino, two cochones living together in a small Nicaraguan town. Tormented and harassed by mostly unseen, offstage townspeople, the two are reduced to a state of fearful siege in their house. When they report their predicament to the local police captain, his response is short: they don't behave like men. (By definition, the men harassing them are behaving like men.) Ramírez's story dramatizes Nicaraguan culture's intolerance and bigotry toward cochones and machismo's implicit violence. Tellingly, the story ends not in murder, or even in violence alone, but in the gang rape of Avelino by the couple's tormenters.

The question of violence is paramount. Every system of exploitation and oppression both *is* violent (by definition) and *requires* violence (force, coercion, compulsion) to continue operating. But this is not to say that all inequalities are the same. Violence, force, and coercion are distributed differently, elaborated variously, in different power systems. When questioned, my informants could not imagine a Nicaraguan equivalent of gay-bashing – and this situation seems logical enough. Bullying, yes; intimidation, sometimes; blackmail, certainly; rough play, frequently. But neither organized, lethal violence nor panicked attacks. In the United States, gay-bashing – physical attacks against homosexuals – bolsters the fragile masculinity and heterosexuality of insecure men. "Homosexual panic," in the context of gay-bashing, has been a legal defense in several trials in the United States (including murder trials), and I suppose we can acknowledge that such a state of panic really does exist: approached by a homosexual (or imagining that they have been approached by one), some men do experience "panic." The panic rests on the principle of homology: a man who has sex with a man is like that man, who is a homosexual. The "panic" erupts when the approached realizes that he is indeed capable of same-sex coitus and is then confronted by the label his actions would impose. Confronted, and doubly so: to be desired by a man raises the question of what that man saw, what he read, in the man who becomes constituted as the object of homosexual desire. And at the same time, if the man realizes that he is capable of performing a homosexual act: to desire a man is to be like the man desired. (Another variation on this: desirable men are apt to be labeled homosexual, a strategy that points desire's arrow in the other direction.) To brutalize what one inwardly, secretly, or subconsciously desires is, of course, a denial.

This state of panic would be impossible in Nicaragua, where assumptions about the nature of intercourse carry no principle of homology and where it is not especially problematic that men are capable of coitus with members of their own sex. Violence is indeed possible – in the form of harassment, censure, stigma, physical intimidation, even rape – but not in the same "panicked" context as in the United States. In Nicaragua, insecurity about one's masculinity or sexuality could be dispelled by mounting – thus sexually subordinating – a cochón. Intercourse in the proper position, more than physical violence, can be a nonthreatening means of subordinating another, hence solidifying one's own masculinity: recall that the penis (*verga*) is itself already seen as a "violent" organ; its operation in intercourse necessarily exercises both pleasure and power principles.

These obscene gestures, offers, and childhood games provide insight into the nature of the sexual practices in question and throw light on the social creation of the cochón. The cochón is but a necessary precipitant of the culture of machismo, or aggressive, competitive masculinity. One man offers to sodomize another, in effect, to make of him a cochón, or if he already is one, to use his services. Thus, men desire to sodomize other men and fear being sodomized by them (Suárez-Orozco 1982). In the same manner, they desire to claim status and prestige and avoid being stigmatized. The routes of sexual use and pleasure thereby illuminate the pathways of male status and sexual power. In a fictionalized version of the same dynamic, Avelino was harassed and gangraped, stigmatized and desired. Boys likewise exhibit their virility by labeling one of their members and mimicking anal intercourse with him. The object of sex/power is the same in either case. Those who consistently lose out in the competition for male status, or who can be convinced to dispose themselves to the sexual urges and status plays of other men, or who dissent from the strictures of manhood, or who, in spite of the stigma, discover pleasure in the passive sexual role or its social status: these men are made into cochones. And those who master the rules of conventional masculinity, or who desire pleasure through their *use* of another (stigmatized by that very pleasure in a sexual position defined as subordinate), are made into machistas.

It is most difficult to get reliable long-range material on the life cycles of cochones. Wrapped in an ambiguous public secrecy, they are both protected and maligned by community gossip. In practice, at the level of neighborhood rumors, this secrecy lends itself to both admissions and denials, accusations and defenses. Some men are clearly defined by that status; others are only tainted with suspicion. Some apparently live out their entire lives in that status; others successfully masculinize themselves by taking a wife and rearing children – though in practice they may (or may not) continue having covert affairs with men. Some develop longstanding covert relationships with particular men. Many live within the closure of secrecy and are not suspected by their neighbors, families, wives, and children. Others become known in male gossip as someone to visit for sexual favors.

Rules in the Social Construction of Sexuality

These processes in the production of sexuality do indeed bear some resemblance to US practices, where male power and status are bound around sexual themes, but the resemblance holds only to a point. Both the homosexual and the cochón are objects in a sexual discourse whose real subject is sexual power. But the structure of that discourse, the meaning of its categories, and the language in which it speaks are decidedly different in each case. To the extent that these processes may be seen at work in our own culture, we may summarize that the object is to label without being labeled, but not to use without being used, for it is the homosexual act itself that is prohibited and not any particular role within the act. Some males in our own milieu, especially adolescents, do in fact attempt to label without being labeled and also use without being used. The difference is that in Anglo-American contexts such conduct is seen as a breach of the rule (or, sometimes, an adolescent suspension of the rule), since homosexual desire itself, without any qualifications, stigmatizes one as a homosexual.

The nature of homosexual transaction in Nicaragua's popular classes seems to bear much greater resemblance to the sexual economy of US prison populations (Blake 1971) – and, by extension, to the milieu of truckstops (Corzine and Kirby 1977) and some types of encounters in public toilets (Humphreys 1970) – where one may indeed both label without being labeled and use without being used. (See also Chauncey's historical account [1989] of sailors in Newport.) Similar rules seem to be in play in either context: passive partners are labeled and stigmatized; active partners are not. The act of intercourse assigns honor to one man, shame to the other. In North American prisons, sex between men becomes a means of exchange because it signifies both pleasure and power in the absence of access to either by other means. But this comparison, although suggestive, should not be overstated or underqualified. Whereas the rules of prison sexuality reflect a deviant and stigmatized subculture, where "normal" rules are suspended or even inverted, the rules of sexuality and stigma in Nicaragua reflect the dominant culture of the popular classes and are thus a normative rather than deviant set of rules and categories.

Thus, the dominant Anglo-American rule would read as follows. A man gains sexual status and honor among other men through and only through his sexual transactions with women. Homosexuals appear as the active refuseniks of that system. In Nicaragua, the rule is built around different principles. A man gains sexual status and honor among other men through his active role in sexual intercourse (either with women or with other men). Cochones are (passive) participants in that system.

As in Anglo-American and Northern European stereotypes of the homosexual, the cochón is commonly ascribed (and sometimes exhibits) such personal characteristics as "effeminacy" and "flamboyance." (I should hasten to add that many cochones exhibit the same temperament as noncochones around them and thus remain as invisible as the majority of homosexuals in the United States.) Feminized by more masculine men, some cochones act out their role in the more extreme form of transvestism. Many others appropriate semitransvestic forms of dress: a shirt just a little too blousy, pants slightly too feminine in color, fit, or texture. Normally, transvestism and near-transvestism receive the reproach of the community. (I once saw a Nicaraguan girl throw dishwater on a cochón who passed by her house in just such a state of near-transvestism.) However, on the special occasions of certain popular religious celebrations, cochones may publicly exhibit their crossdressing with the goodwill and even encouragement of the whole community.

These festivities represent a special niche in the religious life of the lower classes: like Mikhail Bakhtin's (1984) carnival, they project the image of a libidinous popular insurrection (Davis 1978) through a spree of stylized rule breaking. For these ritual occasions, the feminization of men semiotically corresponds to the themes of inversion and reversal that are the core of several popular religious festivities; men dress as women, people take on the costumes of animals, animals challenge human authority, lower classes challenge elite power, and so on (Lancaster 1988b: 38–51). In Masaya's Carnaval, Managua's Coming and Going of Santo Domingo, and other such rituals, the cochón is granted a reprieve from his secrecy and surreption, given a "political" voice, and cast in a central role in popular religious festivities. The transvestic cochones' appearance in these festivities in no sense "scandalizes" public opinion (as does the "coming out" of homosexuals in the United States), for the cochón is supported there by a wider language of travesty, reversal, and parody.

The popular imagination, then, takes up the cochón in an ambiguous way that imbues him with two different meanings. He is usually an object of amusement and contempt, a passive participant put to the use of others. On special occasions, though, the cochón becomes a subject who offers his parodic commentary on a whole array of social and sexual relations. Frequently taunting machistas and mocking civil-religious authority along the way, the transvestic cochón becomes the polysemic voice of discontent in these processions. In his inversion, object becomes subject, and silence bursts out with a voice that discerns the real powers of the powerless and the used. Through the alchemy of popular ritual, the cochón represents the larger point of view of the dispossessed classes in revolt against established authority.

Again, this representative quality of the cochón points to a striking contrast with Anglo-American homosexuals. At their most politically conscious, homosexuals organize themselves into a subculture, a subeconomy, a single-issue politics, all of whose logic is quite singular. Although Managua's cochones pass in and out of an urban demimonde, it can hardly be said that they inhabit a subculture. At his most political, the cochón also represents a very different sort of being than the homosexual: through the polymorphousness of metaphor, carnival speaks to a multiplication of meanings and social entanglements, not to their compartmentalization and impoverishment.

Where Nicaragua's sex categories and sexual transactions most strikingly parallel Western European and North American rules is not in any deviant subculture of the present but in sexual categories and practices widespread in the past, before progressive rationalization in the institutions of religion, law, medicine, and psychiatry had refined a category, the homosexual, out of traditional folk constructs (Trumbach 1977; Weeks 1977). Like its traditional Western parallels (e.g., "bugger," "sodomite," "faggot"), the cochón represents a stigmatized sexual identity, as yet still minimally administered by the institutions of rational sexual categorization and control, still more or less under the rule of popular categories and controls. But even here the cultural tradition in which we encounter the cochón is different from the Anglo-European tradition, whose folk terms often designate the *active*, not passive, category of practice, identity, and stigma. Even as a traditional or nonrationalized construct, the cochón lives in a different cultural stream than do "buggers" and "sodomites."

Cochones, Homosexuality, and the Revolution

From the beginning, revolutionary sectors proved divided on sexual and moral questions. Before the Sandinista triumph of 1979, Christian base communities sometimes held criticism and self-criticism sessions – in the style of the early Christian church – when members were under suspicion of "sexual sins." Nothing could have seemed more bizarre than these "sex trials" to young Sandinista militants drawn from college campuses and influenced by the international New Left of the 1960s. After the revolution, AMNLAE and its feminist supporters were frequently at loggerheads with the Popular Church on issues such as abortion, sterilization, and contraception. And within the Frente Sandinista itself, there were wide divergences of opinion: one could subscribe to a more puritanical current (influenced by local conventionality as well as by Soviet and Cuban Marxism) or to a relatively cosmopolitan leftist current (influenced by New Left Marxism as well as by a more militant reading of revolutionary Christianity).

The Sandinista revolution and its accompanying changes introduced a variety of contradictory changes in the culture's understanding of sexual practices. It may be that the image of Carnaval captures and perpetuates the image of revolt so necessary in the imagination of the populace that would be revolutionary, but the consolidation of a revolutionary state is anything but an extended carnival. Certainly, in its early years the revolution constrained homosexual practice. The nature of socialist revolution, and perhaps particularly that variety influenced by liberation theology, entails a strong normative or corporatist component. The

"New Man" and the "New Society" are envisioned as hardworking, diligent, and studious, pure and without corruption. The aspect of machismo that the New Man embodies is the ascetic side, not the hedonistic one. The cult of the New Man, then, produced a cultural atmosphere in which homosexual practice (and sexual transgression in general) was at least publicly regarded as more suspect than before, tainted with the image of indulgence or corruption, and was perhaps even somewhat less readily available.

More concretely, the revolution for a time tried to strengthen the moral force of the community, especially through the neighborhood CDS. Through such organizations, and through the sensibility of revolution generally, the gaze of the community was particularly strong. At the peak of CDS activism, the semiprivate, semipublic status of the cochón was rendered more problematic. Especially in areas of public morality and public order, a variety of activities, such as prostitution, were actively curbed by the Sandinista Police and the CDS. According to some of my informants, Managua once sported an elite and tourist-oriented nightlife, including perhaps a dozen assorted homosexual bars, exclusive gay clubs, drag shows, and male stripper acts. These apparently serviced Managua's middle-class homosexuals, some of its lower-class cochones, and gay tourists from other countries. They are gone now, and what remains is a small handful of much more discreet bars.

Such closures have affected the traditional cochón much less than the Western-oriented gay or homosexual of professional or middle-class origins. (The rationale for my distinction between these categories will become apparent shortly.) As one Sandinista activist from a working-class barrio (who alternately and in his mind synonymously described himself as a cochón, homosexual, or gay) put it, "It is true that there are fewer bars now, but most of the ones that existed before served only the affluent, not the poor. You had to be rich to get into those nightclubs. It is not so much that they have been closed down by the police or the CDS as that they have moved to Miami with the rich people."

More alienated and less revolutionary cochones spoke of going to live in Miami or especially San Francisco; others spoke of carving out a broader tolerance within the revolutionary process. Not all of the effects of the revolution on cochones were restrictive. While maintaining a discreet sexual profile, many participated in the revolutionary process, some rising to positions of great authority in the CDS, the FSLN, and even the government proper. The informant quoted above, for instance, was elected to the post of barrio director in his community – the highest position in the local CDS. Having fewer family responsibilities and dependents appears to have freed many politically conscious cochones to work for the revolution. In the process, some have gained recognition and status in the community, much as priests derive charisma from a life of celibacy and service. As another informant – a schoolteacher – pointed out: "Cochones were very active in the Sandinista movement from the very beginning. Some people say it's because we're smarter than other people. I don't think it's that. I think it's because we have a different perspective, and we see things differently." How so, I wondered? "We experience oppression more intensely and more intimately than most people. So naturally we identified with the vanguard of the oppressed."

In Nicaragua, the traditional categories remain the dominant popular ones, but they are now coexisting and competing with Western perceptions of homosexuality.

Sexual education in the schools, social contact with *internacionalistas* from the United States and Western Europe, and greater access to international ideas and philosophies all facilitate the acquisition of Western sexual models, especially in the urban, middle-class sectors that look to the United States and Western Europe for educational and cultural values. But changes are also under way – at a slower pace, and in uncharted directions – for a broader section of the urban working class.

In some sections of Managua one now hears such terms as *homosexual* and *heterosexual*. For certain members of a narrow stratum of urban elites, these terms are not so misleading. Many of Managua's sexually active youth, even some of working-class origins (like the barrio director quoted above), also now call themselves "homosexual," "bisexual," or "gay." New syncretisms are indeed slowly emerging, but in practice the dominant logic of the sexual system remains traditional, native, and popular. That is, despite a trend toward greater politicization and organization among a loose network of urban cochones, in popular discourse a cochón remains defined by anal-passive sexual practices (and is, moreover, strongly associated with transvestism). Moreover, the social bearing and political direction of even politicized cochones is to some extent an open question. Greater pride and self-esteem are indeed expressed, and it is often called "gay pride" (*orgullo gay*). But the casual importation of scientific and even political sexual terminologies confuses casual foreign observers in much the same way that the casual use of those terms in social science confuses issues and assimilates real differences. What a Nicaraguan most probably means when he calls himself "gay" is very different from what a homosexual in the United States has in mind when he uses the same term, even though the two may find themselves in broad agreement on certain narrow particulars. New words such as *homosexual* and *gay* typically enter the popular vocabulary as synonyms for familiar categories and practices rather than as new concepts in themselves. This is especially true in the popular classes; and many Nicaraguans, even in Managua, remain quite unfamiliar with these newly introduced words. The frequent misuse of such terms, when they occur, indicates that traditional values still prevail. "Es dicho que él es un *sexual*" (They say that he is a *sexual*) was the way one informant put it to me, referring to a man many thought to be a cochón.

The remarkable conservatism of culture lies in its ability to animate new words with old ideas.[6] Although it is doubtful that one could speak of a "purely" native model anymore in Managua, it is clear that the traditional logic of sexuality remains intact for the massive lower classes. It is not enough to say that most urban cochones call themselves "gay," "homosexual," or "bisexual." (As one informant put it, when asked for definitions, "A homosexual is a cochón; a heterosexual is an hombre-hombre. That means he can fuck women or men.") It would be more compelling evidence of systematic culture change if men who prefer homosexual intercourse but were previously defined as hombres-hombres took up new self-labeling strategies. More compelling yet would be the appropriation of new terms *and* new logics by the population at large. And a real sea change in Nicaragua's sexual culture would be marked not by the importation of a new sexual lexicon – which might just as easily be imbued with "archaic" as with "modern" meanings – but by the introduction of new terms along with the proliferation of specialized bureaucratic instruments of sexual regulation to which those terms correspond (e.g., psychology, sex education) and the development of a homosexual subculture based on a wider variety of less stereotyped roles and practices. But these conditions clearly have not been met . . . .

What is a Homosexual?

There is no *essence* of homosexuality whose historical unfolding can be illuminated. There are only changing patterns in the organization of desire whose specific config-uration can be decoded.

(Jeffrey Weeks, *Sexuality and Its Discontents*)

Marilyn Strathern (1981: 682) uses the phrase "No such thing as a woman" to stress certain theoretical points on the nature of gender studies: if womanhood is conceived in terms of fundamentally different logics in different cultures, then the universal category *woman*, taken as an already known universal, hinders any anthropological attempt at understanding the definition, construction, and mean-ing of womanness in those cultures. Quite literally, then, for anthropology there can be no such thing as a priori woman or a priori man; rather, anthropology's task is to inquire into the various ways cultures elaborate meaning and practice. Here, I follow Strathern's lead and attempt to make similar points in treating the nature and construction of the traditional Nicaraguan category of the cochón. We may speculate that this category is the result of a syncretism between Iberian and indigenous sexual role systems. Moreover, based on my conversations with other Latin Americanists, it seems that the cochón exemplifies something of the sexual rules that are generally found in many Latin American countries, where the essential elements of the cochón appear under different names and with somewhat different definitions (Carrier 1976; Parker 1984, 1985, 1991; Williams 1986: 147–51).

Labels such as *homosexual* or *heterosexual*, along with Northern European and Anglo-American assumptions about stigma, fail to account for the Nicaraguan sexual constructs that ultimately produce the cochón. Theoretically, this sort of difficulty crimps attempts at writing a general history or anthropology of homo-sexuality (or, for that matter, of heterosexuality and even sexuality in general), for such projects must be hedged from the outset with myriad qualifications and circumlocutions (Weeks 1981: 97). Perhaps it does not seem so astonishing anymore to point out that the term *homosexual* (or some immediate equivalent), used to define a person's identity, does not translate into every language. It might still seem more scandalous to point out that *heterosexual* is itself by no means a universal category. But with these realizations come an even more systematic dislodging of Western categorical assumptions. Deprived of the easy language of our own sexual system, and dealing with practices culturally remote from our own, the analyst might find himself or herself compelled to take up various ellipses and periphrases. Thus, in an empirical description of what two people were doing with their bodies, instead of an unproblematic reference to "homosexual acts," the analyst might substitute "what we would call 'homosexual acts.'" Ungainly? No doubt. But having deconstructed the homosexual or heterosexual as persons, the acts themselves have also been undone. What is (what we would call) a homosexual act? The almost tautological answer: Two men engaging in (what we would call) intercourse. That is, a penis in another man's mouth, or anus, or hand or stationed at some other strategic location on the body; at any rate, two male bodies engaged in some activity defined by one or both as pleasurable in a carnal sense. But indeed, what do the two bodies mean, how are they conceived and understood? What does the act mean to them in the context of their culture? Is it taboo, and if so, what sort of infraction does it entail? Or is it mandatory, and if so, by what code? Moreover: What is a man? How is he defined? Is he defined simply by the presence of a penis, or by a web of practices and meanings that locate him in the male sphere? Indeed, what is a penis? Is it an instrument of pleasure, of power, or is it not an instrument at all? Such interrogations take us beyond "the misleading light of the obvious" (Matthieu 1978) – which turns out to be our own common sense, reified as Nature.

Such a calculated circumlocution – "what we would call homosexual" – at least permits a more self-conscious discourse: with relative economy, it allows the bundling of types of sex acts across cultures for comparison and contrast with each other; simultaneously, this operation provides us with critical leverage to understand our own practices as relative and produced; finally, it reminds us that the interest in types is, after all, our own, and that whatever the benefits of this typological analysis by us and for us, the distinctions may not be meaningful (or may not carry the same meaning) in the cultures in question.

At every turn, then, we are always running up against the unintelligibility of foreign practices to our concepts and categories – and vice versa. The best that can be done is to write a limited, circumscribed, and qualified history or anthropology of homosexuality. To write the alternative, a general history or anthropology of homosexuality, one has to posit at least one of two propositions: either (1) that homosexuality and heterosexuality are secured in Nature as distinct biological entities (the difference grounded, presumably, in genetic, hormonal, or developmental differences between homosexuals and heterosexuals), or (2) that culture everywhere and always defines sexual pleasure, sexual practices, and sexual identity in pretty much the same terms, categories, and meanings, *and*, moreover, that some interaction between culture and biology everywhere thus secures the same essential rules of personal development from infancy to adulthood.

Some practitioners of gay studies take the position that homosexuals exist, a priori, across human cultures and throughout human history, *even in cultures that do not necessarily recognize them as such*. It seems to me that one cannot maintain such a position without positing a homosexual/heterosexual distinction in nature, in biology, as an irreducible and eternal essence. And that nature, that biology, must be understood not as an "open" system (e.g., pleasure may be defined and produced in the human body by innumerable strategies) but as a "closed" one (human bodies come prewired: a majority can really appreciate only the arousal of the other sex; a minority can really enjoy only homosexual pleasure).[7]

The majority of biological research on homosexuality traffics in its own mystification – most strikingly, the old-fashioned assumption that male homosexuals are (genetically, hormonally, physiologically, dispositionally) more female than nonhomosexual men are, and lesbians more male than nonlesbian women are. (Thus the search for female hormones in homosexual men and male hormones in lesbians.) Since no significant innate, genetic, hormonal, or biological differences have ever been demonstrated between homosexuals and heterosexuals (where those terms are in currency), and since even the hypothetical discovery of some minor difference would fail to establish cause and effect (biology? socialization?), to posit a "natural" distinction between homosexuality and heterosexuality is to fall prey to the very cultural logic (and its naturalistic alibi) that produces such a categorical distinction in the first place. The second proposition, on closer inspection, is ultimately grounded in the first: it apprehends culture as a reflection of biology, folkloristically understood.[8] If the historical and cross-cultural data demonstrate anything, it is that the distinction between heterosexuality and homosexuality – like the idea of "sexuality" itself as an uncontextualized biological pleasure – is a relatively recent Western cultural product. And these difficulties cannot be resolved by distinguishing identity from orientation – with orientation as essential and biological, and identity as secondary and cultural – for in practice one finds not one orientation, not two, but dozens. Even if we confine ourselves to Western societies, there is no reason to assume that all men reach their homosexuality or heterosexuality by means of the same psychological-developmental route; as Kenneth Lewes (1988: 69–94) argues in his reinterpretation of Freud, not all homosexualities are necessarily the same, just as not all heterosexualities are identical. Lewes discerns at least a dozen possible destinations of sexual development, a dozen distinct, successful modes of resolving the conflicts of the Oedipus complex, six of which are heterosexual and six of which are homosexual. If it is no longer possible to speak of a monistic homosexuality or heterosexuality in the West, what, then, is one to make of persons whose sexual experience is not grouped under a rubric that arbitrarily discerns two modes of intercourse and assigns everyone an identity as either heterosexual or homosexual? Of cultures whose family organization is based on different principles? Of cultures that prescribe (and proscribe) lists of sexual practices very different from our own, and do so by different logics?

Other cultures *are* different. They maintain different understandings of masculinity and femininity, different conceptions of the body and its engagement in the world and with other bodies. But the cochón is by no means as exotic a phenomenon as the cross-gendered (Whitehead 1981) or gender-mixed (Callender and Kochems 1983) Native American *berdache*, nor are his practices as far from Anglo-American and Northern European notions of homosexuality as are the mandatory homosexual initiation rites practiced in parts of Melanesia (Herdt 1981, 1982). Indeed, it is the very similarity between the cochón and the Anglo-American homosexual that makes the two appear, at first glance, to be readily interchangeable: both are adult males with a stigmatized sexual identity. Only on close inspection can we see that the processes of producing identity and stigma differ radically: governed by different rules, each case produces a markedly different existential state. We could say, in Wittgensteinian terms, that machismo is a different game, governed by different rules; or we could say, in Marxist terms, that it represents a different sexual economy, a different mode in the production of sex/gender; or, in Foucauldian terms, we could say that Nicaraguan sexuality represents a discursive (and intercursive) practice radically different from Anglo-American sexuality.

The necessity of drawing such distinctions is far from settled in the current literature. John Boswell (1980) discerns "gay people" in premodern Europe,

Gilbert Herdt (1981: 3, 321) finds "homosexual adults" in the highlands of Papua New Guinea, and Walter Williams (1986) has more recently reiterated the old thesis that the berdache is a Native American gay in drag. Nonetheless, anthropology and sociology have been growing more sensitive to phenomeno-logical differences when they exist at these great historical and cultural distances (see especially Greenberg 1988). Until now, though, the nuances that distinguish, say, the cochón from the homosexual, typically have been glossed over by the misleading terminologies of the latter. June Nash (1979: 141) identifies persons who appear to be the Bolivian equivalents of Nicaraguan cochones as "men with homosexual tendencies," and Cuba's Santería cult is sometimes described as a native niche for an otherwise unproblematic Cuban homosexuality (Arguelles and Rich 1984: 688). At best, modifications of that terminology have been suggested: for instance, "selective homophobia" to identify the stigmatization of the "passive homosexual" (Murphy 1984), or, in Barry Adam's (1987) description of Nicaraguan practices, "homosexuality without a gay world." (See also Brandes's discussion of the passive role in homosexual intercourse in Andalusia [1981: 232–4].)

Such terminology, even when modified, obscures more than it clarifies. Nicaragua's cochones are ontologically different from Anglo-American homosexuals. Both are clearly stigmatized, but they are stigmatized in different ways, according to different rules. Nor is it, as it is often maintained, that in Latin America homophobia is substantially the same as that which one encounters in Northern Europe and the United States, though more severe in its operations. It is not that homophobia is more intense in a culture of machismo, but that it is a different sort of thing altogether. Indeed, the word *homophobia*, meaning a fear of homosexuals or homosexual intercourse, is quite inappropriate in a milieu where unlabeled men desire and actively seek intercourse with labeled men. An altogether different word is necessary to identify the praxis implicit in machismo, whereby men may simul-taneously desire to use, fear being used by, and stigmatize other men.

No inner psychology, no desiring subject, no autonomous individual – in short, no a priori entity, sexual or otherwise – precedes social intercourse and awaits its influence. However it is defined, desire – like gender, color, or class – exists not *within* us, but *between* us. Desire is not part of "nature," nor is it "opposed to" or "beyond" meaning; it is always meaningful, and it operates no less semiotically than language itself does. That it is often felt as an "inner," "subjective" experi-ence by no means diminishes its "outer," "social" character, for desire is always a relation between two *relata*; as such it is constitutive of as well as constituted by the subject of desire. And in this constitution of subjectivity, the desiring subject is traversed, even in his innermost experience of desire, by social forces: not simply (at the most superficial level) by the prohibitions, rules, and recommendations of sanctioned desire, but more significantly, by values, erotics, and evaluations that are part of and made possible by *social language* and by conflicts over them that are no less social in nature. "Inner desire," then, no less than "thinking to oneself," is a social act carried out in and through a social language.[9] Desire is thus always part of the cultural, economic, and ideological world of social relations and social conflicts. It is not simply that these relations and conflicts act on some interior and preexisting sexuality "from the outside" but that they constitute it "from the inside" as well. Which is to say (contrary to common sense): sexual history is possible only to the extent that desire is thoroughly historicized, and sexual anthropology only to the extent that its subject is effectively relativized.[10]

If these criteria allow us to distinguish various systems of sexual signification and power, they may also allow us to generalize a limited (though potentially endless) number of systems based on the operation of similar rules (Greenberg 1988: 25). Nicaragua's sexual system, with its active-honor and passive-shame dichotomy, exemplifies rules governing male sexual relations not only for much of Latin America generally but also for cultures throughout the Mediterranean and the Middle East. Numerous and widely variegated subtypes no doubt obtain, but with its series of dichotomies – penile-anal, active-passive, honor-stigma – this sexual pattern, which is found in peasant societies across much of the world, clearly stands opposed to the system of sexuality predominant in Northern Europe and its offspring cultures, especially in the Anglophone world.[11] Although the Northern European system has undergone successive degrees of intensification and rationalization, its original peculiarity seems to rest on its blanket condemnation of all same-sex practices and, perhaps, active ones in particular (Trumbach 1977).

The provisional models offered here (and elaborated elsewhere (Lancaster 1988a: 121–2)) do not directly address female same-sex practices. In Nicaragua, as in many peasant societies throughout the world, there is little popular interest in categorizing or regulating female same-sex relations, and little exists in the popular lexicon to account for it. There were scattered references to lesbianism in the various newspaper articles I have cited, but in all my conversations the subject of lesbianism never came up unless I raised it. (And even when the subject was raised, some of my informants – men and women – genuinely appeared to know nothing about the matter.) Surely, Nicaraguans can censure female same-sex improprieties, but without the refined and specialized vocabulary through which they speak of the cochón. The culture of machismo, which speaks so directly to male practices, can speak only indirectly or inversely of female ones.

Sexual Politics? Sexual Communities?

Resentment, bitterness, alienation; a recognition of the arbitrariness of power and privilege: such sentiments underlie all oppositional politics, all states of outsiderness and marginality. Those underpinnings are indeed equally present among Nicaragua's cochones and Anglo-American homosexuals. "Things are not always what they seem" is as good a maxim as any for characterizing the double awareness of the oppositional personality. Certainly, it is a maxim that has long characterized the homosexual sensibility in America. And that sensibility is by no means absent from discussions and small talk among Nicaragua's cochones. These oppositions to power, this awareness of the density of oppression, dispersed across the system of social relations, *might* provide the basis for a self-conscious politicized movement of cochones on a significant scale, as they did for US homosexuals. However, they have not yet, and it is not clear whether, when, or how they shall. As I have attempted to show, the very construction of machismo and sexual practices in Nicaragua disables that possibility, and by a logic different from that which constructs masculinity and sexuality in the United States. In the United States, the type of sexual community that provides the social base for homosexual politics is predicated on two social premises: (1) that all homosexual acts of whatever sort are equally stigmatized, and (2) that all men who participate in those acts are defined and stigmatized as homosexual. Such premises are not only absent from Nicaragua but are also quite alien to Nicaraguan popular cultural assumptions.

At the peak of revolutionary tourism in Nicaragua, gay and lesbian activists were numerous among the internacionalistas visiting from the United States and Western Europe. On more than one occasion (and with various degrees of success), some activists attempted to stimulate the formation of a variety of gay self-help groups, educational clubs, and political organizations. Such efforts have always seemed suspect to me: duplicating the logic of colonialism, they invariably posit the US or Western European activist as "teacher" (and never as "student") of some dependent population. As a consequence, such efforts proceed from the peculiar assumption that cochones need a "vanguard from without" to plant the seeds of radical political organization and to clarify, represent, and refine *for them* their implicit political point of view. One of the key limitations of these efforts was the essentialist assumption that homosexuality and lesbianism (somehow merrily integrated by sleight of hand) constitute an international fabric, a universal phenomenon affected by only minor variations in style and expression and afflicted to various degrees by the same homophobia. The task of the teacher, then, would always be to reveal the Truth of (homo/hetero)sexuality, as imported from beyond the borders of Nicaraguan culture. Now I am not saying that gays are not in a unique position, among North Americans and Europeans, to sympathize with and understand the plight of cochones in Nicaragua (it seems to me that they are, though not in any exclusive way), but sympathy, sensitivity, and understanding need not envelop the cochón within the boundaries of Western homosexuality, unreflexively understood. Such activist efforts, and my skepticism toward them, prompted this chapter, with its emphasis on the distinction between cochones and homosexuals; only much later did I come to realize the crucial role of the cochón in centering and grounding machismo as a system. These considerations imply yet more open-ended interrogations: on the question of homosexuality in the United States; on the successes and failures of gay rights politics here; and on the applicability of such gay rights politics in Nicaragua. For if it is agreed that the injurious treatment of the cochón demands a political response, the question becomes, What politics? How defined?

In broad strokes, the possibilities for a radical politicization of the cochón in Nicaragua are not so different from the possibilities of radically politicizing homosexuality in the United States. What is required in either case is a revolution in connotators. On the US side: By what logic and for what reasons does one act belong to the Natural, the other to the Unnatural? How is privilege inscribed by an arbitrary marking of human beings, and how might that system of writing be undone? On the Nicaraguan side: By what necessity is the penis "active" and the anus (or vagina) "passive" in sexual intercourse? Intercourse could just as easily be imagined the other way around. Or any participant in any position could be seen as an "active" partner in intercourse. And why should the feminine be associated with passivity in general, and why should both be denigrated by comparison with masculinity/activity? Indeed, why should risk taking be masculine and planning feminine, if that description distorts each? How is it that the penis is a *violent* organ, and what system of social relations does this conception support?

In narrower strokes: There is no reason why the politicization of the cochón should follow a path resembling the politicization of the homosexual, with its history- and culture-bound definition, identity, and subculture, either as that politicization has already occurred or as it might occur in the future. The cochón's milieu is different; his history is different; the rules that govern the system are different and require different approaches. . . .

The Double Gesture

Jacques Derrida describes as the general strategy of deconstruction "to avoid both simply *neutralizing* the binary oppositions of metaphysics and simply *residing* within the closed field of these oppositions, thereby confirming it." . . .

Obscurantism is often a danger of deconstructionist projects, especially those that emphasize the second gesture over the first. I do not wish to declare, hastily, the negation of hetero/homo, which is, after all, very much a lived reality *for us*. Nor do I wish to leave us with a language by means of which it would be impossible to speak economically of homosexual acts in other cultures – for the project of radical deconstruction *requires* other configurations, other meanings, to provide the critical leverage by means of which we cast our own meanings, practices, structures, and systems into relief. One cannot even readily identify *sexuality as a system* in the West until its categories and operations have been relativized by contact with other systems, other possibilities.

This chapter differentiates apparent similarities in two sexual systems; it diagrams the rules that define the stigmatized Nicaraguan sexual category, the cochón, and contrasts it with the North American homosexual. The cochón is not just one refraction of a larger, universal homosexual category (embedded in Nature – or perhaps, in Unnature), nor is the English term *homosexual* an appropriate translation of that concept – which must, indeed, remain fundamentally untranslatable. This method of semiotic differentiation is in keeping with prevailing deconstructionist and Marxist approaches in sexuality studies (D'Emilio 1983: 4; Greenberg 1988; Weeks 1985), but it also represents a straightforward application of basic Boasian principles to the question of sex: to wit, that what is meaningful about culture is internal, not external, and that cultural meaning resides in specific milieus, not in aggregations of cultures assembled in the light of unproblematic commonsense categories. Indeed, considered this way, cultural relativism was from its inception a doubly deconstructive practice: we can see readily enough that the beliefs and practices of other people are in a sense arbitrary (since they are not like our own); by studying them in some detail, we come to see that our own understandings and practices are no more privileged by Nature. Thus, to study the cochón – as a category, as a discourse, as a practice of machismo – is also to deconstruct our own universalized category, the homosexual; an act may be called *homosexual* if it involves two men (if labeling such things is what we do), but what is significant and meaningful about that act lies beyond any a priori assumptions about the nature of homosexual activity.

Seen in these terms, the specific configuration of sex, power, and stigma traced in Nicaragua's popular classes is indeed jarringly different from the predominant configuration in the United States. But it is not dissimilar from other configurations. Our critical method need not lend itself only to the endless production of distinctions; it can also elaborate typologies based on the operation of similar rules. For instance, I have provisionally proposed an Anglo Northern European or bourgeois sexuality and a circum-Mediterranean/Latin American or peasant sexuality.

To renounce abstract universalism, to thus articulate differences, and to thereby generalize limited typologies is, of course, not a passive duplication of reality. The construction of models is always a *motivated* activity. Typologies become dangerous when they are reified and when the motivated nature of their construction is forgotten. I hope that my analysis has pushed the principles of neither differentiation nor similarity past the point of their intelligibility and utility. Surely, meaning lives in given, distinct cultural milieus that are wondrously varied; certainly, some milieus are more like each other than they are like certain others. But cultures, although distinct, are not altogether discrete; they do not come in hermetically sealed tubes. Living cultural systems, like language systems, interact at their margins with the many other systems on their horizon. No culture has ever been unaware of other cultures, and this awareness allows its members both to portray themselves as unique and to borrow practices from abroad. Nicaragua's traditional sexual system – like that of the United States, and like all others – is itself a cultural hybrid (in this case, Spanish and indigenous: that is, mestizo), and the process of borrowing while remaining distinct continues. This syncretism supports a sometimes open, sometimes closed arena of disagreement, conflict, and change. And as a field of power, the sexual system is not arbitrarily separable from other arenas of power. So, while maintaining a picture of the traditional and still conventional mode of sexuality in Nicaragua, I have also attempted to describe today's situation as a configuration of power and resistance, tradition and change, internal agreements and conflicts in the context of a class system, a gender system, and a revolution, and at the confluence of various interacting and competing sexual modes. . . .

This topography of the body, its accesses and privileges, is at once a map of pleasure and power. And the relationship of the cochón to power, as to the grammar of sex, constitutes a cultural ensemble different from that configuration which we call the homosexual. The object choice of the homosexual isolates him from male power, except insofar as he can serve as a negative example and thus mark off the circuitry of power; a breaker of rules, he is positioned outside the operational rules of normative (hetero)sexuality. The object choice of the cochón casts him in the role of object to machismo's subjectivity; that is, it puts him in a stigmatized but by no means marginal relation to sex/power. Each is defined by a play of sex/power, but the homosexual is a marginalized subject, divested of power, around whom power flows, whereas the cochón is an object through whom power flows and who is therefore, paradoxically, the locus of power's investment in itself.

Notes

This chapter represents something of an ethnography within an ethnography. Its earliest draft was presented at the 1986, 85th Annual Meeting of the American Anthropological Association in Philadelphia. An outline of my arguments appeared in *Signs* 12/1 (1986):

188–92, and a version substantially shorter than the present chapter appeared in *Ethnology* 27/2 (1988): 111–25. For their comments on earlier drafts, I am grateful to Marie Boutte, Samuel Colón, Sue Estroff, Robert Fernea, Byron Good, Richard Parker, Leonard Plotnicov, Jim Quesada, Nancy Scheper-Hughes, and Marilyn Strathern.

1 Called "the festival of disguises," Carnaval is a religious celebration held annually in the large agricultural market town of Masaya. It marks the climax of a series of religious festivals in that town, and not the approach of Lent. An important presence among the elaborate masks and disguises of Carnaval is that of the cochones, who don female attire and parade alongside other participants in the day's procession.

2 My spelling throughout conforms to the only spelling I have ever seen in print, in a *Nuevo diario* editorial (December 6, 1985).

3 Working with a network of *pasivos* or cochones, Adam (1987) provides an overview very similar to the analysis I am developing here.

4 I was not "out" – openly gay – in Erasmus Jiménez. At first, this strategy was to ensure that I could establish good relations with my informants, who, I imagined, would not approve. Later, it became problematic to me just how I would articulate my own understanding of my own sexuality to my informants – as this chapter demonstrates. Covertly, and through various circumlocutions, a few men from the neighborhood attempted to establish sexual liaisons with me; more generally, I encountered cochones in "neutral" and relatively "anonymous" settings such as the marketplace. In either case, for the most part these men assumed that I was an hombre-hombre. If I described myself to them as homosexual or gay, their sexual interest was generally diminished greatly.

5 As Boswell observes (1989: 33–4), fellatio can be considered an "active" behavior; if anything, it is the fellated who is "passive."

6 For example, Potter and Potter (1990: 251–69) show in some detail how the patrilineal system reproduced itself (in its specifically patriarchal form) in China during – and despite – forty years of revolutionary, collectivist efforts designed to eliminate it.

7 For theoretical discussions of "innatist" versus "constructionist" positions, see Boswell 1989; Halperin 1989; and Padgug 1989.

8 At the bottom of naturalistic heterosexism lies a series of premises, each more fallacious than the last:

(a) A paramount project of both biology and culture is to secure the reproduction of the species or the group and (more to the point) the reproduction of one's own genetic material. Stated this way, the idea of some inner "biologic" of culture would seem straightforward and innocent enough. It would seem to place some conception of "material needs" at the heart of culture. But we are already well on the way to a series of other planks: competition for maximization as a biological principle; survival of the fittest as an evolutionary fact rather than business dogma; evolution as "progress" (toward a goal); cultural change as a form of evolution; and so on, ad nauseam. Traveling a similar path, Malinowski ultimately arrived at a conception of culture as an extended gut. But this manifestly social "naturalism" reads into both biology and culture a Darwinian imperative, an active force, a metaphysical drive. Thus reified, natural selection becomes an active process rather than a contingent result: the telos of history, the logos underlying culture. In such an idealist biology and metaphysical materialism, culture becomes nothing more than biology's afterthought: a means of securing for biology what biology cannot secure for itself.

(b) Homosexual acts proper do not produce offspring. This is true enough, but neither do most heterosexual acts.

(c) Homosexual (and heterosexual) *persons* really do exist, in a cross-cultural and transhistorical sense, defined by their preference for homosexual (or heterosexual) intercourse. This plank has no evidence whatsoever, and the bulk of sophisticated ethnographic data weighs against it. Indeed, what of societies where homosexual practice is conceived as a normal (classical Greece) or even mandatory (parts of Melanesia) aspect of every man's life experience?

(d) Homosexual persons, then, are less likely to reproduce themselves than hetero-sexual persons are. This coupling of (b) and (c) ignores all sorts of possibilities and must be considered unimaginative at best. True enough: in our society, self-identified homo-sexuals (and lesbians) are less likely to bear offspring than are persons not self-identified as gay. But the bulk of closeted homosexuals *are* married and *do* produce children. And at the same time, self-identified gays (and lesbians) who want children have availed themselves of a variety of means of producing them, outside (as well as within) the confines of heterosexual marriage. In the end, the simple fact that one prefers inter-course of a homosexual sort by no means obviates the possibilities of reproduction – in this or any other society.

(e) This vital reproductive project requires (or, rather, historically *required*) that everyone (or at least most people) be engaged in a heterosexual union organized for the purposes of reproduction – a biological and material necessity that means that culture everywhere has expressed a preference for heterosexual over homosexual. Actu-ally, as Greenberg (1988: 10) has pointed out, "Even if sexual partners were chosen entirely at random at each mating, without regard to sex, birthrates would remain high enough to sustain population growth." It may well be the case that *most* societies prefer heterosexual union to homosexual union – although (1) the question of union (mar-riage) is distinct from sexual intercourse preferences, and (2) this presumed "prefer-ence" for heterosexual union depends in large part on how one raises the question. As Lévi-Strauss (1969) has shown, marriage does not exist to secure the production of children but to extend the field of one's social and political alliances *between* men *through* women. And as Rubin (1975), following Lévi-Strauss, has argued, one could explain the apparent preference of cultures for heterosexual marriage, then, without any recourse whatsoever to biology; that is, it becomes an entirely social and political question. Departing from Rubin, one might question whether cultures' apparent preference for heterosexual marriage implicitly entails a preference for heterosexual over homosexual intercourse. There is no reason to assume it would, unless one defaults to the series of deductions outlined here, which are really a modernized reading of Leviticus and which would no doubt make the pope glad, since at every step it assumes that sex exists for purposes of procreation and that any other sexual activity is a misuse of what Nature (God) has given us.

9 Here I am applying the linguistic methods of the Bakhtin school to the problem of desire. See Medvedev and Bakhtin 1978; Vološinov 1986.

10 Misunderstandings and misrepresentations of this principle (sexual relativism) abound – as much on the "constructionist" side of the debate as on the "essentialist" one. On the constructionist side: it has been altogether too tempting a gesture to reify "social acts" as "social facts," thus capitulating to the totalitarian logic of functionalism (Weeks 1981: 8). Peculiar statements frequently center on the principle of *rules* versus *violations of the rule*, with scenarios that presuppose a view of culture more absolutist than creative, more programmed than practical. On the other side, rule violations are sometimes cited by those holding an "essentialist" view as evidence of an innate propensity – a natural tendency – in some distinct (if unlabeled) minority toward a homosexual orientation.

Much of the debate has revolved around the misleading question of "sexual plasti-city" (see Greenberg 1988: 486–7), with allied disputes regarding all the familiar antinomies: biology versus culture, individual behavior versus social conventions, and subjective desires versus cultural rules. At stake ultimately – and from various and contradictory angles – is the question of freedom versus determinism. "Construction-ists" have sometimes implicitly rested their theoretical arguments on the assumption that human sexuality is inherently polymorphous and malleable. If sexual response is infinitely plastic, then it can be shaped only by culture. "Culture," thus abstracted from practice and reified, becomes an active and dictatorial force in human affairs rather than an arena of practice, conflict, and change. If the relativist/constructionist position maintains that all human beings are inherently malleable and that culture is a "program" that controls perception and experience, it remains far behind theoretical advances in semiotics. That erotic response in the human race is highly varied is undeniable; that erotic response in any given human being – who necessarily lives in his or her own time, his or her own society, his or her own life, and his or her own existential dilemmas – is highly plastic: that is a completely different idea, and it is not a secure proposition at all. To blur these propositions is to confuse analytical domains.

Actually, sexuality as a social system needs to be theorized as neither more nor less "plastic" than language is (understood as a Bakhtinian "dialogue," not as a Saussurean "structure"). To argue by analogy: the facility for language is made possible by the human brain and connected with the physiology of the vocal apparatus. The human brain is most decidedly a biological organ instantiated in each individual human being; the vocal cords, tongue, and palate, too, belong to our anatomy. Is language, therefore, "rooted" in individual biology? Is it in any significant sense "constrained" by anatomy? Is it the expression of biological or individual essences? Certainly not. As a social-practical phenomenon, language cannot be reduced to biology, anatomy, or the individual. Questions of language are questions of meaning. The biological and anatomical mechanics of speech are not relevant to the meaning of any given speech act or any given discourse, text, or language. Even though the capacity for and necessity of language are both "wired" into the grooves of the brain, no language is explicable in terms of biological imperatives. However, as inadequate as are biological and essentialist views of language, the structuralist or functionalist view of language merely replaces one determinism with another. Its determinism, too, is inadequate – for whatever else language is, it is more a zone of "dialogue" than of homogenous "structure." Even though each language entails normative rules, a stable syntax, a logical grammar – in short, a hypothetical "structure" – speech acts may indeed violate all the tenets of linguistic structure and still remain intelligible linguistic phenomena. Language, though structured, naturally entails disagreements, conflicts, misunderstandings, and ambiguities; though regular, it is very much an *open* (not closed) system; though rulelike, it is not rendered unintelligible by the breaking of rules. The rules of language, then, do not determine what we say; they only circumscribe it. Nor, for that matter, does knowing a language (and thinking in it) preclude learning a second language (although some will have more trouble than others) or even losing one's facility in the first language (given enough time).

The same holds true for sex. The anatomy of the conscious body affords the potential for a large but theoretically limited range of sexual acts. This range of sex acts might be viewed as the sexual equivalent of phonemes in language. Sexual acts in themselves, like phonetic sounds in and of themselves, are meaningless. Sexual meaning occurs when sexual acts are grouped into vocabularies, are imbued with other associations, are appropriated by a sexual grammar. In short, they are meaningful only in a social context – but this is not to say that they are necessarily under the totalitarian control of a cultural program, for what could be more "dialogical," more "interdiscursive," than sex? One could imagine, instead, a series of concentric circles (rather than a hierarchical or deterministic scheme): (a) an individual's sexual practices and narratives, which represent both a lifetime of social intercourse with other people *and* an engagement with and *within* (b) a wider horizon, not of a specific narrative, but of plural, competing, and often conflicting social narratives about sexual practices, which is itself engaged in a dialectical relationship with (c) a larger political economy of gender and sexuality. (And, of course, even this third sphere is embedded in a larger social environment.) Meaning in any of these spheres is never either entirely "determined" or "free"; rather, the meaning of any individual or collective erotic life is precisely the living process of exchange between these zones, which range from the "micro" to the "macro" – and which are traversed by various degrees of autonomy and control, freedom and determinism, rebellion and conformity, power and love. (See Medvedev and Bakhtin 1978: 26–8.) . . .

11 For instance, some Middle Eastern cultures cast these active-passive rules in terms of active adults and passive youths (Trumbach 1977: 8). (See also Foucault's discussion of "the antinomy of the boy" in Greek antiquity (1986: 221). The cochón is an adult though stigmatized male. Nicaraguan and Middle Eastern practices could be seen as variations on the larger type (active-passive rules), or each could be classified as an independent type. The typologies one draws up, then, will depend on one's purpose in classifying practices and what features one deems important (see Greenberg 1988: 490–3).

References

Adam, Barry D. 1987. "Homosexuality Without a Gay World: The Case of Nicaragua." *ARGOH Newsletter* 9/3: 6–10.

Adams, Richard N. 1956. "Cultural Components of Central America." *American Anthropologist* 58: 881–907.

——. 1957. *Cultural Surveys of Panama-Nicaragua-Guatemala – El Salvador – Honduras.* Scientific Publications no. 33. Washington, DC: Pan American Sanitary Bureau, Regional Office of the World Health Organization.

Arguelles, Lourdes, and B. Ruby Rich. 1984. "Homosexuality, Homophobia, and Revolution: Notes Toward an Understanding of the Cuban Lesbian and Gay Male Experience, Part I." *Signs* 9/4: 683–99.

Bakhtin, Mikhail M. 1984. *Rabelais and His World.* Bloomington: Indiana University Press.

Blake, James. 1971. *The Joint.* New York: Doubleday.

Boswell, John. 1980. *Christianity, Social Tolerance, and Homosexuality: Gay People in Western History from the Beginning of the Christian Era to the Fourteenth Century.* Chicago: University of Chicago Press.

——. 1989. "Revolutions, Universals, and Sexual Categories." In Martin Duberman, Martha Vicinus, and George Chauncey, Jr. (eds.) *Hidden from History: Reclaiming the Gay and Lesbian Past.* New York: Meridian, pp. 17–36.

Brandes, Stanley. 1981. "Like Wounded Stags: Male Sexual Ideology in an Andalusian Town." In Sherry Ortner and Harriet Whitehead (eds.) *Sexual Meanings: The Cultural Construction of Gender and Sexuality.* Cambridge: Cambridge University Press, pp. 216–39.

Callender, Charles, and Lee M. Kochems. 1983. "The North American Berdache." *Current Anthropology* 24/4: 1–76.

Carrier, J. M. 1976. "Family Attitudes and Mexican Male Homosexuality." *Urban Life* 5/3: 359–75.

Certeau, Michel de. 1984. *The Practice of Everyday Life.* Berkeley and Los Angeles: University of California Press.

Chauncey, George, Jr. 1989. "Christian Brotherhood or Sexual Perversion? Homosexual Identities and the Construction of Sexual Boundaries in the World War I Era." In Martin Duberman, Martha Vicinus, and George Chauncey, Jr. (eds.) *Hidden From History: Reclaiming the Gay and Lesbian Past.* New York: Meridian, pp. 294–317.

Corzine, Jay, and Richard Kirby. 1977. "Cruising and Truckers: Sexual Encounters in a Highway Rest Area." *Urban Life* 6/2: 171–92.

Davis, Natalie Zemon. 1978. "Women on Top: Symbolic Inversion and Political Disorder in Early Modern Europe." In Barbara A. Babcock, ed., *The Reversible World: Symbolic Inversion in Art and Society.* Ithaca: Cornell University Press, pp. 147–90.

D'Emilio, John. 1983. *Sexual Politics, Sexual Communities: The Making of a Homosexual Minority in the United States, 1940–1970.* Chicago: University of Chicago Press.

Foucault, Michel. 1980 [1976]. *The History of Sexuality*, Vol. 1, An Introduction. Translated by R. Hurley. New York: Random House, Vintage Books.

——. 1986 [1984]. *The History of Sexuality.* Vol. 2, *The Use of Pleasure.* Translated by R. Hurley. New York: Random House, Vintage Books.

Goffman, Erving. 1959. *The Presentation of Self in Everyday Life.* Garden City, NY: Doubleday.

Greenberg, David F. 1988. *The Construction of Homosexuality.* Chicago: University of Chicago Press.

Halperin, David M. 1989. "Sex Before Sexuality: Pederasty, Politics, and Power in Classical Athens." In Martin Duberman, Martha Vicinus, and George Chauncey, Jr. (eds.) *Hidden from History: Reclaiming the Gay and Lesbian Past.* New York: Meridian, pp. 37–53.

Herdt, Gilbert H. 1981. *Guardians of the Flutes: Idioms of Masculinity.* New York: McGraw-Hill.

——. 1982. "Fetish and Fantasy in Sambia Initiation." In Gilbert H. Herdt (ed.) *Rituals of Manhood: Male Initiation in Papua New Guinea.* Berkeley and Los Angeles: University of California Press, pp. 44–98.

Humphreys, Laud. 1970. *Tearoom Trade: Impersonal Sex in Public Places.* Chicago: Aldine.

Jameson, Fredric. 1972. *The Prison-House of Language: A Critical Account of Structuralism and Russian Formalism.* Princeton: Princeton University Press.

Kardiner, Abram. 1954. "The Flight from Masculinity." In *Sex and Morality.* New York: Bobbs-Merrill.

Katz, Jonathan Ned. 1990. "The Invention of Heterosexuality." *Socialist Review* 20/1: 7–33.

Lancaster, Roger N. 1986. "Comment on Arguelles and Rich's 'Homosexuality, Homophobia, and Revolution: Notes Toward an Understanding of the Cuban Lesbian and Gay Male Experience, Part II.'" *Signs* 12/1: 188–92.

——. 1988a. "Subject Honor and Object Shame: The Construction of Male Homosexuality and Stigma in Nicaragua." *Ethnology* 27/2: 111–25.

——. 1988b. *Thanks to God and the Revolution: Popular Religion and Class Consciousness in the New Nicaragua.* New York: Columbia University Press.

Lévi-Strauss, Claude. 1969. *The Elementary Structures of Kinship.* Boston: Beacon.

Lewes, Kenneth. 1988. *The Psychoanalytic Theory of Male Homosexuality.* New York: New American Library.

Matthieu, Nicole-Claude. 1978. "Man-Culture and Woman-Nature?" *Feminist Studies International Quarterly* 1: 55–65.

Mead, Margaret. 1963 [1935]. *Sex and Temperament in Three Primitive Societies.* New York: Morrow Quill.

Medvedev, P. N., and Mikhail M. Bakhtin. 1978 [1928]. *The Formal Method of Literary Scholarship: A Critical Introduction to Sociological Poetics.* Translated by Albert J. Wehrle. Baltimore: Johns Hopkins University Press.

Murphy, M. 1984. "Masculinity and Selective Homophobia: A Case from Spain." *ARGOH Newsletter* 5: 6–12.

Nash, June. 1979. *We Eat the Mines and the Mines Eat Us: Dependency and Exploitation in Bolivian Tin Mines.* New York: Columbia University Press.

Padgug, Robert. 1989. "Sexual Matters: Rethinking Sexuality in History." In Martin Duberman, Martha Vicinus, and George Chauncey Jr. (eds.) *Hidden from History: Reclaiming the Gay and Lesbian Past.* New York: Meridian, pp. 54–64.

Parker, Richard. 1984. "The Body and the Self: Aspects of Male Sexual Ideology in Brazil." Paper presented at the Eighty-third annual meeting of the American Anthropological Association, Denver.

——. 1985. "Masculinity, Femininity, and Homosexuality: On the Anthropological Interpretation of Sexual Meanings in Brazil." *Journal of Homosexuality* 11: 155–63.

——. 1991. *Bodies, Pleasures, and Passions: Sexual Culture in Contemporary Brazil.* Boston: Beacon.

Potter, Sulamith Heins, and Jack M. Potter. 1990. *China's Peasants: The Anthropology of a Revolution.* Cambridge: Cambridge University Press.

Rubin, Gayle. 1975. "The Traffic in Women: Notes on the 'Political Economy' of Sex." In Rayna N. Reiter (ed.) *Toward an Anthropology of Women.* New York: Monthly Review Press, pp. 157–210.

Ruse, Michael. 1988. *Homosexuality: A Philosophical Inquiry.* Oxford: Basil Blackwell.

Sahlins, Marshall. 1977. "Colors and Cultures." In Janet L. Dolgin, David S. Kemnitzer, and David M. Schneider (eds.) *Symbolic Anthropology: A Reader in the Study of Symbols and Meanings.* New York: Columbia University Press, pp. 165–80.

Strathern, Marilyn. 1981. "Culture in a Netbag: The Manufacture of a Subdiscipline in Anthropology." *Man,* n.s. 16: 665–88.

Suárez-Orozco, Marcelo M. 1982. "A Study of Argentine Soccer: The Dynamics of Fans and Their Folklore." *Journal of Psychoanalytic Anthropology* 5: 7–28.

Trumbach, Randolph. 1977. "London's Sodomites: Homosexual Behavior and Western Culture in the Eighteenth Century." *Journal of Social History* 11: 1–33.

Vološinov, V. N. 1986 [1929]. *Marxism and the Philosophy of Language.* Translated by Ladislav Matejka and I. R. Titunik. Cambridge: Harvard University Press.

Weeks, Jeffrey. 1977. *Coming Out: Homosexual Politics in Britain from the Nineteenth Century to the Present.* London: Quartet.

——. 1981. *Sex, Politics, and Society: The Regulation of Sexuality since 1800.* New York: Longman.

——. 1985. *Sexuality and Its Discontents: Meanings, Myths, and Modern Sexualities.* London: Routledge and Kegan Paul.

Whitehead, Harriet. 1981. "The Bow and the Burden Strap: A New Look at Institutionalized Homosexuality in Native North America." In Sherry Ortner and Harriet Whitehead (eds.) *Sexual Meanings: The Cultural Construction of Gender and Sexuality.* Cambridge: Cambridge University Press, pp. 80–115.

Williams, Walter L. 1986. *The Spirit and the Flesh: Sexual Diversity in American Indian Culture.* Boston: Beacon.

4

The Democratic Body: Prostitution and Citizenship in Classical Athens

David Halperin

You see these people here, the ones who occupy the brothels and admittedly practise that activity – well, even they, whenever it happens that they are driven to it by need, nevertheless make some attempt to shield themselves from disgrace and shut their doors. Now if someone were to ask you, as you were walking along the street, what such a person was doing at that moment, you would immediately name the deed, without seeing what was going on and without knowing who it was who had gone inside, but since you know for a fact what the person's chosen trade is, you know perfectly well what that person is doing.[1]

This passage from a speech ("Against Timarchus") delivered by the Attic orator Aeschines in 346/5 BC holds a number of surprises in store for the modern student of ancient Greek prostitution. First of all, both the prostitute and the hypothetical client postulated by Aeschines are male. That the *client* is male may occasion relatively little astonishment: prostitution then, as now, catered almost exclusively to men. The gender of the *prostitute*, however, is perhaps more unexpected; in fact, prostitution in classical Athens routinely engaged young men and boys as well as women of various ages.

Youth seems to have been a more stringent requirement for male than for female prostitutes. Ancient authors, to be sure, preserve no lack of malicious gossip about the miserable and impoverished old age of once-glamorous courtesans who, half-starved and unable to command high prices, can no longer afford to be choosy about their dwindling customers, and many ancient texts describe the elaborate artifices – ranging from wigs to hair dye to elevator heels to a facial powder made from white lead – by which female prostitutes typically attempt to conceal their age and to disguise assorted physical shortcomings. But mature age did not necessarily prohibit a woman from earning a living as a prostitute: male tastes varied (two Hellenistic epigrams by Asclepiades portray female prostitutes dedicating, severally, a purple horsewhip, reins, and a golden spur to Aphrodite), and a sexual market for older women is at least treated as a plausible possibility by the fourth-century BC comic poet Xenarchus.[2] Males, by contrast, were generally thought

Reprinted from *South Atlantic Quarterly* 88/1 (Winter 1989), pp. 149–60.

desirable only between the onset of puberty and the arrival of the beard. In particular, the *hôra* (or youthful "prime") of males – a slender zone between boyhood and manhood comprising what we now call late adolescence and corresponding roughly to the life-stage of American undergraduates – represented the peak of a male's sexual attractiveness and exercised, while it lasted, an apparently irresistible charm on older residents of classical Athens, both male and female, free and slave. Once the frontier between youth and manhood had been crossed, however, a male became visibly *exôros* ("past his prime") – as many an ancient lover remarks with alternating bitterness and relief – and, in Aeschines' words, "no one will give him anything for it any more."[3] An older male who wished, for whatever reason, to attract either women or men had to do his best to look young, and any adult male who actually did (or, what was worse, tried to) look younger than his years was liable to be suspected of pathic desires or adulterous intentions.[4] Male prostitution in classical Athens was largely the province of those below the age of majority.

Aeschines also reveals that male prostitution in Athens was not an especially clandestine or disreputable affair. To *be* a prostitute was hardly a noble vocation for a male, but to *hire* one did not cover you with shame. The very nonchalance with which the orator invites his audience to picture a male brothel implies that such an establishment was a fairly familiar and recognizable feature of the urban landscape. And it apparently conducted its business openly, unprotected from the knowing gaze of passersby. . . .

The apparent extent, visibility, and ordinariness of male prostitution help to illumine another aspect of classical Athenian society: the ubiquity of pederasty. The male desire for sexual contact with comely youths was evidently not confined, as is sometimes alleged, to a tiny, eccentric, and supposedly pro-Spartan aristocracy at Athens, nor was it the exclusive property of a handful of articulate and prolific intellectuals (although in later antiquity it came to be closely identified with Socraticism). Male prostitution evidently supported, and was in turn supported by, a broadly based pederastic constituency; the explicitly sexual ends and mercenary means favored by the members of that constituency distinguished them, at least in tone if not in substance, from the romantic, conspicuously high-minded, and tirelessly self-promoting admirers of the Athenian *jeunesse dorée* celebrated in the writings of Plato and other Socratics (as well as by Aeschines)[5] and defended – with some embarrassment, to be sure – by the more chauvinistic classical handbooks on the ground of their putative educational aims. But the erotic excitement and bittersweet longing aroused in Athenian men (whether low- or high-minded) by handsome youths do not seem to have been primarily, or essentially, of a philosophic nature and, when frustrated, evidently required something besides a platonic outlet.

Particular districts of Athens may have been especially favored by male prostitutes. . . . But prostitutes do not seem to have lodged only in special ghettos where citizens with no interest in patronizing them would never stumble upon them. On the contrary, prostitution seems rather to have been an ordinary feature of daily life in classical Athens.

And no wonder: it was extremely difficult and hazardous for a male resident of Athens in the classical period to gain sexual access to any person of citizen status. The female relations of Athenian citizens, as well as their male and female slaves, were protected from sexual assault by the laws against *hybris* ("outrage" or "infliction of shame"); free Athenian women were also shielded from the advances of a would-be seducer by the laws against *moikheia*, which was a more serious crime than rape: *moikheia* signified consenting but unauthorized sex with a citizen's wife, mother, sister, daughter, or concubine kept "with a view to free children." As such, *moikheia* represented a concept similar to that of "adultery" (by which the word is often translated) but considerably broader, applying to sex with any female under the legal guardianship of a citizen – which is to say any woman of citizen status who was not herself a prostitute. (Athenian women were lifelong statutory minors and were therefore *always* in the legal custody of a male relation.) Citizen women were also protected by the social custom of secluding them, to the greatest extent possible, in the interior domestic space of the Greek household and of keeping a close watch on their activities and movements.

Citizen youths were likewise protected from sexual assault by the laws against *hybris*, but the preservation of their sexual integrity had to proceed by a different set of legal and social strategies. That was partly because they could not be sexually impregnated, and so what happened to them had fewer immediate consequences for the integrity of their families as well as for the eventual transmission of property and ancestral identity within the family; it was also because they moved in the exterior realm of public space, inhabited by men, to which different rules had to be applied.[6] An elaborate system of laws and social customs accordingly restricted sexual access to the young males of citizen families, preventing slaves from courting free boys, insulating citizen youths from the sexual overtures of their fathers' friends, protecting students and athletes from abuse by their teachers and trainers, regulating access to schoolrooms and gymnasia, and thwarting encounters between youths and their male elders before dawn, after dark, and in the absence of third parties.

Whereas unauthorized sexual contact with a woman of citizen status was always a serious crime, sexual contact with a citizen youth did not necessarily require the consent of his guardian and was, at least in principle, obtainable. But numerous obstacles remained. The pederastic ethos of classical Athens denied the junior member of a male couple a share in the *erôs* (or "sexual passion") assumed to animate his older lover: the youth was expected to submit – if, that is, he chose to submit at all – to the enflamed desire of his suitor solely out of a feeling of mingled esteem, gratitude, and affection (or *philia*); like a good Victorian wife, he was supposed to suffer and be still.[7] A youth therefore did not have the sexual motive that women supposedly had to yield to the entreaties of a male lover; furthermore, it was disgraceful for him to appear to be too easily seduced. He had to be won by an elaborate ritual of courtship, which could be lengthy, arduous, highly competitive (good-looking young men were celebrated for their beauty), and possibly quite expensive. Those who could not or would not lavish the requisite time and effort on such demanding affairs but who sought sexual contact with boys and young men could find in male prostitutes a more ready, if less edifying, means of gratifying their sexual *prohairesis* (or "preference"), as Aeschines calls it.[8] . . .

Any male of citizen status whose body had at any time been hired out to anyone for sexual use automatically forfeited, by virtue of that very transaction, many of his citizen rights. . . .

The logic behind the disenfranchisement of citizen prostitutes emerges from the democratic ideology of the Athenian state and from the cultural poetics of manhood underlying it. The transition at Athens to a radical democracy based on universal male suffrage required a series of measures designed to uphold the dignity and autonomy of every (male) citizen, whatever his economic circumstances. For only on that basis could every citizen participate on equal terms in the corporate body of the community and share in its rule. Economic disparities could not, of course, be eliminated, nor were serious efforts made to eliminate them. But a limit could be set to the political and social consequences of such inequities, a zone marked out where their influence might not extend. The body of the male citizen constituted that zone.

At the boundaries of a citizen's body the operation of almost all social and economic power halted.[9] One of the earliest constitutional regulations of the emerging democracy stipulated that a citizen could not be enslaved for debt (although he still might be temporarily disenfranchised), which is to say that his body could not become the target of economic, physical, or sexual violence. Nor could a citizen be tortured to produce evidence in a court of law, as slaves and foreigners might be: his body was thus exempt as well from judicial violence. The body of a citizen was sacrosanct; foreigners and slaves might be manhandled in various ways, but a citizen might not. Freedom from servility, exemption from torture, and corporeal inviolability were markers that distinguished citizens from slaves and from foreign residents in Athens. To violate the bodily sanctity of a citizen by treating him as one would a slave, by manhandling him, or even by placing a hand on his body without his consent was not only to insult him personally but to assault the corporate integrity of the citizen body as a whole and to offend its fiercely egalitarian spirit. It was an act of *hybris*, or "outrage," in short, which signified the violation of a status distinction, the attempted reduction of a person to a status below the one he or she actually occupied. *Hybris* was thus the antidemocratic crime par excellence, and it called down upon the offender the full wrath of the democratic judicial system.

Prostitution is spoken of, especially in the case of males, as hiring oneself out "for *hybris*" (*eph' hybrei*) – meaning, "for other people to treat as they please," to use one's body for the purposes of *their* own pleasure. It was understood, for example, that a man went to prostitutes partly in order to enjoy sexual pleasures that were thought degrading to the person who provided them and that he could not therefore easily obtain from his wife or boyfriend (such as insertive oral sex). The liability to be subjected to degrading sexual acts made prostitutes impure in the Athenian imagination – hence unfit to perform sacred duties on behalf of the city – and, similarly, the length of time required for a man to purify himself ritually after sexual contact with a prostitute was, at least in some places throughout the ancient Greek world, longer than the period required for purification after intercourse with a wife.[10] For males, engaging in prostitution was equivalent to choosing to be the victim of what would have been, if one's surrender had not been voluntary, *hybris*.[11] And so it signified a refusal of the constitutional safeguards of one's bodily integrity provided by the Athenian democracy, a forfeiture of one's birthright as an Athenian to share on an equal basis with one's fellow citizens in the government of the city. It was, next to enslavement, the worst degradation a citizen could suffer, equivalent to voluntary effeminization.

Anyone who prostituted himself – whether out of economic necessity or greed (sexual desire is never mentioned as a possible motive) – indicated by that gesture that his autonomy was for sale to whoever wished to buy it. The city as a collective entity was vulnerable in the person of such a citizen, vulnerable to penetration, corruption, foreign influence. No person who prostituted himself could be allowed to speak before the people in the public assembly because his words might not be his own; he might have been hired to say them by someone else, someone whose interests did not coincide with those of Athens. The acceptance of money for sexual favors violated the ideal of self-sufficiency which, paradoxically enough, constituted the basis of mutual trust among members of the citizen collective, who had to assume that their common interests as equal and full sharers in the privileges of democracy guaranteed their common purpose in advancing the welfare of the city, even when they disagreed with one another. But a prostitute gave up those interests; he showed a willingness to serve (in the worst way) the pleasure, the interests of his client – he proved himself the instrument of another person's pleasure, not an autonomous actor in his own right. Such a person threatened the coherence of democracy from within and had to be disenfranchised.

The institution of the democracy at Athens brought with it, then, the social production and distribution to the citizens of a new kind of body – a free, autonomous, and inviolable body undifferentiated by distinctions of wealth, class, or status: a democratic body, the site and guarantee of personal and political independence. That, of course, was the ideal; the reality of economic hardship and social dependency was quite different, and the poor often found themselves performing the sorts of menial duties routinely assigned to slaves and therefore being assimilated to slaves in the estimation of their more fortunate neighbors.[12] But the *reality* of economic and social life was not the point of the democratic reforms: the democracy was not expected to function perfectly or to extend its benefits indifferently to everyone in practice. The fourth-century BC Attic orator Demosthenes specifically denies that Solon's legislation was intended to prevent citizens from engaging in prostitution altogether; on the contrary, he says, Solon did not ban prostitution outright because he did not wish to burden further those already so poor as to have no other means of earning a living.[13] In this respect, the goal of the democratic legislation was not moral or practical but symbolic: it was designed not to alter the facts of Athenian social life or to reform individual Athenians but to disseminate among the citizens of Athens a new collective self-understanding, an image of themselves as free and autonomous and equal participants in the shared rule of the city precisely insofar as they were all (rich and poor alike) – *in principle*, at least – equally lords over their own bodies. That corporeal sovereignty came to represent to Athenian citizens the ultimate line of defense of their social and political integrity. And so anyone who abandoned it surrendered in effect his principal, if not his sole, political means of recuperating whatever other losses to his dignity he might unavoidably suffer through enforced social or economic dependency.

In another sense, however, prostitution at Athens – far from being repressed by democracy – was the creation of democracy. But now it is a question not of male but of female prostitution. Among the reforms credited in the classical period to Solon, the architect of Athenian democracy, is the institution of (state?) brothels, staffed by slave women at a price that put them within the reach of all citizens. The assumption underlying that institution would seem to be that a society is not democratic so long as sexual pleasure remains an exclusive perquisite of the well-to-do. Solon accordingly earned the gratitude of a nameless character in *The*

Brothers by the late fourth/early third-century BC comic poet Philemon: the speaker is evidently one of the young men rescued from "erotic necessity" by Solon's leveling of sexual inequities.

> But you found a law for the use of everyone; for you were the first, Solon, they say, to discover this practice – a democratic one, by Zeus, and a saving one (I'm an appropriate person to say so, Solon!): seeing the city full of young men and seeing them under the compulsion of nature misbehaving in ways they should not, you bought and stationed women in various public locations, equipped for all alike. They stand there naked, so you won't be deceived: what you see is what you get. You don't happen to feel quite yourself; you have something bothering you: how so? The door is wide open. One obol, and in you hop. There isn't a bit of prudishness or nonsense, and she doesn't shy away from you, but goes straight to it, just as you like and in whatever way you like. You come out: tell her to go to hell, she's nothing to do with you.[14]

From the proceeds of the brothels he had established, Solon built a temple to Aphrodite Pandemos, "Aphrodite of the entire people," to commemorate his achievement – and, no doubt, to drive home its democratic message: sexual pleasure belongs to all the citizens.

The disenfranchisement of male prostitutes and the cheap provision of female prostitutes beg to be seen together as complementary aspects of a single democratizing initiative intended to shore up the masculine dignity of the poorer citizens – to prevent them from being effeminized by poverty – and to promote a new collective image of the citizen body as masculine and assertive, as master of its pleasures, and as perpetually on the superordinate side of a series of hierarchical and roughly congruent distinctions in status: master vs. slave, free vs. unfree, dominant vs. submissive, active vs. passive, insertive vs. receptive, customer vs. prostitute, citizen vs. noncitizen. Rather than outlaw prostitution on the part of Athenian citizens, the democratic constitution of Athens sought to establish the political and ideological *incompatibility* of citizenship and prostitution, thereby incorporating prostitution (albeit in a negative way) into the symbolic codes of Athenian political and personal life.

Notes

This essay represents an excerpt from a longer discussion of both male and female prostitution in ancient Greece, originally commissioned for a special issue of *Storia e Dossier*, edited by Guido Ruggiero, and forthcoming there (without notes or scholarly references) in Italian translation. A fuller version of this essay appears in my *One Hundred Years of Homosexuality and Other Essays on Greek Love* (New York: Routledge, 1990). I wish to thank John J. Winkler for much help and encouragement as well as Cynthia B. Patterson for valuable and friendly criticism.

1 Aeschines Rhetor 1.74.
2 *Greek Anthology* 5.202, 203; Xenarchus frag. 4.9 Edmonds.
3 Aeschines Rhetor 1.95.
4 See Maud W. Gleason, "The Semiotics of Gender: Physiognomy and Self-Fashioning in the Second Century c.e.," in *Before Sexuality: The Construction of Erotic Experience in the Ancient Greek World*, ed. David M. Halperin, John J. Winkler, and Froma I. Zeitlin (Princeton: Princeton University Press, 1990).

5 Aeschines Rhetor 1.132–35.

6 See Michel Foucault, *The History of Sexuality*, vol. 2, trans. Robert Hurley (New York, 1985), pp. 197–8.

7 See David M. Halperin, "Plato and Erotic Reciprocity," *Classical Antiquity* 5 (1986): 60–80, esp. 63–6.

8 Aeschines Rhetor 1.195.

9 In this paragraph I shall be summarizing the arguments advanced by John J. Winkler, "Laying Down the Law: The Oversight of Men's Sexual Behavior in Classical Athens," in Halperin et al., *Before Sexuality*.

10 I owe this information to the forthcoming work of Professor Susan Guettel Cole of the University of Illinois at Chicago, whom I wish to thank for allowing me to refer to it here.

11 See K. J. Dover, *Greek Homosexuality* (London, 1978), pp. 103–4.

12 See Mark Golden, "Slavery and Homosexuality at Athens," *Phoenix* 38 (1984): 308–24, esp. 310 n. 9.

13 Demosthenes 22.30–31.

14 Philemon frag. 4 Edmonds. I have based my translation on that of Charles Burton Gulick, trans., *Athenaeus: The Deipnosophists* (London, 1937), 6, pp. 77–9.

Part II

Social Sciences

Although the sciences of man took their modern configuration late in the nineteenth century, it was not until late in the twentieth that social theorists began to recognize that the "man" under scrutiny is a gendered construction. That recognition reflects the impact of feminism on disciplines whose mission it has been to analyze the fundamental and determinant structures of social life. Unlike psychoanalysis, which aims to reveal the workings of the individual psyche, the social sciences (as defined by leading thinkers such as Rousseau, Marx, Durkheim, and Weber) aim to demystify the world of institutions and social relations. And they do so by focusing on four different kinds of patriarchal structures: economic relations, patterns of social organization, forms of political authority, and ideology.

Until the work of feminist pioneers such as Margaret Mead and Simone de Beauvoir, most social scientists took it for granted that men represent the dominant class in the vast majority of human cultures. Moreover, the classic texts of social science are every bit as masculinist as the societies they study. Yet the works of these critics – and those of a generation of feminist social scientists who came of age in the 1970s – initiated a major revision of social science by criticizing its sexism and analyzing distinctively female social relations, practices, and spheres of activity. They also demonstrated that forms of male domination are inextricably linked to economic and political institutions, ideologies, and class formations. Whereas feminist sociology has tended to concentrate on women, the diverse collection of essays in this part of the *Reader* all shift the focus back to men, to analyze the means by which patriarchal relations are sustained and naturalized. Each essay takes a particular aspect of patriarchal society to be paradigmatic or foundational. For Geertz, it is the cockfight, understood as both a material practice and a metaphor, that authorizes the renegotiation of masculinity in Bali through the wagering of money and status. For Pateman, it is the workings of a modern, liberal, civil society produced when a paternal form of patriarchy is transformed into a fraternal one. For Kimmel, it is the triumph in nineteenth-century America of the Self-Made Man. And for Carrigan et al., it is the social, economic, and libidinal power granted to a particular form of heterosexualized masculinity, which they dub hegemonic.

Despite the considerable differences among these critical approaches, all represent a reaction against what Carrigan et al. describe as the functionalist sex-role theory developed in the 1930s by Talcott Parsons, which attempted to elucidate the underlying principles by which societies are maintained and reproduced. Focusing on normative groups rather than individuals, Parsons's influential theory presumed societies to be "self-equilibrating systems" and rejected a more traditional historical sociology that emphasized power relations and social and ideological struggle (Callinicos: 41). As Carrigan et al. argue, this approach is both conservative and ahistorical because of its naturalization of traditional "sex roles" and its inability to account for deviance or social change. In the reactionary political climate of the 1950s, functionalism easily became complicit with other political and ideological forces dedicated to the containment of women and the demonization of sexual minorities.

Parsonian functionalism was challenged in the late 1960s by a resurgence of Marxist theory and the influence of revolutionary social movements for racial justice, decolonization, and women's liberation on academic research. And while no single theorist is responsible for overthrowing sex-role theory, Gayle Rubin is probably the one most frequently cited as a founder of feminist social science, especially her groundbreaking 1975 essay, "The Traffic in Women: Notes on the 'Political Economy' of Sex." Critiquing key texts in anthropology (Lévi-Strauss), psychoanalysis (Freud), and Marxism, Rubin argues that patriarchal relations worldwide are strictly dependent upon the exchange of women between men. Because "men have been sexual subjects – exchangers – and women sexual semi-objects – gifts – for much of human history, then many customs, clichés, and personality traits seem to make a great deal of sense." The bipolar system of gender thus "exacerbates the biological differences between the sexes" to produce "a socially imposed division" that is the foundation of all human societies (Rubin: 174–9).

Most of the essays in this section owe a significant debt to Rubin's work. Even Geertz, whose piece antedates Rubin's by three years, can be seen to break with sex-role theory and thus to make a first step toward pluralizing and problematizing notions of masculinity. Although frequently anthologized, Geertz's essay on the Balinese cockfight has not been considered for its contribution to the study of masculinity, and its inclusion here suggests previously unexamined implications for his argument. By imagining the cockfight as a drama, a "metaphor," a "means of expression" and communication among men, Geertz argues that it is a crucial site in Balinese culture for working out distinctively masculine anxieties about power and status. Moreover, by recognizing the unmistakably phallic implications of "the deep psychological identification of Balinese men with their cocks," he denaturalizes masculine rituals by linking them to economic and social structures.

In contradistinction to Geertz, the other essays in this section all reflect the influence of feminism or the men's movement. Like "Deep Play," Carol Pateman's well-known feminist work on citizenship is recontextualized here as an essay about masculinity. Arguing that modern civil society is organized around a fraternal contract that "gives the appearance of freedom to sexually ascriptive domination and subjection," Pateman exposes the masculine identity of the individual defined by contract law. She notes, however, that this abstract individual cannot be universalized by fiat, that the abstract man of liberal republicanism cannot simply be translated into a general humanity inclusive of both men and women. Liberal feminism, in particular, she concludes, will need to "come to grips with the deeper problems of *how* women are to take an equal place in the patriarchal civil order." Kimmel's history, in contrast, imagines multiple forms of masculinity engaged in struggle for dominance within American culture. Focusing on literary as well as social texts, he analyzes the contradictions and anxieties associated with the triumph of the Self-made Man in the early years of the American Republic. Carrigan et al. attempt to evaluate and to provide a historical account of the impact of "men's studies" on the social sciences. Their goal, to arrive at an adequate understanding of masculinity within a broader system of gender relations, can only be attained by approaching masculinity as a plural rather than a monolithic category and by linking its study to related research on women and gay men.

By analyzing the dynamics and persistence of various patriarchal institutions, these writers uncover the social structures that produce admittedly diverse masculinities. They also bear witness to a dramatic change in the social sciences since the 1960s, a change that marks a return, after the heyday of Parsonian functionalism, to the classical tradition of social theory intent on demystifying the histories of structures, systems, and subjects that are usually taken for granted. By reviving this critical tradition in the context of feminist and lesbian/gay/queer studies, the social theorists of masculinity are illuminating the workings of patriarchal societies in new and provocative ways.

Bibliography

Callinicos, Alex. 1999. *Social Theory: A Historical Introduction*. New York: New York University Press.

Rubin, Gayle. 1975. "The Traffic in Women: Notes on the 'Political Economy' of Sex." In Rayna R. Reiter (ed.) *Toward an Anthropology of Women*. New York: Monthly Review Press, pp. 157–210.

5

Deep Play: Notes on the Balinese Cockfight

Clifford Geertz

. . .

Of Cocks and Men

Bali, mainly because it is Bali, is a well-studied place. Its mythology, art, ritual, social organization, patterns of child rearing, forms of law, even styles of trance, have all been microscopically examined for traces of that elusive substance Jane Belo called "The Balinese Temper."[1] But, aside from a few passing remarks, the cockfight has barely been noticed, although as a popular obsession of consuming power it is at least as important a revelation of what being a Balinese "is really like" as these more celebrated phenomena.[2] As much of America surfaces in a ball park, on a golf links, at a race track, or around a poker table, much of Bali surfaces in a cock ring. For it is only apparently cocks that are fighting there. Actually, it is men.

To anyone who has been in Bali any length of time, the deep psychological identification of Balinese men with their cocks is unmistakable. The double en- tendre here is deliberate. It works in exactly the same way in Balinese as it does in English, even to producing the same tired jokes, strained puns, and uninventive obscenities. Bateson and Mead have even suggested that, in line with the Balinese conception of the body as a set of separately animated parts, cocks are viewed as detachable, self-operating penises, ambulant genitals with a life of their own.[3] And while I do not have the kind of unconscious material either to confirm or discon- firm this intriguing notion, the fact that they are masculine symbols par excellence is about as indubitable, and to the Balinese about as evident, as the fact that water runs downhill.

The language of everyday moralism is shot through, on the male side of it, with roosterish imagery. *Sabung*, the word for cock (and one which appears in inscrip- tions as early as AD 922), is used metaphorically to mean "hero," "warrior," "champion," "man of parts," "political candidate," "bachelor," "dandy,"

Reprinted from *Rethinking Popular Culture: Contemporary Perspectives in Cultural Studies*, ed. Chan- dra Mukerji and Michael Schudson (Berkeley and Los Angeles: University of California Press, 1991), pp. 243–51, 253–63, 265–6, 269–75. Originally published in *Daedalus*, Journal of the American Academy of Arts and Sciences, 101/1 (1972), pp. 1–37.

"lady-killer," or "tough guy." A pompous man whose behavior presumes above his station is compared to a tailless cock who struts about as though he had a large, spectacular one. A desperate man who makes a last, irrational effort to extricate himself from an impossible situation is likened to a dying cock who makes one final lunge at his tormentor to drag him along to a common destruction. A stingy man, who promises much, gives little, and begrudges that, is compared to a cock which, held by the tail, leaps at another without in fact engaging him. A marriageable young man still shy with the opposite sex or someone in a new job anxious to make a good impression is called "a fighting cock caged for the first time."[4] Court trials, wars, political contests, inheritance disputes, and street arguments are all compared to cockfights.[5] Even the very island itself is perceived from its shape as a small, proud cock, poised, neck extended, back taut, tail raised, in eternal challenge to large, feckless, shapeless Java.[6]

But the intimacy of men with their cocks is more than metaphorical. Balinese men, or anyway a large majority of Balinese men, spend an enormous amount of time with their favorites, grooming them, feeding them, discussing them, trying them out against one another, or just gazing at them with a mixture of rapt admiration and dreamy self-absorption. Whenever you see a group of Balinese men squatting idly in the council shed or along the road in their hips down, shoulders forward, knees up fashion, half or more of them will have a rooster in his hands, holding it between his thighs, bouncing it gently up and down to strengthen its legs, ruffling its feathers with abstract sensuality, pushing it out against a neighbor's rooster to rouse its spirit, withdrawing it toward his loins to calm it again. Now and then, to get a feel for another bird, a man will fiddle this way with someone else's cock for a while, but usually by moving around to squat in place behind it, rather than just having it passed across to him as though it were merely an animal.

In the houseyard, the high-walled enclosures where the people live, fighting cocks are kept in wicker cages, moved frequently about so as to maintain the optimum balance of sun and shade. They are fed a special diet, which varies somewhat according to individual theories but which is mostly maize, sifted for impurities with far more care than it is when mere humans are going to eat it, and offered to the animal kernel by kernel. Red pepper is stuffed down their beaks and up their anuses to give them spirit. They are bathed in the same ceremonial preparation of tepid water, medicinal herbs, flowers, and onions in which infants are bathed, and for a prize cock just about as often. Their combs are cropped, their plumage dressed, their spurs trimmed, and their legs massaged, and they are inspected for flaws with the squinted concentration of a diamond merchant. A man who has a passion for cocks, an enthusiast in the literal sense of the term, can spend most of his life with them, and even those, the overwhelming majority, whose passion though intense has not entirely run away with them, can and do spend what seems not only to an outsider, but also to themselves, an inordinate amount of time with them. "I am cock crazy," my landlord, a quite ordinary *afficionado* by Balinese standards, used to moan as he went to move another cage, give another bath, or conduct another feeding. "We're all cock crazy."

The madness has some less visible dimensions, however, because although it is true that cocks are symbolic expressions or magnifications of their owner's self, the narcissistic male ego writ out in Aesopian terms, they are also expressions – and rather more immediate ones – of what the Balinese regard as the direct inversion, aesthetically, morally, and metaphysically, of human status: animality.

The Balinese revulsion against any behavior regarded as animal-like can hardly be overstressed. Babies are not allowed to crawl for that reason. Incest, though hardly approved, is a much less horrifying crime than bestiality. (The appropriate punishment for the second is death by drowning, for the first being forced to live like an animal.[7]) Most demons are represented – in sculpture, dance, ritual, myth – in some real or fantastic animal form. The main puberty rite consists in filing the child's teeth so they will not look like animal fangs. Not only defecation but eating is regarded as a disgusting, almost obscene activity, to be conducted hurriedly and privately, because of its association with animality. Even falling down or any form of clumsiness is considered to be bad for these reasons. Aside from cocks and a few domestic animals – oxen, ducks – of no emotional significance, the Balinese are aversive to animals and treat their large number of dogs not merely callously but with a phobic cruelty. In identifying with his cock, the Balinese man is identifying not just with his ideal self, or even his penis, but also, and at the same time, with what he most fears, hates, and ambivalence being what it is, is fascinated by – "The Powers of Darkness."

The connection of cocks and cockfighting with such Powers, with the animalistic demons that threaten constantly to invade the small, cleared-off space in which the Balinese have so carefully built their lives and to devour its inhabitants, is quite explicit. A cockfight, any cockfight, is in the first instance a blood sacrifice offered, with the appropriate chants and oblations, to the demons in order to pacify their ravenous, cannibal hunger. No temple festival should be conducted until one is made. (If it is omitted, someone will inevitably fall into a trance and command with the voice of an angered spirit that the oversight be immediately corrected.) Collective responses to natural evils – illness, crop failure, volcanic eruptions – almost always involve them. And that famous holiday in Bali, "The Day of Silence" (*Njepi*), when everyone sits silent and immobile all day long in order to avoid contact with a sudden influx of demons chased momentarily out of hell, is preceded the previous day by large-scale cockfights (in this case legal) in almost every village on the island.

In the cockfight, man and beast, good and evil, ego and id, the creative power of aroused masculinity and the destructive power of loosened animality fuse in a bloody drama of hatred, cruelty, violence, and death. It is little wonder that when, as is the invariable rule, the owner of the winning cock takes the carcass of the loser – often torn limb from limb by its enraged owner – home to eat, he does so with a mixture of social embarrassment, moral satisfaction, aesthetic disgust, and cannibal joy. Or that a man who has lost an important fight is sometimes driven to wreck his family shrines and curse the gods, an act of metaphysical (and social) suicide. Or that in seeking earthly analogues for heaven and hell the Balinese compare the former to the mood of a man whose cock has just won, the latter to that of a man whose cock has just lost.

The Fight

Cockfights (*tetadjen; sabungan*) are held in a ring about fifty feet square. Usually they begin toward late afternoon and run three or four hours until sunset. About nine or ten separate matches (*sehet*) comprise a program. Each match is precisely like the others in general pattern: there is no main match, no connection between individual matches, no variation in their format, and each is arranged on a completely ad hoc basis. After a fight has ended and the emotional debris is cleaned away – the bets have been paid, the curses cursed, the carcasses possessed – seven, eight, perhaps even a dozen men slip negligently into the ring with a cock and seek to find there a logical opponent for it. This process, which rarely takes less than ten minutes, and often a good deal longer, is conducted in a very subdued, oblique, even dissembling manner. Those not immediately involved give it at best but disguised, sidelong attention; those who, embarrassedly, are, attempt to pretend somehow that the whole thing is not really happening.

A match made, the other hopefuls retire with the same deliberate indifference, and the selected cocks have their spurs (*tadji*) affixed – razor-sharp, pointed steel swords, four or five inches long. This is a delicate job which only a small proportion of men, a half-dozen or so in most villages, know how to do properly. The man who attaches the spurs also provides them, and if the rooster he assists wins, its owner awards him the spur-leg of the victim. The spurs are affixed by winding a long length of string around the foot of the spur and the leg of the cock. For reasons I shall come to presently, it is done somewhat differently from case to case, and is an obsessively deliberate affair. The lore about spurs is extensive – they are sharpened only at eclipses and the dark of the moon, should be kept out of the sight of women, and so forth. And they are handled, both in use and out, with the same curious combination of fussiness and sensuality the Balinese direct toward ritual objects generally.

The spurs affixed, the two cocks are placed by their handlers (who may or may not be their owners) facing one another in the center of the ring.[8] A coconut pierced with a small hole is placed in a pail of water, in which it takes about twenty-one seconds to sink, a period known as a *tjeng* and marked at beginning and end by the beating of a slit gong. During these twenty-one seconds the handlers (*pen-gangkeb*) are not permitted to touch their roosters. If, as sometimes happens, the animals have not fought during this time, they are picked up, fluffed, pulled, prodded, and otherwise insulted, and put back in the center of the ring and the process begins again. Sometimes they refuse to fight at all, or one keeps running away, in which case they are imprisoned together under a wicker cage, which usually gets them engaged.

Most of the time, in any case, the cocks fly almost immediately at one another in a wing-beating, head-thrusting, leg-kicking explosion of animal fury so pure, so absolute, and in its own way so beautiful, as to be almost abstract, a Platonic concept of hate. Within moments one or the other drives home a solid blow with his spur. The handler whose cock has delivered the blow immediately picks it up so that it will not get a return blow, for if he does not the match is likely to end in a mutually mortal tie as the two birds wildly hack each other to pieces. This is particularly true if, as often happens, the spur sticks in its victim's body, for then the aggressor is at the mercy of his wounded foe.

With the birds again in the hands of their handlers, the coconut is now sunk three times after which the cock which has landed the blow must be set down to show that he is firm, a fact he demonstrates by wandering idly around the ring for a coconut sink. The coconut is then sunk twice more and the fight must recommence.

During this interval, slightly over two minutes, the handler of the wounded cock has been working frantically over it, like a trainer patching a mauled boxer between rounds, to get it in shape for a last, desperate try for victory. He blows in its mouth, putting the whole chicken head in his own mouth and sucking and blowing, fluffs it, stuffs its wounds with various sorts of medicines, and generally tries anything he can think of to arouse the last ounce of spirit which may be hidden somewhere within it. By the time he is forced to put it back down he is usually drenched in chicken blood, but, as in prize fighting, a good handler is worth his weight in gold. Some of them can virtually make the dead walk, at least long enough for the second and final round.

In the climactic battle (if there is one; sometimes the wounded cock simply expires in the handler's hands or immediately as it is placed down again), the cock who landed the first blow usually proceeds to finish off his weakened opponent. But this is far from an inevitable outcome, for if a cock can walk, he can fight, and if he can fight, he can kill, and what counts is which cock expires first. If the wounded one can get a stab in and stagger on until the other drops, he is the official winner, even if he himself topples over an instant later.

Surrounding all this melodrama – which the crowd packed tight around the ring follows in near silence, moving their bodies in kinesthetic sympathy with the movement of the animals, cheering their champions on with wordless hand motions, shiftings of the shoulders, turnings of the head, falling back en masse as the cock with the murderous spurs careens toward one side of the ring (it is said that spectators sometimes lose eyes and fingers from being too attentive), surging forward again as they glance off toward another – is a vast body of extraordinarily elaborate and precisely detailed rules.

These rules, together with the developed lore of cocks and cockfighting which accompanies them, are written down in palm-leaf manuscripts (*lontar; rontal*) passed on from generation to generation as part of the general legal and cultural tradition of the villages. At a fight, the umpire (*saja komong; djuru kembar*) – the man who manages the coconut – is in charge of their application and his authority is absolute. I have never seen an umpire's judgment questioned on any subject, even by the more despondent losers, nor have I ever heard, even in private, a charge of unfairness directed against one, or, for that matter, complaints about umpires in general. Only exceptionally well trusted, solid, and, given the complexity of the code, knowledgeable citizens perform this job, and in fact men will bring their cocks only to fights presided over by such men. It is also the umpire to whom accusations of cheating, which, though rare in the extreme, occasionally arise, are referred; and it is he who in the not infrequent cases where the cocks expire virtually together decides which (if either, for, though the Balinese do not care for such an outcome, there can be ties) went first. Likened to a judge, a king, a priest, and a policeman, he is all of these, and under his assured direction the animal passion of the fight proceeds within the civic certainty of the law. In the dozens of cockfights I saw in Bali, I never once saw an altercation about rules. Indeed, I never saw an open altercation, other than those between cocks, at all.

This crosswise doubleness of an event which, taken as a fact of nature, is rage untrammeled and, taken as a fact of culture, is form perfected, defines the cockfight as a sociological entity. A cockfight is what, searching for a name for something not vertebrate enough to be called a group and not structureless enough to be called a crowd, Erving Goffman has called a "focused gathering" – a set of persons engrossed in a common flow of activity and relating to one another in terms of that flow.[9] Such gatherings meet and disperse; the participants in them fluctuate; the activity that focuses them is discrete – a particulate process that reoccurs rather than a continuous one that endures. They take their form from the situation that evokes them, the floor on which they are placed, as Goffman puts it; but it is a form, and an articulate one, nonetheless. For the situation, the floor is itself created, in jury deliberations, surgical operations, block meetings, sit-ins, cockfights, by the cultural preoccupations – here, as we shall see, the celebration of status rivalry – which not only specify the focus but, assembling actors and arranging scenery, bring it actually into being.

In classical times (that is to say, prior to the Dutch invasion of 1908), when there were no bureaucrats around to improve popular morality, the staging of a cockfight was an explicitly societal matter. Bringing a cock to an important fight was, for an adult male, a compulsory duty of citizenship; taxation of fights, which were usually held on market day, was a major source of public revenue; patronage of the art was a stated responsibility of princes; and the cock ring, or *wantilan*, stood in the center of the village near those other monuments of Balinese civility – the council house, the origin temple, the marketplace, the signal tower, and the banyan tree. Today, a few special occasions aside, the newer rectitude makes so open a statement of the connection between the excitements of collective life and those of blood sport impossible, but, less directly expressed, the connection itself remains intimate and intact. To expose it, however, it is necessary to turn to the aspect of cockfighting around which all the others pivot, and through which they exercise their force, an aspect I have thus far studiously ignored. I mean, of course, the gambling.

Odds and Even Money

The Balinese never do anything in a simple way that they can contrive to do in a complicated one, and to this generalization cockfight wagering is no exception.

In the first place, there are two sorts of bets, or *toh*.[10] There is the single axial bet in the center between the principals (*toh ketengah*), and there is the cloud of peripheral ones around the ring between members of the audience (*toh kesasi*). The first is typically large; the second typically small. The first is collective, involving coalitions of bettors clustering around the owner; the second is individual, man to man. The first is a matter of deliberate, very quiet, almost furtive arrangement by the coalition members and the umpire huddled like conspirators in the center of the ring; the second is a matter of impulsive shouting, public offers, and public acceptances by the excited throng around its edges. And most curiously, and as we shall see most revealingly, *where the first is always, without exception, even money, the second, equally without exception, is never such.* What is a fair coin in the center is a biased one on the side.

The center bet is the official one, hedged in again with a webwork of rules, and is made between the two cock owners, with the umpire as overseer and public witness.[11] This bet, which, as I say, is always relatively and sometimes very large, is never raised simply by the owner in whose name it is made, but by him together with four or five, sometimes seven or eight, allies – kin, village mates, neighbors, close friends. He may, if he is not especially well-to-do, not even be the major contributor; though, if only to show that he is not involved in any chicanery, he must be a significant one....

The side bets are, however, something else altogether. Rather than the solemn, legalistic pactmaking of the center, wagering takes place rather in the fashion in which the stock exchange used to work when it was out on the curb. There is a fixed and known odds paradigm which runs in a continuous series from ten-to-nine at the short end to two-to-one at the long: 10–9, 9–8, 8–7, 7–6, 6–5, 5–4, 4–3, 3–2, 2–1. The man who wishes to back the *underdog cock* (leaving aside how favorites, *kebut*, and underdogs, *ngai*, are established for the moment) shouts the short-side number indicating the odds he wants *to be given*. That is, if he shouts *gasal*, "five," he wants the underdog at five-to-four (or, for him, four-to-five); if he shouts "four," he wants it at four-to-three (again, he putting up the "three"); if "nine," at nine-to-eight, and so on. A man backing the favorite, and thus considering giving odds if he can get them short enough, indicates the fact by crying out the color-type of that cock – "brown," "speckled," or whatever.[12]

As odds-takers (backers of the underdog) and odds-givers (backers of the favorite) sweep the crowd with their shouts, they begin to focus in on one another as potential betting pairs, often from far across the ring. The taker tries to shout the giver into longer odds, the giver to shout the taker into shorter ones.[13] The taker, who is the wooer in this situation, will signal how large a bet he wishes to make at the odds he is shouting by holding a number of fingers up in front of his face and vigorously waving them. If the giver, the wooed, replies in kind, the bet is made; if he does not, they unlock gazes and the search goes on.

The side betting, which takes place after the center bet has been made and its size announced, consists then in a rising crescendo of shouts as backers of the underdog offer their propositions to anyone who will accept them, while those who are backing the favorite but do not like the price being offered, shout equally frenetically the color of the cock to show they too are desperate to bet but want shorter odds....

The two betting systems, though formally incongruent, are not really contradictory to one another, but are part of a single larger system in which the center bet is, so to speak, the "center of gravity," drawing, the larger it is the more so, the outside bets toward the short-odds end of the scale. The center bet thus "makes the game," or perhaps better, defines it, signals what, following a notion of Jeremy Bentham's, I am going to call its "depth."

The Balinese attempt to create an interesting, if you will, "deep," match by making the center bet as large as possible so that the cocks matched will be as equal and as fine as possible, and the outcome, thus, as unpredictable as possible. They do not always succeed. Nearly half the matches are relatively trivial, relatively uninteresting – in my borrowed terminology, "shallow" – affairs. But that fact no more argues against my interpretation than the fact that most painters, poets, and playwrights are mediocre argues against the view that artistic effort is directed toward profundity and, with a certain frequency, approximates it. The image of artistic technique is indeed exact: the center bet is a means, a device, for creating "interesting," "deep" matches, *not* the reason, or at least not the main reason, *why* they are interesting, the source of their fascination, the substance of their depth.

The question of why such matches are interesting – indeed, for the Balinese, exquisitely absorbing – takes us out of the realm of formal concerns into more broadly sociological and social-psychological ones, and to a less purely economic idea of what "depth" in gaming amounts to.[14]

Playing with Fire

Bentham's concept of "deep play" is found in his *The Theory of Legislation*.[15] By it he means play in which the stakes are so high that it is, from his utilitarian standpoint, irrational for men to engage in it at all. If a man whose fortune is a thousand pounds (or ringgits) wagers five hundred of it on an even bet, the marginal utility of the pound he stands to win is clearly less than the marginal disutility of the one he stands to lose. In genuine deep play, this is the case for both parties. They are both in over their heads. Having come together in search of pleasure they have entered into a relationship which will bring the participants, considered collectively, net pain rather than net pleasure. Bentham's conclusion was, therefore, that deep play was immoral from first principles and, a typical step for him, should be prevented legally.

But more interesting than the ethical problem, at least for our concerns here, is that despite the logical force of Bentham's analysis men do engage in such play, both passionately and often, and even in the face of law's revenge. For Bentham and those who think as he does (nowadays mainly lawyers, economists, and a few psychiatrists), the explanation is, as I have said, that such men are irrational – addicts, fetishists, children, fools, savages, who need only to be protected against themselves. But for the Balinese, though naturally they do not formulate it in so many words, the explanation lies in the fact that in such play, money is less a measure of utility, had or expected, than it is a symbol of moral import, perceived or imposed.

It is, in fact, in shallow games, ones in which smaller amounts of money are involved, that increments and decrements of cash are more nearly synonyms for utility and disutility, in the ordinary, unexpanded sense – for pleasure and pain, happiness and unhappiness. In deep ones, where the amounts of money are great, much more is at stake than material gain: namely, esteem, honor, dignity, respect – in a word, though in Bali a profoundly freighted word, status.[16] It is at stake symbolically, for (a few cases of ruined addict gamblers aside) no one's status is actually altered by the outcome of a cockfight; it is only, and that momentarily, affirmed or insulted. But for the Balinese, for whom nothing is more pleasurable than an affront obliquely delivered or more painful than one obliquely received – particularly when mutual acquaintances, undeceived by surfaces, are watching – such appraisive drama is deep indeed.

This, I must stress immediately, is *not* to say that the money does not matter, or that the Balinese is no more concerned about losing five hundred ringgits than fifteen. Such a conclusion would be absurd. It is because money *does*, in this hardly unmaterialistic society, matter and matter very much that the more of it one risks, the more of a lot of other things, such as one's pride, one's poise, one's dispassion, one's masculinity, one also risks, again only momentarily but again very publicly as well. In deep cockfights an owner and his collaborators, and, as we shall see, to a lesser but still quite real extent also their backers on the outside, put their money where their status is.

It is in large part *because* the marginal disutility of loss is so great at the higher levels of betting that to engage in such betting is to lay one's public self, allusively and metaphorically, through the medium of one's cock, on the line. And though to a Benthamite this might seem merely to increase the irrationality of the enterprise that much further, to the Balinese what it mainly increases is the meaningfulness of it all. And as (to follow Weber rather than Bentham) the imposition of meaning on life is the major end and primary condition of human existence, that access of significance more than compensates for the economic costs involved.[17] Actually, given the even-money quality of the larger matches, important changes in material fortune among those who regularly participate in them seem virtually nonexistent, because matters more or less even out over the long run. It is, actually, in the smaller, shallow fights, where one finds the handful of more pure, addict-type gamblers involved – those who *are* in it mainly for the money – that "real" changes in social position, largely downward, are affected. Men of this sort, plungers, are highly dispraised by "true cockfighters" as fools who do not understand what the sport is all about, vulgarians who simply miss the point of it all. They are, these addicts, regarded as fair game for the genuine enthusiasts, those who do understand, to take a little money away from – something that is easy enough to do by luring them, through the force of their greed, into irrational bets on mismatched cocks. Most of them do indeed manage to ruin themselves in a remarkably short time, but there always seems to be one or two of them around, pawning their land and selling their clothes in order to bet, at any particular time.[18]

This graduated correlation of "status gambling" with deeper fights and, inversely, "money gambling" with shallower ones is in fact quite general. Bettors themselves form a sociomoral hierarchy in these terms. As noted earlier, at most cockfights there are, around the very edges of the cockfight area, a large number of mindless, sheer-chance-type gambling games (roulette, dice throw, coin-spin, pea-under-the-shell) operated by concessionaires. Only women, children, adolescents, and various other sorts of people who do not (or not yet) fight cocks – the extremely poor, the socially despised, the personally idiosyncratic – play at these games, at, of course, penny ante levels. Cockfighting men would be ashamed to go anywhere near them. Slightly above these people in standing are those who though they do not themselves fight cocks, bet on the smaller matches around the edges. Next, there are those who fight cocks in small, or occasionally medium matches, but have not the status to join in the large ones, though they may bet from time to time on the side in those. And finally, there are those, the really substantial members of the community, the solid citizenry around whom local life revolves, who fight in the larger fights and bet on them around the side. The focusing element in these focused gatherings, these men generally dominate and define the sport as they dominate and define the society. When a Balinese male talks, in that almost venerative way, about "the true cockfighter," the *bebatoh* ("bettor") or *djuru kurung* ("cage keeper"), it is this sort of person, not those who bring the mentality of the pea and-shell game into the quite different, inappropriate context of the cockfight, the driven gambler (*potét*, a word which has the secondary meaning of thief or reprobate), and the wistful hanger-on, that they mean. For such a man, what is really going on in a match is something rather closer to an *affaire d'honneur* (though, with the Balinese talent for practical fantasy, the blood that is spilled is only figuratively human) than to the stupid, mechanical crank of a slot machine.

What makes Balinese cockfighting deep is thus not money in itself, but what, the more of it that is involved the more so, money causes to happen: the migration of the Balinese status hierarchy into the body of the cockfight. Psychologically an Aesopian representation of the ideal/demonic, rather narcissistic, male self, sociologically it is an equally Aesopian representation of the complex fields of tension set up by the controlled, muted, ceremonial, but for all that deeply felt, interaction of those selves in the context of everyday life. The cocks may be surrogates for their owners' personalities, animal mirrors of psychic form, but the cockfight is – or more exactly, deliberately is made to be – a simulation of the social matrix, the involved system of cross-cutting, overlapping, highly corporate groups – villages, kingroups, irrigation societies, temple congregations, "castes" – in which its devotees live.[19] And as prestige, the necessity to affirm it, defend it, celebrate it, justify it, and just plain bask in it (but not, given the strongly ascriptive character of Balinese stratification, to seek it), is perhaps the central driving force in the society, so also – ambulant penises, blood sacrifices, and monetary exchanges aside – is it of the cockfight. This apparent amusement and seeming sport is, to take another phrase from Erving Goffman, "a status bloodbath."[20]

The easiest way to make this clear, and at least to some degree to demonstrate it, is to invoke the village whose cockfighting activities I observed the closest – the one in which the raid occurred and from which my statistical data are taken.

Like all Balinese villages, this one – Tihingan, in the Klungkung region of southeast Bali – is intricately organized, a labyrinth of alliances and oppositions. But, unlike many, two sorts of corporate groups, which are also status groups, particularly stand out, and we may concentrate on them, in a part-for-whole way, without undue distortion.

First, the village is dominated by four large, patrilineal, partly endogamous descent groups which are constantly vying with one another and form the major factions in the village. Sometimes they group two and two, or rather the two larger ones versus the two smaller ones plus all the unaffiliated people; sometimes they operate independently. There are also subfactions within them, subfactions within the subfactions, and so on to rather fine levels of distinction. And second, there is the village itself, almost entirely endogamous, which is opposed to all the other villages round about in its cockfight circuit (which, as explained, is the market region), but which also forms alliances with certain of these neighbors against certain others in various supravillage political and social contexts. The exact situation is thus, as everywhere in Bali, quite distinctive; but the general pattern of a tiered hierarchy of status rivalries between highly corporate but various based groupings (and, thus, between the members of them) is entirely general.

Consider, then, as support of the general thesis that the cockfight, and especially the deep cockfight, is fundamentally a dramatization of status concerns, the following facts, which to avoid extended ethnographic description I shall simply pronounce to be facts – though the concrete evidence, examples, statements, and numbers that could be brought to bear in support of them, is both extensive and unmistakable:

1 A man virtually never bets against a cock owned by a member of his own kingroup. Usually he will feel obliged to bet for it, the more so the closer the kin tie and the deeper the fight. If he is certain in his mind that it will not win, he may just not bet at all, particularly if it is only a second cousin's bird or if the fight is a shallow one. But as a rule he will feel he must support it and, in deep games, nearly always does. Thus the great majority of the people calling "five" or "speckled" so demonstratively are expressing their allegiance to their kinsman, not their evaluation of his bird, their understanding of probability theory, or even their hopes of unearned income.

2 This principle is extended logically. If your kingroup is not involved you will support an allied kingroup against an unallied one in the same way, and so on through the very involved networks of alliances which, as I say, make up this, as any other, Balinese village.

3 So, too, for the village as a whole. If an outsider cock is fighting any cock from your village, you will tend to support the local one. If, what is a rarer circumstance but occurs every now and then, a cock from outside your cockfight circuit is fighting one inside it, you will also tend to support the "home bird."

4 Cocks which come from any distance are almost always favorites, for the theory is the man would not have dared to bring it if it was not a good cock, the more so the further he has come. His followers are, of course, obliged to support him, and when the more grand-scale legal cockfights are held (on holidays, and so on) the people of the village take what they regard to be the best cocks in the village, regardless of ownership, and go off to support them, although they will almost certainly have to give odds on them and to make large bets to show that they are not a cheapskate village. Actually, such "away games," though infrequent, tend to mend the ruptures between village members that the constantly occurring "home games," where village factions are opposed rather than united, exacerbate.

5 Almost all matches are sociologically relevant. You seldom get two outsider cocks fighting, or two cocks with no particular group backing, or with group backing which is mutually unrelated in any clear way. When you do get them, the game is very shallow, betting very slow, and the whole thing very dull, with no one save the immediate principals and an addict gambler or two at all interested.

6 By the same token, you rarely get two cocks from the same group, even more rarely from the same subfaction, and virtually never from the same sub-subfaction (which would be in most cases one extended family) fighting. Similarly, in outside village fights two members of the village will rarely fight against one another, even though, as bitter rivals, they would do so with enthusiasm on their home grounds.

7 On the individual level, people involved in an institutionalized hostility relationship, called *puik*, in which they do not speak or otherwise have anything to do with each other (the causes of this formal breaking of relations are many: wife-capture, inheritance arguments, political differences) will bet very heavily, sometimes almost maniacally, against one another in what is a frank and direct attack on the very masculinity, the ultimate ground of his status, of the opponent.

8 The center bet coalition is, in all but the shallowest games, *always* made up by structural allies – no "outside money" is involved. What is "outside" depends upon the context, of course, but given it, no outside money is mixed in with the

main bet; if the principals cannot raise it, it is not made. The center bet, again especially in deeper games, is thus the most direct and open expression of social opposition, which is one of the reasons why both it and matchmaking are surrounded by such an air of unease, furtiveness, embarrassment, and so on.

9 The rule about borrowing money – that you may borrow *for* a bet but not *in* one – stems (and the Balinese are quite conscious of this) from similar considerations: you are never at the *economic* mercy of your enemy that way. Gambling debts, which can get quite large on a rather short-term basis, are always to friends, never to enemies, structurally speaking.

10 When two cocks are structurally irrelevant or neutral so far as *you* are concerned (though, as mentioned, they almost never are to each other) you do not even ask a relative or a friend whom he is betting on, because if you know how he is betting and he knows you know, and you go the other way, it will lead to strain. This rule is explicit and rigid; fairly elaborate, even rather artificial precautions are taken to avoid breaking it. At the very least you must pretend not to notice what he is doing, and he what you are doing.

11 There is a special word for betting against the grain, which is also the word for "pardon me" (*mpura*). It is considered a bad thing to do, though if the center bet is small it is sometimes all right as long as you do not do it too often. But the larger the bet and the more frequently you do it, the more the "pardon me" tack will lead to social disruption.

12 In fact, the institutionalized hostility relation, *puik*, is often formally initiated (though its causes always lie elsewhere) by such a "pardon me" bet in a deep fight, putting the symbolic fat in the fire. Similarly, the end of such a relationship and resumption of normal social intercourse is often signalized (but, again, not actually brought about) by one or the other of the enemies supporting the other's bird.

13 In sticky, cross-loyalty situations, of which in this extraordinarily complex social system there are of course many, where a man is caught between two more or less equally balanced loyalties, he tends to wander off for a cup of coffee or something to avoid having to bet, a form of behavior reminiscent of that of American voters in similar situations.[21]

14 The people involved in the center bet are, especially in deep fights, virtually always leading members of their group – kinship, village, or whatever. Further, those who bet on the side (including these people) are, as I have already remarked, the more established members of the village – the solid citizens. Cockfighting is for those who are involved in the everyday politics of prestige as well, not for youth, women, subordinates, and so forth.

15 So far as money is concerned, the explicitly expressed attitude toward it is that it is a secondary matter. It is not, as I have said, of no importance; Balinese are no happier to lose several weeks' income than anyone else. But they mainly look on the monetary aspects of the cockfight as self-balancing, a matter of just moving money around, circulating it among a fairly well-defined group of serious cockfighters. The really important wins and losses are seen mostly in other terms, and the general attitude toward wagering is not any hope of cleaning up, of making a killing (addict gamblers again excepted), but that of the horseplayer's prayer: "Oh, God, please let me break even." In prestige terms, however, you do not want to break even, but, in a momentary, punctuate sort of way,

win utterly. The talk (which goes on all the time) is about fights against such-and-such a cock of So-and-So which your cock demolished, not on how much you won, a fact people, even for large bets, rarely remember for any length of time, though they will remember the day they did in Pan Loh's finest cock for years.

16 You must bet on cocks of your own group aside from mere loyalty consider-ations, for if you do not people generally will say, "What! Is he too proud for the likes of us? Does he have to go to Java or Den Pasar [the capital town] to bet, he is such an important man?" Thus there is a general pressure to bet not only to show that you are important locally, but that you are not so important that you look down on everyone else as unfit even to be rivals. Similarly, home team people must bet against outside cocks or the outsiders will accuse them – a serious charge – of just collecting entry fees and not really being interested in cockfighting, as well as again being arrogant and insulting.

17 Finally, the Balinese peasants themselves are quite aware of all this and can and, at least to an ethnographer, do state most of it in approximately the same terms as I have. Fighting cocks, almost every Balinese I have ever discussed the subject with has said, is like playing with fire only not getting burned. You activate village and kingroup rivalries and hostilities, but in "play" form, coming dangerously and entrancingly close to the expression of open and direct interpersonal and intergroup aggression (something which, again, almost never happens in the normal course of ordinary life), but not quite, because, after all, it is "only a cockfight."

More observations of this sort could be advanced, but perhaps the general point is, if not made, at least well-delineated, and the whole argument thus far can be usefully summarized in a formal paradigm:

THE MORE A MATCH IS . . .
1 Between near status equals (and/or personal enemies)
2 Between high status individuals

                         THE DEEPER THE MATCH.
THE DEEPER THE MATCH . . .
1 The closer the identification of cock and man (or, more properly, the deeper the match the more the man will advance his best, most closely-identified-with cock).
2 The finer the cocks involved and the more exactly they will be matched.
3 The greater the emotion that will be involved and the more the general absorp-tion in the match.
4 The higher the individual bets center and outside, the shorter the outside bet odds will tend to be, and the more betting there will be overall.
5 The less an "economic" and the more a "status" view of gaming will be involved, and the "solider" the citizens who will be gaming.[22]

Inverse arguments hold for the shallower the fight, culminating, in a reversed-signs sense, in the coin-spinning and dice-throwing amusements. For deep fights there are no absolute upper limits, though there are of course practical ones, and there are a great many legendlike tales of great Duel-in-the-Sun combats between lords and princes in classical times (for cockfighting has always been as much an elite concern as a popular one), far deeper than anything anyone, even aristocrats, could produce today anywhere in Bali.

Indeed, one of the great culture heroes of Bali is a prince, called after his passion for the sport, "The Cockfighter," who happened to be away at a very deep cockfight with a neighboring prince when the whole of his family – father, brothers, wives, sisters – were assassinated by commoner usurpers. Thus spared, he returned to dispatch the upstart, regain the throne, reconstitute the Balinese high tradition, and build its most powerful, glorious, and prosperous state. Along with everything else that the Balinese see in fighting cocks – themselves, their social order, abstract hatred, masculinity, demonic power – they also see the archetype of status virtue, the arrogant, resolute, honor-mad player with real fire, the ksatria prince.[23]

Feathers, Blood, Crowds, and Money

"Poetry makes nothing happen," Auden says in his elegy of Yeats, "it survives in the valley of its saying . . . a way of happening, a mouth." The cockfight, too, in this colloquial sense, makes nothing happen. Men go on allegorically humiliating one another and being allegorically humiliated by one another, day after day, glorying quietly in the experience if they have triumphed, crushed only slightly more openly by it if they have not. *But no one's status really changes.* You cannot ascend the status ladder by winning cockfights; you cannot, as an individual, really ascend it at all. Nor can you descend it that way.[24] All you can do is enjoy and savor, or suffer and withstand, the concocted sensation of drastic and momentary movement along an aesthetic semblance of that ladder, a kind of behind-the-mirror status jump which has the look of mobility without its actuality.

Like any art form – for that, finally, is what we are dealing with – the cockfight renders ordinary, everyday experience comprehensible by presenting it in terms of acts and objects which have had their practical consequences removed and been reduced (or, if you prefer, raised) to the level of sheer appearances, where their meaning can be more powerfully articulated and more exactly perceived. The cockfight is "really real" only to the cocks – it does not kill anyone, castrate anyone, reduce anyone to animal status, alter the hierarchical relations among people, or refashion the hierarchy; it does not even redistribute income in any significant way. What it does is what, for other peoples with other temperaments and other conventions, *Lear* and *Crime and Punishment* do; it catches up these themes – death, masculinity, rage, pride, loss, beneficence, chance – and, ordering them into an encompassing structure, presents them in such a way as to throw into relief a particular view of their essential nature. It puts a construction on them, makes them, to those historically positioned to appreciate the construction, meaningful – visible, tangible, graspable – "real," in an ideational sense. An image, fiction, a model, a metaphor, the cockfight is a means of expression; its function is neither to assuage social passions nor to heighten them (though, in its playing-with-fire way it does a bit of both), but, in a medium of feathers, blood, crowds, and money, to display them.

The question of how it is that we perceive qualities in things – paintings, books, melodies, plays – that we do not feel we can assert literally to be there has come, in recent years, into the very center of aesthetic theory.[25] Neither the sentiments of the artist, which remain his, nor those of the audience, which remain theirs, can account for the agitation of one painting or the serenity of another. We attribute grandeur, wit, despair, exuberance, to strings of sounds; lightness, energy, violence, fluidity to blocks of stone. Novels are said to have strength, buildings eloquence, plays momentum, ballets repose. In this realm of eccentric predicates, to say that the cockfight, in its perfected cases at least, is "disquietful" does not seem at all unnatural, merely, as I have just denied it practical consequence, somewhat puzzling.

The disquietfulness arises, "somehow," out of a conjunction of three attributes of the fight: its immediate dramatic shape; its metaphoric content; and its social context. A cultural figure against a social ground, the fight is at once a convulsive surge of animal hatred, a mock war of symbolical selves, and a formal simulation of status tensions, and its aesthetic power derives from its capacity to force together these diverse realities. The reason it is disquietful is not that it has material effects (it has some, but they are minor); the reason that it is disquietful is that, joining pride to selfhood, selfhood to cocks, and cocks to destruction, it brings to imaginative realization a dimension of Balinese experience normally well-obscured from view. The transfer of a sense of gravity into what is in itself a rather blank and unvarious spectacle, a commotion of beating wings and throbbing legs, is effected by interpreting it as expressive of something unsettling in the way its authors and audience live, or, even more ominously, what they are. . . .

What sets the cockfight apart from the ordinary course of life, lifts it from the realm of everyday practical affairs, and surrounds it with an aura of enlarged importance is not, as functionalist sociology would have it, that it reinforces status discriminations (such reinforcement is hardly necessary in a society where every act proclaims them), but that it provides a metasocial commentary upon the whole matter of assorting human beings into fixed hierarchical ranks and then organizing the major part of collective existence around that assortment. Its function, if you want to call it that, is interpretive: it is a Balinese reading of Balinese experience, a story they tell themselves about themselves. . . .

Notes

1 J. Belo, "The Balinese Temper," in *Traditional Balinese Culture*, ed. J. Belo (New York, 1970) (originally published in 1935), pp. 85–110.

2 The best discussion of cockfighting is G. Bateson and M. Mead's *Balinese Character: A Photographic Analysis* (New York, 1942), pp. 24–5, 140; but it, too, is general and abbreviated.

3 Ibid., pp. 25–6. The cockfight is unusual within Balinese culture in being a single-sex public activity from which the other sex is totally and expressly excluded. Sexual differentiation is culturally extremely played down in Bali and most activities, formal and informal, involve the participation of men and women on equal ground, commonly as linked couples. From religion, to politics, to economics, to kinship, to dress, Bali is a rather "unisex" society, a fact both its customs and its symbolism clearly express. Even in contexts where women do not in fact play much of a role – music, painting, certain

agricultural activities – their absence, which is only relative in any case, is more a mere matter of fact than socially enforced. To this general pattern, the cockfight, entirely of, by, and for men (women – at least *Balinese* women – do not even watch), is the most striking exception.

4 C. Hooykaas, *The Lay of the Jaya Prana* (London, 1958), p. 39. The lay has a stanza (no. 17) with the reluctant bridegroom use. Jaya Prana, the subject of a Balinese Uriah myth, responds to the lord who has offered him the loveliest of six hundred servant girls: "Godly King, my Lord and Master / I beg you, give me leave to go / such things are not yet in my mind; / like a fighting cock encaged / indeed I am on my mettle / I am alone / as yet the flame has not been fanned."

5 For these, see V. E. Korn, *Het Adatrecht van Bali*, 2d edn. (The Hague, 1932), index under *toh*.

6 There is indeed a legend to the effect that the separation of Java and Bali is due to the action of a powerful Javanese religious figure who wished to protect himself against a Balinese culture hero (the ancestor of two Ksatria castes) who was a passionate cock-fighting gambler. See C. Hooykaas, *Agama Tirtha* (Amsterdam, 1964), p. 184.

7 An incestuous couple is forced to wear pig yokes over their necks and crawl to a pig trough and eat with their mouths there. On this, see J. Belo, "Customs Pertaining to Twins in Bali," in *Traditional Balinese Culture*, p. 49; on the abhorrence of animality generally, Bateson and Mead, *Balinese Character*, p. 22.

8 Except for unimportant, small-bet fights (on the question of fight "importance," see below) spur affixing is usually done by someone other than the owner. Whether the owner handles his own cock or not more or less depends on how skilled he is at it, a consideration whose importance is again relative to the importance of the fight. When spur affixers and cock handlers are someone other than the owner, they are almost always quite close relative – a brother or cousin – or a very intimate friend of his. They are thus almost extensions of his personality, as the fact that all three will refer to the cock as "mine," say "I" fought So-and-So, and so on, demonstrates. Also, owner-handler-affixer triads tend to be fairly fixed, though individuals may participate in several and often exchange roles within a given one.

9 E. Goffman, *Encounters: Two Studies in the Sociology of Interaction* (Indianapolis, 1961), pp. 9–10.

10 This word, which literally means an indelible stain or mark, as in a birth-mark or a vein in a stone, is used as well for a deposit in a court case, for a pawn, for security offered in a loan, for a stand-in for someone else in a legal or ceremonial context, for an earnest advanced in a business deal, for a sign placed in a field to indicate its ownership is in dispute, and for the status of an unfaithful wife from whose lover her husband must gain satisfaction or surrender her to him. See Korn, *Het Adatrecht van Bali*; Th. Pigeaud, *Javaans-Nederlands Handwoordenboek* (Groningen, 1938); H. H. Juynboll, *Oudja-vaansche-Nederlandsche Woordenlijst* (Leiden, 1923).

11 The center bet must be advanced in cash by both parties prior to the actual fight. The umpire holds the stakes until the decision is rendered and then awards them to the winner, avoiding, among other things, the intense embarrassment both winner and loser would feel if the latter had to pay off personally following his defeat. About 10 percent of the winner's receipts are subtracted for the umpire's share and that of the fight sponsors.

12 Actually, the typing of cocks, which is extremely elaborate (I have collected more than twenty classes, certainly not a complete list), is not based on color alone, but on a series of independent, interacting, dimensions, which include – besides color – size, bone thickness, plumage, and temperament. (But *not* pedigree. The Balinese do not breed cocks to any significant extent, nor, so far as I have been able to discover, have they ever done so. The *asil*, or jungle cock, which is the basic fighting strain everywhere the sport

is found, is native to southern Asia, and one can buy a good example in the chicken section of almost any Balinese market for anywhere from four or five ringgits up to fifty or more.) The color element is merely the one normally used as the type name, except when the two cocks of different types – as on principle they must be – have the same color, in which case a secondary indication from one of the other dimensions ("large speckled" v. "small speckled," etc.) is added. The types are coordinated with various cosmological ideas which help shape the making of matches, so that, for example, you fight a small, headstrong, speckled brown-on-white cock with flat-lying feathers and thin legs from the east side of the ring on a certain day of the complex Balinese calendar, and a large, cautious, all-black cock with tufted feathers and stubby legs from the north side on another day, and so on. All this is again recorded in palm-leaf manuscripts and endlessly discussed by the Balinese (who do not all have identical systems), and a full-scale componential-cum-symbolic analysis of cock classifications would be extremely valuable both as an adjunct to the description of the cockfight and in itself. But my data on the subject, though extensive and varied, do not seem to be complete and systematic enough to attempt such an analysis here. For Balinese cosmological ideas more generally see Belo, *Traditional Balinese Culture*, and J. L. Swellengrebel, ed., *Bali: Studies in Life, Thought, and Ritual* (The Hague, 1960).

13 For purposes of ethnographic completeness, it should be noted that it is possible for the man backing the favorite – the odds-giver – to make a bet in which he wins if his cock wins or there is a tie, a slight shortening of the odds (I do not have enough cases to be exact, but ties seem to occur about once every fifteen or twenty matches). He indicates his wish to do this by shouting *sapih* ("tie") rather than the cock-type, but such bets are in fact infrequent. . . .

14 Besides wagering there are other economic aspects of the cockfight, especially its very close connection with the local market system which, though secondary both to its motivation and to its function, are not without importance. Cockfights are open events to which anyone who wishes may come, sometimes from quite distant areas, but well over 90 percent, probably over 95, are very local affairs, and the locality concerned is defined not by the village, nor even by the administrative district, but by the rural market system. Bali has a three-day market week with the familiar "solar-system"-type rotation. Though the markets themselves have never been very highly developed, small morning affairs in a village square, it is the microregion such rotation rather generally marks out – ten or twenty square miles, seven or eight neighboring villages (which in contemporary Bali is usually going to mean anywhere from five to ten or eleven thousand people) from which the core of any cockfight audience, indeed virtually all of it, will come. Most of the fights are in fact organized and sponsored by small combines of petty rural merchants under the general premise, very strongly held by them and indeed by all Balinese, that cockfights are good for trade because "they get money out of the house, they make it circulate." Stalls selling various sorts of things as well as assorted sheer-chance gambling games (see below) are set up around the edge of the area so that this even takes on the quality of a small fair. This connection of cockfighting with markets and market sellers is very old, as, among other things, their conjunction in inscriptions (R. Goris, *Prasasti Bali*, 2 vols. (Bandung, 1954)) indicates. Trade has followed the cock for centuries in rural Bali, and the sport has been one of the main agencies of the island's monetization.

15 The phrase is found in the Hildreth translation, International Library of Psychology (1931), note to p. 106; see L. L. Fuller, *The Morality of Law* (New Haven, 1964), p. 6 ff.

16 Of course, even in Bentham, utility is not normally confined as a concept to monetary losses and gains, and my argument here might be more carefully put in terms of a denial that for the Balinese, as for any people, utility (pleasure, happiness . . .) is merely identifiable with wealth. But such terminological problems are in any case secondary to the essential point: the cockfight is not roulette.

17 M. Weber, *The Sociology of Religion* (Boston, 1963). There is nothing specifically Balinese, of course, about deepening significance with money, as Whyte's description of corner boys in a working-class district of Boston demonstrates: "Gambling plays an important role in the lives of Cornerville people. Whatever game the corner boys play, they nearly always bet on the outcome. When there is nothing at stake, the game is not considered a real contest. This does not mean that the financial element is all-important. I have frequently heard men say that the honor of winning was much more important than the money at stake. The corner boys consider playing for money the real test of skill and, unless a man performs well when money is at stake, he is not considered a good competitor." W. F. Whyte, *Street Corner Society*, 2nd edn. (Chicago, 1955), p. 140.

18 The extremes to which this madness is conceived on occasion to go – and the fact that it is considered madness – is demonstrated by the Balinese folk tale *I Tuhung Kuning*. A gambler becomes so deranged by his passion that, leaving on a trip, he orders his pregnant wife to take care of the prospective newborn if it is a boy but to feed it as meat to his fighting cocks if it is a girl. The mother gives birth to a girl, but rather than giving the child to the cocks she gives them a large rat and conceals the girl with her own mother. When the husband returns, the cocks, crowing a jingle, inform him of the deception and, furious, he sets out to kill the child. A goddess descends from heaven and takes the girl up to the skies with her. The cocks die from the food given them, the owner's sanity is restored, the goddess brings the girl back to the father, and reunites him with his wife. The story is given as "Geel Komkommertje" in J. Hooykaas-van Leeuwen Boomkamp, *Sprookjes en Verhalen van Bali* (The Hague, 1956), pp. 19–25.

19 For a fuller description of Balinese rural social structure, see C. Geertz, "Form and Variation in Balinese Village Structure," *American Anthropologist* 61 (1959): pp. 94–108; "Tihingan, A Balinese Village," in R. M. Koentjaraningrat, *Villages in Indonesia* (Ithaca, 1967), pp. 210–43; and, though it is a bit off the norm as Balinese villages go, V. E. Korn, *De Dorpsrepubliek tnganan Pagringsingan* (Santpoort, Netherlands, 1933).

20 Goffman, *Encounters*, p. 78.

21 B. R. Berelson, P. F. Lazersfeld, and W. N. McPhee, *Voting: A Study of Opinion Formation in a Presidential Campaign* (Chicago, 1954).

22 As this is a formal paradigm, it is intended to display the logical, not the causal, structure of cockfighting. Just which of these considerations leads to which, in what order, and by what mechanisms, is another matter – one I have attempted to shed some light on in the general discussion.

23 In another of Hooykaas-van Leeuwen Boomkamp's folk tales ("De Gast," *Sprookjes en Verhalen van Bali*, pp. 172–80), a low caste *Sudra*, a generous, pious, and carefree man who is also an accomplished cockfighter, loses, despite his accomplishment, fight after fight until he is not only out of money but down to his last cock. He does not despair, however – "I bet," he says, "upon the Unseen World."

His wife, a good and hard-working woman, knowing how much he enjoys cockfighting, gives him her last "rainy day" money to go and bet. But, filled with misgivings due to his run of ill luck, he leaves his own cock at home and bets merely on the side. He soon loses all but a coin or two and repairs to a food stand for a snack, where he meets a decrepit, odorous, and generally unappetizing old beggar leaning on a staff. The old man then asks for food, and the hero spends his last coins to buy him some. The old man then asks to pass the night with the hero, which the hero gladly invites him to do. As there is no food in the house, however, the hero tells his wife to kill the last cock for dinner. When the old man discovers this fact, he tells the hero he has three cocks in his own mountain hut and says the hero may have one of them for fighting. He also asks for the hero's son to accompany him as a servant, and, after the son agrees, this is done.

The old man turns out to be Siva and, thus, to live in a great palace in the sky, though the hero does not know this. In time, the hero decides to visit his son and collect the promised cock. Lifted up into Siva's presence, he is given the choice of three cocks. The first crows: "I have beaten fifteen opponents." The second crows, "I have beaten twenty-five opponents." The third crows, "I have beaten the king." "That one, the third, is my choice," says the hero, and returns with it to earth.

When he arrives at the cockfight, he is asked for an entry fee and replies, "I have no money; I will pay after my cock has won." As he is known never to win, he is let in because the king, who is there fighting, dislikes him and hopes to enslave him when he loses and cannot pay off. In order to insure that this happens, the king matches his finest cock against the hero's. When the cocks are placed down, the hero's flees, and the crowd, led by the arrogant king, hoots in laughter. The hero's cock then flies at the king himself, killing him with a spurstab in the throat. The hero flees. His house is encircled by the king's men. The cock changes into a Garuda, the great mythic bird of Indic legend, and carries the hero and his wife to safety in the heavens.

When the people see this, they make the hero king and his wife queen and they return as such to earth. Later their son, released by Siva, also returns and the hero-king announces his intention to enter a hermitage. ("I will fight no more cockfights. I have bet on the Unseen and won.") He enters the hermitage and his son becomes king.

24 Addict gamblers are really less declassed (for their status is, as everyone else's, inherited) than merely impoverished and personally disgraced. The most prominent addict gambler in my cockfight circuit was actually a very high caste *satria* who sold off most of his considerable lands to support his habit. Though everyone privately regarded him as a fool and worse (some, more charitable, regarded him as sick), he was publicly treated with the elaborate deference and politeness due his rank....

25 For four, somewhat variant, treatments, see S. Langer, *Feeling and Form* (New York, 1953); R. Wollheim, *Art and Its Objects* (New York, 1968); N. Goodman, *Languages of Art* (Indianapolis, 1968); M. Merleau-Ponty, "The Eye and the Mind," in his *The Primacy of Perception* (Evanston, Ill., 1964), pp. 159–90....

6

Toward a New Sociology of Masculinity

Tim Carrigan, Bob Connell, and John Lee

The upheaval in sexual politics of the past twenty years [since the mid-1960s] has mainly been discussed as a change in the social position of women. Yet change in one term of a relationship signals change in the other. From very early in the history of women's liberation it was clear that its politics had radical implications for men. A small "men's liberation" movement developed in the 1970s among heterosexual men. Gay men became politicized as the new feminism was developing, and gay liberation politics have continued to call into question the conventional understanding of what it is to be a man. Academic sex-role research, though mainly about women in the family, was easily extended to the "male role." From several different directions in the 1970s, critiques and analyses of masculinity appeared. Quite strong claims about the emergence of a new area of study, and a new departure in sexual politics, were made. The purpose of this article is to bring together these attempts, evaluate them, and propose an alternative.

We think it important to start with the "prehistory" of this debate – early attempts at a sociology of gender, the emergence of the "sex-role" framework, and research on masculinity *before* the advent of women's liberation. In this dusty literature are the main sources of the framework that has governed most recent writing on masculinity. It includes an agenda about modernization, a characteristic blindness about power, and a theoretical incoherence built into the "sex-role" paradigm. There are also, in some nearly forgotten writing, pointers to a much more powerful and interesting analysis.

Approaching the recent literature, we were concerned with three things: its empirical discoveries, its political assumptions and implications, and its theoretical framework. Its empirical content turns out to be slight. Though most social science is indeed about men, good-quality research that brings *masculinity* into focus is rare. Ironically, most recent studies are not up to the standard set by several researchers in the 1950s. There is, however, a notable exception, a new body of work on the history of homosexual masculinity, which has general implications for our understanding of the historical construction of gender categories.

Reprinted from *The Making of Masculinities: The New Men's Studies*, ed. Harry Brod (Boston: Allen & Unwin, 1987), pp. 63–9, 72–80, 83–97.

The political meaning of writing about masculinity turns mainly on its treatment of power. Our touchstone is the essential feminist insight that the overall relationship between men and women is one involving domination or oppression. This is a fact about the social world that must have profound consequences for the character of men. It is a fact that is steadily evaded, and sometimes flatly denied, in much of the literature about masculinity written by men – an evasion wittily documented by Ehrenreich in *The Hearts of Men*.[1]

There are, however, some accounts of masculinity that have faced the issue of social power, and it is here that we find the bases of an adequate theory of masculinity. But they too face a characteristic danger in trying to hold to feminist insights about men, for a powerful current in feminism, focusing on sexual exploitation and violence, sees masculinity as more or less unrelieved villainy and all men as agents of the patriarchy in more or less the same degree. Accepting such a view leads to a highly schematic view of gender relations, and leads men in particular into a paralyzing politics of guilt. This has gripped the "left wing" of men's sexual politics since the mid 1970s.

It is necessary to face the facts of sexual power without evasion but also without simplification. A central argument of this is that the theoretical bases for doing so are now available, and a strong radical analysis of masculinity has become possible. Three steps open this possibility up. First, the question of sexual power has to be taken more seriously and pursued *inside* the sex categories. In particular the relations between heterosexual and homosexual men have to be studied to understand the constitution of masculinity as a political order, and the question of what forms of masculinity are socially dominant or hegemonic has to be explored. The writings of gay liberation theorists already provide important insights about this problem. Second, the analysis of masculinity needs to be related as well to other currents in feminism. Particularly important are those that have focused on the sexual division of labor, the sexual politics of workplaces, and the interplay of gender relations with class dynamics. Third, the analysis needs to use those developments in social theory in the last decade or so that offer ways past the dichotomies of structure versus individual, society versus the person, that have plagued the analysis of gender as much as the analysis of class. These developments imply a focus on the historical production of social categories, on power as the ability to control the production of people (in both the biological and psychological senses), and on large-scale structures as both the objects and effects of collective practice. In the final section of this article we sketch a sociology of masculinity that draws on these sources.

We hope for a realistic sociology of masculinity, built on actual social practices rather than discussion of rhetoric and attitudes. And we hope for a realistic politics of masculinity, neither fatuously optimistic nor defeatist. We see such an enterprise as part of a radical approach to the theory of gender relations in general, made possible by convergences among feminism, gay liberation, contemporary socialism, psychoanalysis, and the history and sociology of practice. The theme of masculinity makes sense only in terms of that larger project. At the same time it is, we think, an important part of it.

Origins

The early sociology of gender and the "sex-role" framework

"The problem of women" was a question taken up by science generally in the second half of the nineteenth century, at first in a mainly biological framework. This was not simply part of the widening scope of scientific inquiry. It was clearly also a response to the enormous changes that had overtaken women's lives with the growth of industrial capitalism. And, toward the end of the century, it was a response to the direct challenge of the women's emancipation movement.

The relationship of the emerging social sciences to this nineteenth- and early twentieth-century discourse on women was profound. In a useful sociology of knowledge investigation of the growth of the discourse, Viola Klein observed that "there is a peculiar affinity between the fate of women and the origins of social science, and it is no mere co-incidence that the emancipation of women should be started at the same time as the birth of sociology."[2] The political stakes were particularly evident in psychological research. The area usually referred to today as "sex-difference research" has been a major component in the development of social science work on gender. In the view of one prominent observer of the field, this work was originally "motivated by the desire to demonstrate that females are inherently inferior to males.... But from 1900 on, the findings of the psychologists gave strong support to the arguments of the feminists."[3]

Rosalind Rosenberg has documented the pioneering, and subsequently forgotten, research by American women into sex differences in the first two decades of the twentieth century. She established the importance of the work of Helen Thompson, Leta Hollingworth, Jessie Taft, Elsie Clews Parsons, and others across a range of disciplines into questions of intelligence, the socialization of women, and American sexual mores. There were serious obstacles in the way of the academic careers of these women, but Rosenberg revealed the influence they had on such later social theorists as W. I. Thomas, Robert Lowie, John Dewey, and Margaret Mead.[4] ...

By midcentury, functionalist sex-role theory dominated the Western sociological discourse on women. The key figure in this development was Talcott Parsons, who in the early 1950s wrote the classic formulation of American sex-role theory, giving it an intellectual breadth and rigor it had never had. The notion of *role* as a basic structural concept of the social sciences had crystallized in the 1930s, and it was immediately applied to questions of gender. Two of Parsons's own papers of the early 1940s talked freely of sex roles. In the course of his argument he offered an interesting account of several options that had recently emerged within the female role. There was, however, little sense of a power relation between men and women; and the argument embedded the issue of sex and gender firmly in the context of the family.[5] ...

At a key point, however, Parsons did make sex-role differentiation the problem, asking how it was to be explained. He rejected the biological-difference argument as utterly incapable of explaining the social pattern of sex roles. Rather, he derived it from a general sociological principle, the imperative of structural differentiation. Its particular form here was explained by the famous distinction between "instrumental" and "expressive" leadership. Parsons treated sex roles as the instrumental / expressive differentiation that operated within the conjugal family. And he treated the conjugal family both as a small group and as the specific agency of the larger society entrusted with the function of socializing the young. Thus he deduced the gender patterning of roles, and their reproduction across generations, from the structural requirements of any social order whatever.

To this tour de force of reasoning Parsons added a sophisticated account of role acquisition, in the sense of how the role gets *internalized*. This is where psychoanalysis, with its account of the production of masculinity and femininity through different patternings of the Oedipal crisis, came into play. In effect, sex role becomes part of the very constitution of the person, through the emotional dynamics of development in the nuclear family.

Thus Parsons analyzed the acquisition of sex roles as a matter of the production, from one generation to the next, of what we might call *gender personalities*. For example:

> Relative to the total culture as a whole, the masculine personality tends more to the predominance of instrumental interests, needs and functions, presumably in whatever social system both sexes are involved, while the feminine personality tends more to the primacy of expressive interests, needs and functions. We would expect, by and large, that other things being equal, men would assume technical, executive and "judicial" roles, women more supportive, integrative and "tension-managing" roles.[6]

This notion provided Parsons then, as it provides role theorists still, with a powerful solution to the problem of how to link person and society. But its ability to do so was based on a drastic simplification. As phrases like "the masculine personality" show, the whole argument is based on a normative standard case. Parsons was not in the least concerned about how many men (or women) are actually like that. Even the options within a sex role that he had cheerfully recognized in the earlier papers had vanished. All that was left in the theory was the normative case on the one hand, and on the other, deviance. Homosexuality, he wrote only a couple of pages after the passage just quoted, is universally prohibited so as to reinforce the differentiation of sex roles.

Apart from being historically false (homosexuality was and is institutionalized in some societies), such a theory fails to register tension and power processes *within* gender relations. Parsons recognizes many forms of "role strain," but basically as a result of problems in the articulation of the different subsystems of society. For instance, in his account the relation between the family and the economy is the source of much of the change in sex roles. The underlying structural notion in his analysis of gender is always differentiation, not relation. Hence his automatic assumption is that the connection between the two sex roles is one of complementarity, not power.

This version of the role framework fitted comfortably with the intense social conservatism of the American intelligentsia in the 1950s, and with the lack of any direct political challenge from women. For functionalist sociology, "the problem of women" was no longer how to explain their social subordination. It was how to understand the dysfunctions and strains involved in women's roles, primarily in relation to the middle-class family. Given the normative emphasis on the family, the sociological focus was strongly on "social problems": the conflicts faced by working wives, "maternal deprivation," divorce rates and juvenile delinquency, and intergenerational family conflict. The sense of conflict is strong in the work of Mirra Komarovsky, who, after Parsons, made the most impressive application of the functionalist framework to sex roles in the 1940s. She developed a general argument about modernization producing a clash between a feminine "home-maker" ideal and a "career girl" ideal. The implications remained vague, but there was much more sense of complexity within sex roles than in Parsons's grand theorizing.[7] . . .

The institutional power that role theory enjoyed in sociology, especially in the United States – where as recently as the mid-1970s Komarovsky could describe it simply as "the generally accepted arsenal of sociological conceptual tools"[8] – ensured that feminist questions would be posed in that framework, at least at the start. Could this framework encompass feminist propositions? Especially could it incorporate the notion of *oppression*, or as it was more often called in this literature, the power differential between men and women? . . .

Some feminist sociologists argued that this was perfectly possible; that role theory had been misapplied, misunderstood, or had not been extended to its full potential.[9] Yet by the late 1970s, other feminist sociologists were arguing that the sex-role framework should be abandoned. Not only had the notion of "role" been shown to be incoherent. The framework continued to mask questions of power and material inequality; or worse, implied that women and men were "separate but equal."[10]

These criticisms underlined a more general problem: the discourse lacked a stable theoretical object. "Sex-role" research could, and did, wobble from psychological argument with biological assumptions, through accounts of interpersonal transactions, to explanations of a macrosociological character, without ever having to resolve its boundaries. The elusive character of a discourse where issues as important as that of oppression could appear, disappear, and reappear in different pieces of writing without anything logically compelling authors to stick with and solve them no doubt lies behind much of the frustration expressed in these criticisms. As we shall see, this underlying incoherence was to have a devastating influence on the sociological literature about men.

The "male role" literature before women's liberation

A sociology of masculinity, of a kind, had appeared before the "sex-role" paradigm. Specific groups of boys and men had become the object of research when their behavior was perceived as a "social problem." Two notable instances are juvenile delinquency and educational underachievement – topics whose significance in the history of sociology can hardly be exaggerated. Studies such as Thrasher's *The Gang* (1927) and Whyte's *Street Corner Society* (1943) talked extensively about masculinity without directly proclaiming sex roles as their object.[11]

Through the 1950s and 1960s the most popular explanation of such social problems was "father absence," especially from poor or black families. The idea of "father absence" had a broader significance, since the historical tendency of capitalism has been to separate home from workplace. Most fathers earning wages or salaries are therefore absent from their families much of the time. This imbalance was the focus of one of the first sociological discussions of the *conflicts* involved in the construction of masculinity. . . .

Other sociologists, including David Riesman, proposed that in the modern male role, expressive functions had been added to the traditional instrumental ones.[12] The idea was clearly formulated by Helen Hacker in a notable paper called "The New Burdens of Masculinity," published in 1957: "As a man, men are now expected to demonstrate the manipulative skill in interpersonal relations formerly reserved for women under the headings of intuition, charm, tact, coquetry, womanly wiles, et cetera. They are asked to bring patience, understanding, gentleness to their human dealings. Yet with regard to women they must still be sturdy oaks."[13]

This argument has become virtually a cliché in more recent writing. Hacker's paper is striking in its emphasis on conflict within masculinity. She pointed out that though the husband was necessarily often absent from his family, he was "increasingly reproached for his delinquencies as father." To compound the problem, men were also under pressure to evoke a full sexual response on the part of women. The result was the growing social visibility of impotence.

Male homosexuality was also becoming increasingly visible, and this was further evidence that "all is not well with men." It is notable that Hacker did not conceive of homosexuality in terms of the current medical model but in relation to the strong differentiation between masculine and feminine social roles. "The 'flight from masculinity' evident in male homosexuality may be in part a reflection of role conflicts. If it is true that heterosexual functioning is an important component of the masculine role in its social as well as sexual aspects, then homosexuality may be viewed as one index of the burdens of masculinity."[14] . . .

Hacker never lost sight of the fact that masculinity exists as a power relation. Her appreciation of the effects of power led her to describe the possible range of masculine types as more restricted than that of feminine types. It also led to the suggestion (reminiscent of Chodorow's later work) that "masculinity is more important to men than femininity is to women."[15]

There is something motherly in Hacker's approach to men. Her feminism, if advanced at the time, certainly seems tame 25 years later. But the striking fact is that most research on masculinity in the meantime has not improved on her analysis. Indeed, much of it has been a good deal more primitive. For instance, *The Male in Crisis* (1970), by the Austrian author Karl Bednarik, suggests that alienation at work, bureaucracy in politics and war, and the commercialization of sexuality all undermine masculinity. Bednarik made some acute observations on the way the commercialization of sexuality connects it with aggressiveness. And his stress on the contradication between the hegemonic male image and the real conditions of men's live is notable. But he never questioned that the traditional image *is* the primordial, true nature of man.[16] Nor did the American Patricia Sexton in her widely quoted book *The Feminized Male* (1969). "What does it mean to be masculine? It means, obviously, holding male values and following male behavior norms. . . . Male norms stress values such as courage, inner direction, certain forms of aggression, autonomy, mastery, technological skill, group solidarity, adventure, and a considerable amount of toughness in mind and body."[17]

In her account, however, the main force pushing American boys away from true masculinity was women. Schoolteachers and mothers, through their control of childrearing and rewarding of conformity and academic success, were making them into sissies. It is not surprising to find that Sexton romanticized working-class boys and their "boy culture," and was hostile to the "visibly feminized" soft men of the New Left and counter culture ("a new lumpen leisure-class of assorted hippies, homosexuals, artistic poseurs, and 'malevolent blacks' ").[18]

But there was something more here: an appreciation of power that had a distinctly feminist flavor. The reason women were engaged in feminizing boys, Sexton argued, was that women have been excluded from all *other* positions of authority. She documented not only the hazards of being male, citing statistics on the higher death and illness rates among men that were soon to become another cliché of the literature. She also recited at length the facts of men's power. Basically the reform she wanted was a change in the sexual division of labor, and in this regard her argument was in line with the feminism of ten years later. But she had no sense that the "male values" and "male norms" she admired are as much effects of the structure of power as the women's behavior she condemned.

Lionel Tiger's *Men in Groups*, published in the same year in Britain, was also a paradigmatic treatment of masculinity. It extensively documented men's control of war, politics, production, and sports, and argued that all this reflected a genetic pattern built into human beings at the time when the human ancestral stock took up cooperative hunting. Greater political participation by women, of the kind argued for by Sexton, would be going against the biological grain.

The notion that there is a simple continuity between biology and the social has been very powerful as ideology. So has another important feature of Tiger's argument, the way *relations* are interpreted as *differences*. The greater social power of men and the sexual division of labor are interpreted as "sexual dimorphism" in behavior. With this, the whole question of social structure is spirited away. Tiger's scientific-sounding argument turns out to be pseudo-evolutionary speculation, overlaying a more sinister political message. Its drift becomes obvious in the book's closing fantasy about masculinity and its concern with "hard and heavy phenomena," with warmongering being part of "the masculine aesthetic," and arguments about what social arrangements are and are not "biologically healthy."[19]

It will be obvious from these cases that there was a reasonably complex and sometimes sophisticated discussion about masculinity going on before the main impact of feminism. It is also clear that this discussion was intellectually disorganized, even erratic. . . .

Toward Redefinition

Sex roles revisited

The very idea of a "role" implies a recognizable and accepted standard, and sex-role theorists posit just such a norm to explain sexual differentiation. Society is organized around a pervasive differentiation between men's and women's roles, and these roles are internalized by all individuals. There is an obvious common-sense appeal to this approach. But the first objection to be made is that it does not actually describe the concrete reality of people's lives. Not all men are "responsible" fathers, nor "successful" in their occupations, and so on. Most men's lives reveal some departure from what the "male sex role" is supposed to prescribe.

The problem here is that the sex-role literature does not consistently distinguish between the expectations made of people and what they in fact do. The framework often sees variations from the presumed norms of male behavior in terms of "deviance," as a "failure" in socialization. This is particularly evident in the functionalist version of sex-role theory, where "deviance" becomes an unexplained, residual, and essentially nonsocial category.

When variation and conflict in the male role are recognized to be more typical, there are two possible explanations for sex-role theorists. Some see this conflict as a result of the blurring of men's and women's roles so that men find they are expected to add expressive elements to their traditional instrumental roles. It is not obvious why men, perhaps allowing for some initial confusion, could not internalize this new male role just as they did the original one. The answer for authors such as Bednarik and Sexton was that these changes in men's lives are going against the grain.[20] Hegemonic masculinity *is* the true nature of men, and social harmony arises from promoting this idea, not impeding it. "Masculinity" in these terms is a nonsocial essence – usually presumed to arise from the biological makeup or genetic programing of men.

In the alternative explanation of role conflict, the focus is more narrowly on the individual. There is variation in masculinity, arising from individual experiences, that produces a range of personalities – ranging in one conception along a dimension from "hard" to "soft," in another from higher to lower levels of androgyny. Conflict arises when society demands that men try to live up to an impossible standard at the hard or gynephobic ends of the scales; this is "dysfunctional." The "male role" is unduly restrictive because hegemonic masculinity does *not* reflect the true nature of men. The assumption is of an essential self whose needs would be better met by a more relaxed existence nearer the soft or androgynous poles. In this argument, masculinity is fundamentally the social pressure that, internalized, prevents personal growth.

The role framework, then, depending on which way one pushes it, can lead to entirely opposite conclusions about the nature of masculinity. One is reminded of the wax nose mentioned by Marc Bloch, which can be bent either to the right or to the left.[21] Role theory in general and sex-role theory in particular lack a stable theoretical object; there is no way that these different lines of argument about masculinity can be forced to meet. As argued in detail elsewhere, this is a consequence of the logical structure of the role framework itself; it is internally incoherent.[22]

As social theory, the sex-role framework is fundamentally static. This is not to say that it cannot recognize social change. Quite the contrary. Change has been a leading theme in the discussion of men's sex roles by authors such as Pleck and Brannon.[23] The problem is that they cannot grasp it as history, as the interplay of praxis and structure. Change is always something that *happens to* sex roles, that impinges on them – whether from the direction of the society at large (as in discussions of how technological and economic change demands a shift to a "modern" male sex role) or from the direction of the asocial "real self" inside the person, demanding more room to breathe. Sex-role theory cannot grasp change as a dialectic arising within gender relations themselves.

This is quite simply inherent in the procedure by which any account of "sex roles" is constructed: generalizing about sexual norms, and then applying this frozen description to men's and women's lives. This is true even of the best role research. Komarovsky in *Blue Collar Marriage* gives a wonderful account of the tangled process of constructing a marriage, the sexual dilemmas, the struggles with in-laws over money and independence, and so on; and then theorizes this as "learning conjugal roles," as if the scripts were just sitting there waiting to be read. Because the framework hypostatizes sex roles, it ultimately takes them for granted; and so remains trapped within the ideological context of what it is attempting to analyze.

The result of using the role framework is an abstract view of the *differences* between the sexes and their situations, not a concrete one of the *relations* between them. As Franzway and Lowe observe in their critique of the use of sex-role theory in feminism, the role literature focuses on attitudes and misses the realities that the attitudes are about.[24] The political effect is to highlight the attitudes and pressures that create an artificially rigid *distinction* between men and women and to play down the *power* that men exercise over women. (As some critics have observed, we do not speak of "race roles" or "class roles" because the exercise of power in these areas of social relations is more immediately evident to sociologists.) Where sex-role analysis does recognize power, it is typically in a very restricted context. Once again, Komarovsky, because her field research is very good, provides a clear example. She recognizes power as a balance within marriage; her analysis of this is subtle and sophisticated. And she reports that in the cases where the wife had achieved dominance within the marriage, it was still not acceptable for this to be shown in public. But she cannot theorize this, though it is a very important point. The notion of the overall social subordination of women, institutionalized in the marital division of labor, but consistent with a fluctuating and occasionally reversed power situation in particular relationships, is not a conception that can be formulated in the language of role theory.

The consequence of the evasion and blurring of issues of power is, we feel, a persistent and serious misjudgment of the position of heterosexual men in the sexual politics of the advanced capitalist countries. The interpretation of oppression as overrigid role requirements has been important in bolstering the idea, widely argued in the "men's movement" literature of the 1970s, that men in general stand to *gain* from women's liberation. This notion is naive at best, and at worst dishonest. The liberation of women must mean a *loss* of power for most men; and given the structuring of personality by power, also a great deal of personal pain. The sex-role literature fairly systematically evades the facts of men's *resistance* to change in the distribution of power, in the sexual division of labor, and in masculinity itself, a point about which we shall have more to say in a moment.

The role framework, then, is neither a conceptually stable nor a practically and empirically adequate basis for the analysis of masculinity. Let us be blunt about it. The "male sex role" does not exist. It is impossible to isolate a "role" that constructs masculinity (or another that constructs femininity). Because there is no area of social life that is not the arena of sexual differentiation and gender relations, the notion of a sex role necessarily simplifies and abstracts to an impossible degree.

What should be put in its place? Partly that question is unanswerable; the only thing that can occupy the conceptual and political place of sex-role theory is sex-role theory itself. It has a particular intellectual pedigree. It is connected with a definite politics (liberal feminism and its "men's movement" offshoot), to which it supplies answers that seem to satisfy. And it is, of course, now institutionalized in academia and plays a very material part in many academic careers. Nothing else will do just that.

But we may still ask for alternatives in another sense. We have argued that the questions that were posed in the language of role theory are real and important questions. If so, they should arise in other approaches to gender relations and sexual politics, though they may take a different shape there....

Gay liberation and the understanding of masculinity

The masculinity literature before women's liberation was frankly hostile to homosexuality, or at best very wary of the issue. What is post-women's liberation is also post-gay liberation. Gay activists were the first contemporary group of men to address the problem of hegemonic masculinity outside of a clinical context. They were the first group of men to apply the political techniques of women's liberation, and to align with feminists on issues of sexual politics – in fact to argue for the importance of sexual politics....

None of the 1970s books about men made a serious attempt to come to grips with gay liberation arguments or to reckon with the fact that mainstream masculinity is heterosexual masculinity. Nor did the "men's movement" publicists ever write about the fact that beside them was another group of men active in sexual politics; or discuss their methods, concerns or problems. The reason is obvious enough. Homosexuality is a theoretical embarrassment to sociobiologists and social-learning theorists alike, and a practical embarrassment to the "men's movement." How they got away with it is another matter. It required them to avert their gaze, not only from gay liberation, but also from contemporary developments in women's liberation (Jill Johnston's *Lesbian Nation* came out in 1973, for instance) and from basic concepts in the analysis of sexuality (notably the theory of bisexuality.[25])

The gay movement has been centrally concerned with masculinity as part of its critique of the political structure of sexuality. In this, it should be noted, the contemporary movement represents a distinct break with previous forms of homosexual activism. It has gone well beyond earlier campaigns for the social rights of homosexual people and the accompanying efforts to foster tolerance in the heterosexual population toward a "sexual minority." Instead, gay liberationists attacked the social practices and psychological assumptions surrounding gender relations, for a prominent theme in their arguments is an attempt to explain the sources of homosexual oppression in these terms. The British gay liberation newspaper *Come Together* declared in 1970: "We recognize that the oppression that gay people suffer is an integral part of the social structure of our society. Women and gay people are both victims of the cultural and ideological phenomenon known as sexism. This is manifested in our culture as male supremacy and heterosexual chauvinism."[26] Activists argued that homosexual people were severely penalized by a social system that enforced the subservience of women to men and that propagated an ideology of the "natural" differences between the sexes. The denial and fear of homosexuality were an integral part of this ideology because homosexuals were seen to contradict the accepted characteristics of men and women, and the complementarity of the sexes that is institutionalized within the family and many other areas of social life.[27]

Not surprisingly, then, the gay movement has been particularly critical of psychiatric definitions of homosexuality as a pathology, and of the concern with "curing" homosexuals, a phenomenon of twentieth-century medicine marked by both theoretical incoherence and practical failure. Activists readily observed the ways in which notions such as "gender inversion" were a transparent rationalization of the prevailing relationships between men and women. For the whole medical model of homosexuality rested on a belief in the biological (or occasionally socially functional) determination of heterosexual masculinity and femininity. The gay liberation tactic in this and many other areas was one of a defiant reversal of the dominant sexual ideology. In affirming a homosexual identity, many gay liberationists embraced the charge of effeminacy and declared that the real problem lay in the rigid social definitions of masculinity. It was society, not themselves, that needed to be cured.[28]

For some, this led to experiments with what was known as "radical drag." An American activist declared, "There is more to be learned from wearing a dress for a day than there is from wearing a suit for life."[29] The point was not to imitate a glamorous image of stereotypical femininity (à la Danny La Rue or Les Girls) but to combine feminine images with masculine ones, such as a dress with a beard. The aim was described as gender confusion, and it was advocated as a means both for personal liberation from the prescriptions of hegemonic masculinity and for subverting the accepted gender categories by demonstrating their social basis, as indicated by its technical name, a "gender fuck." Radical drag was hardly an effective strategy for social change, but it contained far more political insight than did the notion of androgyny that was beginning to be popularized by sex-role theorists at about the same time. . . .

The most general significance of the gay liberation arguments (and no doubt a central reason for the "men's movement" ignoring them) was that they challenged the assumptions by which heterosexuality is taken for granted as the natural order of things. It is, for example, a fundamental element of modern hegemonic masculinity that one sex (women) exists as potential sexual object, while the other sex (men) is negated as a sexual object. It is women, therefore, who provide heterosexual men with sexual validation, whereas men exist as rivals in both sexual and other spheres of life. The gay liberation perspective emphasized that the institutionalization of heterosexuality, as in the family, was achieved only by considerable effort, and at considerable cost not only to homosexual people but also to women and children. It is, then, precisely within heterosexuality as it is currently organized that a central dimension of the power that men exercise over women is to be found.

The gay movement's theoretical work, by comparison with the "sex-role" literature and "men's movement" writings, had a much clearer understanding of the reality of men's power over women, and it had direct implications for any consideration of the hierarchy of power among men. Pleck was one of the few writers outside gay liberation to observe that the homosexual / heterosexual dichotomy acts as a central symbol in *all* rankings of masculinity. Any kind of powerlessness, or refusal to compete, among men readily becomes involved with the imagery of homosexuality.[30]

What emerges from this line of argument is the very important concept of *hegemonic masculinity*, not as "the male role," but as a particular variety of masculinity to which others – among them young and effeminate as well as homosexual men – are subordinated. It is particular groups of men, not men in general, who are oppressed within patriarchal sexual relations, and whose situations are related in different ways to the overall logic of the subordination of women to men. A consideration of homosexuality thus provides the beginnings of a dynamic conception of masculinity as a structure of social relations.

Gay liberation arguments further strengthen a dynamic approach to masculinity by providing some important insights into the historical character of gender relations. Homosexuality is a historically specific phenomenon, and the fact that it is socially organized becomes clear once we distinguish between homosexual *behavior* and a homosexual *identity*. While some kind of homosexual behavior may be universal, this does not automatically entail the existence of self-identified or publicly labeled homosexuals. In fact, the latter are unusual enough to require a historical explanation. Jeffrey Weeks and others have argued that in Western Europe, male homosexuality did not gain its characteristically modern meaning and social organization until the late nineteenth century.[31] That period witnessed the advent of new medical categorizations, homosexuality being defined as a pathology by the German psychiatrist Westphal in 1870. There were also new legal prescriptions, so that all male homosexual behavior was subject to legal sanctions in Britain by the end of the century (one of the first victims of these laws being Oscar Wilde). Such medical and legal discourses underlined a new conception of the homosexual as a specific type of person in contrast to the older one of homosexuality as merely as potential in the lustful nature of all men – or indeed a potential for disorder in the cosmos.[32] Correspondingly, men with same-sex preferences had more reason than previously to think of themselves as separate and distinct; and the homosexual subculture of the time in cities such as London gained its recognizably modern form. . . .

The emerging history of male homosexuality, then, offers the most valuable starting point we have for constructing a historical perspective on masculinity at large. The technical superiority of the work of gay historians over the histories of masculinity and the "male role," to be found in works like Hoch, Dubbert, Stearns, and Pleck and Pleck, is so marked as to be embarrassing. Conceptually, gay history moves decisively away from the conception underlying those works, that the history of masculinity is the story of the modulation, through time, of the expressions of a more or less fixed entity.[33]

The history of homosexuality obliges us to think of masculinity not as a single object with its own history but as being constantly constructed within the history of an evolving social structure, a structure of sexual power relations. It obliges us to see this construction as a social struggle going on in a complex ideological and political field in which there is a continuing process of mobilization, marginalization, contestation, resistance, and subordination. It forces us to recognize the importance of violence, not as an expression of subjective values or of a type of masculinity, but as a constitutive practice that helps to make all kinds of masculinity – and to recognize that much of this violence comes from the state, so the historical construction of masculinity and femininity is also struggle for the control and direction of state power. Finally it is an important corrective to the tendency, in left-wing thought especially, to subordinate the history of gender to the history of capitalism. The making of modern homosexuality is plainly connected to the development of industrial capitalism, but equally clearly has its own dynamic.

Outline of a Social Analysis of Masculinity

Men in the framework of gender relations

The starting point for any understanding of masculinity that is not simply biologistic or subjective must be men's involvement in the social relations that constitute the gender order. In a classic article Rubin has defined the domain of the argument as "the sex/gender system," a patterning of social relations connected with reproduction and gender division that is found in all societies, though in varying shapes.[34] This system is historical, in the fullest sense; its elements and relationships are constructed in history and are all subject to historical change.[35] It is also internally differentiated, as Mitchell argued more than a decade ago [before the mid-1970s].[36] Two aspects of its organization have been the foci of research in the past decade [since the mid-1970s]: the division of labor and the structure of power. (The latter is what Millett originally called "sexual politics"[37] and is the more precise referent of the concept "patriarchy.") To these we must add the structure of cathexis, the social organization of sexuality and attraction – which as the history of homosexuality demonstrates is fully as social as the structures of work and power.

The central fact about this structure in the contemporary capitalist world (like most other social orders, though not all) is the subordination of women. This fact is massively documented and has enormous ramifications – physical, mental, interpersonal, cultural – whose effects on the lives of women have been the major concerns of feminism. One of the central facts about masculinity, then, is that men in general are advantaged through the subordination of women.

To say "men in general" is already to point to an important complication in power relations. The global subordination of women is consistent with many particular situations in which women hold power over men, or are at least equal. Close-up research on families shows a good many households where wives hold authority in practice.[38] The fact of mothers' authority over young sons has been noted in most discussions of the psychodynamics of masculinity. The intersections of gender relations with class and race relations yield many other situations where rich white heterosexual women, for instance, are employers of working-class men, patrons of homosexual men, or politically dominant over black men.

To cite such examples and claim that women are therefore not subordinated in general would be crass. The point is, rather, that contradictions between local situations and the global relationships are endemic. They are likely to be a fruitful source of turmoil and change in the structure as a whole.

The overall relation between men and women, further, is not a confrontation between homogeneous, undifferentiated blocs. Our argument has perhaps established this sufficiently by now; even some role theorists, notably Hacker,[39] recognized a range of masculinities. We would suggest, in fact, that the fissuring of the categories of "men" and "women" is one of the central facts about patriarchal power and the way it works. In the case of men, the crucial division is between hegemonic masculinity and various subordinated masculinities.

Even this, however, is too simple a phrasing, as it suggests a masculinity differentiated only by power relations. If the general remarks about the gender system made above are correct, it follows that masculinities are constructed not just by power relations but by their interplay with a division of labor and with patterns of emotional attachment. For example, as Bray has clearly shown, the character of men's homosexuality, and of its regulation by the state, is very different in the mercantile city from what it was in the precapitalist countryside.[40]

The differentiation of masculinities is psychological – it bears on the kind of people that men are and become – but it is not only psychological. In an equally important sense it is institutional, an aspect of collective practice. In a notable recent study of British printing workers, Cynthia Cockburn has shown how a definition of compositors' work as hypermasculine has been sustained despite enormous changes in technology.[41] The key was a highly organized practice that drove women out of the trade, marginalized related labor processes in which they remained, and sustained a strongly marked masculine "culture" in the workplace. What was going on here, as many details of her study show, was the collective definition of a hegemonic masculinity that not only manned the barricades against women but at the same time marginalized or subordinated other men in the industry (e.g., young men, unskilled workers, and those unable or unwilling to join the rituals). Though the details vary, there is every reason to think such processes are very general. Accordingly we see social definitions of masculinity as being embedded in the dynamics of institutions – the working of the state, of corporations, of unions, of families – quite as much as in the personality of individuals.

Forms of masculinity and their interrelationships

... The ability to impose a particular definition on other kinds of masculinity is part of what we mean by "hegemony." Hegemonic masculinity is far more complex than the accounts of essences in the masculinity books would suggest. It is not a "syndrome" of the kind produced when sexologists like Money reify human behavior into a "condition,"[42] or when clinicians reify homosexuality into a pathology. It is, rather, a question of how particular groups of men inhabit positions of power and wealth, and how they legitimate and reproduce the social relationships that generate their dominance.

An immediate consequence of this is that the culturally exalted form of masculinity, the hegemonic model so to speak, may only correspond to the actual characters of a small number of men. On this point at least the "men's liberation" literature had a sound insight. There is a distance, and a tension, between collective ideal and actual lives. Most men do not really act like the screen image of John Wayne or Humphrey Bogart; and when they try to, it is likely to be thought comic (as in the Woody Allen movie *Play It Again, Sam*) or horrific (as in shootouts and "sieges"). Yet very large numbers of men are complicit in sustaining the hegemonic model. There are various reasons: gratification through fantasy, compensation through displaced aggression (e.g., poofter-bashing by police and working-class youths), and so on. But the overwhelmingly important reason is that most men benefit from the subordination of women, and hegemonic masculinity is centrally connected with the institutionalization of men's dominance over women. It would hardly be an exaggeration to say that hegemonic masculinity is hegemonic so far as it embodies a successful strategy in relation to women.

This strategy is necessarily modified in different class situations, a point that can be documented in the research already mentioned on relationships inside families. A contemporary ruling-class family is organized around the corporate or professional career of the husband. In a typical case the well-groomed wife is subordinated not by being under the husband's thumb – he isn't in the house most of the time – but by her task of making sure his home life runs on wheels to support his self-confidence, his career advancement, and their collective income. In working-class homes, to start with, there is no "career"; the self-esteem of men is eroded rather than inflated in the workplace. For a husband to be dominant in the home is likely to require an assertion of authority without a technical basis; hence a reliance on traditional ideology (religion or ethnic culture) or on force. The working man who gets drunk and belts his wife when she doesn't hold her tongue, and belts his son to make a man of him, is by no means a figure of fiction.[43]

To think of this as "working-class authoritarianism" and see the ruling-class family as more liberal would be to mistake the nature of power. Both are forms of patriarchy; and the husbands in both cases are enacting a hegemonic masculinity. But the situations in which they do so are very different, their responses are not exactly the same, and their impact on wives and children is likely to vary a good deal.

The most important feature of this masculinity, alongside its connection with dominance, is that it is heterosexual. Though most literature on the family and masculinity takes this entirely for granted, it should not be. Psychoanalytic evidence goes far to show that conventional adult heterosexuality is constructed, in the individual life, as one among a number of possible paths through the emotional forest of childhood and adolescence. It is now clear that this is also true at the collective level, that the pattern of exclusive adult heterosexuality is a historically constructed one. Its dominance is by no means universal. For this to become the hegemonic form of masculine sexuality required a historic redefinition of sexuality itself, in which undifferentiated "lust" was turned into specific types of "perversion" – the process documented, from the underside, by the historians of homosexuality already mentioned. A passion for beautiful boys was compatible with hegemonic masculinity in Renaissance Europe, emphatically not so at the end of the nineteenth century. In this historical shift, men's sexual desire was to be focused more closely on women – a fact with complex consequences for them – while groups of men who were visibly not following the hegemonic pattern were more specifically labeled and attacked. So powerful was this shift that even men of the ruling classes found wealth and reputation no protection. It is interesting to contrast the experiences of the Chevalier d'Eon, who managed an active career in diplomacy while dressed as a woman (in a later era he would have been labeled a transvestite), with that of Oscar Wilde a hundred years later.

"Hegemony," then, always refers to a historical situation, a set of circumstances in which power is won and held. The construction of hegemony is not a matter of pushing and pulling between ready-formed groupings but is partly a matter of the *formation* of those groupings. To understand the different kinds of masculinity demands, above all, an examination of the practices in which hegemony is constituted and contested – in short, the political techniques of the patriarchal social order.

This is a large enterprise, and we can note only a few points about it here. First, hegemony means persuasion, and one of its important sites is likely to be the commercial mass media. An examination of advertising, for instance, shows a number of ways in which images of masculinity are constructed and put to work: amplifying the sense of virility, creating anxiety and giving reassurance about being a father, playing games with stereotypes (men washing dishes), and so on.[44] Studying versions of masculinity in Australian mass media, Glen Lewis points to an important qualification to the usual conception of media influence.[45] Commercial television in fact gives a lot of airplay to "soft" men, in particular slots such as hosts of daytime quiz shows. What comes across is by no means unrelieved *machismo*; the inference is that television companies think their audiences would not like that.

Second, hegemony closely involves the division of labor, the social definition of tasks as either "men's work" or "women's work," and the definition of some kinds of work as more masculine than others. Here is an important source of tension between the gender order and the class order, as heavy manual labor is generally felt to be more masculine than white-collar and professional work (though perhaps not management).[46] Third, the negotiation and enforcement of hegemony involves the state. The criminalization of male homosexuality as such was a key move in the construction of the modern form of hegemonic masculinity. Attempts to reassert it after the struggles of the last twenty years [since the mid-1960s], for instance by fundamentalist right-wing groups in the United States, are very much addressed to the state – attempting to get homosexual people dismissed as public school teachers, for instance, or erode court protection for civil liberties. Much more subtly, the existence of a skein of welfare rules, tax concessions, and so on that advantage people living in conventional conjugal households and disadvantage others[47] creates economic incentives to conform to the hegemonic pattern. To argue that masculinity and femininity are produced historically is entirely at odds with the view that sees them as settled by biology, and thus as presocial categories. It is also at odds with the now common view of gender, which sees it as a social elaboration, amplification, or perhaps exaggeration of the biological fact of sex – where biology says "what" and society says "how." Certainly, the biological facts of maleness and femaleness are central to the matter; human reproduction is a major part of what defines the "sex/gender system." But all kinds of questions can be raised about the nature of the *relation* between biology and the social. The facts of anatomical and physiological variation should caution us against assuming that biology presents society with clear-cut categories of people. More generally, it should not be assumed that the relation is one of *continuity*.

We would suggest that the evidence about masculinity, and gender relations at large, makes more sense if we recognize that the social practice of gender arises – to borrow some terminology from Sartre – in *contradiction* to the biological statute.[48] It is precisely the property of human sociality that it transcends biological determination. To transcend is not to ignore: the bodily dimension remains a presence within the social practice. Not as a "base," but as an *object of practice*. Masculinity invests the body. Reproduction is a question of strategies. Social relations continuously take account of the body and biological processes and interact with them. "Interact" should be given its full weight. For our knowledge of the biological dimension of sexual difference is itself predicated on the social categories, as the startling research of Kessler and McKenna makes clear.[49]

In the field of this interaction, sexuality and desire are constituted, being both bodily pain and pleasure, and social injunction and prohibition. Where Freud saw the history of this interaction only as a strengthening prohibition by an undifferentiated "society," and Marcuse as the by-product of class exploitation,[50] we must now see the construction of the unconscious as the field of play of a number of historically developing power relations and gender practices. Their interactions constitute masculinities and femininities as particular patterns of cathexis.

Freud's work with his male patients produced the first systematic evidence of one key feature of this patterning. The repressions and attachments are not necessarily homogeneous. The psychoanalytic exploration of masculinity means diving through layers of emotion that may be flagrantly contradictory. For instance in the "Wolf Man" case history,[51] the classic of the genre, Freud found a promiscuous heterosexuality, a homosexual and passive attachment to the father, and an identification with women, all psychologically present though subject to different levels of repression. Without case-study evidence, many recent authors have speculated about the degree of repression that goes into the construction of dominant forms of masculinity: the sublimated homosexuality in the cult of sports, repressed identification with the mother, and so on. Homosexual masculinity as a pattern of cathexis is no less complex, as we see for instance in Genet. If texts like *Our Lady of the Flowers* are, as Sartre claims, masturbatory fantasies,[52] they are an extraordinary guide to a range and pattern of cathexes – from the hard young criminal to Divine herself – that show, among other things, Genet's homosexuality is far from a mere "inversion" of heterosexual object choice.

In this perspective the unconscious emerges as a field of politics. Not just in the sense that a conscious political practice can address it, or that practices that do address it must have a politics, as argued (against Freud) by the Red Collective in Britain.[53] More generally, the organization of desire is the domain of relations of power. When writers of the books about men ejaculate about "the wisdom of the penis" (H. Goldberg, who thinks the masculine ideal is a rock-hard erection), or when they dilate on its existential significance ("a firm erection on a delicate fellow was the adventurous juncture of ego and courage" – Mailer), they have grasped an important point, though they have not quite got to the root of it. What is at issue here is power over women. This is seen by authors such as Lippert, in an excellent paper exploring the connections of the male-supremacist sexuality of American automobile workers with the conditions of factory work. Bednarik's suggestion about the origins of popular sadism in the commercialization of sex and the degradation of working life is a more complex case of how the lines of force might work.[54]

The psychodynamics of masculinity, then, are not to be seen as a separate issue from the social relations that invest and construct masculinity. An effective analysis will work at both levels; and an effective political practice must attempt to do so too. . . .

Notes

1 B. Ehrenreich, *The Hearts of Men: American Dreams and the Flight from Commitment* (London: Pluto, 1983).

2 V. Klein, *The Feminine Character: History of an Ideology* (London: Routledge & Kegan Paul, 1971), p. 17.

3 L. Tyler, *The Psychology of Human Differences* (New York: Appleton Century Crofts, 1965), p. 240.

4 R. Rosenberg, *Beyond Separate Spheres: Intellectual Roots of Modern Feminism* (New Haven and London: Yale University Press, 1982).

5 T. Parsons, "Age and Sex in the Social Structure of the United States," in *Essays in Sociological Theory* (New York: Free Press, 1964), pp. 89–103; and, in the same volume, "The Kinship System of the Contemporary United States," pp. 177–96.

6 T. Parsons and R. F. Bales, *Family, Socialization and Interaction Process* (London: Routledge & Kegan Paul, 1953), p. 101.

7 M. Komarovsky, "Cultural Contradictions and Sex Roles," *American Journal of Sociology* 52 (November 1946): 184–9; and Komarovsky, "Functional Analysis of Sex Roles," *American Sociological Review* 15 (August 1950): 508–16.

8 M. Komarovsky, *Dilemmas of Masculinity* (New York: Norton, 1976), p. 7.

9 See, for example, M. Komarovsky, "Presidential Address: Some Problems in Role Analysis," *American Sociological Review* 38 (December 1973): 649–62; M. Millman, "Observations on Sex Role Research," *Journal of Marriage and the Family* 33 (November 1971): 772–6; and E. Peal, "'Normal' Sex Roles: An Historical Analysis," *Family Process* 14 (September 1975): 389–409.

10 See, for example, A. R. Edwards, "Sex Roles: A Problem for Sociology and for Women," *Australian and New Zealand Journal of Sociology* 19 (1983): 385–412; S. Franzway and J. Lowe, "Sex Role Theory, Political Cul-de-sac?," *Refractory Girl* 16 (1978): 14–16; M. Gould and R. Kern-Daniels, "Toward a Sociological Theory of Gender and Sex," *American Sociologist* 12 (November 1977): 182–9; and H. Z. Lopata and B. Thorne, "On the Term 'Sex Roles,'" *Signs* 3 (Spring 1978): 718–21.

11 F. M. Thrasher, *The Gang* (Chicago: University of Chicago Press, 1927); W. F. Whyte, *Street Corner Society* (Chicago: University of Chicago Press, 1943).

12 D. Riesman, *The Lonely Crowd* (Garden City, NY: Doubleday Anchor, 1953).

13 H. M. Hacker, "The New Burdens of Masculinity," *Marriage and Family Living* 19 (August 1957): 229.

14 Ibid., p. 231.

15 Ibid., p. 231.

16 K. Bednarik, *The Male in Crisis* (New York: Knopf, 1970).

17 P. Sexton, *The Feminized Male* (New York: Random House, 1969), p. 15.

18 Ibid., p. 204.

19 L. Tiger, *Men in Groups* (London: Nelson, 1969), p. 209.

20 Bednarik, *Male in Crisis;* Sexton, *Feminized Male.*

21 M. Bloch, *The Historian's Craft* (Manchester: University Press, 1984).

22 R. W. Connell, "The Concept of 'Role' and What To Do With It," *Australian and New Zealand Journal of Sociology* 15 (1979): 7–17; reprinted in Connell, *Which Way Is Up?* (Sydney: Allen and Unwin, 1983), ch. 10.

23 J. H. Pleck, "The Male Sex Role: Definitions, Problems and Sources of Change," *Journal of Social Issues* 32 (1976): 155–64; J. H. Pleck, *The Myth of Masculinity* (Cambridge: MIT Press, 1981); and D. S. David and R. Brannon, *The Forty-Nine Percent Majority* (Reading, Mass.: Addison-Wesley, 1976).

24 Franzway and Lowe, "Sex Role Theory."

25 J. Johnston, *Lesbian Nation* (New York: Simon and Schuster, 1973).

26 A. Walter, ed., *Come Together* (London: Gay Men's Press, 1980), p. 49.

27 M. Mieli, *Homosexuality and Liberation* (London: Gay Men's Press, 1980); D. Fernbach, *The Spiral Path* (London: Gay Men's Press, 1981).

28 R. Bayer, *Homosexuality and American Psychiatry* (New York: Basic Books, 1981).

29 Mieli, *Homosexuality and Liberation*, p. 193.

30 J. H. Pleck, "Men's Power with Women, Other Men and Society: A Men's Movement Analysis," in E. H. Pleck and J. H. Pleck, eds., *The American Man* (Englewood Cliffs, NJ: Prentice-Hall, 1980).

31 J. Weeks, *Coming Out* (London: Quartet, 1977); J. Weeks, *Sex, Politics and Society* (London: Longman, 1981); and K. Plummer, ed., *The Making of the Modern Homosexual* (London: Hutchinson, 1981).

32 A. Bray, *Homosexuality in Renaissance England* (London: Gay Men's Press, 1982).

33 P. Hoch, *White Hero, Black Beast* (London: Pluto Press, 1979); T. L. Dubbert, *A Man's Place* (Englewood Cliffs, NJ: Prentice-Hall, 1979); P. N. Stearns, *Be a Man* (New York: Holmes & Meier, 1979); Pleck and Pleck, *American Man*.

34 G. Rubin, "The Traffic in Women: Notes on the 'Political Economy' of Sex," in *Toward an Anthropology of Women*, ed. R. Reiter (New York: Monthly Review Press, 1975), pp. 157–210.

35 R. W. Connell, "Theorising Gender," *Sociology* 19 (May 1985): 260–72.

36 J. Mitchell, *Woman's Estate* (Harmondsworth, England: Penguin Books, 1971).

37 K. Millett, *Sexual Politics* (New York: Doubleday, 1970).

38 G. Dowsett, "Gender Relations in Secondary Schooling," *Sociology of Education* 58 (January 1985): 34–48.

39 Hacker, "New Burdens of Masculinity."

40 Bray, *Homosexuality in Renaissance England*.

41 C. Cockburn, *Brothers: Male Dominance and Technological Change* (London: Pluto, 1983).

42 J. Money, "Sexual Dimorphism and Homosexual Gender Identity," *Psychological Bulletin* 74 (1970): 425–40.

43 See, for example, Kessler et al., "Gender Relations in Secondary Schooling"; and V. Johnson, *The Last Resort* (Ringwood: Penguin, 1981).

44 R. Atwan, D. McQuade, and J. W. Wright, *Edsels, Luckies and Frigidaires* (New York: Delta, 1979).

45 G. Lewis, *Real Men Like Violence* (Sydney: Kangaroo Press, 1983).

46 A. Tolson, *The Limits of Masculinity* (London: Tavistock, 1977).

47 C. V. Baldock and B. Cass, eds., *Women, Social Welfare and the State* (Sydney: Allen and Unwin, 1983).

48 R. W. Connell "Class, Patriarchy and Sartre's Theory of Practice," *Theory and Society* 11 (1982): 305–20.

49 S. J. Kessler and W. McKenna, *Gender: An Ethnomethodological Approach* (New York: Wiley, 1978).

50 S. Freud, "Civilization and its Discontents," *Standard Edition of the Complete Psychological Works*, vol. 21 (London: Hogarth, 1930); and H. Marcuse, *Eros and Civilization* (London: Sphere Books, 1955).

51 S. Freud, "From the History of an Infantile Neurosis," *Standard Edition of the Complete Psychological Works*, vol. 17 (London: Hogarth, 1918).

52 J. P. Sartre, *Saint Genet* (London: W. H. Allen, 1964).

53 Red Collective, *The Politics of Sexuality in Capitalism* (London: Red Collective/PDC, 1978).

54 Goldberg, *Hazards of Being Male:* N. Mailer, *The Prisoner of Sex* (London: Weidenfeld and Nicolson, 1971); J. Lippert, "Sexuality as Consumption," in Snodgrass, *For Men Against Sexism*, pp. 207–213; Bednarik, *Male in Crisis*.

7

The Fraternal Social Contract

Carole Pateman

The sons form a conspiracy to overthrow the despot, and in the end substitute a social contract with equal rights for all...Liberty means equality among the brothers (sons)... Locke suggests that the fraternity is formed not by birth but by election, by contract... Rousseau would say it is based on will.

(Norman O. Brown, *Love's Body*)

The stories of the origins of civil society found in the classic social contract theories of the seventeenth and eighteenth centuries have been repeated many times. More recently, John Rawls and his followers have given new lease of life to the story of the contract that generates political right. But in all the telling of the tales, and in the discussion and argument about the social contract, we are told only half the story. Political theorists present the familiar account of the creation of civil society as a universal realm that (at least potentially) includes everyone and of the origins of political right in the sense of the authority of government in the liberal state, or Rousseau's participatory polity. But this is not the "original" political right. There is silence about the part of the story which reveals that the social contract is a fraternal pact that constitutes civil society as a patriarchal or masculine order. To uncover the latter, it is necessary to begin to tell the repressed story of the genesis of patriarchal political right which men exercise over women.

Most discussions of contract theory accept uncritically the claim that the stories successfully show why the authority of the state is legitimate; but the critical failure to recognize the social contract as fraternal pact is of a different kind. Only half the story appears in commentaries on the classic texts or in contemporary Rawlsian arguments, because modern political theory is so thoroughly patriarchal that one aspect of its origins lies outside the analytical reach of most theorists. Political theorists argue about the individual, and take it for granted that their subject matter concerns the public world, without investigating the way in which the "individual", "civil society" and "the public" have been constituted as patriarchal categories in opposition to womanly nature and the "private" sphere. The civil body politic created through the fraternal social contract is fashioned after only one of the two bodies of humankind.

Reprinted from *The Disorder of Women: Democracy, Feminism and Political Theory* (Cambridge: Polity Press, 1989), pp. 33–57.

The patriarchal character of civil society is quite explicit in the classic texts – if they are read from a feminist perspective. In this chapter, I can draw attention to only a few of the implications of such a reading and to some of most obvious omissions in standard discussions of contract theory.[1] For instance, civil society is public society, but it is not usually appreciated that feminist arguments refer to a different sense of the separation of "public" and "private" from that typically found in discussions of civil society.

The meaning of "civil society" in the contract stories, and as I am using it here, is constituted through the "original" separation and opposition between the modern, public – civil – world and the modern, private or conjugal and familial sphere: that is, in the new social world created through contract, everything that lies beyond the domestic (private) sphere is public, or "civil", society. Feminists are concerned with *this* division. In contrast, most discussions of civil society and such formulations as "public" regulation versus "private" enterprise presuppose that the politically relevant separation between public and private is drawn *within* "civil society" as constructed in the social contract stories. That is to say, "civil society" has come to be used in a meaning closer to that of Hegel, the social contract theorists' greatest critic, who contrasts the universal, public state with the market, classes and corporations of private, civil society.

Hegel, of course, presents a threefold division between family, civil society, state – but the separation between the family and the rest of social life is invariably "forgotten" in arguments about civil society. The shift in meaning of "civil", "public" and "private" goes unnoticed because the "original" creation of civil society through the social contract is a patriarchal construction which is also a separation of the sexes. Political theorists have repressed this part of the story from their theoretical consciousness – though it is implicit in the assumption that civil life requires a natural foundation – and thus liberals and (non-feminist) radicals alike deal only with the liberal understanding of civil society, in which "civil" life becomes private in opposition to the public state.

Perhaps the most striking feature of accounts of the contract story is the lack of attention paid to fraternity, when liberty and equality are so much discussed. One reason for the neglect is that most discussions pass over the insights about fraternity found in Freud's versions of the contract story. Fraternity is central to socialism, and nineteenth- and twentieth-century liberalism, as a recent study has shown, relies heavily on fraternity as a crucial bond integrating individual and community. However, discussions of fraternity do not touch upon the constitution of the "individual" through the patriarchal separation of private and public, nor upon how the division within the (masculine) "individual" includes an opposition between fraternity and reason. Fraternity comes to the fore in liberals' attempts to formulate a more sociologically adequate account of the individual than is found in the abstract conceptions of classic liberal contract theory. But for feminists explicit recourse to liberal or socialist fraternal bonds merely exposes the patriarchal character of ostensibly universal categories and calls attention to the fundamental problem of whether and how women could be fully incorporated into a patriarchal civil world.

A feminist reading of the contract stories is also important for another reason. The contemporary feminist movement has brought the idea of patriarchy into popular and academic currency, but confusion abounds about its meaning and implications and recently some feminists have argued that the term is best avoided.

"Patriarchy" is, to my knowledge, the only term with which to capture the specificities of the subjection and oppression of *women* and to distinguish this from other forms of domination. If we abandon the concept of patriarchy, the problem of the subjection of women and sexual domination will again vanish from view within individualist and class theories. The crucial question, therefore, is the sense in which it can be said that our own society is patriarchal.

Two popular feminist claims about patriarchy add to the confusion. The first is that the literal meaning of "patriarchy", rule by fathers, is still relevant. To insist that patriarchy is nothing more than paternal rule is itself a patriarchal interpretation, as an examination of the classic texts reveals. The second claim is that patriarchy is a timeless, human universal, which obviously rules out the possibility that men's domination of women takes different forms in different historical periods and cultures. More precisely, neither claim about patriarchy can acknowledge that our own momentous transition from the traditional to the modern world – a transition which the contract stories encapsulate theoretically – involved a change from a traditional (paternal) form of patriarchy to a new *specifically modern* (or fraternal) form: patriarchal civil society. . . .

Patriarchal political theory had little in common with the ancient tradition of patriarchalism that took the family as the general model for social order and made claims about the emergence of political society from the family, or the coming together of many families. In *Patriarchalism in Political Thought*, Schochet emphasizes that patriarchal theory was formulated explicitly as a justification for political authority and political obedience, and – as he also stresses – it was systematized in opposition to the social contract theories that were developing at the same time and challenging (one half of) the patriarchalists' most fundamental assumptions.[2] Patriarchalism developed, and was "defeated", in a specific historical and theoretical context.

The standard interpretation of the conflict between the patriarchalists and the contract theorists treats it as a battle over paternal rule and focuses on the irreconcilable differences between the two doctrines over the political right of fathers and the natural liberty of sons. The patriarchalists claimed that kings and fathers ruled in exactly the same way (kings were fathers and vice versa); that family and polity were homologous; that sons were born naturally subject to their fathers; and that political authority and obedience and a hierarchy of inequality were natural. The contract theorists rejected all these claims: they argued that paternal and political rule were distinct; that family and polity were two different and separate forms of association; that sons were born free and equal and, as adults, were as free as their fathers before them; that political authority and obligation were conventional and political subjects were civil equals.[3] It is true that in this particular controversy the patriarchalists were defeated. The theoretical assumptions of the contract theorists were an essential part of the transformation of the traditional order and the world of father-kings into capitalist society, liberal representative government and the modern family.

However, this familiar version of the story in which the sons gain their natural liberty, make the contract and create liberal civil society, or Rousseau's participatory civil order, is only half the tale. It is a patriarchal reading of the texts which identifies patriarchy with paternal rule; it therefore omits the story of the real origin of political right. Patriarchalism has two dimensions: the paternal (father/ son) and the masculine (husband/wife). Political theorists can represent the outcome of the theoretical battle as a victory for contract theory because they are silent about the sexual or conjugal aspect of patriarchy, which appears as non-political or natural and so of no theoretical consequence. But a feminist reading of the texts shows that patriarchalism was far from defeated. The contract theorists rejected paternal right, but they absorbed and simultaneously transformed conjugal, masculine patriarchal right.

To see how this came about – and hence to take a necessary first step towards elucidating some of the characteristics of modern patriarchy – it is necessary to begin with the patriarchal story of monarchical fatherhood exemplified in the writings of Sir Robert Filmer. Although Filmer's father is overthrown in the story of the social contract, his sons receive a vital inheritance that is, paradoxically, obscured by the doctrine of paternal right.

Filmer's aim was to show the awful error of the contract theorists' claim that men were by nature free and equal, a claim he saw as the "main foundation of popular sedition".[4] Filmer argued that all law was of necessity the product of the will of one man. All titles to rule devolved from the original divine grant of kingly right to Adam, the first father. . . .

Filmer's view of the origin of political right seems, therefore, to be unmistakable: it derives from fatherhood. But patriarchy, even in its classical formulation, is more complex than its literal meaning suggests. Fatherly power is only one dimension of patriarchy, as Filmer himself reveals. Filmer's apparently straightforward statements obscure the foundation of patriarchal right. Paternal power is not the origin of political right. The genesis of political power lies in Adam's conjugal or sex right, not in his fatherhood. Adam's political title is granted *before* he becomes a father. Sons, as Filmer caustically reminds Hobbes, do not spring up like mushrooms. If Adam was to be a father, Eve had to become a mother and if Eve was to be a mother, then Adam must have sexual access to her body. In other words, sexual or conjugal right must *necessarily precede* the right of fatherhood.

Filmer makes it clear that Adam's political right is originally established in his right as a husband over Eve: "God gave to Adam . . . the dominion over the woman", and "God ordained Adam to rule over his wife, and her desires were to be subject to his".[5] However, sexual or conjugal right then fades from view in Filmer's writings. After proclaiming that Adam's first dominion or political right is over a woman, not another man (son), Filmer then subsumes conjugal right under the power of fatherhood. Eve and her desires are subject to Adam but, Filmer continues, "here we have the original grant of government, and the fountain of all power placed in the Father of all mankind". Recall that in the Bible story in the Book of Genesis, Eve is created only after Adam and the animals have been placed on earth. Moreover, she is not created *ab initio* but *from* Adam, who is thus in a sense her parent. Filmer is able to treat all political right as the right of a father because the patriarchal father has the creative powers of both a mother and a father. He is not just one of two parents; he is *the* parent.

The patriarchal image of political fathers (here in Locke's words) is that of "nursing Fathers tender and careful of the publick weale".[6] The patriarchal story is about the procreative power of a father who is complete in himself. His procreative power both gives and nurtures physical life and creates and maintains political right. Filmer is able to dismiss Adam's power over Eve so easily because, in the story, women are procreatively and politically irrelevant. The reason Adam has dominion over "the woman" is, according to Filmer (here following a very ancient notion), that "the man...is the nobler and principal agent in generation".[7] Women are merely empty vessels for the exercise of the father's sexual and procreative power. The original political right which God gives to Adam is, so to speak, the right to fill the empty vessel. . . .

Filmer could present the natural freedom of women as the *reductio ad absurdum* of the contract argument because there was no controversy between the patriarchalists and contrast theorists about women's subjection. The contract theorists' aim was theoretical parricide, not the overthrow of the sexual right of men and husbands. Both sides agreed, first, that women (wives), unlike sons, were born and remained naturally subject to men (husbands); and, second, that the right of men over women was *not political*. Locke, for example, concurred with Filmer's view that a wife's subjection has a "Foundation in Nature". The husband is naturally "the abler and the stronger", so he must rule over his wife.[8] Rousseau, the vehement critic of the fraudulent liberal social contract that brings into being a corrupt civil society of inequality and domination, is no less insistent that women must be "subjected either to a man or to the judgements of men and they are never permitted to put themselves above these judgements". When a woman becomes a wife, she acknowledges her husband as "a master for the whole of life".[9]

The contract theorists' "victory" hinged on the separation of paternal from political power, so they could not, like Filmer, subsume sexual under paternal – that is, political – rule. Instead, the social contract story hides original political right by proclaiming sexual or conjugal right as *natural*. Men's dominion over women is held to follow from the respective natures of the sexes, and Rousseau spells out this claim in detail in Book V of *Emile*. Locke has no quarrel with Filmer about the *legitimacy* of sexual, patriarchal right; rather, he insists that it is not political. Eve's subordination

> can be no other Subjection than what every Wife owes her Husband, . . . Adam['s]
> . . . can only be a Conjugal Power, not Political, the Power that every Husband hath to
> order the things of private Concernment in his Family, as Proprietor of the Goods and
> Land there, and to have his Will take place before that of his wife in all things of their
> common Concernment.[10]

Both sides in the seventeenth-century controversy – unlike contemporary political theorists – were well aware that the new doctrine of natural freedom and equality had subversive implications for *all* relationships of power and subordination. The patriarchalists claimed that the doctrine was so absurd that the problems it raised of justifying, say, the power of a husband over his wife were immediately shown to be figments of the contract theorists' disordered imaginations. But if the contract theorists were content with conjugal patriarchy, the individualist language of their attack on paternal right meant that they had (as Sir Robert Filmer argued) opened the thin ends of numerous revolutionary wedges, including a feminist wedge. Women almost at once seized on the contradiction of an "individualism" and a "universalism" which insisted that women were born into subjection and that their subjection was natural and politically irrelevant. By the end of the seventeenth century, for example, Mary Astell was asking: "If all Men are born Free, how is it that all Women are born Slaves?"[11]

The difficulty for the contract theorists was that given their premises, an answer to the question was impossible. Logically, there is no reason why a free and equal female individual should always (contract to) subordinate herself to another free and equal (male) individual upon marriage. The difficulty, however, was easily overcome. Political theorists, whether liberal or socialist, absorbed masculine right into their theories and "forgot" the story of the origin of patriarchal power. Natural subjection was seen in terms of paternal power and three centuries of feminist criticism – whether written by women whose names never appear in political theory textbooks, by the cooperative or utopian socialists, or by the otherwise acceptable philosopher, John Stuart Mill – was suppressed and ignored.

The standard view that the rise of social contract theory and the development of civil society was also a defeat for patriarchalism has meant that some vital questions about the construction of the civil body politic have never been asked. One problem about the social contract that has received some attention is the question of exactly who makes the agreement. Many commentators talk uncritically of "individuals" sealing the pact, but Schochet, for example, points out that in the seventeenth century it was taken for granted that fathers of families entered the social contract.

When I first began to think about these matters from a feminist perspective, I assumed that the social contract was a patriarchal contract because it was made by fathers whose agreement was taken to bind their families. Certainly, "individuals", in the universal sense in which the category is usually used to mean anyone and everyone, do not make the social contract. Women have no part in it: as natural subjects they lack the requisite capacities and abilities. The "individuals" of the stories are *men*, but they do not act as fathers. After all, the stories tell of the defeat of the father's political power. Men no longer have a political place as fathers. But fathers are also husbands – Locke's friend Tyrrell wrote that wives were "concluded by their Husbands"[12] – and, from yet another viewpoint, the participants in the social contract are sons or brothers. The contract is made by brothers, or a *fraternity*. It is no accident that fraternity appears historically hand in hand with liberty and equality, nor that it means exactly what it says: brotherhood.

If "patriarchy" is all too often interpreted literally, "fraternity" is usually treated as if its literal meaning had no relevance today and as if the terms in the revolutionary slogan, "Liberty, Equality, Fraternity", unquestionably applied to us all, not only to men joined by fraternal bonds. Bernard Crick has recently pointed out that fraternity has been relatively little analysed, even though, he says, "fraternity with liberty is humanity's greatest dream".[13] When it is mentioned, fraternity is usually presented as an expression of community; it is seen as "at bottom, a certain type of social co-operation . . . a relation between a group of equals for the utmost mutual help and aid".[14] . . .

The fact that the social contract is not an agreement between individuals, fathers or husbands, but a fraternal pact, becomes particularly clear in Freud's versions of the social contract story. Freud's account of the murder of the primal father by his sons is not usually considered in discussions of the social contract. Yet, as Brown states, "the battle of books re-enacts Freud's primal crime."[15] And Rieff treats

Freud's myth of the parricide as a version of the social contract, to be considered as part of the same tradition as the theories of Hobbes, Locke or Rousseau.[16] The best warrant of all is available for this interpretation. In *Moses and Monotheism* Freud refers to the pact made by the brothers after their dreadful deed as "a sort of social contract".[17] ...

Freud's story of the parricide is important because he makes explicit what the classic tales of theoretical murder leave obscure: the motive for the brothers' collective act is not merely to claim their natural liberty and right of self-government, but *to gain access to women*. In the classic theorists' state of nature the "family" already exists and men's conjugal right is deemed a natural right.[18] Freud's primal father, his *patria potestas*, keeps all the women of the horde for himself. The parricide eliminates the father's political right, and also his *exclusive* sexual right. The brothers inherit his patriarchal, masculine right and share the women among themselves. No man can be a primal father ever again, but by setting up rules that give all men equal access to women (compare their equality before the laws of the state) they exercise the "original" political right of dominion over women that was once the prerogative of the father.

Freud writes of the brothers' "renunciation of the passionately desired mothers and sisters of the horde."[19] This is misleading. The fraternity do not renounce the women, but each gives up the desire to put himself in the place of the father. As part of the fraternal social contract the brothers institute what Freud calls the law of exogamy or kinship. In historically specific terms, the brothers create the modern system of marriage law and family and establish the modern order of conjugal or sexual right. The "natural foundation" of civil society has been brought into being through the fraternal social contract.

The separation of "paternal" from political rule, or the family from the public sphere, is also the separation of women from men through the subjection of women to men. The brothers establish their own law and their own form of sexual or conjugal dominion. The fraternal social contract creates a new, modern patriarchal order that is presented as divided into two spheres: civil society or the universal sphere of freedom, equality, individualism, reason, contract and impartial law – the realm of men or "individuals"; and the private world of particularity, natural subjection, ties of blood, emotion, love and sexual passion – the world of women, in which men also rule.

In short, the contract constitutes patriarchal civil society and the modern, ascriptive rule of men over women. Ascription and contract are usually seen as standing at opposite poles, but the social contract is sexually ascriptive in both form (it is made by brothers) and content (the patriarchal right of a fraternity is established). Civil individuals have a fraternal bond because, *as men*, they share a common interest in upholding the contract which legitimizes their masculine patriarchal right and allows them to gain material and psychological benefit from women's subjection.

One important question raised by the contract stories is exactly how the "foundation in nature", which upholds the subjection of women, should be characterized. Locke tells us that the strength and ability of the man (husband) is the natural basis of the wife's subordination: a view which becomes absorbed into patriarchal liberalism, but also opens the way for liberal feminism. Feminists began to criticize the argument from strength long ago,[20] and although the claim is still heard today, historically it has become less and less plausible to rely on strength as the criterion for masculine political right. Contemporary liberal feminists, following the lead of much earlier writers like Mary Astell and Mary Wollstonecraft, have attacked the alleged lesser ability and capacity of women as an artifact of defective education, as a matter of deliberate social contrivance, not a fact of nature.

The difficulty for the liberal feminist argument is that education cannot be equal while men and women remain differentially positioned within their "separate spheres", but the patriarchal division between the private family and public, civil society is a central structural principle of liberalism. Moreover, the problem runs deeper than a liberal perspective suggests. Liberal feminism assumes that the relevant political problem is to show that women possess the capacities men possess and can do what men can do. However, this also assumes that there is no political significance to the fact that women have one natural ability which men lack: women, but not men, are able to give birth.

Now, it may be claimed that this provides no "foundation in nature" for women's subjection because birth (unlike child-rearing) is ultimately irrelevant to the development of the capacities of civil beings. The difficulty with this argument is that it, too, ignores the story of the "origin" of patriarchal political right, and thus the importance of birth for patriarchal civil society. The ability to give birth, both actually and metaphorically, is central to patriarchal theory.

Filmer's argument shows that Adam's right of domination over Eve is the right to become a father: a right to demand sexual access to Eve's body and to insist that she give birth. Eve's procreative, creative capacity is then denied and appropriated by *men* as the ability to give *political birth*, to be the "originators" of a new form of political order. Adam and the participants in the fraternal social contract gain an amazing patriarchal ability and become the "principal agents" in political generation. More-over, in patriarchal argument birth also symbolizes and encapsulates all the reasons why it has been claimed that women must be bodily removed from civil society.[21] ...

Women are "opposite" to and outside the fraternal social contract and its civil law in two senses. First, they are "originally", necessarily, excluded from an agreement through which the brothers inherit their legacy of patriarchal sex right and legitim-ize their claim over women's bodies and ability to give birth. Second, the civil law encapsulates all that women lack. The civil law stems from a reasoned agreement that it is to the rational mutual advantage of the participants to the contract to constrain their interactions and desires through a law equally applicable to all. Women's passions render them incapable of making such a reasoned agreement or of upholding it if made. In other words, the patriarchal claim that there is a "foundation in nature" for women's subjection to men is a claim that women's bodies must be governed by men's reason. The separation of civil society from the familial sphere is also a division between men's reason and women's bodies. ...

The fraternal social contract is a specifically modern reformulation of this patriarchal tradition. The father is dead, but the brothers appropriate the ability specific to women; they, too, can generate new political life and political right. The social contract is the point of origin, or birth, of civil society, and simultaneously its separation from the (private) sphere of real birth and the disorder of women. The brothers give birth to an artificial body, the body politic of civil society; they create Hobbes's "Artificial Man, we call a Commonwealth", or Rousseau's "artificial and collective body", or the "one Body" of Locke's "Body Politick".

The "birth" of the civil body politic, however, is an act of reason; there is no analogue to a bodily act of procreation. The social contract, as we are all taught, is not an actual event. The natural paternal body of Filmer's patriarchy is metaphorically put to death by the contract theorists, but the "artificial" body that replaces it is a construct of the mind, not the creation of a political community by real people. Whereas the birth of a human child can produce a new male or female, the creation of civil society produces a social body fashioned after the image of only one of the two bodies of humankind. Or, more exactly, the civil body politic is fashioned after the image of the male "individual" who is constituted through the separation of civil society from women. This individual has some singular – and largely unrecognized – aspects precisely because his defining characteristics are thrown into relief only through the contrast with the womanly nature that has been excluded from civil society.

The abstract character of the individual in liberal contract theory has been criticized from the left ever since Rousseau's initial attack. But because the critiques invariably pass silently over the separation of male reason from female body in the original creation of the civil individual, one of his most notable features has also silently been incorporated by the critics. The "individual" is disembodied. For three centuries the figure of the individual has been presented as universal, as the embodiment of all, but it is only because he is disembodied that the "individual" can appear universal. Like the new body politic he, too, is "artificial": he is nothing more than a "man of reason".[22] . . .

Ironically, the disembodiment necessary to maintain the political fiction of the universal civil individual poses profound problems for fraternity. For individualist liberals the problems are part of their wider difficulties over the self, and involve an opposition within the individual between fraternity and reason. The opposition between reason and fraternity is an opposition between the public and the private. But this is not the patriarchal opposition between "private" and "public", between family (women) and civil society (men); instead, the relevant division between public and private is the other opposition to which I referred earlier: the opposition located within "civil society" as I am using the term.[23] For liberals relying on a social view of the self or for socialist critics of liberalism the problems arise because in the 1980s an emphasis on fraternity begins to reveal the patriarchal character of their theories. To preserve universality, "*the* individual" must be abstracted even from his masculinity and fraternity, so that the individual has no body and, hence, no sex.

The creation of the "individual" presupposes the division of rational civil order from the disorder of womanly nature. It might thus seem that the civil individual and the body politic made in his image would be unified. Indeed, they are so presented in liberal theory, but its critics from Rousseau onward argue that the individual and civil society are inherently divided, one from the other and within themselves. The individual is torn between *bourgeois* and *citoyen*, or between *Homo economicus* and *Homo civicus*, and civil society is divided between private interest and the public universal interest, or between "civil" society and state. The point about such critiques, however, is exactly that they are concerned with extrafamilial social life and with the individual as an inhabitant of the public world.

The liberal opposition between private and public (like the patriarchal opposition between the sexes) appears in a variety of guises: for example, society, economy and freedom stand against state, public and coercion. Liberals see these dualities as posing important problems of freedom, since the private sphere of civil society must be protected from the coercive intrusions of the state, and they now spend a good deal of time and effort trying to sort out where the dividing line plausibly can be drawn. Their critics, on the other hand, argue that the opposition between private and public poses an insoluble problem; that it is an unbridgeable structural fissure at the centre of liberalism. I agree with the critics; but the criticism does not go far enough because it takes no account of the "original" patriarchal division and thus leaves the critics' own conception of the "individual" and "civil society" untouched.

In *Knowledge and Politics*, Robert Unger presents a comprehensive discussion and critique of the liberal dichotomies, but even his analysis of the division between fact and theory, values and rules, desire and reason, ignores the fact that it also represents the opposition between the sexes. The "self" is implicitly taken to be masculine. The reference to "men" must be taken literally when he writes: "The dichotomy of the public and private life is still another corollary of the separation of understanding and desire...When reasoning [men] belong to a public world....When desiring, however, men are private beings."[24] In Unger's account, the "desire" and associated disorder represented by women and their private world has been "forgotten". The "self" has become that of the male individual in civil society, an individual torn between the claims of public interest ("reason") and private or subjective interest ("desire"). The opposition between women, bodies, passion, and men, reason, rational advantage, is repressed and replaced by the dichotomy between the individual's private interest and the claims of the public interest or universal law.

In this form, the dichotomy is also expressed as an opposition between the fraternity and reason of civil individuals. The only ties between the individuals of liberal contract theory are those of self-interest. The individual is, as it were, a collection of pieces of property that can, through rational calculation of the mind, be made the subject of contract. The individual thus enters into only certain kinds of relationships and this limitation gives rise to another familiar difficulty within liberal theory: that of presenting a coherent conception of citizenship or the political. The liberal individual's political bonds with other citizens are merely another expression of the pursuit of self-interest; *Homo civicus* is absorbed into, or is nothing more than one face of, the "private" *Homo economicus*. However, this view of the individual as citizen – as public or civil individual – systematically undermines one of the most significant expressions of fraternity.

Liberal individuals interact in a benign public world. They compete one with the other, but the competition is regulated and the rules are fair; the only coercion required is to enforce the rules. Hence the division between private and public as an opposition between society and state is often presented as between freedom and coercion. Currently this position is associated with the New Right, but in the past *le doux commerce* could be offered as the antithesis of violence and the idealist liberals, claiming to have reconciled the oppositions, could assert that will, not force, is the basis of the state.

On the other hand, it is also clear that the individual can be required to protect his protection (as Hobbes put it) by something more than mere obedience to the law. He may have to surrender his body in defence of the state. Indeed, this has always been seen as the ultimate act of loyalty and allegiance, the truly exemplary act of citizenship. However, it is also an act which will never be to the rational advantage of a liberal individual, as Hobbes's logical working out of radical individualism reveals. In the clash between private and public interest, the private claim always has the rational advantage. It is not in the individual's self-interest to be a soldier; thus reason is torn apart from the fraternity on which citizenship, in the last analysis, depends. Of all the male clubs and associations, it is in the military and on the battlefield that fraternity finds its most complete expression.

The opposition between the figure of the soldier and the figure of the individual, or between fraternity and reason, is unique to liberal civil society. In many respects the fraternal contract story transforms ancient patriarchal themes into a specifically modern theory, but the conception of a liberal individual breaks with older traditions in which citizenship has involved a distinctive form of activity and has also been closely tied to the bearing of arms. Feminist scholars are now showing that from ancient times there has been an integral connection between the warrior and conceptions of self-identity, sexuality and masculinity, which have all been bound up with citizenship. The peculiarity of the liberal individual is that although he is male he is also defined – unlike either his predecessors in the traditional world or the "individuals" that appear in social-liberal and socialist theory – in opposition to the political and the masculine passions that underlie the defence of the state by arms. . . .

The explicit use of "fraternity" in both social-liberal and socialist attempts to reintegrate the civil individual and the community (or to reintegrate the liberal division between private and public) means that the patriarchal character of civil society begins to come to the surface. Moreover, the masculine attributes of the individual begin to be exposed. The universalism of the category of the "individual" can be maintained only as long as the abstraction from the body is maintained. "The individual" is a fiction: individuals have one of two bodies, masculine or feminine. But how can the feminine body become part of a (liberal or socialist) fraternal body politic?

Citizenship has now been extended formally to women, raising the substantive problem of how we can become civil "individuals" made in the masculine image. The importance, in practice, of the intimate connection between masculinity, citizenship and bearing arms became explicit when women, taking the universalism of the principles of civil society at face value, demanded to be enfranchised. The "jewel" in the armoury of the anti-suffragists was the argument from physical force.[25] Women, it was claimed, were naturally unable and unwilling to bear arms or use violence, so that if they became citizens, the state would inevitably be fatally weakened.

Now that women are enfranchised (and are even prime ministers) the same patriarchal view of citizenship is still found. In the British House of Commons in 1981, in a debate on the Nationality Bill, Enoch Powell argued that a woman should not pass on her citizenship to her child because "nationality, in the last resort, is tested by fighting. A man's nation is the nation for which he will fight." The difference between men and women, which must be expressed in citizenship, is that between "fighting on the one hand and the creation and preservation of life on the other".[26] It is true that women are now included as members of the armed forces but they are still excluded from combat units, which exemplify fraternities in action.[27]

"Men are born free": the rejection of (masculine) natural subjection generated the revolutionary claim that will, not force, is the basis of the state. One of the major successes of the fraternal contract story is the way it has helped to obscure coercion and violence in civil society and the manner in which "will" is determined within relations of domination and subjection. Critics of contract theory have said a good deal about the inequality of parties to contracts and exploitation, but less about the consequences of contract and subordination. Only rarely have they discussed how contract gives the appearance of freedom to sexually ascriptive domination and subjection. Contract also hides the figure of the armed man in the shadows behind the civil individual. Foucault has counterposed a "military dream" of a society against the original contract (what is presented as the original pact in the familiar stories), but the two are not so far apart as they may seem.

Foucault writes that the military dream looked, "not to the state of nature, but to the meticulously subordinated cogs of a machine, not to the primal social contract, but to permanent coercions, not to fundamental rights, but to indefinitely progressive forms of training, not to the general will but to automatic docility."[28] Automatic docility and the disciplines of the body portrayed by Foucault are part of the consequences of the fraternal social contract. Foucault states that "the development and generalization of disciplinary mechanisms constituted the other, dark side" of the development of a "formally egalitarian juridical framework". However, it is less that the disciplines "distort the contractual link systematically"[29] than that discipline in civil society, *which is also patriarchal discipline*, is typically established through contract. The forms of subjection specific to civil society are, as Foucault emphasizes, developed by the complicity of subordinates as well as by force – complicity made all the easier (as, importantly, is resistance) when consciousness is informed by patriarchal forms of liberty and equality. For example, when "individuals" have a free choice of marriage partner, publicly recognized by a free contract, it is made harder to acknowledge that the marriage contract is a political fiction which ceremonially recognizes the patriarchal subjection of a wife and the masculine privileges of a husband.[30]

The modern discipline of the body is aided by political theory that has already separated reason from the body and the reason of men from the bodies of women. Foucault ignores the significant fact that the "military dream" is a dream of men, whereas the fraternal social contract is also a dream of women. But the women's dream cannot be fulfilled, although the ostensibly universal categories of the contract make it always enticing. The history of liberal feminism is the history of attempts to generalize liberal liberties and rights to the whole adult population; but liberal feminism does not, and cannot, come to grips with the deeper problems of *how* women are to take an equal place in the patriarchal civil order.

Now that the feminist struggle has reached the point where women are almost formal civil equals, the opposition is highlighted between equality made after a male image and the real social position of women *as women*. Women have never, of course, been excluded entirely from civil life – the two spheres of the modern civil order are not separate in reality – but our inclusion has been singular. In a world presented as conventional, contractual and universal, women's civil position is ascriptive, defined by the natural particularity of being women; patriarchal subordination is socially and legally upheld throughout civil life, in production and citizenship as well as in the family. Thus to explore the subjection of women is also to explore the fraternity of men. Recent feminist research has begun to uncover – despite the important divisions between men of different classes and races (and associations and clubs where fraternity is given explicit expression are usually so divided) – how men, *as men*, maintain the power and privileges of their patriarchal right throughout the whole of socio-political life.

The fraternal social contract story shows that the categories and practices of civil society cannot simply be universalized to women. The social contract is a modern patriarchal pact that establishes men's sex right over women, and the civil individual has been constructed in opposition to women and all that our bodies symbolize, so how can we become full members of civil society or parties to the fraternal contract?

The contradictory answer is that women in civil society must disavow our bodies and act as part of the brotherhood – but since we are never regarded as other than women, we must simultaneously continue to affirm the patriarchal conception of femininity, or patriarchal subjection.[31] The peculiar relation between civil society and women and our bodies is illustrated by the fact that few legal jurisdictions have abolished the right of a husband to use his wife's body against her will, that coercive sexual relations ("sexual harassment") are part of everyday working life; that women's bodies are sold in the capitalist market;[32] that women, until 1934 in the USA and 1948 in Britain, lost their citizenship if they married foreigners; that only in 1983 did all British women citizens win the right to pass on their citizenship to their husbands and so enable them to live in Britain;[33] and that welfare policies still do not fully recognize women's status as individuals.

The theoretical and social transformation required if women and men are to be full members of a free, properly democratic (or properly "civilized") society is as far-reaching as can be imagined. The meaning of "civil society" (in both senses discussed here) has been constructed through the exclusion of women and all that we symbolize. To "rediscover" a patriarchal conception of civil society will do little to challenge men's patriarchal right. To create a properly democratic society, which includes women as full citizens, it is necessary to deconstruct and reassemble our understanding of the body politic. This task extends from the dismantling of the patriarchal separation of private and public, to a transformation of our individuality and sexual identities as feminine and masculine beings. These identities now stand opposed, part of the multi-faceted expression of the patriarchal dichotomy between reason and desire. The most profound and complex problem for political theory and practice is how the two bodies of humankind and feminine and masculine individuality can be fully incorporated into political life. How can the present of patriarchal domination, opposition and duality be transformed into a future of autonomous, democratic differentiation?

The traditional patriarchy of the fathers was long ago transformed into the fraternal, modern patriarchy of civil society. Perhaps there is hope, since these observations could be written only under the shadow of the owl of Minerva's wings. Alternatively, perhaps the time for optimism is past; feminism may have re-emerged at a point in the crisis of patriarchy in which the figure of the armed man – now armed not with the sword but with plastic bullets, cluster bombs, chemical, biological and nuclear weapons – has totally obliterated the figure of the civil individual. Perhaps, as Mary O'Brien suggests, "the brotherhood have gone quite mad and lost control of their creations in some cosmic sorcerers' apprenticeship."[34]

Notes

1 A more extensive and detailed feminist reading of the contract stories and of their significance for the marriage contract and other contracts, such as that between prostitute and client, is presented in my book, *The Sexual Contract* (Polity Press, Cambridge, 1988; Stanford University Press, Stanford, 1988)....

2 G. Schochet, *Patriarchalism in Political Thought: The Authoritarian Family and Political Speculation and Attitudes Especially in Seventeenth Century England* (Basil Blackwell, Oxford, 1975).

3 This brief summary highlights the essential points of conflict between the protagonists, and thus glosses over the differences among theorists on both sides. Hobbes, for instance, saw paternal and political rule as homologous, but rejected patriarchal claims about paternity.

4 Sir R. Filmer, *Patriarchia and Other Political Works*, ed. P. Laslett (Basil Blackwell, Oxford, 1949), p. 54....

5 Filmer, *Patriarchia*, pp. 241, 283.

6 J. Locke, *Two Treatises of Government*, ed. P. Laslett, 2nd edn. (Cambridge University Press, Cambridge, 1967), II, §110.

7 Filmer, *Patriarchia*, p. 245.

8 Locke, *Two Treatises*, I, §47; II, §82.

9 J.-J. Rousseau, *Emile, or On Education*, tr. A. Bloom (Basic Books, New York, 1979), pp. 370, 404.

10 Locke, *Two Treatises*, I, §48.

11 M. Astell, *Some Reflections Upon Marriage* (Source Book Press, New York, 1970), p. 107 (from the 1730 edn., first published 1700). On analogies drawn between the marriage contract and social contract and powers of husbands and kings, see M. Shanley, "Marriage Contract and Social Contract in Seventeenth Century English Political Thought", *Western Political Quarterly*, 32(1), (1979), pp. 79–91.

12 Cited by Schochet, *Patriarchalism in Political Thought*, p. 202. I have discussed liberty, equality and the social contract in *The Problem of Political Obligation*, 2nd edn. (Polity Press, Cambridge, 1985; University of California Press, Berkeley, CA, 1985).

13 B. Crick, *In Defence of Politics*, 2nd edn. (Penguin Books, Harmondsworth, Middlesex, 1982), p. 228.

14 E. Hobsbawm, "The Idea of Fraternity", *New Society*, November 1975, cited in M. Taylor, *Community, Anarchy and Liberty* (Cambridge University Press, Cambridge, 1982), p. 31....

15 N. O. Brown, *Love's Body* (Vintage Books, New York, 1966), p. 4. I am grateful to Peter Breiner for drawing my attention to Brown's interpretation in *Love's Body*. A similar point is made, though its implications for patriarchy are not pursued, by M. Hulliung, "Patriarchalism and Its Early Enemies", *Political Theory*, 2 (1974), pp. 410–19. Hulliung (p. 416) notes that there is no reason why the parricide "cannot just as well be turned into a morality play on behalf of... democratic ideals" and that "the assassins are 'brothers' towards each other, and brothers are equal".

16 P. Rieff, *Freud: The Mind of the Moralist* (Methuen, London, n.d.), ch. VII.

17 S. Freud, *Moses and Monotheism*, tr. K. Jones (Vintage Books, New York, 1939), p. 104....

18 Again, Hobbes is an exception. There are no families in his radically individualist state of nature; women are as strong as men. However, he merely assumes that in civil society women will always enter a marriage contract that places them in subjection to their husbands.

19 Freud, *Moses and Monotheism*, p. 153.

20 For example, Mary Astell sarcastically remarks (*Reflections Upon Marriage*, p. 86) that if "Strength of Mind goes along with Strength of Body, [then] 'tis only for some odd Accidents which Philosophers have not yet thought worthwhile to enquire into, that the Sturdiest Porter is not the wisest Man!" Or consider William Thompson, *Appeal of One Half of the Human Race, Women, Against the Pretensions of the Other Half, Men, to Retain them in Political, and Thence in Civil and Domestic, Slavery* (Source Book Press, New York, 1970; originally published 1825), p. 120: "If strength be the superior title to happiness, let the knowledge and skill of man be employed in adding to the pleasurable sensations of horses, elephants, and all stronger animals. If strength be the title to happiness, let all such qualifications for voters as the capacity to read and write, or any *indirect* means to insure intellectual aptitude be abolished; and let the simple test for the exercise of political rights, both by men and women, be the capacity of carrying 300lbs weight."

21 This helps to explain why we do not have "a philosophy of birth"; see M. O'Brien, *The Politics of Reproduction* (Routledge & Kegan Paul, London, 1981), especially ch. 1....

22 For his history, see G. Lloyd, *The Man of Reason; "Male" and "Female" in Western Philosophy* (Methuen, London, 1984). On the Cartesian "drama of parturition", see S. Bordo, "The Cartesian Masculinization of Thought", *Signs*, 11(3), (1986), pp. 439–56....

23 This division between private and public is constituted in the second stage of the familiar story of the social contract (Locke's theory shows this clearly); see my book, *The Problem of Political Obligation*, ch. 4; and ch. 6 of my *The Disorder of Women: Democracy, Feminism and Political Theory* (Polity Press, Cambridge, 1989).

24 R. M. Unger, *Knowledge and Politics* (Free Press, New York, 1976), p. 45. Unger has little to say about women or the family, but his comments (like those on the division of labour) illustrate that his critique is not the "total critique" at which he aims. He notes, for example, that the family "draws men back into an association that competes with loyalties to all other groups" (p. 264) – but it "draws back" only those who go into civil society....

25 The description comes from B. Harrison, *Separate Spheres: The Opposition to Women's Suffrage in Britain* (Holmes & Meier, New York, 1978), ch. 4. Women were once an essential part of armies, but by the First World War "the once integral place of women in Western armies had faded from memory" (like so much else about women!); see B. C. Hacker, "Women and Military Institutions in Early Modern Europe: A Reconnaissance", *Signs*, 6(4), (1981), pp. 643–71 (the quotation is from p. 671).

26 Cited in *Rights*, 4(5), (1981), p. 4.

27 On women, the military and combat, see J. Stiehm, "The Protected, The Protector, The Defender", *Women's Studies International Forum*, 5 (1982), pp. 367–76; and "Reflections on Women and Combat", Postscript to *Bring Me Men and Women: Mandated Change at the US Air Force Academy* (University of California Press, Berkeley, CA, 1981).

28 M. Foucault, *Discipline and Punish: The Birth of the Prison*, tr. A. Sheridan (Vintage Books, New York, 1979), p. 169.

29 Foucault, *Discipline and Punish*, pp. 222–3.

30 See C. Pateman, "The Shame of the Marriage Contract", in J. Stiehm, ed., *Women's View of the Political World of Men* (Transnational Publishers, Dobbs Ferry, NY, 1984).

31 Mrs Thatcher provides a fascinating illustration. On the one hand she is "the best man in the Cabinet", the victor of the Falklands War, accomplice of Reagan's state terrorism against Libya, and is photographed with weapons. On the other hand she talks to the press about "feminine" matters (such as having her hair tinted), draws headlines like "Four Years on and looking Ten Years Younger", and uses the language of good housekeeping to talk about cuts in social welfare spending (see A. Carter, "Masochism for the Masses", *New Statesman*, 3 June 1983, pp. 8–10).

32 For a critique of a contractarian defence of prostitution, see my "Defending Prostitution: Charges Against Ericsson", *Ethics*, 93 (1983), pp. 561–5, and *The Sexual Contract*, ch. 7.

33 The right is still hedged with immigration restrictions that make it hard for black British women to exercise it; for an account of the interaction of sex and race in British law, see Women, Immigration and Nationality Group, *Worlds Apart: Women Under Immigration and Nationality Law* (Pluto Press, London, 1985). For the USA, see V. Sapiro, "Women, Citizenship and Nationality: Immigration and Naturalization Policies in the United States", *Politics and Society*, 13(1) (1984), pp. 1–26.

34 O'Brien, *The Politics of Reproduction*, p. 205.

8

The Birth of the Self-made Man

Michael Kimmel

Nothing conceivable is so petty, so insipid, so crowded with paltry interests – in one word, so anti-poetic – as the life of a man in the United States.

(Alexis de Tocqueville, *Democracy in America*, 1832)

On April 16, 1787, a few weeks before the opening of the Constitutional Convention, the first professionally produced play in American history opened in New York. *The Contrast*, a five-act comedy by Royall Tyler, centered around two men – one, a disingenuous womanizing fop, and the other, a courageous American army officer – and the woman for whose affections they competed.[1] Tyler parodied the dandy's pretensions at the same time that he disdained the superficial vanities of women, contrasting both with an ideal of chaste and noble love. A patriotic play, *The Contrast* offered a kind of Declaration of Independence of Manners and Morals a decade after the original Declaration had spelled out political and economic rights and responsibilities.

The Contrast posed the most challenging question before the newly independent nation: What kind of nation were we going to be? The sharply drawn differences between the two leading male characters, Billy Dimple and Colonel Manly, allowed the playwright to set (in names worthy of Dickens) the Old World against the New. Dimple was a feminized fop, an Anglophilic, mannered rogue who traveled to England and returned a dandy. "The ruddy youth, who washed his face at the cistern every morning, and swore . . . eternal love and constancy, was now metamorphosed into a flippant, pallid, polite beau, who devotes the morning to his toilet, reads a few pages of Chesterfield's letters [on the art of seduction], and then minces out to put the infamous principles in practice on every woman he meets."[2] His rival, the virtuous Colonel Manly, is a former military officer, modeled after George Washington, fresh from the victory over the British – a man loyal to his troops and to honor and duty. Dimple and Manly compete for the hand of Maria, daughter of Mr. Van Rough, a successful urban businessman who is looking to solidify his newly prosperous economic position with a marriage to the well-positioned Dimple. Van Rough's motto is "Money makes the mare go; keep your eye upon the main chance."[3]

Reprinted from *Manhood in America: A Cultural History* (New York: Free Press, 1996), pp. 13–19, 21–3, 25–34, 36, 39–42, 367–75, 377.

While audiences were quick to see the political choices before them – pitting ill-gained wealth and dubious morality against hard work and civic virtue – Tyler was also presenting another contrast, the answer to a different set of questions: What kind of men would populate this new nation? What vision of manhood would be promoted? What would it mean to be a man in the newly independent United States? Dimple, Manly, and Van Rough offered the audience a contrast among three types of men, three versions of manhood; each embodied different relationships to his work, to his family, to his nation. The signal work in the history of American theater is also one of the earliest meditations on American manhood.

When we first meet Maria Van Rough in the play's opening scene, she is disconsolate, extolling the manly virtues that her fiancé, Dimple, lacks:

> The manly virtue of courage, that fortitude which steels the heart against the keenest misfortunes, which interweaves the laurel of glory amidst the instruments of torture and death, displays something so noble, so exalted, that in despite of the prejudices of education I cannot but admire it, even in a savage.

Maria sees Dimple as "a depraved wretch, whose only virtue is a polished exterior; who is actuated by the unmanly ambition of conquering the defenseless; whose heart, insensible to the emotions of patriotism, dilates at the plaudits of every unthinking girl; whose laurels are the sighs and tears of the miserable victims of his specious behavior."[4]

Enter Colonel Manly. When he and Maria meet by accident in the second act, they are smitten, but Manly's virtue precludes any action on his part.[5] As the play builds to the inevitable confrontation between Dimple and Manly, Tyler provides brief exchanges between the two men (and their manservants) to maintain the audience's interest. In one exchange they parry over the question of whether aristocratic wealth saps virility. Manly warns that no one "shall convince me that a nation, to become great, must first become dissipated. Luxury is surely the bane of a nation: Luxury! which enervates both soul and body, . . . which renders a people weak at home and accessible to bribery, corruption and force from abroad."

Dimple responds by describing the pleasures of seduction. "There is not much pleasure when a man of the world and a finished coquette meet, who perfectly know each other; but how delicious it is to excite the emotions of joy, hope, expectation, and delight in the bosom of a lovely girl who believes every tittle of what you say to be serious!" (We learn later that Dimple's disquisition was more than theoretical, as he has seduced all three of the play's leading women.) Manly's retort is angry and virtuous. "The man who, under pretensions of marriage, can plant thorns in the bosom of an innocent, unsuspecting girl is more detestable than a common robber, in the same proportion as private violence is more despicable than open force."[6]

Finally, Dimple is exposed as a phony and denounced by all. Even in defeat, though, he asks that those assembled consider "the contrast between a gentleman who has read Chesterfield and received the polish of Europe and an unpolished, untravelled American." Manly gets Maria's hand and also has the last word, closing the play with what he has learned, that "probity, virtue, honour, though they should not have received the polish of Europe, will secure to an honest American the good graces of his fair countrywomen."[7]

Maria's father, Mr. Van Rough, presents still another masculine archetype; indeed, each of the three – Dimple, Manly, and Van Rough – embodies one of the three dominant ideals of American manhood available at the turn of the nineteenth century.[8] Despite the play's focus on the other two, it is Van Rough who would come to dominate the new country in a new century. Dimple represents what I will call the Genteel Patriarch. Though Tyler's critical characterization sets Dimple out as a flamboyant fop, the Genteel Patriarch was a powerful ideal through the early part of the nineteenth century. It was, of course, an ideal inherited from Europe. At his best, the Genteel Patriarch represents a dignified aristocratic manhood, committed to the British upper-class code of honor and to well-rounded character, with exquisite tastes and manners and refined sensibilities. To the Genteel Patriarch, manhood meant property ownership and a benevolent patriarchal authority at home, including the moral instruction of his sons. A Christian gentleman, the Genteel Patriarch embodied love, kindness, duty, and compassion, exhibited through philanthropic work, church activities, and deep involvement with his family. For an illustration of the Genteel Patriarch, think of Thomas Jefferson at Monticello, George Washington, John Adams, or James Madison.

Colonel Manly embodies a second type of manhood – the Heroic Artisan.[9] This archetype was also inherited from Europe, despite Royall Tyler's attempt to Americanize him. Independent, virtuous, and honest, the Heroic Artisan is stiffly formal in his manners with women, stalwart and loyal to his male comrades. On the family farm or in his urban crafts shop, he was an honest toiler, unafraid of hard work, proud of his craftsmanship and self-reliance. With a leather apron covering his open shirt and his sleeves rolled up, Boston silversmith Paul Revere, standing proudly at his forge, well illustrates this type.

The newcomer to this scene is Mr. Van Rough, the wealthy entrepreneur, whose newly acquired financial fortune leads to his social aspirations of marrying his daughter to the well-placed aristocratic Dimple. Van Rough represents the Self-Made Man, a model of manhood that derives identity entirely from a man's activities in the public sphere, measured by accumulated wealth and status, by geographic and social mobility. At the time, this economic fortune would have to be translated into permanent social standing – Van Rough must try to become Mr. Smooth. Since a man's fortune is as easily unmade as it is made, the Self-Made Man is uncomfortably linked to the volatile marketplace, and he depends upon continued mobility. Of course, Self-Made Men were not unique to America; as the natural outcome of capitalist economic life, they were known as *nouveaux riches* in revolutionary France (and also known as *noblesse de robe*, as well as other, less pleasant, terms, in the preceding century), and they had their counterparts in every European country. But in America, the land of immigrants and democratic ideals, the land without hereditary titles, they were present from the start, and they came to dominate much sooner than in Europe.

In the growing commercial and, soon, industrial society of the newly independent America, the Self-Made Man seemed to be born at the same time as his country. A man on the go, he was, as one lawyer put it in 1838, "made for action, and the bustling scenes of moving life, and not the poetry or romance of existence."[10] Mobile, competitive, aggressive in business, the Self-Made Man was also temperamentally restless, chronically insecure, and desperate to achieve a solid grounding for a masculine identity.

Royall Tyler hoped that the republican virtue of the Heroic Artisan would triumph over the foppish Genteel Patriarch, just as democratic America defeated the aristocratic British. But it was not to be: it was the relatively minor character, Van Rough, who would emerge triumphant in the nineteenth century, and the mobility and insecurity of the Self-Made Man came to dominate the American definition of manhood.

This book [*Manhood in America*] is the story of American manhood – how it has changed over time and yet how certain principles have remained the same.[11] I believe some of its most important characteristics owe their existence to the timing of the Revolution – the emergence of the Self-Made Men at that time and their great success in the new American democracy have a lot to do with what it is that defines a "real" man even today.

Let's look at the Self-Made Man's first appearance on the historical stage, which will help us limn the shifts in the definitions of manhood in the first half of the nineteenth century. An old standard rooted in the life of the community and the qualities of a man's character gave way to a new standard based on individual achievement, a shift in emphasis "from service to community and cultivation of the spirit to improvement of the individual and concern with his body."[12] From a doctrine of "usefulness" and "service" to the preoccupation with the "self," American manhood got off to a somewhat disturbing start.

Part of this start, the American Revolution, brought a revolt of the sons against the father – in this case, the Sons of Liberty against Father England.[13] And this introduced a new source of tension in the act of resolving an old one. The relatively casual coexistence of the Genteel Patriarch and the Heroic Artisan had been made possible by the colonies' relationship with England. Many Genteel Patriarchs looked to England not just for political and economic props but also for cultural prescriptions for behavior. Patriarchs had the right to lead their country by virtue of their title. The American colonies had few noblemen, like Sir William Randolph, but they had plenty of substitutes, from upper-class political elites to Dutch landed gentry in New York and the large plantation owners in Virginia and around Chesapeake Bay. There was little tension between them and the laborers who worked for or near them. The real problem was that as long as the colonies remained in British hands, it seemed to all that manly autonomy and self-control were impossible. Being a man meant being in charge of one's own life, liberty, and property.

Being a man meant also not being a boy. A man was independent, self-controlled, responsible; a boy was dependent, irresponsible, and lacked control. And language reflected these ideas. The term *manhood* was synonymous with "adulthood." Just as black slaves were "boys," the white colonists felt enslaved by the English father, infantilized, and thus emasculated.

The American Revolution resolved this tension because, in the terms of the reigning metaphor of the day, it freed the sons from the tyranny of a despotic father. The Declaration of Independence was a declaration of manly adulthood, a manhood that was counterposed to the British version against which American men were revolting. Jefferson and his co-authors accused the king of dissolving their representative assemblies because they had opposed "with manly firmness, his invasions on the rights of the people." (Of course, the rebellion of the sons did not eliminate the need for patriarchal authority. George Washington was immediately hailed as the Father of our Country, and many wished he would become king.)

By contrast, British manhood and, by extension, aristocratic conceptions of manhood (which would soon come to include the Genteel Patriarch) were denounced as feminized, lacking manly resolve and virtue, and therefore, ruling arbitrarily. Critiques of monarchy and aristocracy were tainted with a critique of aristocratic luxury as effeminate. John Adams posed the question about how to prevent the creation of a new aristocracy in a letter to Thomas Jefferson in December 1819. "Will you tell me how to prevent riches becoming the effects of temperance and industry? Will you tell me how to prevent riches from producing luxury? Will you tell me how to prevent luxury from producing effeminacy, intoxication, extravagance, vice and folly?"[14] . . .

. . . Billy Dimple's time was slowly passing, and Colonel Manly could never be as dominant as Cincinnatus. Instead, the economic boom of the new country's first decades produced the triumph of the Self-Made Men, the Van Roughs, men who were neither aristocratic fops nor virtuous drones – far from it. These Self-Made Men built America.

Between 1800 and 1840 the United States experienced a market revolution. Freed from colonial dependence, mercantile capitalism remade the nation. America undertook the construction of a national transportation system and developed extensive overseas and domestic commerce. Between 1793 and 1807 American exports tripled, while between 1800 and 1840 the total amount of free labor outside the farm sector rose from 17 to 37 percent.[15] The fiscal and banking system expanded rapidly; from eighty-nine banks in 1811 to 246 five years later and 788 by 1837. The economic boom meant westward expansion as well as dramatic urban growth.

Such dramatic economic changes were accompanied by political, social, and ideological shifts. Historian Nancy Cott notes that the period 1780–1830 witnessed a demographic transition to modern patterns of childbirth and childcare, development of uniform legal codes and procedures, expansion of primary education, the beginning of the democratization of the political process, and the "invention of a new language of political and social thought." Democracy was expanding, and with it, by the end of the first half of the century, America was "converted to acquisitiveness," a conversion that would have dramatic consequences for the meanings of manhood in industrializing America. In the third decade of the century, between 1825 and 1835, a bourgeoisie worthy of the name came into being in the Northeast, a self-consciously self-made middle class.[16]

The emerging capitalist market in the early nineteenth century both freed individual men and destabilized them. No longer were men bound to the land, to their estates, to Mother England, or to the tyrannical father, King George. No longer did their manhood rest on their craft traditions, guild memberships, or participation in the virtuous republic of the New England small town. America was entering a new age, and men were free to create their own destinies, to find their own ways, to rise as high as they could, to write their own biographies. God had made man a "moral free agent," according to revivalist minister Charles Finney in a celebrated sermon in 1830. The American Adam could fashion himself in his own image. This new individual freedom was as socially and psychologically unsettling as it was exciting and promising. To derive one's identity, and especially one's identity as a man, from marketplace successes was a risky proposition.

Yet that is precisely what defined the Self-Made Man: success in the market, individual achievement, mobility, wealth. America expressed political autonomy; the Self-Made Man embodied economic autonomy. This was the manhood of the rising middle class. The flip side of this economic autonomy is anxiety, restlessness, loneliness. Manhood is no longer fixed in land or small-scale property ownership or dutiful service. Success must be earned, manhood must be proved – and proved constantly. . . .

The era's most perceptive visitor – perhaps the most observant visitor in our history – was a young French nobleman, Alexis de Tocqueville. When Tocqueville arrived in America in 1830, he was instantly struck by the dramatically different temperament of the American, a difference he attributed to the difference between aristocracies and democracies. Unlike his European counterpart, Tocqueville observed, the American man was a radical democrat – equal and alone, masterless and separate, autonomous and defenseless against the tyranny of the majority. Each citizen was equal, and "equally impotent, poor and isolated." In Europe caste distinctions between nobles and commoners froze social positions but also connected them; "aristocracy links everybody, from peasant to king, in one long chain." Democracy meant freedom but disconnection; it "breaks the chain and frees every link." American democracy also meant a great sliding towards the center; all Americans tended to "contract the ways of thinking of the manufacturing and trading classes."[17]

Tocqueville's dissection of the double-edged quality of the democratic personality remains as incisive today as it was in the early nineteenth century. The middle-class man was an anxious achiever, constantly striving, casting his eyes nervously about as he tried, as Mr. Van Rough put it in *The Contrast*, to "mind the main chance." The American man was "restless in the midst of abundance." In a passage that eloquently defines this restlessness of the Self-Made Man, Tocqueville writes:

> An American will build a house in which to pass his old age and sell it before the roof is on; he will plant a garden and rent it just as the trees are coming into bearing; he will clear a field and leave others to reap the harvest; he will take up a profession and leave it, settle in one place and soon go off elsewhere with his changing desires. . . . [H]e will travel five hundred miles in a few days as a distraction from his happiness.[18]

Like Dickens, Tocqueville also found the American marked by a "strange melancholy"; every American "is eaten up with a longing to rise, but hardly any of them seem to entertain very great hopes or to aim very high." The American man was a man in a hurry but with not very far to go.[19]

Even the term *self-made man* was an American neologism, first coined by Henry Clay in a speech in the US Senate in 1832. Defending a protective tariff that he believed would widen opportunities for humble men to rise in business, he declared that in Kentucky "almost every manufactory known to me is in the hands of enterprising, self-made men, who have whatever wealth they possess by patient and diligent labor."[20]

The term immediately caught on. Rev. Calvin Colton noted in 1844 that America "is a country where men start from a humble origin, and from small beginnings gradually rise in the world, as the reward of merit and industry. . . . One has as good a chance as another, according to his talents, prudence, and personal exertions.... [T]his is a country of *self-made men* [in which] work is held in the highest respect [while] the idle, lazy, poor man gets little pity in his poverty."[21] By the 1840s and 1850s a veritable cult of the Self-Made Man had appeared, as young men devoured popular biographies and inspirational homilies to help future self-made men create themselves. John Frost's *Self Made Men in America* (1848), Charles Seymore's *Self-Made Men* (1858) and Freeman Hunt's *Worth and Wealth* (1856) and *Lives of American Merchants* (1858) provided self-making homilies, packaged between brief biographies of poor boys who had made it rich.

The central characteristic of being self-made was that the proving ground was the public sphere, specifically the workplace. And the workplace was a man's world (and a native-born white man's world at that). If manhood could be proved, it had to be proved in the eyes of other men. From the early nineteenth century until the present day, most of men's relentless efforts to prove their manhood contain this core element of homosociality. From fathers and boyhood friends to our teachers, co-workers, and bosses, it is the evaluative eyes of other men that are always upon us, watching, judging. It was in this regime of scrutiny that such men were tested. "Every man you meet has a rating or an estimate of himself which he never loses or forgets," wrote Kenneth Wayne in his popular turn-of-the-century advice book, *Building the Young Man* (1912). "A man has his own rating, and instantly he lays it alongside of the other man." Almost a century later, another man remarked to psychologist Sam Osherson that "[b]y the time you're an adult, it's easy to think you're always in competition with men, for the attention of women, in sports, at work."[22]

In the early decades of the nineteenth century, the Self-Made Man competed with the two other archetypes from Tyler's play. The Genteel Patriarch had to be displaced, and the Heroic Artisan had to be uprooted and brought into the new industrial marketplace. In the rush of the new century, Self-Made Men did indeed triumph, but neither the patriarch nor the laborer disappeared overnight.

First, the Genteel Patriarch. While the richest tenth of all Americans held slightly less (49.6 percent) than half the wealth in 1774, they held 73 percent in 1860, and the richest 1 percent more than doubled their share of the wealth, from 12.6 to 29 percent, and then to about 50 percent by mid-century. The period 1820–1860 was "probably the most unequal period in American history."[23] But these new wealthy were no longer the landed aristocracy but the new merchants and industrialists.[24] Economically, Van Rough simply blew away Billy Dimple.

American culture followed suit. Gone were the powder, wigs, and richly ornamented and colorfully patterned clothing that had marked the old gentry; the new man of commerce wore plain and simple clothing "to impart trust and confidence in business affairs."[25] Countless pundits recast the Genteel Patriarch as a foppish dandy as they railed against Europe, against traditional feudal society, against historical obligation.[26] Even older, venerated Genteel Patriarchs were not immune to the feminization of the landed gentry. Jefferson himself was castigated as dandified, the product of aristocratic and chivalric Virginia, "America's Athens." He was accused of "timidity, whimsicalness," "a wavering of disposition" and a weakness for flattery, a man who "took counsel in his feelings and imagination," and the Jeffersonians were condemned for their "womanish resentment" against England and their "womanish attachment to France."[27]

Leading the charge against the Genteel Patriarch was Ralph Waldo Emerson, who signaled the shifting taste in his seminal essay "The American Scholar" (1837). Emerson "enshrined psychic self-sovereignty as the essential manly virtue," according to literary critic T. Walter Herbert, and the theme of his essays "of self-reliant struggle from humble origins to high position became the ruling narrative of manly worth, supplanting that of the well-born lad demonstrating his superior breeding in the exercise of responsibilities that were his birthright."[28] Nathaniel Hawthorne even suggested that a young man could be crippled by inheriting "a great fortune." Here was a "race of non-producers," warned S. C. Allen in 1830, a "new sort of aristocracy, of a more uncompromising character than the feudal, or any landed aristocracy can ever be."[29] ...

Meanwhile, the Heroic Artisan was losing his independence, which he so dearly prized. He "looks the whole world in the face / For he owes not any man," as Henry Wadsworth Longfellow put it in "The Village Blacksmith" (1844).[30] Disciplined and responsible, the Heroic Artisan believed that "independent men of relatively small means were both entitled to full citizenship and best equipped to exercise it." A firm believer in self-government, the Heroic Artisan was the embodiment of Jeffersonian liberty; the virtuous "yeoman of the city," as he had called them. Before the Civil War nine of every ten American men owned their own farm, shop, or small crafts workshop. About half of all workmen were employed in shops of ten or fewer; four-fifths worked in shops of no more than twenty. His body was his own, his labor a form of property.[31] ...

The cement of this republican virtue was the coupling of economic autonomy to political community and workplace solidarity. This combination is the essence of *producerism*, an ideology that claimed that virtue came from the hard work of those who produce the world's wealth. Producerism held that there was a deep-rooted conflict in society between the producing and the nonproducing classes and that work was a source of moral instruction, economic success, and political virtue. "We ask that every man become an independent proprietor, possessing enough of the goods of this world, to be able by his own moderate industry to provide for the wants of his body," wrote Orestes Brownson in his tract "The Laboring Classes" (1840). The doctrines of producerism resurface constantly through the century as rural and urban workingmen, from the Populists to the Knights of Labor and early union organizers, cast their resistance to proletarianization in terms of preservation of economic autonomy and political community.[32]

The British historian E. P. Thompson's explorations of the emergence of the British working class revealed an easy flow between the workplace and leisure in the British villages of the pre-Industrial Revolution, even in the actual length and organization of the working day.[33] In their workshops, apprentices, journeymen, and master craftsmen integrated work and leisure. Customers would appear, contract for specific tasks, and socialize and wait while it was being done; when no customers appeared, masters and journeymen would continue to train young apprentices while jugs of hard cider were constantly passed around. At leisure the Heroic Artisan was communitarian, participating regularly in "evenings of drink, merriment, and ceremony that were part of longstanding premodern traditions" and that provided ample opportunities for artisans to meet in a mood of "mutual self-esteem and exaltation."[34]

Workplace solidarity and ease of movement between work and leisure also spilled over into the organization of the trades. Many trades resembled fraternal orders in which artisans developed modest welfare systems for their sick and needy brethren or for the families of deceased brethren. Each volunteer fire department, for example, was its own fraternal society with its own insignias, mottoes, "freshly minted traditions," "fiercely masculine rituals," and sacred emblems like the fire hose, company crest, and fire chief's trumpet.[35]

These independent artisans, craftsmen, and small shopkeepers were on the defensive throughout the first half of the century. Each of the periodic economic crises had struck these artisans especially hard. Older skills became obsolete and factory employment grew – from an average of eight women and men to anywhere between fifty and five hundred men.[36] Masters increased the scale, pace, and routine of production, hiring young strangers, with whom they shared only contractual relations, rather than the sons of their neighbors.[37] Real wages of skilled workers declined, and workplace autonomy seemed to be disappearing everywhere. New forms of labor control, including the putting-out system, sweated labor, and wages, all eroded the virtuous republic. . . .

Many workingmen tried to combat this trend by organizing the nation's first workingmen's political parties, there to redress their economic and political grievances in parties like the Mechanics Union of Trade Associations (1827), the Workingmen's Party (1828), and the Equal Rights Party (1833). These organizations' rhetoric was saturated with equations of autonomy and manhood. Loss of autonomy was equated with emasculation; economic dependence on wages paid by an employer was equivalent to social and sexual dependency. The factory system was "subversive of liberty," according to one worker in the fledgling National Trades Union in 1834, "calculated to change the character of a people from bold and free to enervated, dependent and slavish." Under such circumstances, held an editorialist in the union newspaper *The Man*, it would have been "unmanly" and undignified, "an abdication of their responsibilities as citizens" if they did *not* organize.[38]

Newspapers like *The Man* inveighed regularly against three groups: women, immigrants, and black slaves. Women had earlier been excluded (of course) from craft guilds and apprenticeships, but the emerging working class supported women's complete exclusion from the public sphere, even though only around 2 percent of all females over the age of ten worked in any type of industry. These formerly independent small shopkeepers and craftsmen opposed women's rights to education, property ownership, and suffrage.[39] It was as if workplace manhood could only be retained if the workplace had only men in it.

And only native-born men at that. Immigration had increased rapidly through the first half of the century, from 140,439 in the 1820s to 599,125 in the 1830s. During the 1840s immigration more than tripled to 1,713,251, and 2,598,214 more immigrants arrived during the 1850s. Anti-immigrant demonstrations and riots followed as the native-born artisans felt increasingly threatened by these less-skilled workers, who were willing to work longer hours for lower wages.[40] In antebellum America Irish immigrants were especially stamped with a problematic masculinity. Imagined as rough and primitive, uncivilized and uncivilizable, the Irish were ridiculed as a subhuman species, born to inferiority and incapable of being true American men.[41]

Of course, not all native-born men were real men. In an arresting book the historian David Roediger argues that, from the moment of its origins, the white working class used black slaves as the economic and moral "other," whose economic dependency indicated emasculation and moral degeneracy. Whiteness, Roediger argues, served as a secondary "wage" for white workers who were resisting the view of wage labor as a form of wage slavery. By asserting their whiteness, workers could compensate for their loss of autonomy; the "status and privileges conferred by race could be used to make up for alienating and exploitative class relationships."[42]

What Roediger describes economically, social historian Eric Lott discusses symbolically in his analysis of blackface minstrel shows in antebellum America. Minstrel shows performed a double mimesis; the minstrel show was, Lott argues, both love and theft. The projection of white men's fears onto black men was simultaneously for "whites insecure about their whiteness" and for men insecure about their manhood. "Mediating white men's relations with other white men, minstrel acts certainly made currency out of the black man himself," he writes. The "pale gaze" of the white audience faced with a caricatured black identity paralleled the "male gaze" of this now conscious audience of men reasserting their manhood through the symbolic appropriation of the black man's sexual potency.[43]

In these literal and symbolic ways the American working class that emerged in the decades before the Civil War was self-consciously white, native-born, and male, rooted as much in racism, sexism, and xenophobia as in craft pride and workplace autonomy – a combination that has haunted its efforts to retrieve its lost dignity and organize successfully against industrial capitalists throughout American history. The rage of the dying class of Heroic Artisans took many forms.

In the 1830s, however, something remarkable happened. The working class saw its salvation in the presidential campaign of one of its own. Andrew Jackson was both the last gasp of Jeffersonian republican virtue and the first expression of the politics of class-based resentment.

Andrew Jackson was not the first American leader to combine virulent hyper-masculinity with vengeful, punitive political maneuvers nor, certainly, was he (nor will he be) the last. But he was one of the most colorful and charismatic of such, and he embodied the hopes and fears of many men. The emotions that seem to have animated Jacksonian American were fear and rage. When Jackson first arrived in the Senate, he was unable to speak because of "the rashness of his feelings," then-Vice President Thomas Jefferson recalled. "I have seen him attempt it repeatedly and as often choke with rage." A "choleric, impetuous" man, according to turn-of-the-century historian Frederick Jackson Turner, Jackson was a "tall, lank, uncouth-looking personage, with long locks of hair hanging over his face and a cue [ponytail] down his back tied in an eel skin; his dress singular, his manners those of a rough backwoodsman."[44]

It is difficult not to see Jackson and the men he stood for in starkly Freudian terms. Here was the fatherless son, struggling without guidance to separate from the mother and, again, for adult mastery over his environment. Terrified of infantilization, of infantile dependency, his rage propelled the furious effort to prove his manhood against those who threatened it, notably women and infanti-lized "others." It was as if America found an adolescent leader to preside over its own adolescence as a nation. Here was "the nursling of the wilds," a "pupil of the wilderness," according to George Bancroft; a man, as Tocqueville put it, "of violent character and middling capacities." Andrew Jackson was the consummate schoolyard bully.[45]

The hero of the War of 1812 and the Creek War of 1813/14, Jackson saw his military exploits as an effort to overcome his own "indolence" and achieve republican purification through violence. He came to power as the champion of the Heroic Artisan, whether rural yeoman farmer or urban artisan, against the effete aristocracy of the Eastern urban entrepreneur and the decadent European-ized landed gentry. One laudatory biography of Jackson from 1820 began with alarm over the "voluptuousness and effeminacy" that was attendant upon the sudden rise of new wealth in America, characteristics that were "rapidly diminish-ing that exalted sense of national glory."[46]

The Heroic Artisans embraced Jackson. He campaigned in 1828, in the words of a campaign song, as one "who can fight" against John Quincy Adams, "who can write," pitting "the plowman" against "the professor."[47] As president his hostility towards paper currency, his opposition to corporate charters, his deep suspicion of public enterprise and public debt – all elements of American produ-cerism – appealed to small planters, farmers, mechanics, and laborers, the "bone and sinew of the country." His administration was saturated with the rhetoric of the violent, short-tempered, impulsively democratic artisanate, especially in his struggle against the savage nature of primitive manhood (Indians) and the effete, decadent institutions that signaled Europeanized overcivilization (the Bank). . . .

Jackson's flight from feminizing influences illustrates a psychodynamic element in the historical construction of American manhood. Having killed the tyrannical father, American men feared being swallowed whole by an infantilizing and insati-able mother – voluptuous, voracious, and terrifyingly alluring. Jackson projected those emotions onto "others" so that by annihilating or controlling them, his own temptations to suckle helplessly at the breast of indolence and luxury could be purged. Jackson's gendered rage at weakness, feminizing luxury, and sensuous pleasure resonated for a generation of symbolically fatherless sons, the first gener-ation of American men born after the Revolution.

Historically, such flight from feminization produced its opposite as the Heroic Artisan became wedded to exclusionary policies that left him increasingly defense-less against unscrupulous capitalist entrepreneurs, just as Jackson's effort to recon-cile simple yeoman values with the free pursuit of economic interest ultimately cleared the path for the expansion of laissez-faire capitalist development. The heroic resistance of the artisan against the feminizing Bank was ironically the mechanism by which he was eventually pushed aside and transformed into a proletarian. . . .

In the last decade before the outbreak of Civil War, it was still unclear which model of manhood would emerge as triumphant. Already the Heroic Artisans were in retreat though they still exerted significant influence in local urban politics. And though Genteel Patriarchs had been discredited politically, at least as a political symbol, they still controlled a significant proportion of the nation's property. Their decline and the Self-Made Man's ascendancy were still in question, as was made abundantly clear in a shocking series of events that took place in May 1849. As with Royall Tyler's *The Contrast*, the stage was set, literally, in the New York City theater. Or rather in the Opera House at Astor Place and the surrounding square and city streets.

In May the celebrated British actor William Macready was preparing to perform *Macbeth* at the tony Astor Place Opera House. At the same time, Edwin Forrest, perhaps the most acclaimed American actor of his era, was taking up theatrical residence at the Broadway Theater for a run of his own. What might have begun as a personal squabble between the two premier actors of their respective countries turned into a clash between the patriotic, xenophobic nationalism of the New York working classes and the contemptuous elitism of the powerful. To the emerging urban elite, the working classes were nothing but gutter rabble, "sanguinary ruffians," filthy and uncouth; those same workingmen branded the bankers and merchants as "the dandies of Uppertendom."[48]

The actors themselves had squared off before. Macready was pompous, elegant, and extraordinarily gifted; an "actor autocrat," according to one critic. Forrest was a man of the people, "born in humble life," who "worked his way up from poverty and obscurity." In short, the man hailed as "the American Tragedian" was a self-made man; and as the *Boston Mail* put it in 1848:

> he is justly entitled to that honor – he has acquired it by his own labors; from a poor boy in a circus he has arisen to be a man of fame and wealth, all of which he has lastingly gained by enterprise and talent, and secured both by economy and temperance.[49]

Stylistically and sartorially, the two men were as different as a leather-aproned artisan and a liveried aristocrat. When Macready played Hamlet, one critic observed, he "wore a dress, the waist of which nearly reached his arms; a hat with a sable plume big enough to cover a hearse; a pair of black silk gloves, much too large for him; a ballet shirt of straw coloured satin," which, combined with his angular facial features, made him appear "positively hideous." Forrest's rugged appearance and muscular acting style stood in sharp contrast; Forrest had, in the words of one London reviewer, "shot up like the wild mountain pine and prairie sycamore, amid the free life and spontaneous growths of the west, not rolled in the garden-bed of cities to a dead level, nor clipped of all proportion by too careful husbandry." The two actors captured the contrast of national cultures and of versions of manhood, pitting, as one critic put it, "the unsophisticated energy of the daring child of nature" against the "more glossy polish of the artificial European civilian."[50]

The two played their parts superbly. Neither especially liked the other, either as an actor or as a man. Macready was struck by the "vehemence and rude force" of Forrest's performances, which favorable critics attributed to Forrest's manly vigor and oracular power. Macready was criticized as a "high-hatted" player, "craven-hearted, egotistical, cold, selfish, inflated," and obsessed with his "aristocratic importance."[51] Forrest had earlier hissed at Macready's performance of *Hamlet* ostensibly because the Englishman, castigated as a "superannuated driveller," had tinkered with the play somewhat, introducing into one scene a "fancy dance" that was excoriated by Forrest as a "pas de mouchoir – dancing and throwing up his handkerchief across the stage."

When Macready and Forrest were each booked to perform in New York in May 1849, both stages were set for an explosive confrontation. The opening night performance of Macready's *Macbeth* was punctuated by noisy demonstrations and efforts by the rowdy throngs in the balconies to disrupt the performance. Tossing rotten eggs, "pennies, and other missiles" and eventually throwing a few chairs, they succeeded in driving Macready from the stage of that "aristocratic, kid-glove Opera House."[52] Disgusted, the stalwart English actor determined to cancel his performances and sail the next night for England. The plebeian crowds were jubilant in their assumed victory. The next day, though, Macready changed his mind after being entreated by several New York notables, including bankers, merchants, and writers like Washington Irving and Herman Melville.

The next night, May 10, thousands of workingmen and young working-class teenagers, known colloquially as B'hoys and renowned for their "virtuous contempt" for all things aristocratic, gathered in front of the Opera House.[53] Ned Buntline, the organizer of the infamous nativist organizations the United Sons of America and the Patriotic Order of Sons of America, whipped the "mobbish nativism" of the crowds to a fever pitch; the group now intended to prevent the performance or at least to disrupt its conclusion. Meanwhile the New York City police, joined by the local battalions of the state militia, were determined to keep the enormous crowd in check. By the end of the performance, as the crowds were whisked away via side exits, tempers were flaring. There was the expected shouting back and forth and even a few projectiles launched in the direction of the police and soldiers. Suddenly and unexpectedly the soldiers opened fire on the crowd. Twenty-two were killed, thirty more wounded, and over sixty more arrested.[54]

The Astor Place riot marked the first time in American history that American troops had ever opened fire on American citizens. To some it signaled the beginning of the great class struggle. A year after Marx and Engels had published *The Communist Manifesto* in Germany, one eyewitness saw the Astor Place riots in these terms:

> [I]t was the rich against the poor – the aristocracy against the people; and this hatred of wealth and privilege is increasing all over the world, and ready to burst out whenever there is the slightest occasion. The rich and well bred are too apt to despise the poor and ignorant; and they must not think it strange if they are hated in return.[55]

Those killed and arrested were all local artisans or small shopkeepers, including printers, clerks, grocers, ship joiners, butchers, plumbers, sailmakers, carpenters, and gunsmiths.[56] And their opponents were the newly moneyed urban entrepreneurs, flexing their political muscles, able to harness military and police power for their side and able to fend off efforts to taint them as aristocratic dandies.

It had taken scarcely twenty years for the Self-Made Man to establish a foothold in the consciousness of American men and to stake a claim for dominance in American politics and culture. He had gone from being the new kid on the block to owning the street. Avoiding the taint of aristocracy and subduing the working classes, the Self-Made Man was now, at mid-century, the dominant American conception of manhood. And in the decades following the Civil War, he would transform the nation.

Notes

1 Royall Tyler, *The Contrast: A Comedy in Five Acts* (Boston: Houghton Mifflin, 1920). Some commentary on the play is offered in Ada Lou Carson and Herbert L. Carson, *Royall Tyler* (Boston: Twayne Publications, 1979). See also Alexander Saxton, *The Rise and Fall of the White Republic: Class Politics and Mass Culture in Nineteenth-Century America* (New York: Verso, 1990), pp. 110–13.
2 Tyler, *The Contrast*, I, 1, p. 27.
3 Ibid., I, 2, p. 35.
4 Ibid., I, 2, pp. 32–3, pp. 38–9.
5 Manly's short soliloquy encapsulates what sociologist Max Weber would call, a century later, the Protestant Ethic. "We are both unhappy; but it is your duty to obey your parent – mine to obey my honour. Let us, therefore, both follow the path of rectitude; and of this we may be assured, that if we are not happy, we shall, at least deserve to be so" (IV, p. 99).
6 Tyler, *The Contrast*, III, 2, pp. 79, 82.
7 Ibid., V, pp. 112, 114–15.
8 My typology of masculine archetypes relies on several earlier efforts to map this terrain. See, e.g., Charles Rosenberg, "Sexuality, Class and Role in Nineteenth-Century America," *American Quarterly* 25, 1976; E. Anthony Rotundo, "Body and Soul: Changing Ideals of American Middle-Class Manhood," *Journal of Social History* 16, 1983, and "Learning About Manhood: Gender Ideals and the Middle-Class Family in Nineteenth-Century America," in *Manliness and Morality: Middle-Class Masculinity in Britain and America, 1800–1940*, ed. J. A. Mangan and James Walvin (New York: St. Martin's Press, 1987); David Leverenz, *Manhood and the American Renaissance* (Ithaca, NY: Cornell University Press, 1989). Rotundo's book *American Manhood: Transformations in Masculinity from the Revolution to the Present Era* (New York: Basic Books, 1993) appeared after this book was substantially completed; however, I have benefited greatly from the various articles which compose many of his chapters.
9 I use the term *artisan* here in a broader sense than just those men involved in urban craft production. What distinguishes the artisan, in my view, is his autonomy, his sense of integrity in manual labor, his calling. Thus, I also include the nation's independent farmers, the celebrated yeomen of Jeffersonian republicanism, who equally embraced the ideals of producerism.
10 Cited in Rotundo, "Learning About Manhood," p. 36.
11 Michael Kimmel, *Manhood in America: A Cultural History* (New York: The Free Press, 1996).
12 Rotundo, "Body and Soul," p. 29.
13 On this image, see, e.g., Jay Fliegelman, *Prodigals and Pilgrims: The American Revolution Against Patriarchal Authority, 1750–1800* (New York: Cambridge University Press, 1982), and David Pugh, *Sons of Liberty: The Masculine Mind in Nineteenth-Century America* (Westport, Conn.: Greenwood Press, 1983).
14 John Adams to Thomas Jefferson, 21 December 1819; in Cappon, ed., *The Adams–Jefferson Letters*, 1959; vol. 2, p. 549. John Hancock also warned against the dangers of luxury, writing: "Suffer not yourselves to be betrayed by the soft arts of luxury and effeminacy, into the pit digged for your destruction. Despise the glare of wealth. That people who pay greater respect to a wealthy villain, than to an honest upright man in poverty, almost deserve to be enslaved; they plainly shew that wealth, however it may be acquired, is in their esteem to be preferred to virtue." Cited in Philip Greven, *The Protestant Temperament: Patterns of Child-Rearing, Religious Experience, and the Self in Early America* (New York: Knopf, 1980), p. 351. . . .

15 See Stephanie Coontz, *The Social Origins of Private Life* (New York: Verso, 1988), pp. 118, 168.

16 Nancy Cott, *The Bonds of Womanhood: Women's Sphere in New England, 1780–1835* (New Haven: Yale University Press, 1977), p. 3; Norman Ware, *The Industrial Worker, 1840–1860* (Boston: Houghton Mifflin, 1924), p. 37. On the emergence of the middle class, see Burton Bledstein, *The Culture of Professionalism: The Middle Class and the Development of Higher Education in America* (New York: Norton, 1976); Karen Halttunen, *Confidence Men and Painted Women: A Study of Middle-Class Culture in America, 1830–1870* (New Haven: Yale University Press, 1982); Mary Ryan, *Cradle of the Middle Class: The Family in Oneida County, New York, 1790–1865* (Cambridge: Cambridge University Press, 1981); Paul Johnson, *A Shopkeeper's Millennium: Society and Revivals in Rochester, New York, 1815–1837* (New York: Hill and Wang, 1978); Paul Boyer, *Urban Masses and Moral Order in America, 1820–1920* (Cambridge, Mass.: Harvard University Press, 1978); David Brion Davis, *The Problem of Slavery in an Age of Revolution, 1770–1823* (Ithaca, NY: Cornell University Press, 1975)...

17 Alexis de Tocqueville, *Democracy in America* [1840], trans. George Lawrence (New York: Anchor, 1969), vol. 1, p. 314.

18 Ibid., vol. 2, p. 536.

19 Ibid., vol. 2, pp. 538, 627. He wrote further that

> He who has set his heart exclusively on the pursuit of worldly welfare is always in a hurry, for he has but a limited time at his disposal...The recollection of the brevity of life is a constant spur to him.... This thought fills him with anxiety, fear and regret and keeps his mind in ceaseless trepidation which leads him to perpetually to change his plans and his abode. (2: 162)

20 Cited in Irvin G. Wyllie, *The Self-Made Man in America* (New Brunswick, NJ: Rutgers University Press, 1954), p. 10.

21 Calvin Colton, *Junius Tracts*, no. 7 (New York, 1844), p. 15. Also cited in Charles Sellers, *The Market Revolution: Jacksonian America, 1815–1846* (New York: Oxford University Press, 1992), p. 238. Freeman Hunt's *Hunt's Merchant Magazine*, founded in 1839, also celebrated the cult of the Self-Made Man.

22 Kenneth Wayne, *Building the Young Man* (Chicago: A. C. McClurg, 1912), p. 18; Sam Osherson, *Wrestling with Love: How Men Struggle with Intimacy, with Women, Children, Parents, and Each Other* (New York: Fawcett, 1992), p. 291.

23 Kim Voss, *The Making of American Exceptionalism: The Knights of Labor and Class Formation in the Nineteenth Century* (Ithaca, NY: Cornell University Press, 1993), p. 36. See also Sellers, *The Market Revolution*, pp. 152, 238; and David Leverenz, "The Last Real Man in America: From Natty Bumppo to Batman," *American Literary History* 3, 1991, p. 757.

24 "It is not the wealthy that rule our legislative councils, in societies, in politics, in town meetings, and the everyday concerns of life; it is not the aristocratic part of our community that have sway over the rest; but it is the educated, the active, the intelligent" was the way one member of the Mechanics Institute put it in 1833. Cited in Sean Wilentz, *Chants Democratic: New York City and the Rise of the American Working Class, 1788–1850* (New York: Oxford University Press, 1984), p. 275.

25 Kathy Peiss, "Of Makeup and Men: The Gendering of Cosmetics," paper presented at a Conference on the Material Culture of Gender, Winterthur Museum, November 1989, p. 4.

26 John Adams, for example, wrote that monarchy would

produce so much Taste and Politeness, so much Elegance in Dress, Furniture, Equipage, so much Musick and Dancing, so much Fencing and Skaiting, so much Cards and Backgammon; so much Horse Racing and Cockfighting, so many Balls and Assemblies, so many Plays and Concerts, that the very imagination of them makes me feel vain, light, frivolous. (cited in Greven, *The Protestant Temperament*, p. 336)

And Ralph Waldo Emerson warned that "[t]he world is full of fops who never did anything and who persuaded beauties and men of genius to wear their fop livery; and these will deliver the fop opinion, that it is not respectable to be seen earning a living; that it is much more respectable to spend without earning" (Ralph Waldo Emerson, *Collected Works*, intro. and notes Robert E. Spiller, text established by Alfred R. Ferguson (Cambridge, Mass.: Belknap Press, 1994), vol. 6, pp. 91–2.

27 See William R. Taylor, *Cavalier and Yankee: The Old South and the American National Character* (New York: George Braziller, 1961), p. 91; other quotes were cited in Bruce Curtis, "The Wimp Factor," in *American Heritage*, November 1989; and Mark Kann, *On the Man Question: Gender and Civic Virtue in America* (Philadelphia: Temple University Press, 1991), p. 246. France itself was increasingly cast as feminized.

28 T. Walter Herbert, *Dearest Beloveds: The Hawthornes and the Making of the Middle-Class Family* (Berkeley: University of California Press, 1993), p. 33.

29 Arthur M. Schlesinger, Jr., *The Age of Jackson* (Boston: Little, Brown, 1953), pp. 23, 167; S. C. Allen is cited on p. 153.

30 The poem is in *Longfellow's Complete Poems* (Cambridge: Riverside Press, 1898).

31 Wilentz, *Chants Democratic*, p. 102; Allan Trachtenberg, *The Incorporation of American Culture: Culture and Society in the Gilded Age* (New York: Hill and Wang, 1982); Daniel Rodgers, *The Work Ethic in Industrial America, 1850–1920* (Chicago: University of Chicago Press, 1978), p. 19....

32 See Orestes Brownson, "The Laboring Classes," *Boston Quarterly*, July 1840, pp. 358–95.

33 Thompson writes that "[s]ocial intercourse and labour are intermingled; the working day lengthens or contracts according to the task – there is no great sense of conflict between labour and 'passing the time of day.'" Cited in Cott, *The Bonds of Womanhood*, p. 60.

34 Howard Rock, *Artisans of the New Republic: The Tradesmen of New York in the Age of Jefferson* (New York: New York University Press, 1984), pp. 319, 129. I will return to this theme of American drinking habits in the next chapter.

35 See Wilentz, *Chants Democratic*, pp. 260–261.

36 Wilentz, *Chants Democratic*, p. 145; Paul Johnson, *A Shopkeeper's Millennium: Society and Revivals in Rochester, New York, 1815–1837* (New York: Hill and Wang, 1978), p. 6; Carroll Smith-Rosenberg, *Disorderly Conduct: Visions of Gender in Victorian America* (New York: Knopf, 1985), p. 83. See also Bruce Laurie, *Artisans into Workers: Labor in Nineteenth-Century America* (New York: Hill and Wang, 1989), esp. p. 38.

37 One English journalist in 1819, who remarked on men whose "only object is to accumulate in the aggregation of which, they are perfectly regardless of the wants of the Journeymen whom they employ"; cited in Wilentz, *Chants Democratic*, p. 167. See also Johnson, *Shopkeeper's Millennium*, pp. 57, 60, and Norman Ware, *The Industrial Worker, 1840–1860* (Boston: Houghton Mifflin, 1924), p. xii....

38 Cited in Laurie, *Artisans into Workers*, p. 64. See also Christopher Lasch, *The True and Only Heaven: Progress and Its Critics* (New York: Norton, 1991), esp. p. 203. In this sense, the working-class movement in America has never been, as Marx predicted, a revolutionary movement headed towards a new future; it was instead a defensive movement to protect the independence and workplace autonomy of the skilled crafts-

man and small shopkeeper from the indignities of proletarianization. It was a movement of retreat to the idealized past of the Heroic Artisan more than it was a progressive movement towards the proletarian socialist state.

39 The statistic and citation come from Alice Kessler-Harris, *Out to Work* (New York: Oxford University Press, 1982), pp. 47, 69. "From the perspective of skilled male workers, pressure to keep women out of certain jobs was the only way of saving their own," she writes. Labor historian Philip S. Foner notes that "[m]any skilled craftsmen saw the entrance of women into the job market as the major source of their problems." See *Women and the American Labor Movement* (New York: Free Press, 1982), p. 13. "As they saw it, the more women workers hired, the more the wages of the skilled male workers would suffer" (p. 12). Women were also systematically excluded from the professions, especially law and medicine. See Kessler-Harris, *Out to Work*, p. 57 and passim. See also Susan Estabrook Kennedy, *If All We Did Was to Weep at Home: A History of White Working-Class Women in America* (Bloomington: Indiana University Press, 1979), and Barbara Mayer Wertheimer, *We Were There: The Story of Working Women in America* (New York: Pantheon, 1977).

40 Ware, *Industrial Worker*, p. 10. Foreign-born employers also were targets of nativist resentment; one early broadside tried to arouse the workers with an appeal to nativism and class-based solidarity:

> Fellow Citizen – LET us support our independence! If we are Mechanics, Laborers, and Artizans – Why should we surrender our opinions, and our rights to the arbitrary mandate of a Tory Employer, and that employer, perhaps a foreign emissary! (cited in Rock, *Artisans*, p. 52).

41 See, e.g., Dale Knobel, *Paddy and the Republic: Ethnicity and Nationality in Antebellum America* (Middletown, Conn.: Wesleyan University Press, 1986).

42 David Roediger, *The Wages of Whiteness: Race and the Making of the American Working Class* (New York: Verso, 1991), p. 13. Contemporaries also saw the connection. "If this is not SLAVERY," as the *New York Evening Post* put it in June 1836, "we have forgotten its definition. Strike the right of associating for the sale of labor from the privileges of a freeman, and you may as well at once bind him to a master," cited in Schlesinger, *The Age of Jackson*, p. 196. Roediger argues that whites came to define blackness as all the things that they, the whites, didn't want to be, while at the same time, the things they secretly wanted, desired, and feared.

43 Eric Lott, *Love and Theft: Blackface Minstrelsy and the American Working Class* (New York: Oxford University Press, 1993), pp. 137, 53, et passim.

44 Frederick Jackson Turner, *The Frontier in American History* [1903] (New York: Holt, Rinehart and Winston, 1947), p. 253.

45 Bancroft, cited in Wilson Carey McWilliams, *The Idea of Fraternity in America* (Berkeley: University of California Press, 1973), p. 250; Tocqueville, *Democracy in America*, p. 278. See also Smith-Rosenberg, *Disorderly Conduct*, pp. 99, 101. As I recall, the bully must constantly be exhorted to pick on someone his own size, but he is also the one who's least secure about his masculinity and therefore has to prove it all the time – especially against those who are smaller and presumably weaker. That was, at least, the gender gospel according to my parents when advising that I not get drawn into fights with our local version.

46 Cited in Ron Takaki, *Strangers from a Different Shore: A History of Asian Americans* (New York: Viking, 1989), p. 94. Biography cited in Michael Paul Rogin, *Fathers and Children*, p. 141.

47 Pugh, *Sons of Liberty*, p. 18. In his senate campaigns and later as president, he promoted "the world of independent producers, secure in their modest competence, proud in

their natural dignity, confirmed in their yeoman character, responsible masters of their fate," as the genuine heroes of the American republic (Meyer, 1957, p. 32)....

48 George G. Foster, *New York by Gas Light: With Here and There a Streak of Sunshine* (New York: Dewitt and Davenport, 1849), p. 101; see also Peter G. Buckley, "To the Opera House: Culture and Society in New York City, 1820–1860," Ph.D. diss., Department of History, SUNY at Stony Brook, 1984. On the link of artisanal republicanism and Anglophobic nativism, see Wilentz, *Chants Democratic*, pp. 315–25.

49 Cited in *Account of the Terrific and Fatal Riot at the Astor Place Opera House* (New York: H. M. Ranney, 1849), p. 10. Other valuable sources on the Astor Place riots include Iver Bernstein, *The New York City Draft Riots* (New York: Oxford University Press, 1990), pp. 149–51; Harry Brinton Henderson III, "Young America and the Astor Place Riot," unpublished MA thesis, Columbia University, 1963.

50 *Account of the Terrific and Fatal Riot*, pp. 56–7.

51 Henderson, "The Astor Place Riot," p. 227.

52 *Account of the Terrific and Fatal Riot*, p. 15.

53 On the B'hoys, see Peter Buckley, "To the Opera House," passim; George Foster, *New York by Gas Light*; and Wilentz, *Chants Democratic*. Riots by young single men in New York were also directed towards upper-class brothels, combining "misogyny against sexually independent women" with class resentment that such women were financially out of the reach of the young men. See Timothy Gilfoyle, "Strumpets and Misogynists: Brothel 'Riots' and the Transformation of Prostitution in Antebellum New York City," *New York History*, January 1987, p. 61. See also Timothy Gilfoyle, *City of Eros: New York City, Prostitution and the Commercialization of Sex, 1790–1920* (New York: Norton, 1992), and Patricia Cline Cohen, "Unregulated Youth: Masculinity and Murder in the 1830s City," *Radical History Review* 52, Winter 1992, esp. p. 44.

54 For accounts of the events of the Astor Place riots, see Buckley, "To the Opera House," passim; *Account of the Terrific and Fatal Riot*, passim; Wilentz, *Chants Democratic*; Henderson, "The Astor Place Riot"; and Bernstein, *The New York City Draft Riots*.

55 *Account of the Terrific and Fatal Riot*, p. 19.

56 Henderson, "The Astor Place Riot," p. 173; *Account of the Terrific and Fatal Riot*, pp. 24–8.

Part III

Representations

"From childhood men have an instinct for representation," Aristotle wrote in *Poetics*, "and in this respect man differs from the other animals [in] that he is far more imitative and learns his first lessons by representing things." Although Aristotle is using man in a generic sense, it is also true that our first lessons about masculinity and femininity are conveyed through representations, which model for us the desired goals and limits of gender identification. This point is less obvious than it may initially seem, for the task of explaining how and why we come to identify with or against any given image has proven to be extremely complex. It is particularly important to address the role of representations in creating and sustaining changing cultural ideas about masculinity, because it has so often claimed the status of a natural and unchanging fact of life. The essays in this section interpret representations of masculinity across a range of visual and literary media. Their methods are varied, as are their conclusions, but all assume that sustained analysis of representations can reveal a great deal about the values and assumptions of the context in which they were produced. These pieces take aesthetic artifacts – and the controversies that have surrounded them – as the most revealing ground to investigate the fantasies, anxieties, and contradictions that underlie any given version of masculinity.

Perhaps the most important collective insight provided by these essays is that representations require interpretation, which is an unavoidably political activity. The work of cultural criticism makes visible the processes whereby representations become meaningful, and the political investments at stake in those meanings. Distinctions of taste or aesthetic value (whether Maxine Hong Kingston or Henry James are great writers, whether the photography of Robert Mapplethorpe is art or pornography) are invariably bound to the politics of sex and gender. For example, Eve Sedgwick argues that James's installation as a fixture of the western literary canon has obscured the homosexual dynamics within his work, even though such a reading is encouraged by the biographical details of his own life. Moreover, her conclusions suggest that the larger enterprise of literary criticism has been impoverished by coy or neglectful approaches to the question of sexuality. King-Kok Cheung proposes that debates over the authenticity of Kingston's representations of Chinese American life have everything to do with the anxieties of male Asian American critics within a culture that has represented them as weak and effeminate. For Robyn Wiegman, Hollywood films reveal the contradictions within 1990s multiculturalism, which grants increased visibility to black masculinity but only in exchange for the reconfirmation of white male hegemony and continued erasure of the feminine. Analyzing Mapplethorpe's photography, Kobena Mercer confronts the political consequences of his own interpretive positions: if he condemns the images as racist (as he did in an earlier version of the essay), he plays into the hands of the religious right; if he celebrates their frank representation of male homosexuality, he risks forgetting their deployment of racial stereotypes. Ambivalence, Mercer concludes, is a necessary part of the critical act.

Mercer's insights about the interpretive process confirm the difficulty of making definitive statements about the relationship between representations and gender identification. As Sedgwick describes the vexed process of identity formation, "to identify *as* must always include multiple processes of identification *with*. It also involves identification *as against*; but even did it not, the relations implicit in *identifying with* are, as psychoanalysis suggests, in themselves quite sufficiently fraught with intensities of incorporation, diminishment, inflation, threat, loss, reparation, and disavowal." Consequently, it is extremely difficult to predict how any given image of masculinity will be received and incorporated. Representations only become meaningful in the interaction between the reader/spectator and the artifact. Interpretation is an ongoing process of taking up, trying on, and adopting or rejecting a set of meanings, rather than a search for a unitary meaning contained within the work itself. Reading as a woman, according to Sedgwick, provides privileged insight about male homosexual panic. Living in a homophobic culture makes it extremely difficult for men to acknowledge the full range of their desires, whereas women's distance from those anxieties grants them greater perspective, whether they be characters such as May Bartram, or critics like Sedgwick herself. The identities of both the artist and the critic matter to the kind of interpretation they will produce, but not in any predictable way. The vagaries of identification are illustrated by Mercer's interpretation of the Mapplethorpe photographs, which will mean something different depending on whether he identifies with them as a gay or a black man, and whether he identifies the photographer as a gay or a white man. It is a virtue of Mercer's critical approach that he recognizes the impossibility of separating the various components of identity (he can never read *only as* a gay or a black man), meaning that identification will always be fluid and open to change. Likewise, as Cheung describes it, much of the controversy surrounding Kingston concerned the fact that, in *China Men*, a woman author had adopted the perspective of male characters. Whereas Kingston identified herself as "the kind of woman who loves men and who can tell their stories," her critics demanded consistency between the author's own gender identity and that of her characters. Cheung shows how that position may give rise to reductive readings of literature and produce an unhelpful impasse between feminists and male critics. For both Cheung and Mercer, the introduction of questions about racial authenticity changes the terms of debate about sex and gender identification.

The essays in this section reveal with particular clarity the fact that there is no unified subject of masculinity. Returning to Aristotle's formulation, if men and women alike learn about masculinity through representations, they are presented with a bewildering array of options. Moreover, the multiple forms masculinity might take inevitably intersect with other variants of identity, so that it becomes impossible to discuss masculinity as such without taking into account its relationship to race, class, national, and sexual identifications. For example, in the male bonding scenarios discussed by Robyn Wiegman, the apparent mutuality of the interracial male relationship erases the fact of black man's ongoing political marginality. As much as the films of the 1980s emphasize their transcendence of racial inequalities, their masculine characters cannot be understood in isolation from the history of race relations in the United States.

Finally, the analysis of representations in a variety of media allows for a discussion of the relationship between form and content. Hollywood films are an important medium for critical interpretation, according to Wiegman, because these widespread popular narratives "function as scenes of instruction for the construction of this nation's most pervasive and contested ideology, 'America.'" Their popularity and seemingly apolitical content actually make them all the more efficient as pedagogical tools to impart lessons about the meaning and value of national identity. The influence of Hollywood narratives has much to do with their medium, for film exerts a powerful hold, both conscious and unconscious, on the vast audiences it reaches. Both Wiegman and Mercer are concerned with the increasing prominence of technologies of vision in contemporary culture. In Mercer's analysis, Mapplethorpe uses photography to evoke and reconfigure the white male gaze that has such a long history of objectifying the black male body, but also to represent a certain reciprocity between the gay male photographer and his subjects. Bringing the black man into visibility effects a powerful reversal of his traditional exclusion from artistic representation. By contrast, Wiegman reads the increased visibility of black men in Hollywood film as a way of masking their continued political invisibility. While the proliferation of images of black–white male friendships might appear to be progress, it brings premature closure to the debate over ongoing racial inequities in America. Literary representation raises a somewhat different set of formal problems. As Sedgwick demonstrates, James's "thematics of absence" leads the reader to the open secret of homosexuality in his fiction. It is insufficient to read only for the words on the page, for gaps and silences are an important component of the text's meaning. The queer reading strategies her work makes possible involve new methodological, as well as thematic, approaches to the interpretation of literature.

The essays in this section provide only a small sample of the wide range of scholarship on representations of masculinity. They are intended to model a selection of methods for approaching representations in different media and to invite comparisons between interpretive strategies. They should not be taken as a definitive resolution to the matter of representations, but as a group that opens up the possibilities of ongoing analysis, and, above all, the importance of continued critical engagement.

Bibliography

Aristotle. *Poetics.*
Mitchell, W. T. J. 1990. "Representations," in *Critical Terms for Literary Study,* ed. Frank Lentricchia and Thomas McLaughlin. Chicago: University of Chicago Press, pp. 11–22.
Sedgwick, Eve. 1990. *Epistemology of the Closet.* Berkeley and Los Angeles: University of California Press.

9

The Beast in the Closet: James and the Writing of Homosexual Panic

Eve Kosofsky Sedgwick

Historicizing Male Homosexual panic

At the age of 25, D. H. Lawrence was excited about the work of James M. Barrie. He felt it helped him understand himself and explain himself. "*Do* read Barrie's *Sentimental Tommy* and *Tommy and Grizel*," he wrote Jessie Chambers. "They'll help you understand how it is with me. I'm in exactly the same predicament."[1]

Fourteen years later, though, Lawrence placed Barrie among a group of writers whom he considered appropriate objects of authorial violence. "What's the good of being hopeless, so long as one has a hob-nailed boot to kick [them] with? *Down with the Poor in Spirit!* A war! But the Subtlest, most intimate warfare. Smashing the face of what one *knows* is rotten."[2]

It was not only in the intimate warfares of one writer that the years 1910 to 1924 marked changes. But Lawrence's lurch toward a brutal, virilizing disavowal of his early identification with Barrie's sexually irresolute characters reflects two rather different trajectories: first, of course, changes in the historical and intellectual context within which British literature could be read; but second, a haltingly crystallized literalization, as *between* men, of what had been in Barrie's influential novels portrayed as exactly "the Subtlest, most intimate warfare" *within* a man. Barrie's novel sequence was also interested, as Lawrence was not, in the mutilating effects of this masculine civil war on women.

I argue that the Barrie to whom Lawrence reacted with such volatility and finally with such virulence was writing out of a post-Romantic tradition of fictional meditations on the subject specifically of male homosexual panic.... The cheapnesses and compromises of this tradition will, however, turn out to be as important as its freshest angularities, since one of the functions of a tradition is to create a path-of-least-resistance (or at the last resort, a pathology-of-least-resistance) for the expression of previously inchoate material.

An additional problem: this tradition was an infusing rather than a generically distinct one in British letters, and it is thus difficult to discriminate it with confi-

Reprinted from *American Literature, American Culture*, ed. Gordon Hutner (New York: Oxford University Press, 1999), pp. 476–80, 484–97.

dence or to circumscribe it within the larger stream of nineteenth-century fictional writing. But the tradition is worth tracing partly on that very account, as well: the difficult questions of generic and thematic embodiment resonate so piercingly with another set of difficult questions, those precisely of sexual definition and embodiment. The supposed oppositions that characteristically structure this writing – the respectable "versus" the bohemian, the cynical "versus" the sentimental, the provincial "versus" the cosmopolitan, the anesthetized "versus" the sexual – seem to be, among other things, recastings and explorations of another pseudo-opposition that had come by the middle of the nineteenth century to be cripplingly knotted into the guts of British men and, through them, into the lives of women. The name of this pseudo-opposition, when it came to have a name, was homosexual "versus" heterosexual.

Recent sexual historiography by, for instance, Alan Bray in his *Homosexuality in Renaissance England* suggests that until about the time of the Restoration, homophobia in England, while intense, was for the most part highly theologized, was anathematic in tone and structure, and had little cognitive bite as a way for people to perceive and experience their own and their neighbors' actual activities.[3] Homosexuality "was not conceived as part of the created order at all," Bray writes, but as "part of its dissolution. And as such it was not a sexuality in its own right, but existed as a potential for confusion and disorder in one undivided sexuality."[4] If sodomy was the most characteristic expression of anti-nature or the anti-Christ itself, it was nevertheless, or perhaps for that very reason, not an explanation that sprang easily to mind for those sounds from the bed next to one's own – or even for the pleasures of one's own bed. Before the end of the eighteenth century, however, Bray shows, with the beginnings of a crystallized male homosexual role and male homosexual culture, a much sharper-eyed and acutely psychologized secular homophobia was current.

I have argued (in *Between Men: English Literature and Male Homosocial Desire*) that this development was important not only for the persecutory regulation of a nascent minority population of distinctly homosexual men but also for the regulation of the male homosocial bonds that structure *all* culture – at any rate, all public or heterosexual culture.[5] This argument follows Lévi-Strauss in defining culture itself, like marriage, in terms of a "total relationship of exchange . . . not established between a man and woman, but between two groups of men, [in which] the woman figures only as one of the objects in the exchange, not as one of the partners";[6] or follows Heidi Hartmann in defining patriarchy itself as "*relations between men*, which have a material base, and which, though hierarchical, establish or create interdependence and solidarity among men that enable them to dominate women."[7] To this extent, it makes sense that a newly active concept – a secular, psychologized homophobia – that seemed to offer a new proscriptive or descriptive purchase on the whole continuum of male homosocial bonds, would be a pivotal and embattled concept indeed.

Bray describes the earliest legal persecutions of the post-Restoration gay male subculture, centered in gathering places called "molly houses," as being random and, in his word, "pogrom"-like in structure.[8] I would emphasize the specifically terroristic or exemplary workings of this structure: because a given homosexual man could not know whether or not to expect to be an object of legal violence, the legal enforcement had a disproportionately wide effect. At the same time, however, an opening was made for a subtler strategy in response, a kind of ideological pincers-movement that would extend manyfold the impact of this theatrical enforcement. As *Between Men* argues, under this strategy (or, perhaps better put, in this space of strategic potential)

> not only must homosexual men be unable to ascertain whether they are to be the objects of "random" homophobic violence, but no man must be able to ascertain that he is not (that his bonds are not) homosexual. In this way, a relatively small exertion of physical and legal compulsion potentially rules great reaches of behavior and filiation.
>
> So-called "homosexual panic" is the most private, psychologized form in which many...western men experience their vulnerability to the social pressure of homophobic blackmail.[9]

Thus, at least since the eighteenth century in England and America, the continuum of male homosocial bonds has been brutally structured by a secularized and psychologized homophobia, which has excluded certain shiftingly and more or less arbitrarily defined segments of the continuum from participating in the overarching male entitlement – in the complex web of male power over the production, reproduction, and exchange of goods, persons, and meanings. I argue that the historically shifting, and precisely the arbitrary and self-contradictory, nature of the way *homosexuality* (along with its predecessor terms) has been defined in relation to the rest of the male homosocial spectrum has been an exceedingly potent and embattled locus of power over the entire range of male bonds, and perhaps especially over those that define themselves, not *as* homosexual, but *as against* the homosexual. Because the paths of male entitlement, especially in the nineteenth century, required certain intense male bonds that were not readily distinguishable from the most reprobated bonds, an endemic and ineradicable state of what I am calling male homosexual panic became the normal condition of the male heterosexual entitlement.

Some consequences and corollaries of this approach to male relationships should perhaps be made more explicit. To begin with, as I suggested earlier, the approach is not founded on an essential differentiation between "basically homosexual" and "basically heterosexual" men, aside from the historically small group of consciously and self-acceptingly homosexual men, who are no longer susceptible to homosexual panic as I define it here. If such compulsory relationships as male friendship, mentorship, admiring identification, bureaucratic subordination, and heterosexual rivalry all involve forms of investment that force men into the arbitrarily mapped, self-contradictory, and anathema-riddled quicksands of the middle distance of male homosocial desire, then it appears that men enter into adult masculine entitlement only through acceding to the permanent threat that the small space they have cleared for themselves on this terrain may always, just as arbitrarily and with just as much justification, be punitively and retroactively foreclosed.

The result of men's accession to this double bind is, first, the acute *manipulability*, through the fear of one's own "homosexuality," of acculturated men; and second, a reservoir of potential for *violence* caused by the self-ignorance that this regime constitutively enforces. The historical emphasis on homophobic enforcement in the armed services in, for instance, England and the United States supports this analysis. In these institutions, where both men's manipulability and their potential for violence are at the highest possible premium, the *pre*scription of the most intimate male bonding and the *pro*scription of (the remarkably cognate) "homosexuality" are both stronger than in civilian society – are, in fact, close to absolute.

My specification of widespread, endemic male homosexual panic as a post-Romantic phenomenon rather than as coeval with the beginnings, under homophobic pressure, of a distinctive male homosexual culture a century or so earlier, has to do with (what I read as) the centrality of the paranoid Gothic[10] as the literary genre in which homophobia found its most apt and ramified embodiment. Homophobia found in the paranoid Gothic a genre of its own, not because the genre provided a platform for expounding an already-formed homophobic ideology – of course, it did no such thing – but through a more active, polylogic engagement of "private" with "public" discourses, as in the wildly dichotomous play around solipsism and intersubjectivity of a male paranoid plot like that of *Frankenstein*. The transmutability of the intrapsychic with the intersubjective in these plots where one man's mind could be read by that of the feared and desired other; the urgency and violence with which these plots reformed large, straggly, economically miscellaneous families such as the Frankensteins in the ideologically hypostatized image of the tight Oedipal family; and then the extra efflorescence of violence with which the remaining female term in these triangular families was elided, leaving, as in *Frankenstein*, a residue of two potent male figures locked in an epistemologically indissoluble clench of will and desire – through these means, the paranoid Gothic powerfully signified, at the very moment of crystallization of the modern, capitalism-marked Oedipal family, the inextricability from that formation of a strangling double bind in male homosocial constitution. Put another way, the usefulness of Freud's formulation, in the case of Dr. Schreber, that paranoia in men results from the repression of their homosexual desire,[11] has nothing to do with a classification of the paranoid Gothic in terms of "latent" or "overt" "homosexual" "types," but everything to do with the foregrounding, under the specific, foundational historic conditions of the early Gothic, of intense male homosocial desire as at once the most compulsory and the most prohibited of social bonds.

To inscribe that vulgar classification supposedly derived from Freud on what was arguably the founding moment of the world view and social constitution that he codified would hardly be enlightening. Still, the newly formulated and stressed "universal" imperative/prohibition attached to male homosocial desire, even given that its claim for universality already excluded (the female) half of the population, nevertheless required, of course, further embodiment and specification in new taxonomies of personality and character. These taxonomies would mediate between the supposedly classless, "personal" entities of the ideological fictions and the particular, class-specified, economically inscribed lives that they influenced; and at the same time, the plethoric and apparently comprehensive pluralism of the taxonomies occluded, through the illusion of choice, the overarching existence of the double bind that structured them all.

Recent gay male historiography, influenced by Foucault, has been especially good at unpacking and interpreting those parts of the nineteenth-century systems of classification that clustered most closely around what current taxonomies construe as "the homosexual." The "sodomite," the "invert," the "homosexual," the "heterosexual" himself, all are objects of historically and institutionally explicable construction.[12] In the discussion of male homosexual *panic*, however – the treacherous middle stretch of the modern homosocial continuum, and the terrain from whose wasting rigors *only* the homosexual-identified man is at all exempt – a different and less distinctly sexualized range of categories needs to be opened up. Again, however, it bears repeating that the object of doing that is not to arrive at a more accurate or up-to-date assignment of "diagnostic" categories, but to better understand the broad field of forces within which masculinity – and thus, *at least* for men, humanity itself – could (can) at a particular moment construct itself.

I want to suggest here that with Thackeray and other early and mid-Victorians, a character classification of "the bachelor" came into currency, a type that for some men both narrowed the venue, and at the same time startingly desexualized the question, of male sexual choice.[13] Later in the century, when a medical and social-science model of "the homosexual man" had institutionalized this classification for a few men, the broader issue of endemic male homosexual panic was again up for grabs in a way that was newly redetached from character taxonomy and was more apt to be described narratively, as a decisive moment of choice in the developmental labyrinth of the generic individual (male). As the unmarried gothic hero had once been, the bachelor became once again the representative man: James wrote in his 1881 *Notebook*, "I take [London] as an artist and as a bachelor; as one who has the passion of observation and whose business is the study of human life."[14] In the work of a writer like ... James ... male homosexual panic was acted out as a sometimes agonized sexual anesthesia that was damaging to both its male subjects and its female nonobjects. The paranoid Gothic itself, a generic structure that seemed to have been domesticated in the development of the bachelor taxonomy, returned in some of these works as a formally intrusive and incongruous, but strikingly persistent, literary element.[15] ...

Reading James Straight

James's "The Beast in the Jungle" (1902) is one of the bachelor fictions of this period that seems to make a strong implicit claim of "universal" applicability through heterosexual symmetries, but that is most movingly subject to a change of Gestalt and of visible saliencies as soon as an assumed heterosexual male norm is at all interrogated. ...

The story is of a man and a woman who have a decade-long intimacy. The woman desires the man but the man fails to desire the woman. In fact ... the man simply fails to desire at all. ... John Marcher, in James's story, does not even know that desire is absent from his life, nor that May Bartram desires him, until after she has died from his obtuseness.

To judge from the biographies of Barrie and James, each author seems to have made erotic choices that were complicated enough, shifting enough in the gender of their objects and, at least for long periods, kept distant enough from *éclaircisse-ment* or physical expression to make each an emboldening figure for a literary discussion of male homosexual panic.[16] ... James had – well, exactly that which we now all know that we know not. ... It is hard to read Leon Edel's account of

James's sustained (or repeated) and intense, but peculiarly furtive,[17] intimacies with [Constance Fenimore Woolson, the] deaf, intelligent American woman author who clearly loved him, without coming to a grinding sense that James felt he had with her above all something, sexually, to prove. And it is hard to read about what seems to have been her suicide without wondering whether the expense of James's heterosexual self-probation . . . was not charged most intimately to this secreted-away companion of so many of his travels and residencies. If this is true, the working-out of his denied homosexual panic must have been only the more grueling for the woman in proportion to James's outrageous gift and his moral magnetism.

If something like the doubly destructive interaction I am sketching here did in fact occur between James and Constance Fenimore Woolson, then its structure has been resolutely reproduced by virtually all the critical discussion of James's writing. James's mistake here, biographically, seems to have been in moving blindly from a sense of the good, the desirability, of love and sexuality, to the automatic impos- ition on himself of a specifically *hetero*sexual compulsion. (I say "imposition on himself," but of course he did not invent the heterosexual specificity of this compulsion – he merely failed, at this point in his life, to resist it actively.) The easy assumption (by James, the society, and the critics) that sexuality and hetero- sexuality are always exactly translatable into one another is, obviously, homopho- bic. Importantly, too, it is deeply heterophobic: it denies the very possibility of *difference* in desires, in objects. One is no longer surprised, of course, at the repressive blankness on these issues of most literary criticism; but for James, in whose life the pattern of homosexual desire was brave enough and resilient enough to be at last biographically inobliterable, one might have hoped that in criticism of his work the possible differences of different erotic paths would not be so raven- ously subsumed under a compulsorily – and hence, never a truely "hetero" – heterosexual model. With strikingly few exceptions, however, the criticism has actively repelled any inquiry into the asymmetries of gendered desire.

It is possible that critics have been motivated in this active incuriosity by a desire to protect James from homophobic misreadings in a perennially repressive sexual climate. It is possible that they fear that, because of the asymmetrically marked structure of heterosexual discourse, *any* discussion of homosexual desires or literary content will marginalize him (or them?) as, simply, *homosexual*. It is possible that they desire to protect him from what they imagine as anachronistic- ally "gay" readings, based on a late twentieth-century vision of men's desire for men that is more stabilized and culturally compact than James's own. It is possible that they read James himself as, in his work, positively refusing or evaporating this element of his eros, translating lived homosexual desires, where he had them, into written heterosexual ones so thoroughly and so successfully that the difference *makes* no difference, the transmutation leaves no residue. Or it is possible that, believing – as I do – that James often, though not always, attempted such a disguise or transmutation, but reliably left a residue both of material that he did not attempt to transmute and of material that could be transmuted only rather violently and messily, some critics are reluctant to undertake the "attack" on James's candor or artistic unity that could be the next step of that argument. Any of these critical motives would be understandable, but their net effect is the usual repressive one of elision and subsumption of supposedly embarrassing material. In dealing with the multiple valences of sexuality, critics' choices should not be limited to crudities of disruption or silences of orthodox enforcement.

Even Leon Edel, who traced out *both* James's history with Constance Fenimore Woolson *and* some of the narrative of his erotic desires for men, connects "The Beast in the Jungle" to the history of Woolson,[18] but connects neither of these to the specificity of James's – or of any – sexuality. The result of this hammeringly tendentious blur in virtually all the James criticism is, for the interpretation of "The Beast in the Jungle," seemingly in the interests of showing it as universally applicable (e.g., about "the artist"), to assume without any space for doubt that the moral point of the story is not only that May Bartram desired John Marcher but that John Marcher *should have desired* May Bartram. . . .

. . . Whoever May Bartram is and whatever she wants (I discuss this more later), clearly at least the story has the Jamesian negative virtue of not pretending to present her rounded and whole. She is an imposing character, but – *and* – a bracketed one. James's bravura in manipulating point of view lets him dissociate himself critically from John Marcher's selfishness – from the sense that there is *no possibility* of a subjectivity other than Marcher's own – but lets him leave himself in place of that selfishness finally an *askesis*, a particular humility of point of view as being *limited* to Marcher's. Of May Bartram's history, of her emotional determinants, of her erotic structures, the reader learns very little; we are permitted, if we pay attention at all, to *know* that we have learned very little. Just as, in Proust, it is always open to any minor or grotesque character to turn out at any time to have a major artistic talent with which, however, the novel does not happen to busy itself, so "The Beast in the Jungle" seems to give the reader permission to imagine some female needs and desires and gratifications that are not structured exactly in the image of Marcher's or of the story's own laws.

It is only the last scene of the story – Marcher's last visit to May Bartram's grave – that conceals or denies the humility, the incompleteness of the story's presentation of her subjectivity. This is the scene in which Marcher's sudden realization that *she* has felt and expressed desire for *him* is, as it seems, answered in an intensely symmetrical, "conclusive" rhetorical clinch by the narrative/authorial prescription: "The escape would have been to love her; then, *then* he would have lived."[19] The paragraph that follows, the last in the story, has the same climactic, authoritative (even authoritarian) rhythm of supplying Answers in the form of symmetrical supplementarities. For this single, this conclusive, this formally privileged moment in the story – this resolution over the dead body of May Bartram – James and Marcher are presented as coming together, Marcher's revelation underwritten by James's rhetorical authority, and James's epistemological askesis gorged, for once, beyond recognition, by Marcher's compulsive, ego-projective certainties. In the absence of May Bartram, the two men, author/narrator and hero, are reunited at last in the confident, shared, masculine knowledge of what she Really Wanted and what she Really Needed. And what she Really Wanted and Really Needed show, of course, an uncanny closeness to what Marcher Really (should have) Wanted and Needed, himself.

Imagine "The Beast in the Jungle" without this enforcing symmetry. Imagine (remember) the story with May Bartram alive.[20] Imagine a possible alterity. And the name of alterity is not *always* "woman." What if Marcher himself had other desires?

The Law of the Jungle

Names . . . *Assingham – Padwick – Lutch – Marfle – Bross – Crapp – Didcock – Wichells* – Putchin – *Brind – Coxeter – Coxster . . . Dickwinter . . . Jakes . . . Marcher –*
(James, Notebook, 1901)

There has so far seemed no reason, or little reason, why what I have been calling "male homosexual panic" could not just as descriptively have been called "male heterosexual panic" – or, simply, "male sexual panic." Although I began with a structural and historicizing narrative that emphasized the pre- and proscriptively defining importance of men's bonds with men, potentially including genital bonds, the books I have discussed have not, for the most part, seemed to center emotionally or thematically on such bonds. In fact, it is, explicitly, a male panic in the face of *hetero*sexuality that many of these books most describe. It is all very well to insist, as I have done, that homosexual panic is necessarily a problem only, but endemically, of nonhomosexual-identified men; nevertheless the lack in these books of an embodied male-homosexual thematics, however inevitable, has had a dissolutive effect on the structure and texture of such an argument. Part, although only part, of the reason for that lack was historical: it was only close to the end of the nineteenth century that a cross-class homosexual role and a consistent, ideologically full thematic discourse of male homosexuality became entirely visible, in developments that were publicly dramatized in – though far from confined to – the Wilde trials.

In "The Beast in the Jungle," written at the threshold of the new century, the possibility of an embodied male-homosexual thematics has, I would like to argue, a precisely liminal presence. It is present as a – as a very particular, historicized – thematics of absence, and specifically of the absence of speech. The first (in some ways the only) thing we learn about John Marcher is that he has a "secret" (358), a destiny, a something unknown in his future. "You said," May Bartram reminds him, "you had from your earliest time, as the deepest thing within you, the sense of being kept for something rare and strange, possibly prodigious and terrible, that was sooner or later to happen" (359). I would argue that to the extent that Marcher's secret has *a* content, that content is homosexual.

Of course the extent to which Marcher's secret has anything that could be called a content is, not only dubious, but in the climactic last scene actively denied. "He had been the man of his time, *the* man, to whom nothing on earth was to have happened" (401). The denial that the secret has a content – the assertion that its contents is precisely a lack – is a stylish and "satisfyingly" Jamesian formal gesture. The apparent gap of meaning that it points to is, however, far from being a genuinely empty one; it is no sooner asserted than filled to a plentitude with the most orthodox of ethical enforcements. To point rhetorically to the emptiness of the secret, "the nothing that is," is, in fact, oddly, *the same gesture* as the attribution to it of a compulsory content about heterosexuality – of the content specifically, "He should [have] desire[d] her."

She was what he had missed. . . . The fate he had been marked for he had met with a vengeance – he had emptied the cup to the lees; he had been the man of his time, *the* man to whom nothing on earth was to have happened. That was the rare stroke – that was his visitation. . . . This the companion of his vigil had at a given moment made out, and she had then offered him the chance to baffle his doom. One's doom, however, was never baffled, and on the day she told him his own had come down she had seen him but stupidly stare at the escape she offered him.

The escape would have been to love her; then, *then* he would have lived. (401).

The "empty" meaning of Marcher's unspeakable doom is thus necessarily, specifically heterosexual; it refers to the perfectly specific absence of a prescribed heterosexual desire. If critics, eager to help James moralize this ending, persist in claiming to be able to translate freely and without residue from that (absent) heterosexual desire to an abstraction of all possibilities of human love, there are, I think, good reasons for trying to slow them down. The totalizing, insidiously symmetrical view that the "nothing" that is Marcher's unspeakable fate is necessarily a mirror image of the "everything" he could and should have had is, specifically, in an *oblique* relation to a very different history of meanings for assertions of the erotic negative.

The "full" meaning of that unspeakable fate, on the other hand, comes from the centuries-long historical chain of substantive uses of space-clearing negatives to void and at the same time to underline the possibility of male homosexual genitality. The rhetorical name for this figure is *preterition*. Unspeakable, unmentionable, *nefandam libidinem*, "that sin which should be neither named nor committed,"[21] the "detestable and abominable sin, amongst Christians not to be named,"

> Whose vice in special, if I would declare,
> It were enough for to perturb the air,

"things fearful to name," "the obscene sound of the unbeseeming words,"

> A sin so odious that the fame of it
> Will fright the damned in the darksome pit,[22]

"the Love that dare not speak its name,"[23] – such *were* the speakable nonmedical terms, in Christian tradition, of the homosexual possibility for men. The marginality of these terms' semantic and ontological status as substantive nouns reflected and shaped the exiguousness – but also, the potentially enabling secrecy – of that "possibility." And the newly specifying, reifying medical and penal public discourse of the male homosexual role, in the years around the Wilde trials, far from retiring or obsolescing these preteritive names, seems instead to have packed them more firmly and distinctly with homosexual meaning.[24]

John Marcher's "secret" (358), "his singularity" (366), "the thing she knew, which grew to be at last, with the consecration of the years, never mentioned between them save as 'the real truth' about him" (366), "the abyss" (375), "his queer consciousness" (378), "the great vagueness" (379), "the secret of the gods" (379), "what ignominy or what monstrosity" (379), "dreadful things . . . I couldn't name" (381): the ways in which the story refers to Marcher's secret fate have the same quasi-nominative, quasi-obliterative structure.

There are, as well, some "fuller," though still highly equivocal, lexical pointers to a homosexual meaning: "The rest of the world of course thought him *queer*, but she, she only, knew how, and above all why, queer; which was precisely what enabled her to dispose the concealing veil in the right folds. She took his *gaiety* from him – since it had to pass with them for gaiety – as she took everything else.... She traced his unhappy *perversion* through reaches of its course into which he could scarce follow it" (367; emphasis added). Still, it is mostly in the reifying grammar of periphrasis and preterition – "such a cataclysm" (360), "the great affair" (360), "the catastrophe" (361), "his predicament" (364), "their real truth" (368), "his inevitable topic" (371), "all that they had thought, first and last" (372), "horrors" (382), something "more monstrous than all the monstrosities we've named" (383), "all the loss and all the shame that are thinkable" (384) – that a homosexual meaning becomes, to the degree that it does become, legible. "I don't focus it. I can't name it. I only know I'm exposed" (372).

I am convinced, however, that part of the point of the story is that the reifying effect of periphrasis and preterition on this particular meaning is, if anything, *more* damaging than (though not separable from) its obliterative effect. To have succeeded – which was not to be taken for granted – in cracking the centuries-old code by which the-articulated-denial-of-articulability always had the possibility of meaning two things, of meaning either (heterosexual) "nothing" or "homosexual meaning," would also always have been to assume one's place in a discourse in which there was *a* homosexual meaning, in which all homosexual meaning meant a single thing. To crack a code and enjoy the reassuring exhilarations of knowingness is to buy into the specific formula, "We Know What That Means." (I assume it is this mechanism that makes even critics who know about the male-erotic pathways of James's personal desires appear to be so untroubled about leaving them out of accounts of his writing.[25] As if this form of desire were the most calculable, the simplest to add or subtract or allow for in moving between life and art!) But if, as I suggested in the first section, men's accession to heterosexual entitlement has, for these modern centuries, always been on the ground of a cultivated and compulsory denial of the *un*know-ability, of the arbitrariness and self-contradictoriness, of homosexual/heterosexual definition, then the fearful or triumphant interpretive formula "We Know What That Means" seems to take on an odd centrality. First, it is a lie. But second, it is the particular lie that animates and perpetuates the mechanism of homophobic male self-ignorance and violence and manipulability.

It is worth, then, trying to discriminate the possible plurality of meanings behind the unspeakables of "The Beast in the Jungle." To point, as I argue that the narrative itself points and as we have so far pointed, simply to *a* possibility of "homosexual meaning," is to say worse than nothing – it is to pretend to say one thing. But even on the surface of the story, the secret, "*the* thing," "the thing she knew," is discriminated, first of all discriminated temporally. There are at least two secrets: Marcher feels that he knows, but has never told anyone but May Bartram (secret number one) that he is reserved for some very particular, uniquely rending fate in the future, whose nature is (secret number two) unknown to himself. Over the temporal extent of the story, both the balance, between the two characters, of cognitive mastery over the secrets' meanings, and the temporal placement, between future and past, of the second secret, shift; it is possible, in addition, that the actual content (if any) of the secrets changes with these temporal and cognitive changes, if time and intersubjectivity are of the essence of the secrets.

Let me baldly, then, spell out my hypothesis of what a series of "full" – that is, homosexually tinged – meanings for the Unspeakable might look like for this story, differing both over time and according to character.

For John Marcher, let us hypothesize, the future secret – the secret of his hidden fate – importantly includes, though it is not necessarily limited to, the possibility of something homosexual. *For Marcher*, the presence or possibility of a homosexual meaning attached to the inner, the future secret, has exactly the reifying, totalizing, and blinding effect we described earlier in regard to the phenomenon of the Unspeakable. Whatever (Marcher feels) may be to be discovered along those lines, it is, in the view of his panic, *one* thing, and the worst thing, "the superstition of the Beast" (394). His readiness to organize the whole course of his life around the preparation for it – the defense against it – remakes his life monolithically in the image of *its* monolith of, in his view, the inseparability of homosexual desire, yielding, discovery, scandal, shame, annihilation. Finally, he has "but one desire left": that *it* be "decently proportional to the posture he had kept, all his life, in the threatened presence of it" (379).

This is how it happens that the outer secret, the secret of having a secret, functions, in Marcher's life, precisely as *the closet*. It is not a closet in which there is a homosexual man, for Marcher is not a homosexual man. Instead, however, it is the closet of, simply, the homosexual secret – the closet of imagining *a* homosexual secret. Yet it is unmistakable that Marcher lives as one who is *in the closet*. His angle on daily existence and intercourse is that of the closeted person,

> the secret of the difference between the forms he went through – those of his little office under government, those of caring for his modest patrimony, for his library, for his garden in the country, for the people in London whose invitations he accepted and repaid – and the detachment that reigned beneath them and that made of all behaviour, all that could in the least be called behaviour, a long act of dissimulation. What it had come to was that he wore a mask painted with the social simper, out of the eye-holes of which there looked eyes of an expression not in the least matching the other features. This the stupid world, even after years, had never more than half-discovered. (367–78)

Whatever the content of the inner secret, too, it is one whose protection requires, for him, a playacting of heterosexuality that is conscious of being only window dressing. "You help me," he tells May Bartram, "to pass for a man like another" (375). And "what saves us, you know," she explains, "is that we answer so completely to so usual an appearance: that of the man and woman whose friendship has become such a daily habit – or almost – as to be at last indispensable" (368–9). Oddly, they not only appear to be but are such a man and woman. The element of deceiving the world, of window dressing, comes into their relationship *only* because of the compulsion he feels to invest it with the legitimating stamp of visible, institutionalized genitality: "The real form it should have taken on the basis that stood out large was the form of their marrying. But the devil in this was that the very basis itself put marrying out of the question. His conviction, his apprehension, his obsession, in short, wasn't a privilege he could invite a woman to share; and that consequence of it was precisely what was the matter with him" (365).

Because of the terrified stultification of his fantasy about the inner or future secret, Marcher has, until the story's very last scene, an essentially static relation to and sense of both these secrets. Even the discovery that the outer secret is already shared with someone else, and the admission of May Bartram to the community it creates, "the dim day constituted by their discretions and privacies" (363), does nothing to his closet but furnish it – camouflage it to the eyes of outsiders, and soften its inner cushioning for his own comfort. In fact, the admission of May Bartram importantly *consolidates and fortifies* the closet for John Marcher.

In my hypothesis, however, May Bartram's view of Marcher's secrets is different from his and more fluid. I want to suggest that – while it is true that she feels desire for him – her involvement with him occurs originally on the ground of her understanding that he is imprisoned by homosexual panic; and her interest in his closet is not at all in helping him fortify it but in helping him dissolve it.

In this reading, May Bartram from the first sees, correctly, that the possibility of Marcher's achieving a genuine ability to attend to a woman – sexually or in any other way – depends as an absolute precondition on the dispersion of his totaliz-ing, basilisk fascination with and terror of homosexual possibility. It is only through his coming out of the closet – whether as *a homosexual man*, or as a man with a less exclusively defined sexuality that nevertheless admits the possibility of desires for other men – that Marcher could even begin to perceive the attention of a woman as anything other than a terrifying demand or a devaluing complicity. The truth of this is already evident at the beginning of the story, in the surmises with which Marcher first meets May Bartram's allusion to something (he cannot remember what) he said to her years before: "The great thing was that he saw in this no vulgar reminder of any 'sweet' speech. The vanity of women had long memories, but she was making no claim on him of a compliment or a mistake. With another woman, a totally different one, he might have feared the recall possibly even of some imbecile 'offer'" (356). The alternative to this, however, in his eyes, is a different kind of "sweetness," that of a willingly shared confine-ment: "her knowledge . . . began, even if rather strangely, to taste sweet to him" (358). "Somehow the whole question was a new luxury to him – that is from the moment she was in possession. If she didn't take the sarcastic view she clearly took the sympathetic, and that was what he had had, in all the long time, from no one whomsoever. What he felt was that he couldn't at present have begun to tell her, and yet could profit perhaps exquisitely by the accident of having done so of old" (358). So begins the imprisonment of May Bartram in John Marcher's closet – an imprisonment that, the story makes explicit, is founded on his inability to perceive or value her as a person beyond her complicity in his view of his own predicament.

The conventional view of the story, emphasizing May Bartram's interest in liberating, unmediatedly, Marcher's heterosexual possibilities, would see her as unsuccessful in doing so until too late – until the true revelation that comes, however, only after her death. If what needs to be liberated is in the first place Marcher's potential for homosexual desire, however, the trajectory of the story must be seen as far bleaker. I hypothesize that what May Bartram would have liked for Marcher, the narrative she wished to nurture for him, would have been a progress from a vexed and gaping self-ignorance around his homosexual possibil-ities to a self-knowledge of them that would have freed him to find and enjoy a sexuality of whatever sort emerged. What she sees happen to Marcher, instead, is the "progress" that the culture more insistently enforces: the progress from a vexed and gaping self-ignorance around his homosexual possibilities, to a completed and rationalized and wholly concealed and accepted one. The moment of Marcher's full incorporation of his erotic self-ignorance is the moment at which the imperatives of the culture cease to enforce him, and he becomes instead the enforcer of the culture.

Section 4 of the story marks the moment at which May Bartram realizes that, far from helping dissolve Marcher's closet, she has instead and irremediably been permitting him to reinforce it. It is in this section and the next, too, that it becomes explicit in the story that Marcher's fate, what was to have happened to him and did happen, involves a change in him from being the suffering object of a Law or judgment (of a doom in the original sense of the word) to being the embodiment of that Law.

If the transition I am describing is, in certain respects, familiarly Oedipal, the structuring metaphor behind its description here seems to be oddly alimentative. The question that haunts Marcher in these sections is whether what he has thought of as the secret of his future may not be, after all, in the past; and the question of passing, of who is passing through what or what is passing through whom, of what residue remains to *be* passed, is the form in which he compulsively poses his riddle. Is the beast eating him, or is he eating the beast? "It hasn't passed you by," May Bartram tells him. "It has done its office. It has made you its own" (389). "It's past. It's behind, she finally tells him, to which he replies, "*Nothing,* for me, is past; nothing *will* pass till I pass myself, which I pray my stars may be as soon as possible. Say, however, . . . that I've eaten my cake, as you contend, to the last crumb – how can the thing I've never felt at all be the thing I was marked out to feel?" (391). What May Bartram sees, that Marcher does not, is that the process of incorporating – of embodying – the Law of masculine self-ignorance, is the one that has the least in the world to do with feeling.[26] To gape at and, rebelliously, be forced to swallow the Law is to feel; but to have it finally stick to one's ribs, become however incongruously a part of one's own organism, is then to perfect at the same moment a new hard-won insentience of it and an assumption of (or subsumption by) an identification with it. May Bartram answers Marcher's question, "You take your 'feelings' for granted. You were to suffer your fate. That was not necessarily to know it" (391). Marcher's fate is to cease to suffer fate, and, instead, to become it. May Bartram's fate, with the "slow fine shudder" that climaxes her ultimate appeal to Marcher, is herself to swallow this huge, bitter bolus with which she can have *no* deep identification, and to die of it – of what is, to her, knowledge, not power. "So on her lips would the law itself have sounded" (389). Or, tasted.

To end a reading of May Bartram with her death, to end with her silenced forever in that ultimate closet, "her" tomb that represents (to Marcher) *his fate,* would be to do to her feminine desire the same thing I have already argued that James M. Barrie, unforgivably, did to Grizel's. That is to say, it leaves us in danger of figuring May Bartram, or more generally the woman in heterosexuality, as only the exact, heroic supplement to the murderous enforcements of male homophobic/homosocial self-ignorance. "The Fox," Emily Dickinson wrote, "fits the Hound."[27] It would be only too easy to describe May Bartram as the fox that most irreducibly fits this particular hound. She seems the woman (don't we all know them?) who has not only the most delicate nose for but the most potent attraction toward men who are at crises of homosexual panic . . . – Though for that matter, won't most women admit that an arousing nimbus, an excessively refluent and dangerous maelstrom of eroticism, somehow attends men in general at such moments, even otherwise boring men?

If one is to avoid the Barrie-ism of describing May Bartram in terms that reduce her perfectly to the residue-less sacrifice John Marcher makes to his Beast, it might be by inquiring into the difference of the paths of her own desire. What does she want – not for him, but for herself – from their relationship? What does she actually get? To speak less equivocally from my own eros and experience, there is a particular relation to truth and authority that a mapping of male homosexual panic offers to a woman in the emotional vicinity. The fact that male heterosexual entitlement in (at least modern Anglo-American) culture depends on a perfected but always friable self-ignorance in men as to the significance of their desire for other men, means that it is always open to women to know something that it is much more dangerous for any nonhomosexual-identified man to know. The ground of May Bartram's and John Marcher's relationship from the first is that she has the advantage of him, cognitively: she remembers, as he does not, where and when and with whom they have met before, and most of all she remembers his "secret" from a decade ago while he forgets having told it to her. This differential of knowledge affords her a "slight irony," an "advantage" (353) – but one that he can at the same time use to his own profit as "the buried treasure of her know-ledge," "this little hoard" (363). As their relationship continues, the sense of power and of a marked, rather free-floating irony about May Bartram becomes stronger and stronger, even in proportion to Marcher's accelerating progress toward self-ignorance and toward a blindly selfish expropriation of her emotional labor. Both the care and the creativity of her investment in him, the imaginative reach of her fostering his homosexual potential as a route back to his truer perception of herself, are forms of gender-political resilience in her as well as of love. They are forms of excitement, too, of real though insufficient power, and of pleasure.

In the last scene of the "The Beast in the Jungle," John Marcher becomes, in this reading, not the finally self-knowing man who is capable of heterosexual love, but the irredeemably self-ignorant man who embodies and enforces heterosexual compulsion. In this reading, that is to say, May Bartram's prophecy to Marcher that "You'll never know now" (390) is *a true one*.

Importantly for the homosexual plot, too, the final scene is also the only one in the entire story that reveals or tests the affective quality of Marcher's perception of another man. "The shock of the face" (399) – this is, in the last scene, the beginning of what Marcher ultimately considers "the most extraordinary thing that had happened to him" (400). At the beginning of Marcher's confrontation with this male figure at the cemetery, the erotic possibilities of the connection between the men appear to be all open. The man, whose "mute assault" Marcher feels "so deep down that he winced at the steady thrust," is mourning profoundly over "a grave apparently fresh," but (perhaps only to Marcher's closet-sharpened suspicions?) a slightest potential of Whitmanian cruisiness seems at first to tinge the air, as well.

His pace was slow, so that – and all the more as there was a kind of hunger in his look – the two men were for a minute directly confronted. Marcher knew him at once for one of the deeply stricken...nothing lived but the deep ravage of the features he showed. He *showed* them – that was the point; he was moved, as he passed, by some impulse that was either a signal for sympathy or, more possibly, a challenge to an opposed sorrow. He might already have been aware of our friend....What Marcher was at all events conscious of was in the first place that the image of scarred passion presented to him was conscious too – of something that profaned the air; and in the second that, roused, startled, shocked, he was yet the next moment looking after it, as it went, with envy. (400–1)

The path traveled by Marcher's desire in this brief and cryptic non-encounter re-enacts a classic trajectory of male entitlement. Marcher begins with the possibility of *desire for* the man, in response to the man's open "hunger" ("which," after-ward, "still flared for him like a smoky torch" (401)). Deflecting that desire under a fear of profanation, he then replaces it with envy, with an *identification with* the man in that man's (baffled) desire for some other, female, dead object. "The stranger passed, but the raw glare of his grief remained, making our friend wonder in pity what wrong, what wound it expressed, what injury not to be healed. What had the man *had*, to make him by the loss of it so bleed and yet live?" (401).

What had the man *had?* The loss by which a man *so bleeds and yet lives* is, is it not, supposed to be the castratory one of the phallus figured as mother, the inevitability of whose sacrifice ushers sons into the status of fathers and into the control (read both ways) of the Law. What is strikingly open in the ending of "The Beast in the Jungle" is how central to that process is man's desire for man – and the denial of that desire. The imperative that there *be* a male figure to take this place is the clearer in that, at an earlier climactic moment, in a female "shock of the face," May Bartram has presented to Marcher her own face, in a conscious revelation that was far more clearly of desire.

It had become suddenly, from her movement and attitude, beautiful and vivid to him that she had something more to give him; her wasted face delicately shone with it – it glittered almost as with the white lustre of silver in her expression. She was right, incontestably, for what he saw in her face was the truth, and strangely, without consequence, while their talk of it as dreadful was still in the air, she appeared to present it as inordinately soft. This, prompting bewilderment, made him but gape the more gratefully for her revelation, so that they continued for some minutes silent, her face shining at him, her contact imponderably pressing, and his stare all kind but all expectant. The end, none the less, was that what he had expected failed to come to him. (386)

To the shock of the female face, Marcher is not phobic but simply numb. It is only by turning his desire for the male face into an envious identification with male loss that Marcher finally comes into *any* relation to a woman – and then it is a relation through one dead woman (the other man's) to another dead woman of his own. That is to say, it is the relation of *compulsory* heterosexuality.

When Lytton Strachey's claim to be a conscientious objector was being exam-ined, he was asked what he would do if a German were to try to rape his sister. "I

should," he is said to have replied, "try and interpose my own body."[28] Not the
gay self-knowledge but the heterosexual, self-ignorant acting out of just this
fantasy ends "The Beast in the Jungle." To face the gaze of the Beast would
have been, for Marcher, to dissolve it.[29] To face the "kind of hunger in the look"
of the grieving man – to explore at all into the sharper lambencies of that encounter – would have been to dissolve the closet. Marcher, instead, to the very end,
turns his back – re-creating a double scenario of homosexual compulsion and
heterosexual compulsion. "He saw the Jungle of his life and saw the lurking
Beast; then, while he looked, perceived it, as by a stir of the air, rise, huge and
hideous, for the leap that was to settle him. His eyes darkened – it was close; and,
instinctively turning, in his hallucination, to avoid it, he flung himself, face down,
on the tomb" (402).

Notes

This essay has profited – though not as fully as I wish I had been able to make it do – from
especially helpful readings by Maud Ellmann, Neil Hertz, H. A. Sedgwick, D. A. Miller, and
Ruth Bernard Yeazell.

1 Lawrence to Jessie Chambers, August 1910, *The Collected Letters of D. H. Lawrence*, ed.
   Harry T. Moore (London: W. H. Heinemann, 1962), vol. 1, p. 63.
2 Ibid., Lawrence to Rolf Gardiner, August 9, 1924, vol. 2, p. 801.
3 Alan Bray, *Homosexuality in Renaissance England* (London: Gay Men's Press, 1982),
   chs. 1–3. Note the especially striking example on pp. 68–9, 76–7.
4 Ibid., p. 25.
5 Eve Kosofsky Sedgwick, *Between Men: English Literature and Male Homosocial Desire*
   (New York: Columbia University Press, 1985), pp. 83–96.
6 Claude Lévi-Strauss, *The Elementary Structures of Kinship* (Boston: Beacon Press,
   1969), p. 115; also quoted and well discussed in Gayle Rubin, "The Traffic in
   Women: Notes Toward the 'Political Economy' of Sex," in *Toward an Anthropology of
   Women*, ed. Rayna Reiter (New York: Monthly Review Press, 1975), pp. 157–210.
7 Heidi Hartmann, "The Unhappy Marriage of Marxism and Feminism: Towards a More
   Progressive Union," in *Women and Revolution: A Discussion of the Unhappy Marriage of
   Marxism and Feminism*, ed. Lydia Sargent (Boston: South End Press, 1981), p. 14;
   emphasis added.
8 Bray, *Homosexuality*, ch. 4.
9 Sedgwick, *Between Men*, pp. 88–9.
10 By "paranoid Gothic" I mean Romantic novels in which a male hero is in a close, usually
   murderous relation to another male figure, in some respects his "double," to whom he
   seems to be mentally transparent. Examples of the paranoid Gothic include, besides
   Frankenstein, Ann Radcliffe's *The Italian*, William Godwin's *Caleb Williams*, and James
   Hogg's *Confessions of a Justified Sinner*. This tradition is discussed more fully in my
   Between Men, chs. 5 and 6.
11 Sigmund Freud, "Psycho-Analytic Notes of an Autobiographical Account of a Case of
   Paranoia (Dementia Paranoides)," in *The Standard Edition of the Complete Psychological
   Works of Sigmund Freud*, trans. and ed. James Strachey et al. (London: Hogarth Press,
   1953–73), vol. 12, pp. 143–77.
12 On this see, along with Bray, *Homosexuality*, such works as John Boswell, *Christianity,
   Social Tolerance, and Homosexuality: Gay People in Western Europe from the Beginning of
   the Christian Era to the Fourteenth Century* (Chicago: University of Chicago Press,

1980); Jonathan Katz, *A Gay/Lesbian Almanac* (New York: Thomas Y. Crowell Co., 1982); Jeffrey Weeks, *Coming Out: Homosexual Politics in Britain from the Nineteenth Century to the Present* (London: Quartet Books, 1977); and Weeks, *Sex, Politics, and Society: The Regulation of Sexuality since 1800* (London: Longman, 1981).

13 For more on bachelors see Frederic Jameson, *Wyndham Lewis: Fables of Aggression* (Berkeley and Los Angeles: University of California Press, 1979), ch. 2; also, cited in Jameson, Jean Borie, *Le Célibataire français* (Paris: Le Sagittaire, 1976); and Edward Said, *Beginnings* (New York: Basic Books, 1975), pp. 137–52.

14 F. O. Matthiessen and Kenneth B. Murdock, eds., *The Notebooks of Henry James* (New York: Oxford University Press, 1947), p. 28.

15 Bachelor literature in which the paranoid Gothic – or more broadly, the supernatural – makes a reappearance includes, besides Du Maurier's *Trilby*, George Eliot's *The Lifted Veil*, Robert Louis Stevenson's *Dr. Jekyll and Mr. Hyde*, numerous Kipling stories such as "In the Same Boat," and numerous James stories such as "The Jolly Corner." . . .

16 The effect of emboldenment should be to some extent mistrusted – not, I think, because the attribution to these particular figures of a knowledge of male homosexual panic is likely to be wrong, but because it is so much easier to be so emboldened about men who are arguably homosexual in (if such a thing exists) "basic" sexual orientation; while what I am arguing is that panic is proportioned not to the homosexual but to the nonhomosexual-identified elements of these men's characters. Thus, if Barrie and James are obvious authors with whom to *begin* an analysis of male homosexual panic, the analysis I am offering here must be inadequate to the degree that it does not work just as well – even better – for Joyce, Milton, Faulkner, Lawrence, Yeats.

17 Leon Edel, *Henry James: The Middle Years: 1882–1895*, vol. 3 of *The Life of Henry James* (New York: J. B. Lippincott, Co., 1962; repr., Avon Books, 1978), makes clear that these contacts – coinciding visits to some cities and shared trips to others (e.g., vol. 3, p. 94), "a special rendezvous" in Geneva (p. 217), a period of actually living in the same house (pp. 215–17) – were conducted with a consistent and most uncharacteristic extreme of secrecy. (James seems also to have taken extraordinary pains to destroy every vestige of his correspondence with Woolson.) Edel cannot, nevertheless, imagine the relationship except as "a continuing 'virtuous' attachment": "That this pleasant and *méticuleuse* old maid may have nourished fantasies of a closer tie does not seem to have occurred to him at this time. If it had, we might assume he would have speedily put distance between himself and her" (p. 217). Edel's hypothesis does nothing, of course, to explain the secrecy of these and other meetings.

18 Edel, *Life of James*, vol. 4, *The Master: 1910–1916*, pp. 132–40.

19 "The Beast in the Jungle," in *The Complete Tales of Henry James*, ed. Leon Edel (London: Rupert Hart-Davis, 1964), 11: 401. All subsequent references to this work are to this edition and are cited parenthetically in the text by page number.

20 Interestingly, in the 1895 germ of (what seems substantially to be) "The Beast in the Jungle," in James's *Notebooks*, p. 184, the woman outlives the man. "It's *the woman's sense of what might [have been] in him* that arrives at the intensity. . . . *She is his Dead Self: he is alive in her and dead in himself* – that is something like the little formula I seem to *entrevoir*. He himself, the man, must, *in* the tale, also materially die – die in the flesh as he has died long ago in the spirit, the *right* one. Then it is that his lost treasure revives most – no longer *contrarié* by his material existence, existence in his false self, his wrong one."

21 Quoted in Boswell, *Christianity*, p. 349 (from a legal document dated 533) and p. 380 (from a 1227 letter from Pope Honorius III).

22 Quoted in Bray, *Homosexuality* – the first two from p. 61 (from Edward Coke's *Institutes* and Sir David Lindsay's *Works*), the next two from p. 62 (from William Bradford's *Plimouth Plantation* and Guillaume Du Bartas's *Divine Weeks*), and the last from p. 22, also from Du Bartas.

23 Lord Alfred Douglas, "Two Loves," from *The Chameleon*, quoted in Byrne R. S. Fone, *Hidden Heritage: History and the Gay Imagination* (New York: Irvington Publishers, 1981), p. 196.

24 For a striking anecdotal example of the mechanism of this, see Beverley Nichols, *Father Figure* (New York: Simon & Schuster, 1972), pp. 92–9.

25 Exceptions that I know of include Georges-Michel Sarotte's discussions of James in *Like a Brother, Like a Lover: Male Homosexuality in the American Novel and Theater from Herman Melville to James Baldwin*, trans. Richard Miller (New York: Doubleday & Co./Anchor, 1978); Richard Hall, "Henry James: Interpreting an Obsessive Memory," *Journal of Homosexuality* 8, no. 3/4 (Spring/Summer 1983), pp. 83–97; and Robert K. Martin, "The 'High Felicity' of Comradeship: A New Reading of Roderick Hudson," *American Literary Realism* 11 (Spring 1978), pp. 100–8.

26 A fascinating passage in James's *Notebooks*, p. 318, written in 1905 in California, shows how a greater self-knowledge in James, and a greater acceptance and *specificity* of homosexual desire, transforms this half-conscious enforcing rhetoric of anality, numbness, and silence into a much richer, pregnant address to James's male muse, an invocation of fisting-as-*écriture*:

> I sit here, after long weeks, at any rate, in front of my arrears, with an inward accumulation of material of which I feel the wealth; and as to which I can only invoke my familiar demon of patience, who always comes, doesn't he?, when I call. He is here with me in front of this cool green Pacific – he sits close and I feel his soft breath, which cools and steadies and inspires, on my cheek. Everything sinks in: nothing is lost; everything abides and fertilizes and renews its golden promise, making me think with closed eyes of deep and grateful longing when, in the full summer days of L[amb] H[ouse], my long dusty adventure over, I shall be able to [plunge] my hand, my arm, in, deep and far, and up to the shoulder – into the heavy bag of remembrance – of suggestion – of imagination – of art – and fish out every little figure and felicity, every little fact and fancy that can be to my purpose. These things are all packed away, now, thicker than I can penetrate, deeper than I can fathom, and there let them rest for the present, in their sacred cool darkness, till I shall let in upon them the mild still light of dear old L[amb] H[ouse] – in which they will begin to gleam and glitter and take form like the gold and jewels of a mine.

27 *Collected Poems of Emily Dickinson*, ed. Thomas H. Johnson (Boston: Little, Brown & Co., 1960), p. 406.

28 Lytton Strachey, quoted in Michael Holroyd, *Lytton Strachey: A Critical Biography* (London: W. H. Heinemann, 1968), vol. 2, p. 179.

29 Ruth Bernard Yeazell makes clear the oddity of having Marcher turn his back on the Beast that is supposed, at this late moment, to represent his self-recognition (in *Language and Knowledge in the Late Novels of Henry James* (Chicago: University of Chicago Press, 1976), pp. 37–8).

10

The Woman Warrior versus The Chinaman Pacific: Must a Chinese American Critic Choose between Feminism and Heroism?

King-Kok Cheung

. . .

Sexual politics in Chinese America reflect complex cultural and historical legacies. The paramount importance of patrilineage in traditional Chinese culture predisposes many Chinese Americans of the older generations to favor male over female offspring (a preference even more overt than that which still underlies much of white America). At the same time Chinese American men, too, have been confronted with a history of inequality and of painful "emasculation." The fact that 90 percent of early Chinese immigrants were male, combined with anti-miscegenation laws and laws prohibiting Chinese laborers' wives from entering the US, forced these immigrants to congregate in the bachelor communities of various Chinatowns, unable to father a subsequent generation. While many built railroads, mined gold, and cultivated plantations, their strenuous activities and contributions in these areas were often overlooked by white historians. Chinamen were better known to the American public as restaurant cooks, laundry workers, and waiters, jobs traditionally considered "women's work."[1]

The same forms of social and economic oppression of Chinese American women and men, in conjunction with a longstanding Orientalist tradition that casts the Asian in the role of the silent and passive Other,[2] have in turn provided material for degrading sexual representations of the Chinese in American popular culture. Elaine H. Kim notes, for instance, that the stereotype of Asian women as submissive and dainty sex objects has given rise to an "enormous demand for X-rated films featuring Asian women and the emphasis on bondage in pornographic materials about Asian women," and that "the popular image of alluring and exotic 'dream girls of the mysterious East' has created a demand for 'Oriental' bath house workers in American cities as well as a booming business in mail order marriages."[3] No less insidious are the inscriptions of Chinese men in popular culture. Frank

Reprinted from *Conflicts in Feminism*, ed. Marianne Hirsch and Evelyn Fox Keller (New York and London: Routledge, 1990), pp. 234–9, 241–51.

Chin, a well-known writer and one of the most outspoken revisionists of Asian American history, describes how the American silver screen casts doubts on Chinese American virility:

> The movies were teachers. In no uncertain terms they taught America that we were lovable for being a race of sissies . . . living to accommodate the whitemen. Unlike the white stereotype of the evil black stud, Indian rapist, Mexican macho, the evil of the evil Dr. Fu Manchu was not sexual, but homosexual. . . . Dr. Fu, a man wearing a long dress, batting his eyelashes, surrounded by muscular black servants in loin clothes, and with his bad habit of caressingly touching white men on the leg, wrist, and face with his long fingernails is not so much a threat as he is a frivolous offense to white manhood. [Charlie] Chan's gestures are the same, except that he doesn't touch, and instead of being graceful like Fu in flowing robes, he is awkward in a baggy suit and clumsy. His sexuality is the source of a joke running through all of the forty-seven Chan films. The large family of the bovine detective isn't the product of sex, but animal husbandry. . . . *He never gets into violent things* [my emphasis].[4]

According to Chin and Jeffery Paul Chan, also a writer, "Each racial stereotype comes in two models, the acceptable model and the unacceptable model. . . . The unacceptable model is unacceptable because he cannot be controlled by whites. The acceptable model is acceptable because he is tractable. There is racist hate and racist love."[5] Chin and Chan believe that while the "masculine" stereotypes of blacks, Indians, and Mexicans are generated by "racist hate," "racist love" has been lavished on Chinese Americans, targets of "effeminate" stereotypes:

> The Chinese, in the parlance of the Bible, were raw material for the "flock," pathological sheep for the shepherd. The adjectives applied to the Chinese ring with scriptural imagery. We are meek, timid, passive, docile, industrious. We have the patience of Job. We are humble. A race without sinful manhood, born to mortify our flesh. . . . The difference between [other minority groups] and the Chinese was that the Christians, taking Chinese hospitality for timidity and docility, weren't afraid of us as they were of other races. They loved us, protected us. Love conquered.[6]

If "racist love" denies "manhood" to Asian men, it endows Asian women with an excess of "womanhood." Elaine Kim argues that because "the characterization of Asian men is a reflection of a white male perspective that defines the white man's virility, it is possible for Asian men to be viewed as asexual and the Asian woman as only sexual, imbued with an innate understanding of how to please and serve." The putative gender difference among Asian Americans – exaggerated out of all proportion in the popular imagination – has, according to Kim, created "resentment and tensions" between the sexes within the ethnic community.[7]

Although both the Asian American and the feminist movements of the late sixties have attempted to counter extant stereotypes, the conflicts between Asian American men and women have been all the more pronounced in the wake of the two movements. In the last two decades [since about 1970] many Chinese American men – especially such writers and editors as Chin and Chan – have begun to correct the distorted images of Asian males projected by the dominant culture. Astute, eloquent, and incisive as they are in debunking racist myths, they are often blind to the biases resulting from their own acceptance of the patriarchal construct of masculinity. In Chin's discussion of Fu Manchu and Charlie Chan and in the perceptive contrast he draws between the stock images of Asian men and those of other men of color, one can detect not only homophobia but perhaps also a sexist preference for stereotypes that imply predatory violence against women to "effeminate" ones. Granted that the position taken by Chin may be little more than a polemicist stance designed to combat white patronage, it is disturbing that he should lend credence to the conventional association of physical aggression with manly valor. The hold of patriarchal conventions becomes even more evident in the following passage:

> The white stereotype of the Asian is unique in that it is the only racial stereotype completely devoid of manhood. Our nobility is that of an efficient housewife. At our worst we are contemptible because we are womanly, effeminate, devoid of all the traditionally masculine qualities of originality, daring, physical courage, creativity. We're neither straight talkin' or straight shootin'. The mere fact that four of the five American-born Chinese-American writers are women reinforces this aspect of the stereotype.[8]

In taking whites to task for demeaning Asians, these writers seem nevertheless to be buttressing patriarchy by invoking gender stereotypes, by disparaging domestic efficiency as "feminine," and by slotting desirable traits such as originality, daring, physical courage, and creativity under the rubric of masculinity.[9]

The impetus to reassert manhood also underlies the ongoing attempt by Chin, Chan, Lawson Inada, and Shawn Wong to reconstruct Asian American literary history. In their groundbreaking work *Aiiieeeee! An Anthology of Asian-American Writers*, these writers and co-editors deplored "the lack of a recognized style of Asian-American manhood." In a forthcoming sequel entitled *The Big Aiiieeeee! An Anthology of Asian American Writers*, they attempt to revive an Asian heroic tradition, celebrating Chinese and Japanese classics such as *The Art of War, Water Margin, Romance of the Three Kingdoms, Journey to the West,* and *Chushingura*, and honoring the renowned heroes and outlaws featured therein.[10]

The editors seem to be working in an opposite direction from that of an increasing number of feminists. While these Asian American spokesmen are recuperating a heroic tradition of their own, many women writers and scholars, building on existentialist and modernist insights, are reassessing the entire Western code of heroism. While feminists question such traditional values as competitive individualism and martial valor, the editors seize on selected maxims, purportedly derived from Chinese epics and war manuals, such as "I am the law," "life is war," "personal integrity and honor is the highest value," and affirm the "ethic of private revenge."[11]

The *Aiiieeeee!* editors and feminist critics also differ on the question of genre. According to Chin, the literary genre that is most antithetical to the heroic tradition is autobiography, which he categorically denounces as a form of Christian confession:

> the fighter writer uses literary forms as weapons of war, not the expression of ego alone, and does not [waste] time with dandyish expressions of feeling and psychological attitudinizing.... A Chinese Christian is like a Nazi Jew. Confession and autobiography celebrate the process of conversion from an object of contempt to

an object of acceptance. You love the personal experience of it, the oozings of viscous putrescence and luminous radiant guilt.... It's the quality of submission, not asser-tion that counts, in the confession and the autobiography. The autobiography com-bines the thrills and guilt of masturbation and the porno movie.[12]

Feminist critics, many of whom are skeptical of either/or dichotomies (in this instance fighting vs. feeling) and are impatient with normative definitions of genre (not that Chin's criteria are normative), believe that women have always appropri-ated autobiography as a vehicle for *asserting*, however tentatively, their subjectivity. Celeste Schenck writes:

> the poetics of women's autobiography issues from its concern with constituting a female subject – a precarious operation, which...requires working on two fronts at once, *both* occupying a kind of center, assuming a subjectivity long denied, *and* maintaining the vigilant, disruptive stance that speaking from the postmodern margin provides – the autobiographical genre may be paradigmatic of all women's writing.[13]

Given these divergent views, the stage is set for a confrontation between "hero-ism" and "feminism" in Chinese American letters.

The advent of feminism, far from checking Asian American chauvinism, has in a sense fueled gender antagonism, at least in the literary realm. Nowhere is this antagonism reflected more clearly than in the controversy that has erupted over Maxine Hong Kingston's *The Woman Warrior*. Classified as autobiography, the work describes the protagonist's struggle for self-definition amid Cantonese sayings such as "Girls are maggots in the rice," "It is more profitable to raise geese than daughters," "Feeding girls is feeding cowbirds" (pp. 51, 54). While the book has received popular acclaim, especially among feminist critics, it has been censured by several Chinese American critics – mostly male but also some female – who tax Kingston for misrepresenting Chinese and Chinese American culture, and for passing fiction for autobiography. Chin (whose revulsion against autobiog-raphy we already know) wrote a satirical parody of *The Woman Warrior;* he casts aspersions on its historical status and places Kingston in the same company as the authors of Fu Manchu and Charlie Chan for confirming "the white fantasy that everything sick and sickening about the white self-image is really Chinese."[14] Jeffery Paul Chan castigates Knopf for publishing the book as "biography rather than fiction (which it obviously is)" and insinuates that a white female reviewer praises the book indiscriminately because it expresses "female anger."[15] Benjamin Tong openly calls it a "fashionably feminist work written with white acceptance in mind."[16] As Sau-ling Wong points out, "According to Kingston's critics, the most pernicious of the stereotypes which might be supported by *The Woman Warrior* is that of Chinese American men as sexist," and yet some Chinese American women "think highly of *The Woman Warrior* because it confirms their personal experi-ences with sexism."[17] In sum, Kingston is accused of falsifying culture and of reinforcing stereotype in the name of feminism.

At first glance the claim that Kingston should not have taken the liberty to infuse autobiography with fiction may seem to be merely a generic, gender-neutral criticism, but as Susan Stanford Friedman has pointed out, genre is all too often gendered.[18] Feminist scholars of autobiography have suggested that women writers often shy away from "objective" autobiography and prefer to use the form to reflect a private world, a subjective vision, and the life of the imagination. *The Woman Warrior*, though it departs from most "public" self-representations by men, is quite in line with such an autobiographical tradition. Yet for a "minority" author to exercise such artistic freedom is perilous business because white critics and reviewers persist in seeing creative expressions by her as no more than cultural history.[19] Members from the ethnic community are in turn upset if they feel that they have been "misrepresented" by one of their own. Thus where Kingston insists on shuttling between the world of facts and the world of fantasy, on giving multiple versions of "truth" as subjectively perceived, her Chinese American detractors demand generic purity and historical accuracy. Perhaps precisely because this author is female, writing amid discouraging realities, she can only forge a viable and expansive identity by refashioning patriarchal myths and invoking imaginative possibilities.[20] Kingston's autobiographical act, far from betokening submission, as Chin believes, turns the self into a "heroine" and is in a sense an act of "revenge" (a word represented in Chinese by two ideographs which Kingston loosely translates as "report a crime") against both the Chinese and the white cultures that undermine her self-esteem. Discrediting her for taking poetic licence is reminiscent of those white reviewers who reduce works of art by ethnic authors to sociohistorical documentary.

The second charge concerning stereotype is more overtly gender-based. It is hardly coincidental that the most unrelenting critics (whose grievance is not only against Kingston but also against feminists in general) have also been the most ardent champions of Chinese American "manhood." Their response is understandable. Asian American men have suffered deeply from racial oppression. When Asian American women seek to expose anti-female prejudices in their own ethnic community, the men are likely to feel betrayed.[21] Yet it is also undeniable that sexism still lingers as part of the Asian legacy in Chinese America and that many American-born daughters still feel its sting. Chinese American women may be at once sympathetic and angry toward the men in their ethnic community: sensitive to the marginality of these men but resentful of their male privilege. . . .

An ongoing effort to revamp Chinese American literary history will surely be more compelling if it is informed by mutual empathy between men and women. To return to an earlier point, I am of two minds about the ambitious attempt of the *Aiiieeeee!* editors to restore and espouse an Asian American heroic tradition. Born and raised in Hong Kong, I grew up reading many of the Chinese heroic epics – along with works of less heroic modes – and can appreciate the rigorous effort of the editors to introduce them to Asian American and non-Asian readers alike.[22] But the literary values they assign to the heroic canon also function as ideology. Having spoken out against the emasculation of Asian Americans in their introduction to *Aiiieeeee!*, they seem determined to show further that Chinese and Japanese Americans have a heroic – which is to say militant – heritage. Their propagation of the epic tradition appears inseparable from their earlier attempt to eradicate effeminate stereotypes and to emblazon Asian American manhood.[23] In this light, the special appeal held by the war heroes for the editors becomes rather obvious. Take, for example, Kwan Kung, in *Romance of the Three Kingdoms*: loud, passionate, and vengeful, this "heroic embodiment of martial self-sufficiency" is antithetical in every way to the image of the quiet, passive, and subservient Oriental houseboy. Perhaps the editors hope that the icon of this imposing Chinese hero will dispel myths about Chinese American tractability.

While acquaintance with some of the Chinese folk heroes may induce the American public to acknowledge that Chinese culture too has its Robin Hood and John Wayne, I remain uneasy about the masculist orientation of the heroic tradition, especially as expounded by the editors who see loyalty, revenge, and individual honor as the overriding ethos which should be inculcated in (if not already absorbed by) Chinese Americans. If white media have chosen to highlight and applaud the submissive and nonthreatening characteristics of Asians, the Asian American editors are equally tendentious in underscoring the militant strain of their Asian literary heritage.[24] The refutation of effeminate stereotypes through the glorification of machismo merely perpetuates patriarchal terms and assumptions.

Is it not possible for Chinese American men to recover a cultural space without denigrating or erasing "the feminine"? Chin contends that "use of the heroic tradition in Chinese literature as the source of Chinese American moral, ethical and esthetic universals is not literary rhetoric and smartass cute tricks, not wishful thinking, not theory, not demagoguery and prescription, but simple history."[25] However, even history, which is also a form of social construct, is not exempt from critical scrutiny. The Asian heroic tradition, like its Western counterpart, must be re-evaluated so that both its strengths and limits can surface. The intellectual excitement and the emotional appeal of the tradition is indisputable: the strategic brilliance of characters such as Chou Yu and Chuko Liang in *Romance of the Three Kingdoms* rivals that of Odysseus, and the fraternal bond between the three sworn brothers – Liu Pei, Chang Fei, and Kuan Yu (Kwan Kung) – is no less moving than that between Achilles and Patrocles. But just as I no longer believe that Homer speaks for humanity (or even all mankind), I hesitate to subscribe wholeheartedly to the *Aiiieeeee!* editors' claim that the Asian heroic canon (composed entirely of work written by men though it contains a handful of heroines) encompasses "Asian universals."

Nor do I concur with the editors that a truculent mentality pervades the Chinese heroic tradition, which generally places a higher premium on benevolence than on force and stresses the primacy of kinship and friendship over personal power. By way of illustration I will turn to the prototype for Kingston's "woman warrior" – Fa Mu Lan (also known as Hua Mulan and Fa Muk Lan). According to the original "Ballad of Mulan" (which most Chinese children, including myself, had to learn by heart) the heroine in joining the army is prompted neither by revenge nor by personal honor but by filial piety. She enlists under male disguise to take the place of her aged father. Instead of celebrating the glory of war, the poem describes the bleakness of the battlefield and the loneliness of the daughter (who sorely misses her parents). The use of understatement in such lines as "the general was killed after hundreds of combats" and "the warriors returned in ten years" (my translation) connotes the cost and duration of battles. The "Ballad of Mulan," though it commits the filial and courageous daughter to public memory, also contains a pacifist subtext – much in the way that the *Iliad* conceals an anti-war message beneath its martial trappings. A re-examination of the Asian heroic tradition may actually reveal that it is richer and more sophisticated than the *Aiiieeeee!* editors, bent on finding belligerent models, would allow.[26]

Kingston's adaptation of the legend in *The Woman Warrior* is equally multivalent. Fa Mu Lan as re-created in the protagonist's fantasy does excel in martial arts, but her power is derived as much from the words carved on her back as from her military skills. And the transformed heroine still proves problematic as a model since she can only exercise her power when in male armor. As I have argued elsewhere, her military distinction, insofar as it valorizes the ability to be ruthless and violent – "to fight like a man" – affirms rather than subverts patriarchal mores.[27] In fact, Kingston discloses in an interview that the publisher is the one who entitled the book "The Woman Warrior" while she herself (who is a pacifist) resists complete identification with the war heroine:

> I don't really like warriors. I wish I had not had a metaphor of a warrior, a person who uses weapons and goes to war. I guess I always have in my style a doubt about wars as a way of solving things.[28]

Aside from the fantasy connected with Fa Mu Lan the book has little to do with actual fighting. The real battle that runs through the work is one against silence and invisibility. Forbidden by her mother to tell a secret, unable to read aloud in English while first attending American school, and later fired for protesting against racism, the protagonist eventually speaks with a vengeance through writing – through a heroic act of self-expression. At the end of the book her tutelary genius has changed from Fa Mu Lan to Ts'ai Yen – from warrior to poet.

Kingston's commitment to pacifism – through re-visioning and re-contextualizing ancient "heroic" material – is even more evident in her most recent book, *Tripmaster Monkey.* As though anticipating the editors of *The Big Aiiieeeee!*, the author alludes recurrently to the Chinese heroic tradition, but always with a feminist twist. The protagonist of this novel, Wittman Ah Sing, is a playwright who loves *Romance of the Three Kingdoms* (one of the aforementioned epics espoused by Chin). Kingston's novel culminates with Wittman directing a marathon show which he has written based on the *Romance.* At the end of the show he has a rather surprising illumination:

> He had made up his mind: he will not go to Viet Nam or to any war. He had staged the War of the Three Kingdoms as heroically as he could, which made him start to understand: The three brothers and Cho Cho were masters of the war; they had worked out strategies and justifications for war so brilliantly that their policies and their tactics are used today, even by governments with nuclear-powered weapons. And they *lost*. The clanging and banging fooled us, but now we know – they lost. Studying the mightiest war epic of all time, Wittman changed – beeen! – into a pacifist. Dear American monkey, don't be afraid. Here, let us tweak your ear, and kiss your other ear.[29]

The seemingly easy transformation of Wittman – who is curiously evocative of Chin in speech and manner – is achieved through the pacifist author's sleight of hand. Nevertheless, the novel does show that it is possible to celebrate the ingenious strategies of the ancient warriors without embracing, wholesale, the heroic code that motivates their behavior and without endorsing violence as a positive expression of masculinity.[30]

Unfortunately, the ability to perform violent acts implied in the concepts of warrior and epic hero is still all too often mistaken for manly courage; and men who have been historically subjugated are all the more tempted to adopt a militant stance to manifest their masculinity. In the notorious Moynihan report on the black family, "military service for Negroes" was recommended as a means to potency:

> Given the strains of the disorganized and matrifocal family life in which so many Negro youth come of age, the Armed Forces are a dramatic and desperately needed change: a world away from women, a world run by strong men of unquestioned authority.[31]

Moynihan believed that placing black men in an "utterly masculine world" will strengthen them. The black men in the sixties who worshipped figures that exploited and brutalized women likewise conflated might and masculinity. Toni Cade, who cautions against "equating black liberation with black men gaining access to male privilege," offers an alternative to patriarchal prescriptions for manhood:

> Perhaps we need to let go of all notions of manhood and femininity and concentrate on Blackhood.... It perhaps takes less heart to pick up the gun than to face the task of creating a new identity, a self, perhaps an androgynous self....[32]

If Chinese American men use the Asian heroic dispensation to promote male aggression, they may risk remaking themselves in the image of their oppressors – albeit under the guise of Asian panoply. Precisely because the racist treatment of Asians has taken the peculiar form of sexism – insofar as the indignities suffered by men of Chinese descent are analogous to those traditionally suffered by women – we must refrain from seeking antifeminist solutions to racism. To do otherwise reinforces not only patriarchy but also white supremacy.

Well worth heeding is Althusser's caveat that when a dominant ideology is integrated as common sense into the consciousness of the dominated, the dominant class will continue to prevail.[33] Instead of tailoring ourselves to white ideals, Asian Americans may insist on alternative habits and ways of seeing. Instead of drumming up support for Asian American "manhood," we may consider demystifying popular stereotypes while reappropriating what Stanford Lyman calls the "kernels of truth" in them that are indeed part of our ethnic heritage. For instance, we need not accept the Western association of Asian self-restraint with passivity and femininity. I, for one, believe that the respectful demeanor of many an Asian and Asian American indicates, among other things, a willingness to listen to others and to resolve conflict rationally or tactfully.[34] Such a collaborative disposition – be it Asian or non-Asian, feminine or masculine – is surely no less valid and viable than one that is vociferous and confrontational....

... The recent shift from feminist studies to gender studies suggests that the time has come to look at women and men together. I hope that the shift will also entice both men and women to do the looking and, by so doing, strengthen the alliance between gender studies and ethnic studies. Lest feminist criticism remain in the wilderness, white scholars must reckon with race and class as integral experiences for both men and women, and acknowledge that not only female voices but the voices of many men of color have been historically silenced or dismissed. Expanding the feminist frame of reference will allow certain existing theories to be interrogated or reformulated.[35] Asian American men need to be wary of certain pitfalls in using what Foucault calls "reverse discourse," in demanding legitimacy "in the same vocabulary, using the same categories by which [they were] disqualified."[36] The ones who can be recruited into the field of gender studies may someday see feminists as allies rather than adversaries, and proceed to dismantle not just white but also male supremacy. Women of color should not have to undergo a self-division resulting from having to choose between female and ethnic identities. Chinese American women writers may find a way to negotiate the tangle of sexual and racial politics in all its intricacies, not just out of a desire for "revenge" but also out of a sense of "loyalty." If we ask them to write with a vigilant eye against possible misappropriation by white readers or against possible offense to "Asian American manhood," however, we will end up implicitly sustaining racial and sexual hierarchies. All of us need to be conscious of our "complicity with the gender ideologies" of patriarchy, whatever its origins, and to work toward notions of gender and ethnicity that are nonhierarchical, nonbinary, and nonprescriptive; that can embrace tensions rather than perpetuate divisions.[37] To reclaim cultural traditions without getting bogged down in the mire of traditional constraints, to attack stereotypes without falling prey to their binary opposites, to chart new topographies for manliness and womanliness, will surely demand genuine heroism.

Notes

...

1 The devaluation of daughters is a theme explored in *The Woman Warrior* (New York: Vintage, 1976); as this book suggests, this aspect of patriarchy is upheld no less by women than by men. The "emasculation" of Chinese American men is addressed in *China Men* (New York: Ballantine, 1980), in which Kingston attempts to reclaim the founders of Chinese America. Subsequent page references to these two books will appear in the text. Detailed accounts of early Chinese immigrant history can be found in Victor G. Nee and Brett De Bary Nee, *Longtime Californ': A Documentary Study of an American Chinatown* (New York: Pantheon, 1973); and Ronald Takaki, *Strangers from a Different Shore: A History of Asian Americans* (Boston: Little, Brown, 1989), pp. 79–131.

2 See Edward Said, *Orientalism* (New York: Vintage, 1979). Although Said focuses on French and British representations of the Middle East, many of his insights also apply to American perceptions of the Far East.

3 "Asian American Writers: A Bibliographical Review," *American Studies International* 22/2 (October 1984): 64.

4 "Confessions of the Chinatown Cowboy," *Bulletin of Concerned Asian Scholars* 4/3 (1972): 66.

5 "Racist Love," *Seeing through Shuck*, ed. Richard Kostelanetz (New York: Ballantine, 1972), pp. 65, 79. Although the cinematic image of Bruce Lee as a Kung-fu master might have somewhat countered the feminine representations of Chinese American men, his role in the only one Hollywood film in which he appeared before he died was, in Elaine Kim's words, "less a human being than a fighting machine" ("Asian Americans and American popular Culture," *Dictionary of Asian American History*, ed. Hyung-Chan Kim (New York: Greenwood Press, 1986), p. 107).

6 "Racist Love," p. 69.

7 "Asian American Writers: A Bibliographical Review," p. 64.

8 "Racist Love," p. 68. The five writers under discussion are Pardee Lowe, Jade Snow Wong, Virginia Lee, Betty Lee Sung, and Diana Chang.

9 Similar objections to the passage have been raised by Merle Woo in "Letter to Ma," *This Bridge Called My Back: Writings by Radical Women of Color*, ed. Cherríe Moraga and Gloria Anzaldúa (New York: Kitchen Table, 1981), p. 145; and Elaine Kim in *Asian American Literature: An Introduction to the Writings and Their Social Context* (Philadelphia: Temple University Press, 1982), p. 189. Richard Yarborough delineates a somewhat parallel conundrum about manhood faced by African American writers in the nineteenth century and which, I believe, persists to some extent to this day; see "Race, Violence, and Manhood: The Masculine Ideal in Frederick Douglass's 'Heroic Slave,'" in *Frederick Douglass: New Literary and Historical Essays*, ed. Eric J. Sundquist (Cambridge, MA: Cambridge University Press, 1990). There is, however, an important difference between the dilemma faced by the African American men and that faced by Asian American men. While writers such as William Wells Brown and Frederick Douglass tried to reconcile the white inscription of the militant and sensual Negro and the white ideal of heroic manhood, several Chinese American male writers are trying to disprove the white stereotype of the passive and effeminate Asian by invoking its binary opposite.

10 *Aiiieeeee! An Anthology of Asian-American Writers* (Washington: Howard University Press, 1974), p. xxxviii; *The Big Aiiieeeee! An Anthology of Asian American Writers* (New York: New American Library, 1991). All the Asian classics cited are available in English translations: Sun Tzu, *The Art of War*, trans. Samuel B. Griffith (London: Oxford University Press, 1963); Shi Nai'an and Luo Guanzhong, *Outlaws of the Marsh [The Water Margin]*, trans. Sidney Shapiro (jointly published by Beijing: Foreign Language Press and Bloomington: Indiana University Press, 1981); Luo GuanZhong, *Romance of the Three Kingdoms*, trans. C. H. Brewitt-Taylor (Singapore: Graham Brash, 1986), 2 vols.; Wu Ch'eng-en, *Journey to the West*, trans. Anthony Yu (Chicago: University of Chicago Press, 1980), 4 vols.; Takeda Izumo, Miyoshi Shoraku, and Namiki Senryu, *Chushingura (The Treasury of Loyal Retainers)*, trans. Donald Keene (New York: Columbia University Press, 1971). I would like to thank Frank Chin for allowing me to see an early draft of *The Big Aiiieeeee!*. For a foretaste of his exposition of the Chinese heroic tradition, see "This is Not an Autobiography," *Genre* 18 (1985): 109–30.

11 The feminist works that come to mind include Paula Gunn Allen, *The Sacred Hoop: Recovering the Feminine in American Indian Traditions* (Boston: Beacon, 1986); Nina Auerbach, *Communities of Women: An Idea in Fiction* (Cambridge: Harvard University Press, 1978); Zillah R. Eisenstein, *The Radical Future of Liberal Feminism* (New York: Longman, 1981); Carol Gilligan, *In a Different Voice: Psychological Theory and Women's Development* (Cambridge: Harvard University Press, 1982); Christa Wolf, *Cassandra: A Novel and Four Essays*, trans. Jan van Heurck (New York: Farrar, 1984). The Chinese maxims appear in the introduction to *The Big Aiiieeeee!* (draft) and are quoted with the editors' permission. The same maxims are cited in Frank Chin, "This Is Not an Autobiography."

12 Chin, "This Is Not An Autobiography," pp. 112, 122, 130.

13 "All of a Piece: Women's Poetry and Autobiography," *Life/Lines: Theorizing Women's Autobiography*, ed. Bella Brodzki and Celeste Schenck (Ithaca: Cornell University Press, 1988), p. 286. See also Estelle Jelinek, ed., *Women's Autobiography: Essays in Criticism* (Bloomington: Indiana University Press, 1980); Donna Stanton, *The Female Autograph* (New York: New York Literary Forum, 1984); Sidonie Smith, *Poetics of Women's Autobiography: Marginality and the Fictions of Self-Representation* (Bloomington: Indiana University Press, 1987).

14 "The Most Popular Book in China," *Quilt 4*, ed. Ishmael Reed and Al Young (Berkeley: Quilt, 1984), p. 12. The essay is republished as the "Afterword" in *The Chinaman Pacific & Frisco R. R. Co.* The literary duel between Chin, a self-styled "Chinatown Cowboy," and Kingston, an undisguised feminist, closely parallels the paper war between Ishmael Reed and Alice Walker.

15 "The Mysterious West," *New York Review of Books*, 28 April 1977: 41.

16 "Critic of Admirer Sees Dumb Racist," *San Francisco Journal*, 11 May 1977: 20.

17 "Autobiography as Guided Chinatown Tour?," *American Lives: Essays in Multicultural American Autobiography*, ed. James Robert Payne (Knoxville: University of Tennessee Press, 1992). . . .

18 "Gender and Genre Anxiety: Elizabeth Barrett Browning and H. D. as Epic Poets," *Tulsa Studies in Women's Literature* 5/2 (Fall 1986): 203–28.

19 Furthermore, a work highlighting sexism within an ethnic community is generally more palatable to the reading public than a work that condemns racism. *The Woman Warrior* addresses both forms of oppression, but critics have focused almost exclusively on its feminist themes.

20 Susanne Juhasz argues that because women have traditionally lived a "kind of private life, that of the imagination, which has special significance due to the outright conflict between societal possibility and imaginative possibility, [Kingston] makes autobiography from fiction, from fantasy, from forms that have conventionally belonged to the novel" ("Towards a Theory of Form in Feminist Autobiography," *International Journal of Women's Studies* 2/1 (1979): 62).

21 Cf. similar critical responses in the African American community provoked by Alice Walker's *The Color Purple* and Toni Morrison's *Beloved*.
   Although I limit my discussion to sexual politics in Chinese America, Asian American women are just as vulnerable to white sexism, as the denigrating stereotypes discussed by Kim earlier suggest. . . .

22 The other modes are found in works as diverse as T'ao Ch'ien's poems (pastoral), Ch'u Yuan's *Li sao* (elegiac), selected writing by Lao Tzu and Chuang Tzu (metaphysical), and P'u Sung-ling's *Liao-Chai Chih I* (Gothic). (My thanks to Shu-mei Shih and Adam Schorr for helping me with part of the romanization.) One must bear in mind, however, that Asian and Western generic terms often fail to correspond. For example, what the *Aiiieeeee!* editors call "epics" are loosely classified as "novels" in Chinese literature.

23 Epic heroes, according C. M. Bowra, are "the champions of man's ambitions" seeking to "win as far as possible a self-sufficient manhood" (*Heroic Poetry* (London: Macmillan, 1952), p. 14). Their Chinese counterparts are no exception.

24 Benjamin R. Tong argues that the uneducated Cantonese peasants who comprised the majority of early Chinese immigrants were not docile but venturesome and rebellious, that putative Chinese traits such as meekness and obedience to authority were in fact "reactivated" in America in response to white racism ("The Ghetto of the Mind," *Amerasia Journal* 1/3 (1971): 1–31). Chin, who basically agrees with Tong, also attributes the submissive and "unheroic" traits of Chinese Americans to Christianity ("This Is Not An Autobiography"). While Tong and Chin are right in distinguishing

the Cantonese folk culture of the early immigrants from the classical tradition of the literati, they underestimate the extent to which mainstream Chinese thought infiltrated Cantonese folk imagination, wherein the heroic ethos coexists with Buddhist beliefs and Confucian teachings (which do counsel self-restraint and obedience to parental and state authority). To attribute the "submissive" traits of Chinese Americans entirely to white racism or to Christianity is to discount the complexity and the rich contradictions of the Cantonese culture and the resourceful flexibility and adaptability of the early immigrants.

25 "This Is Not an Autobiography," p. 127.

26 Conflicting attitudes toward Homeric war heroes are discussed in Katherine Callen King, *Achilles: Paradigms of the War Hero from Homer to the Middle Ages* (Berkeley: University of California Press, 1987). Pacifist or at least anti-killing sentiments can be found in the very works deemed "heroic" by Chin and the editors. *Romance of the Three Kingdoms* not only dramatizes the senseless deaths and the ravages of war but also betrays a wishful longing for peace and unity, impossible under the division of "three kingdoms." Even *The Art of War* sets benevolence above violence and discourages actual fighting and killing: "To subdue the enemy without fighting is the acme of skill" (p. 77).

27 "'Don't Tell': Imposed Silences in *The Color Purple* and *The Woman Warrior*," *PMLA* (March 1988): 166. I must add, however, that paradoxes about manhood inform Chinese as well as American cultures. The "contradictions inherent in the bourgeois male ideal" is pointed out by Yarborough: "the use of physical force is, at some levels, antithetical to the middle-class privileging of self-restraint and reason: yet an important component of conventional concepts of male courage is the willingness to use force" ("Race, Violence, and Manhood: The Masculine Ideal in Frederick Douglass's 'Heroic Slave'"). Similarly, two opposing ideals of manhood coexist in Chinese culture, that of a civil scholar who would never stoop to violence and that of a fearless warrior who would not brook insult or injustice. Popular Cantonese maxims such as "a superior man would only move his mouth but not his hands" (i.e. would never resort to physical combat) and "he who does not take revenge is not a superior man" exemplify the contradictions.

28 Interview conducted by Kay Bonetti.

29 *Tripmaster Monkey: His Fake Book* (New York: Knopf, 1989), p. 348.

30 I am aware that a forceful response to oppression is sometimes necessary, that it is much easier for those who have never encountered physical blows and gunshots to maintain faith in nonviolent resistance. My own faith was somewhat shaken while watching the tragedy of Tiananmen on television; on the other hand, the image of the lone Chinese man standing in front of army tanks reinforced my belief that there is another form of heroism that far excels brute force.

31 Lee Rainwater and William L. Yancey, *The Moynihan Report and the Politics of Controversy* (Cambridge: MIT Press, 1967), p. 88 (p. 42 in the original report by Daniel Patrick Moynihan).

32 "On the Issue of Roles," *The Black Woman: An Anthology*, ed. Toni Cade (York, ON: Mentor-NAL, 1970), p. 103; see also Bell Hooks, *Ain't I a Woman: Black Women and Feminism* (Boston: South End Press, 1981), pp. 87–117.

33 *Lenin and Philosophy and Other Essays* (New York: Monthly Review Press, 1971), pp. 174–83.

34 Of course, Asians are not all alike, and most generalizations are ultimately misleading. Elaine Kim pointed out to me that "It's popularly thought that Japanese strive for peaceful resolution of conflict and achievement of consensus while Koreans – for material as much as metaphysical reasons – seem at times to encourage combativeness in one another" (personal correspondence, quoted with permission). Differences within each national group are no less pronounced. . . .

35 Donald Goellnicht, for instance, has argued that a girl from a racial minority "experiences not a single, but a double subject split; first, when she becomes aware of the gendered position constructed for her by the symbolic language of patriarchy; and second, when she recognizes that discursively and socially constructed positions of racial difference also obtain . . . [that] the 'fathers' of her racial and cultural group are silenced and degraded by the Laws of the Ruling Fathers" ("Father Land and/or Mother Tongue: The Divided Female Subject in *The Woman Warrior* and *Obasan*," paper delivered at the MLA Convention, 1988).

36 *The History of Sexuality*, vol. 1, trans. Robert Hurley (New York: Vintage, 1980), p. 101.

37 Teresa de Lauretis, *Technologies of Gender: Essays on Theory, Film, and Fiction* (Bloomington: Indiana University Press, 1987), p. 11.

11

Skin Head Sex Thing: Racial Difference and the Homoerotic Imaginary

Kobena Mercer

In this article I want to explore the experience of aesthetic ambivalence in visual representations of the black male nude. The photographs of Robert Mapplethorpe provide a salient point of entry into this complex "structure of feeling" as they embody such ambivalence experienced at its most intense.[1]

My interest in this aspect of Mapplethorpe's work began in 1982, when a friend lent me his copy of *Black Males*. It circulated between us as a kind of illicit object of desire, albeit a highly problematic one. We were fascinated by the beautiful bodies, as we went over the repertoire of images again and again, drawn in by the desire to look and enjoy what was given to be seen. We wanted to look, but we didn't always find what we wanted to see: we were shocked and disturbed by the racial discourse of the imagery, and above all, we were angered by the aesthetic equation that reduced these black male bodies to abstract visual "things," silenced in their own right as subjects, serving only to enhance the name and reputation of the author in the rarefied world of art photography. But still we were stuck, unable to make sense of our own implication in the emotions brought into play by Mapplethorpe's imaginary.

I've chosen to situate the issue of ambivalence in relation to these experiences because I am now involved in a partial revision of arguments made in an earlier reading of Mapplethorpe's work.[2] This revision arises not because those arguments were wrong, but because I've changed my mind, or rather I should say that I still can't make up my mind about Mapplethorpe. In returning to my earlier essay I want to suggest an approach to ambivalence not as something that occurs "inside" the text (as if cultural texts were hermetically sealed or self-sufficient), but as something that is experienced across the relations between authors, texts, and readers, relations that are always contingent, context-bound, and historically specific.

Posing the problem of ambivalence and undecidability in this way not only underlines the role of the reader, but also draws attention to the important, and equally undecidable, role of context in determining the range of different readings that can be produced from the same text. In this respect, it is impossible to ignore

Reprinted from *How Do I Look? Queer Film and Video*, ed. Bad Object Choices (Seattle: Bay Press, 1991), pp. 169–71, 174–5, 177–85, 187–90, 206–10 (illustrations omitted).

the crucial changes in context that frame the readings currently negotiated around Mapplethorpe and his work. Mapplethorpe's death in 1989 from AIDS, a major retrospective of his work at the Whitney Museum in New York, the political "controversy" over federal arts policy initiated by the fundamentalist Right in response to a second Mapplethorpe exhibition organized by the Institute of Contemporary Art in Philadelphia – these events have irrevocably altered the context in which we perceive, argue about, and evaluate Mapplethorpe's most explicitly homoerotic work.

The context has also changed as a result of another set of contemporary developments: the emergence of new aesthetic practices among black lesbian and gay artists in Britain and the United States. Across a range of media, such work problematizes earlier conceptions of identity in black cultural practices. This is accomplished by entering into the ambivalent and overdetermined spaces where race, class, gender, sexuality, and ethnicity intersect in the social construction and lived experiences of individual and collective subjectivities. Such developments demand acknowledgment of the historical contingency of context and in turn raise significant questions about the universalist character of some of the grand aesthetic and political claims once made in the name of cultural theory. Beginning with a summary of my earlier argument, I want to identify some of the uses and limitations of psychoanalytic concepts in cultural theory before mapping a more historical trajectory within which to examine the constitutive ambivalence of the identifications we actually inhabit in living with difference.

Revising

The overriding theme of my earlier reading of Mapplethorpe's photographs was that they inscribe a process of objectification in which individual black male bodies are aestheticized and eroticized as objects of the gaze. Framed within the artistic conventions of the nude, the bodies are sculpted and shaped into artifacts that offer an erotic source of pleasure in the act of looking. Insofar as what is represented in the pictorial space of the photograph is a "look," or a certain "way of looking," the pictures say more about the white male subject behind the camera than they do about the black men whose beautiful bodies we see depicted. This is because the invisible or absent subject is the actual agent of the look, at the center and in control of the apparatus of representation, the I/eye at the imaginary origin of the perspective that marks out the empty space to which the viewer is invited as spectator. This argument was based on a formal analysis of the codes and conventions brought to bear on the pictorial space of the photographs, and, equally important, on an analogy with feminist analyses of the erotic objectification of the image of women in Western traditions of visual representation.

Three formal conventions interweave across the photographic text to organize and direct the viewer's gaze into its pictorial space: a sculptural code, concerning the posing and posture of the body in the studio enclosure; a code of portraiture concentrated on the face; and a code of lighting and framing, fragmenting bodies in textured formal abstractions. All of these help to construct the *mise-en-scène* of fantasy and desire that structures the spectator's disposition toward the image. As all references to a social or historical context are effaced by the cool distance of the detached gaze, the text enables the projection of a fantasy that saturates the black male body in sexual predicates.

These codes draw from aspects of Mapplethorpe's oeuvre as a whole and have become the signs by which we recognize his authorial signature. Their specific combination, moreover, is punctuated by the technical perfection – especially marked in the printing process – that also distinguishes Mapplethorpe's presence as an author. Considering the way in which the glossy allure of the photographic print becomes consubstantial with the shiny texture of black skin, I argued that a significant element in the pleasures the photographs make available consists in the fetishism they bring into play. Such fetishism not only eroticizes the visible differ-ence the black male nude embodies, it also lubricates the ideological reproduction of racial otherness as the fascination of the image articulates a fantasy of power and mastery over the other.

Before introducing a revision of this view of racial fetishism in Mapplethorpe's photographs, I want to emphasize its dependence on the framework of feminist theory initially developed in relation to cinematic representation by Laura Mul-vey.[3] Crudely put, Mulvey showed that men look and women are looked at. The position of "woman" in the dominant regimes of visual representation says little or nothing about the historical experiences of women as such, because the female subject functions predominantly as a mirror image of what the masculine subject wants to see. The visual depiction of women in the *mise-en-scène* of heterosexual desire serves to stabilize and reproduce the narcissistic scenario of a phallocentric fantasy in which the omnipotent male gaze sees but is never seen. What is important about this framework of analysis is the way it reveals the symbolic relations of power and subordination at work in the binary relations that structure dominant codes and conventions of visual representations of the body. The field of visibility is thus organized by the subject/object dichotomy that associates mascu-linity with the activity of looking and femininity with the subordinate, passive role of being that which is looked at.

In extrapolating such terms to Mapplethorpe's black nudes, I suggested that because both artist and models are male, a tension arises that transfers the frisson of difference to the metaphorically polarized terms of racial identity. The black/ white duality overdetermines the subject/object dichotomy of seeing and being seen. This metaphorical transfer underlines the erotic investment of the gaze in the most visible element of racial difference – the fetishization of black skin. The dynamics of this tension are apparently stabilized within the pictorial space of the photographs by the ironic appropriation of commonplace stereotypes – the black man as athlete, as savage, as mugger. These stereotypes in turn serve to regulate and fix the representational presence of the black subject, who is thereby "put into his place" by the power of Mapplethorpe's gaze.

The formal work of the codes essentializes each model into the homogenized embodiment of an ideal type. This logic of typification in dominant regimes of racial representation has been emphasized by Homi Bhabha, who argues that "an important feature of colonial discourse is its dependence on the concept of 'fixity' in the ideological construction of otherness."[4] The scopic fixation on black skin thus implies a kind of "negrophilia," an aesthetic idealization and eroticized investment in the racial other that inverts and reverses the binary axis of the fears and anxieties invested in or projected onto the other in "negrophobia." Both positions, whether they devalue or overvalue the signs of racial difference, inhabit the representational space of what Bhabha calls colonial fantasy. Although I would now qualify the theoretical analogies on which this analysis of Mapplethorpe's work was based, I would still want to defend the terms of a psychoanalytic reading of racial fetishism, a fetishism that can be most tangibly grasped in a photograph such as *Man in a Polyester Suit* (1980).

The scale and framing of this picture emphasizes the sheer size of the black dick. Apart from the hands, the penis and the penis alone identifies the model as a black man. As Frantz Fanon said, diagnosing the figure of "the Negro" in the fantasies of his white psychiatric patients, "One is no longer aware of the Negro, but only of a penis: the Negro is eclipsed. He is turned into a penis. He *is* a penis."[5] The element of scale thus summons up one of the deepest mythological fears and anxieties in the racist imagination, namely that all black men have huge willies. In the fantasmatic space of the supremacist imaginary, the big black phallus is a threat not only to the white master (who shrinks in impotence from the thought that the subordinate black male is more potent and sexually powerful than he), but also to civilization itself, since the "bad object" represents a danger to white womanhood and therefore miscegenation and racial degeneration.

The binarisms of classical racial discourse are emphasized in Mapplethorpe's photograph by the jokey irony of the contrast between the black man's private parts and the public respectability signified by the business suit. The oppositions exposed/hidden and denuded/clothed play upon the binary oppositions nature/culture and savage/civilized to bring about a condensation of libidinal investment, fear, and wish-fulfillment in the fantasmatic presence of the other. The binarisms repeat the assumption that sex is the essential "nature" of black masculinity, while the cheap, tacky polyester suit confirms the black man's failure to gain access to "culture." The camouflage of respectability cannot conceal the fact that, in essence, he originates, like his prick, from somewhere anterior to civilization. What is dramatized in the picture is the splitting of levels of belief, which Freud regarded as the key feature of the logic of disavowal in fetishism.[6] Hence, the implication: "*I know* it's not true that all black men have big penises, *but still*, in my photographs they do."

It is precisely at this point, however, that the concept of fetishism threatens to conceal more than it reveals about the ambivalence the spectator experiences in relation to the "shock effect" of Mapplethorpe's work. Freud saw the castration anxiety in the little boy's shock at discovering the absence of a penis in the little girl (acknowledged and disavowed in the fetish) as constitutive of sexual difference. The clinical pathology or perversion of the fetishist, like a neurotic symptom, unravels for classical psychoanalysis the "normal" developmental path of Oedipal heterosexual identity: it is the point at which the norm is rendered visible by the pathological. The concept of fetishism was profoundly enabling for feminist film theory because it uncovered the logic of substitution at work in all regimes of representation, which make present for the subject what is absent in the real. But although analogies facilitate cognitive connections with important cultural and political implications, there is also the risk that they repress and flatten out the messy spaces in between. As Jane Gaines has pointed out concerning feminist film theory, the inadvertent reproduction of the heterosexual presumption in the orthodox theorization of sexual difference also assumed a homogeneous racial and ethnic context, with the result that racial and ethnic differences were erased from or marginalized within the analysis.[7] Analogies between race and gender in representation reveal similar ideological patterns of objectification, exclusion, and "othering." In Mapplethorpe's nudes, however, there is a subversive homoerotic dimension in the substitution of the black male subject for the traditional female archetype. This subversive dimension was underplayed in my earlier analysis: my use of the theoretical analogy minimized the homosexual specificity of Mapplethorpe's eroticism, which rubs against the grain of the generic high art status of the traditional female nude.

To pose the problem in another way, one could approach the issue of ambivalence by simply asking: do photographs like *Man in a Polyester Suit* reinscribe the fixed beliefs of racist ideology, or do they problematize them by foregrounding the intersections of difference where race and gender cut across the representation of sexuality? An unequivocal answer is impossible or undecidable, it seems to me, because the image throws the question back onto the spectator, for whom it is experienced precisely as the shock effect. What is at issue is not primarily whether the question can be decided by appealing to authorial intentions, but rather the equally important question of the role of the reader and how he or she attributes intentionality to the author: The elision of homoerotic specificity in my earlier reading thus refracts an ambivalence not so much on the part of Mapplethorpe the author, or on the part of the text, but on my part as a reader: More specifically, it refracted the ambivalent "structure of feeling" that I inhabit as a black gay male reader in relation to the text. Indeed, I've only recently become aware of the logical slippage in my earlier reading, which assumed an equivalence between Mapplethorpe as the individual agent of the image and the empty, anonymous, and impersonal ideological category I described as "the white male subject" to which the spectator is interpellated. Paradoxically, this conflation undermined the very distinction between author-function and ideological subject-position that I drew from Michel Foucault's antinaturalist account of authorship.[8]

In retrospect I feel this logical flaw arose as a result of my own ambivalent positioning as a black gay spectator. To call something fetishistic implies a negative judgment, to say the least. I want to take back the unavoidably moralistic connotation of the term, because I think what was at issue in the rhetoric of my previous argument was the encoding of an ambivalent structure of feeling, in which anger and envy divided the identifications that placed me somewhere always already inside the text. On the one hand, I emphasized objectification because I felt identified with the black males in the field of vision, an identification with the other that might best be described in Fanon's terms as a feeling that "I am laid bare. I am overdetermined from without. I am a slave not of the 'idea' that others have of me but of my own appearance. I am being dissected under white eyes. I am *fixed*.... Look, it's a Negro."[9] But on the other hand, and more difficult to disclose, I was also implicated in the fantasy scenario as a gay subject. That is to say, I was identified with the author insofar as the objectified black male was also an image of the object chosen by my own fantasies and erotic investments. Thus, sharing the same desire to look as the author-agent of the gaze, I would actually occupy the position that I said was that of the "white male subject."

I now wonder whether the anger in that earlier reading was not also the expression and projection of a certain envy. Was it not, in this sense, an effect of a homosexual identification on the basis of a similar object-choice that invoked an aggressive rivalry over the same unattainable object of desire, depicted and represented in the visual field of the other? According to Jacques Lacan, the mirror-stage constitutes the "I" in an alienated relation to its own image, as the image of the infant's body is "unified" by the prior investment that comes from the look of the mother, always already in the field of the other.[10] In this sense, the element of aggressivity involved in textual analysis – the act of taking things apart – might merely have concealed my own narcissistic participation in the pleasures of Mapplethorpe's texts. Taking the two elements together, I would say that my ambivalent positioning as a black gay male reader stemmed from the way in which I inhabited two contradictory identifications at one and the same time. Insofar as the anger and envy were an effect of my identifications with both object and subject of the gaze, the rhetorical closure of my earlier reading simply displaced the ambivalence onto the text by attributing it to the author.

Rereading

If this brings us to the threshold of the kind of ambivalence that is historically specific to the context, positions, and experiences of the reader, it also demonstrates the radically polyvocal quality of Mapplethorpe's photographs and the way in which contradictory readings can be derived from the same body of work. I want to suggest, therefore, an alternative reading that demonstrates this textual reversibility by revising the assumption that fetishism is necessarily a bad thing.

By making a 180-degree turn, I want to suggest that the articulation of ambivalence in Mapplethorpe's work can be seen as a subversive deconstruction of the hidden racial and gendered axioms of the nude in dominant traditions of representation. This alternative reading also arises out of a reconsideration of poststructuralist theories of authorship. Although Romantic notions of authorial creativity cannot be returned to the central role they once played in criticism and interpretation, the question of agency in cultural practices that contest the canon and its cultural dominance suggests that it really *does* matter who is speaking.

The question of enunciation – who is speaking, who is spoken to, what codes do they share to communicate? – implies a whole range of important political issues about who is empowered and who is disempowered in the representation of difference. It is enunciation that circumscribes the marginalized positions of subjects historically misrepresented or underrepresented in dominant systems of representation. To be marginalized is to have no place from which to speak, since the subject positioned in the margins is silenced and invisible. The contestation of marginality in black, gay, and feminist politics thus inevitably brings the issue of authorship back into play, not as the centered origin that determines or guarantees the aesthetic and political value of a text, but as a question about agency in the cultural struggle to "find a voice" and "give voice" to subordinate experiences, identities, and subjectivities. A relativization of authoritative poststructuralist claims about decentering the subject means making sense of the biographical and autobiographical dimension of the context-bound relations between authors, texts, and readers without falling back on liberal humanist or empiricist common sense. Quite specifically, the "death of the author" thesis demands revision because the death of the author in *our* case inevitably makes a difference to the kinds of readings we make.

Comments by Mapplethorpe, and by some of the black models with whom he collaborated, offer a perspective on the questions of authorship, identification, and enunciation. The first of these concerns the specificity of Mapplethorpe's authorial identity as a gay artist and the importance of a metropolitan gay male culture as a context for the homoeroticism of the black male nudes.

In a British Broadcasting Corporation documentary in 1988, Lynne Franks pointed out that Mapplethorpe's work is remarkable for its absence of voyeurism. A brief comparison with the avowedly heterosexual scenario in the work of photographers such as Edward Weston and Helmut Newton would suggest similar aesthetic conventions at the level of visual fetishization; but it would also highlight the significant differences that arise in Mapplethorpe's homoeroticism. Under Mapplethorpe's authorial gaze there is a tension within the cool distance between subject and object. The gaze certainly involves an element of erotic objectification, but like a point-of-view shot in gay male pornography, it is reversible. The gendered hierarchy of seeing/being seen is not so rigidly coded in homoerotic representations, since sexual sameness liquidates the associative opposition be- tween active subject and passive object. This element of reversibility at the level of the gaze is marked elsewhere in Mapplethorpe's oeuvre, most notably in the numerous self-portraits, including the one of him with a bullwhip up his bum, in which the artist posits himself as the object of the look. In relation to the black male nudes and the s&m pictures that preceded them, this reversibility creates an ambivalent distance measured by the direct look of the models, which is another salient feature of gay male pornography. In effect, Mapplethorpe implicates himself in his field of vision by a kind of participatory observation, an ironic ethnography whose descriptive clarity suggests a reversible relation of equivalence, or identifi- cation, between the author and the social actors whose world is described. In this view, Mapplethorpe's homoeroticism can be read as a form of stylized repor- tage that documented aspects of the urban gay subcultural milieu of the 1970s. One can reread Mapplethorpe's homoerotica as a kind of photographic documen- tary of a world that has profoundly changed as a result of AIDS. This reinterpret- ation is something Mapplethorpe drew attention to in the BBC television interview:

> I was part of it. And that's where most of the photographers who move in that direction are at a disadvantage, in that they're not part of it. They're voyeurs moving in. With me it was quite different. Often I had experienced some of those experiences which I later recorded, myself, firsthand, without a camera.... It was a certain moment, and I was in a perfect situation in that most of the people in the photo- graphs were friends of mine and they trusted me. I felt almost an obligation to record those things. It was an obligation for me to do it, to make images that nobody's seen before and to do it in a way that's *aesthetic*.

In this respect, especially in the light of the moral and ethical emphasis by which Mapplethorpe locates himself as a member of an elective community, it is import- ant to acknowledge the ambivalence of authorial motivation suggested in his rationale for the black male nude studies:

At some point I started photographing black men. It was an area that hadn't been explored intensively. If you went through the history of nude male photography, there were very few black subjects. I found that I could take pictures of black men that were so subtle, and the form was so photographical.

On the one hand, this could be interpreted as the discovery and conquest of "virgin territory" in the field of art history; but alternatively, Mapplethorpe's acknowledgment of the exclusion and absence of the black subject from the canonical realm of the fine art nude can be interpreted as the elementary starting point of an implicit critique of racism and ethnocentrism in Western aesthetics. . . .

Once grounded in the context of contemporary urban gay male culture in the United States, the shocking modernism that informs the ironic juxtaposition of elements drawn from the repository of high culture – where the nude is indeed one of the most valued genres in Western art history – can be read as a subversive recoding of the normative aesthetic ideal. In this view, it becomes possible to reverse the reading of racial fetishism in Mapplethorpe's work, not as a repetition of racist fantasies but as a deconstructive strategy that lays bare psychic and social relations of ambivalence in the representation of race and sexuality. This deconstructive aspect of his homoeroticism is experienced, at the level of audience reception, as the disturbing shock effect.

The Eurocentric character of the liberal humanist values invested in classical Greek sculpture as the originary model of human beauty in Western aesthetics is paradoxically revealed by the promiscuous intertextuality whereby the filthy and degraded form of the commonplace racist stereotype is brought into the domain of aesthetic purity circumscribed by the privileged place of the fine art nude. This doubling within the pictorial space of Mapplethorpe's black nudes does not reproduce either term of the binary relation between "high culture" and "low culture" as it is: it radically decenters and destabilizes the hierarchy of racial and sexual difference in dominant systems of representation by folding the two together within the same frame. It is this ambivalent intermixing of textual references, achieved through the appropriation and articulation of elements from the "purified" realm of the transcendental aesthetic ideal and from the debased and "polluted" world of the commonplace racist stereotype, that disturbs the fixed positioning of the spectator. One might say that what is staged in Mapplethorpe's black male nudes is the return of the repressed in the ethnocentric imaginary. The psychic-social boundary that separates "high culture" and "low culture" is transgressed, crossed, and disrupted precisely by the superimposition of two ways of seeing, which thus throws the spectator into uncertainty and undecidability, precisely the experience of ambivalence as a structure of feeling in which one's subject-position is called into question.

In my previous argument, I suggested that the regulative function of the stereotype had the upper hand, as it were, and helped to "fix" the spectator in the ideological subject-position of the "white male subject." Now I'm not so sure. Once we recognize the historical and political specificity of Mapplethorpe's practice as a contemporary gay artist, the aesthetic irony that informs the juxtaposition of elements in his work can be seen as the trace of a subversive strategy that disrupts the stability of the binary oppositions into which difference is coded. In social, economic, and political terms, black men in the United States constitute one of the "lowest" social classes: disenfranchised, disadvantaged, and disempowered as a distinct collective subject in the late capitalist underclass. Yet in Mapplethorpe's photographs, men who in all probability came from this class are elevated onto the pedestal of the transcendental Western aesthetic ideal. Far from reinforcing the fixed beliefs of the white supremacist imaginary, such a deconstructive move begins to undermine the foundational myths of the pedestal itself.

The subaltern black social subject, who was historically excluded from dominant regimes of representation – "invisible men" in Ralph Ellison's phrase – is made visible within the codes and conventions of the dominant culture whose ethnocentrism is thereby exposed as a result. The mythological figure of "the Negro," who was always excluded from the good, the true, and the beautiful in Western aesthetics on account of his otherness, comes to embody the image of physical perfection and aesthetic idealization in which, in the canonical figure of the nude, Western culture constructed its own self-image. Far from confirming the hegemonic white, heterosexual subject in his centered position of mastery and power, the deconstructive aspects of Mapplethorpe's black male nude photographs loosen up and unfix the common-sense sensibilities of the spectator, who thereby experiences the shock effect precisely as the affective displacement of given ideological subject-positions.

To shock was always the key verb of the avant-garde in modernist art history. In Mapplethorpe's work, the shock effected by the promiscuous textual intercourse between elements drawn from opposite ends of the hierarchy of cultural value decenters and destabilizes the ideological fixity of the spectator. In this sense, his work begins to reveal the political unconscious of white ethnicity. It lays bare the constitutive ambivalence that structures whiteness as a cultural identity whose hegemony lies, as Richard Dyer suggests, precisely in its "invisibility."[11]

The splitting of the subject in the construction of white identity, entailed in the affirmation and denial of racial difference in Western humanism, is traced in racist perception. Blacks are looked down upon and despised as worthless, ugly, and ultimately unhuman creatures. But in the blink of an eye, whites look up to and revere the black body, lost in awe and envy as the black subject is idolized as the embodiment of the whites' ideal. This schism in white subjectivity is replayed daily in the different ways black men become visible on the front and back pages of tabloid newspapers, seen as undesirable in one frame – the mugger, the terrorist, the rapist – and highly desirable in the other – the athlete, the sports hero, the entertainer. Mapplethorpe undercuts this conventional separation to show the recto-verso relation between these contradictory "ways of seeing" as constitutive aspects of white identity. Like a mark that is legible on both sides of a sheet of paper, Mapplethorpe's aesthetic strategy places the splitting in white subjectivity under erasure: it is crossed out but still visible. In this sense, the anxieties aroused in the exhibition history of Mapplethorpe's homoerotica not only demonstrate the disturbance and decentering of dominant versions of white identity, but also confront whiteness with the otherness that enables it to be constituted as an identity as such. . . .

Different Degrees of Othering

Coming back to Mapplethorpe's photographs, in the light of this task of making "whiteness" visible as a problem for cultural theory, I want to suggest that the positioning of gay (white) people in the margins of Western culture may serve as a perversely privileged place from which to reexamine the political unconscious of modernity. By negotiating an alternative interpretation of Mapplethorpe's authorial position, I argued that his aesthetic strategy lays bare and makes visible the "splitting" in white subjectivity that is anchored, by homology, in the split between "high culture" and "low culture." The perverse interaction between visual elements drawn from both sources begins to subvert the hierarchy of cultural value, and such subversion of fixed categories is experienced precisely as the characteristic shock effect.

Broadening this theme, one can see that representations of race in Western culture entail different degrees of othering. Or, to put it the other way around: different practices of racial representation imply different positions of identification on the part of the white subject. Hollywood's iconic image of the "nigger minstrel" in cinema history, for example, concerns a deeply ambivalent mixture of othering and identification. The creation of the minstrel mask in cinema, and in popular theater and the music hall before it, was really the work of white men in blackface. What is taking place in the psychic structures of such historical representations? What is going on when whites assimilate and introject the degraded and devalorized signifiers of racial otherness into the cultural construction of their own identity? If imitation implies identification, in the psychoanalytic sense of the word, then what is it about whiteness that makes the white subject want to be black?

"I Wanna Be Black," sang Lou Reed on the album *Street Hassle* (1979), which was a parody of a certain attitude in postwar youth culture in which the cultural signs of blackness – in music, clothes, and idioms of speech – were the mark of "cool." In the American context, such a sensibility predicated on the ambivalent identification with the other was enacted in the bohemian beatnik subculture and became embodied in Norman Mailer's literary image of "the White Negro" stalking the jazz clubs in search of sex, speed, and psychosis. Like a photographic negative, the white negro was an inverted image of otherness, in which attributes devalorized by the dominant culture were simply revalorized or hypervalorized as emblems of alienation and outsiderness, a kind of strategic self-othering in relation to dominant cultural norms. In the museum without walls, Mailer's white negro, who went in search of the systematic derangement of the senses, merely retraced an imaginary pathway in the cultural history of modernity previously traveled by Arthur Rimbaud and Eugène Delacroix in nineteenth-century Europe. There is a whole modernist position of "racial romanticism" that involves a fundamental ambivalence of identifications. At what point do such identifications result in an imitative masquerade of white ethnicity? At what point do they result in ethical and political alliances? How can we tell the difference?[12]

My point is that white ethnicity constitutes an "unknown" in contemporary cultural theory: a dark continent that has not yet been explored. One way of

opening it up is to look at the ambivalent coexistence of the two types of identification, as they figure in the work of (white) gay artists such as Mapplethorpe and
Jean Genet. In *Un Chant d'amour* (1950), Genet's only foray into cinema, there is
a great deal of ambivalence, to say the least, about the black man, the frenzied and
maniacal negro seen in the masturbatory dance through the scopophilic gaze of
the prison guard. In another context, I wrote "The black man in Genet's film is
fixed like a stereotype in the fetishistic axis of the look.... subjected to a pornographic exercise of colonial power."[13] Yes, I know... but. There is something else
going on as well, not on the margins but at the very center of Genet's film. The
romantic escape into the woods, which is the liberated zone of freedom in which
the lover's utopian fantasy of coupling is enacted, is organized around the role of
the "dark" actor, the Tunisian, the one who is not quite white. In this view, the
ambivalence of ethnicity has a central role to play in the way that Genet uses race to
figure the desire for political freedom beyond the prisonhouse of marginality. Once
located in relation to his plays, such as *The Balcony* and *The Blacks*, Genet's textual
practice must be seen as his mode of participation in the "liberation" struggles of
the postwar era.

The word *liberation* tends to stick in our throats these days because it sounds so
deeply unfashionable; but we might also recall that in the 1950s and 1960s it was
precisely the connections between movements for the liberation from colonialism
and movements for the liberation from the dominant sex and gender system that
underlined their radical democratic character. In the contemporary situation, the
essentialist rhetoric of categorical identity politics threatens to erase the connect-
edness of our different struggles. At its worst, such forms of identity politics play
into the hands of the Right as the fundamentalist belief in the essential and
immutable character of identity keeps us locked into the prisonhouse of marginality in which oppressions of race, class, and gender would have us live. By historicizing the imaginary identifications that enable democratic agency, we might
rather find a way of escaping this ideological bantustan.

Instead of giving an answer to the questions that have been raised about the
ambivalence of ethnicity as a site of identification and enunciation, I conclude by
recalling Genet's wild and adventurous story about being smuggled across the
Canadian border by David Hilliard and other members of the Black Panther Party
in 1968. He arrived at Yale University to give a May Day speech, along with Allen
Ginsberg and others, in defense of imprisoned activist Bobby Seale. Genet talks
about this episode in *Prisoner of Love*, where it appears as a memory brought to
consciousness by the narration of another memory, about the beautiful fedayyin, in
whose desert camps Genet lived between 1969 and 1972. The memory of
his participation in the elective community of the Palestinian freedom fighters
precipitates the memory of the Black Panther "brotherhood," into which he was
adopted – this wretched, orphaned, nomadic homosexual thief. I am drawn to this
kind of ambivalence, sexual and political, that shows through, like a stain, in his
telling:[14]

> In white America the Blacks are the characters in which history is written. They are the
> ink that gives the white page its meaning.... [The Black Panthers' Party] built the
> black race on a white America that was splitting.... The Black Panthers' Party wasn't
> an isolated phenomenon. It was one of many revolutionary outcrops. What made it

stand out in white America was its black skin, its frizzy hair and, despite a kind of uniform black leather jacket, an extravagant but elegant way of dressing. They wore multicoloured caps only just resting on their springy hair; scraggy moustaches, sometimes beards; blue or pink or gold trousers made of satin or velvet, and cut so that even the most shortsighted passer-by couldn't miss their manly vigour.

Under what conditions does eroticism mingle with political solidarity? When does it produce an effect of empowerment? And when does it produce an effect of disempowerment? When does identification imply objectification, and when does it imply equality? I am intrigued by the ambivalent but quite happy coexistence of the fetishized big black dick beneath the satin trousers and the ethical equivalence in the struggle for postcolonial subjectivity. Genet's affective participation in the political construction of imagined communities suggests that the struggle for democratic agency and subjectivity always entails the negotiation of ambivalence. Mapplethorpe worked in a different context, albeit one shaped by the democratic revolutions of the 1960s, but his work similarly draws us back into the difficult questions that Genet chose to explore, on the "dark side" of the political uncon-scious of the postcolonial world. The death of the author doesn't necessarily mean mourning and melancholia, but rather mobilizing a commitment to countermem-ory. In the dialogue that black gay and lesbian artists have created in contemporary cultural politics, the exemplary political modernism of Mapplethorpe and Genet, "niggers with attitude" if there ever were, is certainly worth remembering as we begin thinking about our pitiful "postmodern" condition. . . .

Notes

1 References are made primarily to *Black Males*, with introduction by Edmund White (Amsterdam: Gallerie Jurka, 1982) and *The Black Book*, with foreword by Ntozake Shange (New York: St. Martin's Press, 1986).

2 Kobena Mercer, "Imaging the Black Man's Sex," in *Photography/Politics: Two*, ed. Pat Holland, Jo Spence, and Simon Watney (London: Comedia/Methuen, 1987), pp. 61–9.

3 Laura Mulvey, "Visual Pleasure and Narrative Cinema," in *Feminism and Film Theory*, ed. Constance Penley (New York: Routledge, 1988), pp. 57–68.

4 Homi Bhabha, "The Other Question: The Stereotype and Colonial Discourse," *Screen* 24/6 (November–December 1983), pp. 18–36.

5 Frantz Fanon, *Black Skin, White Masks* (London: Paladin, 1970), 120.

6 Sigmund Freud, "Fetishism" (1927), *The Standard Edition of the Complete Psychological Works of Sigmund Freud*, ed. James Strachey (London: Hogarth Press, 1953–74), vol. 21 (1961), pp. 147–57.

7 Jane Gaines, "White Privilege and Looking Relations: Race and Gender in Feminist Film Theory," *Screen* 29/4 (Autumn 1988), pp. 12–27.

8 Michel Foucault, "What Is an Author?" in *Language, Counter-Memory, Practice*, ed. Donald F. Bouchard (Ithaca, NY: Cornell University Press, 1977), pp. 113–38; see also Roland Barthes, "The Death of the Author," in *Image-Music-Text* (New York: Hill and Wang, 1977), pp. 142–8.

9 Fanon, *Black Skin, White Masks*, p. 82.

10 Jacques Lacan, "The Mirror Stage as Formative of the Function of the I," in *Ecrits: A Selection* (London: Tavistock, 1977), pp. 1–7.

11 Richard Dyer, "White," *Screen* 29/4 (Autumn 1988), pp. 44–64.

12 See Norman Mailer, "The White Negro: Superficial Reflections on the Hipster," in *Advertisements for Myself* (New York: Putnam, 1959), pp. 337–58. The fantasy of wanting to be black is discussed as a masculinist fantasy in Suzanne Moore, "Getting a Bit of the Other: The Pimps of Postmodernism," in *Male Order: Unwrapping Masculinity*, ed. Rowena Chapman and Jonathan Rutherford (London: Lawrence and Wishart, 1988), pp. 165–92.

13 See "Sexual Identities: Questions of Difference," a panel discussion with Kobena Mercer, Gayatri Spivak, Jacqueline Rose, and Angela McRobbie, *Undercut* 17 (Spring 1988), pp. 19–30.

14 Jean Genet, *Prisoner of Love* (London: Picador, 1989), p. 213.

12

Bonds of (In)Difference

Robyn Wiegman

In the prologue to the 1980 bestseller *The Lords of Discipline*, Will McLean, the white narrator, presents the purpose of his story: "I want to tell you how it was. I want precision. I want a murderous, stunning truthfulness. I want to find my own singular voice for the first time" (Conroy 1980: 6). The articulation of his own "singular voice," a voice which, by implication, has been denied, characterizes the recurrent representational gesture of the post-civil rights era, where a white masculine perspective poses as truth teller, origin of a solitary and seemingly marginal voice that must now provide the precision missing in *other* versions of the "story." This story, as the novel and its 1983 film version depict, is the story of "America," that infinitely rhetorical figure that secures itself through multiple historicizing narratives of geopolitical destiny and chosen peoples. But like every mythological text that functions to weld disparities together, "America" is tenuous, its mythic plan of liberation "a thousand points of light" above a gaping abyss.[1] That this abyss seems to be stretching out before us in more complicated, encompassing, and less easily resisted ways, bringing with it what many recognize as a political and philosophical crisis, constitutes the prevailing mark of the contemporary period. Such a crisis pressures both cultural critique and political organization, and has made it nearly impossible to continue articulating the contestatory nature of "America" along the lines of dissent used in the 1960s. As we head for the twenty-first century, it is the decade of the 1980s that has come to feel like the final subversion of the twentieth century's high hopes of radical politics, and it is to its various reconfigurations of race and gender that this chapter turns.

But why use "feel like" in the preceding sentence, instead of a visual metaphor to coincide with the broad contours of this project? Can we not say that the 1980s "looks like" a subversion of the political aims of civil rights and feminism, thereby understanding its representational field as a return to earlier, more conservative methods of deployment? The basic presupposition of my argument here is that we cannot, precisely because the subversion at work in the 1980s took place in the transformation of its visual terrain *toward* more clearly inclusive representational images, images that seemed to offer, indeed demand, recognition of an America

Reprinted from *American Anatomies: Theorizing Race and Gender* (Durham: Duke University Press, 1995), pp. 115–34, 138–46, 224–9.

where things, particularly in the wake of civil rights, had definitively changed. In the massive organization of the social gaze through visual technologies, most importantly film and television, in fact, US culture in the 1980s began to answer more fully than ever before the critique of racial segregation. By locating such a critique as an ensemble of representative bodies in media production, the 1980s cannot also claim to have reshaped in politically progressive ways the status of these bodies in the economic and social spheres.[2] Instead, the decade marks a massive retrenchment of political gains for minoritized groups as an integrationist aesthetics (both political and representational) emerged as the strategic and contradictory means for reframing and securing the continuity of white racial supremacy. The disciplinary specularity of lynching and castration ... gave way (though not entirely) to other practices of surveillance and containment, and the long struggle for African-American representational inclusion in popular and political culture alike took center stage as the primary visible economy subtending the production of race.

This means that mass-mediated visual technologies increasingly became the primary locus for race's rhetorical (or performative) deployment, binding together the historical production of the body as a visible geography with the specular apparatuses of late-twentieth-century life. In the process, a proliferating inclusion of African-American characters and cultural contexts in mainstream film and television, at least from a 1950s perspective, could be heralded by some as evidence of a profound transformation of US culture, an eclipse of its historical emphasis on segregationist exclusion. But, while such inclusion has been applauded as an advance toward the fulfillment of "America" and while we may welcome the transgression of segregatory logic, the modes and manners through which this inclusion has been achieved are certainly not without their own political problems, as Kobena Mercer and Isaac Julien, among others, have been concerned to point out.[3] In the frantic move toward representational integration, in both popular culture and the literary canon, the question of political power has been routinely displaced as a vapid fetishization of the visible has emerged to take its place. This fetishization attaches a heightened commodity value to blackness in the wake of civil rights, translating the difficult demands of Afrocentric political critique into strategies for expanding capital's consumer needs. Such a commodity status is not without irony in the broad historical scope of race in this country, where the literal commodification of the body under enslavement is now simulated in representational circuits that produce and exchange subjectivities through the visible presence of multicultural skin.

By securing the visible, epidermal iconography of difference to the commodity tableau of contemporary technologies, the integrationist aesthetic works by apprehending political equality as coterminous with representational presence, thereby undermining political analyses that pivot on the exclusion, silence, or invisibility of various groups and their histories. Given the logic of white supremacy, very little presence is in fact required for the necessary threshold of difference to be achieved. Cinematic depictions of an integrated American landscape, for instance, typically rely on a multiplicity of Anglo-American players as the framework of difference, and racial transcendence is inscribed on the often singular bodies of African-American (or other non-Eurocentric) characters. While the integrationist narrative now current in US culture makes claims toward equal representation, the marketing of inclusion is always implicitly bounded by this border-controlling logic, and white supremacy is able to continue its operation within a seemingly expanded but clearly restrictive social field.

A particularly powerful example of this, and the representational scenario on which this chapter dwells, is that offered by interracial male bonding narratives, whose massive deployment in popular US culture in the decade of the 1980s is witnessed by this cursory list: the films *Stir Crazy* (1980), *Nighthawks* (1981), *48 Hours* (1982), *The Lords of Discipline* (1983), *Trading Places* (1983), *Enemy Mine* (1985), *White Nights* (1985), *Iron Eagle* (1986), *Running Scared* (1986), *Streets of Gold* (1986), *Big Shots* (1987), *Hamburger Hill* (1987), *Lethal Weapon* I (1987) and II (1989), *Cry Freedom* (1988), *Off Limits* (1988), *Shoot to Kill* (1988); the TV shows *Miami Vice, Sonny Spoon, The A Team, J. J. Starbuck* (the TV remake of the *Defiant Ones*) (all 1987), *Magnum P. I., Hill Street Blues,* and *In the Heat of the Night*.[4] While the male bonding structure can be used as the framework for ethical, physical, moral, sexual, or political struggle in all-male group arrangements, its primary figuration, as anyone familiar with contemporary Hollywood film can tell, focuses on a sole interracial couple, most often narrativized within the action genre, and featuring what Donald Bogle calls "huckfinn fixation," where "a trusty black . . . possess[es] the soul the white man searches for" (Bogle: 1989: 140). Implicit in this narrative scenario is the discourse of sexual difference, where the white male occupies the traditionally masculine position of rugged self-assertion, while the African-American male assumes the emotional, feminine sphere. Such an application of the binary grid of gender to the field of masculine relations continues to serve, as it has in the past, an important function in adjudicating racial differences among men.

It is significant that in a number of contemporary interracial male bonding narratives, the discourse of sexual difference does not simply reiterate the historical appointment of the African-American male as the feminine, but works instead to fully inculcate him into the province of the masculine, marking such a masculinization as the precise measurement of "America"'s democratic achievement. The fear of masculine sameness that underwrites the castration and lynching scenario of an earlier era thus emerges in a number of narrative scenarios of the late twentieth century as a positive and necessary cultural assertion. Such necessity can be read as a form of response to the phallicized discourse of Black Power, where the analysis of the specular project of lynching and castration was articulated . . . as both a demand and a warning: "[w]e shall have our manhood . . . or the earth will be leveled by our attempts to gain it" (Cleaver 1968: 66). In their increasing appeal to the mutuality of masculine sameness, male bonding narratives of the 1980s became a crucial site for negotiating this threat of militant black masculinity, offering a particularly compelling revision of the US cultural terrain.

Although this articulation of masculine relations most often forged the image of the African-American male within instead of opposed to the masculine, such a reconfiguration is not necessarily evidence for or part of the process of meaningful social change. That is, in aligning black men with the masculine, popular culture transforms the historical contestations between black and white men into the image of democratic fraternity, marking "America" as an exclusive masculine realm and further ensconcing the elisions at work in the popular phrase "blacks and women." Such elisions are, of course, crucial to the ongoing articulation of white supremacist and patriarchal logic in the contemporary era, as they work to fragment the realm of political opposition by reiterating the binary arrangements that underwrite the regimes of both bodily scripted hierarchies. In this regard, we might understand the use of the discourse of sexual difference to fashion the representational economy that governs African-American men, whether in terms of feminization or masculinization, as having the rhetorical effect in the twentieth century not only of homogenizing the complexities of their social positioning but also of reproducing the cleavage of gender within the category African-American itself.[5] Interracial male bonding narratives reinscribe this cleavage by routinely defining the representational world of female exclusion as the precondition for racism's transcendence. In such a narrative scenario, economic, social, and political differences among men are ultimately displaced by the prevailing framework of gender.

The Brotherhood of the Ring

The Lords of Discipline provides a telling portrait of the historical changes implicit in the shift from a segregationist to an integrationist representational mode by taking the military and its complicity with Jim Crow as the context in which the new "stunning truthfulness" of American culture can be born. To establish the tableau of masculine bonds that historically underwrite the mythology of military masculinity, the film presents the doctrinaire General Durrell (G. D. Spradlin), whose rhetoric explains, "America is fat . . . sloppy, immoral and she needs men of iron to set her on the right path again." Entrance into this "superior breed" that can right the effeminate ways of America is marked by the wearing of a ring, "the sacred symbol of the Institute and its ideals." The significance of this ring as the symbolic bond between men – fashioned across a discourse of masculinity, national identity, and power – displaces, even as it invokes, the heterosexual matrimonial union, marking relations among men as a privileged nonsexual domain. The seeming necessity for this privileged domain ("America is fat") and the racial conflicts within it point to a crisis within the cultural construction of the masculine, a crisis that evinces itself in the proliferation of interracial male bonding narratives in the 1980s.[6]

While the novel and its film version (dir. Frank Roddam) both explore this world of the "brotherhood of the ring, the fellowship of the line," the differences in their narrative structures highlight an increasing emphasis on race as a nodal point in exploring and articulating relations among men in the post-civil rights era. In the novel, the narrative of the sacred ring, of (white) honor and masculinity, is interwoven with the narrative of the ring's more traditional association, heterosexual matrimony. Here, Will McLean's struggle as a rebel in the institution and his subsequent role as the protector of the first black cadet, Tom Pearce, is juxtaposed with his affair with Annie Kate Gervais, a woman from a poor southern family who is impregnated by Tradd St. Croix, Will's best friend and academy roommate. Sexual difference, and the various trajectories of reproduction and responsibility through which masculinity is coded, thus takes a central role in the novel, becoming a primary means through which differences among white men, based on their ethical and moral responses to others, are crafted. In playing out these differences within a highly charged configuration of race and gender, the narrative emphasizes McLean's ethical regard for both poor white women and historically excluded black men.

But where the novel may foreground questions of the ethical within the hierarchies of both race and gender, it is significant that the film omits entirely the narrative of pregnancy and betrayal, focusing solely on the conflicts and tensions wrought by the presence of racial differences. This change is an interesting reconfiguration, suggesting that race has superseded sexual difference as a cultural priority, at least in the register of 1980s popular culture. But we can also read the film's narrative transformation as a consolidation of race and gender, since the elimination of Annie Gervais does not evacuate the symbolics of sexual difference altogether. Instead, it tellingly shifts such symbolics (through the matrimonial metaphor, for instance) from the white female to the black male, from heterosexual to homosocial bonds. Such a translation of the locus of sexual difference in this and other interracial male bonding scenarios inaugurates a narrative trajectory in which the black male, in being representationally condensed with the feminine, must subsequently be rescued from it. Such a complicated narrative symbolic – aligning the black male with the feminine in order to liberate him from it – clearly redraws the representational, not to mention disciplinary, practices of an earlier era. However, it does so in ways that disturbingly refigure, indeed recuperate white masculine hegemony in the post-civil rights years.

In *The Lords of Discipline*, set in Charleston, South Carolina, in 1964, the rescue of the black male from the feminine takes place in the context of an integrationist event: his entrance as the first African-American cadet into the institute. This entrance threatens the sacred circle of the ring by exposing how the institute's most prized ethos, masculinity, rests on an assumption of white racial superiority. Even Bear (Robert Prosky), the officer who assigns McLean (David Keith) to protect Pearce (Mark Breland) from racist attacks, admits, "Yeah, I'm a racist. I'd like nothing better than to see Mr. Pearce move his black ass right out of here... [but] Pearce is one of my lambs and all of my lambs get an even break." Bear's attitude paradoxically affirms racism at the same time it establishes a seemingly democratic perspective, one that promises fair treatment in the face of gross bigotry. This paradox governs the film, shaping as well the perspective of the central hero, McLean, whose rebellion against the corruption of the institute nonetheless becomes the means for fulfilling its goal of setting America "on the right path again." The contradictions embedded in McLean's heroic white masculinity are perhaps best revealed in his answer to the question, "Was it worth it...four years down the drain for a nigger?" "It wasn't for the nigger. It was never for the nigger." This phrase, reverberating not only throughout this film but across the many cultural texts that feature interracial male bonds, demonstrates how the integration of the black male into the sacred circle of the masculine – an integration that significantly rescues him from the historical elision with the feminine – is never "for the nigger," but for the white man so that, as Tradd St. Croix (Mitchell Lichtenstein) says to McLean, "*you* could be a hero."

The ideological project of *The Lords of Discipline*, its construction of an interracial male bond as the precondition for asserting the white male's heroic marginality, is evinced most strongly in the symbolic and narrative relations governing Pearce, the black cadet whose desire for "democratic" opportunity brings upon him the wrath of "The Ten," a secret group of cadets dedicated to preserving the white legacy of the institute. The Ten use a variety of means, including torture, to police and instantiate a normative masculinity among the new cadets, driving out those deemed weak and unprepared for the rigors of military manhood. But the entrance of the first black cadet brings a new focus to the group, one through which blackness, as linked to sexual difference, is cast as equally excessive to the institute's ideal of masculinity.[7] In this context, it is not surprising that for the first half of the film, Pearce's masculinity is in question, and hence the various modes of harassment inflicted on him test the limits not simply of his convictions, but of his ability to survive the feminizing threat of castration. In an early scene, for instance, he is forced to perform pull-ups with a saber strategically placed to pierce his crotch should his strength fail. Later, he finds a burning effigy in his room, hung lynch style and summoning the historic equation of lynching with castration. Then in the final torture scene, where he finally promises to leave the institute, gasoline has been poured over his genitals and The Ten stand poised to set him on fire.

But this is no narrative of the black man's defeat through corporeal dismember-ment, as castration is the symbolic figure belonging to the segregationist, not integrationist era. And the crucial element of the integrationist narrative is the white man's intercession into the scene of genital mutilation, an intercession that preserves the black male's social and corporeal signification as male. In *The Lords of Discipline*, Pearce's struggle for racial equality is thus contingent on McLean's disruption of The Ten's torture, and it is significant that such disruption emerges through the invocation of his masculine bonds with a different group of white men: "I'm putting our friendship on the line," McLean tells his friends, "Now, how about it?" Thus pitting a renegade white male group against the Klan-like society of The Ten, the film posits racial equality as an issue between white men – and, more important, between a white supremacist cultural order and its reconsti-tution as democratic possibility. In this way, the integrationist rhetoric of the film reconstructs the historic injustices of segregation by fashioning a new tradition of action and authority through which white masculine power can exert itself. Indeed, the final words spoken by Pearce, addressed to McLean – "thank you, sir" – reinforce both the subserviency of his representation and the emergent and importantly reconfigured hegemony of the white male role.

The historical irony of this narrative turn is a powerful indication of the need to negotiate masculine relations in the contemporary era, a need inaugurated during radical decades of the twentieth century by moves away from segregationist toward integrationist representational and cultural practices.... [T]he articulation of the African-American male as a threat to the white woman and white civilization and the transformation of this discursive tableau by black revolutionary politics have shifted the conditions under which the category black male is now culturally produced. To a great extent, as I will explore in the following pages, it is through the circulating specter of the African-American male that the white masculine renegotiates its own "singular voice," establishing a system in which the question of race and racial equality can only be answered through a struggle posed between and for white men. In the seeming equality of a post-1960s society, the "brother-hood of the ring" remains a white construct, one through which the historical struggle for racial equality as a hallmark of "America" was, and continues to be, "never for the nigger."

Negotiating the Masculine

Given the consequences of this production of "America," it is perhaps no surprise that the two "classic" bonding films – *The Defiant Ones* (dir. Stanley Kramer, 1958) and *In the Heat of the Night* (dir. Norman Jewison, 1967) – straddle some of the most turbulent years of racial protest and violence in US history, interpreting that history in ways that say a great deal about the political investments of African-American male representation: on one hand, the darkly hopeful Huck Finn dream of two men on the run from white civilization (and white women) and, on the other, the integration narrative that links black and white across the discourse of cultural law and order. These two images of outlaw and officer are stock roles in interracial male bonding narration in the second half of the twentieth century, and in this they represent the mutually exclusive but ideologically conflated indexes of the African-American male's contradictory social position. Alternately aligned with margin and center, the African-American male traverses the boundaries of "difference," moving from criminal excess to central authority and thereby rearticulating his image in defiance of the segregationist codes to which he was heir.

In constructing African-American male representation within a framework that can accommodate his movement between margin and center – as outlaw and lawman, black and male – contemporary interracial male bonding narratives use his traversal of seemingly rigid categories of cultural (dis)empowerment as the vehicle for the white man's own rhetorical extrication from the role of "oppressor," making possible a rearticulation of the locus of cultural power and domination that seems to negate the historical supremacy ascribed to the white male. Through the representational framework of bonds with black men, the white masculine is cast as an oscillating and at times indeterminate formation, one marked by the relations of domination but no longer central to their articulation. As a consequence, the overdetermination of phallic authority within the interracial male bond can serve as the privileged emblem of nonhierarchical structures, reining black men into the ideological orbit of patriarchal relations while casting the white male as both victim of the social order and its potential hero. Through such narratives, the white masculine voice that has been attacked and silenced in the wake of black and feminist discourses can make claims for its own cultural exclusion, reasserting its "singular voice for the first time."

Such a representational strategy participates in the process of "remasculinization" that Susan Jeffords cites as central to contemporary modes of US cultural production, where "[w]ith the advent of women's rights, civil rights, the 'generation gap,' and other alterations in social relations . . . the stability of the ground on which patriarchal power rests was challenged" (Jeffords: 1989: xi–xii). This challenge resulted not in a complete negation of the patriarchal project but in large-scale renegotiations of structures of power in the 1970s and 1980s. As Jeffords defines it, the primary mechanism for this renegotiation is "a revival of the images, abilities, and evaluations of men and masculinity" – a remasculinization most apparent, she contends, in contemporary filmic and televisual depictions of the Vietnam War where the masculine "place[s] itself . . . [as] a social group in need of special consideration. No longer the oppressor, men came to be seen, primarily through the image of the Vietnam veteran, as themselves oppressed" (1989: xii, 169). John Wheeler's summation of the war is perhaps most telling: "the Vietnam veteran was the nigger of the 1970s" (Wheeler 1984: 16), he writes, a formulation which, as Jeffords notes, clears the space of cultural marginalization of its historical occupants and reoccupies it with the seemingly decentered masculine voices that had once held sway in US culture. This articulation of the masculine as a category of oppression elides the specificity of racial violence attendant to all African-Americans, rejuvenating the masculine not simply in the context of, but in the service of white supremacy as well.[8] In the figuration of the vet as nigger, we witness the integrationist strategy in which the implicit feminization of race found throughout nineteenth- and twentieth-century US life is superseded by a supreme and supremely coveted masculinization.

The remasculinization project Jeffords describes emerges as one bound to a double rhetorical move: by recasting the masculine as the newly marginalized position in US culture and shifting the historically oppressed toward the center, an image of social relations can be constructed that posits the white masculine, in the guise of the veteran, "as emblematic of the condition of all American men, not just those who went to war" (Jeffords 1989: 135). According to Jeffords, this homogenization of the masculine as a newly defined category of difference, competing in the cultural marketplace against other kinds of identity-based interests, operates through the mythos of male bonding where the masculine "poses survival – finally the survival of masculinity itself – as depending on the exclusion of women and the feminine, a world in which men are not significantly different from each other and boundaries of race, class … and ethnicity are [seemingly] overcome" (p. 168). While the discourse of sexual difference functions as the primary mechanism for regenerating the failure of masculinity signified by Vietnam, the cultural crisis evinced by the war and the recuperatory practices currently at work to negotiate its effects are not limited solely to gender, but work across the various categories of difference that give shape and substance to US hierarchical arrangements.[9]

For these reasons, we can read contemporary proliferations of interracial male bonding narratives as equally powerful and often overlapping instances of the remasculinization process Jeffords sets forth, where the ideological investments of regenerating the masculine are done to rearticulate dominant relations not just between men and women but, significantly, among men themselves. In such a process, the African-American male's inclusion in the separate world of the masculine is accomplished by detaching him from the historical context of race and installing him instead within the framework of gender. Here, the homosocial bond's assertion of a stridently undifferentiated masculine space can function to veil its simultaneous rejuvenation of racial hierarchies. Through these mechanizations, the African-American male's access to masculine power, contingent on his bodily presence as visible difference, disturbingly ignores contemporary modes of social and economic disempowerment. This diffusion of the hierarchical realms of race and gender demonstrates that it is the masculine that most strenuously (re)constructs the cultural status of the African-American male, making his greatest enemy not the feminine as the male bonding narrative often depicts but, through the brotherhood of the ring, the masculine itself.

The Lineage of Forefathers

The emphasis in bonding narratives on the rearticulation of the white masculine's "singular voice" constructs a new mythology of origins, one through which the white masculine perspective is cast as the originary term in the eradication of racism and hence as the potential site for democracy's achievement. In important ways, such a narrative strategy addresses the contemporary concerns about history, identity, and difference recently collected under the term "multiculturalism" by foregrounding the crisis attending the white masculine position, now pressured to relinquish its historical centrality to a diverse array of counternarratives. In the male bonding scenario, the multicultural comes to be figured in the contact between the white male and his racially different brother, and the narrative of their meeting, friendship, and most often tragic split offers a reconstructed conclusion to the painful history that Western imperialism has spawned. It is this reconstruction that addresses past conquests performed by and in the service of white men, simultaneously drawing global history as a drama, once again, that pivots on the actions of white men. The new mythology of origins, as we will see, is new only to the extent that it begins in the recognition of a national or global history of violence and disempowerment based on race. Its conclusion, as in *The Lords of Discipline*, establishes masculine sameness between men while consigning African-American male subjectivity to the contours of white masculinity.

In utilizing the narrative strategy of acknowledgment followed by negation-through-integration, *The Lords of Discipline* gave way in 1985 to *Enemy Mine* (dir. Wolfgang Petersen), a film overtly obsessed with the global history of imperialism and slavery that characterizes human activity on earth. Instead of forging its obsession as a critique of Western economic interests, the film narrates the imperialist's confrontation with cultural differences by offering the white male a new mythology of origins, one in which his historical position of privilege is exchanged for a heroic place alongside the oppressed. Here, the threat often attributed to multiculturalism of eradicating the history and achievements of white (and) masculine "civilization" is warded off by a glorious embrace of difference that preserves the centrality of the white male as it offers the specular assurance that race and gender have been represented and addressed. Such a strategy, akin in my mind to the political effectivity found in the quest to transform – through inclusion – the canon, maintains the emphasis on white and masculine sameness, forcing the historical relationship between margin and center to be leveled by a pervasive neocolonial ideology. In short, the white and Western foundation remains. This is not to say that multiculturalism has no radical pedagogical potential, but that its political effect is finally neither pure nor secure. Indeed, its claim to eradicate the systemic inadequacies of US education may be another way for white Americans, in particular, to grasp difference in its most abstract and disembodied form, a grasping that has as its political consequence a further taming of those "differences" historically aligned with the margins.

It is just this kind of taming that seems to be at work in *Enemy Mine*, though the body of the other – if I can use a phrase so laced with imperial ideology – is anything but abstract. In fact, in refashioning the traditional interracial male bonding scenario as an intergalactic sci-fi story, *Enemy Mine* presents the dark buddy as quite literally an alien. A reptilian figure, Jerry (played by Louis Gossett Jr.) stands in stark contrast to Willis Davidge (Dennis Quaid), the alien's altogether human, white, and male counterpart. In casting the black actor as alien and his white bonding buddy as human, the film conjures up a long tradition of black stereotypes in US culture, where African Americans have been cast in the role of the white man's nonhuman other, the dark beast, the alien outsider who threatens the sanctity of the cultural order.[10] Such a representation repeats the now-classic structure of the colonial encounter: corporeal essence is defined and symbolized according to the logic of the visible, and hierarchical arrangements are naturalized in the dyadic relationship between identity and difference. Within this structure, the alien body can only take its narrative place within an overarching contradiction, becoming the site for the nostalgic dream of bonding across incommensurate difference, while serving as the very signpost – the corporeal evidence – that sanctions, indeed reassures us, that the dream and its miscegenating potential remain impossibilities.

If the film presents difference along the lines of a human/alien contrast, what textual specificities underwrite my assumption that the film is in fact a racial allegory? Is Gossett's own racial categorization ample cause for reading nonhuman alterity as a symbol of blackness, thereby understanding the film as marking blackness as alien to humanity, indeed as alien to the "human" itself? The opening words of the film, spoken in voice-over by the white male, help sort this out by shaping the narrative context, the latter part of the twenty-first century, as a neocolonial racial encounter. As Davidge, whose quest throughout the movie is the transformation of this "enemy" into "mine," tells us, "the nations of the Earth were finally at peace working together to explore and colonize the distant reaches of space. Unfortunately we weren't alone out there. A race of nonhuman aliens called the Dracs were claiming squatters' rights to some of the richest star systems in the galaxy. Well, they weren't going to get it without a fight." In positing the nonhuman as a difference of "race," Davidge's description simultaneously asserts Earth's transcendence of its violent imperialist struggles and defines space as the new arena for the exertion of colonial control – a representational scenario in which a "healed" human culture can disavow its historical inequities by reconstituting the imperialist tableau in an extraterrestrial domain. In the process, the casting of Gossett as the Drac (named Jerry by Davidge later in the film) must be viewed as hardly coincidental, for it is precisely his "blackness" that functions as the absent presence throughout the film.

While the film appears to offer a confrontation with new, unknown life – the fantasy of science fiction – its pursuit of the mythology of the interracial male bond, set now in the space world of the twenty-first century, is all pervasive. In this scripting of the bond, Davidge and Jerry become stranded on an uncolonized planet where they are forced to learn to overcome their "races'" untamed hostility toward one another for the sake of mutual survival and to articulate, as they say, a "love [that] might unite them." The overtones here of the matrimonial metaphor aptly mark the interplay of race and gender at work in the film and carry us into that now familiar discursive landscape where the black male figure is positioned *vis-à-vis* the white male within both the very space and symbolic locus of the feminine. But this positioning is neither simple nor direct. Indeed, the film goes to great lengths to translate the alien's evocation of the feminine into a post-gender sphere. Like the difference of race that underlies the alien's alterity, however, the Drac's relation to the feminine is only initially veiled. This veiling takes its most overt form in the Drac's characterization as androgynous, but it is an androgyny that, as we will see, simultaneously invokes the feminine and presents it as the very difference from which the human must finally rescue the alien.

The great rescue from the feminine takes place during a birthing scene, where the androgynous Drac (whose swelling belly the film has visually charted), encounters complications and must turn to Davidge for help. Here, as the alien lies groaning in the throes of childbirth, the process of birthing as a function of the feminine is simultaneously asserted and disavowed:

> *Drac*: Something is wrong.
> *Human*: Oh no...you're going to be all right. Women always get nervous before labor.
> *Drac*: I AM NOT A WOMAN.

In Davidge's naming of the Drac as woman and in the Drac's adamant denial, this interracial bonding scene replays, albeit in the intergalactic register, the complex representational history governing black men in US culture. Though the layers of narrative reframing make the race/gender axis the unspoken absence of this science fiction, it is in the disparity between the discursive negation of the feminine and the corporeal figuration of the Drac as pregnant that racial alterity is joined to gender. And while it is the white male who consigns the Drac to the feminine, the alien's translation of the film's pretense of androgyny to not-woman demonstrates in broad allegorical strokes the contestation framing black male representation in the post-civil rights years.

Ultimately, the ideological movement of the film is uninterested in the significance of the black male's disavowal, and it is to the white man's intercession in black male feminization that the narrative quickly turns. Before "Jerry" dies, with the child kicking beneath the scaly folds of the belly, Davidge is instructed: "You must open me. Don't be afraid, my friend." While Davidge is initially horrified at both the instructions and "Jerry's" death, he tears open the pregnant womb with his fingers, pulling the baby from the dead body. By birthing Zammis, Davidge appropriates the feminine activity of reproduction to himself without any question of gender confusion: the possibility of his "being woman" is eradicated in the construction of birth as a masculine activity of tearing. This intercession significantly rescues the alien from the potential castration implicit in birthing (remember, there was no disavowal that the Drac was not a man), and hence makes possible the symbolic interchange between and reduction of androgyny to the masculine. The category "women" has thus been superseded in this film by the white masculine, which overcomes, in a simultaneous move, the threats of racial and sexual difference by "occupying" through this reproductive scenario the alien position altogether.

Through this series of interchanges and the narrative's subsequent plotting, *Enemy Mine* reconstructs the colonial encounter by rendering the white man's intercession as the very means for saving the alien culture. Following Jerry's death, Davidge works to fulfill his "sacred vow" to raise the child, Zammis, and to

eventually return it to its home planet. In this process, Davidge becomes em-
broiled with other humans who, through the labor of enslaved Dracs, begin
colonizing the far side of the planet. By saving Zammis from colonization and
enslavement – and liberating all the Dracs from the labor camp – Davidge eventually earns himself a place in the Draconian song of lineage. As the voice-over at the
conclusion states: "[a]nd so Davidge brought Zammis and the Dracs home. He
fulfilled his vow and recited the line of Zammis's *forefathers* [emphasis added]
before the holy council on Dracon. And when, in the fullness of time, Zammis
brought its own child before the Holy Council, the name of Willis Davidge was
added to the line." In this resolution, the colonial relationship between human
and Drac is thus seemingly undone when the human (read: white man) enters the
alien (read: black man) discourse, making himself both its savior and forebear. If
the narrative force of the androgynous as vehicle for white masculinization had not
been clear before, its overt equation is now complete, as Draconian history and
memory emerge as a lineage of "forefathers."

But what of Jerry? Significantly, his role in procreation has been eradicated,
displaced by the primacy of white paternity. This narrative resolution quite stun-
ningly recalls the slave economy of the Old South, where the black male's position
in reproduction is denied as paternity is signified almost exclusively in the figure of
the white male. But this is the Old South with all of its complicated twists, for this
white father is also the quintessential abolitionist, and it is in the dream wish of
abolition that the full eradication of the black male is achieved. In the era of
integrationist aesthetics, this outcome – this redrawing of white masculine hegemony as the ethical commitment to end racist injustice – is part of the anxious quest
to own the margins, even if the center is beginning to heave. In giving birth to the
Other (Zammis), Davidge confirms, in a necessary recreation of white masculine
hegemony, his own status as savior of alien discourses, while also confirming that
those alien discourses are themselves not alien to the white masculine. In such a
scenario, gender as an initially ambiguous and transitory state veils the underlying
struggle *within* the broad contours of the masculine by positing difference in
sexual terms and thereby obscuring the alien's affinity to the masculine itself.[11]

The narrative trajectory of *Enemy Mine* thus addresses the fear of masculine
sameness through a complicated process of signification: in aligning difference –
both racial and sexual – with the alien, the white male's quest for a reinvigorated
place in history begins with his ability to dissociate the alien from the feminine
before inserting himself into alien culture as its forefather. The integrationist
narrative of the black male's defeminization (his adamant refusal of being
woman) becomes, then, the very vehicle for the white male's new role as protector
and historian of the cultural (and colonial) margins. The film's emphasis on the
Drac's physical difference, his reptilian features and bisexual reproductive capacities, evokes the damning bestiality and femininity simultaneously inscribed in segregationist narratives – and it demands, for the final mutuality of the interracial male
bond, a rescue of the alien from the body. In so doing, in intercepting Jerry from
the castrating birth of his femininity, and in revealing, through his paternal relation
to Zammis, the racial in-difference of this colonial relation, *Enemy Mine* achieves
the full force of integration's effect: the reconstruction of the white masculine,
which, appropriating cultural difference through the alien, can proceed to embody,
without corporeal threat, all difference within itself. Where *The Lords of Discipline*

fully disposes of the narrative of gender and inscribes the white man as the leader in the struggle for civil rights, *Enemy Mine* occupies all positions of difference, the white man "fulfill[ing] his vow" in a sweeping recuperation that is the mark of the contemporary period.

America

But why not read *Enemy Mine* as a critique of white masculine hegemony in which the white male's connection to "the Other" is rearticulated as an anti-colonial bond? After all, Davidge does heed the call to fight the colonial incursion through which Dracs are turned into slaves. Is there nothing politically portentous about a film that depicts the white male as recognizing his own imbrication in issues of racism and colonialism? Are there, in short, only recuperative strategies at work in cultural narratives of interracial male bonds? While it may be difficult, given my reading of *Enemy Mine*, to view these questions as something more than rhetorical dead ends, it would be problematical to entirely dismiss the utopianism that underlies the figuration of interracial bonding. For the dream of the post-colonial, post-segregationist moment, of the possibility of bonding across racial difference, is no politically insignificant wish. In a nation whose self-identity is so deeply formed around the democratic – around the inculcation of difference into the framework of a citizen "same" – the confrontation in which difference is articulated and some fundamental affinity or similarity affirmed has long been the political hope for hierarchical subversion.

The question on which my readings of these films turn, however, concerns the possibility of difference to maintain its autonomy, the possibility for a *mutuality of difference* to stand as the fundamentally ethical relationship, a moment of kinship, if you will, that does not settle back into the body of the same. This is a seemingly impossible hope in the context of mainstream cultural production, particularly Hollywood film, since its version of the relationship between identity and difference is so territorially tied in the contemporary era to the representational propulsion of integration. Not that African-American characters are populating filmic productions in any equitable way, but the marketing logic of film (like television) is at pains to negotiate the multiculturalism of US culture and that culture's historic reliance on the ideological supremacy of everything white, heterosexual, and male. It is this negotiation and the theoretical apparatuses we employ to read, understand, and plot to subvert it that interest me, in both a pedagogical and a political vein. These films do function as scenes of instruction for the construction of this nation's most pervasive and contested ideology, "America." As such, the realm of the popular, of popular cinematic productions, cannot be dismissed as either simple or vulgar, as mere perversions of a truer consciousness that lies elsewhere. Instead, popular cinema, like the host of interracial buddy narratives it has spawned, partakes in the very meaning of "America": that rhetoric of nation, narrative of origin, and abstracted locus of supposedly equal entitlements.

Indeed, it is the inability of "America" to function as a transhistorical sign that necessitates its reiterative production. And it is at the site of interracial male bonds that popular culture in the 1980s most repetitively struggled to rehabilitate "America" from its segregationist as well as its imperialist past. In the bonds'

quest for a self-enclosed, racially undifferentiated masculine space, cultural production casts its net around a reconfiguration of "America," providing narrative
trajectories that pivot on the confrontation with difference and its ultimate shim-
mering transcendence. This confrontation and transcendence is itself the narrative
trope of "America," its most prized and evoked ontology. But in the need for its
representational replay, we witness one of the ways the contemporary crisis of the
masculine expresses itself: caught in its most complex contradiction – between the
assertion of masculine sameness and the (re)construction of difference in the face
of that sameness – the interracial male bonding narrative embodies the oscillation
of "America," constructing on one hand the ideological dream of cohesion, of an
essential, uniform masculine identity, while forging, on the other, discriminations
that qualify and specify the boundaries of that identity.

In the broad terrain of "America," the tension produced through this contradiction allows for various discourses to gain visibility in US culture – the inculcation of seemingly marginalized voices acting as the necessary proof of
"America's" democratic possibility. In this process, where the materiality of cultural relations are superseded by the dreamscape of "America's" production, we
encounter what Sacvan Bercovitch calls the "American form," that transformation
of "what might have been a confrontation of alternatives into an alternation of
opposites" (1986: 438). Bercovitch's description characterizes, to a certain scary
extent, the dynamic of US culture production, where the conflation of identity and
history into binary oppositions – in Bercovitch's terms, fusion or fragmentation,
myth or material existence – enables the apparent opposition to be absorbed by
and set to work for its antithesis. As such, heterogenous elements can be homogenized in the enunciation of a seemingly larger cultural identity, one that incorporates the radical multiplicity inherent in the disparate cultural identities that have
converged on the Native Indian soil of North America. As Bercovitch writes,
"[t]echnology and religion, individualism and social progress, spiritual, political
and economic values – all the fragmented aspects of life and thought...
flowed into 'America,' the symbol of cultural consensus" (1981: 27). In this
process, of course, consensus is radically displaced by its symbolic production,
which in turn functions as the simulacra of consensus.

"America," in other words, becomes the repository for its own ideological and
rhetorical ideals, the means for the reification of "nation." But it is not only so-
called dominant discourses that partake in this reification, for the process of
articulating "America" has been a crucial component in the construction and
negotiation of counterdiscourses as well. In the case of civil rights struggle, for
instance (whether for race, gender, or sexual "preference"), the historic argument
for inclusion has always been set within the overarching sign of "America": equal
rights equals the achievement of America's democratic ideals. In the contemporary
era, we are witnessing how this idea of rights can be turned into the means for
garnering protection for the historically privileged, so that whites, men, and
heterosexuals can claim – and have been winning their claims in court – their
right to exclude and discriminate. As Bercovitch has discussed, "[t]he same ideals
that at one point nourish [or challenge] the system may later become the basis of a
new revolutionary [or conservative] consensus, one that invokes those ideas on
behalf of an entirely different way of life" (1986: 431). As such, the question of
politics in the contemporary era cannot continue to rely on mid-century strategies

of cultural dissent, for the framework of inclusion, visibility, and rights has become, in the mythology of "American" consensus, the very means for appropriating the radical portent of 1960s politics into the reconstructed image of "America's" post-segregationist content.

In the transformation and reappropriation of cultural discourses of identity and difference, we can perhaps see how narratives of interracial male bonds – while not essentially conservative – can nonetheless facilitate this process of reiterating "America," manipulating the very racial and sexual tensions that propelled political movements three decades ago. By refiguring the center as margin, these narratives offer images of a completed social revolution, creating a post-1960s egalitarianism that absorbs the threat of racial dissonance into a reconstructed mythology of US cultural relations, a mythology that is itself enacted through marginalized appeals to the ideological ideal of "America." Because of this appeal to the actualization of "America," the hegemonic response to challenge can be measured through economic, social, and political gains that reaffirm dominant cultural values, redistributing certain components of cultural power (enhancing the size of the black middle class, for instance) without wholly changing the social contract through which that power is articulated.

The importance of this reconstruction as a new narrative of "America" cannot be underestimated, as the proliferation of bonding scenarios in the contemporary period also works within the politics of US-defined global arrangements. The remapping of race relations supports ideologically the imperialistic moves by the United States, simultaneously creating a powerful self-image as a purified moral center, while fashioning itself as vanguard of human rights and dignity to the "third world." Ironically, *Enemy Mine*'s narrative explanation of a peaceful human community in conflict with aliens over squatters' rights recreates the relations of exploitation attending America's contemporary activities. As a precondition for movement beyond the geographical borders of nation (or Earth-as-nation in *Enemy Mine*), it becomes necessary to assert moral superiority based on an already-secured political position. In *Enemy Mine* this means that difference as the grounds for hierarchical relations is located in the star systems. Thus the film enacts a symbolic replay of US culture in the 1980s in which Cold War politics forge a disavowal of internal racial hierarchies through the representation of hierarchy elsewhere. . . .

The Positive Image

. . . [T]he image of the black male as . . . citizen and father is . . . not a new narrative strategy within scenarios of the interracial male bond. Its more traditional configuration – the black male as cop, symbolic father of the cultural order – is a major trope in popular US narration of the past twenty years. In what was perhaps the first of its kind, *In the Heat of the Night* (1967), for instance, the African-American male is a homicide detective, his knowledge and training essential to the restoration of order in a small Mississippi town.[12] Such a construction of the black officer as fighting not with brawn but with intelligence helps to settle that era's fear of racial violence by locating black masculinity on the side of cultural law and order. In the contemporary era, the black cop figure functions in much the same way, establishing masculinity as the necessary force for the protection of US culture and containing, in the process, the specter of open black rebellion. By extending a strenuous masculinity to black men, the black cop figure can work to transform his potential subversion of US culture into affirmation, protection, and appeal – through presence and visibility – to democratic enunciations. This transformation is remarkably facilitated within configurations of the interracial male bond in which the loyalty between black and white men can outweigh the cultural power imbalances between them, where "the love [that] might unite them" can evince an America where "things have changed."

As guardian of law and order, the black police figure plays out the role of cultural father, a role crucial to the remasculinization project of contemporary decades in which, in the face of a cultural economy that had been radically disrupted, the resurrection of the father in his many cultural guises is essential to the reestablishment of the masculine as the site for healing and wholeness. Through the black father figure, dominant discourses provide images of individual African-American males that offer the appearance of a reconfigured US culture. While this reconfiguration can be witnessed in material practices as strategies of inclusion (affirmative action and the often tokenistic use of African-Americans as visible presences in otherwise all-white institutions), white supremacy is not necessarily dislodged but rather disguised and repressed. Most disturbing is the fact that while images of the interracial male bond and its rhetoric of democracy allow greater visibility for some black male actors and politicians, the same is not true for African-American women whose representational visibility has in fact decreased in the cultural obsession with narrations of differences among men. Indeed, as the threat of racial difference is worked through the remasculinization project, the political, economic, legal, and social status of African-American women will pay the heaviest price in the cultural rehabilitation of the white masculine.

Where her exiled image haunts most interracial bonding narratives – *The Defiant Ones, In the Heat of the Night, Shoot to Kill* – it is significant that the popular 1987 film, *Lethal Weapon* (dir. Richard Donner), manipulates the image of the black woman as evidence of US cultural achievement; no longer the traditional stereotypes of mammy or whore, here, in a film featuring the black male as both father and police officer, she is offered the seemingly egalitarian roles of wife and daughter. In a grand reversal of cultural stereotypes, the African-American woman now occupies the traditional images of the white woman: tied completely to the bourgeois family, she exists both as the housewife Trish Murtaugh (Darlene Love) whose "bad cooking" becomes a joke between men and as the virginal daughter Rianne Murtaugh (Traci Wolfe) who must be saved by them. While for some readers the representation of black women in the more traditional roles of wife, mother, and virginal daughter might signal a positive representational shift, offering as it does black access to the realm of bourgeois culture widely denied until the civil rights era, it would be a mistake to view such representation as evidence of the black woman's real advancement in the struggle for race and gender equality. Indeed, as Robert Stam and Louise Spence write, "[t]he insistence on 'positive images' . . . obscures the fact that 'nice' images might at times be as pernicious as overtly degrading ones, providing a bourgeois facade for paternalism, a more pervasive racism" (1983: 3). The bourgeois facade of *Lethal Weapon* operates, in fact, to tie the black woman to a heterosexual economy in which her body functions not only, in the role of wife, as the plot space for the establishment of a normative (hetero)sexuality but also, in the role of virginal daughter, as the landscape across which interracial masculine bonds can be both formed and maintained.

Most specifically, by focusing its action on the interracial relation of Roger Murtaugh (Danny Glover) and Martin Riggs (Mel Gibson), *Lethal Weapon* seeks to override the potential disruption caused by race by establishing bourgeois culture as the signifier of racial *in*difference while constructing gender as the only significant, and seemingly natural, category of differentiation. All notions of historically constructed differences among black and white are thus recast as a function of capitalist attainment, and the spectacle of middle-class life provides the representation of America with an embodiment of its own democratic ideals. While the alignment of the black female with the representational space most often reserved for white women inculcates her into this democratic ethos, it is the relationship between black and white men that functions as the film's pivotal site for democratic wholeness: the black woman achieves her status only through the black male's connection to, and reaffirmation of, hegemonic power itself. Thus, in *Lethal Weapon*, the image of the black woman circulates in an economy of masculine power where racial differences among men are seemingly eradicated and the democratic rhetoric that has often historically accompanied US patriarchal power is reinscribed.

Like other interracial cop scenarios, *Lethal Weapon* is constructed on a basic pattern. By initially depicting the contrary lives of Murtaugh and Riggs, who are thrown together as partners against their wishes, the film charts their growing respect and affection for one another. Displacing racial difference into less volatile forms such as age, lifestyle, and mental health, *Lethal Weapon* begins in contrast: while Murtaugh enjoys a bath in his well-decorated home with his wife and children singing happy birthday to him, Riggs is shown lying in bed smoking a cigarette, his mobile home wracked by debris. Suicidal because of the recent death of his wife, Riggs is psychically lost, the squalor of his environment indicative of his alienation from the commodified heterosexual norm that the black family represents. In an interesting reversal of paternalistic ideology, it is the white male who, debilitated by grief, can be restored to life only through the aid of the black "father" – the figure responsible, in the film's resolution, for drawing the alienated white male back into the folds of sanity and the bourgeois family. Earlier cinematic versions of African-Americans as alienated outsiders are refused in the narrative economy of *Lethal Weapon*, which provides a representation that shifts the terms of US racial structures: the white male is both victimized – by fate (his wife's death), by his peers (who think he's crazy), and by himself (his suicidal tendencies) – and significantly rehabilitated from such victimization with the help of a black man. At its deepest level, *Lethal Weapon*'s evocation of a world beyond race enables the white male to regain identity and power across a seemingly egalitarian representation of the black bourgeoisie.

We Do This My Way

Most important perhaps, it is Riggs, a martial arts specialist, who emerges as central in the duo's quest to unravel a suspicious suicide. When Murtaugh's daughter, Rianne, is abducted by the men who orchestrated the suicide, Riggs goes on the offensive: "We do this my way," he tells Murtaugh. "You shoot, you shoot to kill. You get as many as you can." In the process, the white male body becomes the privileged emblem of masculinity in the film, a privileging that begins in the initial scenes where, in contrast to Murtaugh in a bubble bath, the camera follows Riggs's naked figure from his bedroom to the kitchen. In viewing the male body from behind, the camera avoids not simply an X rating, but the castration implicit in the voyeuristic look at male genitalia outside a scene of sexual activity, that is, outside erection and the displacement of desire onto the presence of the female body. In denying the sight of the penis, the film both represses the construction of the spectator's gaze within a homosexual economy of desire and reinscribes the penis as the phallus: Riggs's entire body, in its muscularity and strength, continually evokes the absent penis. Because, as Neale writes, "there is no cultural or cinematic convention which would allow the male body to be presented," the penis itself becomes unrepresentable except as the phallus (1983: 14).

In this representational process, "male" sexuality – the sighting of sex/genitalia – is transformed into a culturally constructed "masculine" sexuality in which the white male body achieves power and privilege in its reconstruction as stand-in for the absent penis. White masculine sexuality thus presents itself within an economy of desire greater than its parts, a desire through which the overdetermined evocation of parts (the phallus that proliferates in the absence of the penis) wards off castration by reconstructing itself everywhere. The film's various moments of looking at Riggs reclining, running, falling, fighting, shooting are affirmations that the threat of castration has not simply been averted but that the body has now become the phallus, literalizing itself in various displays of phallic authority as the "lethal weapon." In a key scene, Riggs, tortured until he becomes unconscious, hangs by rope from the ceiling when suddenly he springs back to life, attacking his captor and strangling the man with his legs. In a symbolic denouncement of castration, Riggs's body evinces its own phallicism, the villain's neck being literally snapped in the powerful crotch of the hero.

The construction of the white masculine body thus pivots on an exchange from its presentation in the opening scene as the site of the voyeuristic gaze to this later evocation of phallic activity and mastery. To deny our contemplation of Riggs's body in a scene of passive nudity or symbolic castration, in other words, enables the masculine body and its power before the gaze of the camera to not simply remain intact, but to exceed itself. This denial of the gaze stands in contrast to the film's articulation of the sexualized female body, which is overwhelmingly white. In the film's opening sequence, against which the credits are run, the white female body is established as the primary object of the voyeuristic gaze, providing the arena of visible difference across which interracial relations will be formed. From an aerial view of downtown San Francisco, the camera slowly focuses on Amanda Hunsaker (Jackie Swanson) who, clad in lace stockings, lingerie, and high heels, moves to the balcony, teeters briefly on its railing, and jumps. As her body crashes on top of a parked car, the voyeuristic gaze is so insistent that we look at it exposed, spread out *facing* the camera, her femininity – and hence her castration – open to view.

The look at Amanda's purely sexualized body, combined with the later narrative of Murtaugh's daughter, Rianne, whose chastity is threatened, establish what

Teresa de Lauretis calls "female-obstacle-boundary-space," that "landscape, stage, or portion of plot-space [where] the female character... represent[s] and literally mark[s] out the place (to) which the hero will cross" (1984: 121, 139). These women's bodies – as virgin (Rianne) and, as we find out later, as whore (Amanda) – evoke the classic construction of female sexuality, even as they invert the racial stereotypes that govern representational economies in US culture. This inversion is crucial to the integrationist narrative, where the sanitary normativity of all the sexual roles within the black family is a necessary precondition for its function as the emotional and moral rehabilitative center for the white male.

To complete the film's emphasis on normative sexuality, Amanda is revealed not only as whore but as lesbian, a revelation that displaces all homosexual tension between the closely bonded men onto white female sexuality. Significantly, the assertion of Amanda's lesbianism is made during a conversation between Riggs and Murtaugh at the police firing range, the woman's lesbianism being framed by images of the men firing their weapons. In this overdetermined phallic setting, Amanda's sexuality reaffirms the masculine as itself the site of heterosexual wholeness; in this way, white female sexuality, while initially charting a heterosexual space, is fully negated as the masculine comes to stand for all culturally accepted sexuality. The narrative of Amanda's sexuality and the images of her body thus function in two ways and, importantly, in this order: first to assert heterosexuality at the film's beginning so that the ensuing scenes of Riggs and Murtaugh naked are read as heterosexual and not homosexual,[13] and, second, to assume the sexual tensions between the men entirely to herself, to the white female and not the male or black female body. In her dual function, the representational paradigm governing the white female is resexualized and racially inverted from virgin/mother to lesbian/whore, so that all sites in this film of unproductive female sexuality leave the space of production entirely to the masculine.

In establishing this racially dichotomized paradigm of sexual difference as the frame of the film, masculine sexuality can appear to be constructed rather homogeneously, with no internal hierarchies or imbalances of power. This illusion is provided by the text of sexual difference, which diffuses and renders secondary the bond's reconstruction of racial difference; through the discourse of sexual difference, the interracial male bond can seal over the frisson of its own construction, enabling all differences among men to be subsumed in the seemingly natural realm of gender. In addition, differences among black and white women can be strengthened, as it is the white woman's death (and her sexually illicit lifestyle) that initiates the narrative drama that threatens both the sanctity and the individual lives of the black family.

While these configurations of race and gender enable the masculine to assume the appearance of homogeneity (and conversely to posit the feminine as the site of disunity and fragmentation), the relations of "looking" established in the film's final scene demonstrate the symbolic significance of the white masculine body as the lethal weapon and the consequent passive position assigned to the black male. Here, in the final confrontation, it is Riggs who does battle with the most hardened criminal, Joshua, while Murtaugh looks on. In his exclusion from the scene of phallic activity, Murtaugh's passive looking confirms his displacement within the field of the masculine, situating Murtaugh in league with the camera's phallicizing of the white male body and marking the black male as physically impotent. Such a construction of the white body as spectacle and the black male as spectator, activator of the look that empowers the white body, demonstrates the underlying representational paradigm of the interracial male bond. In this construction, the white masculine body retains its privilege as the primary site of power while the black masculine role is forced to the margins of the scene; Murtaugh's plea, "Let me take him," and Riggs's response, "No, back off," evince the narrative's inflection of this economy, where the lethal weapon of the white masculine body articulates itself as the central term.

While such a hierarchicalized articulation poses a threat to the democratic enunciations of the interracial bond, it is significant that in this scene the black male is allowed to symbolically take on the power of the white phallus, to appropriate its evocation of masculine sexuality and power. In a configuration of bodies recalling, through inversion, Ralph Ellison's "The Birthmark," the white male, at the conclusion of the fight, leans against Murtaugh, constructing them as one: the white male poses in front of Murtaugh, functioning as his symbolic phallus. When Joshua wrests a weapon from another officer and prepares to shoot, Murtaugh and Riggs respond by drawing their guns. Positioned together, the black male sheltering the white with his raincoat and his body, they shoot Joshua simultaneously. In this way, the scene charts the mastery of the white male body (its ultimate phallic authority) while displacing it in the fusion of an interracial configuration. Ellison's image of the castrated black male functioning as the phallus of his white assailant is thus reconstructed in the cultural production of the 1980s as the black male drawing his own phallic power through the appropriation of the white phallus, an inversion that is symptomatic of contemporary strategies of racial recuperation in US culture.

In characterizing the white male body as the lethal weapon, the film renegotiates its presentation of a world beyond racial difference, evincing within the remasculinization project that marks *Lethal Weapon* a subtle internal hierarchy. Indeed, Riggs's rehabilitation within the space of the black family is countered by his numerous acts of preserving it. In an early scene in the film, it is Riggs who saves Murtaugh's life, forcing the black male to apologize: "[l]ook, sorry about all that shit I said out there. You saved my life. Thank you." The privileging of Riggs is inscribed again when he is the first to escape from his captor, breaking into Murtaugh's torture chamber where the criminals are threatening to rape Rianne. Seconds before Riggs's entrance, the leader tries to silence the irate Murtaugh: "[s]pare me, son. There're no more heroes in the world." But, of course, there are heroes again, as Riggs's immediate appearance evinces, and it is no accident that the hero who comes bursting through the door, the hero who throws the body of his captor on top of an onrushing villain, the hero whose body is the lethal weapon that restores order to this post-1960s world, is white.[14]

An Endangered Species

In positing a racially healed America, *Lethal Weapon* and similar male bonding narratives of the 1980s demonstrate the rhetorical practices of contemporary US cultural production, practices that incorporate the images of black men in popular representation even as those who live under its categorical sign are increasingly displaced by social, political, and economic processes of exclusion. While the visibility of the African-American player in a narrative offering egalitarian possibility seemingly redistributes masculine power, its primary political effect is not only a reaffirmation of the masculine as the basis of cultural power but also a confirmation of the centrality of white supremacy. The remasculinization process functions, in other words, to disrupt *racial* challenges to white supremacy by negotiating that difference through an appeal to masculinity and gender solidarity, thereby making race itself appear to be a settled site on the cultural "frontier." Most crucially, in presenting this story of post-civil rights egalitarianism, the "singular voice" that emerges is that of the white masculine, which has spoken itself not "for the nigger" but for himself, so that he "could be [the] hero."[15]

While configurations of the interracial male bond seem obsessively drawn to these narrative typologies – routinely inverting the historical relationships between identity and cultural marginality – their repetitions are significant not as details of contemporary Hollywood film, but in their circulation within broader negotiatory mechanisms in US culture. David Duke, founder of the National Association for the Advancement of White People and contender for governor of Louisiana in 1991, demonstrates the extreme moment in cultural articulations of white masculine disenfranchisements in the post-civil rights years, articulations that have resulted in increasing support for his (and other similar) political aspirations. Regardless of the extent to which the Republican Party wished to dismiss Duke as eccentric to its overall agenda during the early stages of the presidential election in 1992, the significance of his inclusion in mainstream politics and the effectiveness of his inversion of the discourse of civil rights demonstrate the contextual parameters within which images of interracial male bonds currently play. Through this nexus, Duke's fusion of white supremacist logic with the rhetoric of cultural marginality serves as the far-right position of insecurity that interracial male bonds, in a more liberally configured public sphere, can subsequently heal. The bourgeois black male, supporter and defender of the family, ensconced in heterosexuality, and in debt (psychically, if not financially) to the heroic white male offers a scenario of cultural acceptance that not only reinscribes the supremacy of father/family/capital/heterosexuality but also implicitly criminalizes the categories of opposition on which these images of cultural centrality and normativity dwell.

In this regard, the gleaming positivity of black men in interracial male configurations serves as both the precondition for and symbolic achievement of integration's possibility, a possibility articulated within the normative categories instantiating the subject in US culture: masculinity, heterosexuality, and Anglo-American ethnicity. In the ascendancy of these normative positions and in the black male's representational inculcation into their systemic logic, integration entails a process of subjective identification, inscribing the black male within an economy of desire and prohibition that finally and paradoxically depends on the disavowal of differences. Such disavowal necessarily invites psychic violence, as the social subject is asked to identify, seemingly against himself, with a tableau of normativity that links race, in a complex and reinforcing pattern, to class, gender, and sexual hegemonies as well.[16] It is this link across categories of difference that binds the integrationist narrative to social determinations seemingly outside the scope of racial discourse. These representations of interracial male bonding level the threat of black male challenge to white supremacist power by reasserting, through the specter of bourgeois and heterosexual conformity, the patriarchal preconditions that have historically structured the illusion of coherence underwriting modern "man."

As this last comment suggests, what we make of the cultural fascination with interracial male bonding narratives is ultimately indicative of more than the integrationist aesthetic and its recuperation of the threat posed by twentieth-century social protest. It points as well to the enduring – and rapidly transforming – problem of vision and modernity, where the incorporation of the subject into visually coded corporeal identities takes center stage as the defining emblem of the public sphere. That these corporealities are predicated on asymmetries between bodies and their seeming ontologies is part of the racism that wends its way in various registers and modes of deployment through the US social formation, making the challenge of social protest not simply difficult – because uncertain – but often quite painful as well. In our seduction into the visual realm of culture, in our desire to find the visible liberating, in our subjective need to reclaim bodies from their abjection and recuperation, we encounter both the threat and the utopic possibility of contemporary social critique. To forge this critique as part of undoing the illusion of "man," of refusing the myth of masculinity's completion in an interracial domain devoid of women, is to expose the continuing rift within whiteness, that materially violent abstraction that perversely gathers strength by offering itself now as a struggling, innocent, and singular voice.

Notes

1 Most people will recognize here my play on George Bush's presidential election theme in 1991 – the thousand points of light connoting for him the volunteering program of self-sacrifice needed to replace government entitlements.

2 In its defiance of broad economic and political transformation, the integrationist strategy functions in contemporary visual culture within the realm of the spectacle, thereby displacing the question of multicultural participation in the economic and productive aspects of film and television. To be sure, Hollywood remains in the hands of predominantly white producers, directors, and actors, even as the rhetoric of integration heralds a cultural visibility of multiplicity.

3 Kobena Mercer and Isaac Julien, like Robert Stam and Louise Spence in "Colonialism, Racism, and Representation," are skeptical about the practices of social integration that interpret the "positive" image as the sign of democratic inclusion (see Mercer and Julien 1988). They emphasize instead how the terms of inclusion and exclusion or positive versus negative carry little political utility for describing and critiquing the various forms that white supremacy can take. Indeed, it is precisely through the use of inclusionary rhetoric and representational positivities that the current recuperative strategies of US cultural production have gained their most damaging political force. See also Marlon Riggs's film *Color Adjustment* in which the history of African Americans on television is traced from within the context of the problematics of the "positive" and "negative" image. From a slightly different perspective, Michele Wallace takes up these issues in *Invisibility Blues* 1–10 (1990b).

4 In presenting this list, I am trying to make a case for the cultural "hegemony" of interracial male bonding narratives in the 1980s, even as I recognize that such narratives, as Leslie Fiedler has suggested in *Love and Death in the American Novel* (1966), are traditional components of the literary canon – that is, nothing wholly new on the

American representational scene. But I would place Fiedler…within the integrationist strategy that these films for me evince, thereby understanding their proliferation in contemporary culture and their mapping in post-1960s cultural criticism as historically linked enterprises.

5 Michele Wallace's work on the implications of sexual difference within black power discourses and organizational structures in *Black Macho and the Myth of the Superwoman* (1990a)…demonstrates the difficulties of forging a political movement against white supremacy when the interconnections of sexism and racism are ignored.

6 Like others engaged in interpretations of contemporary popular culture, I am anxious about our critical methodologies, especially the conditions under which we choose texts as paradigmatic examples of broader cultural forces and meanings. Such anxieties…are not new, though the realm of the popular, given its sheer proliferation of texts, renders insufficient the traditional practices of literary criticism where our faith in canonicity and author study, for instance, help to alleviate the epistemological questions that underwrite this particular discipline and its modern anxieties. Not that literary study can protect itself from such issues any longer, but it seems to me that a chapter such as this one particularly begs the question of how and for what political purposes the critic pursues a historicizing cultural narrative. Certainly the films that I discuss bear no intrinsic "value" as cultural objects, and I am under no illusion that the narrative I am constructing from them is the only or even the most salient interpretative possibility attending their cultural production. Indeed, it seems to me that a likely alternative approach might look at the disparity between the recuperative politics of interracial male bonding scenarios and the reception of such narratives by minoritized viewers for whom representational presence is itself understood, in the context of the everyday, as politically enabling.

7 The association between blackness and the feminine is initially drawn through the film's mapping of social space, as Pearce shares a room with the most effeminate character, Poteete (Malcolm Danare), who will eventually be driven by The Ten to suicide. In his proximity to Pearce, the overweight, high-voiced, and routinely crying Poteete is a significant, if short-lived character, becoming both the representative of femininity and the measurement against which Pearce's masculinity will ultimately be drawn.

8 Several Supreme Court cases of the late 1980s evince this resurrection of the white male as the new victim of US cultural practices. The June 1989 decision conferring the right of affirmative action appeal to white firefighters in Birmingham, Alabama, is only one indication of the New Right's efforts to abolish civil rights legislation by claiming it discriminates against white men.

9 It is no accident that numerous representations of the interracial male bond are linked to the image of the vet or that the actors in popular Vietnam movies reappear in other bonding films. For instance, the central actors of the "classic" Vietnam war movie *Platoon* (dir. Oliver Stone, 1986), Tom Berenger and William Defoe, are recycled into two later interracial bonding pictures, *Shoot to Kill* (dir. Robert Spottiswoode) and *Off Limits* (dir. Christopher Crowe) alongside two African-American actors who have appeared in a number of bonding films, Sidney Poitier and Gregory Hines.

10 See in particular Donald Bogle, *Toms, Coons, Mulattoes, Mammies, and Bucks* (1989); Thomas Cripps, *Slow Fade to Black* (1977); and Daniel J. Leab, *From Sambo to Superspade* (1975).

11 At the same time, it allows the alien to speak the words that naturalize human reproduction through the romance of heterosexual union: "you humans have separated your sexes into two separate halves for the joy of that bridged union."…

12 In 1988, NBC produced a sequel to *In the Heat of the Night*, which inaugurated a mid-season series that ran throughout the early 1990s. The sequel depicts Virgil Tibbs returning to Sparta to serve as its detective. Quickly Tibbs becomes involved in the

investigation of a white woman's murder, a murder conveniently – and stereotypically – pinned on a black male who is also conveniently and stereotypically lynched in his cell. In unraveling the murder, Tibbs must confront the racist echelon of the town as the murderer turns out to be the son of the oldest, finest, and wealthiest family. The major difference between this and the earlier version is not the depiction of Tibbs, but that of his white counterpart who, in the ethos of the 1980s, is no longer a bigot but a man who himself picked cotton alongside blacks as a child – a man whose fondest war buddy is black. This "humanization" of the white southerner evinces the strategy under examination here where the interracial male bond is necessary to the recuperation of the white male who must see himself transformed from victimizer/oppressor to partner – even if hesitant – in cultural and racial change.

13 The importance of disaffiliating the male bond from the threat of homosexuality is inscribed overtly in *Shoot to Kill*, where the male protagonists, Warren Stantin (Sidney Poitier) and Jonathan Knox (Tom Berenger), become trapped on a snow-packed mountain at dusk. Knox creates an igloo in the snow and the men spend the night there. As Stantin starts to show signs of frostbite, Knox removes his own shirt and crawls on top of Stantin's body to generate heat; in doing so, he cracks a joke about "country boys," they laugh, and the threat of homosexuality is simultaneously foregrounded and averted.

14 This is no less true of the 1988 film *Cry Freedom*, which tells the story of the struggle against apartheid in South Africa by recounting white journalist Donald Woods's (Kevin Kline) relationship with black rebel Steve Biko (Denzel Washington). Although the film is set in South Africa and directed by the British-born Richard Attenborough, it is in every way an American movie, not simply because of its use of American actors but more importantly because of its reliance on the representational trope common to contemporary American cultural production, that of the interracial male bond. Here, as in *White Nights*, "the West" is upheld as the site of freedom and egalitarianism and reinforced through scenes depicting the terror of the South African regime. In a reenactment of all the films under discussion here, *Cry Freedom* casts the white male as the defender of black liberty who risks his life for the salvation of the other: it is Woods who must escape South Africa with the manuscript he has been writing about Biko's life and political leadership; it is the white family that remains intact soaring through billowing white clouds to freedom in the final scene, a scene that is followed by a list of names, dates, and official reasons for the deaths of blacks held in detention by South African officials. The disparity between the narrative resolution of the white family's odyssey and that of the real victims of apartheid ironically demonstrates the ideological politics governing the representation of the interracial bond. One can only wonder, in fact, why Biko's story was not considered sufficient enough for a film about apartheid.

15 My readings of contemporary interracial male bonding films as recuperative practices for the historically shifting dimensions of white supremacy is not meant to dismiss the importance of Anglo-American interest in subverting the cultural primacy of white skin. But it is to foreground the difference between narratives of white heroism, cast now within a defining framework of antiracism, and the kinds of difficult and necessary negotiations attending any white figure involved in the struggle against white supremacy. Interracial male bonding narratives too often recreate the imperialistic gesture by simply appropriating a visible economy of difference to refashion Anglo-American centricity.

16 The 1993 film *Philadelphia* (dir. Jonathan Demme) offers an interesting contrast to interracial male bonding films of the 1980s, foregrounding the interplay between homosexuality and African-American ethnicity that earlier Hollywood productions struggled so hard to veil. Here, of course, the African-American male acts as the

normative sexual character, and it is from within his biases and prejudices that the film's liberal discourse of homosexuality is defined.

References

Bercovitch, Sacvan. 1981. "The Rites of Ascent: Rhetoric, Ritual, and the Ideology of American Consensus." *The American Self: Myth, Ideology and Popular Culture*, ed. Sam B. Girgus. Albuquerque: University of New Mexico Press, pp. 5–42.

——1986. "Afterword." *Ideology and Classic American Literature*, ed. Bercovitch and Myra Jehlen. New York and Cambridge: Cambridge University Press, pp. 418–42.

Bogle, Donald. 1989. *Toms, Coons, Mulattoes, Mammies, and Bucks: An Interpretative History of Blacks in American Films*, rev. edn. New York: Continuum.

Cleaver, Eldridge. 1968. *Soul on Ice*. New York: Dell.

Conroy, Pat. 1980. *The Lords of Discipline*. Reprinted New York and Toronto: Bantam, 1982.

Cripps, Thomas. 1977. *Slow Fade to Black: The Negro in American Film 1900–1942*. New York: Oxford University Press.

de Lauretis, Teresa. 1984. *Alice Doesn't: Feminism, Semiotics, Cinema*. Bloomington: Indiana University Press.

Fiedler, Leslie. 1966. *Love and Death in the American Novel* [1960]. Reprint, New York: Stein & Day.

Jeffords, Susan. 1989. *The Remasculinization of America: Gender and the Vietnam War*. Bloomington: Indiana University Press.

Leab, Daniel J. 1975. *From Sambo to Superspade: The Black Experience in Motion Pictures*. Boston: Houghton Mifflin.

Merio Kobena, and Isaac Julien. 1988. "Introduction: De Margin and De Centre." *Screen* 29/4 (Autumn): 2–10.

Neale, Steve, 1983. "Masculinity as Spectacle: Reflections on Men and Mainstream Cinema." *Screen* 24/6 (Nov.–Dec.): 2–16.

Stam, Robert, and Louise Spence. 1983. "Colonialism, Racism and Representation." *Screen* 24/2 (Mar.–Apr.): 2–20.

Wallace, Michele, 1990a. *Black Macho and the Myth of the Superwoman*. 1979. Reprint, London and New York: Verso.

——1990b. *Invisibility Blues: From Pop to Theory*. London and New York: Verso.

Wheeler, John. 1984. *Touched with Fire: The Future of the Vietnam Generation*. New York: Avon.

Part IV

Empire and Modernity

The theoretical insights about gender, imperialism, and modernity provided by the following essays arise from a productive convergence of
political and intellectual history over the last half of the twentieth century.
During this period, a surge of movements for national liberation brought
about the demise of European colonialism and changes in the global
distribution of power. The process of decolonization provided the conditions of possibility for the emergence of the interdisciplinary field of postcolonial studies. In the most general sense, postcolonial studies investigates
the effects of western colonialism and its aftermath. Its theoretical origins
are generally attributed to the publication of Edward Said's landmark
study, *Orientalism* (1978), which documents a lengthy tradition of constructing the "Orient" as the imaginary antithesis of the West. At the
heart of Said's analysis is the fundamental relationship between knowledge and power, between the constitution of Orientalism as a field of
academic study and the economic and military operations of western imperialism. As it has engaged in productive alliances with deconstruction,
Marxism, psychoanalysis, cultural and gender studies, postcolonial criticism
challenged the organization and assumptions of knowledge across many
disciplines.

Questions of gender were introduced to postcolonial studies by feminist
scholars such as Gayatri Spivak, Chandra Mohanty, Trinh T. Minh-Ha, and
Rey Chow. In her influential essay, "Can the Subaltern Speak?" (1988)
Spivak asked about the possibilities and limitations for representing the
subaltern woman, who was marginalized by both patriarchy and colonial
power. Concluding that the subaltern was, by definition, voiceless, she
charged intellectuals with the responsibility for speaking on her behalf.
In her articles, "French Feminism in an International Frame" (1987) and
"Three Women's Texts and a Critique of Imperialism" (1985), Spivak criticized western feminism for eliding the figure of the Third World woman.
Mohanty extends these provocations in "Under Western Eyes: Feminist
Scholarship and Colonial Discourses," which disputes the one-dimensional
representation of the native as a passive victim in texts written by western
feminists. The alignment between feminism and postcolonialism was subject to further critique in Sara Suleri's 1992 essay, "Woman Skin Deep:

Feminism and the Postcolonial Condition," which cautioned against an overly sentimental or opportunistic embrace of the subaltern woman within an expanding field of oppositional criticism. As scholars became increasingly enamored of marginality, Suleri saw the Third World woman as an easy symbol of oppression that served the intellectual's professional interests while ignoring the lived experiences of women within formerly colonized nations.

Turning the force of its inquiry upon the neglected figure of the gendered subaltern, feminist postcolonial criticism has, for the most part, been concerned exclusively with women. The study of masculinity within the colonial and postcolonial context follows a somewhat different trajectory, which begins with the work of the Martinican psychiatrist and intellectual, Frantz Fanon. Fanon occupies an important position in this section because his writings, which provide some of the founding insights of postcolonial theory, are particularly attentive to the debilitating effects of colonialism on non-white men. His first book, *Black Skin, White Masks* (1952), thus situates the problem of masculinity as one of the originary preoccupations of anti-colonial thought. Fanon's training as a psychiatrist in French-occupied Algeria formed a basis for his powerful meditations on the psychological effects of colonialism on both colonizer and colonized. Because of his concern with the impact of colonialism on the psyche, Fanon is acknowledged as a precursor of psychoanalytically-informed postcolonial criticism in a work such as Homi Bhabha's *The Location of Culture* (1994), a book that is, in turn, credited for reintroducing Fanon into the canon of postcolonial studies. Psychoanalysis allows access to the phantasmatic dimensions of colonialism, the fantasies of racial and gendered inferiority which inevitably accompany the political and sociological aspects of empire. Understanding and deconstructing these fantasies is an integral component of Fanon's attempt to articulate an anti-colonial nationalism.

As the essay by Daniel Boyarin in this section attests, Fanon is particularly important to scholars of masculinity because of his concern with gender in the analysis of revolutionary conflict. At the same time, contemporary critics have been forced to contend with the problem of Fanon's sexism. Boyarin ascribes Fanon's misogyny and homophobia to his own unstable position within the colonial order. Boyarin's comparative analysis of Freud and Fanon describes the divided self of psychoanalysis as a prototype for the "other within" of colonial subjectivity. That is, Boyarin attributes Freud's recollection of mistaking his own mirror image for another's in "The Uncanny" – a misrecognition that provides one of the founding insights of his psychoanalytic theory – to his ambiguous racial status as a Jew in nineteenth-century Europe. So too, Fanon's analysis of colonial psychology is premised on a self-division or double consciousness resulting from the imperial situation. According to Boyarin, both Freud and Fanon experienced the anxiety of racial inferiority as the threat of feminization. He reads the troubling denigration of women and homosexuals in their work as a compensatory strategy to regain masculine authority.

The articulation of masculinity and power in the rhetoric of colonialism had an inevitable impact on the configuration of revolutionary nationalisms. Reacting against a colonial system that disempowers non-western men by proclaiming their effeminacy, indigenous nationalisms have often been formulated in terms of reclaiming a lost masculine potency. Fanon is at once a product and a critic of a colonial order that relies on the exclusion of women. The inherent gendering of imperial power leads him to ask "What does the black man want?" in an echo of the Freudian question, "What does woman want?" Fanon's attention to the black man's frustrated masculinity is a corrective to the rhetoric of imperial conquest that depicts him as passive and feminized. Boyarin shows the destructive consequences of that discourse on women, who may fare no better within a newly-formed nation state than they did under colonialism. His attention to how women are adversely affected by different groups of men struggling to claim masculinity, attests to the importance of a systematic approach to understanding masculinity and femininity as relational terms that cannot be adequately studied in isolation from one another or from the political contexts that enframe them.

The essay by R. W. Connell provides a useful historical overview of the gendering of imperial power. Connell effectively demonstrates the impact of modern capitalism and the nation state on Western European formations of masculinity, and the radiating consequences of that gendering as the effects of European and American imperialism spread throughout the rest of the globe. Dominant images of masculinity are perpetuated not simply in the form of institutions and social conventions but through cultural representations, which claim a powerful hold on the fantasy life of both colonizer and colonized. Richard Dyer analyzes how Hollywood film romanticized the project of colonial domination by depicting the white man's benevolent intervention in the non-western world. Dyer's work places particular emphasis on the body as a microcosm for imperial conquest. The statuesque physique of the white male protagonist is emblematic of his superiority over the dark-skinned people who need his help.

Whereas the muscular, aggressive forms of masculinity that US and Western European cultures contributed to the colonial context have been well documented by Connell, Dyer, and others, we know less about the gender order that those forms replaced and how precolonial masculinities resurfaced in national resistance movements. Among scholars of masculinity, research devoted to the traditions of formerly colonized nations may reveal very different conceptions of gender than those imposed by the occupying power. Revathi Krishnaswamy's "The Economy of Colonial Desire" documents tensions between competing forms of masculinity within colonial India. When British colonizers imposed a stereotypic effeminacy on Indian men, they did so in the context of a long-standing affirmation of androgyny within traditional Hinduism. Krishnaswamy argues that effeminacy – most commonly understood as a strategy used by the colonizer to disempower the colonized – can also be a mode of resistance, a refusal to assimilate dominant British forms of masculinity by returning to indigenous traditions. Inspired by Boyarin's insights about Jewish effeminacy, Krishnaswamy uncovers a Hinduism that valued "femininity-in-masculinity." This precolonial foundation enabled Gandhi to articulate an Indian nationalism that drew on premodern Christianity, positive images of Hindu androgyny, and dynamic womanhood to create a countermodel of revolutionary masculinity.

Krishnaswamy's essay detects a traditionally effeminate passivity at the heart of Gandhian strategies for non-violent, anticolonial resistance. By contrast, Julie Peteet's ethnographic research on Palestinian attitudes towards violence reveals a context in which beatings represent a form of masculine resistance against a more powerful occupying force. Read as a pair, Krishnaswamy and Peteet show how widely divergent understandings of masculinity can emerge in response to conditions of colonization. In desperate times, Peteet argues, Palestinians have turned the Israeli tactic of publicly administered corporeal punishment into a symbol of honorable sacrifice for the collective good. The masculinity of the heavily armed Israeli soldiers who attack unarmed young men is called into question. Women who stand at the sidelines of such violence are not seen as innocent bystanders but agents whose witnessing is an act of political activism. Completed in the early 1990s, Peteet's research on gendered resistance has an unfortunate timeliness in light of the escalating conflict between Israelis and Palestinians at the beginning of the twenty-first century.

Together, the essays in this section demonstrate that a focus on masculinity reorders the terms we use to think about empire by revealing that gender division is not a by-product of colonialism, but a constitutive aspect of its power. An approach to masculinity informed by postcolonial criticism need not (and should not) limit itself to elaborating the gender dichotomies established by the colonial power, or the resistance to them, for colonized cultures are neither blank slates nor do they provide neat analogues for western gender configurations. These essays model a variety of strategies for explaining how gender has been harnessed to colonial power and anti-imperialist resistance movements, as well as attending to the alternative gender formations displaced during the era of colonial occupation.

Bibliography

Bhabha, Homi. 1994. *The Location of Culture.* New York and London: Routledge.
Minh-Ha, Trihn T. 1989. *Woman, Native, Other.* Bloomington: Indiana University Press.
Mohanty, Chandra Talpade. 1991. "Under Western Eyes: Feminist Scholarship and Colonial Discourses," in C. T. Mohanty, A. Russo, and L. Torres (eds.) *Third World Women and the Politics of Feminism.* Bloomington: Indiana University Press, pp. 51–80.
Nandy, Ashis. 1983. *The Intimate Enemy: Loss and Recovery of Self Under Colonialism.* Delhi: Oxford University Press.
Said, Edward W. 1978. *Orientalism: Western Conceptions of the Orient.* New York: Vintage.
Sinha, Mrinalini. 1995. *Colonial Masculinity: The Manly Englishman and the Effeminate Bengali in the Late Nineteenth Century.* Manchester: Manchester University Press.
Sharpe, Jenny. 1993. *Allegories of Empire: The Figure of Woman in the Colonial Text.* Minneapolis: University of Minnesota Press.
Spivak, Gayatri. 1985. "Three Women's Texts and a Critique of Imperialism." *Critical Inquiry* 12: 242–61.

——.1987. "French Feminism in an International Frame," in *In Other Worlds: Essays in Cultural Politics*. New York: Methuen, pp. 134–53.

——.1988. "Can the Subaltern Speak?," in Cary Nelson and Lawrence Grossberg (eds.) *Marxism and the Interpretation of Culture*. Urbana: University of Illinois Press, pp. 271–313.

Stoler, Ann Laura. 1995. *Race and the Education of Desire: Foucault's History of Sexuality and the Colonial Order of Things*. Durham: Duke University Press.

Suleri, Sara. 1992. "Feminism Skin Deep." *Critical Inquiry* 18 (Summer): 756–69.

13

The Fact of Blackness

Frantz Fanon

"Dirty nigger!" Or simply, "Look, a Negro!"

I came into the world imbued with the will to find a meaning in things, my spirit filled with the desire to attain to the source of the world, and then I found that I was an object in the midst of other objects.

Sealed into that crushing objecthood, I turned beseechingly to others. Their attention was a liberation, running over my body suddenly abraded into nonbeing, endowing me once more with an agility that I had thought lost, and by taking me out of the world, restoring me to it. But just as I reached the other side, I stumbled, and the movements, the attitudes, the glances of the other fixed me there, in the sense in which a chemical solution is fixed by a dye. I was indignant; I demanded an explanation. Nothing happened. I burst apart. Now the fragments have been put together again by another self.

As long as the black man is among his own, he will have no occasion, except in minor internal conflicts, to experience his being through others. There is of course the moment of "being for others," of which Hegel speaks, but every ontology is made unattainable in a colonized and civilized society. It would seem that this fact has not been given sufficient attention by those who have discussed the question. In the *Weltanschauung* of a colonized people there is an impurity, a flaw that outlaws any ontological explanation. Someone may object that this is the case with every individual, but such an objection merely conceals a basic problem. Ontology – once it is finally admitted as leaving existence by the wayside – does not permit us to understand the being of the black man. For not only must the black man be black; he must be black in relation to the white man. Some critics will take it on themselves to remind us that this proposition has a converse. I say that this is false. The black man has no ontological resistance in the eyes of the white man. Overnight the Negro has been given two frames of reference within which he has had to place himself. His metaphysics, or, less pretentiously, his customs and the sources on which they were based, were wiped out because they were in conflict with a civilization that he did not know and that imposed itself on him.

The black man among his own in the twentieth century does not know at what moment his inferiority comes into being through the other. Of course I have

Reprinted from *Black Skin, White Masks*, trans. Charles Lam Markmann (New York: Grove Press, 1967), pp. 109–24, 126–40.

talked about the black problem with friends, or, more rarely, with American Negroes. Together we protested, we asserted the equality of all men in the world. In the Antilles there was also that little gulf that exists among the almost-white, the mulatto, and the nigger. But I was satisfied with an intellectual understanding of these differences. It was not really dramatic. And then....

And then the occasion arose when I had to meet the white man's eyes. An unfamiliar weight burdened me. The real world challenged my claims. In the white world the man of color encounters difficulties in the development of his bodily schema. Consciousness of the body is solely a negating activity. It is a third-person consciousness. The body is surrounded by an atmosphere of certain uncertainty. I know that if I want to smoke, I shall have to reach out my right arm and take the pack of cigarettes lying at the other end of the table. The matches, however, are in the drawer on the left, and I shall have to lean back slightly. And all these movements are made not out of habit but out of implicit knowledge. A slow composition of my *self* as a body in the middle of a spatial and temporal world – such seems to be the schema. It does not impose itself on me; it is, rather, a definitive structuring of the self and of the world – definitive because it creates a real dialectic between my body and the world.

For several years certain laboratories have been trying to produce a serum for "denegrification"; with all the earnestness in the world, laboratories have sterilized their test tubes, checked their scales, and embarked on researches that might make it possible for the miserable Negro to whiten himself and thus to throw off the burden of that corporeal malediction. Below the corporeal schema I had sketched a historico-racial schema. The elements that I used had been provided for me not by "residual sensations and perceptions primarily of a tactile, vestibular, kinesthetic, and visual character,"[1] but by the other, the white man, who had woven me out of a thousand details, anecdotes, stories. I thought that what I had in hand was to construct a physiological self, to balance space, to localize sensations, and here I was called on for more.

"Look, a Negro!" It was an external stimulus that flicked over me as I passed by. I made a tight smile.

"Look, a Negro!" It was true. It amused me.

"Look, a Negro!" The circle was drawing a bit tighter. I made no secret of my amusement.

"Mama, see the Negro! I'm frightened!" Frightened! Frightened! Now they were beginning to be afraid of me. I made up my mind to laugh myself to tears, but laughter had become impossible.

I could no longer laugh, because I already knew that there were legends, stories, history, and above all *historicity*, which I had learned about from Jaspers. Then, assailed at various points, the corporeal schema crumbled, its place taken by a racial epidermal schema. In the train it was no longer a question of being aware of my body in the third person but in a triple person. In the train I was given not one but two, three places. I had already stopped being amused. It was not that I was finding febrile coordinates in the world. I existed triply: I occupied space. I moved toward the other...and the evanescent other, hostile but not opaque, transparent, not there, disappeared. Nausea....

I was responsible at the same time for my body, for my race, for my ancestors. I subjected myself to an objective examination, I discovered my blackness, my ethnic characteristics; and I was battered down by tom-toms, cannibalism, intellectual deficiency, fetishism, racial defects, slave-ships, and above all else, above all: "Sho' good eatin'."

On that day, completely dislocated, unable to be abroad with the other, the white man, who unmercifully imprisoned me, I took myself far off from my own presence, far indeed, and made myself an object. What else could it be for me but an amputation, an excision, a hemorrhage that spattered my whole body with black blood? But I did not want this revision, this thematization. All I wanted was to be a man among other men. I wanted to come lithe and young into a world that was ours and to help to build it together.

But I rejected all immunization of the emotions. I wanted to be a man, nothing but a man. Some identified me with ancestors of mine who had been enslaved or lynched: I decided to accept this. It was on the universal level of the intellect that I understood this inner kinship – I was the grandson of slaves in exactly the same way in which President Lebrun was the grandson of tax-paying, hard-working peasants. In the main, the panic soon vanished.

In America, Negroes are segregated. In South America, Negroes are whipped in the streets, and Negro strikers are cut down by machine-guns. In West Africa, the Negro is an animal. And there beside me, my neighbor in the university, who was born in Algeria, told me: "As long as the Arab is treated like a man, no solution is possible."

. . .

My body was given back to me sprawled out, distorted, recolored, clad in mourning in that white winter day. The Negro is an animal, the Negro is bad, the Negro is mean, the Negro is ugly; look, a nigger, it's cold, the nigger is shivering, the nigger is shivering because he is cold, the little boy is trembling because he is afraid of the nigger, the nigger is shivering with cold, that cold that goes through your bones, the handsome little boy is trembling because he thinks that the nigger is quivering with rage, the little white boy throws himself into his mother's arms: Mama, the nigger's going to eat me up.

All round me the white man, above the sky tears at its navel, the earth rasps under my feet, and there is a white song, a white song. All this whiteness that burns me....

I sit down at the fire and I become aware of my uniform. I had not seen it. It is indeed ugly. I stop there, for who can tell me what beauty is?

Where shall I find shelter from now on? I felt an easily identifiable flood mounting out of the countless facets of my being. I was about to be angry. The fire was long since out, and once more the nigger was trembling.

"Look how handsome that Negro is! . . ."

"Kiss the handsome Negro's ass, madame!"

Shame flooded her face. At last I was set free from my rumination. At the same time I accomplished two things: I identified my enemies and I made a scene. A grand slam. Now one would be able to laugh.

The field of battle having been marked out, I entered the lists.

What? While I was forgetting, forgiving, and wanting only to love, my message was flung back in my face like a slap. The white world, the only honorable one, barred me from all participation. A man was expected to behave like a man. I was expected to behave like a black man – or at least like a nigger. I shouted a greeting to the world and the world slashed away my joy. I was told to stay within bounds, to go back where I belonged.

They would see, then! I had warned them, anyway. Slavery? It was no longer even mentioned, that unpleasant memory. My supposed inferiority? A hoax that it was better to laugh at. I forgot it all, but only on condition that the world not protect itself against me any longer. I had incisors to test. I was sure they were strong. And besides. . . .

What! When it was I who had every reason to hate, to despise, I was rejected? When I should have been begged, implored, I was denied the slightest recognition? I resolved, since it was impossible for me to get away from an *inborn complex*, to assert myself as a BLACK MAN. Since the other hesitated to recognize me, there remained only one solution: to make myself known.

In *Anti-Semite and Jew*, Sartre says: "They [the Jews] have allowed themselves to be poisoned by the stereotype that others have of them, and they live in fear that their acts will correspond to this stereotype. . . . We may say that their conduct is perpetually overdetermined from the inside."[2]

All the same, the Jew can be unknown in his Jewishness. He is not wholly what he is. One hopes, one waits. His actions, his behavior are the final determinant. He is a white man, and, apart from some rather debatable characteristics, he can sometimes go unnoticed. He belongs to the race of those who since the beginning of time have never known cannibalism. What an idea, to eat one's father! Simple enough, one has only not to be a nigger. Granted, the Jews are harassed – what am I thinking of? They are hunted down, exterminated, cremated. But these are little family quarrels. The Jew is disliked from the moment he is tracked down. But in my case everything takes on a *new* guise. I am given no chance. I am overdetermined from without. I am the slave not of the "idea" that others have of me but of my own appearance.

I move slowly in the world, accustomed now to seek no longer for upheaval. I progress by crawling. And already I am being dissected under white eyes, the only real eyes. I am *fixed*. Having adjusted their microtomes, they objectively cut away slices of my reality. I am laid bare. I feel, I see in those white faces that it is not a new man who has come in, but a new kind of man, a new genus. Why, it's a Negro!

I slip into corners, and my long antennae pick up the catch-phrases strewn over the surface of things – nigger underwear smells of nigger – nigger teeth are white – nigger feet are big – the nigger's barrel chest – I slip into corners, I remain silent, I strive for anonymity, for invisibility. Look, I will accept the lot, as long as no one notices me!

"Oh, I want you to meet my black friend. . . . Aimé Césaire, a black man and a university graduate. . . . Marian Anderson, the finest of Negro singers. . . . Dr. Cobb, who invented white blood, is a Negro. . . . Here, say hello to my friend from Martinique (be careful, he's extremely sensitive). . . ."

Shame. Shame and self-contempt. Nausea. When people like me, they tell me it is in spite of my color. When they dislike me, they point out that it is not because of my color. Either way, I am locked into the infernal circle.

I turn away from these inspectors of the Ark before the Flood and I attach myself to my brothers, Negroes like myself. To my horror, they too reject me. They are almost white. And besides they are about to marry white women. They will have children faintly tinged with brown. Who knows, perhaps little by little. . . .

I had been dreaming.

"I want you to understand, sir, I am one of the best friends the Negro has in Lyon."

The evidence was there, unalterable. My blackness was there, dark and unarguable. And it tormented me, pursued me, disturbed me, angered me.

Negroes are savages, brutes, illiterates. But in my own case I knew that these statements were false. There was a myth of the Negro that had to be destroyed at all costs. The time had long since passed when a Negro priest was an occasion for wonder. We had physicians, professors, statesmen. Yes, but something out of the ordinary still clung to such cases. "We have a Senegalese history teacher. He is quite bright.... Our doctor is colored. He is very gentle."

It was always the Negro teacher, the Negro doctor; brittle as I was becoming, I shivered at the slightest pretext. I knew, for instance, that if the physician made a mistake it would be the end of him and of all those who came after him. What could one expect, after all, from a Negro physician? As long as everything went well, he was praised to the skies, but look out, no nonsense, under any conditions! The black physician can never be sure how close he is to disgrace. I tell you, I was walled in: No exception was made for my refined manners, or my knowledge of literature, or my understanding of the quantum theory.

I requested, I demanded explanations. Gently, in the tone that one uses with a child, they introduced me to the existence of a certain view that was held by certain people, but, I was always told, "We must hope that it will very soon disappear." What was it? Color prejudice.

> It [colour prejudice] is nothing more than the unreasoning hatred of one race for another, the contempt of the stronger and richer peoples for those whom they consider inferior to themselves and the bitter resentment of those who are kept in subjection and are so frequently insulted. As colour is the most obvious outward manifestation of race it has been made the criterion by which men are judged, irrespective of their social or educational attainments. The light-skinned races have come to despise all those of a darker colour, and the dark-skinned peoples will no longer accept without protest the inferior position to which they have been relegated.[3]

I had read it rightly. It was hate; I was hated, despised, detested, not by the neighbor across the street or my cousin on my mother's side, but by an entire race. I was up against something unreasoned. The psychoanalysts say that nothing is more traumatizing for the young child than his encounters with what is rational. I would personally say that for a man whose only weapon is reason there is nothing more neurotic than contact with unreason.

I felt knife blades open within me. I resolved to defend myself. As a good tactician, I intended to rationalize the world and to show the white man that he was mistaken.

In the Jew, Jean-Paul Sartre says, there is

> a sort of impassioned imperialism of reason: for he wishes not only to convince others that he is right; his goal is to persuade them that there is an absolute and unconditioned value to rationalism. He feels himself to be a missionary of the universal; against the universality of the Catholic religion, from which he is excluded, he asserts

the "catholicity" of the rational, an instrument by which to attain to the truth and establish a spiritual bond among men.[4]

. . .

With enthusiasm I set to cataloguing and probing my surroundings. As times changed, one had seen the Catholic religion at first justify and then condemn slavery and prejudices. But by referring everything to the idea of the dignity of man, one had ripped prejudice to shreds. After much reluctance, the scientists had conceded that the Negro was a human being; *in vivo* and *in vitro* the Negro had been proved analogous to the white man: the same morphology, the same histology. Reason was confident of victory on every level. I put all the parts back together. But I had to change my tune.

That victory played cat and mouse; it made a fool of me. As the other put it, when I was present, it was not; when it was there, I was no longer. In the abstract there was agreement: The Negro is a human being. That is to say, amended the less firmly convinced, that like us he has his heart on the left side. But on certain points the white man remained intractable. Under no conditions did he wish any intimacy between the races, for it is a truism that "crossings between widely different races can lower the physical and mental level. . . . Until we have a more definite knowledge of the effect of race-crossings we shall certainly do best to avoid crossings between widely different races."[5]

For my own part, I would certainly know how to react. And in one sense, if I were asked for a definition of myself, I would say that I am one who waits; I investigate my surroundings, I interpret everything in terms of what I discover, I become sensitive.

In the first chapter of the history that the others have compiled for me, the foundation of cannibalism has been made eminently plain in order that I may not lose sight of it. My chromosomes were supposed to have a few thicker or thinner genes representing cannibalism. In addition to the *sex-linked*, the scholars had now discovered the *racial-linked*.[6] What a shameful science!

But I understand this "psychological mechanism." For it is a matter of common knowledge that the mechanism is only psychological. Two centuries ago I was lost to humanity, I was a slave forever. And then came men who said that it all had gone on far too long. My tenaciousness did the rest; I was saved from the civilizing deluge. I have gone forward.

. . .

The Jew and I: Since I was not satisfied to be racialized, by a lucky turn of fate I was humanized. I joined the Jew, my brother in misery.

An outrage!

At first thought it may seem strange that the anti-Semite's outlook should be related to that of the Negro-phobe. It was my philosophy professor, a native of the Antilles, who recalled the fact to me one day: "Whenever you hear anyone abuse the Jews, pay attention, because he is talking about you." And I found that he was universally right – by which I meant that I was answerable in my body and in my heart for what was done to my brother. Later I realized that he meant, quite simply, an anti-Semite is inevitably anti-Negro.

You come too late, much too late. There will always be a world – a white world – between you and us. . . . The other's total inability to liquidate the past once and for all. In the face of this affective ankylosis of the white man, it is understandable that I could have made up my mind to utter my Negro cry. Little by little, putting out pseudopodia here and there, I secreted a race. And that race staggered under the burden of a basic element. What was it? *Rhythm!* Listen to our singer, Léopold Senghor:

> It is the thing that is most perceptible and least material. It is the archetype of the vital element. It is the first condition and the hallmark of Art, as breath is of life: breath, which accelerates or slows, which becomes even or agitated according to the tension in the individual, the degree and the nature of his emotion. This is rhythm in its primordial purity, this is rhythm in the masterpieces of Negro art, especially sculpture. It is composed of a theme – sculptural form – which is set in opposition to a sister theme, as inhalation is to exhalation, and that is repeated. It is not the kind of symmetry that gives rise to monotony; rhythm is alive, it is free.... This is how rhythm affects what is least intellectual in us, tyrannically, to make us penetrate to the spirituality of the object; and that character of abandon which is ours is itself rhythmic.[7]

Had I read that right? I read it again with redoubled attention. From the opposite end of the white world a magical Negro culture was hailing me. Negro sculpture! I began to flush with pride. Was this our salvation?

I had rationalized the world and the world had rejected me on the basis of color prejudice. Since no agreement was possible on the level of reason, I threw myself back toward unreason. It was up to the white man to be more irrational than I. Out of the necessities of my struggle I had chosen the method of regression, but the fact remained that it was an unfamiliar weapon; here I am at home; I am made of the irrational; I wade in the irrational. Up to the neck in the irrational. And now how my voice vibrates!

> Those who invented neither gunpowder nor the compass
> Those who never learned to conquer steam or electricity
> Those who never explored the seas or the skies
> But they know the farthest corners of the land of anguish
> Those who never knew any journey save that of abduction
> Those who learned to kneel in docility
> Those who were domesticated and Christianized
> Those who were injected with bastardy....

Yes, all those are my brothers – a "bitter brotherhood" imprisons all of us alike. Having stated the minor thesis, I went overboard after something else.

> ...But those without whom the earth would not be
>   the earth
> Tumescence all the more fruitful
> than
> the empty land
> still more the land
> Storehouse to guard and ripen all
> on earth that is most earth
> My blackness is no stone, its deafness
> hurled against the clamor of the day

> My blackness is no drop of lifeless water
> on the dead eye of the world
> My blackness is neither a tower nor a cathedral
> It thrusts into the red flesh of the sun
> It thrusts into the burning flesh of the sky
> It hollows through the dense dismay of its own
> pillar of patience.[8]

Eyah! the tom-tom chatters out the cosmic message. Only the Negro has the capacity to convey it, to decipher its meaning, its import. Astride the world, my strong heels spurring into the flanks of the world, I stare into the shoulders of the world as the celebrant stares at the midpoint between the eyes of the sacrificial victim.

. . .

Yes, we are – we Negroes – backward, simple, free in our behavior. That is because for us the body is not something opposed to what you call the mind. We are in the world. And long live the couple, Man and Earth! Besides, our men of letters helped me to convince you; your white civilization overlooks subtle riches and sensitivity. Listen:

Emotive sensitivity. *Emotion is completely Negro as reason is Greek.*[9] Water rippled by every breeze? Unsheltered soul blown by every wind, whose fruit often drops before it is ripe? Yes, in one way, the Negro today is richer *in gifts than in works.*[10] But the tree thrusts its roots into the earth. The river runs deep, carrying precious seeds. And, the Afro-American poet, Langston Hughes, says:

> I have known rivers
> ancient dark rivers
> my soul has grown deep
> like the deep rivers.

The very nature of the Negro's emotion, of his sensitivity, furthermore, explains his attitude toward the object perceived with such basic intensity. It is an abandon that becomes need, an active state of communion, indeed of identification, however negligible the action – I almost said the personality – of the object. A rhythmic attitude: The adjective should be kept in mind.[11]

So here we have the Negro rehabilitated, "standing before the bar," ruling the world with his intuition, the Negro recognized, set on his feet again, sought after, taken up, and he is a Negro – no, he is not a Negro but the Negro, exciting the fecund antennae of the world, placed in the foreground of the world, raining his poetic power on the world, "open to all the breaths of the world." I embrace the world! I am the world! The white man has never understood this magic substitution. The white man wants the world; he wants it for himself alone. He finds himself predestined master of this world. He enslaves it. An acquisitive relation is established between the world and him. But there exist other values that fit only my forms. Like a magician, I robbed the white man of "a certain world," forever after lost to him and his. When that happened, the white man must have been rocked backward by a force that he could not identify, so little used as he is to such reactions. Somewhere beyond the objective world of farms and banana trees and rubber trees, I had subtly brought the real world into being. The essence of the world was my fortune. Between the world and me a relation of coexistence was established. I had discovered the primeval One. My "speaking hands" tore at the hysterical throat of the world. The white man had the anguished feeling that I was escaping from him and that I was taking something with me. He went through my pockets. He thrust probes into the least circumvolution of my brain. Everywhere he found only the obvious. So it was obvious that I had a secret.

. . .

I made myself the poet of the world. The white man had found a poetry in which there was nothing poetic. The soul of the white man was corrupted, and, as I was told by a friend who was a teacher in the United States, "The presence of the Negroes beside the whites is in a way an insurance policy on humanness. When the whites feel that they have become too mechanized, they turn to the men of color and ask them for a little human sustenance." At last I had been recognized, I was no longer a zero.

I had soon to change my tune. Only momentarily at a loss, the white man explained to me that, genetically, I represented a stage of development: "Your properties have been exhausted by us. We have had earth mystics such as you will never approach. Study our history and you will see how far this fusion has gone." Then I had the feeling that I was repeating a cycle. My originality had been torn out of me. I wept a long time, and then I began to live again. But I was haunted by a galaxy of erosive stereotypes: the Negro's *sui generis* odor . . . the Negro's *sui generis* good nature . . . the Negro's *sui generis* gullibility. . . .

I had tried to flee myself through my kind, but the whites had thrown themselves on me and hamstrung me. I tested the limits of my essence; beyond all doubt there was not much of it left. It was here that I made my most remarkable discovery. Properly speaking, this discovery was a rediscovery.

I rummaged frenetically through all the antiquity of the black man. What I found there took away my breath. In his book *L'Abolition de l'esclavage* Schoelcher presented us with compelling arguments. Since then, Frobenius, Westermann, Delafosse – all of them white – had joined the chorus: Ségou, Djenné, cities of more than a hundred thousand people; accounts of learned blacks (doctors of theology who went to Mecca to interpret the Koran). All of that, exhumed from the past, spread with its insides out, made it possible for me to find a valid historic place. The white man was wrong, I was not a primitive, not even a half-man, I belonged to a race that had already been working in gold and silver two thousand years ago. And too there was something else, something else that the white man could not understand. Listen:

> What sort of men were these, then, who had been torn away from their families, their countries, their religions, with a savagery unparalleled in history?
>
> Gentle men, polite, considerate, unquestionably superior to those who tortured them – that collection of adventurers who slashed and violated and spat on Africa to make the stripping of her the easier.
>
> The men they took away knew how to build houses, govern empires, erect cities, cultivate fields, mine for metals, weave cotton, forge steel.
>
> Their religion had its own beauty, based on mystical connections with the founder of the city. Their customs were pleasing, built on unity, kindness, respect for age.

No coercion, only mutual assistance, the joy of living, a free acceptance of discipline.

Order – Earnestness – Poetry and Freedom.

From the untroubled private citizen to the almost fabulous leader there was an unbroken chain of understanding and trust. No science? Indeed yes; but also, to protect them from fear, they possessed great myths in which the most subtle observation and the most daring imagination were balanced and blended. No art? They had their magnificent sculpture, in which human feeling erupted so unrestrained yet always followed the obsessive laws of rhythm in its organization of the major elements of a material called upon to capture, in order to redistribute, the most secret forces of the universe....[12]

Monuments in the very heart of Africa? Schools? Hospitals? Not a single good burgher of the twentieth century, no Durand, no Smith, no Brown even suspects that such things existed in Africa before the Europeans came....

But Schoelcher reminds us of their presence, discovered by Caillé, Mollien, the Cander brothers. And, though he nowhere reminds us that when the Portuguese landed on the banks of the Congo in 1498, they found a rich and flourishing state there and that the courtiers of Ambas were dressed in robes of silk and brocade, at least he knows that Africa had brought itself up to a juridical concept of the state, and he is aware, living in the very flood of imperialism, that European civilization, after all, is only one more civilization among many – and not the most merciful.[13]

I put the white man back into his place; growing bolder, I jostled him and told him point-blank, "Get used to me, I am not getting used to anyone." I shouted my laughter to the stars. The white man, I could see, was resentful. His reaction time lagged interminably....I had won. I was jubilant.

"Lay aside your history, your investigations of the past, and try to feel yourself into our rhythm. In a society such as ours, industrialized to the highest degree, dominated by scientism, there is no longer room for your sensitivity. One must be tough if one is to be allowed to live. What matters now is no longer playing the game of the world but subjugating it with integers and atoms. Oh, certainly, I will be told, now and then when we are worn out by our lives in big buildings, we will turn to you as we do to our children – to the innocent, the ingenuous, the spontaneous. We will turn to you as to the childhood of the world. You are so real in your life – so funny, that is. Let us run away for a little while from our ritualized, polite civilization and let us relax, bend to those heads, those adorably expressive faces. In a way, you reconcile us with ourselves."

Thus my unreason was countered with reason, my reason with "real reason." Every hand was a losing hand for me. I analyzed my heredity. I made a complete audit of my ailment. I wanted to be typically Negro – it was no longer possible. I wanted to be white – that was a joke. And, when I tried, on the level of ideas and intellectual activity, to reclaim my negritude, it was snatched away from me. Proof was presented that my effort was only a term in the dialectic:

But there is something more important: The Negro, as we have said, creates an anti-racist racism for himself. In no sense does he wish to rule the world: He seeks the abolition of all ethnic privileges, wherever they come from; he asserts his solidarity with the oppressed of all colors. At once the subjective, existential, ethnic idea of *negritude* "passes," as Hegel puts it, into the objective, positive, exact idea of *proletariat.* "For Césaire," Senghor says, "the white man is the symbol of capital as the Negro is that of labor.... Beyond the black-skinned men of his race it is the battle of the world proletariat that is his song."

That is easy to say, but less easy to think out. And undoubtedly it is no coincidence that the most ardent poets of negritude are at the same time militant Marxists.

But that does not prevent the idea of race from mingling with that of class: The first is concrete and particular, the second is universal and abstract; the one stems from what Jaspers calls understanding and the other from intellection; the first is the result of a psychobiological syncretism and the second is a methodical construction based on experience. In fact, negritude appears as the minor term of a dialectical progression: The theoretical and practical assertion of the supremacy of the white man is its thesis; the position of negritude as an antithetical value is the moment of negativity. But this negative moment is insufficient by itself, and the Negroes who employ it know this very well; they know that it is intended to prepare the synthesis or realization of the human in a society without races. Thus negritude is the root of its own destruction, it is a transition and not a conclusion, a means and not an ultimate end.[14]

When I read that page, I felt that I had been robbed of my last chance. I said to my friends, "The generation of the younger black poets has just suffered a blow that can never be forgiven." Help had been sought from a friend of the colored peoples, and that friend had found no better response than to point out the relativity of what they were doing. For once, that born Hegelian had forgotten that consciousness has to lose itself in the night of the absolute, the only condition to attain to consciousness of self. In opposition to rationalism, he summoned up the negative side, but he forgot that this negativity draws its worth from an almost substantive absoluteness. A consciousness committed to experience is ignorant, has to be ignorant, of the essences and the determinations of its being.

Orphée Noir is a date in the intellectualization of the *experience* of being black. And Sartre's mistake was not only to seek the source of the source but in a certain sense to block that source:

> Will the source of Poetry be dried up? Or will the great black flood, in spite of everything, color the sea into which it pours itself? It does not matter: Every age has its own poetry; in every age the circumstances of history choose a nation, a race, a class to take up the torch by creating situations that can be expressed or transcended only through Poetry; sometimes the poetic impulse coincides with the revolutionary impulse, and sometimes they take different courses. Today let us hail the turn of history that will make it possible for the black men to utter "the great Negro cry with a force that will shake the pillars of the world" (Césaire).[15]

And so it is not I who make a meaning for myself, but it is the meaning that was already there, pre-existing, waiting for me. It is not out of my bad nigger's misery, my bad nigger's teeth, my bad nigger's hunger that I will shape a torch with which to burn down the world, but it is the torch that was already there, waiting for that turn of history.

In terms of consciousness, the black consciousness is held out as an absolute density, as filled with itself, a stage preceding any invasion, any abolition of the ego by desire. Jean-Paul Sartre, in this work, has destroyed black zeal. In opposition to historical becoming, there had always been the unforeseeable. I needed to lose myself completely in negritude. One day, perhaps, in the depths of that unhappy romanticism. . . .

In any case I *needed* not to know. This struggle, this new decline had to take on an aspect of completeness. Nothing is more unwelcome than the commonplace: "You'll change, my boy; I was like that too when I was young . . . you'll see, it will all pass."

The dialectic that brings necessity into the foundation of my freedom drives me out of myself. It shatters my unreflected position. Still in terms of consciousness, black consciousness is immanent in its own eyes. I am not a potentiality of something, I am wholly what I am. I do not have to look for the universal. No probability has any place inside me. My Negro consciousness does not hold itself out as a lack. It *is*. It is its own follower.

. . .

The Negro is a toy in the white man's hands; so, in order to shatter the hellish cycle, he explodes. I cannot go to a film without seeing myself. I wait for me. In the interval, just before the film starts, I wait for me. The people in the theater are watching me, examining me, waiting for me. A Negro groom is going to appear. My heart makes my head swim.

The crippled veteran of the Pacific war says to my brother, "Resign yourself to your color the way I got used to my stump; we're both victims."[16]

Nevertheless with all my strength I refuse to accept that amputation. I feel in myself a soul as immense as the world, truly a soul as deep as the deepest of rivers, my chest has the power to expand without limit. I am a master and I am advised to adopt the humility of the cripple. Yesterday, awakening to the world, I saw the sky turn upon itself utterly and wholly. I wanted to rise, but the disemboweled silence fell back upon me, its wings paralyzed. Without responsibility, straddling Nothingness and Infinity, I began to weep.

Notes

1 Jean Lhermitte, *L'Image de notre corps* (Paris, Nouvelle Revue critique, 1939), p. 17.
2 *Anti-Semite and Jew* (New York: Grove Press, 1960), p. 95.
3 Sir Alan Burns, *Colour Prejudice* (London: Allen & Unwin, 1948), p. 16.
4 *Anti-Semite and Jew*, pp. 112–13.
5 Jon Alfred Mjoen, "Harmonic and Disharmonic Race-crossings," The Second International Congress of Eugenics (1921), *Eugenics in Race and State*, vol. II, p. 60, quoted in Burns, *Colour Prejudice*, p. 120.
6 In English in the original. (Translator's note.)
7 "Ce que l'homme noir apporte," in Claude Nordey, *L'Homme de couleur* (Paris: Plon, 1939), pp. 309–10.
8 Aimé Césaire, *Cahier d'un retour au pays natal* (Paris: Présence Africaine, 1956), pp. 77–8.
9 My italics – F.F.
10 My italics – F.F.
11 Léopold Senghor, "Ce que l'homme noir apporte," in Nordey, *L'Homme de couleur*, p. 205.
12 Aimé Césaire, Introduction to Victor Schoelcher, *Esclavage et colonisation* (Paris: Presses Universitaires de France, 1948), p. 7.

13 Ibid., p. 8.
14 Jean-Paul Sartre, *Orphée Noir*, preface to *Anthologie de la nouvelle poésie nègre et malgache* (Paris: Presses Universitaires de France, 1948), pp. xl ff.
15 Ibid., p. xliv.
16 *Home of the Brave* [play by Arthur Laurents (New York: Random House, 1946)].

14

The History of Masculinity

R. W. Connell

I have stressed that masculinities come into existence at particular times and places, and are always subject to change. Masculinities are, in a word, historical . . . But so far the argument has lacked historical depth and an appropriate scale.

To understand the current pattern of masculinities we need to look back over the period in which it came into being. Since masculinity exists only in the context of a whole structure of gender relations, we need to locate it in the formation of the modern gender order as a whole – a process that has taken about four centuries. The local histories of masculinity recently published provide essential detail, but we need an argument of broader scope as well.

It is mainly ethnographic research that has made the scale of the issue, and the vital connections, clear: the unprecedented growth of European and North American power, the creation of global empires and a global capitalist economy, and the unequal encounter of gender orders in the colonized world. I say "connections" and not "context", because the fundamental point is that masculinities are not only shaped by the process of imperial expansion, they are active in that process and help to shape it.

Popular culture tells us this without prompting. Exemplars of masculinity, whether legendary or real – from Paul Bunyan in Canada via Davy Crockett in the United States to Lawrence "of Arabia" in England – have very often been men of the frontier. A game I played as a boy in Australia was, extraordinarily enough, a ritual of imperial expansion in North America, shipped across the Pacific in comic-book and Hollywood images of masculinity: a replay of frontier warfare between "Cowboys and Indians". We cannot understand the connection of masculinity and violence at a personal level without understanding that it is also a global connection. European/American masculinities were deeply implicated in the world-wide violence through which European/American culture became dominant.

What follows is, inevitably, only a sketch of a vastly complex history. Yet it seems important to get even rough bearings on a history so charged with significance for our current situation.

Reprinted from *Masculinities* (Berkeley: University of California Press, 1995), pp. 185–203, 253–5.

The Production of Masculinity in the Formation of the Modern Gender Order

In the period from about 1450 to about 1650 (the "long" sixteenth century, in the useful phrase of the French historian Fernand Braudel) the modern capitalist economy came into being around the North Atlantic, and the modern gender order also began to take shape in that region. Four developments seem particularly important for the making of those configurations of social practice that we now call "masculinity".

First was the cultural change that produced new understandings of sexuality and personhood in metropolitan Europe. When medieval Catholicism, already changing, was disrupted by the spread of Renaissance secular culture and the Protestant reformation, long-established and powerful ideals for men's lives were also disrupted. The monastic system crumbled. The power of religion to control the intellectual world and to regulate everyday life began its slow, contested, but decisive decline.

On the one hand, this opened the way for a growing cultural emphasis on the conjugal household – exemplified by no less a figure than Martin Luther, the married monk. Marital heterosexuality displaced monastic denial as the most honoured form of sexuality. The cultural authority of compulsory heterosexuality clearly followed this shift.

On the other hand, the new emphasis on individuality of expression and on each person's unmediated relationship with God led towards individualism and the concept of an autonomous self. These were cultural prerequisites for the idea of masculinity itself, . . . a type of person whose gendered character is the reason for his (or her, in the case of masculine women) actions. Classical philosophy from Descartes to Kant, as Victor Seidler has argued, construed reason and science through oppositions with the natural world and with emotion. With masculinity defined as a character structure marked by rationality, and Western civilization defined as the bearer of reason to a benighted world, a cultural link between the legitimation of patriarchy and the legitimation of empire was forged.[1]

The second development was the creation of overseas empires by the Atlantic seaboard states – Portugal and Spain, then the Netherlands, France and England. (The overland empires of Russia and the United States, and the overseas empires of Germany, Italy and Japan, came in a second round of imperialism.)

Empire was a gendered enterprise from the start, initially an outcome of the segregated men's occupations of soldiering and sea trading. When European women went to the colonies it was mainly as wives and servants within households controlled by men. Apart from a few monarchs (notably Isabella and Elizabeth), the imperial states created to rule the new empires were entirely staffed by men, and developed a statecraft based on the force supplied by the organized bodies of men.

The men who applied force at the colonial frontier, the "conquistadors" as they were called in the Spanish case, were perhaps the first group to become defined as a masculine cultural type in the modern sense. The conquistador was a figure displaced from customary social relationships, often extremely violent in the search for land, gold and converts, and difficult for the imperial state to control. (The hostility between the royal authorities and Hernan Cortés, the Spanish conqueror of Mexico, was notorious.) Loss of control at the frontier is a recurring theme in the history of empires, and is closely connected with the making of masculine exemplars.

An immediate consequence was a clash over the ethics of conquest, and a demand for controls. Bartolomé de Las Casas's famous denunciation of the bloodbath that resulted from the uncontrolled violence of the Spanish conquerors, in his *Very Brief Relation of the Destruction of the Indies*, is thus a significant moment in the history of masculinity. "Insatiable greed and ambition, the greatest ever seen in the world, is the cause of their villainies." Las Casas's rhetoric was literally correct. This was something new in the world, and his own work was the first extended critique of an emerging gender form.[2]

The third key development was the growth of the cities that were the centres of commercial capitalism, notably Antwerp, London and Amsterdam, creating a new setting for everyday life. This was both more anonymous, and more coherently regulated, than the frontier or the countryside.

The main gender consequences of this change became visible only in the seventeenth and eighteenth centuries, but for brevity I will note them here. The changed conditions of everyday life made a more thoroughgoing individualism possible. In combination with the "first industrial revolution" and the accumulation of wealth from trade, slaving and colonies, a calculative rationality began to permeate urban culture. This was the development picked up in Max Weber's thesis about the "Protestant ethic", and it is interesting to notice the gendered character of the "spirit of capitalism". Weber's prime exhibit was Benjamin Franklin, and he quoted this passage:

> The most trifling actions that affect a man's credit are to be regarded. The sound of your hammer at five in the morning, or eight at night, heard by a creditor, makes him easy six months longer; but if he sees you at a billiard-table, or hears your voice at a tavern, when you should be at work, he sends for his money the next day...

A man, literally, is meant. The entrepreneurial culture and workplaces of commercial capitalism institutionalized a form of masculinity, creating and legitimating new forms of gendered work and power in the counting-house, the warehouse and the exchange.

But this was not the only transformation of gender in the commercial cities. The same period saw the emergence of sexual subcultures. The best documented are the Molly houses of early eighteenth-century London, "Molly" being a slang term used for effeminate men who met in particular houses and taverns, and whose gender practices included cross-dressing, dancing together and sexual intercourse with each other.

Historians of the period have noted a shift in medical ideologies of gender, from an earlier period when gender anomalies were freely attributed to hermaphroditic bodies, to a later period when a clear-cut dichotomy of bodies was presumed and anomalies therefore became a question of gender deviance. The requirement that one must have a personal identity as a man or a woman, rather than simply a location in the social order as a person with a male or female (or hermaphroditic) body, gradually hardened in European culture. Mary Wollstonecraft's perception of the social bases of women's gendered character, in contrast to that of men, provided the core argument of her *Vindication of the Rights of Woman* at the end of the eighteenth century.[3]

The fourth development was the onset of large-scale European civil war. The sixteenth- and seventeenth-century wars of religion, merging into the dynastic wars of the seventeenth and eighteenth centuries, did more than relocate a few kings and bishops. They disturbed the legitimacy of the gender order. The World Turned Upside Down by revolutionary struggles could be the gender as well as the class order. In the English-speaking countries it was the Quakers, a religious-cum-political sect emerging from the upheavals of the English civil war, who made the first public defence of equality in religion for women. They not only proclaimed the principle, but actually gave women a significant organizing role in practice.

This challenge was turned back (though its memory lingered). The patriarchal order was consolidated by another product of the European civil wars, the strong centralized state. In the era of absolute monarchy the state provided a larger-scale institutionalization of men's power than had been possible before. The professional armies constructed in the religious and dynastic wars, as well as in imperial conquest, became a key part of the modern state. Military prowess as a test of honour was in medieval Europe a class theme of knighthood – the connection mocked in Cervantes' *Don Quixote*. It increasingly became an issue of masculinity and nationalism, a transition visible in Shakespeare's most chauvinistic play:

> On, on, you Noblish English,
> Whose blood is fet from Fathers of Warre-proofe:
> Fathers, that like so many *Alexanders*,
> Have in these parts from Morne till Even fought
> And sheath'd their Swords, for lack of argument.[4]

With the eighteenth century, in seaboard Europe and North America at least, we can speak of a gender order in which masculinity in the modern sense – gendered individual character, defined through an opposition with femininity and institutionalized in economy and state – had been produced and stabilized. For this period we can even define a hegemonic type of masculinity and describe some of its relations to subordinated and marginalized forms.

Though cultural change in the cities has caught the attention of historians, it was the class of hereditary landowners, the gentry, who dominated the North Atlantic world of the eighteenth century. George Washington was a notable example of the class and its hegemonic form of masculinity. Based in land ownership, gentry masculinity was involved in capitalist economic relations (production for the market, extraction of rents) but did not emphasize strict rational calculation in the manner of the merchants.

Nor was it based on a concept of the isolated individual. Land ownership was embedded in kinship; the lineage as much as the individual was the social unit. British politics in the age of Walpole and the Pitts, for instance, generally followed family lines with the state apparatus controlled by great families through patronage. British rule in India and North America was organized on much the same lines.

Gentry masculinity was closely integrated with the state. The gentry provided local administration (through justices of the peace, in the British system) and staffed the military apparatus. The gentry provided army and navy officers, and often recruited the rank and file themselves. At the intersection between this direct involvement in violence and the ethic of family honour was the institution of the duel. Willingness to face an opponent in a potentially lethal one-to-one combat was a key test of gentry masculinity, and it was affronts to honour that provoked such confrontations.

In this sense the masculinity of the gentry was emphatic and violent. Yet the gender order as a whole was not as strongly regulated as it later became. Thus a French gentleman, the Chevalier d'Eon, could be switched from masculine to feminine gender without being socially discredited (though remaining an object of curiosity for the rest of her life). Licence in sexual relationships, especially with women of the lower classes, was a prerogative of rank. It was even to a degree celebrated, by the "libertines". It seems that homosexual relationships were being increasingly understood as defining a specific type of men, though in the writings of the Marquis de Sade they are still an aspect of libertinage in general.

Gentry masculinity involved domestic authority over women, though the women were actively involved in making and maintaining the network of alliances that tied the gentry together – the strategies lovingly dissected in Jane Austen's novels.

Gentry masculinity involved a much more brutal relationship with the agricultural workforce, still the bulk of the population. The social boundary here was marked by the code of honour, which was not applied outside the gentry. Control was exerted by evictions, imprisonment, the lash, transportation and hangings. Applying this violent discipline was not a specialized profession. It was an ordinary part of local administration, from the English countryside, and George Washington's slave estate in Virginia, to the new colony at the Antipodes – where Samuel Marsden, the "Flogging Parson", became a well-known justice of the peace.[5]

Transformations

The history of European/American masculinity over the last two hundred years can broadly be understood as the splitting of gentry masculinity, its gradual displacement by new hegemonic forms, and the emergence of an array of subordinated and marginalized masculinities. The reasons for these changes are immensely complex, but I would suggest that three are central: challenges to the gender order by women, the logic of the gendered accumulation process in industrial capitalism, and the power relations of empire.

The challenge from women is now well documented. The nineteenth century saw a historic change in gender politics, the emergence of feminism as a form of mass politics – a mobilization for women's rights, especially the suffrage, in public arenas. This was closely connected to the growth of the liberal state and its reliance on concepts of citizenship.

Yet women's challenges to the gender order were not confined to the suffrage movement, which had a limited reach. Gentry and middle-class women were active in reforms of morals and domestic customs in the early nineteenth century which sharply challenged the sexual prerogatives of gentry men. Working-class women contested their economic dependence on men as the factory system evolved. Middle-class women again challenged men's prerogatives through the temperance movement of the late nineteenth century. The conditions for the maintenance of patriarchy changed with these challenges, and the kind of masculinity which could be hegemonic changed in response.

With the spread of industrial economies and the growth of bureaucratic states (whether liberal or autocratic), the economic and political power of the land-owning gentry declined. This was a slow process, and effective rear-guard actions were fought. For instance the Prussian gentry, the Junkers, kept control of the German state into the twentieth century. In the course of the transition, some of the forms of gentry masculinity were handed on to the men of the bourgeoisie. The historian Robert Nye has given us a remarkable example: the transfer of a prickly code of honour, centring on the institution of the duel, to the bourgeoisie in France. The number of duels fought in France actually rose in the later nineteenth century, and a profession of duelling-master developed to induct men into the code and teach the techniques of sword-fighting.[6]

Though some men died in duels, this was basically a symbolic definition of masculinity through violence. Real warfare became increasingly organized. The mass armies of the revolutionary and Napoleonic wars became standing conscript armies with permanent officer corps. Such corps, at first recruited from the gentry, became repositories of gentry codes of masculinity, the Prussian officer corps being the most famous example. (Hitler's generals in the 1940s were still mostly drawn from this background.) But the social context was changed. The new officer corps were professionalized, trained at military schools.

Violence was now combined with rationality, with bureaucratic techniques of organization and constant technological advance in weaponry and transport. Armed forces were reorganized to bring them under the control of a centre of technical knowledge, the General Staff, an institution created by the Prussians and copied in fear by the other Great Powers. If Las Casas's writings can be regarded as a key document of early modern masculinity, perhaps the equivalent for the nineteenth century is Carl von Clausewitz's classic *On War*, proclaiming a social technology of rationalized violence on the largest possible scale. Clausewitz was one of the reformers who created the new Prussian army.[7]

It was the social technique of bureaucratically rationalized violence, as much as sheer superiority of weapons, that made European states and settlers almost invincible in the colonial wars of the nineteenth century. But this technique risked destroying the society that sustained it. The vast destructiveness of the Great War led to revolutionary upheaval in 1917–23. In much of Europe the capitalist order was stabilized, after a decade of further struggle, only by fascist movements.

In gender terms, fascism was a naked reassertion of male supremacy in societies that had been moving towards equality for women. To accomplish this, fascism promoted new images of hegemonic masculinity, glorifying irrationality (the "triumph of the will", thinking with "the blood") and the unrestrained violence of the frontline soldier. Its dynamics soon led to a new and even more devastating global war.[8]

The defeat of fascism in the Second World War cut off this turn in hegemonic masculinity. But it certainly did not end the bureaucratic institutionalization of violence. Hitler himself had modernized his armed forces and was an enthusiast for high-technology weapons; in that respect fascism supported rationalization. The Red Army and United States armed forces which triumphed in 1945 continued to multiply their destructive capability, as the nuclear arsenal built up. In China, Pakistan, Indonesia, Argentina, Chile and much of Africa, less technologically advanced armies remain central to the politics of their respective states. There are currently about twenty million in the world's armed forces, the vast majority being men, with their organization modelled on the armies of the North Atlantic powers.[9]

The growing significance of technical expertise in the military paralleled developments in other parts of the economy. The nineteenth century saw the foundation of mass elementary schooling, and the twentieth century has added public secondary and university systems. Research institutes were invented and the research capabilities of corporations and government departments have been hugely expanded. Labour markets have been transformed by the multiplication of professions with claims to expertise. Information industries have expanded geometrically. Currently one of the two richest persons in the United States is a specialist in computer programming, a man whose company designed the operating system for the computer I am using to write this text (plus a few million other computers).[10]

These trends have seen another split in hegemonic masculinity. Practice organized around dominance was increasingly incompatible with practice organized around expertise or technical knowledge. Management was divided from professions, and relations between the two became a chronic problem in corporations and in the state. (The correct use of experts – "on tap or on top" – is a classic issue in management science; while the idea of "management science" itself reveals the prestige of expertise.) Factional divisions opened in both capitalist ruling classes and communist elites between those willing to coerce workers (conservatives/ hard-liners), and those willing to make concessions on the strength of technological advance and economic growth (liberals/reformers).

A polarity thus developed within hegemonic masculinity between dominance and technical expertise. In this case, however, neither version has succeeded in displacing the other. They currently coexist as gendered practices, sometimes in opposition and sometimes meshing. As alternative versions of hegemonic masculinity they can be called upon by advertising and political campaigns – "tough on crime" vs. "information superhighway", to take examples from current United States politics....

As hegemonic masculinity in the metropole became more subject to rationalization, violence and licence were, symbolically and to some extent actually, pushed out to the colonies. On the frontier of white settlement regulation was ineffective, violence endemic and physical conditions harsh. Industries such as mining offered spectacular profits on a chancy basis. A very imbalanced sex ratio allowed a cultural masculinization of the frontier.

Jock Phillips's study of New Zealand . . . draws the contrast between two groups of men and two cultural accounts of masculinity: the brawling single frontiersman and the settled married pioneer farmer. The distinction is familiar on the Western frontier in North America. It is a striking fact that even before this frontier closed, with military defeat of the native peoples and the spread of white settlement across the continent, frontiersmen were being promoted as exemplars of masculinity.

The novels of James Fenimore Cooper and the Wild West show of Buffalo Bill Cody were early steps in a course that led eventually to the Western as a film genre and its self-conscious cult of inarticulate masculine heroism. The historian John MacKenzie has called attention to the similar cult of the hunter in the late nineteenth-century British empire. Wilderness, hunting and bushcraft were welded into a distinct ideology of manhood by figures such as Robert Baden-Powell, the founder of the scouting movement for boys, and Theodore Roosevelt in the United States.[11]

The scouting movement celebrated the frontier, but it was actually a movement for boys in the metropole. Here it took its place in a long series of attempts to foster particular forms of masculinity among boys. Other moments in this history include the nineteenth-century reform of the British elite public school, in the period after Dr Arnold; the Church of England Boys' Brigade directed at working-class youth; the German youth movement at the turn of the century; the Hitler Youth, turned into a mass institution when the Nazis came to power in Germany; and widespread attempts at military training of secondary school boys through army cadet corps, still operating in Australia when I was in high school in 1960. (I rose to the rank of corporal, and learned to fire the Lee-Enfield rifle, a state-of-the-art weapon during the Boer War.)

The striking thing about these movements was not their success, always limited, but the persistence with which ideologists of patriarchy struggled to control and direct the reproduction of masculinity. It is clear that this had become a significant problem in gender politics.[12]

Why was this a problem? Some turn-of-the-century ideologists, as Jeffrey Hantover noted in a study of the Boy Scouts of America, expressed a fear that boys would be feminized through too much influence by women. This directs us to changes in the organization of domestic life. Pressure from women against gentry masculinity had been part of the historical dynamic that led to a key institution of bourgeois culture, the ideology and practice of "separate spheres". This defined a domestic sphere of action for women, contrasted with a sphere of economic and political action for men.

The division was supported by an ideology of natural difference between women and men, which was not only promoted by male ideologists (for instance, it was a theme of the duelling cult in France), but was widely acceptable to nineteenth-century feminists as well. The women's sphere was, in ordinary practice, subordinate to the men's. But within that sphere bourgeois women might act as employers of servants and managers of business (with advisors such as Mrs Beeton), and could often count on considerable autonomy. And it was in that sphere that the rearing of young boys was located.[13]

At much the same time hegemonic masculinity was purged in terms of sexuality. As gay historians have shown, the late nineteenth century was the time when "the homosexual" as a social type became clearly defined. This involved both a medical and a legal demarcation. At earlier periods of history, sodomy had been officially seen as an act which might be undertaken by any man who gave way to evil. Homosexual desire was now viewed as defining a particular type of man, the "invert" in the most common medical view. New laws criminalized homosexual contact as such (called "gross indecency" in the 1885 Labouchère Amendment in England), and routine police surveillance of "perverts" followed.

From the point of view of hegemonic masculinity, the potential for homoerotic pleasure was expelled from the masculine and located in a deviant group, symbolically assimilated to women or to beasts. There was no mirror-type of "the heterosexual". Rather, heterosexuality became a required part of manliness. The contradiction between this purged definition of masculinity, and the actual conditions of emotional life among men in military and paramilitary groups reached crisis level in fascism. It helped to justify, and possibly to motivate, Hitler's murder of Ernst Röhm, the homosexual leader of the Storm-troopers, in 1934.[14]

The gradual displacement of the gentry by businessmen and bureaucrats in the metropolitan countries was paralleled by the transformation of peasant populations into industrial and urban working classes. This change too had its gender dimension. The factory system meant a sharper separation of home from workplace, and the dominance of money wages changed economic relations in the household. The expansion of industrial production saw the emergence of forms of masculinity organized around wage-earning capacity, mechanical skills, domestic patriarchy and combative solidarity among wage earners.

Women were, in fact, a large part of the original workforce in the textile factories of the Industrial Revolution, and were also present in coal mining, printing and steelmaking. They were involved in industrial militancy, sometimes were leaders of strikes, as Mary Blewett has shown for the weavers of Fall River, Massachusetts. The expulsion of women from heavy industry was thus a key process in the formation of working-class masculinity, connected with the strategy of the family wage and drawing on the bourgeois ideology of separate spheres. The craft union movement can be seen as the key institutionalization of this kind of masculinity.[15]

But only part of the working class was ever unionized, or commanded a family wage. The creation of this respectable, orderly masculinity had, as its dialectical opposite, the development of rough, disorderly masculinities among the marginalized "dangerous classes". The fear this aroused even among revolutionary socialists can be felt in Friedrich Engels's savage remarks on the urban poor:

> The *lumpenproletariat*, this scum of depraved elements from all classes, with headquarters in the big cities, is the worst of all the possible allies. This rabble is absolutely venal and absolutely brazen . . . Every leader of the workers who uses these scoundrels as guards or relies on them for support proves himself by this action alone a traitor to the movement.

Such groups have attracted little attention as yet from historians of gender, though their presence is documented by historians of class in studies of "outcast London", of the "new unionism" of the late nineteenth century, and of workplaces such as wharves and markets which employed casual labour.[16]

Outside the metropole, the economic logic of empire led to extraordinary population shifts as labour forces were moved from one continent to another. This meant the emigration of "free" settlers to New Zealand, Australia, Canada and Algeria, but violent enslavement or coercive employment in many other cases. They include the shipping of an African slave workforce to Brazil, the Caribbean and North America; the shipping of indentured labour from India to the

Caribbean, parts of Africa, Malaya and Fiji; the shipping of Chinese labour to build North American railroads, and convict labour from England and Ireland to Australia.

The legacy of these population movements has commonly been a racial hierarchy, of considerable importance – both symbolically and practically – for the construction of masculinities.... [B]lack masculinity has commonly been pictured as a sexual and social threat in dominant white cultures. This gender ideology has fuelled harsh policing and political racism in settings ranging from the United States to South Africa to contemporary France.

The realities of masculinity in transplanted labour forces have been shaped by the conditions of settlement, which commonly involved poverty and heavy labour as well as the disruption of families and communities. Some of the resulting complexities can be seen in Chandra Jayawardena's study of sugar workers in British Guiana in the 1950s, descendants of a labour force transplanted from India in the later nineteenth century. Their beliefs and social practices emphasized equality and social solidarity, "mati" or mateship. Heavy drinking – always in groups – expressed this solidarity. Disputes about offences to honour arose among these men, called "eye-pass" disputes; but they had a very different logic from the duelling disputes among the French bourgeoisie. They were not based on claims to individual distinction but on the collective rejection of such claims, which would have broken up the community of poor labourers. Here masculine assertion occurred in the cause of equality, not competition.[17]

In colonies where conquered populations were not displaced or massacred but were made into a subordinated labour force on the spot – most of Latin America, India and South-East Asia and parts of Africa – the gender consequences involved a reshaping of local culture under the pressure of the colonizers. The British in India constructed different images of masculinity for different peoples under their rule, for instance, contrasting effeminate Bengalis with fierce Pathans and Sikhs. Like the ideology of white military masculinity discussed earlier, this imagery probably had a role in recruitment and social control.

It is a familiar suggestion that Latin American machismo was a product of the interplay of cultures under colonialism. The conquistadors provided both provocation and model, Spanish Catholicism provided the ideology of female abnegation, and economic oppression blocked other sources of authority for men. As Walter Williams has shown, Spanish colonialism also involved a violent and sustained assault on the customary homosexuality of native cultures. This has influenced contemporary expressions of masculinity. In Mexico, for instance, the public presentation of masculinity is aggressively heterosexual, though the practice is often bisexual.[18]

The history of masculinity, it should be abundantly clear, is not linear. There is no master line of development to which all else is subordinate, no simple shift from "traditional" to "modern". Rather we see, in the world created by the European empires, complex structures of gender relations in which dominant, subordinated and marginalized masculinities are in constant interaction, changing the conditions for each others' existence and transforming themselves as they do.

With that banal but necessary historical point in mind, let us turn to the current state of play.

The Present Moment

The idea that we live at the moment when a traditional male sex role is softening is as drastically inadequate as the idea that a true, natural masculinity is now being recovered. Both ideas ignore most of the world. To grasp what is going on in this global network of gender institutions and relationships requires a very different perspective.

On a global scale, the most profound change is the export of the European/American gender order to the colonized world. There is every reason to think this trend is accelerating. As the world capitalist order becomes more complete, as more local production systems are linked in to global markets and local labour brought into wage systems, local versions of Western patriarchal institutions are installed. These include corporations, state bureaucracies, armies and mass education systems. I have already indicated the scale of Westernized armies in the contemporary world. Education sectors are somewhat bigger (in the developing countries as a whole there are approximately 140 teachers for every 100 soldiers). Corporate sectors are bigger again.

This provides a solid institutional base for changes in gender ideology and imagery, and changes in everyday practice. The export of European/American gender ideology can be seen in the mass media of the developing world. A notable example is the promotion of Xuxa in Brazil as an icon of femininity – a blonde model who has become remarkably popular, and remarkably rich, through a television programme for children. (In the same country, street children who don't have television sets have been murdered by male death squads.) Gender regimes are also being transformed in everyday practice. For instance, indigenous customs of same-sex eroticism, as far apart as Brazil and Java, are converging on the Western urban model of "gay identity".[19]

For the first time in history, there is a prospect of all indigenous gender regimes foundering under this institutional and cultural pressure. Some gender configurations have already gone. One example is the Confucian tradition of male homosexuality in China, the "passions of the cut sleeve" (so called from the story of an emperor who cut off the sleeve of his robe rather than disturb his sleeping lover). Another is the tradition of heterosexual eroticism and women's sexual freedom in Polynesian Hawaii. To say they are gone is perhaps too mechanical. Both these traditions were deliberately destroyed under the influence of Western homophobia and missionary puritanism.[20]

Replacing the diversity of gender orders is an increasingly coordinated, increasingly visible global gender order. European/American gender arrangements are hegemonic in this system. A dramatic demonstration is provided by the recent history of Eastern Europe. As the Stalinist regimes collapsed and market economies were installed, Western ideologies of gender were installed with them and state guarantees of equality for women (which were never consistently applied but had some practical force) have been lost.

However, the global gender order is not homogeneous, not just a matter of cloning European/American culture. Feminist research on women workers in the global factory of modern multinational production has shown differentiated positions being constructed: for electronics assembly workers in Malaysia, prostitutes in the Philippines and Thailand, garment workers in Mexico.[21]

The same is certainly true for men, though this has been less studied. In Japan, for instance, the modernization programme of the Meiji regime in the late nineteenth century led to a large expansion of the education system and competition for access to administrative and clerical jobs. This in turn led to the emergence of the "salaryman", the deferential but competitive servant of the corporate oligarchs who dominate the Japanese economy. (The term dates from the First World War, though it has only been noticed by English-speaking countries in the last two decades.) This is a notable example of a class-specific form of masculinity which is only conceivable in a global capitalist economy but is also culturally and politically specific.[22]

We should also register the strength of reactions against the Western gender order. The most dramatic, in the last two decades [since the early 1970s], has been in those parts of the Islamic world where political independence has been followed by a reassertion of men's patriarchal authority. Men who have forced women to wear the veil and withdraw from public arenas are pursuing a gender politics through the same gestures as an anti-colonial politics. (This is not a necessary part of Islam; the largest Islamic country in the world, Indonesia, pays no attention to the veil.)[23]

The men of the metropolitan countries are, collectively the main beneficiaries of the contemporary world order. The most striking feature of their historical situation is the vastly increased power, over the natural world and over the services of other people, that the accumulation and concentration of wealth has delivered to them. The scale of the concentration should be registered. On recent calculations, the richest fifth of the world's population receives 83 percent of total world income; the poorest fifth receives only 1.4 percent. (And national-level studies show the distribution of wealth is substantially more unequal than the distribution of income.)[24]

This amplified power is realized in a number of ways. As consumption of resources (such as oil and ores from the rest of the world), it sustains a level of material comfort previously available only to aristocracies. As investment in technology, it has eliminated most heavy labour from production processes in the rich countries and . . . has restructured occupational hierarchies. The material uses and pleasures of male bodies have thus changed dramatically.

At the same time the wealth of the metropolitan countries sustains elaborate service industries. In these industries the symbolic meanings of masculinity are elaborated – notably in mass media, commercial sport and transportation (fast cars and heavy trucks being vehicles of masculinity in every sense). Metropolitan wealth and technology also sustain masculinized armed forces which have reached a terrifying level of destructiveness, from time to time visited on Third-World opponents (Vietnam, Cambodia, Afghanistan, Iraq).

Given these circumstances alone, we should not be surprised to find among the men of the rich countries a widespread awareness of change in gender arrangements. . . . What is perhaps more surprising is a sense of change out of control, of dislocation in gender relations. This too is evidently widespread.[25]

The enormous growth of the material power of the men in metropolitan countries has been accompanied, I would argue, by an intensification of crisis tendencies in the gender order. . . . They have resulted, clearly enough, in a major loss of legitimacy for patriarchy, and different groups of men are now negotiating this loss in very different ways.

The clearest sign of this loss, and the most striking feature of the present moment in the gender order of the rich countries, is the open challenge to men's privileges made by feminism. By virtue of these countries' wealth and control of mass communications, this challenge circulated globally as soon as it was made. It has been pursued in different ways. "Western" feminism is now engaged in a complex and tense negotiation with "Third-World" feminism about the legacy of colonialism and racism.[26]

As I have suggested already, the challenge to hegemonic heterosexuality from lesbian and gay movements is logically as profound as the challenge to men's power from feminism, but has not been circulated in the same way. Most heterosexual men are able to marginalize this challenge, to regard it as an issue concerning a minority and not affecting them.

The oppositional movements have opened up a range of possibilities for gender relations which is also historically new. Jeffrey Weeks and others have pointed to the recent multiplication of sexual subcultures and sexual identities. . . . [T]he stabilization of gay communities and gay social identity in metropolitan cities means that the gender order now contains a kind of permanent alternative. The very straight gay is at present a loyal opposition, to be sure, but hegemonic heterosexuality cannot now monopolize the imagination in the way it once did.[27]

The expansion of possibilities is not only a question of growing variety in current sexual practice. There has also been a flowering of utopian thinking about gender and sexuality, a sense of expanded historical possibilities for the longer term. A genre such as feminist science fiction may sound exotic, but when one compares it with the male-supremacist "space westerns" that used to monopolize science fiction (and are still being churned out), the leap of imagination is very clear. Utopian thinking about sexuality and gender is found in other genres too, among them film, painting, poetry, reggae and rock.[28]

The men of the metropolitan countries thus inhabit a paradoxical moment of history. More than any category of people before them, they collectively have the power – the accumulated resources, the physical and social techniques – to shape the future. More possible futures than were ever recognized have been opened up through the work of feminist and sexual liberation movements and through utopian thinking.

But the category "men" in the rich countries is not a *group* capable of deliberating and choosing a new historical direction. The differences within this category, as we have seen, are profound. To the extent the members of this category share an interest, as a result of the unequal distribution of resources across the world, and between men and women within the rich countries, it would lead them to reject utopian change and defend the status quo.

In this situation their own gender becomes an inescapable issue. The meaning of masculinity, the variety of masculinities, the difficulties of reproducing masculinity, the nature of gender and the extent of gender inequality all come into question and are furiously debated. I suggest that the growth of interest in masculinity at this point in history is not accidental. The issue will not go away, though media attention to such exotic manifestations as the mythopoetic men's movement will doubtless fade.

These circumstances have produced a wider range of politics addressing masculinity, more attempts to define masculinity and influence its reproduction, than have existed before.

Notes

1 On reason, masculinity and classical philosophy, see Seidler 1989, ch. 2. Fromm 1942 opened up some of the themes sketched here.

2 Las Casas 1992 [1552]: 31. This is not to say his critique was couched in gender terms; it was phrased in the language of Catholic evangelism and political morality.

3 For the quotation from Franklin, Weber 1976 [1904–5]: 49. For the Molly houses, Bray 1982, ch. 4. On bodies and genders, Trumbach 1991; on fixed identity, Foucault 1980b; and on the formation of gendered character, Wollstonecraft 1975 [1792].

4 *Henry V,* Act III, scene i. Henry's speech is class-stratified; this is the part addressed to the nobility. Hence "noblish", usually corrected to "noblest", may contain an echo of "noblesse". Shakespeare, like Cervantes, was also adept at deflating the ideology of valour:

> Can Honour set too a legge? No: or an arme? No: Or take away the greefe of a wound? No. Honour hath no skill in Surgerie, then? No. What is Honour? A word. What is that word Honour? Ayre: a trim reckoning. (*Henry IV, Part I*, Act V, scene i)

For the Quaker story, see Bacon 1986, ch. 1.

5 This sketch of gentry masculinity is put together from a wide range of sources, principally British, American and Australian. For d'Eon, see Kates 1991; on the duel, Kiernan 1988. For gentry relations with the agricultural workforce in the Antipodes, Connell and Irving 1992, ch. 2. Curiously the most famous theorist of libertinage, a member of this class, took what was already an old-fashioned view of sodomy as an expression of generalized enthusiasm for evil: de Sade 1966 [1785].

6 Nye 1993.

7 Clausewitz 1976 [1832]. On the Prussian officer corps, see Wheeler-Bennett 1953, and on the General Staff concept, Dupuy 1977.

8 On masculine imagery in the origins of German fascism, see Theweleit 1987; for its development by the Nazi leadership, see, for example, Manvell and Fraenkel 1960.

9 These Statistics, and others in the chapter, relate to the early 1990s. Eds.

10 Bill Gates, part-owner of Microsoft Corporation and estimated by *Forbes* magazine (19 October 1992) to be worth 6.3 billion dollars. . . .

11 Phillips 1987; for similar themes in the United States, see Stein 1984. On the "hunter", see MacKenzie 1987. Marsh 1990 cautions that this imagery could be very remote from the reality of metropolitan life.

12 Several of these movements are documented in Mangan and Walvin 1987.

13 Hantover 1978. This sketch of the ideology and practice of "separate spheres" is of course an enormous oversimplification; for the complex details, in middle-class England, see the wonderful study by Davidoff and Hall 1987.

14 Weeks 1977, D'Emilio and Freedman 1988. The sexual politics of the Röhm purge is noted in Orlow 1969, 1973, ch. 3.

15 Blewett 1990. On the family wage and expulsions of women from industry, see Seccombe 1986, Cockburn 1983.

16 Engels 1969 [1870]: 163. A classic of class-analytic research on the urban poor is Stedman Jones 1971, who notes a softening of Engels's attitude to the poor when they looked like candidates for being organized.
17 Jayawardena 1963.
18 For British constructions of Bengali masculinity, see Sinha 1987. For...the Spanish colonial assault on the berdache and its long-term consequences, Williams 1986: ch. 7.
19 For the remarkable story of Xuxa, see Simpson 1993. On the emergence of gay identity in Brazil, see Parker 1985, in Java, see Oetomo 1990.
20 Hinsch 1990; Ortner 1981.
21 Fuentes and Ehrenreich 1983.
22 Kinmonth 1981.
23 For this dynamic in Algeria, see Knauss 1987.
24 For these estimates, see United Nations Development Programme 1992.
25 For all its flakiness as research, Hite 1981 at least documents this....
26 For an account of this negotiation, see Bulbeck 1988.
27 Weeks 1986. Further evidence of the stabilization of the alternative is in Herdt 1992.
28 I have in mind work such as Le Guin 1973, Piercy 1976.

References

Bacon, Margaret Hope. 1986. *Mothers of Feminism: The Story of Quaker Women in America*. San Francisco: Harper & Row.

Blewett, Mary H. 1990. "Masculinity and mobility: the dilemma of Lancashire weavers and spinners in late-nineteenth-century Fall River, Massachusetts", pp. 164–77 in *Meanings for Manhood: Constructions of Masculinity in Victorian America*, ed. Mark C. Carnes and Clyde Griffen. Chicago: University of Chicago Press.

Bray, Alan. 1982. *Homosexuality in Renaissance England*. London: Gay Men's Press.

Bulbeck, Chilla. 1988. *One World Women's Movement*. London: Pluto Press.

Clausewitz, Carl von. 1976 [1832]. *On War*. Princeton: Princeton University Press.

Cockburn, Cynthia. 1983. *Brothers: Male Dominance and Technological Change*. London: Pluto Press.

Connell, R. W. and T. H. Irving. 1992. *Class Structure in Australian History*, 2nd edn. Melbourne: Longman Cheshire.

Davidoff, Leonore and Catherine Hall. 1987. *Family Fortunes: Men and Women of the English Middle Class*. London: Hutchinson.

D'Emilio, John and Estelle B. Freedman. 1988. *Intimate Matters: A History of Sexuality in America*. New York: Harper & Row.

Dupuy, T. N. 1977. *A Genius for War: The German Army and General Staff, 1807–1945*. London: Macdonald & Jane's.

Engels, Friedrich. 1969 [1870]. Preface to "The Peasant War in Germany", pp. 158–65 in Karl Marx and Friedrich Engels, *Selected Works*, vol. 2. Moscow: Progress.

Foucault, Michel. 1980b. *Introduction to Herculine Barbin: Being the Recently Discovered Memoirs of a Nineteenth-Century French Hermaphrodite*. New York: Pantheon.

Fromm, Erich. 1942. *The Fear of Freedom*. London: Routledge & Kegan Paul.

Fuentes, Annette and Barbara Ehrenreich. 1983. *Women in the Global Factory*. Boston: South End Press.

Hantover, Jeffrey P. 1978. "The boy scouts and the validation of masculinity". *Journal of Social Issues* 34: 184–95.

Herdt, Gilbert H. (ed.) 1992. *Gay Culture in America: Essays from the Field*. Boston: Beacon Press.

Hinsch, Bret. 1990. *Passions of the Cut Sleeve: The Male Homosexual Tradition in China.* Berkeley: University of California Press.

Hite, Shere. 1981. *The Hite Report on Male Sexuality.* New York: Knopf.

Jayawardena, Chandra. 1963. *Conflict and Solidarity in a Guianese Plantation.* London: Athlone Press.

Kates, Gary. 1991. "D'Eon returns to France: gender and power in 1777", pp. 167–94 in *Body Guards: The Cultural Politics of Gender Ambiguity*, ed. Julia Epstein and Kristina Straub. New York: Routledge.

Kiernan, V. G. 1988. *The Duel in European History: Honour and the Reign of Aristocracy.* Oxford: Oxford University Press.

Kinmonth, Earl H. 1981. *The Self-Made Man in Meiji Japanese Thought: From Samurai to Salary Man.* Berkeley: University of California Press.

Knauss, Peter R. 1987. *The Persistence of Patriarchy: Class, Gender and Ideology in Twentieth Century Algeria.* New York: Praeger.

Las Casas, Bartolomé de. 1992 [1552]. *The Devastation of the Indies: A Brief Account.* Baltimore: Johns Hopkins University Press.

Le Guin, Ursula. 1973. *The Left Hand of Darkness.* London: Panther.

MacKenzie, John M. 1987. "The imperial pioneer and hunter and the British masculine stereotype in late Victorian and Edwardian times", pp. 176–98 in *Manliness and Morality: Middle-Class Masculinity in Britain and America, 1800–1940*, ed. J. A. Mangan and James Walvin. Manchester: Manchester University Press.

Mangan, J. A. and James Walvin (eds.) 1987. *Manliness and Morality: Middle-Class Masculinity in Britain and America, 1800–1940.* Manchester: Manchester University Press.

Manvell, Roger and Heinrich Fraenkel. 1960. *Doctor Goebbels: His Life and Death.* London: Heinemann.

Marsh, Margaret. 1990. "Suburban men and masculine domesticity, 1870–1915", pp. 111–27 in *Meanings for Manhood: Constructions of Masculinity in Victorian America*, ed. Mark C. Carnes and Clyde Griffen. Chicago: University of Chicago Press.

Nye, Robert A. 1993. *Masculinity and Male Codes of Honor in Modern France.* New York: Oxford University Press.

Oetomo, Dede. 1990. "Patterns of bisexuality in Indonesia". Universitas Airlangga, Faculty of Social and Political Sciences.

Orlow, Dietrich. 1969, 1973. *The History of the Nazi Party*, 2 vols. Pittsburgh: University of Pittsburgh Press.

Ortner, Sherry B. 1981. "Gender and sexuality in hierarchical societies: the case of Polynesia and some comparative implications", pp. 360–409 in *Sexual Meanings: The Cultural Construction of Sexuality*, ed. S. B. Ortner and H. Whitehead. Cambridge: Cambridge University Press.

Parker, Richard. 1985. "Masculinity, femininity, and homosexuality: on the anthropological interpretation of sexual meanings in Brazil". *Journal of Homosexuality* 11: 155–63.

Phillips, J. O. C. 1987. *A Man's Country? The Image of the Pakeha Male, A History.* Auckland: Penguin.

Piercy, Marge. 1976. *Woman on the Edge of Time.* New York: Knopf.

Sade, Donatien Alphonse-Françoise, Marquis de. 1966 [1785]. *The 120 Days of Sodom, and Other Writings.* New York: Grove Press.

Seccombe, Wally. 1986. "Patriarchy stabilized: the construction of the male breadwinner wage norm in nineteenth-century Britain". *Social History* 2: 53–75.

Seidler, Victor J. 1989. *Rediscovering Masculinity: Reason, Language and Sexuality.* London: Routledge.

Simpson, Amelia. 1993. *Xuxa: The Mega-Marketing of Gender, Race and Modernity.* Philadelphia: Temple University Press.

Sinha, Mrinalini. 1987. "Gender and imperialism: colonial policy and the ideology of moral imperialism in late nineteenth-century Bengal", pp. 217–31 in *Changing Men: New Directions in Research on Men and Masculinity*, ed. Michael S. Kimmel. Newbury Park, CA: Sage.

Stedman Jones, Gareth. 1971. *Outcast London: A Study in the Relationship between Classes in Victorian Society.* Oxford: Clarendon Press.

Stein, Howard F. 1984. "Sittin' tight and bustin'" loose: contradiction and conflict in mid-western masculinity and the psycho-history of America". *Journal of Psychohistory* 11: 501–12.

Theweleit, Klaus. 1987. *Male Fantasies.* Cambridge: Polity Press.

Trumbach, Randolph. 1991. "London's Sapphists: from three sexes to four genders in the making of modern culture", pp. 112–41 in *Body Guards: The Cultural Politics of Gender Ambiguity*, ed. Julia Epstein and Kristina Straub. New York: Routledge.

United Nations Development Programme. 1992. *Human Development Report.* New York: Oxford University Press.

Weber, Max. 1976 [1904–5]. *The Protestant Ethic and the Spirit of Capitalism.* New York: Scribner.

Weeks, Jeffrey. 1977. *Coming Out: Homosexual Politics in Britain, from the Nineteenth Century to the Present.* London: Quartet.

——.1986. *Sexuality.* London: Horwood & Tavistock.

Wheeler-Bennett, John. 1953. *Nemesis of Power: The German Army in Politics, 1918–1945.* London: Macmillan.

Williams, Walter L. 1986. *The Spirit and the Flesh: Sexual Diversity in American Indian Culture.* Boston: Beacon Press.

Wollstonecraft, Mary. 1975 [1792]. *Vindication of the Rights of Woman.* Harmondsworth: Penguin.

15

The White Man's Muscles

Richard Dyer

Until the 1980s, it was rare to see a white man semi-naked in popular fictions. The art gallery, sports and pornography offered socially sanctioned or cordoned-off images, but the cinema, the major visual narrative form of the twentieth century, only did so in particular cases. This was not so with non-white male bodies. In the Western, the plantation drama and the jungle adventure film, the non-white body is routinely on display. Dance numbers with body-baring chorus boys (up to and including Madonna's videos) most often used non-white (including "Latin") dancers. Paul Robeson, the first major African-American acting star (as opposed to featured player), appeared torso-naked or more for large sections in nearly all his films, on a scale unimaginable with white male stars. The latter might be glimpsed for a brief shot washing or coming out of a swimming pool or the sea (at which point they instantly put on a robe), but a star like Rudolph Valentino (in any case Latin and often cast as a non-white) or a film like *Picnic* (1955) stand out as exceptions,[1] together with two genres: the boxing film (not really discussed here) and the adventure film in a colonial setting with a star possessed of a champion or built body.

This latter form is found in three cycles. One is the Tarzan films, beginning in 1912 with *Tarzan of the Apes*, continuing through forty-six further features, along with two television series and several Tarzan lookalikes (e.g. *King of the Jungle* (1927 and 1933) and Bomba the Jungle Boy (1949–)).[2] A second is the series of Italian films produced between 1957 and 1965 centred on heroes drawn from classical antiquity played by US bodybuilders, a cycle that has come to be known as the peplum.[3] Third, since the mid-1970s, there have been vehicles for such muscle stars as Arnold Schwarzenegger, Sylvester Stallone, Claude Van Damme and Dolph Lundgren.[4]

The two common features of these films – a champion/built body and a colonial setting – set terms for looking at the naked white male body. The white man has been the centre of attention for many centuries of Western culture, but there is a problem about the display of his body, which gives another inflection to the general paradox, already adumbrated, of whiteness and visibility. A naked body is a vulnerable body. This is so in the most fundamental sense – the bare body has no protection from the elements – but also in a social sense. Clothes are bearers of

Reprinted from *White* (New York and London: Routledge, 1997), pp. 145–53, 155–65, 230–1 (illustrations omitted).

prestige, notably of wealth, status and class: to be without them is to lose prestige. Nakedness may also reveal the inadequacies of the body by comparison with social ideals. It may betray the relative similarity of male and female, white and non-white bodies, undo the remorseless insistences on difference and concomitant power carried by clothes and grooming. The exposed white male body is liable to pose the legitimacy of white male power: why should people who look like that – so unimpressive, so like others – have so much power?

At the same time, there is value in the white male body being seen. On the one hand, the body often figures very effectively as a point of final explanation of social difference. By this argument, whites – and men – are where they are socially by virtue of biological, that is, bodily superiority. The sight of the body can be a kind of proof. On the other hand, the white insistence on spirit, on a transcendent relation to the body, has also led to a view that perhaps non-whites have better bodies, run faster, reproduce more easily, have bigger muscles, that perhaps indeed "white men can't jump", a film title that has both a literal, basketball reference and an appropriately heterosexual, reproductive connotation. The possibility of white bodily inferiority falls heavily on the shoulders of those white men who are not at the top of the spirit pile, those for whom their body is their only capital. In the context particularly of white working-class or "underachieving" masculinity, an assertion of the value and even superiority of the white male body has especial resonance (see Tasker 1993; Walkerdine 1986). The built body in colonial adventures is a formula that speaks to the need for an affirmation of the white male body without the loss of legitimacy that is always risked by its exposure, while also replaying the notion that white men are distinguished above all by their spirit and enterprise....

Tarzan, Hercules, Rambo[5] and the other heroes of the films in question here are all played by actors with champion and/or built physiques. The first Tarzans, and the stars of an earlier (c. 1912–26) Italian muscle cycle, were drawn from the strong man acts of the variety stage. Thereafter, however, sports proper generally provided the performers. Of the Tarzans, James Peirce (1926) was an All-American centre on the Indiana University Football Team, and Frank Merill (1928 and 1929) a national gym champion; Johnny Weissmuller (twelve films between 1932 and 1948) had five Olympic gold medals for swimming; Buster Crabbe (1933) was also an Olympic swimmer, Herman Brix (1935 and 1938) an Olympic shot putter, Glenn Morris (1938) an Olympic decathlon champion, Denny Miller (1960) a UCLA basketball star and Mike Henry (three films between 1967 and 1968) a star line-backer for the Los Angeles Rams. Although Lex Barker (1949–55), Jock Mahoney (1962–3) and Ron Ely (TV 1966–8) were beefy rather than sculpted, Gordon Scott (1955–60) was clearly a bodybuilder, while Miles O'Keefe (1981) and Wolf Larson (TV 1991–3) are manifest creatures of the Nautilus age. The stars of the peplum and recent muscleman films are also obviously gym products. In two notable cases they are explicitly champions of bodybuilding: Steve Reeves (the most famous peplum star) won the Mr America contest in 1947 and Mr Universe in 1950 and Arnold Schwarzenegger was seven times Mr Olympia.

Tarzan since the 1950s, the peplum heroes and Schwarzenegger, Stallone et al. have bodybuilt bodies. The bodies of earlier Tarzans were winners, and hence amenable to being understood in terms of white superiority, but the heightened muscularity of the built body carries further connotations of whiteness.

Bodybuilding as an activity has a relatively good track record in terms of racial equality. From the 1950s on, non-white men – and especially those of African descent – became major figures in bodybuilding competitions.[6] Yet the dominant images of the built body remain white. Kenneth Dutton (1995: 232) points out that black bodybuilders are rare on the cover of *Muscle and Fitness*, the body-building magazine now most responsible for establishing and promulgating the image of the sport. They feature inside, as, given their pre-eminence in the field, they must, but a cover fixes an image of the world evoked by a magazine, even for those who don't buy it – the covers of *Muscle and Fitness* tend to define built bodies as white. The treatment of non-white bodybuilders by the movies is no better. There is no king of the jungle of African descent, no really major non-white muscle stars.[7] The peplum used two spectacularly built black bodybuilders, Paul Wynter and Serge Nubret, the latter now one of the best known figures in bodybuilding, but they were never the heroes, only, as I discuss below, helpers or foes.[8]

Bodybuilding in popular culture articulates white masculinity.[9] The body shapes it cultivates and the way it presents them draw on a number of white traditions. First, bodybuilding makes reference to classical – that is, ancient Greek and Roman – art (cf. Doan and Dietz 1984: 11–18; Wyke 1996). Props or montages often explicitly relate body shape and pose to classical antecedents, as does writing about bodybuilding.[10] The standard posing vocabulary was elaborated at the end of the nineteenth century in conscious emanation of the classic statuary then so prized in the visual culture. Eugen Sandow, the first bodybuilding star, affirmed for himself a lineage back to the Greeks and Romans in his 1904 manual *Bodybuilding, or Man in the Making*.[11] By this time, the Caucasian whiteness of the classical world was taken for granted, down to the pleasure taken in the literal (hue) whiteness that its statues now have (the Victorians were scandalised to be told that Greek statues were once coloured (Jenkyns 1980: 146–54)). Second, bodybuilding now more often invokes a US, and *a fortiori* Californian, life-style, with a characteristic emphasis on ideas of health, energy and naturalness. Dutton (1995: 17) locates bodybuilding's US-ness in its concatenation of labour and leisure, pain and con-sumerism:

> The combination of an affluent consumer society and the Protestant work ethic has been reflected in activities which paradoxically combine disciplined asceticism on the one hand and narcissistic hedonism on the other.

The USA is of course a highly multiracial society, but the idea of being an "American" has long sat uneasily with ideas of being any other colour than white. Third, bodybuilding has sometimes adopted the image of the barbarian, drawn principally from comic books. Schwarzenegger's earliest vehicles were *Conan the Barbarian* (1982) and *Conan the Destroyer* (1984), and there is a host of largely straight-to-video movies based on this theme, including *The Barbarians* (1987) starring the Paul brothers, who called themselves the Barbarians for their bodybuilding performances. The primitivism and exoticism of this – to say nothing of the fact that "the barbarians" are generally credited with the destruction of classical civilisation – might suggest that this is a rather non-white image. However, not only is the casting (and in the comics the drawing) of the hero always white, it very often mobilises a sub-Nietzschian rhetoric of the Übermensch[12] that, however inaccurately, is strongly associated with Hitlerism and crypto-fascism. Finally, body-building does also sometimes draw on Christian imagery. The activity itself involves pain, bodily suffering, and with it the idea of the value of pain. This may be echoed in film in images of bodybuilders crucified. Leon Hunt has discussed the importance of crucifixion scenes in epic films, combining as they do "passivity offset by control, humiliation offset by nobility of sacrifice, eroticism offset by religious connotations of transcendence" (1993: 73). Though infrequent, the recourse to crucifixion can be a key moment in establishing the moral superiority of not specifically Christian characters: Conan in *Conan the Barbarian*, Rambo in *Rambo II* (1985).

Classicism, Californianism, barbarianism and crucifixionism are specific, strongly white representational traditions. Equally, many of the formal properties of the built body carry connotations of whiteness: it is ideal, hard, achieved, wealthy, hairless and tanned.

The built body presents itself not as typical but as ideal. It suggests our vague notions of the Greek gods and the Übermensch. Organised as competition, body-building encourages discussion of the best body. Kenneth Dutton's study of the tradition roots it in a characteristically Western investment in perfectibility, in the possibility of humans developing themselves here on earth. In *Pumping Iron* (1976), Schwarzenegger describes bodybuilding as "the dream of physical perfec-tion and the agonies you go through to attain it". Whiteness is an aspirational structure, requiring ideals of human development. All the rhetoric of bodybuilding is founded on this and most vividly seen in the aspirational motifs of the posing vocabulary, bodies forever striving upwards.

The built body is hard and contoured, often resembling armour. Bodybuilding has three goals: mass (muscle size), definition (the clarity with which one muscle group stands out from another) and proportion (the visual balance between all the body's muscle groups). The first two of these present a look of hardness: the skin stretched over pumped up muscle creates a taut surface, the separation of groups seems, as bodybuilding jargon has it, to "cut" into the body as into stone. Definition and proportion also emphasise contour, of individual muscle groups and of the body as a whole. Posing conventions, maximising size, tightening for definition, relating muscle groups to one another, further highlight these qualities; the use of oil (or often in films water or sweat) on the body emphasises it as a surface and hence its shape; relatively hard, three-quarter angle lighting brings out muscle shape; posing against cycloramas or shooting against skylines presents the overall body contour.

Looking like a statue again invokes the classical; men against the horizon are a cliché of aspirational propaganda. Moreover, a hard, contoured body does not look like it runs the risk of being merged into other bodies. A sense of separation and boundedness is important to the white male ego. Klaus Theweleit's study (1987) of the German Freikorps suggests a model of white male identity in which anxieties about the integrity and survival of the self are expressed through fantas-mic fears of the flooding, invading character of women, the masses and racial inferiors. Only a hard, visibly bounded body can resist being submerged into the horror of femininity and non-whiteness.

The built body is an achieved body, worked at, planned, suffered for. A massive, sculpted physique requires forethought and long-term organisation; regimes of graduated exercise, diet and scheduled rest need to be worked out and strictly adhered to; in short, building bodies is the most literal triumph of mind over matter, imagination over flesh. Some pepla (e.g. *La schiava di Roma, La guerra di Troia, La battaglia di Maratona*), and many contemporary muscleman films, include sequences showing such disciplined physical preparation. They are especially common in Stallone's films, notably *Rocky IV* (1985), which intercuts Rocky's down-home, improvisatory training routines with his Soviet opponent's hi-tech, body-as-machine processes. Schwarzenegger's films contain nothing so agonised, and he has been cast as a machine in the *Terminator* films (1984 and 1991) rather than as a machine's opponent. Schwarzenegger, as a multiple Mr Olympia winner, is always already a champion physique; Stallone's body is not so certified, his narratives involve him in proving himself physically. Schwarzenegger's body is simply massive, his characteristic facial expression genial, his persona one of Teutonic confidence; Stallone's muscles look tortured into existence, with veins popping out and strained skin, his eyes and mouth express vulnerability, iconic images have him bruised (*Rocky*) or scarred (*Rambo*).[13] Schwarzenegger and Stallone are variations on achievement. Their bodies, like those of all muscle heroes, carry the signs of hard, planned labour, the spirit reigning over the flesh.

The built body is a wealthy body. It is well fed and enormous amounts of leisure time have been devoted to it. The huge, firm muscles of Gordon Scott, Steve Reeves or Arnold Schwarzenegger make the simplest contrast with the thin or slack bodies of the native peoples in their films. Such muscles are a product and sign of affluence.

Finally, bodybuilders have hairless (shaved when not naturally so) and tanned bodies. Both of these are done in order to display the muscles more clearly, but they have further connotations. Body hair is animalistic; hairlessness connotes striving above nature. The climax of *Gli amori di Ercole* has Hercules fighting a giant ape, who has previously behaved in a King Kong-ish way towards Hercules's beloved Dejanira, stroking her hair and when she screams making as if to rape her; close-ups contrast Hercules's smooth, hairless muscles with the hairy limbs of this racist archetype.[14]

The modern bodybuilder tans. Although Sandow used white powder to make his body look more Greek sculptural, contemporary bodybuilding guru Robert Kennedy advises: "To stand out on stage at a physique event, one must be really well tanned" (1983: 139). Tanning, which only white people do, connotes typically white privileges: leisure (having the time to lie about acquiring a tan), wealth (buying that time, acquiring an artificial tan or travelling to the sun) and a healthy life style (the California/Australia myth that no amount of melanoma statistics seem to dim).

These bodies with their white connotations are on display in colonialist adventure films. Few are about the settlement in and maintenance of rule over foreign lands. Yet the heroes are also not usually indigenous inhabitants of the land in which the action takes place. They relate to it as a postcolonial.

Muscle heroes are not indigenous. Tarzan, though he lives in the jungle, is not of the jungle. The peplum heroes, initially located in ancient Greece or Rome, soon roamed very far and wide in time and space. The widespread use of a widely recognised "Vietnam" iconography (lush, glistening, dense jungle, camouflage gear, hi-tech hand weaponry, napalm-style fire)[15] in 1980s muscle films (e.g. *Commando* (1985) and *Predator* (1987), both with Schwarzenegger, Stallone's Rambo films, Chuck Norris's work,[16] the *American Ninja* series 1985– with Michael Dudikoff, *Sword of Bushida* (1990) with Richard Norton, *Men of War* (1994) with Dolph Lundgren) invokes the most vividly remembered fighting in a foreign land of recent Western history. This invocation, associating the muscle image with the Vietnam experience, is carried over into other contemporary muscle films.

In all cases, the hero is up against foreignness, its treacherous terrain and inhabitants, animal and human. The latter are quite often his adversaries, but by no means always. There are good and bad, instinctual and wily, stupid and wise, primitive and orientalist natives, in any combination. The colonialist structure of the heroes' relation to the native is aid as much as antagonism: he sorts out the problems of people who cannot sort things out for themselves. This is the role in which the Western nations liked to cast themselves in relation to their former colonies. The claim that had always been made, that imperial possession brought, and was even done in order to bring, benefits to the natives, informed policy since the 1950s, headed by the idea of the USA as world policeman, sharpened by cold war rivalry over political/economic influence. Aid is the watchword alike of foreign policy towards the Third World and the muscleman hero. . . .

The Tarzan films are clearly rooted in colonialism, but with a twist. Very many involve a journey of white people from without into Africa. The difficulty of the terrain, its unfamiliarity and its dangers (savage beasts, precipitous mountain passes, tumultuous rivers, thick jungle) provide the opportunity for the exercise of the white spirit, indomitable, organised. The native people may have some specialised knowledge useful to the whites, but otherwise are either serviceable to carry things or else one more aspect of the land's perils. All this is the familiar basis for the thrills of the jungle adventure story. But Tarzan is already in the jungle. Apart from the Elmo Lincoln films and *Greystoke, the Legend of Tarzan* (1984), which tell the story of how he comes to be there (born of Scottish parents who die soon after), it is simply a given that Tarzan lives in the jungle. Sometimes he helps the whites, but very often he defends the jungle against them, for they have come to find treasure or, most often, despoil nature (for example, killing elephants for tusks, capturing animals who are Tarzan's helpers). Politically, Tarzan is a green.[17] Not infrequently, he defends native people against whites whose actions would destroy their way of life.

Tarzan, then, is identified with the jungle. He is at one with the animals. In his unadorned near-nakedness, he is natural man. Some of the comic strips, and the Weissmuller films especially, show him merging with the shapes and shadows of the jungle. Yet he is also superior to nature, he is king of the jungle. Just as elephants and chimpanzees come to the rescue at his call, or even because they sense instinctually that he is in peril, so too are lions and crocodiles swiftly despatched at his hands. Likewise, he is a friend to good natives (though never going so far as to live with them), but an invincible enemy of the bad, and in either case, he is physically, mentally and morally their superior.

The theme of nature, Tarzan's greenness, is not a mere mask for this colonialist relation. The treatment of nature is a central aspect of colonial enterprise. The latter is understood to involve mastery and ordering, but also a depredation that distances the white man from nature. A lament for a loss of closeness to nature has run through a very great deal of white culture. With Tarzan, however, one can have colonial power and closeness to nature. Tarzan is indubitably white – even those who do not know the story of his Scottish aristocratic parentage and the notion of heredity so important in the novels (see Bristow 1991: 213–18; Newsinger 1986) will register his whiteness in the films in his sports- or gym-created body, its contrast to the other, darker native male bodies and, very often, the unabashed reference to him as a "white ape". Yet this white man is more in harmony with nature than the indigenous inhabitants. With Tarzan, the white man can be king of the jungle without loss of oneness with it.

Tarzan films effect an imaginary reconciliation between the enjoyment of colonial power and the ecological price of colonialism. The Rambo films do something similar, only more torturously. As Yvonne Tasker has pointed out (1993: 98ff.), the films themselves are greatly at variance to the wider image of Rambo as a straightforward gung-ho American patriot. Rather, he is a patriot without, it seems, a country. The first film has him returning, much decorated, from Vietnam, to find himself rejected as an uncouth trouble-maker. The film is set in the US North West, but as Rambo is pursued into the forest it begins to look as if it is Vietnam. Rambo wins against the enemies in this foreign land – but it is his home country. In the first sequel, he rescues soldiers missing in action in Vietnam after the war, actions revealed to be against actual (as opposed to declared) policy; the actions of the military bureaucracy not only seek to undermine his success but put Rambo himself at risk. He is a product of their finest training yet is none the less expendable. In *Rambo III* he is a one-man intervention in the Soviet occupation of Afghanistan, doing the job (of destroying the arch enemy of US ideals, communism) that the US government should be doing. Thus he repeatedly upholds basic American values against the actuality of America.

Equally significant as this structural pattern is the way he dresses and fights. His spirit is evident in both his resourcefulness, that is, the intelligent, improvisatory use of his environment, and his endurance, his capacity to withstand pain and torture. Rambo's actions, as well as Stallone's tortured muscles, both express this. Yet the resourcefulness also involves him in adopting non-white techniques. Like Tarzan, he becomes more absorbed into nature than the locals, most memorably in *Rambo II*, where he sinks himself deep into a mud bank, only his eyes visible, before rearing out to kill one of the US marines set on his trail. His fighting attire includes a ritualistically donned headband, suggesting his half-Native American parentage, while his weapons of choice include a huge serrated knife and a powered bow and arrow. The latter also invoke Native Americans, though in hi-tech versions. Rambo repeatedly and explicitly espouses a love of America, yet he dresses and fights for America by going generically native (that is, conflating Native American with, in the second and third films, the know-how of good Orientals). "America" can only be redeemed through bypassing the historical reality of the white USA, by returning to what can be conceptualised as coming before and without the USA. The Rambo films leave off at the impossibility of redemption by such contradictory means, ending with Rambo in tears

(*First Blood*), Rambo walking off into a barren landscape (*Rambo II*), Rambo driving off screen, leaving the camera to dwell on the people he has saved (*Rambo III*).

The Rambo films have qualms, to a degree rare, I think, in other 1980s and 1990s muscle films. In other of the Vietnam iconography films, the misgivings, let alone the impossible knot of contradictions in loving a country that doesn't exist, are not present, although the theme of being at once emotionally central – male, white, heterosexual, powerful – and yet betrayed by bureaucrats and politicians is still very much in evidence.

Tarzan, Hercules, Rambo and the rest show us ideal, hard, achieved, wealthy, hairless and tanned white male bodies set in a colonialist relation, of aid as much as antagonism, to lands and peoples that are other to them. This body in this setting constructs the white man as physically superior, yet also an everyman, built to do the job of colonial world improvement.

The body is distinguished from those around it: hard not slack, well-fed not emaciated, cut not indulgently fat, aspirationally posed not curved over or hanging back. It does sometimes happen that the built white hero is pitted against a built non-white body, but, since the former invariably wins, this only affirms the ultimate superiority of the white man's body. At the climax of *Tarzan and the Great River* (1967), Tarzan (Mike Henry) fights Barcuna (Rafer Johnson), the black leader who wants to control the country's main water supply (a key issue in the politics of development). Johnson has a fine physique, but less cut, less evidently worked at, than Henry's. In cross-cutting, the latter is shot from below, Johnson from above, a standard aggrandising/diminishing rhetoric. Tarzan/Henry wears a tailored loincloth (and is earlier seen in a Western suit), whereas Barcuna/Johnson wears a leopard skin and mumbo-jumbo adornments. In other words, not only does the outcome of the confrontation prove Tarzan's bodily superiority, but casting, shooting and dress bespeak it throughout. The same contrast of attire is often found in the peplum. In *Maciste nella terra dei ciclopi*, Maciste (Gordon Mitchell) wears a cloth peplum (suggesting in fabric as well as tailoring an advanced level of human development), as compared to his unnamed black adversary (Paul Wynter), who wears a leopard skin loincloth (attire based on a primitive level of development, hunted not manufactured, draped not tailored). In this case, the adversary, Wynter, a Mr Universe, has a finer physique than the hero, but attire and defeat undercut it.

The hero's body is superior, but his skin colour – tanned white – also signals him an everyman. Tanning does not suggest a desire or readiness to be racially black – a tanned white body is always indubitably just that. At the same time, it also implies that white people are capable of attractive variation in colour, whereas blacks who lighten and otherwise whiten their appearance are mocked for the endeavour and are generally held to have failed. The tanned built body affirms whiteness as a particular yet not a restricted identity, something heightened by comparison with the other bodies in the films. Tarzan is lighter than the natives, but darker than other white men; on two book covers by the same artist he has lighter skin when battling an ape, darker when coming upon a white woman, flexible within these extremes of male darkness and female lightness. The peplum, which does not so often have non-white characters, none the less plays on skin colour. The hero is always darker than all white women, whether they be good (and blonde) or bad (and brunette), a fact encapsulated in the common pose of the woman's white hand resting against the broad expanse of the hero's tanned pectorals. He is also darker than other white men, especially bad ones, orientalist rulers whose pasty complexions are of a piece with their decadence, primitives whose underground or cave dwellings have kept their skins from sunlight. The hero, so often first seen standing in the sun against the horizon or even, as in *Maciste nella terra dei ciclopi*, apparently born in a ray of sunshine, is the antithesis of this whiteness that shrinks from the life-giving sun. Even good white men are seldom as dark as the hero. Yet the hero is never equated with racial blackness: when even good, and physically spectacular, black men are present, the films are at great pains to stress the hero's superiority to them. White male heroism is thus constructed as both unmistakably yet not particularistically white. The muscle hero is an everyman: his tan bespeaks his right to intervene anywhere.

The emphasis in the peplum on the spectacle of the body also represents masculinity and colonialism in terms of relations between bodies. The economic, military and technological realities of colonialism disappear in a presentation of white bodily superiority as explanation of the colonising position. At its simplest this becomes the resolution of colonial conflict as a one-to-one fight between the hero and an antagonist, be the latter the leading warrior of the society, its ruler or a usurper (three versions of embodied power). Whatever the narrative specifics, the hero's better body wins out over the inferior oriental or primitive one. The example given above from *Tarzan and the Great River*, or Arnie's final stripped to the waist confrontation at the climax of *Commando*, reduce the political struggle over, respectively, natural resources or US foreign policy to a contest of bare flesh and may the best body win.

This pattern is often heightened by pitting the hero's body against the technology of his antagonists. It is they, the object of the hero's colonialist sorting out, who have recourse to elaborate weaponry and massed militia, which the hero confronts with his bare body alone. An especially vivid image of this is the climax of *La battlaglia di Maratona*, where Philippides (Steve Reeves) wears only a white loincloth as compared to the heavy armour of his opponents and where he has only his body to set against their elaborate machineries of war. Yet his built white body triumphs over their black-clad, technologically sophisticated ones. The colonial encounter, and white supremacy, is thus naturalised by being realised and achieved in the body.

The built white body is not the body that white men are born with; it is the body made possible by their natural mental superiority. The point after all is that it is built, a product of the application of thought and planning, an achievement. It is the sense of the mind at work behind the production of this body that most defines its whiteness. This makes the white man better able to handle his body, to improvise with what is to hand, to size up situations; no matter how splendid the physiques of non-white bodybuilders, they are never granted this quality (and thus the fact that their bodies too were produced ones is forgotten). The hero's physique may be fabulous, but what made it, and makes it effective, is the spirit within.

In short, the built body and the imperial enterprise are analogous. The built body sees the body as submitted to and glorified by the planning and ambition of the mind; colonial worlds are likewise represented as inchoate terrain needing the skill, sense and vision of the coloniser to be brought to order. The muscle hero has landscaped his body with muscles and he controls them superbly and sagely; the lands of the muscle film are enfeebled or raw bodies requiring discipline. The built white male body and colonial enterprise act as mirrors of each other, and both, even as they display the white man's magnificent corporeality, tell of the spirit within. . . .

Notes

1 On Valentino, see Studlar 1989, Hansen 1991, Dyer 1992 and Leconte 1996; on *Picnic*, see Cohan 1991.

2 On Tarzan films, see Essoe 1968, Lacassin 1982, Nesteby 1982, Torgovnick 1990, Morton 1993 and Fury 1994.

3 The cycle runs from the 1957 *Le fatiche di Ercole* to 1965, with the odd straggler such as *Combate de gigantes* (1966); the most complete account is in Cammarota 1987. The term "peplum" (plural "pepla") was coined by French critics in the early 1960s; it derives from a Latinised Greek word meaning a woman's tunic but here refers to the short skirt or kilt worn by the heroes. "Peplum" is generally understood to refer to the 1958–65 Italian cycle, but is also sometimes used to refer to an earlier Italian one, from *Quo Vadis?* (1912) and especially *Cabiria* (1914) to c.1926, or even to all adventure films set in "ancient times", including Hollywood films such as *The Ten Command-ments, Ben Hur, Cleopatra* and *Conan the Barbarian*. Here however "peplum" refers only to the 1957–65 cycle.

4 Two studies of these films are Tasker 1993 and Jeffords 1994.

5 The Rambo films are *First Blood* (1982), *Rambo: First Blood Part II* (1985) and *Rambo III* (1988). I shall refer to them as *First Blood, Rambo II* and *Rambo III* respectively.

6 Webster (1979: 105) does note that before this there had been a view that "the high calves of the negro races prevented full and proportionate development", suggesting – as have comparable arguments about ballet – a particular biological discourse aimed at preserving the whiteness of activities concerned with producing body images supposedly founded on "classical" precedent.

7 The exception is Bruce Lee, significantly, in the US context, Asian not black African.

8 The earlier cycle had introduced (in *Cabiria* (1914)) the character of Maciste, helper to the unmuscular hero, as a Nubian slave (played by an Italian, Bartolomeo Pagano). So popular was he that he became the most loved character of this and the later cycle – but his blackness was forgotten.

9 See Holmlund (1989) for a discussion of the way femininity and blackness are negoti-ated in the *Pumping Iron* films.

10 Note also that the Tarzan of the books is described in explicitly classical terms; see Holtsmark 1981.

11 On Sandow, see Chapman 1994.

12 Notably in the use in bodybuilding competitions of the opening of Richard Strauss's symphonic poem based on Nietzsche, *Also sprach Zarathustra*. . . .

13 On the role of pain in the Rambo films, see Warner 1992.

14 On *King Kong* as a racist archetype, see Lott 1995.

15 The films are not necessarily set in Vietnam. On "Vietnam" in 1980s action cinema, see Tasker 1993: *passim.*

16 See Williams 1990.

17 This was the subject of an essay by John Tinkler, written for my MA course. . . .

References

Bristow, Joseph (1991) *Empire Boys: Adventures in a Man's World*, London: Harper-Collins.

Chapman, David (1994) *Sandow the Magnificent: Eugen Sandow and the Beginnings of Bodybuilding*, Urbana: University of Illinois Press.

Cohan, Steve (1991) "Masquerading as the American Male: *Picnic*, William Holden and the Spectacle of Masculinity in Hollywood Film", *Camera Obscura* 25–6: 42–72.

Doan, William and Dietz, Craig (1984) *Photoflexion: A History of Bodybuilding Photography*, New York: St Martin's Press.

Dutton, Kenneth R. (1995) *The Perfectible Body*, London: Cassell.

Dyer, Richard (1992) "The Son of the Sheik", in *Only Entertainment*, London: Routledge, pp. 99–102.

Fury, David (1994) *Kings of the Jungle: An Illustrated Reference to Tarzan on Screen and Television*, Jefferson NC: McFarland.

Hansen, Miriam (1991) "Pleasure, ambivalence, fascination: Valentino and female spectatorship", in Christine Gledhill (ed.) *Stardom: Industry of Desire*, London: British Film Institute, pp. 259–82.

Holmlund, Christine (1989) "Visible Difference and Flex Appeal: The Body, Sex, Sexuality, and Race in the *Pumping Iron* films", *Cinema Journal* 28(4): 38–51.

Holtsmark, Erling B. (1981) *Tarzan and Tradition: Classical Myth in Popular Literature*, Westport, CT: Greenwood Press.

Hunt, Leon (1993) "What Are Big Boys Made Of?: *Spartacus, El Cid* and the Male Epic", in Pat Kirkman and Janet Thumin (eds) *You Tarzan: Masculinity, Movies and Men*, London: Lawrence & Wishart, pp. 65–83.

Jeffords, Susan (1994) *Hard Bodies: Hollywood Masculinity in the Reagan Era*, New Brunswick, NJ: Rutgers University Press.

Jenkyns, Richard (1980) *The Victorians and Ancient Greece*, Oxford: Basil Blackwell.

Kennedy, Robert (1983) *Beef It! Upping the Muscle Mass*, New York: Sterling.

Lacassin, Francis (1982) *Tarzan, ou le Chevalier crispé*, Paris: Veyrier.

Leconte, Loredana (1996) "Fascino Latino: L'invenzione di Rodolfo Valentino", in Giannino Malossi (ed.) *Latin Lover: A sud della passione*, Milan: Charta, pp. 81–93.

Lott, Tommy L. (1995) "King Kong Lives: Racist Discourse and the Negro-Ape Metaphor", in Ron Platt (ed.) *Next of Kin: Looking at the Great Apes*, Cambridge, MA: MIT List Visual Arts Center, pp. 37–43.

Morton, Walt (1993) "Tracking the Sign of Tarzan: Trans-media Representation of a Pop-Culture Icon", in Pat Kirkman and Janet Thumin (eds) *You Tarzan: Masculinity, Movies and Men*, London: Lawrence & Wishart, pp. 106–25.

Nesteby, James R. (1982) "The Tarzan Formula for Racial Stereotyping", in *Black Images in American Films 1896–1954*, New York: University Press of America, pp. 137–47.

Newsinger, John (1986) "Lord Greystoke and Darkest Africa: the Politics of the Tarzan Stories", *Race and Class* 28(2): 59–71.

Studlar, Gaylyn (1989) "Discourses of Gender and Ethnicity: The Construction and De(con)struction of Rudolph Valentino as Other", *Film Criticism* 13(2): 18–35.

Tasker, Yvonne (1993) *Spectacular Bodies: Gender, Genre and the Action Cinema*, London: Routledge.

Theweleit, Klaus (1987) *Male Fantasies*, Cambridge: Polity.

Torgovnick, Marianna (1990) "Taking Tarzan Seriously", in *Gone Primitive: Savage Intellects, Modern Lives*, Chicago: University of Chicago Press, pp. 42–72.

Walkerdine, Valerie (1986) "Video Replay: Families, Films and Fantasy", in Victor Burgin, James Donald and Cora Kaplan (eds) *Formations of Fantasy*, London: Methuen, pp. 167–89.

Warner, William (1992) "Spectacular Action: Rambo and the Popular Pleasures of Pain", in Lawrence Grossberg, Cary Nelson and Paula Treichler (eds) *Cultural Studies*, New York: Routledge, pp. 672–88.

Webster, David (1979) *Barbells and Beefcake: An Illustrated History of Bodybuilding*, Irvine (GB): Webster.

Williams, Tony (1990) "*Missing in Action*: The Vietnam Construction of the Movie Star", in Linda Dittmar and Gene Michaud (eds) *From Hanoi to Hollywood: The Vietnam War in American Film*, New Brunswick, NJ: Rutgers University Press, pp. 129–44.

Wyke, Maria (1996) "Herculean Muscle!: the Classicizing Rhetoric of Bodybuilding", *Arion* 4(3).

16

What Does a Jew Want? or, The Political Meaning of the Phallus

Daniel Boyarin

In his essay "The 'Uncanny'" (1919), Freud recounts a moment when he looks accidentally at a mirror and imagines he sees someone else: "I can still recollect that I thoroughly disliked his appearance. ... Is it not possible, though, that our dislike of [the double is] a vestigial trace of the archaic reaction which feels the 'double' to be something uncanny?" (1919: 248n).[1] Strangely no matter how many uses and stagings of the uncanny he describes, Freud always returns it to castration. He even connects Rank's account of the "double" with dreams, within which castration represents "a doubling or multiplication of a genital symbol" (p. 235). After listing example after example of uncanny moments having nothing to do with castration,[2] Freud concludes: "We have now only a few remarks to add, for animism, magic and sorcery, the omnipotence of thoughts, man's attitude to death, involuntary repetition and the castration complex comprise practically all the factors which turn something frightening into something uncanny" (p. 243). Something in Freud's world was clearly pressing in this direction with remarkable insistence.

In a later text, *Moses and Monotheism* (1939), Freud argues that circumcision "makes a disagreeable, uncanny impression, which is to be explained no doubt by its recalling the dreaded castration" (p. 91; see also 1919: 247–8). Reversing the terms of Freud's interpretation in both of these accounts, I argue that castration recalls a dreaded *circumcision* – dreaded because this act cripples a male by turning him into a Jew. If we read these two "uncanny" moments together, circumcision and Freud's glimpse of himself in the mirror, we might conclude that in seeing himself in the mirror, Freud had the same uncanny feeling that he claims an anti-Semite experiences when looking at a Jew. We cannot claim that Freud meant this disagreeable, uncanny impression to recur only among gentiles (contra Geller 1993: 57, 1992: 438). In my reading, the "appearance" Freud disliked reflects the cultural "trauma" of circumcision. The conceptual implications of this trauma take us far beyond the immediate concerns of psychobiography (see Kofman 1985: 32).

Reprinted from *The Psychoanalysis of Race*, ed. Christopher Lane (New York: Columbia University Press), pp. 211–13, 218–31, 233–6.

This paper interprets the moment when Freud grasped the misrecognition – the doubling of self – informing his Jewish self-alienation.[3] I argue that this misrecognition marks a precise historical moment making psychoanalysis possible,[4] and that the doubling of self ("less than one and double" in Bhabha's aphorism) generates a series of potentially toxic political symptoms in Freud and Fanon, which critics have not interpreted in quite the way I do here. These symptoms include bizarre moments of misogyny in both writers, Fanon's homophobia, and Freud's ambivalence – to say the least – about his own homoerotic desires. But especially relevant for the present study are the strange figurings of "Mulattos" in Freud's work and of "Jews" in Fanon's, which highlight Freud's racism and Fanon's anti-Semitism.

Ann Pellegrini partly anticipates this argument when she writes: "To represent the predicament of the black [male] subject, Fanon turns repeatedly to the machinery of sexual difference. The femininity he puts into play is white femininity. Fanon's strategy for revealing 'racial' difference may not really be so far from Freud's strategy for concealing it" (1997a: 109). While I clarify that colonized subjects have a certain knowledge of lack that has liberating effects, I do not idealize this knowledge. Instead, I expose Freud's and Fanon's attempt to unknow that which sexually and racially they already perceived on a cultural level.[5] I illustrate this "attempt to unknow" by advancing episodic readings of Freud's essay on Little Hans and Fanon's study *Black Skin, White Masks.* Although my essay interprets biographical information about Freud and Fanon, I explore the conceptual and political implications of blind spots in their work, arguing in the process that these blind spots have profound significance for a psychoanalysis of race.

Before Fanon, Freud seemed to realize that the "colonized as constructed by colonialist ideology is the very figure of the divided subject [that] psychoanalytic theory [posits] to refute humanism's myth of the unified self" (Parry 1987: 29). In a profound sense, "humanism's myth" is a colonial myth. It follows that psychoanalysis is *au fond* not so much a Jewish science as a science of the doubled colonized subject – more perhaps than its practitioners have realized or conceded. This doubling of self is endemic to the colonial psyche. As James C. Scott observes, "When the script is rigid and the consequences of a mistake large, subordinate groups may experience their conformity as a species of manipulation. Insofar as the conformity is tactical it is surely manipulative. This attitude again requires a division of the self in which one self observes, perhaps cynically and approvingly, the performance of the other self" (1990: 33).

In this respect, it is no accident that psychoanalysis has proven most productive in theorizing colonialism: Fanon's psychology of colonial subjectivity strongly develops insights that already exist in Freud's text. The recognition, raised to exquisite lucidity by Fanon, that the "other within" is the doubled self of colonialism, suggests a new significance for psychoanalysis as an instrument that interprets Jewish history. This recognition surfaces neither as applied psychoanalysis nor as psychohistory, but as a symptom of the crisis shared by Jews and other postcolonial ("modernizing") peoples, whose double consciousness gives them particular insight.[6] Freud himself seemed to have intimated this relationship. He once described the subject's internal alterity as "the State within the State," a pejorative phrase for the German state's twin others: women and Jews (Geller 1993: 56). For colonial subjects such as Freud and Fanon, the cultural world, their identity, and their allegiances double: They live "lives in between," in Leo Spitzer (the younger's) evocative term. . . .

Freud Reads Fanon, or, The Misogyny of the Colonized Male

More than once, Freud used metaphors of race and colonization for psychological ideas. Attempting to situate fantasy (like a hybrid) between preconscious and unconscious systems, Freud used one of the most revealing of these metaphors, writing of "individuals of mixed race who, taken all round, resemble white men, but who betray their coloured descent by some striking feature or other, and on that account are excluded from society and enjoy none of the privileges of white people" (1915: 191). This brief and deeply enigmatic metaphor discloses Freud's rapt engagement with the question of "race," and the way that race and sexuality were for him inseparable. The "dark continent" of women's sexuality is not "merely" metaphor, but the figure of a nexus between race and gender that Freud's text insinuates. In David Kazanjian's formulation, these are "statements that open his argument onto a wide sociohistorical field" (1993: 102). Precisely what sociohistorical field opens here? How does Freud enfold gender, race, sexuality, and colonization, and how does he position himself racially in these contexts?

An early disciple of Freud's and the founder of psychoanalysis in India, G. Bose, once sent Freud a portrait of an English gentleman, remarking that he imagined that was what Freud looked like. Freud responded that Bose had not paid attention to certain "racial" differences between him and the English – that is, his Jewishness (Seshadri-Crooks 1994: 185, 211 n. 19). As this anecdote suggests, Freud's origins as *Ostjude* impeded his aspirations as a bourgeois European; he was both the object and the subject of racism. From the colonized's perspective, Freud might look like a white man; from his perspective, and that of dominating white Christians, he was a Jew, every bit as racially marked as the Indian. In the racist imaginary of the late nineteenth century, Jews most often appeared as mulattos. The best denotation for the "race" of the European Jew seems to be off-white.[7] *Ecru Homo.*

Two modalities of reading the "race" of Freud's discourse have emerged in recent years: One – the "colonial" – would read this passage, and by extension Freud's other "ethnological" comments and texts, as the product of a "white" man commenting on "black" men (Bhabha, 1994: 89; Kazanjian 1993: 103–5). The other would read "white" and "black" here as barely disguised ciphers for Aryan and Jew (Gilman 1991: 175, 1993b: 21). In the first reading, Freud is the colonizer; in the second, the colonized.

These disparate ways of reading Freud on race are not exclusive, but two aspects of the European Jew's racial anomalousness: Jews are not white/not quite, to borrow Bhabha's felicitous formulation for other colonial subjects. Freud was at once the other and the metropolitan, the "Semite" among "Aryans" and the Jew desperately constructing his whiteness by othering colonized blacks.[8] The results of this conflicted condition are virtually indistinguishable in Freud's texts because Jews were genuinely racialized (as African Americans are in the United States) and, paradoxically, because he identified with his oppressors. For Freud, "the repugnance of the Aryan for the Semite" was *not* an example of "the narcissism of minor differences" but an example parallel to that of the "white races for the coloured." Indeed, this "repugnance" contrasts with the narcissism of the minor difference (Freud 1921: 101; contra Gilman 1993a: 21, 22, and *passim*).[9]

Jewishness functioned racially in Austro-Germany as "blackness" does in the United States. The "one drop" theory prevailed for Jewishness. Thus a typical anti-Semite of Freud's time stated: "Jewishness is like a concentrated dye; a minute quantity suffices to give a specific character – or at least, some traces of it – to an incomparably greater mass" (quoted in Gilman 1991: 175). Another representative nineteenth-century savant referred to "the African character of the Jew," while Houston Stewart Chamberlain, Wagner's son-in-law and Hitler's hero, wrote that the Jews are a mongrel race that had interbred with Africans.[10] The Jew was literally a mulatto, as W. E. B. Du Bois found out one night in Slovenia when a taxi driver took him to the Jewish ghetto (Gilroy 1993: 212). Since Freud feared that some feature would betray his thinking as "of Jewish descent" and his discourse as merely a "Jewish science," the "individuals of mixed race," in his metaphor, are certainly Jews. Nonetheless, we cannot deny that he also wrote about "whites" and "coloured";[11] we cannot simply dismiss the "colonial" reading of Freud.[12] Freud's ambiguous use of "race" is no accident: his position between white and black greatly contributed to his psychological and ethnological theories.

Like Freud, Fanon produces surprising metaphors of "race." "The Jew" plays as disturbing and enigmatic a role in Fanon's text as "blacks" do in Freud's.[13] In this respect, we should read Freud's deposition about "individuals of mixed race" alongside Fanon's: "All the same, the Jew can be unknown in his Jewishness. He is not wholly what he is. One hopes, one waits. His actions, his behavior are the final determinant. He is a white man, and, apart from some rather debatable characteristics, he can sometimes go unnoticed" (1967: 115). Each man fantasizes that the other Other can (almost) "pass." This assumption prevails in Freud's reading of Little Hans: that circumcision cannot be erased but forever marks the Jewish male as appropriate object of contempt, with his evident envy of mulattos who "taken all around resemble white men"! For Fanon, the ineradicability of blackness stands explicitly against the Jew's ability to be unknown as Jewish. Yet both men also acknowledge that passing does not entirely work. Fanon fantasizes that "no anti-Semite . . . would ever conceive of the idea of castrating the Jew." His argument is symptomatic, for he could not be more mistaken historically. Owing to fantasies of Jewish desire for Christian women, castrations of Jews are not unknown (Fabre-Vassas 1994).[14] Fanon's utterance reveals envy for the Jew's imaginary phallus.

The processes of Jewish modernization and Westernization, known collectively as the "Emancipation," closely resemble the dislocating effects suffered by colonial subjects educated in Europe.[15] We can pursue these analogies by comparing the two groups' cultural/linguistic predicaments: "Every colonized people – in other words, every people in whose soul an inferiority complex has been created by the death and burial of its local cultural originality – finds itself face to face with the language of the civilizing nation; that is, with the culture of the mother country" (Fanon 1967: 18). "Any Jew wishing to escape his material and moral isolation was forced, whether he liked it or not, to learn a foreign language" (Anzieu 1986:

203).[16] Fanon would have understood the anguish of Arthur Schnitzler, who described the colonized Jew's double bind thus: "[A Jew] had the choice of being counted as insensitive, obtrusive and fresh; or of being oversensitive, shy and suffering from feelings of persecution. And even if you managed somehow to conduct yourself so that nothing showed, it was impossible to remain completely untouched; as for instance, a person may not remain unconcerned whose skin has been anesthetized but who has to watch, with his eyes open, how it is scratched by an unclean knife, even cut into until the blood flows" (Schnitzler 1970: 67).

Freud, of course, called Schnitzler his *Doppelgänger* (Bolkosky 1986: 1). Marthe Robert has also eloquently delineated the situation of German Jewish intellectuals at the *fin de siècle*. She describes them as divided subjects, trying as hard as they could to wear German masks but inevitably revealing their Jewish skins: their interpellation as Jews. The very condition of doubled consciousness, and not of some essential nature, marks such subjects as Jews. For the effort to "efface" – and embrace – Jewishness is a response to being denounced by specific cultural formations. Many Jewish jokes of the time, including much of Freud's *Jokebook*, understand this paradox well. The harder such Jews tried to efface their Jewishness, the more they were rejected (Robert 1976: 17). In a passage whose sting and content recall Fanon's writing, one such Jew writes (already in the 1830s): "It's a kind of miracle! I've experienced it a thousand times, and yet it still seems new to me. Some find fault with me for being a Jew; others forgive me; still others go so far as to compliment me for it; but every last one of them thinks of it" (Ludwig Börne, quoted in Robert 1976: 18; on Börne, see Gilman 1986: 148–67).

Freud knew Börne very well. In 1919 he wrote to Ferenczi, "I received Börne as a present when I was very young, perhaps for my thirteenth birthday. I read him avidly, and some of these short essays have always remained very clearly in my memory, not of course the cryptomnesic one. When I read this one again I was amazed to see how much in it agrees practically word for word with things I have always maintained and thought. He could well have been the real source of my originality" (quoted in Freud et al. 1985: 73). Indeed, Börne is perhaps a prototype of the split colonial subject. Fanon echoed him over a century later: "Shame. Shame and self-contempt. Nausea. When people like me, they tell me it is in spite of my color. When they dislike me, they point out that it is not because of my color. Either way, I am locked into the infernal circle" (1967: 115).

As Fanon describes the psychology of the colonized, the echo of Jewish conditions in central/western Europe since the late nineteenth century recurs. Generally, the prescriptions for solving the "Jewish problem," whether proposed by "evolved" Jews or by anti-Semites, involved a version of the civilizing mission. Thus Walter Rathenau saw "as the sole cure the integration of the Jew into German education (*Bildung*)" (Gilman 1986: 223; Cuddihy 1987: 25; see also Spitzer 1989: 26; Berkowitz 1993. 2–3, 99). Even more pointed are the ideas of another assimilated Jew, Ernst Lissauer, who held that "the Jew, like Nietzsche's Superman, is progressing from a more primitive stage of development, characterized by religious identity, to a higher stage of development, characterized by the present identification with cultural qualities of the German community, to eventually emerge whole and complete" (quoted in Gilman 1986: 225). Gilman remarks clearly on the analogies between this situation and that of colonialism: "By observing the Ostjude, says the Western Jew, we can learn where we have come from, just as Hegel uses the African black as the sign of the progress of European civilization" (1986: 253).

The more "educated" the subject is, the more acute its dis-ease (Fanon 1967: 9–23).[17] Börne returns to the Frankfurt Ghetto after seven years away, and "everything is so dark and so limited" (quoted in Gilman 1986: 150). "The Antilles Negro who goes home from France . . . tells his acquaintances, 'I am so happy to be back with you. Good Lord, it is hot in this country, I shall certainly not be able to endure it very long'" (Fanon 1967: 37).[18]

Language also marked the extent of this split: consider the abandonment of Creole/Yiddish "jargon" for French/"High" German (Fanon 1967: 27–8; Hutton 1990). An internal hierarchy emerged, elevating the more "civilized" subject of the Antilles/Vienna above the still "native, uncivilized" subjects of Dahomey or the Congo/Warsaw (Fanon 1967: 25–6). The German-speaking Jew who applied anti-Semitic stereotypes to the Yiddish-speaking *Ostjude* is an uncanny analog to the "evolved" colonial subject, with his contempt for his native people, language, and culture. For the German-speaking Viennese Jew, the *Ostjude* was what the "Unto Whom" ("the ignorant, illiterate, pagan Africans . . . unto whom God swore in his wrath," etc.) were to a Europeanized Yoruba such as Joseph May (quoted in Spitzer 1989: 42).[19] We can imagine the effect of such internalized representations on the transplanted Freud, whose mother spoke only Galician Yiddish all her life (Hutton 1990: 11; *contra* Anzieu 1986: 204 and *passim*). I contend that the experience of a self doubling back on itself, observing itself, is psychoanalysis's primal encounter with the decentered self.

I suggest not that disadvantaged subjects – whether gay, female, colonized, black, or Jewish – have a politically privileged access to "truth" but that their disadvantage is a condition of their access to such understanding. Thus David Halperin claims that "the aim . . . is to treat homosexuality as a position from which one can know, to treat it as a legitimate *condition* of knowledge. Homosexuality, according to this Foucauldian vision of *un gai savoir*, 'a gay science,' is not something to be gotten right but an eccentric positionality to be exploited and explored: a potentially privileged site for the criticism and analysis of cultural discourses" (1995: 61). As we can see from Freud's dilemma, disavowing one's "eccentric positionality" – which Lacan figured suggestively, but problematically, as a disavowal of castration – erases the epistemological advantage of the "post-colonial subject" *vis-à-vis* the white male's imaginary possession of the phallus.[20] Put another way, Freud's closeted Jewishness (and I use this term for all of its historical and discursive, paranoiac effects) has a toxic effect precisely when the closet emerged historically. Unclosseting this identity would not result in an automatic dissolving of the toxic energy of the anti-Semitic, misogynistic, and homophobic imaginary (Dean 1995). Rather, "coming out" is perhaps a prophylactic, a way of defending one's self from full participation in the most noxious forms of that discourse. In this respect, Freud hides in, and sometimes emerges from, the queer and Jewish closets of his time (Boyarin 1994b).

Doubled consciousness has had calamitous effects on postcolonial subjects. It has precipitated the Negrophobia of the (modernizing) Jew and the anti-Semitism of the (postcolonial) Negro. These phobias, rather than being analogous, are part of the same historical process. The pathological implications of this doubly liminal situation ("not yet/no longer wholly") devastatingly appear in the gender discourses of these colonized subjects – that is, in their misogyny, homophobia, and self-contempt:

> What does a man want?
> What does the black man want?
> At the risk of arousing the resentment of my colored brothers, I will say that the black is not a man. (Fanon 1967: 8)

These "pathologies" also appear as universal concepts in psychoanalysis: as sublation and attempted sublimation.[21]

The racial other lacks the phallus; "he" is always castrated. While the situation of racial others (the Jew, the black) is productive of knowledge (like Halperin's *gai savoir*), these combinations of race and gender have misogynistic and homophobic effects. The dominating European culture often represented blacks as "feminine"; the myth of hypervirility does not properly counter this point. As Fanon repeatedly claimed, "The Negro *is* the genital" (1967: 180; my emphasis). In this respect, maleness equates with possessing the phallus, while it is the condition of "Woman" to *be* the phallus. The same appears true for the Negro.

Differing slightly from its perception of blacks, European cultures represented male Jews as "female." Geller put this succinctly: "In the Central European cultural imagination, male Jews are identified with men without penises, that is, as women" (1993: 52). Gilman also provides the following startling evidence for this claim:

> The clitoris was seen as a "truncated penis." Within the turn-of-the-century understanding of sexual homology, this truncated penis was seen as an analogy not to the body of the idealized male, with his large, intact penis, but to the circumcised ("truncated") penis of the Jewish male. This is reflected in the popular fin de siècle Viennese view of the relationship between the body of the male Jew and the body of the woman. The clitoris was known in the Viennese slang of the time simply as the "Jew" (*Jud*). The phrase for female masturbation was "playing with the Jew." (Gilman 1993b: 38–9)

The black man is a penis; the male Jew is a clitoris. Neither has the phallus.

This understanding might have generated a powerful critique of gendered and sexual meanings in Freud's and Fanon's oppressive cultures; it almost did. But while Freud and Fanon had the critical knowledge to conduct this critique, and saw much else from this perspective, neither could ultimately depart from their Eurocentric perspectives and demystify the phallus *tout court*. Freud's and Fanon's projects partly entail getting the phallus for their respective male selves/peoples; the homophobia circulating in their texts makes these projects symptomatic.[22] The phallus is the ultimate white mask or *laissé passer*. We can now sharpen our interpretation of Freud's reaction to his father's story of "passively" picking up his hat when a Christian anti-Semite knocked it off his head. McGrath argues that Freud understood this hat as a symbol for the phallus: "the knocking off his father's hat could have directly symbolized to him the emasculation of Jakob Freud" (1986: 64).

The Phallus as White Mask

Writers of the Négritude movement embraced "feminization": "*Emotion is completely Negro as reason is Greek*" (Senghor, quoted in Fanon 1967: 127). Fanon, however, experienced his negritude as "castration" and was unwilling to accept it: "with all my strength I refuse to accept that amputation" (p. 140). On that note, he began a chapter on "The Negro and Psychopathology" and went devastatingly "wrong" in treating gender within the colonized people. His errors are perhaps symptomatic of the situation facing male *post*colonial subjects. Indeed, this blindness in a seer like Fanon makes it doubly instructive, representing the male subject of a colonial discourse who cannot escape his desire to be white/uncircumcised. Here the Freudian/Lacanian reading of lack as figured in the discourse of a particular culture is powerfully diagnostic of cultural effects, but only if we read this figuration as the product of a particular culture. Otherwise, and in all versions of psychoanalysis, the diagnosis threatens to collapse into the disease. Fanon's symptomatic chapter on the sexuality of women reveals this collapse.

In this chapter, Fanon develops his notorious arguments about (white) women's psychology. "Basically, does this *fear* of rape not itself cry out for rape? Just as there are faces that ask to be slapped, can one not speak of women who ask to be raped?" (p. 156).[23] After producing this grotesque misogyny concerning the psychosexuality of "white women," Fanon writes of the woman of color, "I know nothing about her" (p. 180), a statement that eerily echoes Freud's claim about the "dark continent" of woman's sexuality (Freud 1926: 212).[24]

In his brilliant and passionate *cri de coeur* against "Negrophobia," Fanon produces both misogyny and homophobia: "The behavior of these women [who are afraid to dance with a Negro] is clearly understandable from the standpoint of imagination. That is because the Negrophobic woman is in fact nothing but a putative sexual partner – just as the Negrophobic man is a repressed homosexual" (1967: 156). Note the telling shift of subject that this sentence encodes grammatically: Fanon tries to theorize the desire and fear of the "Negrophobic woman," but she is "nothing but a putative sexual partner," the object of someone else's desire. Thus the colonized male, who in a situation of partial decolonization begins to look at himself from the white man's perspective, recovers his "maleness" (as defined by the dominant culture) by pathologizing his male and female enemies as feminine. Put another way, the colonizer's misogyny and homophobia become internalized in complicated ways, then projected by the colonized against women and gays.[25] It is not I who have these despised characteristics; it is they!

This defense prevails in Fanon's text particularly when he denies the existence of "homosexuality" in Martinique. Here his homophobia is a great deal more extreme than is Freud's. There are berdaches (my term) in Martinique, but they lead "normal sex lives" (Fanon's phrase): "they can take a punch like any 'he-man' and they are not impervious to the allures of women" (p. 180; his scare quotes). "Fault, guilt, refusal of guilt, paranoia – one is back in homosexual territory" (p. 183). Precisely when Fanon retorts to the racist pronouncement that every Negro is sensual, he dramatically avows: "I have never been able, without revulsion, to hear a *man* say of another man: 'He is so sensual!' ... Imagine a woman saying of another woman: 'She's so terribly desirable – she's darling . . .' " (p. 201; original emphasis).

Here the psychic mechanism is clear: The colonizers render us effete; we will assert our value by rejecting everything that stinks of effeminacy, homosexuality, and the female. Freud's self-described "overcoming of his homosexual cathexis" is surely cut from the same psychic cloth, as is his psychic "bedrock" that repudiates femininity (Fuss 1994: 30).[26] Paula Hyman has sharply formulated this process:

> Challenging elements of the Western model that rigidly limited the public role of women and spiritualized them as mothers, eastern European immigrants and their children contested the boundaries between domestic and public life that characterized middle-class gender norms. As they integrated into middle-class American culture, however, immigrant Jewish men and their sons – like their predecessors in Western societies – played out their ambivalence about their own identity as Jews in non-Jewish societies in gendered terms. (Hyman 1995: 8–9)

As a consequence: "Jewish men, first in the countries of western and central Europe and later in America, constructed a *modern* Jewish identity that devalued women, the Other within the Jewish community" (Hyman 1995: 134–5; my emphasis).

. . . [O]nly misogyny and homophobia gave Freud and Fanon the whiteness they sought. From this analysis, the misogyny, homophobia, and racism of both thinkers is a dimension of racial self-hatred. According to Gilman, this structure projects the racist stereotype of one's "own" group onto its other members (1986: 1–21): the *Ostjude*, the Congolese, women, homosexuals. If we see colonized blacks and Jews as Europeans saw them – as, in some sense, members of a single group – this much is clear: we must also consider Freud's racism toward "primitives," like Fanon's toward Jews, for its elements of self-hatred.

Fanon's account of Negrophobia as a product of homosexual desire resembles Freud's interpretation of Daniel Schreber's paranoia, with its anti-Semitic components as a product of homosexuality.[27] Yet Fanon does not seem to cite Freud so much as reproduce the thought processes that led Freud to his conclusions.[28] In this way, the internalized self-contempt that the colonized male feels for his disempowered situation (represented in Jews by the affect surrounding circumcision, and in the Negro by his representation as penis) powerfully determines colonial misogyny and homophobia: the situation of both Jew and Negro is misrecognized as feminine. This mechanism entails a form of intrapsychic splitting, in which the colonized establishes a partial identification with the colonizer.[29] The colonized begins to see himself from the eyes of his oppressor and tries to reject what he considers contemptible by projecting all of this onto the white man's other Others: the Jew onto the black, the black onto the Jew, and both onto women and homosexuals.

Fanon reveals the grounds of this structure as clearly as Freud does. Drawing synecdochically on the "Negro of the Antilles," he claims to write about "every colonized man," and concludes that the colonized person wishes to achieve a "universal" status: the black to become white, etc. (1967: 18; see Spitzer 1989: 37). This is a highly symptomatic moment in Fanon's work, which ignores the colonized's possible deep contempt for the colonizer (see also Bhabha 1985: 162). Comparing this situation to that of *fin-de-siècle* Viennese Jews suggests a more illuminating, less universal reading. After all, only the "emancipated" Jew wishes to become gentile and thus views his circumcision with contempt.[30] As Seshadri-Crooks remarks: "If [premodern] Jews as a minority loathed their difference, then conversion could be a simple option. But that didn't happen." In traditional Jewish culture, only the circumcised male was deemed "whole" (Boyarin and Boyarin 1995). To this extent, circumcision did not produce anxiety or self-contempt but was instead a sign of resistance and a deliberate (private) setting apart of oneself from the dominant culture. As I have argued elsewhere (Boyarin 1994c), even if traditional Jewish male subjects in late antiquity perceived themselves as "feminine," in part because of their circumcision, this did not imply a lack or deprivation for them but a gain: such a perspective insists that the foreskin is a blemish and that circumcision, far from being a mutilation, adorns the male body.

We can take this perspective "straight" and as a parody of gentile claims of superiority over Jews. The best analogy I have found is a text purportedly by a Bengali that Jenny Sharpe interprets, in which two Bengalis converse on why the English would benefit from learning Bengali. This text "restages the colonizers' privileging of racial purity and their own superior intellect in a manner that turns the language of purity and superiority against them" (1989: 145; but see her properly skeptical glosses on this text). In premodern Jewish descriptions that the uncircumcised penis is ugly, gross, impure, and in the Bengali reverse discourse about their superior language, we see parodic rejections of the dominant culture's claims, to which Scott refers as "hidden transcripts."

Scott argues eloquently against assumptions of hegemony here, claiming instead that the appearance of hegemony is only a "public script" serving the interests of colonizer and colonized in situations of near-total domination: "In this respect, subordinate groups . . . contribut[e] to a sanitized official transcript, for that is one way they cover their tracks" (1990: 87). He also claims that "genuine" hegemony occurs only in situations where the oppressed or dominated party hope one day to dominate – not over their present oppressors but over others – e.g., in age-graded systems of domination. I suggest that the condition of incipient decolonization, represented for Jews by their *fin-de-siècle* transitional emancipation status, and for Fanon by his education in France, is precisely such an "expectation that one will eventually be able to exercise the domination that one endures today." According to Scott, that would be "a strong incentive serving to legitimate patterns of domination" (1990: 82) and thus an occasion for turning the hidden transcript of contempt for the oppressor into self-contempt. In this way, the moment of decolonization on the political level ("emancipation" for the Jews) ironically fosters hegemony. For instance, an early-twentieth-century American Jewish professor remarked of his coreligionists in Eastern Europe that their bodies are bound but their spirits are free; for those of the West, however, the opposite was true (see also Guha 1989).

Here circumcision for the Jewish colonial subject resembles a moment of displaced castration (Geller 1993). When looking into a mirror, Freud experiences his circumcision as "uncanny," and, closeted behind the mask of white scientist, sets out to explain – almost to justify – anti-Semitism. To the extent that Jewish

psychoanalysts read circumcision in this way, they glaringly inscribe their ambivalent understanding of Jewish male difference, an ambivalence that American
culture records in Alexander Portnoy's and Woody Allen's "psychoanalytic" discourse. Freud is a paradigm for this ambivalent subjectivity, one of the strongest
symptoms of which is his thought's frequent, but not ubiquitous, misogyny,
racism, and homophobia (Gilman 1993b: 23). The incongruity of this prejudice
alongside the best of Freud's thought leads me to interpret its recurrence as a type
of lapse (Fuss 1994: 36).

Freud's master complex, the Oedipus/castration complex, is the most dramatic
example of this sociopsychic process. Let me repeat Freud's statement. "The
castration complex is the deepest unconscious root of anti-semitism; for even in
the nursery little boys hear that a Jew has something cut off his penis – a piece of
his penis, they think – and this gives them the right to despise Jews. And there is no
stronger unconscious root for the sense of superiority over women" (1909: 198–
9). ... Freud claims that boys hearing of circumcision is the unconscious root of
misogyny, anti-Semitism – and, at a deeper level – Jewish self-hatred, to react
against suggestions of Jews' "castration" and "feminization." Gilman reads this as
the development of normal Jews who "overcome their anxiety about their own
bodies by being made to understand that the real difference is not between their
circumcised penises and those of uncircumcised males, but between themselves
and castrated females" (1993b: 87); I would add that the same paradigm determines the colonized Jew's misogyny.[31]

I am not denying that other factors contributed to these ideologies and representations in Freud and Fanon. In Freud's case, we must reckon with the general
upsurge in misogyny that came to a crisis in *fin-de-siècle* Europe, as Bram Dijkstra
has fully diagnosed in *Idols of Perversity* (1986). For Fanon, the influence of Freud
is certainly undeniable. For both as well, elements of misogyny and homophobia
inherited from their "traditional" cultures preexist them. It is not, however,
sufficient to argue that Freud and Fanon were men of their times and cultures;
we must ask why – and for what *structural* reasons – they accepted and rejected
various ideological motifs in their respective cultures. These men were radical
rejectors of common wisdom. Why did they occasionally become so conventional?
Their sociopsychological situations as men "in between" – as neither "native" nor
fully Western – suggests one explanation. Postcolonial theory, and specifically
Fanon's elaboration of the colonized male subject, has helped us uncover this
aspect of psychoanalysis's cultural unconscious.

In the context of postcolonial theory, Freud's universalized theories of subjectivity, all of them centered on the phallus – the Oedipus complex, the castration
anxiety, and penis envy – seem an elaborate defense against the feminization of
Jewish men. Freud's naturalization of misogyny is also a way for him to appropriate
the phallus for himself as a circumcised male. His theories allowed him to claim that
the "real" difference is not between the Jewish and gentile penis but between
having and not having a penis. The binary opposition phallus/castration conceals
the same third term that Freud conceals in his mystification of Little Hans's identity:
the circumcised penis. Both the "*idealization* of the phallus, whose integrity is
necessary [to] edif[y] the entire psychoanalytical system" (Johnson 1987: 225),
and the flight to Greek cultural models and metaphors signal this production's

inmixing when psychoanalysis theorizes the affect of colonized people. We might say that the Oedipus complex is Freud's "family romance," in the exact sense of the term. Although this issue is not reducible to Freud or merely a question of psychobiography, Freud seems to fantasize unconsciously that he is not the circumcised Schelomo, son of Jakob, but the uncircumcised and virile Greek Oedipus, son of Laius (see Anzieu 1986: 195), just as he earlier fantasized that he was Hannibal, son of Hamilcar, not the son of his "unheroic" Jewish father. Fanon also writes of "a bilateral process, an attempt to acquire – by internalizing them – assets that were originally prohibited [by the colonizers]" (1967: 59–60). Such was Freud's sublated penis become phallus (Lacan 1985: 82), not as an asset that he owned but as one he sought to acquire: a mask (the product of a mimicry) as abject and subversive as that of white masks for black skins.

. . . Freud shows that the liminal racial position he occupied generates knowledge and unknowing. Freud's narrative of sexual differentiation as *nonbiological* in its foundations is a good deal more liberatory than is, for instance, Karen Horney's contention that people are born male or female (see also Ramas 1980: 480–1). In this respect, the castration complex represents an astonishing theoretical advance over naturalized views of sexual difference. Yet Freud's greatest insight – that sexual difference is made and not born – is also his darkest moment of misogyny; it emerges out of the same point in his discourse, as does his interpretation of words like *heimlich*, which are fundamentally equivocal. We must reject crude readings of Freud that caricature him merely as a white male woman-hater, but we cannot simply ignore the gender effects of Freud's castration discourse. The point is certainly not to disqualify Freud's contribution by locating it in a particular social circumstance; instead, by identifying its moments of blindness and insight, I clarify why Freud's thesis sometimes becomes incoherent, unnecessary, or otherwise unhelpful. There is, for instance, a signal blindness in Freud's unwillingness to figure sexual difference in any other way than by the phallus, which, as Lacan *correctly* interpreted, is symbolically equivalent to the Name-of-the-Father. Why was a thinker who was in many ways able to break with his culture's paradigms quite unable to do so here?

It is as if a gap emerged between Freud's figuring his affect as "defense against castration" and as "a slyly hidden opposition to his own Jewishness" (Le Rider 1995: 31). This clarifies "the divided subject posited by psychoanalytic theory . . . refut[ing] humanism's myth of the unified self," and the same subject's concomitant misogyny, homophobia, and racism (Parry 1987: 29). We now have a paradigm by which to explain the curious way in which Freud's texts support the most radical and reactionary sociopolitical projects. . . .

. . . Freud's conflicted social position produced the internal divisions of his subject position, resulting in both his discourse's Janus-like duality, at once radical and reactionary, and his understanding of the subject's divisions. I have attempted to show how these divisions manifest themselves, pointing out their wider implications for a psychoanalytic approach to racial conflicts. In light of these divisions, the peculiarly American developments of ego psychology, which mobilize only the most reactionary aspects of Freud's thinking on sex and gender, would appear as a desperate attempt to resolve the paradoxes of such postcolonial subjectivities as that of the European Jewish refugee.

Notes

The essay was originally dedicated to Tony Kushner, with love.

1 Susan Shapiro is writing a book on the uncanny as a trope for the Jew.
2 Freud's interpretation of Hoffman's *The Sandman* remains just that – a compelling interpretation, not an explanation or proof of the centrality of castration in the uncanny.
3 I wonder how akin Freud's mirror is to Stephen Dedalus's description of Irish art as "the cracked looking-glass of a servant" (Joyce 1961: 6).
4 W. E. B. Du Bois's *The Souls of Black Folk* laid the intellectual foundations for this chapter. For a brilliant reading, see Gilroy, 1993.
5 Mosse's account of the contrast between Friedländer and Hirschfeld, both Jewish and homosexual, is instructive: "For Friedländer [who converted], the Jews were assigned the very stereotype which society had created for homosexuals.... Magnus Hirschfeld, homosexual and Jew, became [a] strong advocate of human rights" (1985: 41).
6 In an illuminating essay, Harpham describes the *conversos* ("forcibly" converted Jews) of early modern Spain as paradigmatic modern subjects (1994: 550–1)....
7 Interestingly, a similar situation seems to obtain for the Irish. As Duffy remarks, "it was inevitable that the Irish would be seen to occupy an ambivalent middle ground between the 'master' and the 'dark' races" (1994: 42–3).
8 For analogous processes in American culture, see Rogin 1992; Gilman, 1994.
9 In *Civilization and its Discontents* (1930: 114), to be sure, it seems that Freud represents hostility to Jews as an example of "the narcissism of minor differences," but a careful reading shows that this is not necessarily the case. See also Pellegrini 1997.
10 Freud had read Chamberlain (Gilman, 1993b: 236). For extensive documentation of the "blackness" of Jews, see Gilman 1986: 172–5 and 1993a: 19–21. For a fascinating explanation of the functions of such discourse, see Cheyette 1995.
11 "Jewish science" was definitely a racist/anti-Semitic term of art, a fact Gilman clarifies in 1995: 112–13.
12 For a very thoughtful version, see Seshadri-Crooks, who asks whether certain descriptions of Freud as contemptuously patronizing of Indian psychoanalysts (including Bose) do not reproduce such a stance, since Bose and his fellows seem unaware of Freud's contempt and patronization (1994: 186). We could also ask a version of this question here. If, as some claim, Freud's work is irretrievably tainted with racism and colonialist ideology, why was someone like Fanon unaware of this corruption?
13 Compare Gilman (1991: 194–209), who goes too far in my opinion in associating the straightforward racism – Nazi sympathies – of Masud Khan with Fanon's complex affect concerning Jews. There is no evidence that Fanon, for all his tragic misrecognition of European anti-Semitism, read Jews as racially inferior, *pace* Gilman (p. 200). On the other hand, we must contrast Fanon's grotesque reading of the Nazi genocide as a "family quarrel" with Césaire's sensitive understanding that colonialism is practice for the internal other's genocide; see Boyarin 1992: 105–7.
14 I am grateful to Jonathan Boyarin for this reference.
15 Cuddihy was perhaps the first to realize that there are significant homologies between Jewish "Emancipation" and the postwar processes of decolonization:

> The fact that Jews in the West are a decolonized and modernizing people, an "underdeveloped people" traumatized – like all underdeveloped countries – by contact with the more modernized and hence "higher" nations of the West goes unrecognized for several reasons. First, because they have been a colony *internal* to the West; second, because decolonization has been gradual and continuous; third, because of the democratic manners of the West (only Max Weber called

them a pariah people, i.e., a ritually segregated guest people); and fourth, because the modernization collision has been politicized and theologized by the charge of "anti-Semitism" (as, in noncontiguous Western colonies, the charge of "imperialism" effectively obscures the real nature of the collision – namely, between modernizing and nonmodernized peoples). (1987: 47)

In "*Épater l'embourgeoisement*" (1994a) I discuss Cuddihy critically and at some length. For all his celebration of the West's civilizing mission, Cuddihy at least identifies the Jews as subject to it. I prefer not to use the term "assimilation," because of its implicit assumption that previously one could speak of an unassimilated or pure cultural situation, on either side. In all but the most exceptional cases, it is now clear that cultures are always to some extent in contact, thus always assimilating. This term does not sufficiently evoke the particular cultural anxieties of the transition from colonial domination to emancipation. Further, "assimilation" implies a stability in the "target culture" to which one is assimilating; in reality, European culture at the time of Jewish Emancipation was greatly in flux. Indeed, it would not be inaccurate to say that Jewish cultural activities played a role in the production of European modernity, just as we are coming to recognize the cultural role of colonialism and the colonies in producing European modernity. See also Boyarin 1992: 82. For the particular application of the term "colonial subject" to the "Western-educated native," see Sharpe 1989: 139–40.

16 Martin Jay has cautioned me, however, that this was true of many groups in Europe in the nineteenth century. Insofar as there were other internal colonies, undoubtedly many of the same processes befell them, each, of course, with its own historical inflections and specificities.

17 My interpretation of Börne is entirely different from that of Arendt, who wrote, "The anti-Jewish denunciations of Marx and Börne cannot be properly understood except in the light of this conflict between rich Jews and Jewish intellectuals" (1958: 54). It is certainly not irrelevant that both Marx and Börne were converted Jews – the limit case of the hybrid and self-alienated Jewish subject.

18 In this essay I will use the term "Negro," following Fanon. Here, obviously, neither "African" nor "African American" will do.

19 I suggest that this split between Ostjuden and Viennese Jews allowed the latter to "maintain a primary identification with the group from which they stemmed" (Spitzer 1989: 38, referring to Rozenblit 1983), i.e., by splitting off good, acculturated, German-speaking Jews from bad, primitive, Yiddish-speaking ones – who were, often their parents or grandparents! The idea of Judaism as a religion enabled this "primary identification." The famous Wien chapter of the Benei Brith is reminiscent of nothing so much as the National Benevolent Society of Yorubas in Sierra Leone (Spitzer 1989: 43; Rozenblit 1983: 150). See also Cuddihy 1987: 176.

20 In other words, I suggest that there are situations in which an imaginary possession of the phallus can be less toxic than a desperate effort to get it. Both, of course, are equally products of a certain relation to the dominant fiction.

21 Compare the kindred argument of Gilman 1993a; see also Fuss 1994: 38.

22 Insofar as Freud is "in the closet" qua Jew and qua "queer," his discourse is oppressive to women, lesbians, and gay men; when he is less closeted, we find the moments of powerful liberatory insight so sharply located by Bersani in the margins of Freud's texts (1986). See also Duffy's sensitive remarks (1994: 21).

23 Morgan gives us a brief and moving account of her response to Fanon and the ways in which he empowered her, in spite of it all (1982: 113). Her strategy, in summary, is to translate what Fanon says about colonized men into discourse about women and to bracket and voluntarily ignore what he says about women.

24 Note that "dark continent" is in English. Freud's search, like Herzl's, was for an "Anglo-Saxon" white-male sublimity.

25 Of course, I am not implying that this is the *only* source of prejudice in "native" peoples. I clarify this later in the essay.

26 I would be somewhat less generous to Fanon than Fuss is here. She reads this statement as "a rejection of the 'primitive = invert' equation that marks the confluence of evolutionary anthropology and sexology," while I see it as an instance of identificatory mimesis of white homophobia, which does not refuse the categories of European sexuality but reifies and "universalizes" them. Fuss's formulation on p. 36 (1994) is more critical.

27 See also the fascinating account of this trope (the anti-Semite as repressed homosexual) in Gilman, 1993b: 196–8, and especially Santner 1996.

28 See also Cheung 1990: 236–8 for a parallel analysis of Chinese-American critical writing and its "lending credence to the conventional association of physical aggression with manly valor" and its "sexist preference for [male] stereotypes that imply predatory violence against women to 'effeminate' ones" (p. 237).

29 Hutton usefully interprets Freud's telling of Yiddish jokes as another form of this splitting: "It involves an interplay between the identity of the 'little Jew' and that of the intellectual or 'outsider' Jew. In telling the joke, Freud or the narrator identifies with both sides, seeing each inside the other" (1990: 14). This is a somewhat more genial description of the process than I have given. See also the telling example discussed in Gilman 1992: 162–3.

30 In the present-day United States, however, circumcision itself has been configured as "universal," although this is certainly changing.

31 I am drawing a distinction here, as throughout my work, between the disenfranchisement of women in the social sphere and misogyny *per se* – the expression of contempt and hatred for women. The two are obviously related but not identical. The former is endemic in Jewish culture; the latter, I argue, sporadic. Moreover, misogyny *per se* grows stronger throughout European Jewish history, reaching its peak in Eastern Europe precisely at the moment of modernization (decolonization).

References

Anzieu, Didier. 1986. *Freud's Self-Analysis* [Paris: 1975]. Trans. Peter Graham. Pref. M. Masud R. Khan. New York: International University Press.

Arendt, Hannah. 1958. *The Origins of Totalitarianism*, 2d edn. Cleveland: Meridian-World.

Berkowitz, Michael. 1993. *Zionist Culture and West European Jewry Before the First World War*. New York: Cambridge University Press.

Bersani, Leo. 1986. *The Freudian Body: Psychoanalysis and Art*. New York: Columbia University Press.

Bhabha, Homi K. 1985. "Signs Taken for Wonders: Questions of Ambivalence and Authority under a Tree Outside Delhi, May 1817." *Critical Inquiry* 12/1: 144–65.

——. 1994. *The Location of Culture*. New York: Routledge.

Bolkosky, Sidney. 1986. "Arthur Schnitzler and the Fate of Mothers in Vienna." *Psychoanalytic Review* 73/1: 1–15.

Boyarin, Daniel. 1994a. "*Épater l'embourgeoisement*: Freud, Gender, and the (De)Colonized Psyche." *Diacritics* 24/1: 17–42.

——.1994b. "Freud's Baby, Fliess's Maybe: Male Hysteria, Homophobia, and the Invention of the Jewish Man." *GLQ* 2/1: 1–33.

——.1994c. "Jewish Masochism: Couvade, Castration, and Rabbis in Pain." *American Imago* 51/1: 3–36.

Boyarin, Jonathan. 1992. "The Other Within and the Other Without." *Storm from Paradise: The Politics of Jewish Memory.* Minneapolis: University of Minnesota Press, pp. 77–98.

Boyarin, Jonathan, and Daniel Boyarin. 1995. "Self-exposure as Theory: The Double Mark of the Male Jew." *Rhetorics of Self-making.* Ed. Debbora Battaglia. Berkeley: University of California Press, pp. 16–42.

Cheung, King-Kok. 1990. "The Woman Warrior Versus the Chinaman Pacific: Must a Chinese American Critic Choose between Feminism and Heroism?" *Conflicts in Feminism.* Ed. Marianne Hirsch and Evelyn Fox Keller. New York: Routledge, pp. 234–51.

Cheyette, Bryan. 1995. "Neither Black Nor White: The Figure of 'the Jew' in Imperial British Literature." In *The Jew in the Text: Modernity and the Politics of Identity.* Ed. Linda Nochin and Tamar Garb. London: Thames and Hudson, pp. 31–41.

Cuddihy, John Murray. 1987. *The Ordeal of Civility: Freud, Marx, Lévi-Strauss, and the Jewish Struggle with Modernity* [1974]. With a New Preface by the Author. Boston: Beacon.

Dean, Tim. 1995. "On the Eve of a Queer Future." *Raritan* 15/1: 116–34.

Dijkstra, Bram. 1986. *Idols of Perversity: Fantasies of Feminine Evil in Fin-de-siècle Culture.* New York: Oxford University Press.

Duffy, Enda. 1994. *The Subaltern Ulysses.* Minneapolis: University of Minnesota Press.

Fabre-Vassas, Claudine. 1994. *La Bête singulière: Les juifs, les chrétiens, et le cochon.* Paris: Gallimard.

Fanon, Frantz. 1967. *Black Skin, White Masks* [1952]. Trans. Charles Lam Markmann. New York: Grove.

Freud, Ernst, Lucie Freud, and Ilse Grubrich-Simitis, eds. 1985. *Sigmund Freud: His Life in Pictures and Words* [1978]. New York: Norton.

Freud, Sigmund. *The Standard Edition of the Complete Psychological Works of Sigmund Freud,* 24 vols. Ed. and trans. James Strachey. London: Hogarth, 1953–74.

——. 1909. *Analysis of a Phobia in a Five-Year-Old Boy (Little Hans).* Vol. 10 of *SE,* pp. 3–149.

——. 1915. "The Unconscious." Vol. 14 of *SE,* pp. 159–215.

——. 1919. "The 'Uncanny.'" Vol. 17 of *SE,* pp. 217–56.

——. 1921. *Group Psychology and the Analysis of the Ego.* Vol. 18 of *SE,* pp. 67–143.

——. 1926. "The Question of Lay Analysis." Vol. 20 of *SE,* pp. 179–258.

——. 1930. *Civilization and Its Discontents.* Vol. 21 of *SE,* pp. 59–145.

Fuss, Diana. 1994. "Interior Colonies: Frantz Fanon and the Politics of Identification." *Diacritics* 24/2–3: 20–42.

Geller, Jay. 1992. "'A Glance at the Nose': Freud's Inscription of Jewish Difference." *American Imago* 49/4: 427–44.

Geller, Jay. 1993. "A Paleontological View of Freud's Study of Religion: Unearthing the Leitfossil Circumcision." *Modern Judaism* 13: 49–70.

Gilman, Sander L. 1986: *Jewish Self-hatred: Anti-Semitism and the Hidden Language of the Jews.* Baltimore: Johns Hopkins University Press.

——. 1991. *The Jew's Body.* New York: Routledge.

——. 1992. "Freud, Race and Gender." *American Imago* 49/2: 155–83.

——. 1993a. *The Case of Sigmund Freud: Medicine and Identity at the Fin de Siècle.* Baltimore: Johns Hopkins UP.

——. 1993b. *Freud, Race, and Gender.* Princeton: Princeton UP.

——. 1994. "Dangerous Liaisons." *Transitions* 64: 41–52.

——. 1995. "Otto Weininger and Sigmund Freud: Race and Gender in the Shaping of Psychoanalysis." In *Jews and Gender: Responses to Otto Weininger.* Ed. Nancy A. Harrowitz and Barbara Hyams. Philadelphia: Temple University Press, pp. 103–20.

Gilroy, Paul. 1991. *There Ain't No Black in the Union Jack: The Cultural Politics of Race and Nation*. With a New Preface by Houston A. Baker, Jr. Chicago: University of Chicago Press.

——. 1993. *The Black Atlantic: Modernity and Double Consciousness*. Cambridge: Harvard University Press.

Guha, Ranajit. 1989. "Dominance Without Hegemony and Its Historiography." *Subaltern Studies* 6. Ed. Guha. Delhi: Oxford UP, 210–309.

Halperin, David M. 1995. *Saint Foucault: Towards a Gay Hagiography*. New York: Oxford University Press.

Harpham, Geoffrey Galt. 1994. "So . . . What *Is* Enlightenment? An Inquisition into Modernity." *Critical Inquiry* 20.3: 524–56.

Hutton, Christopher. 1990. "Freud and the Family Drama of Yiddish." *Studies in Yiddish Linguistics*. Ed. Paul Wexler. Tübingen: Niemeyer, pp. 9–22.

Hyman, Paula E. 1995. *Gender and Assimilation in Modern Jewish History: The Roles and Representation of Women*. The Samuel & Althea Stroum Lectures in Jewish Studies. Seattle: University of Washington Press.

Johnson, Barbara. 1987. "The Frame of Reference: Poe, Lacan, Derrida." *The Purloined Poe*. Ed. John P. Muller and William J. Richards. Baltimore: Johns Hopkins University Press, pp. 213–51.

Joyce, James. 1961. *Ulysses* [1922]. New York: Random House.

Kazanjian, David. 1993. "Notarizing Knowledge: Paranoia and Civility in Freud and Lacan." *Qui Parle* 7/1: 102–39.

Kofman, Sarah. 1985. *The Enigma of Woman*. Trans. Catherine Porter. Ithaca: Cornell University Press.

Lacan, Jacques. 1985. "The Meaning of the Phallus." *Feminine Sexuality: Jacques Lacan and the école freudienne*. Ed. Juliet Mitchell and Jacqueline Rose. Trans. Rose. New York: Norton, pp. 74–85.

Le Rider, Jacques. 1995. "The 'Otto Weininger Case' Revisited." In *Jews and Gender: Responses to Otto Weininger*. Ed. Nancy A. Harrowitz and Barbara Hyams. Philadelphia: Temple University Press, pp. 21–33.

McGrath, William J. 1986. *Freud's Discovery of Psychoanalysis: The Politics of Hysteria*. Ithaca: Cornell University Press.

Morgan, Robin. 1982. "The Politics of Sado-masochist Fantasies." *Against Sadomasochism: A Radical Feminist Analysis*. Ed. Robin Ruth Linden et al. San Francisco: Frog in the Well, pp. 109–23.

Mosse, George. L. 1985. *Nationalism and Sexuality: Middle-Class Morality and Sexual Norms in Modern Europe*. Madison: University of Wisconsin Press.

Parry, Benita. 1987. "Problems in Current Theories of Colonial Discourse." *Oxford Literary Review* 9: 27–58.

Pellegrini, Ann. 1997a. *Performance Anxieties: Staging Psychoanalysis, Staging Race*. New York: Routledge.

——. 1997b. "Whiteface Performances: 'Race,' Gender, and Jewish Bodies." *Jews and Other Differences: The New Jewish Cultural Studies*. Ed. D. Boyarin and J. Boyarin. Minneapolis: University of Minnesota Press, pp. 108–49.

Ramas, Maria. 1980. "Freud's Dora, Dora's Hysteria: The Negation of a Woman's Rebellion." *Feminist Studies* 6.3: 472–510.

Robert, Marthe. 1976. *From Oedipus to Moses: Freud's Jewish Identity*. Trans. Ralph Manheim. Garden City, NY: Doubleday.

Rogin, Michael. 1992. "Blackface, White Noise: The Jewish Jazz Singer Finds His Voice." *Critical Inquiry* 18: 417–53.

Rozenblit, Marsha. 1983. *The Jews of Vienna, 1867–1914: Assimilation and Community*. Albany: SUNY Press.

Santner, Eric. 1996. *My Own Private Germany: Daniel Paul Schreber's Secret History of Modernity.* Princeton: Princeton University Press.

Schnitzler, Arthur. 1970. *My Youth in Vienna.* Trans. Catherine Hutter. New York: Holt, Rinehart, and Winston.

Scott, James C. 1990. *Domination and the Arts of Resistance: Hidden Transcripts.* New Haven: Yale University Press.

Seshadri-Crooks, Kalpana. 1994. "The Primitive as Analyst: Postcolonial Feminism's Access to Psychoanalysis." *Cultural Critique* 28: 175–218.

——. 1998. "The Comedy of Domination: Psychoanalysis and the Conceit of Whiteness." In *The Psychoanalysis of Race.* Ed. Christopher Lane. New York: Columbia University Press, pp. 353–79.

Sharpe, Jenny. 1989. "Figures of Colonial Resistance." *Modern Fiction Studies* 35/1: 137–55.

Spitzer, Leo. 1989. *Lives In-Between: Assimilation and Marginality in Austria, Brazil, and West Africa, 1780–1945.* Studies in Comparative World History. New York: Cambridge University Press.

17

The Economy of Colonial Desire

Revathi Krishnaswamy

The Masks of Masculinity

"The East is East and the West is West and never the twain shall meet," claimed Rudyard Kipling in "The Ballad of East and West," and then went on to imagine the ground on which this impossible meeting may become possible: "when two strong men stand face to face, though they come from the ends of the earth."[1] Kipling's vision of colonial intimacy intriguingly predicates cultural and racial difference on a metaphoric distinction between male strength and male weakness rather than on the more conventional demarcation between masculinity and femininity. Masculinity is not only a foundational notion of modernity, but it is also the cornerstone in the ideology of moral imperialism that prevailed in British India from the late nineteenth century onward. The cult of masculinity rationalized imperial rule by equating an aggressive, muscular, chivalric model of manliness with racial, national, cultural, and moral superiority.

Modern masculinity was elaborated not only through an increasingly stricter demarcation between the sexes but also through a systematic "unmanning" of minorities within and foreigners without Europe. According to this model, the ideal appearance of the English male (the tall, strong, clean-cut English man) specifically excluded those who were stunted, narrow-chested, excitable, easily wearied, or inefficient – qualities associated with women, the lower classes, Jews, Papists, Spaniards, the French, and colored peoples. Eschewing the "feminine" virtues of early Christianity – meekness, mildness, and martyrdom – the ideal of manliness emerging in eighteenth-century Europe combined a Greek aesthetics of the body with Roman militarism and medieval chivalry. Johann Joachim Winckelmann (1717–68), archaeologist and art historian, was most influential in manufacturing an aesthetics of male beauty derived from descriptions of Greek sculpture. He represented the ideal male body as one that is harmonious in proportions and projected strength as well as restraint. Anthropologists then used this aesthetic criteria to identify differences between whites and non whites ("primitives"). Through cranial measurements and facial comparisons they exalted physical beauty as an attribute of superior European species. In the 1790s Winck-

Reprinted from *Effeminism: The Economy of Colonial Desire* (Ann Arbor: University of Michigan Press, 1998), pp. 15–27, 29, 31–52, 171–7.

elmann's ideal of beauty was used as a standard by Peter Camper to classify races. The equation between manly beauty and virtue that emerged through these comparisons and classifications became an important aspect of modern masculinity. Such a link between body and soul, outer and inner, physical and moral, was more firmly cemented in the new eighteenth-century sciences of physiognomy, anthropology, and modern medicine. Thus, Johann Kaspar Lavatar, founding practitioner of the science of physiognomy, adopted Winckelmann's aesthetics to identify explicitly beauty with virtue and ugliness with vice. For Lavatan beauty was a product of cleanliness, love of work, and moderation. A similar sentiment is evident in the educational tract *Emile* (1762), in which Rousseau declares that wisdom and understanding would inevitably follow from physical robustness and good health.[2]

If masculine beauty was an expression of white European racial, moral and cultural superiority, ugliness was evidence of nonwhite, non-European inferiority. The disorderly appearance attributed to diverse groups of foreigners and social misfits referred not only to physical deformity, but it also implied lack of mental discipline and emotional moderation. Modern medicine and psychology played a powerful role in solidifying the link between body and soul through the very process of designating and defining as diseased those who did not fit in. Among the most common "diseases" attributed to the Other in the eighteenth and nineteenth centuries was nervousness. Nervousness, linked to the body, had been considered a sickness even during the seventeenth century, as evident in the views expressed by the famous English physician Thomas Sydenham, who believed that women, because of their delicate constitution, were more prone to nervousness and mental diseases than men.[3] But in the following two centuries, encouraged by the eighteenth-century cult of sensibility and by Romanticism, there was an enormous fascination with nervous disorder throughout Europe. As more physicians began to study the nervous system, illnesses that has earlier been attributed to foul vapors or bad humors were now attributed to weak nerves. In fact, shattered nerves were blamed for the predicaments of modernity, for cultural and political decay, for rapid economic and social change. Although seen as a mental illness, nervousness nevertheless affected the entire body through muscular contortions. In addition to maintaining good physical health through exercise and sports, nervous disorders could be warded off by reining in one's imagination, passions, and fantasies. A fanciful imagination, it was believed, could drive a man to excesses, especially sexual excesses in the form of masturbation, frequent intercourse, or homosexuality, all of which would inevitably distort both body and mind.

Thus, toward the end of the nineteenth century a paranoid British culture pictured itself under siege by immigrant hordes of physically undesirable, morally degenerate aliens. It was feared that the mongrelization of the white race would lead to the disintegration of the empire itself. To counter these fears Victorian myths of manhood and of the empire as a vast paternalistic enterprise were manufactured, feeding the notion that character was key to maintaining racial and cultural superiority. Accordingly, the definition of manliness in British public schools shifted first from Thomas Arnold's notion of "godliness and goodlearning," in the 1830s, to the vigorous "muscular Christianity" of the mid-Victorian period, associated with men such as Charles Kingsley and Thomas Hughes, and, finally, to the "athleticism" of the 1870s, which, popularized by writers like Samuel

Smiles and Lord Baden-Powell (a close friend of Kipling), fed the recruiting campaigns for imperial projects in the late nineteenth century.[4] Baden-Powell may be considered the architect of the idea that English character was a defense against external threat. The Boy Scouts he founded became what Michael Rosenthal terms the "character factory," an institutionalized site for the production of "boy nature" – a class construct designed for the lower classes in order to refashion them to conform to middle-class interests. The Boy Scout code of character aimed at instant denial of individualism, thought, and emotion, in favor of corporate loyalty and group identity. The Boy Scout emphasis on pluck and determination translated skills on the cricket field to the battlefields of empire.[5]

The trope of chivalry also constituted a privileged locus of colonial self-image – one whose ideological origins may be traced back to the aristocracy of medieval and Renaissance Europe. The ideology of knighthood was instrumental in making and maintaining structures of power based on class (ruler and vassal in feudal society), gender (lady and knight in courtly love tradition), and religion (the Christians against the Islamic infidels as in the Crusades). The code of chivalry mediated these relations of power and dependence by setting up reciprocal bonds of duty and obligation. But, while chivalry reproduced and reinforced the knight's class and gender status, it also acted as a safety valve, providing young males of aspiring lower social strata with opportunities for upward mobility. Such a concept of chivalry, as Rajeswari Sunder Rajan points out, proved to be eminently adaptable to the context of colonization:

> large numbers of young British men – administrators, soldiers, traders, educationalists, missionaries – found themselves unexpectedly authorized in the exercise of power over masses of Indians. But they also discovered that they had to undergo rites of initiation into the exercise of this power. The colonizer's racial superiority, however flagrant skin color or the trappings of power may have rendered it, had also to be demonstrated by acts of valor and authority.[6]

This expectation, Sunder Rajan goes on to suggest, provided the legitimating narrative for colonial legislation on behalf of Indian women, who were cast as the hapless victims of a barbaric Indian patriarchy. The deficiency of Indian males in adequately embodying the chivalric ideal of manhood, the British argued, not only stunted interracial bonds but actually made India unfit for self-rule. The British believed that their exposure to a bracing, self-strengthening physical and moral climate at "home" (and in the frontier regions of India) made them natural leaders, while Indian men, lacking such exposure, remained weak and ineffectual. In fact, the distinction between male strength and weakness inscribed in Kipling's "Ballad of East and West" raises a larger question that increasingly haunts Anglo-India: (how) is it possible for (manly) English and (effeminate) Indian men to be friends?

Read against the grain, Kipling's infamous observation about strong men from the ends of the earth allows us to identify the British Raj as a "homosocial" space constituted by contending male fears, frustrations, and fascinations.[7] The entire structure of colonial homosociality, however, rests on the ideologeme of effeminacy. Effeminacy represents a critical and contentious idiom through which the racial and sexual ideologies of empire are mediated. Ashis Nandy describes the critical change in consciousness that colonialism produced in India as follows:

The polarity defined by the antonymous *purusatva* (the essence of masculinity), and *naritva* (the essence of femininity) was gradually supplanted, in the colonial culture of politics, by the antonyms of *purusatva* and *klibatva* (the essence of hermaphroditism). Femininity-in-masculinity was perceived as the final negation of a man's political identity, a pathology more dangerous than femininity itself.[8]

I shall use the term *effeminism* to refer to the racialized construction of "femininity-in-masculinity" as a pathological condition. While tracing the production of effeminacy in various nineteenth-century discourses, it will be my contention that Indian effeminacy should not be regarded simply as a false construct, an untrue stereotype, or an inverted projection, but should be seen, rather, as a misvalued and distorted recognition of something real in Indian culture. In other words, I am suggesting that there was indeed some basis for viewing Hindu society as effeminate, for not only did dominant strands of Hinduism reverse the Western equation of passivity with femininity and activity with masculinity, but androgyny, inspired by the medieval Bhakti movement, remained a forceful spiritual ideal for Hindu men at least until the first half of the nineteenth century. Let me hasten to add that neither of these views necessarily implies a pro-woman or feminist stance, because Hinduism generally devalued female activity to male stasis, while androgyny was held out as a liberating ideal primarily for men rather than for women. By the second half of the nineteenth century, however, a dramatic shift had occurred in the culture of colonial India: androgyny had been largely discredited as a positive spiritual ideal, and few Hindu men were able to escape the negative self-image of effeminacy.[9] It was Gandhian nationalism that finally revived, reformed, and elaborated androgyny as an alternative to colonial masculinity, thereby providing Indians with a powerful political plank from which to fight colonialism.

My second argument...is based on the assumption that we need to study the ways in which a stereotype frames and limits the stereotyped as well as the stereotyper. Otherwise, we run the risk of reifying the omnipotent image of colonialism by granting it total hegemony over representation....[E]ffeminism not only enabled British colonialism in India, but it also estranged colonial authority and bracketed colonial hegemony in certain important respects....

...I will be using the term *effeminacy* in three distinct yet related contexts. My first and most obvious application of the term relates to its historical use in colonial India as a derogatory label applied specifically to the elite, Hindu, Bengali male – and gradually, by extension, to all Indian men – to suggest that they are physically, intellectually, and morally, soft, frail, weak or cowardly, in short, "like a woman." My second use of the term *effeminacy* emphasizes a corollary of the first: the implied devaluation and disempowerment of women and femininity. As such, I am concerned not only with the dynamics of colonial masculine desire but also with its differential effects on white and brown women. Finally, I use the term in a rather restricted, perhaps radical sense to denote the experience of biculturality or cultural androgyny that colonialism inevitably involved for both colonizer and colonized. Used in this sense, *effeminacy* becomes a kind of "mimicry," a production of "hybridity" that carries with it an explosive potential for resistance or subversion.[10] I shall elaborate each of these contexts by briefly tracing the historical production of effeminism.

Effeminism

There is considerable evidence to show that from the early years of colonial rule
Europeans viewed Orientals in general and Indians in particular as a passive and
indolent people. Thus, Robert Orme, the eighteenth-century British historian,
declares: "breathing in the softest climates, having so few wants and receiving even
the luxuries of other nations with little labour from their own soil, the Indian must
have become the most effeminate inhabitant of the globe."[11] Many colonial texts
use the word *effeminate* to describe the inhabitants of the Indian subcontinent.
The word, George Mosse tells us, came into general usage in England during the
eighteenth century, indicating an unmanly softness and delicacy.[12] Ketaki Dyson
points out that the delicate physical features, dresses, and personal decorations of
Oriental men were commented on in great detail by Anglo-Indians.[13] Descriptions
of first landings on Indian shores attest to the dramatic way in which the dark male
body must have impinged on the colonizing imagination. William Hodges, a
professional artist under the patronage of Warren Hastings, records his first
impression of "delicately framed" men with feminine hands and "mild, tranquil,
and sedulously attentive" manners. Some of the men, Hodges observes, are
"wholly naked," while others wear "long muslin dresses," their "black faces
adorned with large gold ear-rings and white turbans." The "rustling of fine
linen, and the general hum of unusual conversation" suggests to Hodges "an
assembly of females."[14] This "spectacular" Oriental body is a product of what
Christine Bolt has called the "hardening of race thinking" through various ideological practices that consolidated race as the most visible category in colonial
society.[15] For Flora Annie Steel, who went out to India with her husband in 1867,
the racial male body becomes an extension of the exoticism of the Indian landscape: "My first entry into India was in a masulah boat through the surf at Madras.
It was exhilarating. Something quite new; something that held all possibilities. A
boat that had not a nail in it; dark-skinned boatmen with no clothes on, who did
not look naked, a surf such as I had never seen before, thundering on the yellow
sands."[16] E. M. Forster's entry into India focuses quite explicitly on the ambiguous beauty of the racial male body: "The last horrid meal on the horrid ship ended
as we reached Bombay, and we went ashore in style in a native boat, an ugly crew
but beautiful skins."[17] This hidden homoerotic look returns to complicate the
ideological and aesthetic configurations of *A Passage to India*, generating some of
the most arresting icons of male nudity in Anglo-Indian literature.

Over time *effeminacy* evolved from a vague adjective used to describe physical
appearance or lifestyle into a powerful ideologeme deployed in many different
discourses and in many varied contexts. Thus, for instance, William Jones, the
Orientalist scholar and translator responsible for the most influential introduction
of a textualized India to Europe in the late eighteenth century, relies heavily upon a
vocabulary of effeminacy to describe and codify Eastern languages and literatures.
In an essay on Oriental poetry Jones describes the Persians as characterized by
"that softness, and love of pleasure, that indolence, and effeminacy, which have
made them an easy prey to all the western and northern swarms."[18] Persian poetry
is said to be greatly influenced by the Indians, who are "soft and voluptuous, but
artful and insincere."[19] This particular strand of Orientalist scholarship provided

indirect support for Anglicist belief in the moral superiority of English by implicitly defining European languages and literatures, especially English, as hard, energetic, rational, and masculine. Thus, contrary to common assumption, Orientalism and Anglicism were not just competing discourses but also complementary discourses in the larger project of colonialism....

...Anglicist belief in the superiority of English rested on a racialized and gendered equation between language and nation. The Rev. George [a clergyman deeply concerned with Britain's civilizing mission] thus argued that "as the mind grows, the language grows, and adapts itself to the thinking of the people. Hence, a highly civilized race, will ever have, a highly accomplished language. The English tongue, is in all senses a very noble one."[20]

The enormously consequential ways in which such Anglicist assumptions entered into the formation of the "science" of modern linguistics in the late nineteenth and early twentieth centuries is a subject that is yet to be adequately addressed. For the purposes of the present discussion, however, I will only note that the gendered rhetoric used by both Orientalists as well as Anglicists continued to inform important strands of linguistics in the early decades of the twentieth century. For example, the influential grammarian and linguist Otto Jespersen argues that English is a "masculine" language since English consonants are "clearly and precisely pronounced."[21] After analyzing the first ten stanzas of Tennyson's *Locksley Hall*, he concludes that "the English language is a methodical, energetic, business-like and sober language, that does not care much for finery and elegance, but does care for logical consistency and is opposed to any attempt to narrow-in life by police regulations and strict rules either of grammar or of lexicon. As the language is, so also is the nation."[22] By contrast, Jespersen pointed to lexical diversity in "primitive languages" and argued that the presence of many words for "cow" in Zulu or for "grey" in Lithuanian, for instance, illustrates the fact that "primitive man did not see the wood from the trees."[23]

Effeminacy could serve both as cause and effect in colonial discourse. Thomas Babington Macaulay, law member for India in the 1830s and author of the infamous "Minute on Indian Education," is perhaps the most cited source on Indian effeminacy.... [He] offers effeminacy as both an explanation and a justification for India's loss of independence to Britain. Elaborating and enriching the notion of effeminacy in another essay, Macaulay made further observations about the inhabitants of Bengal:

> The physical organization of the Bengalee is feeble even to effeminacy. He lives in a constant vapour bath. His pursuits are sedentary, his limbs delicate, his movements languid. During many ages he has been trampled upon by men of bolder and more hardy breeds. Courage, independence, veracity, are qualities to which his constitution and his situation are equally unfavourable. His mind bears a singular analogy to his body. It is weak even to helplessness for purposes of manly resistance; but its suppleness and its tact move the children of sterner climates to admiration, not unmingled with contempt....

Through a phantasmatic proliferation of analogies Macaulay's passage reduces a jumble of geographic, physiological, ethnographic, and anthropological observations into the single overarching category of effeminacy that, nevertheless, remains an idiosyncratic and contradictory construct: feeble but delicate, weak yet resilient, cowardly but courageous, contemptuous yet admirable, the effeminate Indian unsettles the binary categories of colonial epistemology. The mildness and softness of the Indian are seen in shifting terms as an index of cultural sophistication and/ or as a mark of racial inferiority – a textual conflict that is also written into James Mill's authoritative *History of British India*. Arguing that the beginnings of civilization are compatible with "great violence" as well as with "great gentleness,"[24] Mill concludes that "the Hindu, like the eunuch, excels in the qualities of a slave."[25]

Macaulay's eloquent observations about the effeminate inhabitants of Bengal, widely shared by subsequent generations of Anglo-Indians, took on a very specific significance in the stereotype of the "effeminate Bengali babu." During the nineteenth century, and especially in the years following the Sepoy Mutiny of 1857, the urban centers of Bengal emerged as sites of anticolonial resistance. The increasingly articulate, politically self-conscious, Western-educated, middle-class Hindu Bengali society demanded a greater role in the colonial administration. The figure of effeminacy consequently takes on certain marked characteristics that reflect the politics of post-Mutiny Raj. From a loosely defined attribute associated with the entire population of Bengal, and by extension to all of India, at times even to all of Asia, effeminacy evolves into an attribute associated very specifically with Western-educated Indians, a large majority of whom were Bengali Hindus. As Mrinalini Sinha points out, the notion of Bengali effeminacy was, on the one hand, restricted quite specifically to the Bengali "babus," while, on the other hand, it was elaborated to include the politically discontented middle class all over India. Indeed, the very word *babu*, Sinha notes, underwent a change in usage that reflects the rearticulation of colonial racial politics in changed material conditions: from being a term used as a title of respect (much like *Mr.* or *Esq.*) in the first half of the century, *babu* began to connote a social-climbing, money-grubbing mentality, until by the late nineteenth century it came to signify "the grandiose pretensions and the economic impotence of the potentially disloyal Anglicized or English-educated Indian."[26] Sinha quotes *The Hobson-Jobson*, a glossary of words and phrases used by the British in India compiled in the 1880s, to show that in the popular imagination the word *babu* had come to designate a "native clerk who writes in English" and that the word was used with "a slight savour of disparagement, as characterizing a superficially cultivated but too often effeminate Bengali."[27]

The stereotypical babu was thus an urban, English-educated, alienated "intellectual." English education, it was widely believed, compounded the Bengali's inherent cowardliness to produce personal malice and political sedition. In September 1888 an editorial in Lahore's *Civil and Military Gazette* – in which Kipling worked as a reporter – declared that "nowhere in any corner of his character has the Bengali a spark of the spirit which has guided Englishmen in taking and ruling India; and upon occasions of legislative difficulty, it is impossible that he could offer, of his own motion, any reasonable advice toward the maintenance of that rule. He is a shrewd judge of all matters regarding his own comfort."[28] This image of the effeminate babu reflects the political challenge newly posed by the Indian middle class to certain exclusive rights and privileges the British enjoyed in India. It also signals a shift in colonial attitudes toward Western-educated Indians, who are no longer seen in Macaulayean terms as mediators between the colonial administration and the rest of the Indian population but, rather, as an unrepresentative and artificial minority capable of expressing nothing but the anomalies of their own situation.

The figure of the Bengali babu in late-nineteenth-century India can be usefully understood in terms of the concept of "ressentiment." This notion was powerfully theorized by Friedrich Nietzsche to explain ethics in general and the Judeo-Christian tradition in particular as a revenge of the slaves upon the masters whereby, through an ideological ruse, the slaves infect the masters with a slave mentality, expressed in the ethos of charity, and rob the masters of their natural vitality and aristocratic insolence. . . . Although in Nietzsche's explanation *ressentiment* is proposed as a psychological mechanism in the service of a critique of Victorian moralism and hypocrisy, its secondary adaptations, as Fredric Jameson points out, show that the concept has a more fundamentally political function:

> First, in a kind of exoteric and vulgar sense, the ideologeme of ressentiment can seem to account in a "psychological" and nonmaterialistic sense for the destructive envy the have-nots feel for the haves, and thus account for the otherwise inexplicable fact of a popular mass uprising against a hierarchical system of which the historian is concerned to demonstrate the essential wholesomeness and organic or communitarian virtue. Meanwhile, in a secondary and more esoteric, "overdetermined" use, ressentiment can also explain the conduct of those who incited an otherwise essentially satisfied popular mass to such "unnatural" disorders: the ideologeme thus designates Nietzsche's "ascetic priests," the intellectuals par excellence – unsuccessful writers and poets, bad philosophers, bilious journalists, and failures of all kinds – whose private dissatisfactions lead them to their vocations as political and revolutionary militants.[29]

Such a formulation of ressentiment is useful for conceptualizing the Bengali babu's role in nineteenth-century colonial politics and for understanding the Bengali elite's struggle for hegemony under conditions of colonial rule. From being openly supportive of imperial authority during the mutiny the Bengali elite moved toward muted criticism of specific colonial policies in the 1870s and 1880s, until finally by the turn of the century it emerged as an aggressive and articulate inciter of public opinion against the British Raj. As its traditional property privileges were gradually destroyed in the second half of the nineteenth century, the Bengali elite scrambled to take advantage of the employment opportunities and other benefits of English education. If this move brought on the ignominy and humiliation of petty bureaucratic or clerical work, it nevertheless proved pivotal to specific Bengali/Indian groups, first in articulating nationalist aspirations and subsequently in establishing class hegemony in an emerging nation-state.

By the end of the nineteenth century, however, effeminacy had become the most powerful signifier of India's cultural decline, and the effeminate babu had become the quintessential embodiment of this degeneracy. Effeminacy came to be seen as one facet of a general pattern of moral shortcoming, a reflection of the diffuse sensuality and debilitating femininity in Indian society. Various pseudoscientific theories were put forth as explanations for India's loss of that virility the ancient Aryans had supposedly shared with their European counterparts. In addition to ecological or environmental factors, biological, economic, social, and religious factors were frequently identified as causes of cultural decline. Bengali effeminacy, for example, was variously attributed to the warm climate, enfeebling diet, mixed Aryan-Dravidian descent, premature maternity, the Hindu caste system, insecure property relations in Hindu society, and matrifocal Hinduism.

An important ingredient of Indian effeminacy was the open-ended, unorganized, polytheistic, matrifocal nature of Hinduism. In contrast to Judeo-Christian monotheism, which seemed robust, reasonable, ordered, and properly male, Hinduism, with its erotic, ecstatic cults, seemed improper, irrational, and feminine. During the early years of the nineteenth century the rise of evangelical influence hardened Anglo-Indian attitudes toward Hinduism into prejudice. Even British Orientalists like William Jones, who idealized the textualized Brahmanical Vedic past, bemoaned the contemporary state of Hindu beliefs. The mythology, iconography, and practice of popular Hinduism, which included promiscuous and androgynous gods like Krishna and Siva, aggressive embodiments of female sexuality such as the goddesses Kali, and the institution of temple dancers, contravened Judeo-Christian conceptions of gender and divinity. By the middle of the nineteenth century, when the evangelical fervor of earlier decades had been replaced by a more pragmatic, muscular Christianity, the colonial government redirected its old religious zeal toward education and social reform. And, since both the colonial government as well as the Indians invoked religious sanction for social practices such as sati and child marriage, it became easy to target Hinduism as a degenerate belief system underlying a morally bankrupt society. . . .

Sigmund Freud, of course, located matriarchal polytheism in the prehistory of mankind: "The matriarchal structure of society was replaced by a patriarchal one . . . This turning from the mother to the father, however, signifies above all a victory of spirituality over the senses – that is to say, a step forward in culture, since maternity is proved by the senses whereas paternity is a surmise based on a deduction and a premise. This declaration in favour of the thought-process, thereby raising it above sense perception, has proved to be a step charged with serious consequences."[30] From this perspective the polytheist could only be an anthropological object; it would take monotheism to make him a subject of history. . . .

From its inception psychoanalysis (wedded to anthropology in the form of ethnopsychology) is imbricated in the ideologies of empire. Highlighting the role of psychoanalysis as an instrument of British colonialism in India, Christiane Hartnack shows how British members of the International Psychoanalytical Association, especially Owen Berkeley-Hill and Claud Dangar Daly, used psychoanalysis to pathologize the Indian male as infantile and effeminate in order to justify colonial rule. She also finds Freud's correspondence with various Indians indicative of an indifference, even aversion, toward India.[31] Whatever feelings Freud may have entertained toward India, his theories of culture certainly pathologize non-Western societies in ways that justified European domination.[32] . . .

The metropolitan production of heterosexuality/homosexuality in nineteenth-century psychological/psychoanalytic, medical, and anthropological discourses interestingly intersects with the colonial elaboration of Indian effeminacy. The first British writer to explicitly identify the East as a homosexual terrain was Sir Richard Burton. Bringing together the conclusions of decades of travel and reading in the celebrated "Terminal Essay" of *Thousand Nights and a Night*

(1885–8), Burton posited the existence of a "Sotadic Zone" running through the tropics and semitropics, representing those regions of the world where "pederasty" is as common as heterosexuality.[33] The word *pederasty* is also used by Freud in an 1897 letter: "It is to be supposed that the element essentially responsible for repression is always what is feminine . . . What men essentially repress is the pederastic element."[34] If normative heterosexual masculinity could be achieved only through a repression of the feminine "pederastic element," Burton's Sotadic Zone is a place populated by failed men.

Throughout the Judeo-Christian tradition sexuality between men had been infamous among those who knew about it at all precisely for having no name. The "unspeakable," "unmentionable," "not to be named among Christian men," are among the terms recorded by Louis Crompton.[35] Clearly, what allows Burton to speak the unspeakable, then, is the historical opportunity made available to him by empire.[36] In other words, homosexuality could be named more safely in an anthropological discourse about the colonized Other. Incidentally, Burton's career came to a sudden end when an elaborate private report he had written on the "eunuch brothels of Karachi" erroneously arrived before the Bombay government. An important aspect of Burton's "theory" of Oriental homosexuality is its emphasis on ecology. Burton insists that the influence of the Sotadic Zone on "the Vice" is "geographical and climatic, not racial."[37] "This insistence," Eve Sedgwick points out, "reflects an important element of the racism that accompanied British imperialism – an element that distinguishes it from American racism: its genetic basis, where asserted, is much less rigidly conceived. Americans are black or white from birth; colonials, on the other hand, can 'go' native for out there is a taint of climate, of moral ethos that, while most readily described in racial terms, is actually seen as contagious."[38]

The influence of Burton's ideas is evident in *The Underworld of India* (1932), a lurid account of the seamy side of Indian life authored by Sir George MacMunn, a veteran of the Indian Army and a prolific writer on matters Indian, who even produced two appreciative commentaries on Kipling's work, *Rudyard Kipling: Craftsman* and *Kipling's Women*. In *The Underworld of India* MacMunn explicitly identifies homosexuality as the hidden hurdle to colonial friendships. In a passage that, read against the grain, could well serve as a gloss to the aborted eroticism between Fielding and Aziz in *A Passage to India*, MacMunn writes:

> While in the West homosexuality or pederasty is the sign of the degenerate or mentally unstable, and accompanies the disappearance of manliness and self-respect, in Asia, it is often the vice of the most resolute characters . . . Unfortunately, the most in other respects reputable of Eastern friends and conferencers may be so inclined, and it is the one hidden cause which stood in the past athwart friendship between Eastern and Western men, till all chance of the failing is ruled out.[39]

In Europe the cluster of associations around homosexuality almost always included effeminacy.[40] But India apparently presented a paradox, for homosexual practices were most commonly attributed not so much to the derided effeminate Bengali but, rather, to the more admired virile and manly "martial" races. What intrigues MacMunn most is that homosexual practices could exist among "the most resolute characters," among those very Indians who symbolized to him "the last words in daring and reckless courage."[41] Homosexual yet manly, heterosexual yet effeminate, Indian masculinity injects a fearful indeterminacy into the economy of colonial desire.

Both Burton and MacMunn are obsessively drawn to the Indian male courtesan, who, rather than the female prostitute, emerges as the most threatening source of cultural contagion. The female prostitute, whose threat to white purity was controlled through the importation of English women to the colony, actually becomes a more predictable (even reassuring) embodiment of India's Otherness. By contrast, the sexualized racial male body functioning as a viable medium of erotic/economic exchange not only remains unassimilated into the gendered configurations of empire but provides a deeply disturbed allegory for the disguised, disembodied homoeroticism in Anglo-Indian narrative.

The ascribed homosexuality of the Orient presents the colonizing male imagination with strange possibilities and unknown dangers. Possibly the most startling erotic motif to emerge in colonial settings is that of male rape. . . .

The culmination of the motif of interracial male rape, as Eve Kosofsky Sedgwick points out, is unfortunately, an account of a real rape in T. E. Lawrence's *Seven Pillars of Wisdom*.[42] Many passages in Lawrence's book are devoted to charting the alien yet compelling geography of male homosociality in Arab culture. Lawrence himself had moved from apparently unfulfilling bonds with English men to bonds with Arab men that had, for political reasons, far more space for fantasy and mystification and, hence, for the illusionistic charisma of will.[43] The rape occurs at a point when Lawrence, taken prisoner as a possible spy, refuses the advances of a Turkish commander, who "half-whispered to the corporal to take me out and teach me everything" . . .

Lawrence experiences a profound loss of the sense of time, of personal identity, and, indeed, of life itself. Sedgwick observes that for Lawrence "the racial and cultural foreignness of the Turks (in relation to 'his' Arabs, as well as to himself) seems an emblem for the wrenching disjunctions in his ability, as a man, to master the map of male homosocial desire . . . For Lawrence, the unprepared-for and hence unmasterable confrontation with yet another, arbitrarily different, brutally contradictory way of carving up the terrain of male bonding, sexuality, and domination, made the self-contradictory grounds of his previously costly and exciting poise too rawly obvious."[44] In a brutal instance of the empire striking back Lawrence's chilling account returns the figure Freud repressed so assiduously in his theories of gender and sexuality – the figure of a man being (ab)used "like a woman." By focusing on the rape of a white man, the account also conceals a different scene of homosexual exploitation in which the subaltern Oriental male is ravished by a lustful European. Such a refiguration of rape is available in the self-censored "kanaya" memoir of E. M. Forster's *The Hill of Devi*.[45] Forster's depiction of homosexual rape provides a more appropriate metaphor for the dynamics of a homosocial colonialism founded on the economic and political exploitation of brown men by white men.

Such direct representations are, however, rare in Anglo-Indian literature, in which the theme of white male penetration and ravishment is more commonly expressed through metaphoric and disguised images of supernatural invasion, possession, regression, and decline. These images are manifested most starkly in the genre of colonial fiction Patrick Brantlinger has called the "Imperial

Gothic."[46] In the demonic universe of the Imperial Gothic, a genre favored by Rudyard Kipling, the sexual and racial anxieties of Victorian and Edwardian imperialism are externalized in the form of supernatural, mystic, or occult forces that threaten the white man's physical and psychological integrity. . . . The pervasiveness of male sexual fear in the Imperial Gothic suggests that, by the end of the nineteenth century, rape may have come to condition the minds of white men almost as much as it had the minds of white women in the colonies.[47]

The homosocial economy of colonialism, however, ensures that empire's master metaphor – rape – is inscribed as a heterosexual violation of the innocent white woman by the dark Indian rapist. Yet, despite the wide currency of the stereotype of the dark rapist, the Indian male, unlike the black male in America, was not portrayed to any marked extent as a phallic figure or as a sexual rival to the white male. While the myth of the black rapist supposes a potent Negro bestiality, the stereotype of the Oriental rapist hinges on an assumption of Asiatic duplicity derived from British perceptions of Hindu degeneracy and Mughal decadence. Thus, in the case of the Indian male sexual aggression itself becomes a symptom of weakness rather than of virility.

Effeminacy as Mimicry

Anglo-India thus found its most seductive metaphor for racial, physical, moral, and cultural weakness not in the vulnerability of womanhood but in the weakness of colonized manhood. Colonialism was justified, naturalized, even legitimized, through an ideological distinction between English manliness and Indian, particularly Bengali, effeminacy. But, as Mrinalini Sinha points out, Bengali effeminacy is not simply the complete opposite of Victorian manliness; rather, like homosexuality, it was constructed as the fallen, failed, bastardized, or incomplete form of manliness.[48] The construction of effeminacy as a distorted or degenerate version of a pure original, Sinha suggests, was extremely effective, because it captured the element of what Homi Bhabha has called "mimicry," or "hybridization." She goes on to argue that the depiction of the Westernized Bengali male as a mimicry of the white male reflects an ideological contradiction, or, in Bhabha's terminology, an "ambivalence," that shaped colonial policy in India. In the early decades of the nineteenth century Thomas Macaulay and others successfully argued for the promotion of Western education and Western values as a means of civilizing the native. But by the late nineteenth century, when Westernized Indians began to question the exclusionary policies of the imperial government, the task of redeeming the native was declared to be an impossible one. . . .

Sinha's elaboration of effeminacy usefully historicizes Bhabha's concept of mimicry, or hybridization, by treating it not as a general theory of subject constitution under colonialism but as an explanation of how a particular segment of the Indian population (elite, educated, Bengali) came to be defined by the exigencies of late-nineteenth-century colonial politics. Sinha also grounds the notion of ambivalence in colonial reality by relating its ideological function to political practices that ensured continued imperial dominance. In doing this, however, she overlooks or minimizes, what I consider to be a crucial aspect of hybridity: the potential for subversion or resistance. . . . Although mimicry imposes a flawed identity on colonized people, who are then obliged to inhabit an uninhabitable zone of ambivalence that grants them neither identity nor difference, Bhabha argues that there is a slippage between identity and difference that throws the "normalizing" authority of colonial discourse into question. The dream of post-Enlightenment civility is alienated from itself because in the colonial state it can no longer parade as a state of nature. Mimicry becomes "at once resemblance and menace."[49] Bhabha recognizes that ambivalences of colonial subjectivity need not always pose a threat to dominant power relations and may, in fact, "exercise them pleasurably and productively."[50] But elsewhere he develops the notion of mimicry less as a self-defeating colonial strategy than as a form of anti-colonial resistance. Mimicry here "marks those moments of civil disobedience within the discipline of civility: signs of spectacular resistance."[51] Hybridity

> unsettles the mimetic or narcissistic demands of colonial power but reimplicates its identifications in strategies of subversion that turn the gaze of the discriminated back upon the eye of power... If discriminatory effects enable the authorities to keep an eye on them, their proliferating difference evades that eye, escapes that surveillance ... It [hybridization] reveals the ambivalence at the source of traditional discourses on authority and enables a form of subversion, founded on that uncertainty, that turns the discursive conditions of dominance into the grounds of intervention.[52] ...

...I shall attempt to selectively deploy Bhabha's rich insights into the play of fantasy and desire in colonial contests to theorize the subversive potential of effeminacy not as an intrinsic or internal effect of colonial mimicry as such but, rather, as a strategy historically available only to elite Indian men in their struggle against colonialism. In so applying his idea of subversive mimicry exclusively to elite Indian men, I am perhaps taking Bhabha far more literally than he intends. My discussion highlights two specific ways in which effeminacy becomes subversive: first, as an "everyday form of resistance"; and second, as a programmatic rescripting affected by Gandhian nationalism. I shall, however, argue that, to the extent effeminacy or cultural hybridity was a specific attribute of urban, Western-educated, elite, mostly Hindu men, both the parodic possibilities of effeminacy in everyday life and the Gandhian deployment of effeminacy actually served to ensure elite male hegemony in an emerging postcolonial order. In other words, I attempt to show that effeminacy was simultaneously a mimicry of subversion that successfully disrupted colonial authority in certain contexts as well as a mimicry of subjugation that kept the lower castes, religious minorities, and women under elite male control. Context, therefore, is decisive in my determination of whether and when effeminacy may be considered subversive.

The subversive potential of mimicry becomes visible in the unexpected, ironic effects of colonial effeminism. The violent intervention of the West into the East, not to mention colonialism's ideological project of remaking the Other in the image of the Self, inevitably needed and produced culturally hybrid subjects among the colonizers as well as the colonized. By the late nineteenth century many Anglo-Indian families with a tradition of colonial service involving long periods of residence in the colony included many who, like Kipling, had been born in India and nurtured by Indians during the initial impressionable years of childhood. The Anglo-Indian practice of sending children away to England for schooling – a practice born as much out of a fear about physical health as about cultural purity and, as in Kipling's case, one that would prove psychologically harrowing – was aimed at erasing or at least diluting the effeminizing influence of colonized culture by instilling the manly virtues of Englishness. The typical product of such practices was, like Kipling, a split subject, a bicultural sahib alienated from manly England and effeminate India alike. This subject position is somewhat different from the "white skin, black mask" position taken up by Lawrence of Arabia. Kipling, unlike Lawrence, tried very hard to repress and deny that part of himself that, without his conscious choice or will, had become Indianized. In fact, one might say that what Kipling really desired but was never sure he possessed was the self-conscious, manipulative hybridity emblematized in Lawrence. Indeed . . . Kipling's characterization of Kim is driven by an anxiety that mimicry, instead of becoming a willed performance of hybridity that reinforces racial difference, might well become a paralyzing, unwilled, mongrelization of identity that would collapse all difference. This is why the syncretic possibilities of Kim must necessarily atrophy into the pseudohybridity of a colonial spy. Colonialism required of every white man a denial of cultural androgyny. "Colonialism," as Ashis Nandy notes, "took away the wholeness of every white man who chose to be a part of the colonial machine and gave him a new self-definition which, while provincial in its cultural orientation, was universal in its geographical scope."[53]

Bound together by mimicry, the Anglicized Indian and the Indianized English man represent mirror images of each other. Yet it was the Indian's hybridity that was systematically stressed and ridiculed, while the biculturality of the Anglo-Indian was silently suppressed. Thus, the quintessential embodiment of cultural hybridity in the post-Mutiny era was the Bengali babu, a figure stereotyped by Kipling as pathologically effeminate, ridiculous, and inauthentic. What Kipling despises most is the babu's inability (his refusal?) to be a proper victim, to stand up boldly, fight in manly fashion, and pay back the tormentor in his own coin. In story after story he mocks the babu for adopting such effeminate tactics as non-cooperation, flattery, obsequiousness, evasion, shirking, irresponsibility, lying, avoidance, and refusal to value face-to-face fights. But at key moments, Kipling's fiction registers a keen awareness of the subversive potential in the babu's passive-aggressive modes of resistance. The crafty babus, Kipling recognizes in disgust, adopt but adapt English ways to suit their own ends; they bow down obsequiously before the white man only to subtly manipulate him for their own purposes. Indeed, . . . Kipling's *Kim* not only exposes the terrifying similarities between the androgynous wonder-boy Kim and his effeminate partner Huree babu, it also contains an implicit acknowledgment of the subversive potential of effeminacy, or cultural hybridity.

The figure of the Westernized Indian, in spite of its pathology and its tragicomic core, may be viewed, Ashis Nandy suggests, as an assimilated form of an other civilization that gate-crashed into India. For what looks like Westernization may actually be a means of domesticating the West, sometimes by reducing the West to the comic or the trivial.[54] The process of cultural osmosis in colonial India was highly complex, not always unidirectional, not always involving conflict, not always producing a sense of loss. The uncanny art of survival perfected by an ancient society experienced in absorbing and adapting foreign influences taught Indians to bend to colonial rule without completely breaking. The performance of effeminacy or the practice of hybridity in everyday life allowed Indians to assimilate and conform while preserving subterraneous spaces of escape and refuge.

My understanding of effeminacy as an "everyday form of resistance" is grounded in recent studies that seek to move away from the conventional focus on extraordinary, often violent, moments of collective protest toward those forms of struggle present in the behaviors and cultural practices of subordinated peoples at times other than those of overt revolt. The writings of James Scott have, most notably, questioned the common assumption that in "normal" times, when there are no dramatic collective upheavals, the relations of power remain largely intact, and the identities and cultural practices of the dominant remain firmly in place.[55] ...

Extending Scott's insights, historians of South Asia have, in recent years, focused on the myriad ways in which the social relations of daily existence in colonial India were enmeshed in and transfigured by contradictions and contestations that seem quite innocent or innocuous. This means, as Douglas Haynes and Gyan Prakash, editors of an important collection of essays on everyday social relations in South Asia, point out, "consciousness" need not be essential to resistance.[56] ... Colonial ideology itself ... differentiated the mimicry of the colonizer from the mimicry of the colonized precisely by claiming self-consciousness, agency, and individual will exclusively for the colonizer while attributing a paralyzing lack of consciousness to the colonized. My point here is not simply to show up the obvious bias in such a claim by pointing to instances of deliberate or willed colonized agency – something already done quite forcefully by Fanon, Bhabha and Irigaray. Rather, it is to suggest that consciousness is neither a necessary nor a sufficient ground of resistance.

To view the babu's effeminacy as a lived or everyday form of passive resistance does not, therefore, imply that he consciously adopted cultural hybridity as a form of protest against the colonizer. Far from it. In fact, the self-image of Indian, especially Bengali, men in the nineteenth century was deeply conditioned by a negative view of effeminacy. Whether they urged their fellow Indians to cultivate a robust physique or advocated violent military resistance to imperial rule, whether they undertook to revitalize Hinduism along the lines of muscular Christianity or attempted to reform the lives of women, many Bengali writers, reformers, political and religious leaders of the time – men like Michael Madhusudan Dutt (1824–73), Dayanand Saraswati (1824–83), Bankim Chandra Chatterjee (1838–94), and Vivekananda (1863–1902) – were simply reacting to being labeled effeminate.

Effeminacy, or rather femininity-in-masculinity, however, had not always been given such a negative scripting in precolonial Hindu society. Although Brahmanical masculinity, which emphasized a hard asceticism, renunciation, and sublimation, and Kshatriya masculinity, which emphasized a hard aggression, pleasure, and good living, remained the dominant contending models of masculinity, a third model that involved androgyny, particularly for men, had evolved out of Puranic traditions and had been held up as a spiritual ideal by various medieval Bhakti movements. Beginning in the eighth and ninth centuries in South India, the Bhakti movements, which involved an impassioned, frequently eroticized intimacy with god, had, by the thirteenth century, spread to most parts of India and remained a powerful force well into the nineteenth century. The emergence of the Bhakti movements also interestingly coincided with the rise of goddess-centered cults, especially in Bengal, where they served as a powerful site of anti-colonial resistance during the nineteenth century. Bhakti, however, stands in clear contrast not only with Brahmanical Vedantic Hinduism but with Tantric Hinduism as well. In Vedanta the worshiper is the godhead; in Tantrism the worshiper can either identify with the goddess or entertain an erotic relationship with her; however, the Bhakti cults (more so in the Vaishnava cults than in the Saivite ones) generally envisioned a male diety and placed the devotee in a paradigmatic-ally feminized position. The bhakta, or devotee (paradigmatically male), visualizes himself as a woman not only because god is male but also because the stance of the ideal devotee is identical with the stance of the ideal woman, for the goal of the bhakta is to become completely open to being penetrated and possessed by the male diety. While this resolutely heterosexual paradigm replicated the conven-tions of male dominance–female subordination and respected the taboos on overt homosexuality, it required the male worshiper to renounce masculinity and em-brace femininity.[57] This requirement, which in extreme and rare cases involved an actual change of sex, more often took the form of transvestism, as in the case of Chaitanya (1486–1538) and Ramakrishna (1836–86), two of the most prominent saints of Bengal, whose spiritual practice combined Bhakti and Tantric traditions.

The bias toward femininity in the stance of the worshiper is also an effect of the nature of the diety when it is visualized as female. Except in Tantrism, in which a fairly straightforward erotic relationship is entertained between male worshiper and female deity, most other forms of goddess worship are driven by a need to avoid an erotic union that is apprehended as an annihilation. To avoid the fate of lascivious demons, beings typically dominated and killed by the goddess, male worshipers sometimes became transvestites or even eunuchs, just like the bhaktas of male deities. Thus, the male worshiper must become female either to unite with a male god or to avoid uniting with a female mother goddess. Even in the Shakta religion, in which the relationship between male devotee and female deity is conceived in nonerotic terms, the male worshiper becomes female in order to serve the goddess.[58]

In an interesting letter to Freud (Nov. 1929) G. Bose, the first Indian Freudian (and one who actively worked to establish the Indian Psychoanalytic Society), wrote about the necessity to rethink castration anxiety in view of goddess worship in India: "The real struggle lies between the desire to be a male and its opposite the desire to be female ... The Oedipus mother is very often a combined parental image and this is a fact of great importance. I have reason to believe that much of the motivation of the 'maternal deity' is traceable to this source."[59] Kalpana Seshadri-Crooks characterizes Freud's response to Bose as "nominal and evasive," because Freud's theory "could not accommodate a mother-worshipping polythe-ist as analyst or subject."[60] Nor could Freud's heteronormatizing theory accom-modate the picture Bose was painting of a male desiring *to be* rather than *to have* a female.

Hindu androgyny, however, was widely understood as a symbolic transcendence of gender division rather than as a lived experience of bisexuality that was tolerated more in local folk traditions than in the pan-Hindu traditions. But even in the symbolic realm androgyny was presented as an ideal primarily for men, not women. In Hindu mythological representations androgyny is a predominantly male phenomenon. Thus, contrary to Ashis Nandy's view, Ardhanarishwara, liter-ally "the lord (iswara) who is half (ardha) woman (nari)" is always regarded as a form of Siva, not a form that represents an equal synthesis of Siva-Parvathi. As in Hindu marriage, when Parvathi fuses with Siva, she generally becomes half of his body, losing half of her own substance, while he usually becomes enriched by her without losing any of his own substance. Similarly the iconography of the linga (phallus) is regarded as a form of Siva alone even though the linga is always surrounded by the yoni, symbolizing the goddess's sexual organ. Again the Hindu conception of shakti or energy as feminine traditionally refers to the energy of the male.[61] Even in the Bhakti movement, despite the active participation of several women saint-poets, there was a greater tendency to present androgyny as an ideal for the male worshiper.[62]

As this ideal of Hindu masculinity weakened and eroded under colonial assault, androgyny got rescripted as effeminacy, and Hindu men felt forced to reform themselves and their religion in the image of a muscular, monotheistic, heterosexual, masculine Protestantism. Here we see a situation of what James Scott characterizes as genuine or total hegemony – a situation where, the oppressed group hopes it will eventually exercise over others (not its present oppressors, though) the domination it endures today, where there are "strong incentives to legitimate patterns of domination," thus cancelling the hidden transcripts of contempt for the oppressor and turning into self-contempt.[63] The shift from a positive notion of androgyny toward a negative image of effeminacy is most sharply dramatized in the difference between Ramakrishna and his star disciple, Vivekananda. Ramakrishna was perhaps the last prominent Hindu saint to embrace androgyny credibly both as a spiritual goal and as a method for achieving transcendence. His performance of Hinduism, involving explicit transvestism and implicit homoeroticism, did not really engage colonialism in a contest of manliness. By contrast, Vivekananda's virile Hinduism, like his hard gendering, was locked in a Manichean battle with colonialism and, consequently, carried with it all the normative trappings of colonial masculinity. Attributing contemporary Hindu weakness or emasculation to loss of textual Brahmanism and social Kshatriyahood – a loss that had robbed Hindus of those original Aryan qualities they shared with Westerners – he tried to turn Hinduism into an organized monotheism (albeit a goddess-centered one), complete with The Book (the Vedas and the Gita), priests (order of monks), and even missionaries.[64] Echoing the novelist Bankim Chandra Chatterjee, this activist monk, who declared manliness to be his "new gospel," preached that the androgynous motifs of Hindu mythology were dissolute, enervating and effeminate.[65] "Who cares what your scriptures say?" he asked defiantly. "I will go into a thousand hells cheerfully if I can arouse my countrymen, immersed in darkness, to stand on their own feet and be men inspired with the spirit of Karma yoga."[66] Attempting to arouse his followers to action, Vivekananda admonished them: "No more weeping, but stand on your feet and be men. It is a man-making religion I want. I want the strength, manhood, kshatravirya or the virility of a warrior."[67] Musing that "the older I grow, the more everything seems to me to lie in manliness,"[68] this stellar student of Ramakrishna prayed, "O Thou Mother of the Universe, vouchsafe manliness unto me – Make me a man!"[69]

The Bengali male's self-perception of effeminacy was also an effect of the struggle for hegemony by an elite community under the conditions of nineteenth-century colonialism. Manhood in colonial society, as Tanika Sarkar shows, was based on a particular relationship to property – a relationship that was gradually eroded for the Bengali middle class in the second half of the nineteenth century. Combined with the gradual decline in the fortunes of the landed classes, Bengali elites were being defined more and more in terms of professional and administrative employment. The majority found their horizons severely contracted by petty clerical work. Indeed, the ignominious experience of petty clerical work, according to Tanika Sarkar, underpinned the self-perception of effeminacy among the Bengali elites. Thus, at a time when the Bengali elite still refrained from direct criticism of colonial rule, it expressed its hegemonic aspirations not by assuming economic and political leadership but by attributing to the male physique all the ravages and despair of colonial rule.[70] Ashis Nandy is therefore quite correct in his perception that most pre-Gandhian reform and protest movements ended up legitimizing the very model of masculinity they sought to resist because they accepted, rather than altered, the terms of colonial discourse.[71]

Effeminacy, as mimicry or hybridization, however, did provide an opportunity for tactical intervention – an opportunity that Gandhi was to use very effectively. . . . In contrast to the early militant phase of Indian nationalism, Gandhian nationalism, Ashis Nandy contends, undermined the imperialist ethos of hyper-masculinity by delinking courage and activism from aggression and violence and making them compatible with certain forms of femininity.[72] Or, as I would like to argue, with certain forms of effeminacy. In other words, I am suggesting that Gandhi strategically drew upon premodern Christianity (he claimed to have taken nonviolence from the Sermon on the Mount) as well as traditional Hindu images of positive androgyny and dynamic womanhood to elaborate an alternative model of masculinity, not femininity. Contrary to Nandy's view, Gandhian androgyny is neither an equal bisexual fusion of male and female nor an asexual transcendence of male and female; rather, what Gandhi devised was a counter-model of masculinity, one that selectively incorporated certain Hindu conceptions of femininity for use by Indian men in their fight against colonialism. Its effect on the material lives of Indian women therefore proved to be both uneven as well as limited.

Contrary to what Nandy implies, Gandhian gender ideology did not radically alter Indian conceptions of womanhood or wholly liberate Indian women from conventional roles. In Gandhian nationalism, as in various forms of anticolonial Hindu militancy and subaltern insurgency, femininity, particularly maternity, serves as an important discursive site for the mobilization of male interests and aspirations. The maternal figure in Hindu iconography incorporates a dialectical tension between the virulent, potently sexual Kali and Durga, her docile, domesticated counterpart. Most varieties of elite Hindu militancy and subaltern insurgency had traditionally embraced the more aggressive symbol of female energy; Gandhi, on the other hand, upheld the domestic ideal, emphasizing moral qualities such as patience, self-sacrifice, and suffering. In challenging nationalist historiography, which typically subsumes female liberation under the grand narrative of national liberation, Indian feminist scholarship has identified the domestic ideal as an important inhibiting factor in Gandhian gender ideology.[73] While Gandhi's maternal domestic ideal clearly inhibited radical change in Indian women's lives, it is important to note that neither elite nor subaltern insurgent movements that worshiped man-eating goddesses did much better. . . . The problematic of the Indian woman as signifier in heterogenous discursive sites, it would appear, must necessarily take into account her function as a transactional token in the homo-social struggle between English imperialism and Indian nationalism. I therefore view Gandhian ideology as an effort to construct an oppositional model of masculinity for Indian men, rather than as an intervention into the lives of Indian women. When viewed this way, Gandhi's selective utilization of femininity makes strategic sense, since it incorporates precisely those qualities imperial culture had devalued as effeminate. What Gandhi managed to do was tap the ambiguities and contradictions that mimicry produced in the economy of effeminism and turn them to political advantage.

Women and Homosocial Colonialism

Absolutely necessary yet eminently dispensable, women are the circuitry through which colonial desire flows, the conduit through which collusions and collisions between colonizing and colonized men are conducted. Nineteenth-century colonial ideology and politics are marked by the historic emergence of womanhood as the most powerful signifier of cultural superiority. Indeed, one of the most common liberal justifications for the extension of colonial rule and for the maintenance of the civilizing mission is the imputed barbarity of the treatment of women within the culture under attack. The social status of women thus became the ultimate and unequivocal measure of civil society. In his influential *History of British India* James Mill, one of the foremost exponents of moral imperialism, contrasts the "exalted" status of British women with the degraded condition of Indian women as a way of establishing the unmanliness of Hindu society.[74] The treatment of widows in Hindu society and the practice of sati became the most spectacularly visible signs of colonized female oppression. By making the treatment of women an important determinant of manhood, and therefore a critical sign of civilization, the imperial project was narrativized in moral terms as a case of "white men rescuing brown women from brown men."[75] From Jules Verne's *Around the World in Eighty Days* (1873) and Flora Annie Steel's *On the Face of the Waters* (1897) to M. M. Kaye's *The Far Pavilions* (1978), the ideological production of a chivalric model of English manhood invariably involves the rescue of the Indian woman, particularly the sati, from the clutches of a barbaric Indian patriarchy.[76] Sati continued to exercise the European imagination long after it was legally abolished in 1929, and, interestingly, sati continues to dominate postcolonial perspectives of India.

In projecting themselves as champions of women, the British were far more concerned with emasculating or effeminizing Indian men than with emancipating women. Feminist historians have shown that nineteenth-century social reforms aimed at improving the lives of Indian women were motivated more by political expediency than by humanitarian concern. Moreover, since colonial lawmakers were acting in accordance with Victorian gender ideologies when legislating over such matters as sati, child marriage, and widow remarriage, in many cases they effectively "rescued" Indian women from one form of male dominance only to subject them to another. Lata Mani has persuasively argued that Indian women were neither the subjects nor the objects of colonial discourses on sati but, rather, the ground upon which colonizing and colonized men confronted and negotiated the moral challenges of colonial rule. Similarly, Mrinalini Sinha's discussion of the 1891 Age of Consent Act, which sought to regulate child marriages in India, shows that the moral principle of female emancipation was not the real concern of legislators, who were always willing to subordinate the women's question to the pursuit of economic and political power. Despite its liberal and humanitarian rhetoric, Sinha shows, the Age of Consent Act became an arena in which English men exhibited their disdain of Bengali manhood, while Bengali men, in turn, tried to reassert their masculinity. To the colonizer the Indian woman was primarily a tool for demonstrating the inferiority of indigenous masculinity. To the colonized she became an instrument for reclaiming their lost manhood, a device for renewing a defunct patriarchy.[77]

While the social reforms that emerged out of the homosocial struggles between English and Indian men incidentally ameliorated the Indian woman's life to an extent, imperial intervention often had a contradictory and ironic effect upon her material life. Not only was she newly subjected to the control of British patriarchy, her subjugation in Indian society was perpetuated, albeit in a modified or altered form. The disarming and disempowering presence of the colonial state shut out Indian men from public political authority and denied them access to the main instruments of state power. Yet out of this general disempowerment the British rulers found a variety of means through which to reempower groups of Indian men at different levels of colonial society. In fact, the colonial construction of the Indian male as effeminate actually led to an intensification of indigenous patriarchal structures as Indian men, denied participation in the public arena, began to exercise increasing authority in the private realm. Through a gradual severance of Hindu social relations and ritual practices from politics, the state produced a depoliticized socioreligious sphere, implicitly defined in terms of contemporary Western distinctions between public and private domains and explicitly defined, especially after the Sepoy Mutiny of 1857, by state assurances of noninterference in the private socioreligious concerns of Indian subjects. In Western political contexts the distinctions between private and public were employed ideologically to emphasize the personal freedoms of the individual. In the colonial context these distinctions juxtaposed the realm of the state's competence not with that of individuals but of Hindu communities. This historical process had some important consequences for gender relations and gender ideology in colonial society. On the one hand, it pushed Indian women ever more deeply into the privatized domain of the home over which Indian men were assured complete and unqualified control. On the other hand, it effeminized Indian men by mystifying and essentializing the newly constituted private domain as the true site of Hindu/Indian identity, which was nevertheless defined in feminine terms as excessive, passive, inert, conservative, dependent, and irrational.[78]

Constituted as the privileged object of colonial salvation, the Indian woman also served as an important site for nineteenth-century English feminist individualism. Rather than contesting the moral superiority and the concomitant desexualization imposed upon them by Victorian patriarchy, early English feminists empowered themselves as "mothers of the race" and as "companionate colonialists."[79] By casting themselves in the role of maternal saviors, they adopted the secluded Indian woman as the object of their own unique female salvationist project and thereby negotiated an acceptable, albeit limited, entry into public life.

The entry of white women in large number into the homosocial arena of colonial India signals the emergence of an anomaly in colonial hierarchy, since the English woman embodies a contradictory combination of sexual subordination and racial domination. These contradictions are most sharply visible during the Sepoy Mutiny of 1857, an important historical moment that constituted the English woman as the innocent sex victim of a degenerate and rapacious Indian male. The tropology of rape highlights in a particularly stark manner the simultan-eous exploitation and exclusion of women in colonial politics. The positioning of white women as sex victims of dark indigenous males allowed English men to crush a challenge to colonial rule ruthlessly by casting themselves in the role of righteous avengers and chivalric protectors. Describing white woman as the "absent center" around which colonial allegories of rape and race revolve, Jenny Sharpe has suggested that "a crisis in British authority is managed through the circulation of the violated bodies of English women as a sign for the violation of colonialism." Sharpe thus finds English womanhood emerging as "an important cultural signifier for articulating a colonial hierarchy of race."[80] Within the inter-pretive parameters of colonial homosociality the rape of English women by Indian men is both intended and interpreted as a political challenge to English men. Indian nationalists shared the masculinist understanding of rape as an assault on men rather than as a violation of women. The "Ravishment Proclamations," issued by Indian nationalists in the aftermath of the Amritsar massacre of 1919 in which unarmed Indians were shot down by the imperial army, equates the sexual humiliation of women with an indirect attack upon men. Tactically deploying the image of the dark rapist against the British, Indian nationalists put out incendiary posters calling for the "dishonor" of English "ladies." The violated white female body could thus serve as a mobilizing site not only for imperialists but for nationalists as well.[81]

By becoming both a public spectacle and an object of white male salvation during the mutiny, the English woman in India ironically came to occupy a position similar to that of the Indian sati, functioning, like her, as a transactional token in the homosocial power struggle between colonizing and colonized men. The question of whether the Indian man could be trusted to exercise political or judicial power over English women dominates debates in post-Mutiny India, debates in which the women themselves often played an active and public role. The Illbert Bill controversy of 1883–4 represents one such important moment in which the sexual vulnerability of the white female body was used to deny Indian men access to political participation. Thus, the presence of the English woman at once emasculated the Indian male and constituted him as a sexual threat.

White male response to the increased visibility of their women in the public life of the colony was typically ambivalent. While the decline in sexual liaisons between British men and Indian women brought on by the arrival of British wives had been viewed approvingly by evangelicals, colonial administrators saw the women, espe-cially after 1857, as obstacles to intimate contact with Indian culture and society. From the administrator's perspective a wife and family made demands upon a man's time and took him away from his colonial duties. The literature of the Raj reflects this attitude toward English women in India. Although most Anglo-Indian novels maintain the decorums of heterosexuality – men marry, have affairs, visit prostitutes – the women involved in colonial transactions, when they are not hollowed out into conduits for interracial male friendships, are typically devalued as distractions to masculine pursuits or marginalized as impediments to male solidarity. Thus, in Kipling's *Kim* (1901) the young hero loquaciously complains, "how can a man follow the Way or the Great Game when he is so always pestered by women?"[82] And in E. M. Forster's *A Passage to India* (1924) Turton, the district collector, retains "a contemptuous affection for the pawns he had moved about for so many years, they must be worth his pains," but is annoyed at the women whom he silently blames for making "everything difficult out here."[83] Turton's feelings are echoed loudly in the literature and historiography of the Raj. And even in recent years English men have blamed the women for the loss of empire.[84]

The Raj, as many have recognized, was founded on an intimate bond between English administrator, soldier, or spy and the Indian men they ruled, subjugated, and controlled.[85] Ashis Nandy points out that the ambivalence of white males often compelled Anglo-Indian women to regard themselves as the "sexual competitors of Indian men, with whom their men had established an unconscious homoeroticized bonding."[86] At the same time, the racial fear of rape that the Sepoy Mutiny had produced led to an intensification of patriarchal controls over English women in India. Consequently, the Anglo-Indian woman often found herself confined in homes, hill stations, cantonments, compounds, and clubs, living a life of segregation that was not very different from that of the Indian woman she deplored.... [T]he intense resentment and rivalry between English and Indian women that such unacceptable contiguity provoked, stage-managed by an interested patriarchy, marks out the extent and limit of late-nineteenth-century British imperial feminism.

The writings of Anglo-Indian women like Flora Annie Steel amply attest to the fact that these women, like their Indian counterparts, found themselves caught in the homosocial crossfire between colonizing and colonized men. While I draw attention to this symbolic or structural similarity in order to highlight the instrumentality of both Indian and English women in colonial society, I hasten to add that it does not warrant an equation between the historical positioning of white and brown women, because English women's access to domestic companionship and social independence, the norms of nineteenth-century feminism, is in fact grounded in and guaranteed by the negative presence of the silent, passive Indian woman. Their histories, neither same nor separate but intersecting, point to contradictions in the categories of race and gender that homosocial colonialism thrived upon.

Notes

1 Rudyard Kipling, "The Ballad of East and West." In *Rudyard Kipling's Verse*, Inclusive Edition (Garden City: Doubleday, Page and Co., 1922), p. 272.

2 George L. Mosse, *The Image of Man: The Creation of Modern Masculinity* (New York: Oxford University Press, 1996), pp. 26–7.

3 My discussion of nervousness draws on George Mosse's (ibid., pp. 60–2).

4 See Norman Vance, "The Ideal of Manliness," in B. Simon and I. Bradley, eds., *The Victorian Public School: Studies in the Development of an Educational Institution* (Dublin:

Gill and Macmillan, 1975), pp. 115–28; also Vance's *The Sinews of the Spirit: The Ideal of Christian Manliness in Victorian Literature and Religious Thought* (Cambridge: Cambridge University Press, 1985); David Newsome, *Godliness and Goodlearning: Four Studies on a Victorian Ideal* (London: John Murray, 1961); and J. A. Mangan, *Athleticism in the Victorian and Edwardian Public Schools* (Cambridge: Cambridge University Press, 1981).

5 Michael Rosenthal, *The Character Factory: Baden Powell's Boy Scouts and the Imperatives of Empire* (New York: Pantheon, 1984).

6 Rajeswari Sunder Rajan, *Real and Imagined Women: Gender, Culture and Postcolonialism* (London: Routledge, 1993), p. 42.

7 I take the term *homosocial* from Eve Kosofsky Sedgwick to designate desire between men that is channeled through women, who are used as exchange objects in transactions that primarily promote the interests of male rivalry and/or male solidarity. And, because homosocial desire operates through enforced heterosexuality, it is generally (though not always) homophobically proscribed (Eve Kosofsky Sedgwick, *Between Men: English Literature and Male Homosocial Desire* (New York: Columbia University Press, 1985)).

8 Ashis Nandy, *The Intimate Enemy: Loss and Recovery of Self under Colonialism* (New York: Oxford University Press, 1983), p. 8.

9 For a fascinating account of a remarkably similar shift that took place in Jewish self-image in *fin-de-siècle* Europe, see Daniel Boyarin, *Unheroic Conduct: The Rise of Heterosexuality and the Invention of the Jewish Man* (Berkeley: University of California Press, 1997).

10 *Mimicry* and *hybridization* are terms used by Homi Bhabha to describe the terrifying ambivalence produced when colonial authority is split by the exorbitant object of discrimination. See Homi Bhabha, "Signs Taken for Wonders: Questions of Ambivalence and Authority under a Tree Outside Delhi, May 1817," *Critical Inquiry* 12/1 (Autumn 1985): 144–65.

11 Robert Orme, *Historical Fragments of the Mogol Empire: Of the Morattoes, and the English Concerns, in Indostan, from the Year M,DC,LIX* (London: Printed for C. Nourse, 1782), p. 472.

12 Mosse, *Image of Man*, 9.

13 Ketaki Dyson, *A Various Universe: A Study of Journals and Memoirs of British Men and Women in the Indian Subcontinent, 1765–1856* (New Delhi: Oxford University Press, 1978), p. 93.

14 William Hodges, *Travels in India* (London, n.p., 1793), pp. 1–2; quoted in Dyson, *Various Universe*, p. 134.

15 Christine Bolt, "Race and the Victorians," in *British Imperialism in the Nineteenth Century*, ed. C. C. Eldridge (New York: Macmillan, 1984), p. 129.

16 Flora Annie Steel, *The Garden of Fidelity* (London: Macmillan, 1929), p. 28.

17 E. M. Forster, *The Hill of Devi and Other Indian Writings*, ed. Elizabeth Heine (London: Edward Arnold, 1983), p. 125.

18 William Jones, *Translations from Oriental Languages* (New Delhi: Pravesh Publications, n.d.), 1: 348.

19 Ibid., 1: 358....

20 Ibid., p. 4.

21 Otto Jespersen, *Growth and Structure of the English Language* (Toronto: Collier-Macmillan, 1938/1968), p. 2.

22 Ibid., p. 16.

23 Otto Jespersen, *Language, its Nature, Development and Origin* (London: George Allen & Unwin, 1922/1969), p. 430....

24 James Mill, *History of British India* (1817; reprint, New Delhi: Associated Publishing House, 1972), vol. 1, p. 486.

25 Ibid., vol. 1, p. 287.
26 Mrinalini Sinha, *Colonial Masculinity: The Manly Englishman and the Effeminate Bengali in the Late Nineteenth Century* (Manchester: Manchester University Press, 1995), p. 17.
27 Ibid., p. 18.
28 *Civil and Military Gazette* 15 (September 1888): 3. . . .
29 *Fredric Jameson, The Political Unconscious: Narrative as Socially Symbolic Act* (Ithaca, NY: Cornell University Press, 1981), pp. 201–2.
30 Sigmund Freud, *Moses and Monotheism: Three Essays*, vol. 23: *The Standard Edition of the Complete Psychological Works of Sigmund Freud*, ed. and trans. James Strachey and Anna Freud (1939; reprint, London: Hogarth, 1955), pp. 112–13. . . .
31 Christiane Hartnack, "Vishnu on Freud's Desk," *Social Research* 57 (1990): 921–49; also "British Psychoanalysts in Colonial India," in *Psychology in Twentieth Century Thought and Society*, ed. Mitchell G. Ash and William Woodward (New York: Cambridge University Press, 1987), pp. 233–57.
32 Homi Bhabha, *The Location of Culture* (London: Routledge, 1994), p. 89. . . .
33 Richard F. Burton, "Terminal Essay," in *A Plain and Literal Translation of the Arabian Nights' Entertainments, Now Entitled The Book of the Thousand Nights and a Night, With Introduction Explanatory Notes on the Manners and Customs of Moslem Men and a Terminal Essay upon the History of the Nights*, Medina Edition (London: Burton Club, 1886), vol. 10, pp. 63–302.
34 *The Complete Letters of Sigmund Freud to Wilhelm Fleiss, 1887–1904*, ed. and trans. Jeffrey Moussaieff Masson (Cambridge, Mass.: Harvard University Press, Belknap Press, 1985), p. 246; quoted in Boyarin, *Unheroic Conduct*, p. 195.
35 Louis Crompton, "Gay Genocide: From Leviticus to Hitler," in *The Gay Academic*, ed. Louie Crew (Palm Springs, Calif.: ETC Publications, 1978), p. 67; quoted in Sedgwick, *Between Men*, p. 94.
36 For a discussion of the sexual opportunities empire made available to the white male, see Richard Hyam, *Sexuality and Empire: The British Experience* (Manchester: Manchester University Press, 1990); for a critique of Hyam, see Mark T. Berger, "Imperialism and Sexual Exploitation," *Journal of Imperial and Commonwealth History* 17/1 (1988): pp. 83–9.
37 Burton, *Thousand Nights*, pp. 206–7.
38 Sedgwick, *Between Men*, p. 183.
39 George MacMunn, *The Underworld of India* (London: Jarrolds, 1933), p. 202; quoted in Benita Parry, *Delusions and Discoveries: Studies on India in the British Imagination, 1880–1930* (Berkeley: University of California Press, 1972), pp. 62–3.
40 Sedgwick, *Between Men*, p. 93.
41 See MacMunn, *Underworld of India*, 201; among recent works that call attention to this aspect of colonial thinking are the following: Lewis D. Wurgaft, *The Imperial Imagination: Magic and Myth in Kipling's India* (Middletown, Conn.: Wesleyan University Press, 1983), p. 50; and Sinha, *Colonial Masculinity*, p. 19. . . .
42 Sedgwick, *Between Men*, p. 193.
43 Edward Said, *Orientalism* (New York: Random House, Vintage Books, 1978), pp. 242–3. . . .
44 Sedgwick, *Between Men*, pp. 196–7.
45 Forster, *The Hill of Devi*.
46 Patrick Brantlinger, *Rule of Darkness: British Literature and Imperialism, 1830–1914* (Ithaca, NY: Cornell University Press, 1988).
47 This point is made by Sedgwick (*Between Men*, 191).
48 Mrinalini Sinha, "Colonial Policy and the Ideology of Moral Imperialism in Late Nineteenth-Century Bengal," in *Changing Men: New Directions in Research on*

Men and Masculinity, ed. Michael S. Kimmel (London: Sage Publications, 1987), p. 230....

49 Homi K. Bhabha, "Of Mimicry and Man: The Ambivalence of Colonial Discourse," *October* 28 (spring 1984): 127.

50 Homi K. Bhabha, "Difference, Discrimination, and the Discourse of Colonialism," in *The Politics of Theory*, ed. Francis Barker et al. (Colchester: University of Essex, 1983): p. 205.

51 Bhabha, "Signs Taken for Wonders," p. 162.

52 Ibid., p. 154....

53 Nandy, *Intimate Enemy*, p. 48.

54 Ibid., pp. 75–6, 108.

55 James C. Scott, *Weapons of the Weak: Everyday Forms of Peasant Resistance* (New Haven: Yale University Press, 1985); see also James C. Scott and Benedict J. Tria Kerkvliet, eds., *Everyday Forms of Peasant Resistance in South-east Asia*, Special Issue of the *Journal of Peasant Studies* 13 (1986): 1–150....

56 Douglas Haynes and Gyan Prakash, eds., *Contesting Power: Resistance and Everyday Social Relations in South Asia* (Berkeley: University of California Press, 1991): p. 3....

57 Wendy Doniger O'Flaherty, *Women, Androgynes, and Other Mythical Beasts* (Chicago: University of Chicago Press, 1980), pp. 88–90.

58 Ibid.

59 Quoted in Kalpana Seshadri-Crooks, "The Primitive as Analyst: Post-colonial Feminism's Access to Psychoanalysis," *Cultural Critique* 28 (1994): 198. Seshadri-Crooks is most illuminating on Bose in general.

60 Ibid., p. 198.

61 It is in this light that the semen itself is sometimes spoken of as female, as shakti. See O'Flaherty, *Women, Androgynes, and Other Mythical Beasts*, pp. 317–18.

62 For a discussion of women in the Bhakti movement, see Revathi Krishnaswamy, "Subversive Spirituality: Woman as Saint-Poet in Medieval India," *Women's Studies International Forum* 16/3 (1993): 139–47.

63 James C. Scott, *Weapons of the Weak*, p. 82.

64 For a Freudian reading of Vivekananda, see Sudhir Kakar, *The Inner World: A Psychoanalytic Reading of Childhood and Society in India* (New Delhi: Oxford University Press, 1981), pp. 160–81. For a more thorough analysis of Ramakrishna and Vivekananda in the context of religion, gender, and colonialism, see Parama Roy, *Indian Traffic: Subjects in Motion in British India* (Berkeley: University of California Press, 1998), esp. the chapter entitled "As the Master Saw Her: Religious Discipleship and Gender Traffic in Nineteenth Century India."

65 Vivekananda, *The Yogas and Other Works*, ed. Nikhilananda (New York: Ramakrishna-Vivekananda Center, 1953), p. 151.

66 Ibid., p. 128.

67 Vivekananda, *Collected Works of Swami Vivekananda*, vol. 3 (Calcutta: Advaita Ashrama, 1970), p. 224.

68 Vivekananda, *The Yogas*, 151.

69 Vivekananda, *Collected Works*, 4: 143.

70 Tanika Sarkar, "The Hindu Wife and the Hindu Nation: Domesticity and Nationalism in Nineteenth-Century Bengal," *Studies in History* 8/2 (1992): 213–35.

71 Nandy, *Intimate Enemy*, pp. 8–9....

72 Ibid., p. 54.

73 For feminist readings of Gandhian nationalism, see Tanika Sarkar, "Politics and Women in Bengal – the Conditions and Meaning of Participation," in *Women in Colonial India: Essays on Survival, Work and the State*, ed. J. Krishnamurthy (Delhi: Oxford University Press, 1989), pp. 231–41; Devaki Jain, "Gandhian Contributions towards a Theory of

'Feminist Ethic,' " in *Speaking of Faith: Cross-Cultural Perspectives in Women, Religion and Social Change*, ed. Devaki Jain and Diana Eck (Delhi: Kali for Women, 1986), pp. 255–70; Madhu Kishwar, "Women in Gandhi," *Economic and Political Weekly* 20/40–1 (1985): 1691–1702, 1753–58; Sujata Patel, "The Construction and Reconstruction of Women in Gandhi," *Economic and Political Weekly* 23/8 (1988): 377–87....

74 James Mill, *History of British India*, vol. 1 (1817; reprint, New Delhi: Associated Publishing House, 1972).

75 Gayatri Chakravorty Spivak, "Can the Subaltern Speak? Speculations on Widow-Sacrifice," *Wedge* 7–8 (winter–spring, 1985): 121.

76 For a discussion of how the ideology of chivalry underwrites representations of sati in the novels of Jules Verne and M. M. Kaye, see Rajeswari Sunder Rajan, *Real and Imagined Women*, pp. 42–4.

77 Lata Mani, "Contentious Traditions: The Debate on Sati in Colonial India," in *Recasting Women: Essays in Colonial Indian History*, ed. Kumkum Sangari and Sudesh Vaid (New Brunswick: Rutgers University Press, 1990), pp. 88–126; Sinha, "Colonial Policy," pp. 221–5; also Sinha, *Colonial Masculinity*, pp. 138–80; see also Sangari and Vaid, *Recasting Women*.

78 Rosalind O'Hanlon, "Issues of Widowhood in Colonial Western India," in *Contesting Power: Resistance and Everyday Social Relations in South Asia*, ed. Douglas Haynes and Gyan Prakash (Berkeley: University of California Press, 1991), pp. 76–9.

79 Barbara Ramusack, "Cultural Missionaries, Maternal Imperialists, Feminist Allies: British Women Activists in India, 1865–1945," *Women's Studies International Forum* 13/4 (1990): 309–21.

80 Jenny Sharpe, *Allegories of Empire* (Minneapolis: University of Minnesota Press, 1993), pp. 8, 4.

81 These posters are cited in the report of the Hunter Committee, which conducted an official inquiry into the events at Amritsar, and in the memoirs of Michael O'Dwyer, then lieutenant-governor of the Punjab. See *Report of the Committee Appointed by the Government of India to Investigate the Disturbances in the Punjab, etc.* (London: n.p., 1920), p. 53; and O'Dwyer, *India as I Knew It, 1885–1925* (London: Constable, 1925), pp. 291–2.

82 Rudyard Kipling, *Kim*, ed. Alan Sandison (Oxford: Oxford University Press, 1987), p. 257.

83 E. M. Forster, *A Passage to India*, ed. Oliver Stallybrass (Harmondsworth: Penguin, 1980), p. 217.

84 Such views can be found in all the following books: Percival Spear, *The Nabobs* (London: Oxford University Press, 1963), 140; Mark Nadis, "Evolution of the Sahib," *Historian*, 19/4 (August 1957): 430; Charles Allen, ed., *Plain Tales from the Raj: Images of British India in the Twentieth Century* (New York: St. Martin's Press, 1976). For a recent expression of the same view, see David Lean, quoted in "Sayings of the Week," *Observer*, February 24, 1985; cited in Helen Callaway, *Gender, Culture, and Empire: European Women in Colonial Nigeria* (Urbana: University of Illinois Press, 1987), p. 3.

85 John McBratney, "Images of Indian Women in Rudyard Kipling: A Case of Doubling Discourse" in *Inscriptions* 3–4 (1988): 53–4.

86 Nandy, *Intimate Enemy*, p. 10.

18

Male Gender and Rituals of Resistance in the Palestinian Intifada: A Cultural Politics of Violence

Julie Peteet

At the time of writing this article,[1] around 40 per cent (approximately 2,100,000) of Palestinians lived under Israeli rule, either in Israel proper (around 645,000), in the West Bank and East Jerusalem (around 938,000), or in the Gaza Strip (around 525,000).[2] From the beginning of the intifada in December 1987 through December 1990, an estimated 106,600 Palestinians were injured.[3] Beatings are not isolated in these statistics, so it is impossible to calculate with any certainty the numbers involved, though one would have been hard pressed to find a young male Palestinian under occupation who had not been beaten or who did not personally know someone who had been.[4] This article examines the attainment and enactment of manhood and masculinity among Palestinian male youths in relation to these beatings and detention in the occupied West Bank. The beatings (and detention) are framed as rites of passage that became central in the construction of an adult, gendered (male) self with critical consequences for political consciousness and agency.

Under the political and military authority of a foreign power, Palestinians possess few, if any, political rights, nor do they possess or have access to technologies of domination. Their powerlessness is all the more pronounced given their occupation by a major military power. The juxtaposition of technologies is striking. Offensively and defensively, Palestinians wield stones, one of the earliest forms of weaponry known to humankind. As part of the natural environment and landscape, the stone bears minimal, if any, application of human technological skills.

The occupying authority continuously displays the potential for and the actuality of violence to stem opposition and to imprint upon the subject population its lack of autonomy. In spite of more than two decades passing and a generation of youths who have known no other way of life, Israel has not been able to "normalize" its power relations with those under occupation. Since the beginning (in

Reprinted from *Imagined Masculinities: Male Identity and Culture in the Modern Middle East*, ed. Mai Ghoussoub and Emma Sinclair-Webb (London: Saqi Books, 2000), pp. 103–24.

1967), resistance has been common.[5] The inability to establish a "naturalness" to occupation has meant a continued recourse to physical violence along with the standard forms of structural violence.

One quickly discerns that beatings are a common occurrence. The anticipation of an encounter with occupation authorities that might lead to a beating influences the daily mobility of young men. They decline evening social invitations that necessitate driving after dark. Military personnel at roadblocks stop cars and randomly pull out men for beating. Parents hesitate to allow adolescent boys to go downtown unaccompanied, or even on short errands, fearing they might be pulled over for an identity check and in the process roughed up. In the alleys of the camps, children now are more careful to stay close to home because, on their daily patrols, soldiers occasionally chase, manhandle and detain them for several hours until their parents pay a stiff fine.

Beatings have thus been a part of the apparatus of domination since the beginning of the occupation, both in public and as an integral part of the interrogation process. How then do pre-intifada and intifada beatings differ? While framing beatings in the context of time periods, one must not draw too distinct a boundary. In the first weeks of fieldwork in a refugee camp in the West Bank, I would pose many of my questions in terms of a distinct set of time frames – "pre-intifada" and "intifada". Finally, one woman kindly, but with some exasperation, told me: "Look, we've been having an intifada here for 40 years, since 1948! The difference now is the rest of the population of the occupied territories is involved, and the continuity of resistance is being sustained! Though this word intifada is new to us, we've been resisting for 40 years."

Before the intifada, beatings were less public, usually taking place while in custody.[6] They were an integral part of an interrogation procedure, designed to break the will of prisoners and to extract confessions as to their alleged deeds and those of their acquaintances and to possible externally-based political backing and material support for resistance against the occupation.[7]

Soon after the launching of the intifada in December 1987, beatings became an explicit policy of the occupation authorities. On 19 January 1988, Defence Minister Yitzhak Rabin announced a new policy of "might, power, and beatings" to quell the uprising. The international witnessing of the public beatings and bone-breaking evoked widespread alarm among Israel's supporters, particularly in the United States. Subsequently, Likud ministers barred the media from the territories. Until the ban (Spring 1988), the beatings were featured prominently on nightly news broadcasts in the USA and Europe. In diminishing the external witnessing of the infliction of pain, the occupying authorities were attempting to create a fictitious reality of non-violent techniques of control for external consumption.

For the Israelis, the beatings were an encoded medium intended to convey a message regarding the consequences of opposition. The young male is a metonym for Palestinian opposition and struggle against domination, the idea and symbols of which must be rooted out and silenced: the Palestinian population must be made acquiescent to the colonizing project. Israeli violence proceeds on the assumption of collective guilt and responsibility among Palestinians. In the occupied territories, violence is directed at individual bodies as representations of a collective transgressive other.[8] This collective other, however, is denied a national identity. The pre-given defining power of the collective Palestinian body, which requires a violently negating intervention, lies precisely in its assertive national identity, which in its very existence denies the mythical Zionist landscape of Palestine. Taussig draws our attention to torture and terror as "ritualized art forms" that "far from being spontaneous, sui generis, and an abandonment of what are often called the values of civilization...have a deep history deriving power and meaning from those very values" (1987: 133). Unbowed males signified an assertive resistance to the colonial project and a Zionist self-identity.

The walking embodiment of power, the Israeli soldier, totes the modern technology of violence: automatic rifle, pistol, grenade, hand-cuffs, tear-gas canisters, and batons. Anthropologist and Israeli army captain Ben-Ari remarked that some soldiers, given their training for warfare, were very uneasy with their task of policing heavily civilian areas (1989: 376).[9] This unease, he suggests, should be understood against the images soldiers had of the uprising. The mass media presentation was one of "mass demonstrations, concentrated rock throwing and tyre burning, and the constant use of Molotov cocktails". Ben-Ari frames the behaviour of soldiers in the territories in terms of the metaphor of masks and disguises. He suggests "that for the limited period of milium (reserve duty) the reservists cease to be the normally identified, circumscribed, constrained members of Israeli society who must be concerned with how they are regarded by themselves and by others" (1989: 378).

Donning masks and disguises facilitates construction of "highly delimited – spatially as well as temporally – episodes during which they become another person" (Ben-Ari 1989: 378–9). Rather than "donning masks" and becoming "an other", I would cast their behaviour as more analogous to what Taussig referred to as "colonial mirroring", where "the terror and tortures they devised mirrored the horror of the savagery they both feared and fictionalized" (1987: 133).

Tolerance of physical abuse of Palestinians was underwritten by a regime of knowledge that cast them as lawless and socially primitive and violent – terrorists, threats to law and order, bands, gangs – and thus as amenable to violent extrajudicial measures. Beyond the pale, Palestinians were cast as possessing a fundamentally different set of morals and knowledge – commonly stated as "they only understand force". Their human status does not correspond to that of others. Israeli military announcements do not use the Hebrew word for "child" when reporting injuries or deaths of Palestinian children in confrontations with the military. The Israeli Palestinian writer Anton Shammas commented that "for twenty years now officially there has been no childhood in the West Bank and Gaza Strip...[A] ten year-old boy shot by military forces is reported to be a 'young man of ten'" (1988: 10). Military discourse bypasses childhood, collapsing male Palestinian life-cycle categories. This regime of knowledge, together with a widespread ideology of the rights of the occupiers to Palestinian land and resources, constitutive of a claim to an Israeli national identity, and a judicial system that tolerated systematic human rights violations, if not indeed encouraged them as Amnesty International (1991) argues, fostered an atmosphere where inflictions of bodily violence flourished.

Whether pre-intifada or intifada, the intent behind the beating was to reconstitute the Palestinian male as a non-resistant, though certainly not consenting, subject of colonization. Stone throwing, tyre burning, demonstrating, or displaying symbols of Palestine, such as the flag or its colours, could bring a swift and violent response. But rather than being mute repositories or sites on which the occupier exhibited and constructed power and affirmed its civilization and identity, the meaning of the beating has been appropriated by the subject in a dialectical and agential manner.

Before moving on to look at the social meaning of violence to the body in the specific context of the intifada, a few remarks on manhood and rites of passage in the Middle East are in order. Masculinity is neither natural nor given. Like femininity, it is a social construct. Herzfeld argues that, in a Cretan village, there is more stress on how rather than on what men do – what counts is "performative excellence" (1985: 16). Gilmore notes that a "critical threshold" is passed by various forms of tests and ordeals (1990: 11). While cautious of the perils of essentializing the category of gender, male or female, it is fairly safe to say, on a reading of the anthropological literature on masculinity in the Arab world[10] and its conflation with the deed, that this conflation conforms to Gilmore's criterion of being "something almost generic . . . a ubiquity rather than a universality" (1990: 2–3).

Arab masculinity (*rujulah*) is acquired, verified and played out in the brave deed, in risk-taking, and in expressions of fearlessness and assertiveness. It is attained by constant vigilance and willingness to defend honour (*sharaf*), face (*wajh*), kin and community from external aggression and to uphold and protect cultural definitions of gender-specific propriety.[11] Since elaborate, well-defined rites of passage to mark transitions from boyhood to adolescence to manhood are difficult to discern, a loose set of rites marking the route to "manhood" must be accompanied by performative deeds to convince and win public approval.

In the Palestinian context, the occupation has seriously diminished those realms of practice that allow men to engage in, display and affirm masculinity by means of autonomous actions.[12] Frequent witnesses to their fathers' beatings by soldiers or settlers, children are acutely aware of their fathers' inability to protect themselves and their children.[13]

Manliness is also closely intertwined with virility and paternity, and with paternity's attendant sacrifices. Denying one's own needs while providing for others is such a signifier. Resistance to occupation and the consequences of such resistance constitute a category of sacrifice with long-term implications for the autonomy and security of the community and larger national collectivity.[14]

Several anthropologists have referred to the concept of honour as a defining frame for masculinity. Abu-Lughod's work on the Egyptian Bedouin emphasizes the notion of control as crucial: control is the lack of "fear of anyone or anything", for to exhibit such fear "implies that it has control over one" (1986: 88). "Real men" are able to exact respect and command obedience from others while they themselves resist submitting to others' control (1986: 88–90). Among the Berbers of Algeria, Bourdieu locates the man of honour in the context of challenge and riposte. A challenge confers honour upon a man, because it is a cultural assumption that the "challenge, as such, requires a riposte and therefore is addressed to a man deemed capable of playing the game of honour" (1977: 11). The challenge provides an opportunity for males to prove their belonging to the world of men. A point to which I shall return later concerns Bourdieu's contention that challenges directed to men who are unable to take them up dishonours the challenger.

I shall also return more generally to some of these questions about the construction of masculinity and rites of passage after an ethnographic discussion of inscriptions of violence on the Palestinian male body.

Bodies on Display

The bodies of those under occupation are continuously called forth to present themselves to outsiders. Visits to families are punctuated by the display of bodies with the marks of bullets and beatings and are social settings for the telling of beatings, shootings, verbal exchanges with settlers and soldiers, and prison stories. After several visits to Um Fadi, I noticed that her children were always in the house or in the walled garden around the house with the gate locked. Once when I had to knock very loudly several times for the children to open, she rushed to open it and explained that she no longer leaves the gate open or allows her children to play in the alleys of the camp. After we were seated in the house and drinking tea, she quietly motioned her 11-year-old son and 13-year-old daughter to come stand in front of us. With the reluctance of children their age, they silently did so. In a subdued and controlled tone, she related how they once were caught by soldiers while playing in the alley. Soldiers regularly patrol the streets and alleys of the camp, and occasionally groups of children throw stones at them. Four soldiers claimed they had been stoned by children in the vicinity and accused Um Fadi's son and daughter. Both were beaten with batons and rifle butts directed at the kidneys, arms and face. When he got up to run, the boy was shot in the side. She asked him to raise his T-shirt to show me the scar. During this telling, several women neighbours were present as well as friends of her children. There was hushed silence as she told the story. The older women would periodically interject, almost inaudibly: "In the name of God – how can they do this to children!", "What can we do?", "What kind of people are these!" The act of telling lends dramatic narrative form to a dialogic process. For the listener, a sense of community is evoked through empathy. Many families have experienced such pain, and for those who have not the possibility looms large.

The physical marks of beatings, rubber bullets and live ammunition constitute crucial elements in dialogue with others, particularly Americans whose near official silence on the matter of Palestinian human rights violations by the occupying authorities is seen as a form of complicity. Given the levels and continuity of US financial support for the occupying power, they consider it all the more appropriate to display the physical signs of their suffering to Westerners. The battered body is a representation fashioned by the Israelis but presented by Palestinians to the West. To the Palestinians, the battered body, with its bruises and broken limbs, is the symbolic embodiment of a twentieth-century history of subordination and powerlessness – of "what we have to endure" – but also of their determination to resist and to struggle for national independence.

A representation created with the intent of humiliating has been reversed into one of honour, manhood and moral superiority. But bodies do more than represent. Torture and beatings are ordeals one undergoes as sacrifices for the struggle (*qadiyyah*). It should be firmly stated that this argument in no way is meant to imply that Palestinians make light of physical violence. It is rather to try to understand how culturally they make sense of it. Displaying physical marks of violence, that one is usually powerless to avoid, stands as a "commentary on suffering" (Keesing 1985; Peteet 1991) but also, I would suggest, as a commentary on sacrifice. As such they are poignant communicative devices. These displays are powerful statements belying claims of a benign occupation and resonate with the honour that comes from unmasking and resisting.

Becoming Men

One sign of things to come – amidst the jokes and nervous laughter there were signs of genuine excitement by some soldiers at the prospect of "teaching them not to raise their heads". (Israeli soldier in the occupied territories, quoted in Peretz 1990: 122)

I first had an inkling of the meaning of the beating and imprisonment as rites of passage when Hussein, 24 years old and resident in Jalazon refugee camp, remarked casually and with a hint of resignation that, on his first evening home from a nine-month stint in prison, a neighbour had come to ask his help in mediating a dispute he was involved in with another neighbour. Hussein pleaded fatigue and the crush of visitors to avoid assuming this mantle of community responsibility, a responsibility that carries with it substantial moral authority. To be a mediator is a position and task usually the preserve of well-respected, older men known for their sagacity and even temperament. Such men are thought to have attained 'aql (reason or social common sense).[15]

Hussein did handle the matter the next day, talking to both parties, eventually hammering out a compromise solution. Like many young men of his generation and experience, he suddenly found himself faced with responsibility for managing community affairs, mainly such tasks as mediation in disputes and participating in popular tribunals to try suspected collaborators.[16]

During visits to Hussein's family, I began to notice the deference paid him by his father, an unusual state of affairs in Arab family relations where sons are usually deferential to their fathers. Much about hierarchy and submission can be read in seemingly mundane, everyday gestures. Seating patterns in Arab culture are spatial statements of hierarchy. Those who stand or sit closest to the door are usually subordinate, younger males, while those farthest from the door and centrally positioned are older, respected men who are able to command obedience. The spatial arrangement of visitors and family members when congregating at Hussein's home did not conform to the traditional pattern. Indeed Hussein often was centrally positioned with his father clearly on the periphery. During conversations where his father was present, along with other family members and friends, his father deferred to Hussein in speech, allowing his son to interrupt him. Hussein's father listened attentively as his son talked for lengthy periods of time before interjecting himself. In short, he gave Hussein the floor. When Hussein would describe his prolonged torture at the hands of the interrogators, his father was quiet, only occasionally to interject, "Prison is a school, a university" and "Prison is for men."

In observing resistance activities in camps, villages and urban neighbourhoods, it was clear the older men played little, if any role. It was the preserve of the young (under 25 years of age), and as such they embodied the prestige and respect that come from, and yet give one access to, leadership positions. It did not take long to realize that Hussein was a member of the local underground leadership. He had spent 19 months in jail on charges of organizing local forms of escalation, such as stone throwing and barricade building. Chased and publicly beaten in the camp's alleyways before being thrown into a jeep, he was then taken to prison and subjected to 18 days of interrogation. Naked, deprived of food, water and sanitation facilities for the first three days, he was subjected to beatings with fists, pipes and rifle butts, which alternated with questioning over an 18-day period.

Once interrogation procedures are completed, prisoners join their fellow inmates in daily prison routine. Palestinian political prisoners are highly organized. Classes are conducted daily in a variety of subjects ranging from foreign languages to maths, science and history. Classes in political theory and practice are the high points in this educational project. For this reason, it is commonplace in contemporary Palestinian discourse to hear the comment, "Prison is a university." A leadership hierarchy emerges, and as young men are released they take up the leadership mantle of those who are newly detained. In this way, young men circulate between prison and leadership positions. This circulation of young men ensures a leadership in spite of the campaign of massive arrests and detention of young males.

Upon his release, Hussein returned home to several days of visitors – kin, friends and neighbours – and new responsibilities in the camp leadership. Within the prisons, recruitment to political organizations flourishes, and leaders of each political faction emerge to lead their followers. From the prison they can have some voice in the daily actions and policies of the intifada as they confer instructions and ideas on prisoners about to be released. Upon returning to their communities, young men like Hussein have acquired the stature to lead. They have withstood interrogation and not given away information or become collaborators. More importantly, however, they return "educated men". Hussein and other released detainees spoke of prison as a place where they learned not only academic subjects, but also about power and how to resist.

Another young man I became acquainted with in the West Bank was Ali. Ali's experience of bodily inflictions of violence began substantially before the intifada. Within a five-year period, he had been detained seventeen times. [He was p]olitically inactive before he was taken away from home in the middle of the night during his last year of high school, [and] the soldiers assured his frightened parents that they would just ask him a few questions and let him go. Handcuffed and blindfolded, he was placed on the floor of a jeep where he was repeatedly kicked and hit with rifle butts. He recalls that the jeep stopped and picked up someone else. Once they started beating the other fellow, and he screamed, Ali realized it was his friend Sami. Sami told him: "Don't cry or shout. Don't let them know it hurts." He told me:

> At first, of course, I was scared to death, and then once you're in that room and they slap your face and start hitting you – that's it, it goes away and you start being a different person. All of a sudden you have a power inside you – a power to resist – you want to resist. You can't help it; you feel very strong, you even want to challenge them, though basically I had nothing to tell them since I had done nothing.

After his release several days later, he returned home. Two weeks later, soldiers appeared again and detained him, this time for about two weeks. Upon his release, he decided to join the underground resistance movement and after several months was active in the local-level leadership. He now had stature in the community as a result of the beatings, arrests and interrogations. He was effective in mobilizing others to join in demonstrations, national celebrations, and the resistance movement on the university campus he later attended.

Physical violence can be construed by its recipients as a "bridge-burning" activity (Gerlach and Hines 1970). One often hears comments such as "I've nothing left to lose" and "I've already paid the price, I might as well be active." Palestinian males need not necessarily do violence to become political agents as Fanon (1969) argued for the Algerian revolution. As its recipients, they acquire masculine and revolutionary credentials. Marks on the body, though certainly unwanted, signal a resistant, masculine subjectivity and agency. The pervasiveness of beatings/detention, their organizational format, and their construal by recipients as entry into the world of masculinity make possible their casting as a rite of passage.

In his classic study of rites of passage, Van Gennep (1961) identified three characteristic stages: separation, marginality, and aggregation. A logic of sequences is apparent in the transformative process of physical violence. In the initial phase, the individual is physically detached from the group. He is either taken from his home and family to the jeep and then the interrogation room, or he is detached from the crowd in public and held by soldiers or settlers who try to keep at a distance those who would intervene. The second, or liminal, stage is a state of marginality and ambiguity and is one fraught with dangers. The young novice exists outside of social time, space, and the categories of the life cycle. Social rules and norms are suspended. Interrogation, with its applications of physical violence, is such a liminal stage during which social hierarchies of age and class are diluted. Oppositions between normal social life and liminality (Turner 1977) can be applied to the one being beaten, especially those in custody who are frequently naked, in a state of humility and without rank or status, and who silently undergo pain and suffering. Imprisonment is also a liminal period because communitas is achieved and expressed in the emergence of new hierarchies that rest on an ability to withstand physical violation and pain, political affiliation and rank, and ability to lead in the prison community.

The final sequence, aggregation or the post-liminal re-entry into normal social life, is verified and enacted by the family and the community at large. The return home is marked by a fairly well-defined celebratory etiquette. Relatives, friends and neighbours visit for several weeks to show respect to the released detainee and his family. Special foods, usually more expensive meat dishes, are prepared by the women of the household both to strengthen the detainee's often poor health as well as to show appreciation and respect for his endurance. New clothes are bought to mark re-entry into the community. The respect shown by deferential gestures to the former prisoner or beaten youth all mark his re-entry into society with a new status of respect and manhood.

In emerging from the beating unbowed and remaining committed to resistance activities, young men exhibit generosity to the point of sacrifice that asserts and validates a masculine self. The infliction of pain reveals, in the most intimate and brutal way, the nature of occupation and strengthens them, they contend, to confront it.

Endowed with the qualities of adulthood, honour and manhood, [their] emergence from the ordeal dovetails with access to power and authority. In a reversal of meaning, the beating empowers the self and informs an agency of resistance. Palestinians, as participants in and as audience to the public spectacle of beatings, have consciously and creatively taken a coherent set of signs and practices of domination and construed them to buttress an agency designed to overthrow political hierarchies.

The Intifada: Tremors in the Construction of Masculinity

The term intifada comes from the Arabic root n-f-d, which indicates a shaking, as in shaking the dust from (Harlow 1989: 32). It implies a shaking off of foreign occupation and ties of economic and administrative linkage. While its eruption was fairly spontaneous, the intifada was the culmination of years of accumulated frustrations and outrage. A decade of grassroots political and social organizing undergirded its direction and ability to sustain itself (Hiltermann 1991). The intifada brought to the forefront of international diplomacy an internally-based Palestinian leadership. Equally, it signalled a generational shake-up. The young, armed only with stones and facing death and pain, were to sweep away the older generation in terms of political relevance and actual leadership. Shaking off also implicates forms of internal domination embodied in age, class and gender hierarchies. The continuity created by life-cycle transitions such as marriage, employment, and reaching the state of *'aql* were destabilized by the actions of young boys.

The assertion that the male under occupation is reconstituted via violence implies that the creation of meaning is a matter of Palestinian control. The transformative power of the ritual lies in the individual who consciously commits himself to political action and in the community's ability to confer adult status. Ritual mediates between relations of violence and domination and political agency by subordinates in such a way as to defy any notion of directional unilineality between oppression and resistance. As Feldman argued in his discussion of political violence in Northern Ireland, "Political agency is not given but achieved on the basis of practices that alter the subject" (1991: 1). Yet it is political practices by boys, many undertaken willingly and often spontaneously rather than given, that lead to further political agency via ritual.

As rites of passage, beatings and imprisonment are procedures that are not controlled or overseen by the family or kin group. It is an individual experience within a collectivity of young men. Thus a critical rite of passage into adulthood, with its corresponding privileges of power/authority/respect, is now accomplished earlier and is initially out of the bounds of the kin group. Indeed, it underscores the powerlessness of the kin group to protect its youth.

To return to Bourdieu's mapping of the relationship between masculinity and honour, we can now pose the question, What happens to the cultural categories and concepts around which honour is organized and expressed when challenge and riposte take place not between members of the same social group, but between a colonial entity, and its apparatus of force, and a subjugated, indigenous population? A man dishonours himself when he challenges a man considered incapable of "taking up the challenge" (Bourdieu 1977: 11). When Israelis pursue and engage Palestinian youths, the cultural interpretation available to Palestinians is to consider the Israelis as lacking in the emotional and moral qualities of manhood. Only men of little honour and thus dubious masculinity would beat unarmed youths while they themselves are armed with and trained in the use of modern implements of warfare. Because little or no effective riposte is possible at the instant, there is no challenge – and the encounter degenerates into mere aggression (Bourdieu 1977: 12). Such aggression deprives its practitioners of claims to honour and morality.

Palestinians construe these aggressions as cowardly and immoral, rather than a challenge. But what has all this to do with manhood? Palestinians have changed the cultural categories of the encounter so that manhood comes from a "riposte" not to a challenge but to what Bourdieu distinguished as "mere aggression". It is against this backdrop of aggression then that Palestinians are reconstructing defining elements of their culture and society. This will take on more meaning when read against the following scene.

Moral Superiority: Affirming Cultural and National Selves

On my way to an office in east Jerusalem, I was rushing to avoid the 1:00 p.m. closure of all commercial activity in the Palestinian sector of the city in observance of the general strike. Children were returning home from school, and shop shutters were hastily rolling down. As I rounded the corner, I saw two jeeps and about six or seven heavily armed soldiers. They had a 10-year-old mentally handicapped boy pressed against the stone wall, were slapping him in the face, shaking him, and yelling in broken Arabic for him to admit throwing a stone at them. Being mentally handicapped, the boy could only whimper and cry – he was incapable of talking. I ran into our office to tell the others that they were beating the boy who lived across the alley. By this time several neighbourhood women, by and large middle-class Jerusalemites, had also appeared. One of these women, fluent in English, calmly walked up to the group, which had now expanded to four jeeps and about fifteen soldiers. She politely asked why they were bothering this boy who was retarded and could barely speak. She kept repeating to the soldiers that the boy could not understand and speak like a normal child. By now, she had a slight mocking smile on her face and appealed to the soldiers with a kind of sarcasm: "Can't you see he's retarded? It takes all of you soldiers and four jeeps to question a retarded boy?" The other women were smirking and exchanging comments on what it was that could possess these people to beat retarded children. Several of the soldiers were clearly embarrassed and physically distanced themselves, turning their backs on the boy and the two soldiers roughing him up. They smiled sheepishly to the women gathered there and shrugged their shoulders as if to say, "What can we do?"

An audience of women defused a potential escalation of violence through mockery and joking. The imbalance of forces is so patently absurd that Palestinians find an almost comic relief in watching soldiers engage in such morally revealing behaviour. In imposing interpretation and meaning on the violence of the occupiers, Palestinians are (re)constituting themselves in a moral sense. Violent encounters where Palestinians are both participants and audiences are public scenes where their moral qualities are dramatically juxtaposed against those of the occupiers.

The reconstitution of a moral self via violence involves both men and women. To some extent, however, a gendered distinction appears in the practice of violence. While women have been active in all arenas, a task assigned to them early in the intifada, and one in tune with cultural notions of female propriety and "natural" concerns and mobility constraints, was to intervene in violent encounters. In other words, women were to witness and defuse rites of violence. A leaflet (*bayan*) distributed on 8 March 1988, and signed "Palestinian Women in the Occupied Territories", said, "Mothers, in camps, villages, and cities, continue confronting soldiers and settlers. Let each woman consider the wounded and imprisoned her own children."[17]

Despite a gendered division of roles, the moral reconstruction consequent to violent acts does indeed permeate gender boundaries. The reconstituting moral self, whether male or female, is a cultural category, in this case one with a national content, constructed as it currently is *vis-à-vis* a foreign other. As the witnessing audience, women provide a running commentary intended to shame soldiers to cease a beating or to stop an arrest. "Don't you people have children?", "Has God abandoned you?" is screamed at soldiers while entreating them to desist. While women's moral self is enacted and affirmed publicly in this act of witnessing, the male being beaten or arrested is also positioned performatively to place himself against another. But how are non-participants positioned such that they also ultimately are enabled to construct a moral self? I would argue that the "telling", punctuated by moral and evaluative judgements that circulate throughout Palestinian society as people visit one another in the course of daily life, is one such event in which a moral constitution of the self unfolds.

Israeli behaviour is considered rude and boorish. Palestinian discussions are punctuated by surprise at their bad manners: "These are supposedly educated people – why do they behave so obnoxiously?" They are regarded as lacking in ethics and morality. Most significantly, they are seen as deficient in empathy with the suffering of others.[18] In contemporary constitutions of self *vis-à-vis* their occupiers, Palestinians have recourse to a "poetics of contrast" (Comaroff and Comaroff 1987: 205). Clear and defining distinctions are drawn between their behaviour and the occupiers'. Palestinians consider themselves polite to others and reserved in public, personal qualities that are central to a Palestinian etiquette. Images of contrast are rhetorical devices that lend meaning to the occupiers' behaviour. The moral nature of these images provides Palestinians with the stuff of which they construct a collective self-image in a situation of subordination and an absence of autonomy.

Transforming Hierarchies: Class and Generation

In the historical encounter, socio-cultural systems are simultaneously transformed and reproduced (Sahlins 1981). Inscriptions of bodily violence and their construal as rites of passage both transform and reproduce certain structural, relational and cultural features of Palestinian society. The intifada has had profound implications for class and generational structures and relations in the occupied territories. While the intifada is a popular uprising, those in the forefront of resistance to occupation are subaltern male youths from the refugee camps, villages and urban popular quarters who are usually under 20 years of age and can be as young as 10.

The power and status of the older generation were eclipsed. Young males took over the tasks previously the preserve of more mature, often notable men. For example, disputes were mediated in new judicial tribunals organized and staffed by the underground leadership. A common lament was that the young were out of control, displaying little or no respect for their parents. It reached such a pitch that several leaflets in 1990 called for parents to reassert control and for youth to heed the voices of their parents and teachers.

The older generation, those over the age of 35, played little, if any, visible role in the daily activities of the intifada. A telling incident occurred one day in a service (shared taxi) ride from Jerusalem to Ramallah. There were six passengers, myself included. As we approached a roadblock manned by soldiers, we could see several other cars stopped with young male passengers being searched and questioned. No one in our car seemed particularly worried or concerned. Our car came to a halt and the soldiers peered in, gave each of us a searching glance, and then motioned the driver to proceed. My husband commented to the rest of the passengers, "Why didn't they ask to see our identity cards or search us?" The other men in the car, none of whom appeared to be younger than 30 or 35, turned around in their seats and looked at him with incredulity. One of them said, "You think you're a boy! They aren't interested in men our age!"

Bodily inscriptions of violence are more prevalent in camps and villages and thus are somewhat class bound. The politically active urban elite, often from notable families, who have traditionally striven for leadership, are not usually exposed to bodily inscriptions of violence, though they may well undergo periods of administrative detention. Indeed, they can be subject to derision for assuming a mantle of leadership when they have not been credentialized by violence. Um Kamel is a 40-year-old mother and activist in a refugee camp. Her husband is in jail serving a ten-year sentence on the grounds of organizing anti-occupation activities. One son has spent considerable periods of time in prison, and a 16-year-old son has been shot twice in the stomach. Twice she has had homes demolished, with only a few hours notice, because of allegations of her sons' political activism. She commented sarcastically of the urban-based leaders: "What do they know of suffering? Who are they to lead? They and their sons aren't beaten and they rarely go to jail. Their sons study here and abroad while our sons are beaten, shot and imprisoned!"

Reproducing Hierarchies: Gender

Contemporary rites of initiation into manhood articulate with and set in dramatic relief the social reproduction of asymmetrical gender arrangements, while a hierarchical male identity and notions of selfhood and political position are reaffirmed in these rites of passage.

Given the casting of the beating as a zone of prestige for young men, what does it mean for women? The number of women beaten, arrested and detained is small, and their status afterwards is more ambiguous than heroic. The number does not index women's level of involvement in the uprising, which has been extensive. It does indicate, however, their less visible role, and the tendency of the Israeli Defence Forces to go for males first. Ambiguity devolves for the women from the shame of having bodily contact with strange men, a stark transgression of the code of modesty and shame. Foremost on everyone's mind is the question of sexual violation. Women who violate the modesty code by engaging in illicit sexual activities (pre-marital sexual relations or adultery after marriage) risk incurring reprisals by kinsmen. But when the violator is a common enemy in whose face one's kinsmen hold no power and few means of recourse, ambiguity sets in. Ambiguity arises from the notion of will and intent. Arab women are seen as possessed of an active sexuality. When transgressions of the sexual code occur, the women can be held responsible. Yet, if a woman's nationalist activity sets in motion a series of events that culminates in a beating and detention, and an interrogation procedure that includes sexual torture, it is difficult to cast her as having violated the modesty code. The nationalist, patriotic cast of her intent and actions precludes the usual cultural interpretation. By the time of the intifada, ambiguity was giving way to a cautious respect for the woman detainee.

While femininity is no more natural than masculinity, physical violence is not as central to its construction. It does not reproduce or affirm aspects of female identity, nor does it constitute a rite of passage into adult female status. Women frame their physical violation as evidence of their equality with men and wield it to press their claims – "We suffer like men, we should have the same rights", quipped one former prisoner who had undergone a lengthy detention and was tortured during interrogation. While the violence visited upon males credentializes masculinity, that visited upon women indicates a potential equality of citizenship (Peteet 1991).

Women experience the phenomenon of beating from a multiplicity of subject positions. The "mother" saving boys from soldiers' blows is one of the most widespread and enduring images to emerge in the intifada. Mothers of the subaltern are extolled as the "mothers of all Palestinians". Known in the camp as "a mother of all youths", Um Kamel explained her actions in intervening in public beatings: "I feel each and every one of those boys is my son. If it was my son, I would want other mothers to try to protect him." The mothers intervene during beatings, at once screaming for the soldiers to stop and pleading with them to show mercy. They hurl insults that highlight the soldiers' denial of the humanity of others: "Have you no compassion and pity?", "Aren't we human beings, too?", "Don't you have mothers and sons – how would your mother feel if you were treated this way; would you like to see your sons beaten like this?", "What kind of a people takes the land of another and then beats them when they protest?" This protective action of middle-aged mothers accomplishes several things: it can create a diversion that allows boys to escape. The noise and confusion it generates can quickly mobilize large groups of passers-by and nearby residents to surround soldiers and try to intervene. But above all, it casts shame on soldiers by scrutinizing their moral qualities in a dramatic, public narrative. Women as mothers of all are a collective moral representation of a community testifying to the abusive nature of occupation.

Thus women are not silent witnesses to everyday violence. Witnessing is itself a form of political activism. When the occasional foreign journalist enters a camp, a delegation comes from abroad, or the anthropologist such as myself comes, the "mothers", those who risked their own safety to protect others, are called forth. Much like the vaunted position of the "mothers of the martyrs" in areas where Palestinian resistance takes the form of armed struggle (Peteet 1991), they are called upon to tell their stories, to assume the position of communal witnesses and tellers of suffering. The experience of a beating may not affirm a feminine identity and selfhood, yet it does evoke some female traits – stoicism and silence, to protect the community.

While beatings reproduce a masculine identity, they also reproduce men's authority and physical domination in the family. Asymmetrical gender relations may be reaffirmed as a result of a young man's assumption of adult tasks and authority that in this case are assumed through violent rites of passage. Young wives and sisters complained that their husbands and brothers returned from interrogation and detention with a new authoritarianism expressed in attempts to assert control over their mobility. Style of dress was another arena of conflict, as women were pressured to wear head scarves. Domestic violence, wives and social workers claimed, was on the rise. Some men who were subjected to beatings and torture return home and inflict violence upon women.

Conclusion

The meaning of the beating is central to new conceptions of manhood and ultimately access to leadership positions. Violence has almost diametrically opposed meanings. For one, it is an index of a fictionalized fear and image of inferiority of a subject population and is intended to control and dishonour; for the others, it is constitutive of a resistant subjectivity that signals heroism, manhood, and access to leadership and authority. Practices that intimately situate Israelis and Palestinians are construed by Palestinians as transformative and agential. How did the experience of physical violence become construed as a rite of passage into manhood with its associated practices? In other words, can we identify a dynamic interplay between meaning and agency? The categories of experience, meaning and agency should not be arranged in a unilinear manner so as to identify a direction of transformation. A more fruitful line of inquiry would cast these categories as existing in a relationship of mutual constitutiveness.

While beatings, bodies and rites of passage are texts and structures of meaning, they are also historically grounded social constructions derived from particular signs and practices that galvanize a community to action. The call to action derives less from the actual structure of the ritual and more from its performative essence, in which the audience plays a crucial role in reversing the meaning intended by the dominant performers. The intifada abruptly and violently signalled an end to what Scott has referred to as the "public transcript . . . the open interaction between subordinates and those who dominate" (1990: 2). Israel's public performances to exact submission are no longer efficacious.

The act of incorporating beatings and imprisonment into a cultural criterion of manhood and assigning them status as a rite of passage is a "trick", if you will, that reverses the social order of meaning and leads to political agency. To let bodily violence stand as constitutive of an inferior and submitting social position and subjectivity without interpretation and challenge would be to submit to the dominant performers' meaning. For the anthropologist, to interpret it otherwise would leave it as a textual rather than an agential problematic.

The occupying authorities, with constant attention directed to detecting ripples of change in Palestinian cultural categories and social relations, have by now caught on to the way applications of bodily violence and imprisonment have empowered a generation committed to resistance. A new element seems to be emerging in their regime of pseudo-knowledge of the subject population. Interrogation procedures now contain a sexual practice designed to thwart the meaning and agency of physical violence as rites of passage to masculinity and manhood. Rape during interrogation is now being more widely discussed among some released prisoners, as is fondling by interrogators with photographs taken of these incidents. Sexual forms of interrogation deprive young men of claims to manhood and masculinity. One cannot return from prison and describe forms of torture that violate the most intimate realm of gendered selfhood. If knowledge of such sexual tortures circulates widely, the power of violence and detention to contribute to a gendered sense of self informing political agency will be diluted.

Notes

1 This article was completed in November 1992 and is here reprinted in an abbreviated form with small modifications by permission of the American Anthropological Association (not for further reproduction). It has been decided not to attempt to "update" the original article or to change tenses throughout to reflect the fact that, with the institution of the Palestinian Authority, there have been changes in the status of some Palestinians. The article first appeared in *American Ethnologist* 21(1) February 1994, and research for it was carried out in the West Bank during 1990. Funding for a year of fieldwork was generously provided by the Fulbright Islamic Civilization Program. The Palestinian Academic Society for the Study of International Affairs (PASSIA) graciously provided institutional support and hospitality. I would like to extend my appreciation to Mary Hegland, Yvonne Jones and William Young for comments on an earlier draft and to the four anonymous reviewers for *American Ethnologist* for their helpful comments and suggestions for revision.

2 See Hajjar and Beinin 1988. This is a primer designed to provide a very basic overview of twentieth-century Palestinian history and society.

3 This encompasses injuries sustained from live ammunition, which includes plastic bullets, rubber bullets, metal marbles and tear gas.

4 The Palestine Human Rights and Information Committee (PHRIC) cautions that the figure of 106,600 should probably be doubled, especially the beatings. They receive their information from hospitals and clinics, and many people do not seek medical care. Moreover, they do not receive figures on beating cases treated in emergency rooms, in local or private clinics, or by the medical communities. The figures from the Gaza Strip for the month of December 1990 indicate 273 reported beatings (66 were of women, 45 of children) (Palestine Human Rights and Information Campaign 1990).

5 See Aronson 1987 (198 days of the occupation).

6 Their actual numbers are somewhat harder to estimate because, with the intifada, human rights organizations began making a concerted attempt to keep monthly and annual figures on human rights violations, breaking them down into distinct categories.

7 Amnesty International (1991) states that in the occupied territories, Palestinian detain-ees are: "typically subjected to forms of torture or ill-treatment, with the aim of obtaining information as well as a confession...Torture or ill-treatment seem to be virtually institutionalized during the arrest and interrogation procedure...The practices relating in particular to interrogation procedures have been officially endorsed or are generally condoned, and therefore effectively encouraged, by the authorities." (p. 45)

Amnesty's report also questions the "fairness of military court trials" because of the prominent role of confessions and "the apparent reluctance by judges to investigate claims of coerced statements" (p. 49). The report states that "the substantial evidence available indicates the existence of a clear pattern of systematic psychological and physical ill-treatment, constituting torture or other forms of cruel, inhuman, or degrad-ing treatment which is being inflicted on detainees during the course of interrogation" (p. 58).

8 Zionist fictionalizing, and I would add, fear of collective Arab sentiment and action, goes far in explaining why the shooting of an Israeli diplomat in London could be presented as justification for the 1982 invasion of Lebanon and yet why Israel has usually insisted on bilateral negotiations with Arab states.

9 See Peretz (1990) for a discussion of the complexity of views among soldiers serving in the occupied territories.

10 Literature devoted explicitly to masculinity in the Arab world is rare, but the topic surfaces in a variety of works, not exclusively but largely based on ethnography in North Africa (Abu-Lughod 1986; Caton 1985, 1987; David and Davis 1989).

11 Unlike masculinity in the Mediterranean, especially Spain, public displays of lust and sexual bravado are not explicit components of Arab manhood. Indeed self-mastery of lust and romantic emotions is crucial to the construction and maintenance of Arab manhood (see Abu-Lughod 1986; Gilmore 1990: 40). In Muslim thought, unregulated sexuality can lead to *fitna* (social chaos).

12 Autonomy is more than simply the ability to provide physical protection. It is also the ability to support one's family through labour. Adequately to explain how the Palestin-ian economy has been harnessed to that of the occupying country, and in the process how labour categories, relations, and patterns have been transformed is beyond the scope of this article.

13 In a study of the dreams of Palestinian children, Bilu (1991) noted that in nightmares of violent encounters between their families and Israeli soldiers or settlers, parents are unable to protect children from violence, whereas in Israeli children's nightmares of violence emanating from Arabs, salvation arrives in the form of fathers, families, and the army. In one case the nightmare is resolved, in the other it is simply a nightmare from which the child can find no escape. A study discussed by Peretz had a similar conclusion. In a study of Palestinian children's dreams, a prominent theme was the presence of soliders in their homes, smashing furniture and beating parents. Peretz commented that: "a major conclusion was that these children regard themselves as victims of violence initiated by armed men and that the family no longer provides security. The father almost never figures in these dreams; according to the analysis, he has lost his authority." (1990: 116) His source is Amos Lavav, "Jewish-Arab Psychoanalysis," *Sof-Shavooa*, weekly supplement to *Maariv International Edition*, 23 December 1988.

14 See Peteet (1991: 105–7) where I argue that, among the Palestinians in Lebanon, rituals of martyrdom for guerrillas were testimonials of their honour and immortality in the collective consciousness. Moreover, their celebratory spirit signalled defiance of death and the subordination it was supposed to overcome.

15 For an extensive discussion of the concept of '*aql*, see Rosen 1984. '*Aql* has been described as the "faculty of understanding, rationality, judiciousness, prudence, and wisdom" (Altorki 1986: 51). Males begin to acquire '*aql* around the age of 20. While

acquisition of this quality has no definable starting date, it does grow with marriage, and most men attain it fully "no earlier than 40, or mature adulthood, when men are perceived to have achieved sufficient capacity to deal with the complex problems of social existence" (Altorki 1986: 52). Milestones along this path to adulthood are circumcision, educational achievements, marriage, income earning, the birth of children, and the acquisition of wisdom that comes from knowledge of one's society and its customs. See Granqvist (1931, 1935, 1947), for a description of circumcisions and weddings in Mandate Palestine.

16 For discussion of Palestinian popular tribunals and popular justice committees during the intifada, see McDowell (1989) and Peretz (1990). A similar process of legal development occurred in Lebanon under the PLO (Peteet 1987).

17 Leaflets are printed several times a month by the underground leadership of the intifada. They contain a listing of the strike days and days of confrontation, and additionally exhort people to boycott Israeli goods, actively to participate in popular committees, in general, to support the uprising.

18 Jewish theologian Mark Ellis suggests that "Holocaust theology" – emergent since the creation of Israel in 1948 – is a self-absorbed phenomenon based on a joining of religious heritage with loyalty to Israel. Such self-absorption diminishes Jewish capacity for empathy with Palestinian suffering (Neimark 1992: 21; see also Lewis 1990).

References

Abu-Lughod, Lila. 1986. *Veiled Sentiments: Honor and Poetry in a Bedouin Society*, Berkeley: University of California Press.

Altorki, Soraya. 1986. *Women in Saudi Arabia: Ideology and Behavior among the Elite*, New York: Columbia University Press.

Amnesty International, Israel and the Occupied Territories. 1991. *The Military Justice System in the Occupied Territories: Detention, Interrogation and Trial Procedures*, New York: Amnesty International.

Aronson, Geoffrey. 1987. *Creating Facts: Israel, Palestinians, and the West Bank*, Washington, DC: Institute for Palestine Studies.

Ben-Ari, Eyal. 1989. "Masks and Soldiering: The Israeli Army and the Palestinian Uprising", *Cultural Anthropology* 4: 372–89.

Bilu, Yoram. 1991. "The Other as Nightmare: The Articulation of Aggression in Children's Dreams in Israel and the West Bank", paper presented at the 90th Annual Meeting of the American Anthropological Association, Chicago.

Bourdieu, Pierre. 1977. *Outline of a Theory of Practice*, Cambridge: Cambridge University Press.

Caton, Steven. 1985. "The Poetic Construction of Self", *Anthropological Quarterly* 58: 141–51.

——.1987: "Power, Persuasion, and Language: A Critique of the Segmentary Model in the Middle East", *International Journal of Middle East Studies* 19: 77–102.

Comaroff, John L. and Comaroff, Jean. 1987. "The Madman and the Migrant: Work and Labor in the Historical Consciousness of a South African People", *American Ethnologist* 14: 191–209.

Davis, Susan, and Davis, Douglas. 1989. *Adolescence in a Moroccan Town*, New Brunswick and London: Rutgers University Press.

Fanon, Frantz. 1969. *The Wretched of the Earth*, Harmondsworth: Penguin Books.

Feldman, Allen. 1991. *Formations of Violence: The Narrative of the Body and Political Terror in Northern Ireland*, Chicago: University of Chicago Press.

Gerlach, Luther, and Hines, Virginia. 1970. *People, Power and Change: Movements of Social Transformation*, Indianapolis: Bobbs-Merrill Educational Publications.

Gilmore, David. 1990. *Manhood in the Making: Cultural Concepts of Masculinity*, New Haven and London: Yale University Press.

Granqvist, Hilma. 1931 and 1935. *Marriage Conditions in a Palestinian Village*, 2 vols., Helsingfors, Finland: Societas Scientiarum Fennica.

——.1947. *Birth and Childhood among the Arabs: Studies in a Muhammadan Village in Palestine*, Helsingfors, Finland: Soderstrom & Co.

Hajjar, Lisa, and Beinin, Joel. 1988. "Palestine for Beginners", *Middle East Report* 154: 17–20.

Harlow, Barbara 1989. "Narrative in Prison: Stories from the Palestinian Intifada", *Modern Fiction Studies* 35: 29–46.

Herzfeld, Michael. 1985. *The Poetics of Manhood: Contest and Identity in a Cretan Mountain Village*, Princeton, NJ: Princeton University Press.

Hiltermann, Joost. 1991. *Behind the Uprising*, Princeton, NJ: Princeton University Press.

Keesing, Roger. 1985. "Kwaio Women Speak: The Micropolitics of Autobiography in a Solomon Island Society", *American Anthropologist* 87: 27–39.

Lewis, Mark. 1990. *Beyond Innocence and Redemption: Confronting the Holocaust and Israeli Power*, San Francisco: Harper & Row.

McDowell, David. 1989. *Palestine and Israel: The Uprising and Beyond*, Berkeley: University of California Press.

Neimark, Marilyn. 1992. "American Jews and Palestine: The Impact of the Gulf War", *Middle East Report* 175: 19–23.

Palestine Human Rights and Information Campaign 1990: *Palestine Human Rights and Information Campaign* 3: 13, Human Rights Update.

Peretz, Don. 1990. *Intifada: The Palestinian Uprising*, Boulder, CO: Westview Press.

Peteet, Julie. 1987. "Socio-political Integration and Conflict Resolution in a Palestinian Refugee Camp", *Journal of Palestine Studies* 16(2): 29–44.

——.1991. *Gender in Crisis: Women and the Palestinian Resistance Movement*, New York: Columbia University Press.

Rosen, Lawrence. 1984. *Bargaining for Reality: The Construction of Social Relations in a Muslim Community*, Chicago: University of Chicago Press.

Sahlins, Marshall. 1981. *Historical Metaphors and Mythical Realities: Structure in the Early History of the Sandwich Islands Kingdom*, Ann Arbor: University of Michigan Press.

Scott, James. 1990. *Domination and the Arts of Resistance: Hidden Transcripts*, New Haven, CT: Yale University Press.

Shammas, Anton. 1988. "A Stone's Throw", *New York Review of Books*, March 31: 10.

Taussig, Michael. 1987. *Shamanism, Colonialism, and the Wild Man: A Study in Terror and Healing*, Chicago: University of Chicago Press.

Turner, Victor. 1977. *The Ritual Process: Structure and Anti-Structure*, Ithaca, NY: Cornell University Press.

Van Gennep, Arnold. 1961. *The Rites of Passage* [1909], Chicago: University of Chicago Press.

Part V

Borders

Scholarship on masculinity is divided between those who believe that it is best understood by examining its idealized or dominant forms and those who look to the margins for its least successful manifestations. All of the authors in this section begin by assuming that the most fruitful site for analyzing, and dismantling, the connection between masculinity and cultural authority is at its seams, where the process of gender construction is most visible. "Borders" is a deliberately broad term that describes the indeterminate zone between two categories that seem to exist in opposition to one another. The following essays exemplify a wide range of scholarship devoted to exploring margins and liminal spaces of all kinds, and their methods might be loosely described as deconstructive. Deconstruction is a reading strategy designed to interrogate the logic of binary oppositions that have dominated western intellectual traditions by seeking points of pressure where those oppositions erode. As a method, it involves identifying a series of polarized terms within a given text, then showing how they break down and collapse into one another. Since such dichotomies as man/woman, white/black, west/east are inevitably asymmetrical, deconstruction calls into question the hierarchies that privilege one term over another. By extension, borders are gray areas where we can see continuities or fusion between categories that seem to be antithetical. Things look different from the margins, where two apparently opposed concepts may bifurcate into three, or an infinity of, possibilities.

The borders of particular interest in this section demarcate the insecure divisions between male and female, femininity and masculinity, heterosexual and homosexual, friend and sodomite. Beginning at the margins, these articles unsettle many of the assumptions that govern dominant understandings of masculinity. In each case, the category of masculinity, which aspires to permanence and universality, is destabilized by attention to its fraying borders. One border zone of particular interest is female masculinity. Judith Halberstam raises an important question about whether masculinity belongs first and foremost to men. She professes to find dominant forms of straight, white masculinity relatively uninteresting, turning instead to the margins where she locates such masculine women as butches, dykes, and androgynes. When female masculinity plays a part in lesbian relationships, men are written out of the equation altogether. By contrast, the Brazilian travesti studied by Don Kulick might be described in terms of male femininity. Male prostitutes who go to extreme measures to create feminine bodies, the travesti nonetheless continue to identify as men. Whereas anthropologists such as Roger Lancaster have carefully documented the differences between western and Latin American systems of sexuality, Kulick argues that far less attention has been paid to the complex range of gender roles necessary to understand the travesti. His fieldwork explores an intriguing context in which gender is divided not into male and female but "men" and "not men." Like Halberstam, Kulick's work shows how studying a marginal subculture can have broad implications for the organization of gender categories, revealing the need for a more expansive and culturally specific approach to masculinity.

A second implication of both arguments is that masculinity is not necessarily heterosexual. By introducing questions of masculinity into their analyses of same-sex relationships, Halberstam and Kulick both dramatically decouple masculinity from straight men. Alan Bray's essay provides a complimentary perspective by putting contemporary understandings of sexual identity into historical context. Somewhat counterintuitively, he proposes that the modern concept of homosexuality protects men who identify as straight by eliminating the possibility that their intimate male friendships might contain elements of erotic attraction. By contrast, the more indeterminate categories of friendship and sodomy in Elizabethan England created profound social anxiety that they might collapse into one another. Moreover, the broader connotations of the term "sodomite" during the Renaissance encompassed a range of "uncivil" activities that extended well beyond taboo sexual acts. According to Bray, the opposition between hetero and homo that presumes to explain an individual's sexual identity is a relatively recent innovation; historical perspective reveals that apparently fixed and permanent identitarian categories actually change over time.

Finally, these articles attempt to unsettle any firm opposition between masculine and feminine, the male and female body. The continuity between biological sex and gender performance is fundamental to Freud's theory of gender differentiation. According to Freud, anatomy is destiny, for gender is an effect of an individual perception of the body. In his memorable formulation, "the ego is first and foremost a bodily ego." Halberstam refutes this assumption by demonstrating that women may claim the attributes of masculinity. The distinction between sex and gender is important to her contention that someone who is biologically female can act as a man. Likewise, Kulick asserts that a man can continue to identify as such despite inhabiting a feminine body often attained through painful and dangerous means. While the bodies of the travesti stubbornly revert to maleness without constant vigilance, as Anne Fausto-Sterling's history of sexual ambiguity reveals, a surprising number of bodies are neither male nor female. Despite the fact that we live in a culture devoted to the idea that there are two sexes, bodies do not always oblige. Biology gives the lie to the cultural demand that a person be either male or female. Fausto-

Sterling provides historical evidence that the concept of sexual differentiation has changed over time; the contemporary dichotomy between male and female is not a universal constant, but a product of social norms that are reinforced by medical practice. At the same time, the masculinist biases of western culture have worked to assimilate and defuse the power of biological indeterminacy over the course of many centuries by forcing intersexed persons to choose one sex or another. She argues that patriarchal interests are upheld by science, which, instead of providing objective access to the truth of sex, employs methods and assumptions that reflect the values of the dominant culture. For example, in the nineteenth century when the proposition that all men are created equal threatened to overthrow the system of racial and gender division so important to the social order, the life sciences claimed to provide definitive proof that in fact some men were superior to others. Arguments for equality between the sexes were met by physicians' insistence on the hierarchical division between male and female. Turning scientific evidence back onto the scientists themselves, Fausto-Sterling documents how gender ambiguity has been erased from history in order to maintain the patriarchal authority premised on a system of sexual difference.

By looking to the borders between men and women, masculinity and femininity, heterosexuality and homosexuality these critics reveal instabilities and fractures in apparently fixed dichotomies. Not only do they privilege the terms that have typically been treated as uninteresting and inferior, but they show the inadequacy of the oppositions themselves. Perhaps the most valuable lesson contained in these essays is about the variability of the human body and its erotic proclivities, which cannot be contained by rigid identitarian categories. Borders are the place where we find a multitude of alternatives, as well as the critical arsenal to deconstruct the oppositions upon which hegemonic masculinities are erected.

Bibliography

Derrida, Jacques. 1976. *Of Grammatology* [1967], trans. Gayatri Chakravorty Spivak. Baltimore: Johns Hopkins University Press.

Freud, Sigmund. 1923. *The Ego and the Id*. Standard Edition of the Complete Psychological Works of Sigmund Freud, trans. James Strachey, vol. 19. London: Hogarth Press.

Laplanche, Jean and Pontalis, J. B. 1973. *The Language of Psychoanalysis* [1967], trans. Donald Nicholson-Smith. London: Hogarth Press.

Silverman, Kaja. 1992. *Male Subjectivity at the Margins*. New York and London: Routledge.

19

Homosexuality and the Signs of Male Friendship in Elizabethan England

Alan Bray

Dreams, Fantasies, and Fears

This essay is a commentary on two images that exercised a compelling grip on the imagination of sixteenth-century England, if the many references to them are a reliable guide to its dreams and fears. One is the image of the masculine friend. The other is the figure called the sodomite. The reaction these two images prompted was wildly different; the one was universally admired, the other execrated and feared: and yet in their uncompromising symmetry they paralleled each other in an uncanny way. Why this was and what it tells us of early modern England is what I have set out to explore here.

This symmetry appears among the shadows, on the edge of social life, in the fears and fantasies of Elizabethan England. But I shall argue that if we press it we will quickly emerge into the daylight, in the very center of early modern England. But we will go by a road, which I hope to lay open in this essay, which the Elizabethans themselves were unwilling to acknowledge was there.

The Sodomite

Elizabethan society was one of those which lacked the idea of a distinct homosexual minority, although homosexuality was nonetheless regarded with a readily expressed horror. In principle it was a crime which anyone was capable of, like murder or blasphemy. This is the New England minister Thomas Shepard in his *The Sincere Convert* of 1641:

> Thy heart is a foul sink of all atheism, sodomy, blasphemy, murder, whoredom, adultery, witchcraft, buggery; so that, if thou hast any good thing in thee, it is but as a drop of rosewater in a bowl of poison; where fallen it is all corrupted.

Reprinted from *Queering the Renaissance*, ed. Jonathan Goldberg (Durham: Duke University Press, 1994), pp. 40–54, 56–61.

It is true thou feelest not all these things stirring in thee at one time . . . but they are in thee like a nest of snakes in an old hedge. Although they break not out into thy life, they lie lurking in thy heart.

It was, according to John Rainolds, not only a "monstrous sin against nature" but also one to which "men's natural corruption and viciousness is prone." It is why it was sometimes attributed to drunkenness and why a sixteenth-century minister accused of sodomy said when first confronted that what he had done he had done in his sleep. The logic is the same as that of Thomas Shepard. It was not part of the individual's nature: it was part of all human nature and could surface when the mind was dulled or sleeping, much as someone might commit murder in a drunken fit or in a dream.[1]

But the Elizabethan "sodomy" differed from our contemporary idea of "homosexuality" in a number of other ways also. It covered more hazily a whole range of sexual acts, of which sexual acts between people of the same sex were only a part. It was closer, rather, to an idea like debauchery. But it differed more fundamentally also in that it was not only a sexual crime. It was also a political and a religious crime and it was this that explains most clearly why it was regarded with such dread, and it is this point that I propose to investigate.

One can see this sharply outlined in the accusations made in Elizabeth's reign against the rebellious nobleman Edward de Vere by his erstwhile fellow conspirators. The picture they draw is of a man who was not only a sodomite but also an enemy of society: a traitor and a man given to lawless violence against his enemies. He was also, they tell us, a habitual liar, an atheist, and a blasphemer. The charge of sodomy was not merely added to the list. It symbolized it. If this man was a rebel against nature, was it surprising that he was also a rebel against society and the truth (or the Truth) that supported it? Sodomy, the jurist Edward Coke wrote, was "crimen laesae majestatis, a sin horrible committed against the king: and this is either against the king celestial or terrestrial." It was one of those horrible crimes according to James I that a king was bound in conscience never to forgive. It was in this way that the ubiquitous association of sodomy with treason and heresy was put together and why one encounters it so commonly in the polemics of Reformation Europe.[2]

The Masculine Friend

The image of the masculine friend was an image of intimacy between men in stark contrast to the forbidden intimacy of homosexuality. It is an image which will be very familiar to students of Elizabethan poetry and drama, where it frequently appears; but the image there is misleading, for when we see how it was used in the tumble of daily life we see something more immediately practical than the literary images at first glance reveal. The "voices of yourselves, your tenants and such other friends as you can procure" was how a northern landowner was asked for his support in an election early in the seventeenth century. "It were pity to lose him" wrote an Elizabethan commander in the Low Countries about the possible loss of an influential supporter "for he is indeed marvelously friended."[3]

It is in this way we see the word *friend* being used in such mundane documents, and behind it is a web of social relations which will be recognized readily by students of Elizabethan society. What it points to is that network of subtle bonds amongst influential patrons and their clients, suitors, and friends at court.

A concept so necessary to social life was far removed from the "uncivil" image of the sodomite, yet there was still between them a surprising affinity, as in some respects they occupied a similar terrain. An illustration of this is the way each required a physical closeness, although after four centuries have passed it is perhaps not immediately obvious how crucial this was to the way friendship worked. One striking expression of this is what it meant in early modern England to be someone's "bedfellow." This was a society where most people slept with someone else and where the rooms of a house led casually one into the other and servants mingled with their masters. Such a lack of privacy usually made who shared a bed with whom into a public fact. It was also a potentially meaningful one, for beds are not only places where people sleep: they are also places where people talk. To be someone's "bedfellow" suggested that one had influence and could be the making of a fortune.

It is in that sense that the Countess of Oxford used the word when she complained about the influence a certain John Hunt was exercising over her son: "Hunt hath impudently presumed to be his bedfellow and otherwise used him most unrespectively." Anne Bacon uses "bed-companion" in the same sense in a letter to Anthony Bacon in 1594: "Your brother...keepeth that bloody Pérez, as I told him then, yea as a coach-companion and bed-companion." But the most striking illustration I know of is an entry Archbishop Laud made in his diary in August 1625: "That night in a dream the Duke of Buckingham seemed to me to ascend into my bed, where he carried himself with much love towards me, after such rest wherein wearied men are wont exceedingly to rejoice; and likewise many seemed to me to enter the chamber who did see this." Archbishop Laud's dream is of his patron the great Duke of Buckingham but the point of the dream is in its conclusion, that the powerful mark of favor he was dreaming of was public. It is in this sense also that we should read the now famous remark of George Villiers when he looked back with gratitude in a letter to James I, to that night when first "the bed's head could not be found between the master and his dog."[4]

The common bed shared in the public eye was only one expression of this. When two men kissed or embraced, the gesture had the same meaning. "But I doubt not so soon as his name shall come into the knowledge of men and his worthiness be sounded in the trump of fame, but that he shall be not only kissed but also beloved of all, embraced of the most, and wondered at of the best." That is the editor of the *Shepheardes Calender* in 1579 introducing its hopeful author, and such a public kiss carried the same meaning as the equally public fact of being a powerful man's bedfellow. At the beginning of Davenant's play *The Cruel Brother* of 1627, one of the characters points to just such public embraces as evidence of a certain Lucio's influence with the duke; and it is in such terms that Thomas Howard recorded Robert Carr's rise to power at the court of James I: "The Prince leaneth on his arm, pinches his cheek, smooths his ruffled garment...We are almost worn out in our endeavours to keep pace with this fellow in his duty and labour to gain favour, but all in vain; where it endeth I cannot guess, but honours are talked of speedily for him." This publicly displayed intimacy is part of what Francis Bacon in his essay

Of Followers and Friends called "countenance," the appearance of a patron's evident favor; and its withdrawal could mean ruin. This is what Henry Howard later advised the now greatly powerful Robert Carr: "There is no better way to pare their nails...than by some withdrawing of your favourable countenance, which I do assure you is a groundyard to their boldness and a discharge of many watchful ears and eyes."[5]

Such kisses and embraces were for such "watchful ears and eyes" as these, as was the common bed Archbishop Laud dreamed of; but the physical intimacy they expressed was not the only sign of a friendship between two men that was recognized by the Elizabethans. It was expected to be matched by an equivalent emotional bond, and this had a part in the conventions of friendship as deep as the physical intimacy I have been describing. One can see this at length in the letters written by Antonio Pérez, the renegade secretary of Philip II, while he was part of the circle around the Earl of Essex during his visit to England in the 1590s. Love between men is the theme of these letters, which are suffused by an understood emotional attachment both between Essex and his servants and among them. Typical of many more is the letter in which a mere note arranging a meeting in the morning becomes an elaborate reflection, as moving now as it was then, on the nature of one man's desire for another. We should not be misled, though, by Pérez's neoplatonic decorations: this is in essence the same language that a great earl uses when he signs a stern note to one of his clients "Your loving master" or a great lord when he closes a message with the injunction to love this messenger, adding significantly that the recipient of the letter should also receive its bearer into his protection. In these letters Pérez was merely using the ubiquitous convention.[6]

One might well wonder, of course, how genuine were such expressions of affection. Antonio Pérez was a man on the make, and those he scattered about rarely convince. But one can see alongside his friendships others which had all the utilitarian functions the Elizabethans expected of friendship and yet did contain within them obviously genuine emotion. The correspondence of Michael Hickes, the patronage secretary of Lord Burghley, and his friend John Stubbe in the Lansdowne Manuscripts is one of these. We see Michael Hickes putting out money on John Stubbe's behalf. We see him trying to obtain payment of a debt due to him. We also see Stubbe asking Hickes to use his influence on behalf of a friend. But these letters document also an intense personal friendship which began when they were students together in Cambridge and in its time included both passion and jealousy. In 1570 we see Hickes writing Stubbe an emotional and jealous letter complaining of his friendship with a friend of their Lincoln's Inn days. Which of the two, he asks angrily, do you love the best? And one can see from a teasing letter Stubbe sent him in 1575 that he was still prickly about the friendship several years later. There are also in these letters evident expressions of affection in quieter times and a glimpse in a late letter of Stubbe of that youth, as he put it, that they spent together.[7] ...

Emotional bonds such as these had their place alongside the physical links of friendship, but in contrast these were directed inward to the participants themselves, not outward to the world at large. They were an assurance that their friendship would remain, in good fortune or bad: a sign and a telling guarantee that they could indeed rely on each other.

Such comments give us a vantage point from which to judge the elegant garments in which friendship was often dressed in Elizabethan England, as much in its daily use as in a poem or a play or a piece of imaginative literature. Typical of the carefully beautiful manner in which it was usually presented is the picture of Euphues's friendship with his friend Philautus in John Lyly's Elizabethan novel *Euphues*:

> But after many embracings and protestations one to another they walked to dinner, where they wanted neither meat, neither music, neither any other pastime; and having banqueted, to digest their sweet confections they danced all that afternoon. They used not only one board but one bed, one book (if so be it they thought not one too many). Their friendship augmented every day, insomuch that the one could not refrain the company of the other one minute. All things went in common between them, which all men accounted commendable.

This is idealized, of course; and there are literary echoes here, especially of Cicero's essay on friendship, *De Amicitia*, and of the numerous ornate treatises on love which popularized Ciceronian and neoplatonic ideas on friendship. Indeed, the same could be said of all the letters between friends I have referred to. But when one looks at the details of this account one sees something surprisingly more mundane. Its material is made up virtually entirely of the conventions I have been writing of: the embraces and the protestations of love, the common bed and the physical closeness, the physical and emotional intimacy. All had their ready parallels in the accustomed conventions of Elizabethan friendship. Its idealization consisted rather in what it left out: its tactful omission of those bonds of mutual interest of which the everyday signs were such conventions. The engaging artifice is part of a tough reality, and the realistic comment to set by it is that of Francis Bacon at the end of his essay on followers and friends when he says that such friendship as there is in this world is in truth between those who have the same material interests, those "whose fortunes" as he puts it "may comprehend the one the other."[8]

But John Lyly was fully right to declare such intimacy to be accepted by all. There was no suggestion at all about it of the possible signs of a sodomitical relationship. When William Prynne edited Archbishop Laud's diary he tried to read into it the sodomitical sin one would expect of the papist in heart that Prynne presented him as being, but when he came to his dream of sleeping with the Duke of Buckingham he merely transcribed it. Its meaning was too obvious to do otherwise. And one would be greatly mistaken to assume a softness toward sodomy on the part of these writers. Sodomy for Tobie Matthew was one of "those crimes which are against nature...ever to be detested and punished," and the sodomite for John Lyly was "a most dangerous and infectious beast." So also when Antonio del Corro preached in London on the sin of the sodomites in Paul's letter to the Romans he elaborated the horror of the sin with all the exuberance of a popular preacher.[9]

The great distance between sodomy and friendship and the nature of that distance is well illustrated by a sodomitical joke Antonio Pérez includes in one of his letters to the Earl of Essex, in which he likens himself to the girlfriend of his newly arrived assistant. One can see that this is a joke but it seems rather a dangerous one, for the Inquisition charged Pérez with being a sodomite as well as a heretic and a traitor; and yet it was quite out of character for him to have added fuel to the charge by a rash remark. But how rash was this remark? The joke rested securely on a real distinction between the joke itself and the actuality. It turned the world upside down. In it, it is the patron who becomes the conventionally weaker part and the servant the powerful: it is Pérez and not the servant who becomes the girl. That was why the joke was only a joke and not to be taken seriously.[10]

In the same way, how seriously could one then take the apparent similarity between the sodomite and the masculine friend? The signs of the one were indeed sometimes also the signs of the other, but the conventions of friendship were set a world away from the wild sin of Sodom by the placid orderliness of the relationships they expressed. The anarchic crime of which Edward Coke wrote was a clearly different thing.

An Unnatural Intimacy

The distinction between the two kinds of intimacy was then apparently sharp and clearly marked: the one was expressed in orderly "civil" relations, the other in subversive; and this simple distinction explains a good deal of what we see. But it does not explain quite all. On occasion one can also come across a document that appears – against all our expectations – to be putting the two together and reading a sodomitical meaning by such a monstrous image into just those conventions of friendship which elsewhere seemed protected from that interpretation.

Rare though they are, these documents are not to be dismissed as mere curiosities, and I propose to look at two such documents closely, for they suggest that this distinction was neither as sharp nor as clearly marked as the Elizabethans would have us believe. They cast by this an unexpectedly bright light on that hidden road I mentioned: the unacknowledged connection between the unmentionable vice of Sodom and the friendship which all accounted commendable.

One of these two documents is a denunciation made in 1601 by a paid informer by the name of William Reynolds, whose subject was a certain Piers Edmonds, a soldier who had been in Ireland with the Earl of Southampton before Southampton joined Essex's ill-fated rebellion of that year. Piers Edmonds, he implies, was likely to have been a rebel as his master had been; and into this implication William Reynolds weaves a story of an unnatural intimacy between the two men that told its own tale.

> I do marvel also what became of Piers Edmonds, called Captain Piers or Captain Edmonds, the Earl of Essex man, born in Strand near me, one which has had many rewards and preferments by the Earl Essex. His villainy I have often complained of.
>
> He dwells in London. He was corporal general of the horse in Ireland under the Earl of Southampton. He ate and drank at his table and lay in his tent. The Earl of Southampton gave him a horse which Edmonds refused a hundred marks for him. The Earl Southampton would coll [embrace] and hug him in his arms and play wantonly with him.
>
> This Piers began to fawn and flatter me in Ireland, offering me great courtesy, telling me what pay, graces and gifts the earls bestowed upon him, thereby seeming to

move and animate me to desire and look for the like favour. But I could never love and affect them to make them my friends, especially Essex, whose mind I ever mistrusted.

Behind this account is the familiar Elizabethan stereotype that the man guilty of "unnatural filthiness" would be also very likely a traitor. But the evidence William Reynolds points to so menacingly – the common tent in which they slept, the embraces William Reynolds saw – were all the conventional signs of friendship; and that the characters in this drama understood them in this way is strongly suggested by the openness of Piers Edmonds's boasting and the public nature of these embraces, for they must indeed have been public if someone like William Reynolds could have been a witness of them.[11]

A document such as this poses an interesting question about what its author is doing, but first the other such document I mentioned. This works in a similar way but is far more famous. The relationship of Edward and Gaveston in Marlowe's play *Edward II* is of a piece with all that I have said of friendship and is the spectacular center of the play, in that it is Edward's love for Gaveston and Gaveston's rise to power which prompt the rebellion of Edward's resentful nobles and his ensuing tragedy and death. Modern critics of the play have recognized that its conventions are those of sixteenth-century, not fourteenth-century, England. But the many who have written of the apparently openly "homosexual" nature of the play have not grasped its irony or that the intense emotion, the passionate language, and the embraces we see between these two men have ready parallels in Elizabethan England in the daily conventions of friendship without being signs of a sodomitical relationship.[12]

When we look for signs of overt sexuality, what we see are rather Edward as a father and his determination to marry Gaveston to his niece. The latter is no incidental detail, nor is it an accident that she is referred to quite simply as the king's niece, as her role is to unite Gaveston and Edward as well as to give Gaveston a wife. . . .

Yet there are in the relationship of Edward and Gaveston dark suggestions of sodomy. It is there in the sexual ambiguity of the opening. When the naked and lovely boy in Gaveston's entertainment for Edward holds a bush "to hide those parts which men delight to see" is it the body of the boy which is being hidden or of the goddess he is playing? It is there in the later comparison of Gaveston to the classical Ganymede, the beautiful youth caught up by Zeus to be his cupbearer. Giles Fletcher could compare Christ's ascension without embarrassment to the fate of Ganymede, but a "ganymede" was also used more crudely as a synonym for a catamite. It is there also in Gaveston's foreign birth and Italianate ways, both of which were associated in Elizabethan England with sodomy. It is there most clearly but most disturbingly in the hideous sodomitical murder of Edward at the end of the play. Yet this one clear statement of Edward's sodomitical sin is put in the hands of a man called Lightborne, whose name is but an Anglicized echo of Lucifer, the father of all lies.[13]

Marlowe describes in this play what could be a sodomitical relationship, but he places it wholly within the incompatible conventions of Elizabethan friendship, in a tension which he never allows to be resolved. The image we see is simultaneously that of both friendship and its caricature.

A Changing Context

Such unlikely texts as these of William Reynolds's denunciation and Christopher Marlowe's play prompt the same question. These texts appear to be bringing together images which were usually kept quite detached from each other. Why, we might well then ask, did their authors think they would be believed? The answer casts a light on the society in which these documents were put together quite as much as it does on the documents themselves. The answer in short is this. As a contemporary would have seen far more readily than we do, some of the conventions of friendship are missing in these accounts and the missing ones are precisely those that ensured that the intimacy of these conventions was read in an acceptable frame of reference; but they were not only missing in these accounts: by the end of the sixteenth century they were also often missing in society at large. It is this that these documents point up.

One of these conventions was the assumption that both masters and their close servingmen would be "gentle," men (as a work published in 1598 entitled *A Health to the Gentlemanly Profession of Seruingmen* puts it) "made of their own metal, even a loaf of their own dough, which being done ... the gentleman received even a gentleman into his service." It is this missing propriety that William Reynolds indirectly alludes to when he describes Piers Edmonds as a man born in the Strand "near me"; another description of Piers Edmonds puts it more bluntly as, "a man of base birth," and the nobles' frequently repeated complaints of Gaveston's "base" birth in *Edward II* make the same point.[14]

A second assumption which is missing is that the bond between a master and such an intimate servingman was personal, not mercenary. Such a servant did not seek a reward, although both master and servant would rightly care for the interests of the other. Rather the relationship was like that of father and son, to which it was habitually compared. ... It is this missing assumption which William Reynolds alludes to in the damning commentary he quietly adds to Piers Edmonds's boasting, beginning with that simple but all important participle "seeming to move and animate me to desire and look for the like favour." His motives were as base as his origins; that is what William Reynolds indirectly is telling his reader.[15]

Gaveston's motives are as suspect as William Reynolds would have us believe Piers Edmonds's were. The opening scene in the play makes that all too clear, as does the image Marlow later has him unconsciously lapse into. It begins with the same – eminently proper – sentiment which Antonio Pérez's servant professed. Its end is brutally different:

> It shall suffice me to enjoy your love,
> Which whiles I have I think myself as great
> As Caesar riding in the Roman streets
> With captive kings at his triumphant car.[16]

The absence of these two reassuring conventions left what remained open to a darker interpretation. What then was it that one was seeing? If someone had acquired a place in society to which he was not entitled by nature and could then perhaps even lord it over those who were naturally his betters, the specter likely to be conjured up in the mind of an Elizabethan was not the orderly relationship of friendship between men but rather the profoundly disturbing image of the sodomite, that enemy not only of nature but of the order of society and the proper kinds and divisions within it. Perhaps, it darkly suggested, it was the signs of *this* that one was seeing? It is this fear that William Reynolds and Christopher Marlowe played on with such skill.

Such documents warn one against making a mistake one might otherwise easily fall into; they clarify that what one is seeing in such a structure of ideas as I have described is not a collective and automatic mentality, of any kind. It is rather a kind of code: the difference between the two lay in that a code was something individuals were still free to manipulate. They may not have done it very often, but the possibility of consciously manipulating the signs of this code, for their own benefit, was always there; and it is not an accident that the two clearest examples I have seen were created by authors whose task was to shape and manipulate meaning: to tell tales.

But this was not merely sleight of hand, and it is this that makes these documents so revealing. These two authors were able to present such credible pictures precisely because the conventions which were so crucially absent in these accounts were also in practice often absent in daily life. It was because contemporaries were often *not* following the ideals of service that Elizabethans wrote their tracts expounding them, as the tracts themselves make clear. A master looking for a useful servant might well prefer the industrious servant who was poor but able and anxious to better himself to the better born one, and the protestations of disinterested service one reads so frequently were often hollow. After the pious protestations of the secretary of Antonio Pérez I quoted earlier, he then coldly sets about adding up how much he is likely to make through his master's influence. Hardly more convincing are the protestations of affection for his dearest friends with which his master himself recommends various rich merchants to the Earl of Essex.[17] . . .

Such cynicism was probably always likely to have been justified, but there is something wider at work here also. A broad hint of this is given in the *Health to the Gentlemanly Profession of Seruingman*, which I quoted from earlier. The decay in the conventions of service, its author tells us, was something that he could still describe. The Lisle letters support that judgment; in them we see the conventions of personal service still very much alive in the 1530s. Why then the change? According to the anonymous author of this work, the change was brought about by the decline in the open-handed "housekeeping" of the great house. It was also due, he tells us, to the replacement of gentlemen retainers by servants drawn from outside the gentry, a change which was referred to by Walter Darell in his conduct book for servingmen published in 1572. The gentleman servingman was being replaced by the gentry with "the rich farmer's son," as Darell puts it, a man who will "drudge in their business."[18]

Behind these complaints lies the sixteenth-century decline in the hordes of retainers in the great houses of an earlier and different England and the conventions of personal service associated with them, a change these tracts closely document. Such great households were by no means extinct in Elizabeth's reign. Lord Burghley was still able to say that it was his disease to have too many servants although there was little he could do about it, and early in the following century we still see the Earl of Northampton taking into his household the sons of his gentry supporters. But servingmen like these were increasingly an anachronism. The able and hard-working secretaries of the Earl of Essex or Lord Burghley, men such as Michael Hickes (who was the son of a mercer), were altogether more suited to their times.[19]

As a social form the personal service of early Tudor England was in decay by the end of the sixteenth century, but as a cultural form it was not; here the language of "friendship," as a set of assumptions and expectations, was still very much alive. There was, though, now a disparity between the two in precisely those elements that protected the intimacy it involved from a charge of sodomy, and it was this that provided a convenient inlet to charges of the kind that were laid at the prison door of the Earl of Southampton and the hapless Piers Edmonds. William Reynolds's account and the picture Christopher Marlowe gives in *Edward II* are in fact more accurate pictures of the ties of friendship in the late sixteenth century than the conventional ideal the Elizabethans were still apt to present, and it was this fact that made these descriptions so frighteningly effective.

The Weapon

To take William Reynolds's allegations as evidence of a covert sexual relationship is to follow a phantom, cunningly made. But they do put in a different light many of the changes of homosexuality we see in early modern England. We cannot say whether there was a sexual relationship between Piers Edmonds and the Earl of Southampton, and the malice of their accuser should make us cautious; but to leave the matter there is to miss the nature of such accusations. They did not need such a sexual relationship. They turned rather on a sharp-eyed recognition that the public signs of a male friendship – open to all the world to see – could be read in a different and sodomitical light to the one intended. But although we cannot say whether there was a sexual relationship between the Earl of Southampton and the man who served under him in Ireland as corporal general of the horse, we can see within the accusation a familiar social outline. This relationship is not alone in that. It is true also of a good many others: of Charles I's bishop John Atherton and Atherton's proctor, who were accused of sodomy in 1640 at the onset of the ruin of the Caroline church; of the Casiodoro de Reina mentioned earlier and the servant who shared his bed, with whom he was accused of sodomy in a tale spread by his enemies in the émigré community; of the popish Earl of Castlehaven, who in 1631, in a prosecution full of anti-Catholic prejudice, was accused of sodomy with his servants; and, indeed, of James I in the famous accusations made against him and companions such as Robert Carr or the Duke of Buckingham. We will misunderstand these accusations if, beguiled by them, we uncritically assume the existence of the sexual relationship which they appear to point to, for the material from which they could be constructed was rather open and public to all. What such accusations have in common is rather the outline of a relationship which at other times an Elizabethan might have called friendship.[20]

This is not to say that they were always inventions. Homosexual relationships did indeed occur within social contexts which an Elizabethan would have called friendship, between masters and servants included. But accusations like those of William Reynolds are not evidence of it; and the ease with which he was able to make his case out of the most everyday of materials should make us wary. We see in them rather the unwelcome difficulty the Elizabethans had in drawing a dividing line between those gestures of closeness among men that they desired so much and those they feared.[21]

But to call someone a sodomite was to do more than invite public censure on what was thought of as a private vice. Its effect involved incomparably more than that. . . .

. . . If [a] man was a sodomite, then was he not likely in all his doings to be the enemy of God's good order, in society as well as in nature? That was the transubstantiation it brought about. It could turn what seemed like gifts into bribes and what seemed like patronage into the support of infamy; it revealed what they really were. If successful, it turned all to ruin, and it could work its alchemy by a manipulation of the signs of friendship which it found so ready to hand.

The Shadow in the Garden

Perhaps there is always a potential ambiguity about intimacy between men. It may be so. But in early modern England such intimacy was peculiarly ambivalent, for the protecting conventions that ensured that it was seen in an acceptable frame of reference were often absent by the end of the sixteenth century. It was a disturbing fact that the Elizabethans preferred not to acknowledge, but when it suited them it provided a weapon that lay close to hand; and it left this intimacy more open and less secure in its meaning than the formal Elizabethan essays on friendship would have us believe.

The ambiguity drew, though, on a tension in Elizabethan England we are not now accustomed to. The intimacy between men in Europe and in North America today is protected to a large extent by the notion of a quite distinct homosexual minority for whom alone homosexual desire is a possibility. This was a shield Elizabethan England did not have and we might well wonder if this cultural difference is the reason why later historians have been so blind to the fearsome weapon its absence provided.

I am inclined to think that it is, but whether or not this is so I would suggest that the study in this essay of the Elizabethan sin of Sodom places it outside a discrete history of sexuality; its shadow was never far from the flower-strewn world of Elizabethan friendship and it could never wholly be distinguished from it. A hard fact which those of power and influence in Elizabethan England preferred not to see; but they were willing, still, to make use of it.

Notes

This article first appeared in *History Workshop Journal* 29 (Spring 1990): 1–19 . . . A shorter version was given at the conference "Homosexuality, Which Homosexuality?" at the Free University of Amsterdam in December 1987 and at the seminar "Society, Belief, and Culture in the Early Modern World" at the Institute of Historical Research; I am grateful to the participants there for their lively discussions of it, which have greatly influenced its final form. Jeremy Clarke, Anna Davin, and others also kindly read the first draft of the essay. I owe a particular debt also to Michel Rey, from whom over many years of discussions I have learned so much of the history of friendship.

1 Thomas Shepard, *The Works of Thomas Shepard* (Boston: Doctrinal Tract and Book Society, 1853), 1: 28, included in the collection of documents of Jonathan Ned Katz, *Gay/Lesbian Almanac* (New York: Harper and Row, 1983), pp. 82–4. "Sodomy" and "buggery" were overlapping (and equally vague). The first was the scholarly word, the second the vulgar, which Shepard is here using for emphasis. John Rainolds, *Th' Overthrow of Stage-Playes* (1599), pp. 10 and 32. Alan Bray, *Homosexuality in Renaissance England* (London: Gay Men's Press and Gay Men's Press Publishers, 1982 and 1988), p. 16. This is cited below as Bray, *Homosexuality*; in each case the page references are the same to each edition. Arthur G. Kinder, *Casiodoro de Reina: Spanish Reformer of the Sixteenth Century* (London: Tamesis Books, 1975), pp. 28, 29, 105, 107, 109. Quotations (here and elsewhere in this essay) are modernized and are given according to the rules in Bray, *Homosexuality*, p. 115; documents not in English are given in translation.

2 Public Record Office, State Papers, 12/151/100–102, 103–104v, 109–109v, 113–113v, 118–119v, and British Museum, Cotton MSS, Titus C VI/5ff. "Nature" here is the order of creation: that in "men's natural corruption" in the quotation from Rainolds is the nature given us by Adam's Fall. Edward Coke, *Twelfth Part of the Reports* (1656), 37. James VI (and I), Βασιλικὸν δῶρον (1887), pp. 37–8. Buggery was usually excluded from a general pardon: J. A. Sharpe, *Crime in Seventeenth-Century England: A County Study* (Cambridge: Cambridge University Press, 1983), pp. 147 and 257. The explanation given in this section of the nature of the "sodomite" in Elizabethan England is set out more fully in Bray, *Homosexuality*, pp. 13–32. There is a criticism of the apparently functionalist form I gave to my analysis in chapter 4 of *Homosexuality*, in Eve Kosofsky Sedgwick, *Between Men: English Literature and Male Homosocial Desire* (New York: Columbia University Press, 1985), pp. 83ff. There is also a careful criticism of my handling of Richard Barnfield's writings in Jonathan Goldberg, "Colin to Hobbinol: Spenser's Familiar Letters," *South Atlantic Quarterly* 88, no. 1 (1989): 107–26. Each of these anticipated in some ways the development in my thinking apparent in this essay, and I would warmly commend them.

3 John K. Gruenfelder, "The Electoral Patronage of Sir Thomas Wentworth, Earl of Strafford, 1614–1640," *Journal of Modern History* 49/4 (1977): p. 557. British Museum, Harl. MSS, 285/173, in John Bruce, ed., *Correspondence of Robert Dudley, Earl of Leycester* (1844), p. 33.

4 Public Record Office, State Papers, 14/65/78 ("unrespectively": disrespectfully). Lambeth Palace Library, 653/318, in Gustav Ungerer, *A Spaniard in Elizabethan England: The Correspondence of Antonio Pérez's Exile* (London: Tamesis Books, 1974 and 1976), 1: 219; he rightly corrects the transcription by James Spedding which I followed in *Homosexuality*, p. 49. James Bliss, ed., *The Works of . . . William Laud* (1853), 3: 170. I have followed William Prynne's translation in *A Breviate of the Life of William Laud* (1644), p. 6; compare Charles Carlton, *Archbishop William Laud* (London and New York: Routledge and Kegan Paul, 1987), p. 152. Longleat House, Portland Papers, 2/44, in Historical Manuscripts Commission, *Calendar of the Manuscripts of the Marquis of Bath* (Dublin, 1907), 2: 71; compare Roger Lockyer, *Buckingham: The Life and Political Career of George Villiers, First Duke of Buckingham, 1592–1628* (London: Longman, 1981), p. 22.

5 Edwin Greenlaw and others, eds., *The Works of Edmund Spenser. A Variorum Edition: The Minor Poems* (Baltimore: Johns Hopkins University Press, 1943), 1: 7. James Maidment and W. H. Logan, eds., *The Dramatic Works of Sir William Davenant* (Edinburgh, 1872), 1: 119–20. Linda Levy Peck, *Northampton: Patronage and Policy at the Court*

of James I (London: George Allen and Unwin, 1982), p. 30. Edward Arber, ed., *A Harmony of the Essays etc of Francis Bacon* (1871), pp. 32–3. Peck, *Northampton*, p. 36.

6 Ungerer, *A Spaniard in Elizabethan England*, especially the letters in the first volume, and Antonio Pérez, *Ant. Perezii ad Comitem Essexium...Epistolarvm. Centuria Vna* in *Cartas de A Perez* (Paris, n.d.); the reference here is to Epistola 75 in the latter. S. L. Adams, "The Gentry of North Wales and the Earl of Leicester's Expedition to the Netherlands, 1585–86," *Welsh History Review* 7/2 (1974–5): 147. Ungerer, *A Spaniard in Elizabethan England*, 1: 417 ("protection": patrocinium).

7 British Museum, Lansdowne MSS, 12/217–217v and 23/179–179v; 107/168–168v; 61/170 (see also 31/40); 12/217–217v (see also 12/117–117v); 21/26; 36/212– 213 (generally see also 25/135 and 107/170–170v). Discussed in Alan G. R. Smith, *Servant of the Cecils: The Life of Sir Michael Hickes, 1543–1612* (London: Jonathan Cape, 1977), pp. 22, 70, 92–6....

8 R. W. Bond, ed., *The Complete Works of John Lyly*, vol. 1 (Oxford, 1902), p. 199. Arber, *Essays of Francis Bacon*, pp. 38–9. This is not to contrast literary with other sources. The same point could be made, in varying degrees, with all the images of friendship.

9 Prynne, *Breviate of the Life of Laud* (1644), p. 6; compare p. 29. *The Confessions of the Incomparable Doctor S. Augustine*, trans. Tobie Matthew (1620), pp. 108–9. Bond, ed., *Works of John Lyly* (1902), 1: 280; this is an addition John Lyly made during his paraphrase of Plutarch (*Plutarch's Moralia*, with translation by F. C. Babbitt, vol. 1, 1927, pp. 54–5). One can see the expressions added to the biblical text in Corro's paraphrase of *Romans* 1: 26–7 in Antonius Corranus, *Dialogvs Theologicvs*, 1574 (English translation Antonie Corranus, *A Theological Dialogve*, 1575) and in Antonius Corranus, *Dialogvs in Epistolam D Pauli ad Romanos*, Frankfurt, 1587, and Antonius Corranus, *Epistola Beati Pavli Apostoli ad Romanos*, 1581, in which Corro gathered his lectures together for publication.

10 Published by Pérez in *Ant. Perezii ad Comitem Essexium*, n.d., as Epistola 60. The original is given in Ungerer, *A Spaniard in Elizabethan England*, 1: 424–5 (which probably would have circulated in manuscript as a literary exercise).

As often in Pérez's writings there is an obscurity here and more than one reading is possible, but the dangerous reading I have given it is certainly one of these possible readings. He was careful to avoid the charge that he was a heretic by the permission he obtained when he visited England to practice catholicism. Ungerer, *A Spaniard in Elizabethan England*, 1: 145. Why would he have taken a different attitude to the charge that he was a sodomite? The one was the mere reflection of the other.

The Inquisition's charges of sodomy are set out in *Colección de Documentos Inéditos para la Historia de España*, vol. 12, D. Miguel Salvá and Pedro Sainz de Baranda, eds., *Documentos Relativos á Antonio Pérez* (Madrid, 1848), pp. 224–36, 255–9, 400–1, and G. Marañon, *Antonio Pérez* (Madrid, 1948), 1: 306–9 and vol. 2, appendix no. 26. See also 1: 310–11. The independent nature of much of this evidence strongly suggests that in this case it was true.

11 Hatfield House, Cecil Papers, 83/62. The letters from Piers Edmonds at 90/76 and 90/77 contain more information about him. Calendared in Historical Manuscripts Commission, *Calendar of the Manuscripts of the Most Hon. the Marquis of Salisbury*, part II, 1906, pp. 93–4 and 99. I have emended the "called Called" of the text and omitted the illegible (or deleted) word that follows.

12 Some critics have read the apparently homosexual relationship as an affirmation of humane values, for example Leonora L. Brodwin, "Edward II: Marlowe's Culminating Treatment of Love," *ELH* 31/2 (1964): 139–55, or Purvis E. Boyette, "Wanton Humour and Wanton Poets: Homosexuality in Marlowe's Edward II," *Tulane Studies in English* 22 (1977): 33–50, or Ronald Huebert, "Tobacco and Boys and Marlowe," *Sewanee Review* 92/2 (1984): 206–24. Others have read it as an obscenity, such as

Wilbur Sanders, *The Dramatist and the Received Idea: Studies in the Plays of Marlowe and Shakespeare* (Cambridge: Cambridge University Press, 1968), pp. 121–42, or William L. Godshalk, *The Marlovian World Picture* (The Hague: Mouton, 1974), pp. 59ff. But the assumption is widespread in what has been written of the play that the play *does* deal with an openly homosexual relationship. The importance of L. J. Mills's early but neglected discussion of the role of friendship in the play has not been fully appreciated: "The Meaning of Edward II," *Modern Philology* 32/1 (1934–35): 11–31; Mills missed the contemporary social and political meaning of "friendship" but he was on the right lines. Another neglected early clue was the importance of caricature in the writings of Marlowe that T. S. Eliot pointed to in his 1919 essay "Christopher Marlowe" (*Selected Essays* (London: Faber and Faber, 1951), pp. 118–25). More recently Simon Shepherd and Jonathan Goldberg have discussed sensitively the language of sodomy in *Edward II* and the Baines note (Simon Shepherd, *Marlowe and the Politics of Elizabethan Theatre* (Brighton: Harvester Press, 1986), pp. 197–207, and Jonathan Goldberg, "Sodomy and Society: The Case of Christopher Marlowe," *Southwest Review* 69/4 (1984): 371–8). And the sexual ambiguity in the play was referred to briefly but perceptively by Anne Barton in a review of Bray, *Homosexuality*, in *London Review of Books* 5/15 (18–31 August 1983): 18.

13 Fredson Bowers, ed., *The Complete Works of Christopher Marlowe*, Cambridge: Cambridge University Press, 1981), pp. 16–17. The opening is an epitome of the play as a whole. The depiction of the friendship between Edward and Gaveston with which it opens can be read as Edward, after the death of his father, building up a body of clients to secure his position, as we then see Gaveston doing in his turn and as Mortimer later says he will do: "Mine enemies will I plague, my friends advance" (Bowers, *Works*, 88). In this familiar Elizabethan context we are then presented with the conventional expressions of such "friendship." It is this that accounts for the close similarity between the queen's description of Edward's intimacy with Gaveston (p. 22) and Thomas Howard's of James I's with Robert Carr, which I quote in the third section of this essay. It is also why Gaveston's protestation of his love for Edward (p. 20) is in the same form as that of the secretary of Antonio Pérez which I quote in section 5.

Gaveston's sexual image (Bowers, *Works*, 15) and Edward's (p. 40), of which much has been made, are part of these conventions; Antonio Pérez uses similarly sexual images in some of his letters to Anthony Bacon (Ungerer, *A Spaniard in Elizabethan England*, 1: 490–3). The link is masculinity, expressed alike in sexual potency as in the bonds that bound men: "Clients love masculine men," wrote Pérez in one of his letters to the Earl of Essex "as wives their husbands": "amant enim clientes sicut vxores maritos viros viriles" (*Ant. Perezii ad Comitem Essexium*, Epistola 61, which is also given in Ungerer, *A Spaniard in Elizabethan England*, 1: 475).

Ganymede: Bowers, *Works*, 29. Giles Fletcher: Will T. Brooke, ed., *Christ's Victory and Triumph* (London: Griffin, Favian, Okeden and Welsh, n.d.), p. 117. Bray, *Homosexuality*, pp. 16, 53, 66, 126. His Italian tastes are emphasized on pp. 16 and 35 and his foreign origins on pp. 21 and 22; on the assumed connection between these and sodomy, see pp. 75–6. Murder: pp. 90–3; I accept the arguments for the view that the murder of Edward as given in Holinshed was enacted in full view of the audience, but my point holds good even if Marlowe felt he could go no further than to allude to it in the references we see in the text.

14 I. M., *A Health to the Gentlemanly Profession of Seruingmen*, 1598, CI–CIV. Cecil Papers 83/97v; calendared in Historical Manuscripts Commission, *Marquis of Salisbury*, part II, 1906, pp. 107–8.

15 Ungerer, *A Spaniard in Elizabethan England*, 2: 47–8.

16 Bowers, *Works of Christopher Marlowe*, p. 20.

17 Jerónimo López and Laurence des Bouverie (Ungerer, *A Spaniard in Elizabethan England*, 1: 327 and 472–3).

18 I. M., *Seruingmen*, 1598. Muriel St. Clare Byrne, ed., *The Lisle Letters* (Chicago and London: University of Chicago Press, 1981), 3: 1–35. Walter Darell, *A Short Discourse of the Life of Seruingmen*, 1578 (in *Studies in Philology* 31/2 (1934): 124).

19 J. E. Neale, *The Age of Catherine de Medici and Essays in Elizabethan History* (London: Jonathan Cape, 1963), p. 153, and Peck, *Northampton*, p. 59.

20 Bray, *Homosexuality*, pp. 14–15, 72; A. Gordon Kinder, *Casiodoro de Reina* (London: Tamesis Books, 1975), pp. 27–37, 58–9, 99–120; Bray, *Homosexuality*, pp. 29–30, 49, 54, 121.

21 Bray, *Homosexuality*, pp. 44–53 and 54–5. I would now be rather more cautious, though, in my comments on Francis Bacon on p. 49. . . .

20

An Introduction to Female Masculinity:
Masculinity without Men

Judith Halberstam

What's the use of being a little boy if you are going to grow up to be a man?
(Gertrude Stein, *Everybody's Autobiography*, 1937)

The Real Thing

What is "masculinity"? This has been probably the most common question that I have faced over the past five years while writing on the topic of female masculinity. If masculinity is not the social and cultural and indeed political expression of maleness, then what is it? I do not claim to have any definitive answer to this question, but I do have a few proposals about why masculinity must not and cannot and should not reduce down to the male body and its effects. I also venture to assert that although we seem to have a difficult time defining masculinity, as a society we have little trouble in recognizing it, and indeed we spend massive amounts of time and money ratifying and supporting the versions of masculinity that we enjoy and trust; many of these "heroic masculinities" depend absolutely on the subordination of alternative masculinities. I claim that far from being an imitation of maleness, female masculinity actually affords us a glimpse of how masculinity is constructed as masculinity. In other words, female masculinities are framed as the rejected scraps of dominant masculinity in order that male masculinity may appear to be the real thing. But what we understand as heroic masculinity has been produced by and across both male and female bodies.

This chapter does not simply offer a conventional theoretical introduction to the enterprise of conceptualizing masculinity without men; rather, it attempts to compile the myths and fantasies about masculinity that have ensured that masculinity and maleness are profoundly difficult to pry apart. I then offer, by way of a preliminary attempt to reimagine masculinity, numerous examples of alternative masculinities in fiction, film, and lived experience. These examples are mostly queer and female, and they show clearly how important it is to recognize

Reprinted from *Female Masculinity* (Durham: Duke University Press, 1998), pp. 1–9, 13–29, 40–1, 279–82.

alternative masculinities when and where they emerge. Throughout this [chapter], I detail the many ways in which female masculinity has been blatantly ignored both in the culture at large and within academic studies of masculinity. This widespread indifference to female masculinity, I suggest, has clearly ideological motivations and has sustained the complex social structures that wed masculinity to maleness and to power and domination. I firmly believe that a sustained examination of female masculinity can make crucial interventions within gender studies, cultural studies, queer studies, and mainstream discussions of gender in general.

Masculinity in this society inevitably conjures up notions of power and legitimacy and privilege; it often symbolically refers to the power of the state and to uneven distributions of wealth. Masculinity seems to extend outward into patriarchy and inward into the family; masculinity represents the power of inheritance, the consequences of the traffic in women, and the promise of social privilege. But, obviously, many other lines of identification traverse the terrain of masculinity, dividing its power into complicated differentials of class, race, sexuality, and gender. If what we call "dominant masculinity" appears to be a naturalized relation between maleness and power, then it makes little sense to examine men for the contours of that masculinity's social construction. Masculinity... becomes legible as masculinity where and when it leaves the white male middle-class body. Arguments about excessive masculinity tend to focus on black bodies (male and female), latino/a bodies, or working-class bodies, and insufficient masculinity is all too often figured by Asian bodies or upper-class bodies; these stereotypical constructions of variable masculinity mark the process by which masculinity becomes dominant in the sphere of white middle-class maleness. But all too many studies that currently attempt to account for the power of white masculinity recenter this white male body by concentrating all their analytical efforts on detailing the forms and expressions of white male dominance. Numerous studies of Elvis, white male youth, white male feminism, men and marriage, and domestications of maleness amass information about a subject whom we know intimately and ad nauseam. This study professes a degree of indifference to the whiteness of the male and the masculinity of the white male and the project of naming his power: male masculinity figures in my project as a hermeneutic, and as a counterexample to the kinds of masculinity that seem most informative about gender relations and most generative of social change....

How else to begin [an essay] on female masculinity but by deposing one of the most persistent of male heroes: Bond, James Bond. To illustrate my point that modern masculinity is most easily recognized as female masculinity, consider the James Bond action film, in which male masculinity very often appears as only a shadow of a more powerful and convincing alternative masculinity. In *Goldeneye* (1995), for example, Bond battles the usual array of bad guys: Commies, Nazis, mercenaries, and a superaggressive violent femme type. He puts on his usual performance of debonair action adventure hero, and he has his usual supply of gadgetry to aid him – a retractable belt, a bomb disguised as a pen, a laser weapon watch, and so on. But there's something curiously lacking in *Goldeneye*, namely, credible masculine power. Bond's boss, M, is a noticeably butch older woman who calls Bond a dinosaur and chastises him for being a misogynist and a sexist. His secretary, Miss Moneypenny, accuses him of sexual harassment, his male buddy betrays him and calls him a dupe, and ultimately women seem not to go for his charms – bad suits and lots of sexual innuendo – which seem as old and as ineffective as his gadgets.

Masculinity, in this rather actionless film, is primarily prosthetic and, in this and countless other action films, has little if anything to do with biological maleness and signifies more often as a technical special effect. In *Goldeneye* it is M who most convincingly performs masculinity, and she does so partly by exposing the sham of Bond's own performance. It is M who convinces us that sexism and misogyny are not necessarily part and parcel of masculinity, even though historically it has become difficult, if not impossible, to untangle masculinity from the oppression of women. The action adventure hero should embody an extreme version of normative masculinity, but instead we find that excessive masculinity turns into a parody or exposure of the norm. Because masculinity tends to manifest as natural gender itself, the action flick, with its emphases on prosthetic extension, actually undermines the heterosexuality of the hero even as it extends his masculinity. So, in *Goldeneye*, for example, Bond's masculinity is linked not only to a profoundly unnatural form of masculine embodiment but also to gay masculinities. In the scene in which Bond goes to pick up his newest set of gadgets, a campy and almost queeny science nerd gives Bond his brand-new accessories and demonstrates each one with great enthusiasm. It is no accident that the science nerd is called Agent Q. We might read Agent Q as a perfect model of the interpenetration of queer and dominant regimes – Q is precisely an agent, a queer subject who exposes the workings of dominant heterosexual masculinity. The gay masculinity of Agent Q and the female masculinity of M provide a remarkable representation of the absolute dependence of dominant masculinities on minority masculinities.

When you take his toys away, Bond has very little propping up his performance of masculinity. Without the slick suit, the half smile, the cigarette lighter that transforms into a laser gun, our James is a hero without the action or the adventure. The masculinity of the white male, what we might call "epic masculinity," depends absolutely, as any Bond flick demonstrates, on a vast subterranean network of secret government groups, well-funded scientists, the army, and an endless supply of both beautiful bad babes and beautiful good babes, and finally it relies heavily on an immediately recognizable "bad guy." The "bad guy" is a standard generic feature of epic masculinity narratives: think only of *Paradise Lost* and its eschatological separation between God and Devil; Satan, if you like, is the original bad guy. Which is not to say that the bad guy's masculinity bars him from the rewards of male privilege – on the contrary, bad guys may also look like winners, but they just tend to die more quickly....

There is also a long literary and cinematic history that celebrates the rebellion of the male. If James Stewart, Gregory Peck, and Fred Astaire represent a few faces of good-guy appeal, James Dean, Marlon Brando, and Robert De Niro represent the bad-guy appeal, and really it becomes quite hard to separate one group from the other. Obviously, bad-boy representations in the 1950s captured something of a white working-class rebellion against middle-class society and against particular forms of domestication, but today's rebel without a cause is tomorrow's investment banker, and male rebellion tends toward respectability as the rewards for conformity quickly come to outweigh the rewards for social rebellion. To paraphrase Gertrude Stein, what's the point of being a rebel boy if you are going to grow up to be a man? Obviously, where and when rebellion ceases to be white middle-class male rebellion (individualized and localized within the lone male or even generalized into the boy gang) and becomes class rebellion or race rebellion, a very different threat emerges.

Tomboys

What happens when boy rebellion is located not in the testosterone-induced pout of the hooligan but in the sneer of the tomboy? Tomboyism generally describes an extended childhood period of female masculinity. If we are to believe general accounts of childhood behavior, tomboyism is quite common for girls and does not generally give rise to parental fears. Because comparable cross-identification behaviors in boys do often give rise to quite hysterical responses, we tend to believe that female gender deviance is much more tolerated than male gender deviance.[1] I am not sure that tolerance in such matters can be measured or at any rate that responses to childhood gender behaviors necessarily tell us anything concrete about the permitted parameters of adult male and female gender deviance. Tomboyism tends to be associated with a "natural" desire for the greater freedoms and mobilities enjoyed by boys. Very often it is read as a sign of independence and self-motivation, and tomboyism may even be encouraged to the extent that it remains comfortably linked to a stable sense of a girl identity. Tomboyism is punished, however, when it appears to be the sign of extreme male identification (taking a boy's name or refusing girl clothing of any type) and when it threatens to extend beyond childhood and into adolescence.[2] Teenage tomboyism presents a problem and tends to be subject to the most severe efforts to reorient. We could say that tomboyism is tolerated as long as the child remains prepubescent; as soon as puberty begins, however, the full force of gender conformity descends on the girl. Gender conformity is pressed onto all girls, not just tomboys, and this is where it becomes hard to uphold the notion that male femininity presents a greater threat to social and familial stability than female masculinity. Female adolescence represents the crisis of coming of age as a girl in a male-dominated society. If adolescence for boys represents a rite of passage (much celebrated in Western literature in the form of the bildungsroman), and an ascension to some version (however attenuated) of social power, for girls, adolescence is a lesson in restraint, punishment, and repression. It is in the context of female adolescence that the tomboy instincts of millions of girls are remodeled into compliant forms of femininity.

That any girls do emerge at the end of adolescence as masculine women is quite amazing. The growing visibility and indeed respectability of lesbian communities to some degree facilitate the emergence of masculine young women. But as even a cursory survey of popular cinema confirms, the image of the tomboy can be tolerated only within a narrative of blossoming womanhood; within such a narrative, tomboyism represents a resistance to adulthood itself rather than to adult femininity. In both the novel and film versions of the classic tomboy narrative *The Member of the Wedding*, by Carson McCullers, tomboy Frankie Addams fights a losing battle against womanhood, and the text locates womanhood or femininity as a crisis of representation that confronts the heroine with unacceptable life options. As her brother's wedding approaches, Frankie Addams pronounces herself mired in a realm of unbelonging, outside the symbolic partnership of the wedding but also alienated from belonging in almost every category that might describe her. McCullers writes: "It happened that green and crazy summer when Frankie was twelve years old. This was the summer when for a long time she had not been a member. She belonged to no club and was a member of nothing in the world. Frankie was an unjoined person who hung around in doorways, and she was afraid."[3] McCullers positions Frankie on the verge of adolescence ("when Frankie was twelve years old") and in the midst of an enduring state of being "unjoined": "She belonged to no club and was a member of nothing in the world." While childhood in general may qualify as a period of "unbelonging," for the boyish girl arriving on the doorstep of womanhood, her status as "unjoined" marks her out for all manner of social violence and opprobrium. As she dawdles in the last light of childhood, Frankie Addams has become a tomboy who "hung around in doorways, and she was afraid."

As a genre, the tomboy film . . . suggests that the categories available to women for racial, gendered, and sexual identification are simply inadequate. In her novel, McCullers shows this inadequacy to be a direct result of the tyranny of language – a structure that fixes people and things in place artificially but securely. Frankie tries to change her identity by changing her name: "Why is it against the law to change your name?" she asks Berenice. Berenice answers: "Because things accumulate around your name," and she stresses that without names, confusion would reign and "the whole world would go crazy." But Berenice also acknowledges that the fixity conferred by names also traps people into many different identities, racial as well as gendered: "We all of us somehow caught. . . . And maybe we wants to widen and bust free. But no matter what we do we still caught." Frankie thinks that naming represents the power of definition, and name changing confers the power to reimagine identity, place, relation, and even gender. "I wonder if it is against the law to change your name," says Frankie, "Or add to it. . . . Well I don't care. . . . F. Jasmine Addams."[4]

Psychoanalysis posits a crucial relationship between language and desire such that language structures desire and expresses therefore both the fullness and the futility of human desire – full because we always desire, futile because we are never satisfied. Frankie in particular understands desire and sexuality to be the most regimented forms of social conformity – we are supposed to desire only certain people and only in certain ways, but her desire does not work that way, and she finds herself torn between longing and belonging. Because she does not desire in conventional ways, Frankie seeks to avoid desire altogether. Her struggle with language, her attempts to remake herself through naming and remake the world with a new order of being, are ultimately heroic, but unsuccessful. McCullers's pessimism has to do with a sense of the overwhelming "order of things," an order that cannot be affected by the individual, and works through things as basic as language, and forces nonmembers into memberships they cannot fulfill.

My [essay] refuses the futility long associated with the tomboy narrative and instead seizes on the opportunity to recognize and ratify differently gendered bodies and subjectivities. . . . [I argue] for the production of new taxonomies, what Eve K. Sedgwick humorously called "nonce taxonomies" in *Epistemology of the Closet*, classifications of desire, physicality, and subjectivity that attempt to intervene in hegemonic processes of naming and defining. Nonce taxonomies are categories that we use daily to make sense of our worlds but that work so well that we actually fail to recognize them. . . . I attempt to bring some of the nonce taxonomies of female masculinity into view, and I detail the histories of the suppression of these categories. . . . I am using the topic of female masculinity to explore a queer subject position that can successfully challenge hegemonic models of gender conformity. Female masculinity is a particularly fruitful site of investigation because it has been vilified by heterosexist and feminist/womanist programs alike; unlike male femininity, which fulfills a kind of ritual function in male homosocial cultures, female masculinity is generally received by hetero- and homonormative cultures as a pathological sign of misidentification and maladjustment, as a longing to be and to have a power that is always just out of reach. Within a lesbian context, female masculinity has been situated as the place where patriarchy goes to work on the female psyche and reproduces misogyny within femaleness. There have been to date remarkably few studies or theories about the inevitable effects of a fully articulated female masculinity on a seemingly fortified male masculinity. Sometimes female masculinity coincides with the excesses of male supremacy, and sometimes it codifies a unique form of social rebellion; often female masculinity is the sign of sexual alterity, but occasionally it marks heterosexual variation; sometimes female masculinity marks the place of pathology, and every now and then it represents the healthful alternative to what are considered the histrionics of conventional femininities.

I want to carefully produce a model of female masculinity that remarks on its multiple forms but also calls for new and self-conscious affirmations of different gender taxonomies. Such affirmations begin not by subverting masculine power or taking up a position against masculine power but by turning a blind eye to conventional masculinities and refusing to engage. Frankie Addams, for example, constitutes her rebellion not in opposition to the law but through indifference to the law: she recognizes that it may be against the law to change one's name or add to it, but she also has a simple response to such illegal activity: "Well, I don't care." I am not suggesting in this book that we follow the futile path of what Foucault calls "saying no to power," but I am asserting that power may inhere within different forms of refusal: "Well, I don't care." . . .

Constructing Masculinities

Within cultural studies itself, masculinity has recently become a favorite topic. I want to try here to account for the growing popularity of a body of work on masculinity that evinces absolutely no interest in masculinity without men. I first noticed the unprecedented interest in masculinity in April 1994 when the DIA Center for the Performing Arts convened a group of important intellectuals to hold forth on the topic of masculinities. On the opening night of this event, one commentator wondered, "Why masculinity, why now?" Several others, male critics and scholars, gave eloquent papers about their memories of being young boys and about their relationships with their fathers. The one lesbian on the panel, a poet, read a moving poem about rape. At the end of the evening, only one panelist had commented on the limitations of a discussion of masculinity that interpreted "masculinity" as a synonym for men or maleness.[5] This lonely intervention highlighted the gap between mainstream discussions of masculinity and men and ongoing queer discussions about masculinity, which extend far beyond the male body. Indeed, in answer to the naive question that began the evening, "Why masculinities, why now?" one might state: Because masculinity in the 1990s has finally been recognized as, at least in part, a construction by female-as well as male-born people.[6]

The anthology that the conference produced provides more evidence of the thoroughgoing association that the editors have made between masculinity and maleness. The title page features a small photographic illustration of a store sign advertising clothing as "Fixings for Men." This illustration has been placed just below the title, *Constructing Masculinity*, and forces the reader to understand the construction of masculinity as the outfitting of males within culture. The introduction to the volume attempts to diversify this definition of masculinity by using Judith Butler's and Eve Sedgwick's contributions to suggest that the anthology recognizes the challenges made by gays, lesbians, and queers to the terms of gender normativity. The editors insist that masculinity is multiple and that "far from just being about men, the idea of masculinity engages, inflects, and shapes everyone."[7] The commitment to the representation of masculinity as multiple is certainly borne out in the first essay in the volume, by Eve Sedgwick, in which she proposes that masculinity may have little to do with men, and is somewhat extended by Butler's essay "Melancholy Gender." But Sedgwick also critiques the editors for having proposed a book and a conference on masculinity that remain committed to linking masculinity to maleness. Although the introduction suggests that the editors have heeded Sedgwick's call for gender diversity, the rest of the volume suggests otherwise. There are many fascinating essays in this anthology, but there are no essays specifically on female masculinity. Although gender-queer images by Loren Cameron and Cathy Opie adorn the pages of the book, the text contains no discussions of these images. The book circles around discussions of male icons such as Clint Eastwood and Steven Seagal; it addresses the complex relations between fathers and sons; it examines topics such as how science defines men and masculinity and the law. The volume concludes with an essay by Stanley Aronowitz titled "My Masculinity," an autobiographically in-flected consideration of various forms of male power.

None of my analysis here is to say that this is an uninteresting anthology or that the essays are somehow wrong or misguided, but I am trying to point out that the editorial statement at the beginning of the volume is less a prologue to what follows and more of an epilogue that describes what a volume on masculinity *should* do as opposed to what the anthology does do. Even when the need for an analysis of female masculinity has been acknowledged, in other words, it seems remarkably difficult to follow through on. What is it then that, to paraphrase Eve Sedgwick's essay, makes it so difficult *not* to presume an essential relation between masculinity and men?[8]

By beginning with this examination of the *Constructing Masculinity* conference and anthology, I do not want to give the impression that the topic of female masculinities must always be related to some larger topic, some more general set of masculinities that has been, and continues to be, about men. Nor do I want to suggest that gender theory is the true origin of gender knowledges. Rather, this conference and book merely emphasize the lag between community knowledges and practices and academic discourses.[9] I believe it is both helpful and important to contextualize a discussion of female and lesbian masculinities in direct opposition to a more generalized discussion of masculinity within cultural studies that seems intent on insisting that masculinity remain the property of male bodies. The continued refusal in Western society to admit ambiguously gendered bodies into functional social relations (evidenced, for example, by our continued use of either/or bathrooms, either women or men) is, I will claim, sustained by a conservative and protectionist attitude by men in general toward masculinity. Such an attitude has been bolstered by a more general disbelief in female masculinity. I can only describe such disbelief in terms of a failure in a collective imagination: in other words, female-born people have been making convincing and powerful assaults on the coherence of male masculinity for well over a hundred years; what prevents these assaults from taking hold and accomplishing the diminution of the bonds between masculinity and men? Somehow, despite multiple images of strong women (such as bodybuilder Bev Francis or tennis player Martina Navratilova), of cross-identifying women (Radclyffe Hall or Ethel Smyth), of masculine-coded public figures (Janet Reno), of butch superstars (k. d. lang), of muscular and athletic women (Jackie Joyner-Kersee), of female-born transgendered people (Leslie Feinberg), there is still no general acceptance or even recognition of masculine women and boyish girls. This [essay] addresses itself to this collective failure to imagine and ratify the masculinity produced by, for, and within women.

In case my concerns about the current discussions of masculinity in cultural studies sound too dismissive, I want to look in an extended way at what happens when academic discussions of male masculinity take place to the exclusion of discussions of more wide-ranging masculinities. While it may seem that I am giving an inordinate amount of attention to what is after all just one intervention into current discussions, I am using one book as representative of a whole slew of other studies of masculinity that replicate the intentions and the mistakes of this one. In an anthology called *Boys: Masculinities in Contemporary Culture*, edited by Paul Smith for a Cultural Studies series, Smith suggests that masculinity must always be thought of "in the plural" as masculinities "defined and cut through by differences and contradictions of all sorts."[10] The plurality of masculinities for Smith encompasses a dominant white masculinity that is crisscrossed by its others, gay, bisexual, black, Asian, and Latino masculinities. Although the recognition of a host of masculinities makes sense, Smith chooses to focus on dominant white masculinity to the exclusion of the other masculinities he has listed. Smith, predictably, warns the reader not to fall into the trap of simply critiquing dominant masculinity or simply celebrating minority masculinities, and then he makes the following foundational statement:

> And it may well be the case, as some influential voices often tell us, that masculinity or masculinities are in some real sense not the exclusive "property" of biologically male subjects – it's true that many female subjects lay claim to masculinity as their property. Yet in terms of cultural and political *power*, it still makes a difference when masculinity coincides with biological maleness.[11]

What is immediately noticeable to me here is the odd attribution of immense power to those "influential voices" who keep telling us that masculinity is not the property of men. There is no naming of these influential voices, and we are left supposing that "influence" has rendered the "female masculinity theorists" so powerful that names are irrelevant: these voices, one might suppose, are hegemonic. Smith goes on to plead with the reader, asking us to admit that the intersection of maleness and masculinity does "still" make a difference. His appeal here to common sense allows him to sound as if he is trying to reassert some kind of rationality to a debate that is spinning off into totally inconsequential discussions. Smith is really arguing that we must turn to dominant masculinity to begin deconstructing masculinity because it is the equation of maleness plus masculinity that adds up to social legitimacy. As I argued earlier in this chapter, however, precisely because white male masculinity has obscured all other masculinities, we have to turn away from its construction to bring other more mobile forms of masculinity to light. Smith's purpose in his reassertion of the difference that male masculinity makes is to uncover the "cultural and political *power*" of this union in order to direct our attention to the power of patriarchy. The second part of the paragraph makes this all too clear:

> Biological men – male-sexed beings – are after all, in varying degrees, the bearers of privilege and power within the systems against which women still struggle. The privilege and power are, of course, different for different men, endlessly diversified through the markers of class, nation, race, sexual preference and so on. But I'd deny that there are any men who are entirely outside of the ambit, let's say, of power and privilege *in relation to women*. In that sense it has to be useful to our thinking to recall that masculinities are not only a function of dominant notions of masculinity and not constituted solely in resistant notions of "other" masculinities. In fact, masculinities exist inevitably in relation to what feminisms have construed as the system of patriarchy and patriarchal relations.[12]

The most noticeable feature of this paragraph is the remarkable stability of the terms "women" and "men." Smith advances here a slightly old-fashioned feminism that understands women as endlessly victimized within systems of male power. Woman, within such a model, is the name for those subjects within patriarchy who have no access to male power and who are regulated and confined by patriarchal structures. But what would Smith say to Monique Wittig's claim that lesbians are not women because they are not involved in the heterosexual matrix that produces sexual difference as a power relation? What can Smith add to Judith Butler's influential theory of "gender trouble," which suggests that "gender is a copy with no original" and that dominant sexualities and genders are in some sense imbued with a pathetic dependence on their others that puts them perpetually at risk? What would Smith say to Jacob Hale's claim that the genders we use as reference points in gender theory fall far behind community productions of alternative genderings?[13] Are butch dykes women? Are male transvestites men? How does gender variance disrupt the flow of powers presumed by patriarchy in relations between men and women? Smith, in other words, cannot take female masculinity into account because he sees it as inconsequential and secondary to much more important questions about male privilege. Again, this sounds more like a plaintive assertion that men *do* still access male power within patriarchy (don't they?), and it conveniently ignores the ways in which gender relations are scrambled where and when gender variance comes into play.

Smith's attempt to shore up male masculinity by dismissing the importance of other masculinities finds further expression in his attempt to take racialized masculinities into consideration. His introductory essay opens with a meditation on the complications of the O. J. Simpson case, and Smith wonders at the way popular discourse on the O. J. case sidesteps issues of masculinity and male domination in favor of race. When he hears a black male caller to a radio talk show link O. J.'s case to an ongoing conspiracy against black men in this country, Smith ponders: "His spluttering about the attempted genocide of black men reminded me, somehow, that another feature of the O. J. case was the way it had started with the prosecution trying to establish the relevance of O. J.'s record as a wife beater."[14] Noting that the callers to the talk show did not have much to say about this leads Smith to wonder whether race can constitute a collective identity but masculinity cannot, and finally he suggests that although "it might be difficult to talk about race in this country, it is even more difficult to talk about masculinity."[15] If you are a white man, it is probably extremely difficult to talk about either race or masculinity let alone both at the same time. But, of course, race and masculinity, especially in the case of O. J., are not separable into tidy categories. Indeed, one might say that the caller's "spluttering" about conspiracies against black men constituted a far more credible race analysis in this case than Smith's articulation of the relations between race and masculinity. For Smith, masculinity in the case of O. J. constitutes a flow of domination that comes up against his blackness as a flow of subordination. There is no discussion here of the injustices of the legal system, the role of class and money in the trial, or the complicated history of relations between black men and white women. Smith uses O. J. as shorthand for a model that is supposed to suggest power and disempowerment in the same location.

I am taking so much time and effort to discount Smith's introduction to *Boys* because there is a casualness to his essay that both indicates his lack of any real investment in the project of alternative masculinities and suggests an unwillingness to think through the messy identifications that make up contemporary power relations around gender, race, and class. The book that Smith introduces also proves to have nothing much to offer to new discussions of masculinity, and we quickly find ourselves, from the opening essay on, in the familiar territory of men, boys, and their fathers. The first essay, for example, by Fred Pfeil, "A Buffalo, New York Story," tells a pitiful tale about father–son relations in the 1950s. In one memorable moment from the memoir, he (Fred) and Dad have cozied up on the couch to watch *Bonanza* while Mom and Sis are doing the dishes in the kitchen. Boy asks Dad "why bad guys were always so stupid," and Dad laughs and explains "because they were bad."[16] The story goes on to detail the innocent young boy's first brushes with his male relatives' racism and his own painful struggle with car sickness. Besides taking apart the dynamics of fathers and sons cozying up together to watch *Bonanza*, there most certainly are a multitude of important things to say about men and masculinity in patriarchy, but Smith and some of his contributors choose not to say them. We could be producing ethnographies on the aggressive and indeed protofascist masculinities produced by male sports fans.[17] Much work still remains to be done on the socialization (or lack thereof) of young men in high schools, on (particularly rich white male) domestic abusers, on the new sexism embodied by "sensitive men," on the men who participate in the traffic in mail-order brides and sex tourism (including a study of privileged white gay masculinity). But studies in male masculinity are predictably not so interested in taking apart the patriarchal bonds between white maleness and privilege; they are much more concerned to detail the fragilities of male socialization, the pains of manhood, and the fear of female empowerment.[18]

Because I have criticized Smith for his apparent lack of investment in the project of producing alternative masculinities, let me take a moment to make my own investments clear. . . . [I]t seems important to state that this [essay], is an attempt to make my own female masculinity plausible, credible, and real. For a large part of my life, I have been stigmatized by a masculinity that marked me as ambiguous and illegible. Like many other tomboys, I was mistaken for a boy throughout my childhood, and like many other tomboy adolescents, I was forced into some semblance of femininity for my teenage years. When gender-ambiguous children are constantly challenged about their gender identity, the chain of misrecognitions can actually produce a new recognition: in other words, to be constantly mistaken for a boy, for many tomboys, can contribute to the production of a masculine identity. It was not until my midtwenties that I finally found a word for my particular gender configuration: butch. . . .

The Bathroom Problem

If three decades of feminist theorizing about gender has thoroughly dislodged the notion that anatomy is destiny, that gender is natural, and that male and female are the only options, why do we still operate in a world that assumes that people who are not male are female, and people who are not female are male (and even that people who are not male are not people!). If gender has been so thoroughly defamiliarized, in other words, why do we not have multiple gender options, multiple gender categories, and real-life nonmale and nonfemale options for embodiment and identification? In a way, gender's very flexibility and seeming fluidity is precisely what allows dimorphic gender to hold sway. Because so few people actually match any given community standards for male or female, in other words, gender can be imprecise and therefore multiply relayed through a solidly binary system. At the same time, because the definitional boundaries of male and female are so elastic, there are very few people in any given public space who are completely unreadable in terms of their gender.

Ambiguous gender, when and where it does appear, is inevitably transformed into deviance, thirdness, or a blurred version of either male or female. As an example, in public bathrooms for women, various bathroom users tend to fail to measure up to expectations of femininity, and those of us who present in some ambiguous way are routinely questioned and challenged about our presence in the "wrong" bathroom. For example, recently, on my way to give a talk in Minneapolis, I was making a connection at Chicago's O'Hare airport. I strode purposefully into the women's bathroom. No sooner had I entered the stall than someone was knocking at the door: "Open up, security here!" I understood immediately what had happened. I had, once again, been mistaken for a man or a boy, and some woman had called security. As soon as I spoke, the two guards at the bathroom stall realized their error, mumbled apologies, and took off. On the way home from the same trip, in the Denver airport, the same sequence of events was repeated.

Needless to say, the policing of gender within the bathroom is intensified in the space of the airport, where people are literally moving through space and time in ways that cause them to want to stabilize some boundaries (gender) even as they traverse others (national). However, having one's gender challenged in the women's rest room is a frequent occurrence in the lives of many androgynous or masculine women; indeed, it is so frequent that one wonders whether the category "woman," when used to designate public functions, is completely outmoded.[19]

It is no accident, then, that travel hubs become zones of intense scrutiny and observation. But gender policing within airport bathrooms is merely an intensified version of a larger "bathroom problem." For some gender-ambiguous women, it is relatively easy to "prove" their right to use the women's bathroom – they can reveal some decisive gender trait (a high voice, breasts), and the challenger will generally back off. For others (possibly low-voiced or hairy or breastless people), it is quite difficult to justify their presence in the women's bathroom, and these people may tend to use the men's bathroom, where scrutiny is far less intense. Obviously, in these bathroom confrontations, the gender-ambiguous person first appears as not-woman ("You are in the wrong bathroom!"), but then the person appears as something actually even more scary, not-man ("No, I am not," spoken in a voice recognized as not-male). Not-man and not-woman, the gender-ambiguous bathroom user is also not androgynous or in-between; this person is gender deviant.

For many gender deviants, the notion of passing is singularly unhelpful. Passing as a narrative assumes that there is a self that masquerades as another kind of self and does so successfully; at various moments, the successful pass may cohere into something akin to identity. At such a moment, the passer has *become*. What of a biological female who presents as butch, passes as male in some circumstances and reads as butch in others, and considers herself not to be a woman but maintains distance from the category "man"? For such a subject, identity might best be described as process with multiple sites for becoming and being. To understand such a process, we would need to do more than map psychic and physical journeys between male and female and within queer and straight space; we would need, in fact, to think in fractal terms and about gender geometries. . . . The stone butch, for example, in her self-definition as a non-feminine, sexually untouchable female, complicates the idea that lesbians share female sexual practices or women share female sexual desires or even that masculine women share a sense of what animates their particular masculinities.

I want to focus on what I am calling "the bathroom problem" because I believe it illustrates in remarkably clear ways the flourishing existence of gender binarism despite rumours of its demise. Furthermore, many normatively gendered women have no idea that a bathroom problem even exists and claim to be completely ignorant about the trials and tribulations that face the butch woman who needs to use a public bathroom. But queer literature is littered with references to the bathroom problem, and it would not be an exaggeration to call it a standard feature of the butch narrative. For example, Leslie Feinberg provides clear illustrations of the dimensions of the bathroom problem in *Stone Butch Blues*. In this narrative of the life of the he-she factory worker, Jess Goldberg, Jess recounts many occasions in which she has to make crucial decisions about whether she can afford to use the women's bathroom. On a shopping outing with some drag queens, Jess tells Peaches: "I gotta use the bathroom. God, I wish I could wait, but I can't." Jess takes a deep breath and enters the ladies' room:

> Two women were freshening their makeup in front of the mirror. One glanced at the other and finished applying her lipstick. "Is that a man or a woman?" She said to her friend as I passed them.
>
> The other woman turned to me. "This is the women's bathroom," she informed me.
>
> I nodded. "I know."
>
> I locked the stall door behind me. Their laughter cut me to the bone. "You don't really know if that is a man or not," one woman said to the other. "We should call security to make sure."
>
> I flushed the toilet and fumbled with my zipper in fear. Maybe it was just an idle threat. Maybe they really would call security. I hurried out of the bathroom as soon as I heard both women leave.[20]

For Jess, the bathroom represents a limit to her ability to move around in the public sphere. Her body, with its needs and physical functions, imposes a limit on her attempts to function normally despite her variant gender presentation. The women in the rest room, furthermore, are depicted as spiteful, rather than fearful. They toy with Jess by calling into question her right to use the rest room and threatening to call the police. As Jess puts it: "They never would have made fun of a guy like that." In other words, if the women were truly anxious for their safety, they would not have toyed with the intruder, and they would not have hesitated to call the police. Their casualness about calling security indicates that they know Jess is a woman but want to punish her for her inappropriate self-presentation.

Another chronicle of butch life, *Throw It to the River*, by Nice Rodriguez, a Filipina-Canadian writer, also tells of the bathroom encounter. In a story called "Every Full Moon," Rodriguez tells a romantic tale about a butch bus conductor called Remedios who falls in love with a former nun called Julianita. Remedios is "muscular around the arms and shoulders," and her "toughness allows her to bully anyone who will not pay the fare."[21] She aggressively flirts with Julianita until Julianita agrees to go to a movie with Remedios. To prepare for her date, Remedios dresses herself up, carefully flattening out her chest with Band-Aids over the nipples: "She bought a white shirt in Divisoria just for this date. Now she worries that the cloth may be too thin and transparent, and that Julianita will be turned off when her nipples protrude out like dice."[22] With her "well-ironed jeans," her smooth chest, and even a man's manicure, Remedios heads out for her date. However, once out with Julianita, Remedios, now dressed in her butch best, has to be careful about public spaces. After the movie, Julianita rushes off to the washroom, but Remedios waits outside for her:

> She has a strange fear of ladies' rooms. She wishes there was another washroom somewhere between the mens' and the ladies' for queers like her. Most of the time she holds her pee – sometimes as long as half a day – until she finds a washroom where the users are familiar with her. Strangers take to her unkindly, especially elder women who inspect her from head to toe.[23]

Another time, Remedios tells of being chased from a ladies' room and beaten by a bouncer. The bathroom problem for Remedios and for Jess severely limits their ability to circulate in public spaces and actually brings them into contact with physical violence as a result of having violated a cardinal rule of gender: one must be readable at a glance. After Remedios is beaten for having entered a ladies' room, her father tells her to be more careful, and Rodriguez notes: "She realized that being cautious means swaying her hips and parading her boobs when she enters any ladies' room."[24]

If we use the paradigm of the bathroom as a limit of gender identification, we can measure the distance between binary gender schema and lived multiple gendered experiences. The accusation "you're in the wrong bathroom" really says two different things. First, it announces that your gender seems at odds with your sex (your apparent masculinity or androgyny is at odds with your supposed femaleness); second, it suggests that single-gender bathrooms are only for those who fit clearly into one category (male) or the other (female). Either we need open-access bathrooms or multigendered bathrooms, or we need wider parameters for gender identification. The bathroom, as we know it, actually represents the crumbling edifice of gender in the twentieth century. The frequency with which gender-deviant "women" are mistaken for men in public bathrooms suggests that a large number of feminine women spend a large amount of time and energy policing masculine women. Something very different happens, of course, in the men's public toilet, where the space is more likely to become a sexual cruising zone than a site for gender repression. Lee Edelman, in an essay about the interpenetration of nationalism and sexuality, argues that "the institutional men's room constitutes a site at which the zones of public and private cross with a distinctive psychic charge."[25] The men's room, in other words, constitutes both an architecture of surveillance and an incitement to desire, a space of homosocial interaction and of homoerotic interaction.

So, whereas men's rest rooms tend to operate as a highly charged sexual space in which sexual interactions are both encouraged and punished, women's rest rooms tend to operate as an arena for the enforcement of gender conformity. Sex-segregated bathrooms continue to be necessary to protect women from male predations but also produce and extend a rather outdated notion of a public/private split between male and female society. The bathroom is a domestic space beyond the home that comes to represent domestic order, or a parody of it, out in the world. The women's bathroom accordingly becomes a sanctuary of enhanced femininity, a "little girl's room" to which one retreats to powder one's nose or fix one's hair. The men's bathroom signifies as the extension of the public nature of masculinity – it is precisely not domestic even though the names given to the sexual function of the bathroom – such as cottage or tearoom – suggest it is a parody of the domestic. The codes that dominate within the women's bathroom are primarily gender codes; in the men's room, they are sexual codes. Public sex versus private gender, openly sexual versus discreetly repressive, bathrooms beyond the home take on the proportions of a gender factory.

Marjorie Garber comments on the liminality of the bathroom in *Vested Interests* in a chapter on the perils and privileges of cross-dressing. She discusses the very different modes of passing and cross-dressing for cross-identified genetic males and females, and she observes that the rest room is a "potential waterloo" for both female-to-male (FTM) and male-to-female (MTF) cross-dressers and transsex-uals.[26] For the FTM, the men's room represents the most severe test of his ability to pass, and advice frequently circulates within FTM communities about how to go unnoticed in male-only spaces. Garber notes: "The cultural paranoia of being caught in the ultimately wrong place, which may be inseparable from the pleasure of 'passing' in that same place, depends in part on the same cultural binarism, the idea that gender categories are sufficiently uncomplicated to permit self-assortment into one of the two 'rooms' without deconstructive reading."[27] It is worth pointing out here (if only because Garber does not) that the perils of passing FTMs in the men's room are very different from the perils of passing MTFs in the women's room. On the one hand, the FTM in the men's room is likely to be less scrutinized because men are not quite as vigilant about intruders as women for obvious reasons. On the other hand, if caught, the FTM may face some version of gender panic from the man who discovers him, and it is quite reasonable to expect and fear violence in the wake of such a discovery. The MTF, by comparison, will be more scrutinized in the women's room but possibly less open to punishment if caught. Because the FTM ventures into male territory with the potential threat of violence hanging over his head, it is crucial to recognize that the bathroom problem is much more than a glitch in the machinery of gender segregation and is better described in terms of the violent enforcement of our current gender system.

Garber's reading of the perilous use of rest rooms by both FTMs and MTFs develops out of her introductory discussion of what Lacan calls "urinary segrega-tion." Lacan used the term to describe the relations between identities and signifiers, and he ultimately used the simple diagram of the rest-room signs "Ladies" and "Gentlemen" to show that within the production of sexual differ-ence, primacy is granted to the signifier over that which it signifies; in more simple terms, naming confers, rather than reflects, meaning.[28] In the same way, the system of urinary segregation creates the very functionality of the categories "men" and "women." Although rest-room signs seem to serve and ratify distinc-tions that already exist, in actual fact these markers produce identifications within these constructed categories. Garber latches on to the notion of "urinary segrega-tion" because it helps her to describe the processes of cultural binarism within the production of gender; for Garber, transvestites and transsexuals challenge this system by resisting the literal translation of the signs "Ladies" and "Gentlemen." Garber uses the figures of the transvestite and the transsexual to show the obvious flaws and gaps in a binary gender system; the transvestite, as interloper, creates a third space of possibility within which all binaries become unstable. Unfortunately, as in all attempts to break a binary by producing a third term, Garber's third space tends to stabilize the other two. In "Tearooms and Sympathy," Lee Edelman also turns to Lacan's term "urinary segregation," but Edelman uses Lacan's diagram to mark heterosexual anxiety "about the potential inscriptions of homosexual desire and about the possibility of knowing or recognizing whatever might constitute 'homosexual difference'."[29] Whereas for Garber it is the transvestite who marks the instability of the markers "Ladies" and "Gentlemen," for Edelman it is not the passing transvestite but the passing homosexual.

Both Garber and Edelman, interestingly enough, seem to fix on the men's room as the site of these various destabilizing performances. As I am arguing here, however, focusing exclusively on the drama of the men's room avoids the much more complicated theater of the women's room. Garber writes of urinary segregation: "For transvestites and transsexuals, the 'men's room' problem is really a challenge to the way in which such cultural binarism is read."[30] She goes on to list some cinematic examples of the perils of urinary segregation and discusses scenes from *Tootsie* (1982), *Cabaret* (1972), and the *Female Impersonator Pageant* (1975). Garber's examples are odd illustrations of what she calls "the men's room problem" if only because at least one of her examples (*Tootsie*) demonstrates gender policing in the women's room. Also, Garber makes it sound as if vigorous gender policing happens in the men's room while the women's room is more of a benign zone for gender enforcement. She notes: "In fact, the urinal has appeared in a number of fairly recent films as a marker of the ultimate 'difference' – or studied indifference."[31] Obviously, Garber is drawing a parallel here between the conventions of gender attribution within which the penis marks the "ultimate difference"; however, by not moving beyond this remarkably predictable description of gender differentiation, Garber overlooks the main distinction between gender policing in the men's room and in the women's room. Namely, in the women's room, it is not only the MTF but *all* gender-ambiguous females who are scrutinized, whereas in the men's room, biological men are rarely deemed out of place. Garber's insistence that there is "a third space of possibility" occupied by the transvestite has closed down the possibility that there may be a fourth, fifth, sixth, or one hundredth space beyond the binary. The "women's room problem" (as opposed to the "men's room problem") indicates a multiplicity of gender displays even within the supposedly stable category of "woman."

So what gender are the hundreds of female-born people who are consistently not read as female in the women's room? And because so many women clearly fail the women's room test, why have we not begun to count and name the genders that are clearly emerging at this time? One could answer this question in two ways: On the one hand, we do not name and notice new genders because as a society we are committed to maintaining a binary gender system. On the other hand, we could also say that the failure of "male" and "female" to exhaust the field of gender variation actually ensures the continued dominance of these terms. Precisely because virtually nobody fits the definitions of male and female, the categories gain power and currency from their impossibility. In other words, the very flexibility and elasticity of the terms "man" and "woman" ensures their longevity. To test this proposition, look around any public space and notice how few people present formulaic versions of gender and yet how few are unreadable or totally ambiguous. The "It's Pat" character on a *Saturday Night Live* skit dramatized the ways in which people insist on attributing gender in terms of male or female on even the most undecidable characters. The "It's Pat" character produced laughs by consistently sidestepping gender fixity – Pat's partner had a neutral name, and everything Pat did or said was designed to be read either way. Of course, the enigma that Pat represented could have been solved very easily; Pat's coworkers could simply have asked Pat what gender s/he was or preferred. This project on female masculinity is designed to produce more than two answers to that question and even to argue for a concept of "gender preference" as opposed to compulsory gender binarism. The human potential for incredibly precise classifications has been demonstrated in multiple arenas; why then do we settle for a paucity of classifications when it comes to gender? A system of gender preferences would allow for gender neutrality until such a time when the child or young adult announces his or her or its gender. Even if we could not let go of a binary gender system, there are still ways to make gender optional – people could come out as a gender in the way they come out as a sexuality. The point here is that there are many ways to depathologize gender variance and to account for the multiple genders that we already produce and sustain. Finally, as I suggested in relation to Garber's arguments about transvestism, "thirdness" merely balances the binary system and, furthermore, tends to homogenize many different gender variations under the banner of "other."

It is remarkably easy in this society not to look like a woman. It is relatively difficult, by comparison, not to look like a man: the threats faced by men who do not gender conform are somewhat different than for women. Unless men are consciously trying to look like women, men are less likely than women to fail to pass in the rest room. So one question posed by the bathroom problem asks, what makes femininity so approximate and masculinity so precise? Or to pose the question with a different spin, why is femininity easily impersonated or performed while masculinity seems resilient to imitation? Of course, this formulation does not easily hold and indeed quickly collapses into the exact opposite: why is it, in the case of the masculine woman in the bathroom, for example, that one finds the limits of femininity so quickly, whereas the limits of masculinity in the men's room seem fairly expansive?

We might tackle these questions by thinking about the effects, social and cultural, of reversed gender typing. In other words, what are the implications of male femininity and female masculinity? One might imagine that even a hint of femininity sullies or lowers the social value of maleness while all masculine forms of femaleness should result in an elevation of status.[32] My bathroom example alone proves that this is far from true. Furthermore, if we think of popular examples of approved female masculinity like a buffed Linda Hamilton in *Terminator* 2 (1991) or a lean and mean Sigourney Weaver in *Aliens*, it is not hard to see that what renders these performances of female masculinity quite tame is their resolute heterosexuality. Indeed, in *Alien Resurrection* (1997), Sigourney Weaver combines her hard body with some light flirtation with co-star Winona Ryder and her masculinity immediately becomes far more threatening and indeed "alien." In other words, when and where female masculinity conjoins with possibly queer identities, it is far less likely to meet with approval. Because female masculinity seems to be at its most threatening when coupled with lesbian desire, . . . I concentrate on queer female masculinity almost to the exclusion of heterosexual female masculinity. I have no doubt that heterosexual female masculinity menaces gender conformity in its own way, but all too often it represents an acceptable degree of female masculinity as compared to the excessive masculinity of the dyke. It is important when thinking about gender variations such as male femininity and female masculinity not simply to create another binary in which masculinity always signifies power; in alternative models of gender variation, female masculinity is not simply the opposite of female femininity, nor is it a female version of male masculinity. . . .

In this [essay] I have tried to chart the implications of the suppression of female masculinities in a variety of spheres: in relation to cultural studies discussions, the suppression of female masculinities allows for male masculinity to stand unchallenged as the bearer of gender stability and gender deviance. The tomboy, the masculine woman, and the racialized masculine subject, I argue, all contribute to a mounting cultural indifference to the masculinity of white males. Gender policing in public bathrooms, furthermore, and gender performances within public spaces produce radically reconfigured notions of proper gender and map new genders onto a utopian vision of radically different bodies and sexualities. By arguing for gender transitivity, for self-conscious forms of female masculinity, for indifference to dominant male masculinities, and for "nonce taxonomies," I do not wish to suggest that we can magically wish into being a new set of properly descriptive genders that would bear down on the outmoded categories "male" and "female." Nor do I mean to suggest that change is simple and that, for example, by simply creating the desegregation of public toilets we will change the function of dominant genders within heteropatriarchal cultures. However, it seems to me that there are some very obvious spaces in which gender difference simply does not work right now, and the breakdown of gender as a signifying system in these arenas can be exploited to hasten the proliferation of alternate gender regimes in other locations. From drag kings to spies with gadgets, from butch bodies to FTM bodies, gender and sexuality and their technologies are already excessively strange. It is simply a matter of keeping them that way....

Notes

1 For an extension of this discussion of tomboys see my article "Oh Bondage Up Yours: Female Masculinity and the Tomboy," in *Sissies and Tomboys: Gender Nonconformity and Homosexual Childhood*, ed. Matthew Rottnek (New York: New York University Press, 1999).

2 For more on the punishment of tomboys see Phyllis Burke, *Gender Shock: Exploding the Myths of Male and Female* (New York: Anchor Books, 1996). Burke analyzes some recent case histories of so-called GID or Gender Identity Disorder, in which little girls are carefully conditioned out of male behavior and into exceedingly constrictive forms of femininity.

3 Carson McCullers, *The Member of the Wedding* [1946] (reprint, New York: Bantam, 1973), p. 1.

4 Ibid., pp. 107, 113, 15....

5 The conference papers were collected in a volume called *Constructing Masculinity*, ed. Maurice Berger, Brian Wallis, and Simon Watson (New York: Routledge, 1996), and the one intervention on behalf of nonmale masculinities was made by Eve Kosofsky Sedgwick.

6 I am using the terms "female born" and "male born" to indicate a social practice of assigning one of two genders to babies at birth. My terminology suggests that these assignations may not hold for the lifetime of the individual, and it suggests from the outset that binary gender continues to dominate our cultural and scientific notions of gender but that individuals inevitably fail to find themselves in only one of two options.

7 Berger, Wallis, and Watson, introduction to *Constructing Masculinity*, p. 7.

8 More and more journals are putting together special issues on masculinity, but I have yet to locate a single special issue with a single essay about female masculinity. The latest journal announcement that found its way to me was from *The Velvet Light Trap: A Critical Journal of Film and Television*. They announced an issue on "New

Masculinities" that featured essays titled "The 'New Masculinity' in *Tootsie*," "On Fathers and Sons, Sex and Death," "Male Melodrama and the Feeling Man," and so forth. This is not to say that such topics are not interesting, only that the "new masculinities" sound remarkably like the old ones. See *The Velvet Light Trap*, "New Masculinities," no. 38 (fall 1996).

9 Berger, Wallis, and Watson, *Constructing Masculinity.*

10 Paul Smith, ed., *Boys: Masculinities in Contemporary Culture* (Boulder, Colo.: Westview Press, 1996), p. 3.

11 Ibid., p. 4.

12 Ibid., pp. 4–5.

13 See Monique Wittig, "The Straight Mind," in *The Straight Mind and Other Essays* (Boston: Beacon Press, 1992); Judith Butler, "Imitation and Gender Insubordination," in *Inside/Out: Lesbian Theories, Gay Theories*, ed. Diana Fuss (New York: Routledge, 1991), pp. 13–31; Jacob Hale, "Are Lesbians Women?" *Hypatia* II 2 (Spring 1996): 94–121.

14 Smith, *Boys*, p. 14.

15 Ibid., p. 1.

16 Ibid., p. 10.

17 Indeed, one such ethnography has been carried out, but significantly it took English soccer hooligans as its topic. See Bill Buford's remarkable *Among the Thugs* (New York: Norton, 1992). A similar work on American male fans would be extremely useful.

18 For verification of such topics of concern just check out the men's sections that are popping up in your local bookstores. More specifically see the work of Michael Kimmel and Victor Seidler: Michael Kimmel, *Manhood in America: A Cultural History* (New York: Free Press, 1996); Victor J. Seidler, *Unreasonable Men: Masculinity and Social Theory* (New York: Routledge, 1994).

19 The continued viability of the category "woman" has been challenged in a variety of academic locations already: Monique Wittig, most notably, argued that "lesbians are not women" in her essay "The Straight Mind," p. 121. Wittig claims that because lesbians are refusing primary relations to men, they cannot occupy the position "woman." In another philosophical challenge to the category "woman," transgender philosopher Jacob Hale uses Monique Wittig's radical claim to theorize the possibility of gendered embodiments that exceed male and female (see Jacob Hale, "Are Lesbians Women?" *Hypatia* II 2 (Spring 1996)). Elsewhere, Cheshire Calhoun suggests that the category "woman" may actually "operate as a lesbian closet" (see Cheshire Calhoun, "The Gender Closet: Lesbian Disappearance under the Sign 'Women,'" *Feminist Studies* 21 I (Spring 1995): 7–34).

20 Leslie Feinberg, *Stone Butch Blues: A Novel* (Ithaca, NY: Firebrand, 1993), p. 59.

21 Nice Rodriguez, *Throw It to the River* (Toronto, Canada: Women's Press, 1993), pp. 25–6.

22 Ibid., p. 33.

23 Ibid., pp. 40–1.

24 Ibid., p. 30.

25 Lee Edelman, "Tearooms and Sympathy, or The Epistemology of the Water Closet," in *Homographesis: Essays in Gay Literary and Cultural Theory* (New York: Routledge, 1994), p. 158.

26 Marjorie Garber, *Vested Interests: Cross-Dressing and Cultural Anxiety* (New York: Routledge, 1992), p. 47. Obviously Garber's use of the term "waterloo" makes a pun out of the drama of bathroom surveillance. Although the pun is clever and even amusing, it is also troubling to see how often Garber turns to punning in her analyses. The constant use of puns throughout the book has the overall effect of making gender crossing sound like a game or at least trivializes the often life-or-death processes involved

in cross-identification. This is not to say gender can never be a "laughing matter" and must always be treated seriously but only to question the use of the pun here as a theoretical method.

27 Garber, *Vested Interests*, p. 47.
28 See Jacques Lacan, "The Agency of the Letter in the Unconscious," in *Ecrits: A Selection*, trans. Alan Sheridan (New York: Norton, 1977), p. 151.
29 Garber, *Vested Interests*, p. 160.
30 Ibid., p. 14.
31 Ibid.
32 Susan Bordo argues this in "Reading the Male Body," *Michigan Quarterly Review* 32 4 (Fall 1993). She writes: "When masculinity gets 'undone' in this culture, the deconstruction nearly always lands us in the territory of the degraded; when femininity gets symbolically undone, the result is an immense elevation of status" (p. 721)....

21

"That Sexe Which Prevaileth"

Anne Fausto-Sterling

The Sexual Continuum

In 1843 Levi Suydam, a twenty-three-year-old resident of Salisbury, Connecticut, asked the town's board of selectmen to allow him to vote as a Whig in a hotly contested local election. The request raised a flurry of objections from the opposition party, for a reason that must be rare in the annals of American democracy: it was said that Suydam was "more female than male," and thus (since only men had the right to vote) should not be allowed to cast a ballot. The selectmen brought in a physician, one Dr. William Barry, to examine Suydam and settle the matter. Presumably, upon encountering a phallus and testicles, the good doctor declared the prospective voter male. With Suydam safely in their column, the Whigs won the election by a majority of one.

A few days later, however, Barry discovered that Suydam menstruated regularly and had a vaginal opening. Suydam had the narrow shoulders and broad hips characteristic of a female build, but occasionally "he" felt physical attractions to the "opposite" sex (by which "he" meant women). Furthermore, "his feminine propensities, such as fondness for gay colors, for pieces of calico, comparing and placing them together and an aversion for bodily labor, and an inability to perform the same, were remarked by many."[1] (Note that this nineteenth-century doctor did not distinguish between "sex" and "gender." Thus he considered a fondness for piecing together swatches of calico just as telling as anatomy and physiology.) No one has yet discovered whether Suydam lost the right to vote.[2] Whatever the outcome, the story conveys both the political weight our culture places on ascertaining a person's correct "sex" and the deep confusion that arises when it can't be easily determined.

European and American culture is deeply devoted to the idea that there are only two sexes. Even our language refuses other possibilities; thus to write about Levi Suydam . . . I have had to invent conventions – s/he and h/er to denote individuals who are clearly neither/both male and female or who are, perhaps, both at once. Nor is the linguistic convenience an idle fancy. Whether one falls into the category of man or woman matters in concrete ways. For Suydam – and still today for

Reprinted from *Sexing the Body: Gender Politics and the Construction of Sexuality* (New York: Basic Books, 2000), pp. 30–44, 273–5 (illustrations omitted).

women in some parts of the world – it meant the right to vote. It might mean being subject to the military draft and to various laws concerning the family and marriage. In many parts of the United States, for example, two individuals legally registered as men cannot have sexual relations without breaking antisodomy laws.[3]

But if the state and legal system has an interest in maintaining only two sexes, our collective biological bodies do not. While male and female stand on the extreme ends of a biological continuum, there are many other bodies, bodies such as Suydam's, that evidently mix together anatomical components convention-ally attributed to both males and females. The implications of my argument for a sexual continuum are profound. If nature really offers us more than two sexes, then it follows that our current notions of masculinity and femininity are cultural conceits. Reconceptualizing the category of "sex" challenges cherished aspects of European and American social organization.

Indeed, we have begun to insist on the male/female dichotomy at increasingly early ages, making the two-sex system more deeply a part of how we imagine human life and giving it the appearance of being both inborn and natural. Now-adays, months before the child leaves the comfort of the womb, amniocentesis and ultrasound identify a fetus's sex. Parents can decorate the baby's room in gender-appropriate style, sports wallpaper – in blue – for the little boy, flowered designs – in pink – for the little girl. Researchers have nearly completed development of technology that can choose the sex of a child at the moment of fertilization.[4] Moreover, modern surgical techniques help maintain the two-sex system. Today children who are born "either/or – neither/both"[5] – a fairly common phenom-enon – usually disappear from view because doctors "correct" them right away with surgery. In the past, however, intersexuals (or hermaphrodites, as they were called until recently) were culturally acknowledged.... (Members of the present-day Intersexual Movement eschew the use of the word *hermaphrodite*. I will try to use it when it is historically proper. Since the word *intersexual* is a modern one, I will not use it when writing about the past.)

How did the birth and acknowledged presence of hermaphrodites shape ideas about gender in the past? How did modern medical treatments of intersexuality develop? How has a political movement of intersexuals and their supporters emerged to push for increased openness to more fluid sexual identities, and how successful have their challenges been? What follows is a most literal tale of social construction – the story of the emergence of strict surgical enforcement of a two-party system of sex and the possibility, as we move into the twenty-first century, of the evolution of a multiparty arrangement.

Hermaphrodite History

Intersexuality is old news. The word *hermaphrodite* comes from a Greek term that combined the names Hermes (son of Zeus and variously known as the messenger of the gods, patron of music, controller of dreams, and protector of livestock) and Aphrodite (the Greek goddess of sexual love and beauty). There are at least two Greek myths about the origins of the first hermaphrodite. In one, Aphrodite and Hermes produce a child so thoroughly endowed with the attributes of each parent that, unable to decide its sex for sure, they name it Hermaphroditos. In the other, their child is an astonishingly beautiful male with whom a water nymph falls in love. Overcome by desire, she so deeply intertwines her body with his that they become joined as one.

If the figure of the hermaphrodite has seemed odd enough to prompt speculation about its peculiar origins, it has also struck some as the embodiment of a human past that predated dualistic sexual division. Early biblical interpreters thought that Adam began his existence as a hermaphrodite and that he divided into two individuals, male and female, only after falling from grace. Plato wrote that there were originally three sexes – male, female, and hermaphrodite – but that the third sex became lost over time.[6]

Different cultures have confronted real-life intersexuals in different ways. Jewish religious texts such as the Talmud and the Tosefta list extensive regulations for people of mixed sex, regulating modes of inheritance and of social conduct. The Tosefta, for example, forbids hermaphrodites from inheriting their fathers' estates (like daughters), from secluding themselves with women (like sons), and from shaving (like men). When they menstruate they must be isolated from men (like women); they are disqualified from serving as witnesses or as priests (like women); but the laws of pederasty apply to them. While Judaic law provided a means for integrating hermaphrodites into mainstream culture, Romans were not so kind. In Romulus's time intersexes were believed to be a portent of a crisis of the state and were often killed. Later, however, in Pliny's era, hermaphrodites became eligible for marriage.[7]

In tracking the history of medical analyses of intersexuality, one learns more generally how the social history of gender itself has varied, first in Europe and later in America, which inherited European medical traditions. In the process we can learn that there is nothing natural or inevitable about current medical treatment of intersexuals. Early medical practitioners, who understood sex and gender to fall along a continuum and not into the discrete categories we use today, were not fazed by hermaphrodites. Sexual difference, they thought, involved quantitative variation. Women were cool, men hot, masculine women or feminine men warm. Moreover, human variation did not, physicians of this era believed, stop at the number three. Parents could produce boys with different degrees of manliness and girls with varying amounts of womanliness.

In the premodern era, several views of the biology of intersexuality competed. Aristotle (384–322 BC), for example, categorized hermaphrodites as a type of twin. He believed that complete twinning occurred when the mother contributed enough matter at conception to create two entire embryos. In the case of intersexuals, there was more than enough matter to create one but not quite enough for two. The excess matter, he thought, became extra genitalia. Aristotle did not believe that genitalia defined the sex of the baby, however. Rather, the heat of the heart determined maleness or femaleness. He argued that underneath their confusing anatomy, hermaphrodites truly belonged to one of only two possible sexes. The highly influential Galen, in the first century AD, disagreed, arguing that hermaphrodites belonged to an intermediate sex. He believed that sex emerged from the opposition of male and female principles in the maternal and paternal seeds in combination with interactions between the left and right sides of the uterus. From the overlaying of varying degrees of dominance between male and female seed on top of the several potential positions of the fetus in the womb, a grid containing from three to seven cells emerged. Depending upon where on the grid an embryo fell, it could range from entirely male, through various intermediate states, to entirely female. Thus, thinkers in the Galenic tradition believed no stable biological divide separated male from female.[8]

Physicians in the Middle Ages continued to hold to the classical theory of a sexual continuum, even while they increasingly argued for sharper divisions of sexual variation. Medieval medical texts espoused the classical idea that the relative heat on the right side of the uterus produced males, the cooler fetus developing on the left side of the womb became a female, and fetuses developing more toward the middle became manly women or womanly men.[9] The notion of a continuum of heat coexisted with the idea that the uterus consisted of seven discrete chambers. The three cells to the right housed males, the three to the left females, while the central chamber produced hermaphrodites.[10]

A willingness to find a place for hermaphrodites in scientific theory, however, did not translate into social acceptance. Historically, hermaphrodites were often regarded as rebellious, disruptive, or even fraudulent. Hildegard of Bingen, a famous German abbess and visionary mystic (1098–1179) condemned any confusion of male and female identity. As the historian Joan Cadden has noted, Hildegard chose to place her denunciation "between an assertion that women should not say mass and a warning against sexual perversions. . . . A disorder of either sex or sex roles is a disorder in the social fabric . . . and in the religious order."[11] Such stern disapproval was unusual for her time. Despite widespread uncertainty about their proper social roles, disapproval of hermaphrodites remained relatively mild. Medieval medical and scientific texts complained of negative personality traits – lustfulness in the masculine femalelike hermaphrodite and deceitfulness in the feminine malelike individual,[12] but outright condemnation seems to have been infrequent.

Biologists and physicians of that era did not have the social prestige and authority of today's professionals and were not the only ones in a position to define and regulate the hermaphrodite. In Renaissance Europe, scientific and medical texts often propounded contradictory theories about the production of hermaphrodites. These theories could not fix gender as something real and stable within the body. Rather, physicians' stories competed both with medicine and with those elaborated by the Church, the legal profession, and politicians. To further complicate matters, different European nations had different ideas about the origins, dangers, civil rights, and duties of hermaphrodites.[13]

For example, in France, in 1601, the case of Marie/Marin le Marcis engendered great controversy. "Marie" had lived as a woman for twenty-one years before deciding to put on men's clothing and registering to marry the woman with whom s/he cohabited. "Marin" was arrested, and after having gone through harrowing sentences – first being condemned to burn at the stake, then having the penalty "reduced" to death by strangling (and we thought *our* death row was bad!!) – s/he eventually was set free on the condition that s/he wear women's clothing until the age of twenty-five. Under French law Marie/Marin had committed two crimes: sodomy and cross-dressing.

English law, in contrast, did not specifically forbid cross-gender dressing. But it did look askance at those who donned the attire of a social class to which they did not belong. In a 1746 English case, Mary Hamilton married another woman after assuming the name "Dr. Charles Hamilton." The legal authorities were sure she had done something wrong, but they couldn't quite put their finger on what it was. Eventually they convicted her of vagrancy, reasoning that she was an unusually ballsy but nonetheless common cheat.[14]

During the Renaissance, there was no central clearinghouse for the handling of hermaphrodites. While in some cases physicians or the state intervened, in others the Church took the lead. For instance, in Piedra, Italy, in 1601, the same year of Marie/Marin's arrest, a young soldier named Daniel Burghammer shocked his regiment when he gave birth to a healthy baby girl. After his alarmed wife called in his army captain, he confessed to being half male and half female. Christened as a male, he had served as a soldier for seven years while also a practicing blacksmith. The baby's father, Burghammer said, was a Spanish soldier. Uncertain of what to do, the captain called in Church authorities, who decided to go ahead and christen the baby, whom they named Elizabeth. After she was weaned – Burghammer nursed the child with his female breast – several towns competed for the right to adopt her. The Church declared the child's birth a miracle, but granted Burghammer's wife a divorce, suggesting that it found Burghammer's ability to give birth incompatible with role of husband.[15]

The stories of Marie/Marin, Mary Hamilton, and Daniel Burghammer illustrate a simple point. Different countries and different legal and religious systems viewed intersexuality in different ways. The Italians seemed relatively nonplussed by the blurring of gender borders, the French rigidly regulated it, while the English, although finding it distasteful, worried more about class transgressions. Nevertheless, all over Europe the sharp distinction between male and female was at the core of systems of law and politics. The rights of inheritance, forms of judicial punishment, and the right to vote and participate in the political system were all determined in part by sex. And those who fell in between? Legal experts acknowledged that hermaphrodites existed but insisted they position themselves within this gendered system. Sir Edward Coke, famed jurist of early modern England wrote "an Hermaphrodite may purchase according to that sexe which prevaileth."[16] Similarly, in the first half of the seventeenth century, French hermaphrodites could serve as witnesses in the court and even marry, providing that they did so in the role assigned to them by "the sex which dominates their personality."[17]

The individual him/herself shared with medical and legal experts the right to decide which sex prevailed but, once having made a choice, was expected to stick with it. The penalty for reneging could be severe. At stake was the maintenance of the social order and the rights of man (meant literally). Thus, although it was clear that some people straddled the male-female divide, the social and legal structures remained fixed around a two-sex system.[18]

The Making of the Modern Intersexual

As biology emerged as an organized discipline during the late eighteenth and early nineteenth centuries, it gradually acquired greater authority over the disposition of ambiguous bodies.[19] Nineteenth-century scientists developed a clear sense of the statistical aspects of natural variation,[20] but along with such knowledge came the authority to declare that certain bodies were abnormal and in need of correction.[21]

The biologist Isidore Geoffroy Saint-Hilaire played a particularly central role in recasting scientific ideas about sexual difference. He founded a new science, which he dubbed *teratology*, for the study and classification of unusual births. Saint-Hilaire and other like-minded biologists set out to study all anatomical anomalies, and they established two important principles that began to guide medical approaches to natural variation. First, Saint-Hilaire argued that "Nature is one whole"[22] – that is, that even unusual or what had been called "monstrous" births were still part of nature. Second, drawing on newly developed statistical concepts, he proclaimed that hermaphrodites and other birth anomalies resulted from abnormal embryonic development. To understand their genesis, he argued, one must understand normal development. Studying abnormal variations could in turn illuminate normal processes. Saint-Hilaire believed that unlocking the origins of hermaphrodites would lead to an understanding of the development of sexual difference more generally. This scientific transposition of the old mythic fascination with hermaphrodites has remained, to this day, a guiding principle of scientific investigation into the biological underpinnings of sex/gender roles and behaviors of nonintersexuals. . . .

Saint-Hilaire's writings were not only of importance to the scientific community, they served a new social function as well. Whereas in previous centuries, unusual bodies were treated as unnatural and freakish, the new field of teratology offered a natural explanation for the birth of people with extraordinary bodies.[23] At the same time, however, it redefined such bodies as pathological, as unhealthy conditions to be cured using increased medical knowledge. Ironically, then, scientific understanding was used as a tool to obliterate precisely the wonders it illuminated. By the middle of the twentieth century, medical technology had "advanced" to a point where it could make bodies that had once been objects of awe and astonishment disappear from view, all in the name of "correcting nature's mistakes."[24]

The hermaphrodite vanishing act relied heavily on the standard scientific technique of classification.[25] Saint-Hilaire divided the body into "sex segments," three on the left and three on the right. He named these zones the "profound portion," which contained ovaries, testicles, or related structures; the "middle portion," which contained internal sex structures such as the uterus and seminal vesicles; and the "external portion," which included the external genitalia.[26] If all six segments were wholly male, he decreed, so too was the body. If all six were female, the body was clearly female. But when a mixture of male and female appeared in any of the six zones, a hermaphrodite resulted. Thus, Saint-Hilaire's system continued to recognize the legitimacy of sexual variety but subdivided hermaphrodites into different types, laying the groundwork for future scientists to establish a difference between "true" and "false" hermaphrodites. Since the "true" hermaphrodites were very rare, eventually a classification system arose that made intersexuality virtually invisible.

In the late 1830s, a physician named James Young Simpson, building on Saint-Hilaire's approach, proposed to classify hermaphrodites as either "spurious" or "true." In spurious hermaphrodites, he wrote, "the genital organs and general sexual configuration of one sex approach, from imperfect or abnormal development, to those of the opposite," while in true hermaphrodites "there actually coexist upon the body of the same individual more or fewer of the genital organs."[27] In Simpson's view, "genital organs" included not only ovaries or testes (the gonads) but also structures such as the uterus or seminal vesicles. Thus, a true hermaphrodite might have testes and a uterus, or ovaries and seminal vesicles.

Simpson's theory presaged what the historian Alice Dreger has dubbed the Age of Gonads. The honor of offering definitive powers to the gonads fell to a German physician named Theodor Albrecht Klebs, who published his ideas in 1876. Like Simpson, Klebs contrasted "true" with what he called "pseudo" – hermaphrodites. He restricted the term *true hermaphrodite* to someone who had both ovarian and testicular tissue in h/her body. All others with mixed anatomies – persons with both a penis and ovaries, or a uterus and a mustache, or testes and a vagina – no longer, in Klebs's system, qualified as true hermaphrodites. But if they were not hermaphrodites, what were they? Klebs believed that under each of these confusing surfaces lurked a body either truly male or truly female. Gonads, he insisted, were the sole defining factor in biological sex. A body with two ovaries, no matter how many masculine features it might have, was female. No matter if a pair of testes were nonfunctional and the person possessing them had a vagina and breast, testes made a body male. The net result of this reasoning, as Dreger has noted, was that "significantly fewer people counted as 'truly' both male and female."[28] Medical science was working its magic: hermaphrodites were beginning to disappear.

Once the gonads became the decisive factor, it required more than common sense to identify an individual's true sex. The tools of science – in the form of a microscope and new methods of preparing tissue for microscopic examination – became essential.[29] Rapidly, images of the hermaphrodite's body disappeared from medical journals, replaced by abstract photographs of thinly sliced and carefully colored bits of gonadal tissue. Moreover, as Alice Dreger points out, the primitive state of surgical techniques, especially the lack of anesthesia and antisepsis, at the end of the nineteenth century meant that doctors could obtain gonadal tissue samples only after death or castration: "Small in number, dead, impotent – what a sorry lot the true hermaphrodites had become!"[30] People of mixed sex all but disappeared, not because they had become rarer, but because scientific methods classified them out of existence.

At the turn of the century (1896, to be exact), the British physicians George F. Blackler and William P. Lawrence wrote a paper examining earlier claims of true hermaphroditism. They found that only three out of twenty-eight previously published case studies complied with the new standards. In Orwellian fashion, they cleansed past medical records of accounts of hermaphroditism, claiming they did not meet modern scientific standards,[31] while few new cases met the strict criterion of microscopic verification of the presence of both male and female gonadal tissue.

Arguing about Sex and Gender

Under the mantle of scientific advancement, the ideological work of science was imperceptible to turn-of-the-century scientists, just as the ideological work of requiring Polymerase Chain Reaction Sex Tests of women athletes is, apparently, to the [International Olympic Committee]. . . . Nineteenth-century theories of intersexuality – the classification systems of Saint-Hilaire, Simpson, Klebs, Blacker, and Lawrence – fit into a much broader group of biological ideas about difference. Scientists and medical men insisted that the bodies of males and females, of whites and people of color, Jews and Gentiles, and middle-class and laboring men differed deeply. In an era that argued politically for individual rights on the basis of human equality, scientists defined some bodies as better and more deserving of rights than others.

If this seems paradoxical, from another point of view it makes good sense. Political theories that declared that "all men are created equal" threatened to do more than provide justification for colonies to overthrow monarchies and establish independent republics. They threatened to undermine the logic behind funda-mental social and economic institutions such as marriage, slavery, or the limiting of the right to vote to white men with property. Not surprisingly, then, the science of physical difference was often invoked to invalidate claims for social and political emancipation.[32]

In the nineteenth century, for example, women active in the movement to abolish slavery in the United States, soon began to insist on their right to speak in public,[33] and by mid-century women in both the United States and England were demanding better educational opportunities and economic rights and the right to vote. Their actions met fierce resistance from scientific experts.[34] Some doctors argued that permitting women to obtain college degrees would ruin their health, leading to sterility and ultimately the degeneration of the (white, middle-class) human race. Educated women angrily organized counterattacks and slowly gained the right to advanced education and the vote.[35]

Such social struggles had profound implications for the scientific categorization of intersexuality. More than ever, politics necessitated two and only two sexes. The issue had gone beyond particular legal rights such as the right to vote. What if, while thinking she was a man, a woman engaged in some activity women were thought to be incapable of doing? Suppose she did well at it? What would happen to the idea that women's natural incapacities dictated social inequity? As the battles for social equality between the sexes heated up in the early twentieth century, physicians developed stricter and more exclusive definitions of hermaphroditism. The more social radicals blasted away at the separations between masculine and feminine spheres, the more physicians insisted on the absolute division between male and female.

Intersexuals Under Medical Surveillance

Until the early nineteenth century, the primary arbiters of intersexual status had been lawyers and judges, who, although they might consult doctors or priests on particular cases, generally followed their own understanding of sexual difference. By the dawn of the twentieth century, physicians were recognized as the chief regulators of sexual intermediacy.[36] Although the legal standard – that there were but two sexes and that a hermaphrodite had to identify with the sex prevailing in h/her body – remained, by the 1930s medical practitioners had developed a new angle: the surgical and hormonal suppression of intersexuality. The Age of Gonads gave way to the even less flexible Age of Conversion, in which medical practitioners found it imperative to catch mixed-sex people at birth and convert them, by any means necessary, to either male or female. . . .

But patients, troubling and troublesome patients, continued to place themselves squarely in the path of such oversimplification. Even during the Age of Gonads, medical men sometimes based their assessment of sexual identity on the overall shape of the body and the inclination of the patient – the gonads be damned. In 1915, the British physician William Blair Bell publicly suggested that sometimes the body was too mixed up to let the gonads alone dictate treatment. The new technologies of anesthesia and asepsis made it possible for small tissue samples (biopsies) to be taken from the gonads of living patients. Bell encountered a patient who had a mixture of external traits – a mustache, breasts, an elongated clitoris, a deep voice, and no menstrual period – and whose biopsy revealed that the gonad was an ovo-testis (a mixture of egg-producing and sperm-producing tissues).

Faced with a living and breathing true hermaphrodite Bell reverted to the older legal approach, writing that "predominating feminine characteristics have decided the sex adopted." He emphasized that one need not rely wholly on the gonads to decide which sex a patient must choose, but that "the possession of a [single] sex is a necessity of our social order, for hermaphrodites as well as for normal subjects."[37] Bell did not abandon, however, the concepts of true and pseudo-hermaphroditism. Indeed, most physicians practicing today take this distinction for granted. But faced with the insistent complexity of actual bodies and personalities, Bell urged that each case be dealt with flexibly, taking into account the many different signs presented by the body and behaviors of the intersexual patient.

But this returned doctors to an old problem: Which signs were to count? Consider a case reported in 1924 by Hugh Hampton Young, "the Father of American Urology."[38] Young operated on a young man with a malformed penis,[39] an undescended testis, and a painful mass in the groin. The mass turned out to be an ovary connected to an underdeveloped uterus and oviducts. Young pondered the problem:

> A normal-looking young man with masculine instincts [athletic, heterosexual] was found to have a . . . functioning ovary in the left groin. What was the character of the scrotal sac on the right side? If these were also undoubtedly female, should they be allowed to remain outside in the scrotum? If a male, should the patient be allowed to continue life with a functioning ovary and tube in the abdomen on the left side? If the organs of either side should be extirpated, which should they be?[40]

The young man turned out to have a testis, and Young snagged the ovary. As his experience grew, Young increasingly based his judgment calls on his patients' psychological and social situations, using sophisticated understandings of the body more as a guide to the range of physical possibilities than as a necessary indicator of sex.

In 1937, Young, by then a professor of urology at Johns Hopkins University, published *Genital Abnormalities, Hermaphroditism and Related Adrenal Diseases*, a book remarkable for its erudition, scientific insight, and open-mindedness. In it he further systematized the classification of intersexes (maintaining Blackler and

Lawrence's definition of true hermaphroditism) and drew together a wealth of carefully documented case histories, both his own and others', in order to demonstrate and study the medical treatment of these "accidents of birth." He did not judge the people he described, several of whom lived as "practicing hermaphrodites" – that is, they had sexual experiences as both men and women.[41] Nor did he attempt to coerce any of them into treatment.

One of Young's cases involved a hermaphrodite named Emma who grew up as a female. With both a large clitoris (one or two inches in length) and a vagina, s/he could have "normal" heterosexual sex with both men and women. As a teenager s/he had sex with a number of girls to whom she was deeply attracted, but at age nineteen s/he married a man with whom s/he experienced little sexual pleasure (although, according to Emma, he didn't have any complaints). During this and subsequent marriages, Emma kept girl friends on the side, frequently having pleasurable sex with them. Young described h/her as appearing "to be quite content and even happy." In conversation, Dr. Young elicited Emma's occasional wish to be a man. Although he assured her that it would be a relatively simple matter, s/he replied, "Would you have to remove that vagina? I don't know about that because that's my meal ticket. If you did that I would have to quit my husband and go to work, so I think I'll keep it and stay as I am. My husband supports me well, and even though I don't have any sexual pleasure with him, I do have lots with my girlfriend." Without further comment or evidence of disappointment, Young proceeded to the next "interesting example of another practicing hermaphrodite."[42]

His case summary mentions nothing about financial motivations, saying only that Emma refused a sex fix because she "dreaded necessary operations,"[43] but Emma was not alone in allowing economic and social considerations to influence her choice of sex. Usually this meant that young hermaphrodites, when offered some choice, opted to become male. Consider the case of Margaret, born in 1915 and raised as a girl until the age of 14. When her voice began to deepen into a man's, and her malformed penis grew and began to take on adult functions, Margaret demanded permission to live as a man. With the help of psychologists (who later published a report on the case) and a change of address, he abandoned his "ultrafeminine" attire of a "green satin dress with flared skirt, red velvet hat with rhinestone trimming, slippers with bows, hair bobbed with ends brought down over his cheeks." He became, instead, a short-haired, baseball-and football-playing teenager whom his new classmates called Big James. James had his own thoughts about the advantages of being a man. He told his half-sister: "It is easier to be a man. You get more money (wages) and you don't have to be married. If you're a girl and you don't get married people make fun of you."[44]

Although Dr. Young illuminated the subject of intersexuality with a great deal of wisdom and consideration for his patients, his work was part of the process that led both to a new invisibility and a harshly rigid approach to the treatment of intersexual bodies. In addition to being a thoughtful collection of case studies, Young's book is an extended treatise on the most modern methods – both surgical and hormonal – of treating those who sought help. Although less judgmental and controlling of patients and their parents than his successors, he nevertheless supplied the next generation of physicians with the scientific and technical bedrock on which they based their practices.

As was true in the nineteenth century, increased knowledge of the biological origins of sexual complexity facilitated the elimination of their signs. Deepening understandings of the physiological bases of intersexuality combined with improvements in surgical technology, especially since 1950, began to enable physicians to catch most intersexuals at the moment of birth.[45] The motive for their conversion was genuinely humanitarian: a wish to enable individuals to fit in and to function both physically and psychologically as healthy human beings. But behind the wish lay unexamined assumptions: first, that there should be only two sexes; second, that only heterosexuality was normal; and third, that particular gender roles defined the psychologically healthy man and woman.[46] These same assumptions continue to provide the rationale for the modern "medical management" of intersexual births.

Notes

1 Quoted in Epstein 1990. Epstein and Janet Golden found the Suydam story and made it available to other scholars.
2 A fact-checker for *The Sciences* called Suydam's town in Connecticut to verify the story. The town official asked to keep the family name quiet, apparently because relatives still live in the area and the story still bothers some local residents.
3 Halley 1991.
4 Kolata 1998.
5 I owe this phrase to Epstein 1990.
6 Young 1937 has a full and highly readable review of hermaphrodites from antiquity to the present.
7 Ibid.
8 This discussion comes from Cadden 1993; Epstein 1990; Epstein and Straub 1991; Jones and Stallybrass 1991; and Park 1990.
9 My account of sex determination and the meanings of gender in the Middle Ages comes from Cadden 1993.
10 In one variation of this idea the uterus had five chambers, with the middle one, again, producing the hermaphrodite.
11 Cadden 1993, p. 213.
12 Ibid., p. 214.
13 Jones and Stallybrass 1991.
14 Ibid.; Daston and Park 1985.
15 Matthews 1959, pp. 247–8. I am indebted to a colleague, Professor Pepe Amor y Vasquez, for bringing this incident to my attention.
16 Quoted in Jones and Stallybrass 1991, p. 105.
17 Quoted in Ibid., p. 90.
18 Several historians note that concerns about homosexuality enhanced the felt need for social regulation of hermaphrodites. In fact, homosexuality itself was sometimes represented as a form of hermaphroditism. Thus intersexuality, although relatively rare, fell (and falls) into a broader category of sexual variation of concern to physicians as well as religious and legal authorities. See discussions in Dreger 1998a, 1998b; Epstein 1990; Epstein and Straub 1991; and Park 1990.
19 Coleman 1971 and Nyhart 1995.
20 Foucault 1970; Poovey 1995; and Porter 1986.
21 Daston 1992.
22 Quoted in Dreger 1988b, p. 33.

23 On earlier treatments of "monstrous births," see Daston and Park 1998; for a modern scientist's evaluation of St.-Hilaire, see Morin 1996.

24 These comments are inspired by Thomson 1996 and Dreger 1998b. For a discussion of how modern reproductive and genetic technology has pushed us even further in the direction of eliminating wondrous bodies, see Hubbard 1990.

25 For a discussion of the social function of classification and of how social ideology produces particular systems of classification, see Schiebinger 1993; and Dreger 1998b.

26 Dreger 1998b.

27 Quoted in Dreger 1998b.

28 Dreger 1998b, p. 146.

29 The microscope was not new, although it underwent continued improvement in the nineteenth century. Just as important was the development of techniques to slice tissues into very thin strips and to stain the tissue to make them distinct under microscopic examination (Nyhart 1995).

30 Dreger 1998b, p. 150.

31 For current estimates using this "modern" system, see Blackless et al. 1999.

32 For well-documented examples of the uses of the science of physical difference, see Russett 1989.

33 Sterling 1991.

34 Newman 1985.

35 Clarke 1873; Howe 1874; for the century-long struggle of women to enter science themselves, see Rossiter 1982 and 1995.

36 Historian Dreger based her book on over 300 cases in the medical literature in Britain and France.

37 Quoted in Dreger 1998b, pp. 161, 1.

38 Newsom 1994.

39 The man suffered from hypospadias, a failure of the urethra to run to the tip of the penis. Men with hypospadias have difficulties with urination.

40 Quoted in Hausman 1995, p. 80.

41 Practicing hermaphrodites differ from bisexuals. Bisexuals are completely male or completely female but not completely heterosexual. *A practicing hermaphrodite*, as Young used the term, meant a person who used his male parts to take the male role in sex with a woman and her female parts to take the female role in sex with a man.

42 Young, 1937, pp. 140, 142.

43 Ibid., p. 139.

44 Dicks and Childers 1934, pp. 508, 510.

45 The latest medical writings speculate about the future use of gene therapy in utero; in theory, such treatments could prevent many of the more common forms of intersexuality. See Donahoe et al. 1991.

46 Evidence for this lack of self-reflection on the part of the medical community may be found in Kessler 1990.

References

Blackless, M., A. Charuvastra, et al. 2000. How sexually dimorphic are we? A review article. *American Journal of Human Biology* 12/2: 151–66.

Cadden, J. 1993. *Meanings of Sex Difference in the Middle Ages: Medicine, Science and Culture.* New York: Cambridge University Press.

Clarke, E. H. 1873. *Sex in Education; Or, a Fair Chance for the Girls.* Boston: James R. Osgood.

Coleman, W. 1971. *Biology in the 19th Century: Problems of Form, Function and Transformation*. New York: Wiley.

Daston, L. 1992. The naturalized female intellect. *Science in Context* 5/2: 209–35.

Daston, L., and K. Park. 1985. Hermaphrodites in Renaissance France. *Critical Matrix* 1/5: 1–19.

——.1998. *Wonders and the Order of Nature, 1150–1750*. New York: Zone Books.

Dicks, G. H., and A. T. Childers. 1934. The social transformation of a boy who had lived his first fourteen years as a girl: A case history. *American Journal of Orthopsychiatry* 4: 508–17.

Donahoe, P. K., D. M. Powell, et al. 1991. Clinical management of intersex abnormalities. *Current Problems in Surgery* 28/8: 513–70.

Dreger, A. D. 1998a. Ambiguous sex – or ambivalent medicine? Ethical issues in the treatment of intersexuality. *Hastings Center Report* (May–June): 24–35.

——. 1998b. *Hermaphrodites and the Medical Invention of Sex*. Cambridge, Mass.: Harvard University Press.

Epstein, J. 1990. Either/or – Neither/both: Sexual ambiguity and the ideology of gender. *Genders* 7: 99–142.

Epstein, J., and K. Straub. 1991. Introduction: The guarded body. In *Body Guards: The Cultural Politics of Gender and Gender Ambiguity*, ed. J. Epstein and K. Straub. New York: Routledge, pp. 1–28.

Foucault, M. 1970. *The Order of Things: An Archeology of the Human Sciences*. New York: Random House.

Halley, J. 1991. Misreading sodomy: A critique of the classification of homosexuals in federal equal protection law. In *Body Guards: The Cultural Politics of Gender and Gender Ambiguity*, ed. J. Epstein and K. Straub. New York: Routledge, pp. 351–77.

Hausman, B. L. 1995. *Changing Sex: Transsexualism, Technology and the Idea of Gender in the 20th Century*. Durham, NC: Duke University Press.

Howe, J. W., ed. 1874. *Sex and Education: A Reply to Dr. E. Clarke's "Sex in Education."* Boston: Roberts Brothers.

Hubbard, R. 1990. *The Politics of Women's Biology*. New York: Routledge.

Jones, A. R., and P. Stallybrass. 1991. Fetishizing gender: Constructing the hermaphrodite in Renaissance Europe. In *Body Guards: The Cultural Politics of Gender and Gender Ambiguity*, ed. J. Epstein and K. Straub. New York: Routledge, pp. 80–111.

Kessler, S. J. 1990. The medical construction of gender: Case management of intersexed infants. *Signs* 16/1: 3–26.

Kolata, G. 1998. Researchers report success in method to pick baby's sex. *New York Times*, September 9, A 1ff.

Matthews, G. T., ed. 1959. 259. A Lansquenet bears a child. News and Rumor. In *Renaissance Europe (The Fugger Newsletters)*. New York: Capricorn Books.

Morin, A. 1996. La tératologie de Geoffroy Saint-Hilaire à nos jours. *Bulletin de l'Association des Anatomistes* 80/248: 17–31.

Newman, L. M., ed. 1985. *Men's Ideas, Women's Realities: Popular Science, 1870–1915*. New York: Pergamon Press.

Newsom, B. 1994. Hugh Hampton Young, M. D., 1870–1945. *Journal of the South Carolina Medical Association* 90/5: 254.

Nyhart, L. 1995. *Biology Takes Form: Animal Morphology and the German Universities, 1800–1900*. Chicago: University of Chicago Press.

Park, K. 1990. Hermaphrodites and lesbians: Sexual anxiety and French medicine, 1570–1621. Talk given at Annual Meeting of the History of Science Society.

Poovey, M. 1995. *Making a Social Body: British Cultural Formation, 1830–1864*. Chicago: University of Chicago Press.

Porter, T. M. 1986. *The Rise of Statistical Thinking, 1820–1900*. Princeton: Princeton University Press.

Rossiter, M. W. 1982. *Women Scientists in America: Struggles and Strategies to 1940*. Baltimore: Johns Hopkins University Press.

——. 1995. *Women Scientists in America: Before Affirmative Action*. Baltimore: Johns Hopkins University Press.

Russett, C. E. 1989. *Sexual Science: The Victorian Construction of Womanhood*. Cambridge, Mass.: Harvard University Press.

Schiebinger, L. 1993. *Nature's Body: Gender in the Making of Modern Science*. Boston: Beacon Press.

Sterling, D. 1991. *Ahead of Her Time: Abby Kelley and the Politics of Antislavery*. New York: Norton.

Thomson, R. G., ed. 1996. *Freakery: Cultural Spectacles of the Extraordinary Body*. New York: New York University Press.

Young, H. H. 1937. *Genital Abnormalities, Hermaphroditism and Related Adrenal Diseases*. Baltimore: Williams and Wilkins.

22

The Gender of Brazilian Transgendered Prostitutes

Don Kulick

Males who enjoy being anally penetrated by other males are, in many places in the world, an object of special cultural elaboration. Anywhere they occur as a culturally recognized type, it is usually they who are classified and named, not the males who penetrate them (who are often simply called "men"). Furthermore, to the extent that male same-sex sexual relations are stigmatized, the object of social vituperation is, again, usually those males who allow themselves to be penetrated, not the males who penetrate them. Anywhere they constitute a salient cultural category, men who enjoy being penetrated are believed to think, talk, and act in particular, identifiable, and often cross-gendered manners. What is more, a large number of such men do in fact behave in these culturally intelligible ways. So whether they are the *mahus, hijras, kathoeys, xaniths,* or *berdaches* of non-Western societies, or the mollies and fairies of our own history, links between habitual receptivity in anal sex and particular effeminate behavioral patterns structure the ways in which males who are regularly anally penetrated are perceived, and they structure the ways in which many of those males think about and live their lives.[1]

One area of the world in which males who enjoy being anally penetrated receive a very high degree of cultural attention is Latin America. Any student of Latin America will be familiar with the effervescent figure of the effeminate male homosexual. Called *maricón, cochón, joto, marica, pajara, loca, frango, bicha,* or any number of other names depending on where one finds him (see Murray and Dynes 1987 and Dynes 1987 for a sampling), these males all appear to share certain behavioral characteristics and seem to be thought of, throughout Latin America, in quite similar ways.[2]

One of the basic things one quickly learns from any analysis of Latin American sexual categories is that sex between males in this part of the world does not necessarily result in both partners being perceived as homosexual. The crucial determinant of a homosexual classification is not so much the fact of sex as it is the role performed during the sexual act. A male who anally penetrates another male is generally not considered to be homosexual. He is considered, in all the various local idioms, to be a "man"; indeed, in some communities, penetrating another male and then bragging about it is one way in which men demonstrate their masculinity to others (Lancaster 1992: 241; cf. Brandes 1981: 234).

Reprinted from *American Anthropologist* 99/3 (1997), pp. 574–84.

Quite different associations attach themselves to a male who allows himself to be penetrated. That male has placed himself in what is understood to be an unmasculine, passive position. By doing so, he has forfeited manhood and becomes seen as something other than a man. This cultural classification as feminine is often reflected in the general comportment, speech practices, and dress patterns of such males, all of which tend to be recognizable to others as effeminate.

A conceptual system in which only males who are penetrated are homosexual is clearly very different from the modern heterosexual/homosexual dichotomy currently in place in countries such as the United States, where popular understanding generally maintains that a male who has sex with another male is gay, no matter how carefully he may restrict his behavior to the role of penetrator.[3] This difference between Latin American and northern Euro-American understandings of sexuality is analyzed with great insight in the literature on male same-sex relations in Latin America, and one of the chief merits of that literature is its sensitive documentation of the ways in which erotic practices and sexual identities are culturally organized.

Somewhat surprisingly, the same sensitivity that informs the literature when it comes to sexuality does not extend to the realm of gender. A question not broached in this literature is whether the fundamental differences that exist between northern Euro-American and Latin American regimes of sexuality might also result in, or be reflective of, different regimes of gender. This oversight is odd in light of the obvious and important links between sexuality and gender in a system where a simple act of penetration has the power to profoundly alter a male's cultural definition and social status. Instead of exploring what the differences in the construction of sexuality might mean for differences in the construction of gender, however, analysis in this literature falls back on familiar concepts. So just as gender in northern Europe and North America consists of men and women, so does it consist of men and women in Latin America, we are told. The characteristics ascribed to and the behavior expected of those two different types of people are not exactly the same in these two different parts of the world, to be sure, but the basic gender categories are the same.

This article contests that view. I will argue that the *sexual division* that researchers have noted between those who penetrate and those who are penetrated extends far beyond sexual interactions between males to constitute the basis of the *gender division* in Latin America. Gender, in this particular elaboration, is grounded not so much in sex (like it is, for example, in modern northern European and North American cultures) as it is grounded in sexuality. This difference in grounding generates a gender configuration different from the one that researchers working in Latin America have postulated, and it allows and even encourages the elaboration of cultural spaces such as those inhabited by effeminate male homosexuals. Gender in Latin America should be seen not as consisting of men and women, but rather of men and not-men, the latter being a category into which both biological females and males who enjoy anal penetration are culturally situated. This specific situatedness provides individuals – not just men who enjoy anal penetration, but everyone – with a conceptual framework that they can draw on in order to understand and organize their own and others' desires, bodies, affective and physical relations, and social roles.

The Body in Question

The evidence for the arguments developed here will be drawn from my fieldwork in the Brazilian city of Salvador, among a group of males who enjoy anal penetration. These males are effeminized prostitutes known throughout Brazil as *travestis* (a word derived from *transvestir*, to cross-dress).[4]

Travestis occupy a strikingly visible place in both Brazilian social space and in the Brazilian cultural imaginary.[5] All Brazilian cities of any size contain travestis, and in the large cities of Rio de Janeiro and São Paulo, travestis number in the thousands. (In Salvador, travestis numbered between about 80 and 250, depending on the time of year.)[6] Travestis are most exuberantly visible during Brazil's famous annual Carnival, and any depiction or analysis of the festival will inevitably include at least a passing reference to them, because their gender inversions are often invoked as embodiments of the Carnival spirit. But even in more mundane contexts and discourses, travestis figure prominently. A popular Saturday afternoon television show, for example, includes a spot in which female impersonators, some of whom are clearly travestis, get judged on how beautiful they are and on how well they mime the lyrics to songs sung by female vocalists. Another weekly television show regularly features Valéria, a well-known travesti. *Tieta*, one of the most popular television *novelas* in recent years, featured a special guest appearance by Rogéria, another famous travesti. And most telling of the special place reserved for travestis in the Brazilian popular imagination is the fact that the individual widely acclaimed to be the most beautiful woman in Brazil in the mid-1980s was . . . a travesti. That travesti, Roberta Close, became a household name throughout the country. She regularly appeared on national television, starred in a play in Rio, posed nude (with demurely crossed legs) in *Playboy* magazine, was continually interviewed and portrayed in virtually every magazine in the country, and had at least three songs written about her by well-known composers. Although her popularity declined when, at the end of the 1980s, she left Brazil to have a sex-change operation and live in Europe, Roberta Close remains extremely well-known. As recently as 1995, she appeared in a nation-wide advertisement for Duloren lingerie, in which a photograph of her passport, bearing her male name, was transposed with a photograph of her looking sexy and chic in a black lace undergarment. The caption read, "Você não imagina do que uma Duloren é capaz" (You can't imagine what a Duloren can do).

Regrettably, the fact that a handful of travestis manage to achieve wealth, admiration, and, in the case of Roberta Close, an almost iconic cultural status says very little about the lives of the vast majority of travestis. Those travestis, the ones that most Brazilians only glimpse occasionally standing along highways or on dimly lit street corners at night or read about in the crime pages of their local newspapers, comprise one of the most marginalized, feared, and despised groups in Brazilian society. In most Brazilian cities, travestis are so discriminated against that many of them avoid venturing out onto the street during the day. They are regularly the victims of violent police brutality and murder.[7] The vast majority of them come from very poor backgrounds and remain poor throughout their lives, living a hand-to-mouth existence and dying before the age of 50 from violence, drug abuse, health problems caused or exacerbated by the silicone they inject into their bodies, or, increasingly, AIDS.

The single most characteristic thing about travestis is their bodies. Unlike the drag performers examined by Esther Newton (1972) and recently elevated to the status of theoretical paragons in the work of postmodernist queer scholars such as Judith Butler (1990), travestis do not merely don female attributes. They incorporate them. Sometimes starting at ages as young as 10 or 12, boys who self-identify as travestis begin ingesting or injecting themselves with massive doses of female hormones in order to give their bodies rounded features, broad hips, prominent buttocks, and breasts. The hormones these boys take either are medications designed to combat estrogen deficiency or are contraceptive preparations designed, like "the pill," to prevent pregnancy. In Brazil such hormones are cheap (a month's supply, which would be consumed by a travesti in a week or less, costs the equivalent of only a few dollars) and are sold over the counter in any pharmacy.

Boys discover hormones from a variety of sources. Most of my travesti friends told me that they learned about hormones by approaching adult travestis and asking them how they had achieved the bodies they had. Others were advised by admirers, boyfriends, or clients, who told them that they would look more attractive and make more money if they looked more like girls.

Hormones are valued by travestis because they are inexpensive, easy to obtain, and fast working. Most hormones produce visible results after only about two months of daily ingestion. A problem with them, however, is that they can, especially after prolonged consumption, result in chronic nausea, headaches, heart palpitations, burning sensations in the legs and chest, extreme weight gain, and allergic reactions. In addition, the doses of female hormones required to produce breasts and wide hips make it difficult for travestis to achieve erections. This can be quite a serious problem, since a great percentage of travestis' clients want to be penetrated by the travesti (a point to which I shall return below). What usually happens after several years of taking hormones is that most individuals stop, at least for a while, and begin injecting silicone into their bodies.

Just as hormones are procured by the individual travestis themselves, without any medical intervention or interference, so is silicone purchased from and administered by acquaintances or friends. The silicone available to the travestis in Salvador is industrial silicone, which is a kind of plastic normally used to manufacture automobile parts such as dashboards. Although it is widely thought to be illegal for industrial outlets to sell this silicone to private individuals, at least one or two travestis in any city containing a silicone manufacturing plant will be well connected enough to be able to buy it. Whenever they sense a demand, these travestis contact their supplier at the plant and travel there in great secrecy to buy several liters. They then resell this silicone (at a hefty profit) to other travestis, who in turn pay travestis who work as *bombadeiras* (pumpers) to inject it directly into their bodies.

Most travestis in Salvador over the age of 17 have some silicone in their bodies. The amount of silicone that individual travestis choose to inject ranges from a few glasses to up to 18 liters. (Travestis measure silicone in liters and water glasses (*copos*), six of which make up a liter.) Most have between two and five liters. The majority have it in their buttocks, hips, knees, and inner thighs. This strategic placement of silicone is in direct deference to Brazilian aesthetic ideals that consider fleshy thighs, expansive hips, and a prominent, teardrop-shaped *bunda* (buttocks) to be the hallmark of feminine beauty. The majority of travestis do *not* have silicone in their breasts, because they believe that silicone in breasts (but not elsewhere in the body) causes cancer, because they are satisfied with the size of the breasts they have achieved through hormone consumption, because they are convinced that silicone injections into the chest are risky and extremely painful, or because they are waiting for the day when they will have enough money to pay for silicone implants (*prótese*) surgically inserted by doctors. A final reason for a general disinclination to inject silicone into one's breasts is that everyone knows that this silicone shifts its position very easily. Every travesti is acquainted with several unfortunate others whose breasts have either merged in the middle, creating a pronounced undifferentiated swelling known as a "pigeon breast" (*peito de pomba*), or whose silicone has descended into lumpy protrusions just above the stomach.

The Body in Process

Why do they do it? One of the reasons habitually cited by travestis seems self-evident. Elizabeth, a 29-year-old travesti with 1½ liters of silicone in her hips and one water-glass of silicone in each breast, explained it to me this way: "To mold my body, you know, be more feminine, with the body of a woman." But why do travestis want the body of a woman?

When I first began asking travestis that question, I expected them to tell me that they wanted the body of a woman because they felt themselves to be women. That was not the answer I received. No one ever offered the explanation that they might be women trapped in male bodies, even when I suggested it. In fact, there is a strong consensus among travestis in Salvador that any travesti who claims to be a woman is mentally disturbed. A travesti is not a woman and can never be a woman, they tell one another, because God created them male. As individuals, they are free to embellish and augment what God has given them, but their sex cannot be changed. Any attempt to do so would be disastrous. Not only do sex-change operations not produce women (they produce, travestis say, only *bichas castradas*, castrated homosexuals), they also inevitably result in madness. I was told on numerous occasions that, without a penis, semen cannot leave the body. When trapped, it travels to the brain, where it collects and forms a "stone" that will continue to increase in size until it eventually causes insanity.

So Roberta Close notwithstanding, travestis modify their bodies not because they feel themselves to be women but because they feel themselves to be "feminine" (*feminino*) or "like a woman" (*se sentir mulher*), qualities most often talked about not in terms of inherent predispositions or essences but rather in terms of behaviors, appearances, and relationships to men.[8] When I asked Elizabeth what it meant when she told me she felt feminine, for example, she answered, "I like to dress like a woman. I like when someone – when men – admire me, you know? . . . I like to be admired, when I go with a man who, like, says: 'Sheez, you're really pretty, you're really feminine.' That . . . makes me want to be more feminine and more beautiful every day, you see?" Similar themes emerged when travestis talked about when they first began to understand that they were travestis. A common response I received from many different people when I asked that question was that they made this discovery in connection with attraction and sexuality. Eighteen-year-old Cintia told me that she understood she was a travesti from the age of 7:

> I already liked girls' things, I played with dolls, played with…girls' things; I only played with girls. I didn't play with boys. I just played with these two boys; during the afternoon I always played with them…well, you know, rubbing penises together, rubbing them, kissing on the mouth. (*Laughs.*)

Forty-one-year-old Gabriela says that she knew that she was a travesti early on largely because "since childhood I always liked men, hairy legs, things like that, you know?" Banana, a 34-year-old travesti, told me "the [understanding that I was a] travesti came after, you know, I, um, 8, 9 years, 10 years old, I felt attracted, really attracted to men."

The attraction that these individuals felt for males is thus perceived by them to be a major motivating force behind their self-production as travestis, both privately and professionally. Travestis are quick to point out that, in addition to making them feel more feminine, female forms also help them earn more money as prostitutes. At night when they work on the street, those travestis who have acquired pronounced feminine features use them to attract the attention of passing motorists, and they dress (or rather, undress) to display those features prominently.

But if the goal of a travesti's bodily modifications is to feel feminine and be attractive to men, what does she think about her male genitals?

The most important point to be clear about is that virtually every travesti values her penis: "There's not a better thing in the whole world," 19-year-old Adriana once told me with a big smile. Any thought of having it amputated repels them. "*Deus é mais*" (God forbid), many of them interject whenever talk of sex-change operations arises. "What, and never cum (i.e., ejaculate, *gozar*) again?!" they gasp, horrified.

Despite the positive feelings that they express about their genitals, however, a travesti keeps her penis, for the most part, hidden, "imprisoned" (*presa*) between her legs. That is, travestis habitually pull their penises down between their legs and press them against their perineums with their underpanties. This is known as "making a cunt" (*fazer uma buceta*). This cunt is an important bodily practice in a travesti's day-to-day public appearance. It is also crucial in another extremely important context of a travesti's life, namely in her relationship to her *marido* (live-in boyfriend). The maridos of travestis are typically attractive, muscular, tattooed young men with little or no education and no jobs. Although they are not pimps (travestis move them into their rooms because they are impassioned (*apaixonada*) with them, and they eject them when the passion wears thin), *maridos* are supported economically by their travesti girlfriends. All these boyfriends regard themselves, and are regarded by their travesti girlfriends, as *homens* (men) and, therefore, as nonhomosexual.

One of the defining attributes of being a *homem* (man) in the gender system that the travestis draw on and invoke is that a man will not be interested in another male's penis. A man, in this interpretative framework, will happily penetrate another male's anus. But he will not touch or express any desire for another male's penis. For him to do so would be tantamount to relinquishing his status as a man.

He would stop being a man and be reclassified as a *viado* (homosexual, faggot), which is how the travestis are classified by others and how they see themselves.

Travestis want their boyfriends to be men, not *viados*. They require, in other words, their boyfriends to be symbolically and socially different from, not similar to, themselves. Therefore, a travesti does not want her boyfriend to notice, comment on, or in any way concern himself with her penis, even during sex. Sex with a boyfriend, consists, for the most part, of the travesti sucking the boyfriend's penis and of her boyfriend penetrating her, most often from behind, with the travesti on all fours or lying on her stomach on the bed. If the boyfriend touches the travesti at all, he will caress her breasts and perhaps kiss her. But no contact with the travesti's penis will occur, which means, according to most travestis I have spoken to, that travestis do not usually have orgasms during sex with their boyfriends.

What surprised me most about this arrangement was that the ones who are the most adamant that it be maintained are the travestis themselves. They respect their boyfriends and maintain their relationships with them only as long as the boyfriends remain "men." If a boyfriend expresses interest in a travesti's penis, becomes concerned that the travesti ejaculate during sex, or worst of all, if the boyfriend expresses a desire to be anally penetrated by the travesti, the relationship, all travestis told me firmly, would be over. They would comply with the boyfriend's request, they all told me, "because if someone offers me their ass, you think I'm not gonna take it?" Afterward, however, they were agreed, they would lose respect for the boyfriend. "You'll feel disgust (*nojo*) toward him," one travesti put it pithily. The boyfriend would no longer be a man in their eyes. He would, instead, be reduced to a *viado*. And as such, he could no longer be a boyfriend. Travestis unfailingly terminate relationships with any boyfriend who deviates from what they consider to be proper manly sexuality.

This absolute unwillingness to engage their own penises in sexual activity with their boyfriends stands in stark contrast to what travestis do with their penises when they are with their clients. On the street, travestis know they are valued for their possession of a penis. Clients will often request to see or feel a travesti's penis before agreeing to pay for sex with her, and travestis are agreed that those travestis who have large penises are more sought after than those with small ones. Similarly, several travestis told me that one of the reasons they stopped taking hormones was because they were losing clients. They realized that clients had begun avoiding them because they knew that the travesti could not achieve an erection. Travestis maintain that one of the most common sexual services they are paid to perform is to anally penetrate their clients.

Most travestis enjoy this. In fact, one of the more surprising findings of my study is that travestis, in significant and highly marked contrast to what is generally reported for other prostitutes, enjoy sex with clients.[9] That is not to say they enjoy sex every time or with every client. But whenever they talk about thrilling, fulfilling, or incredibly fun sex, their partner is always either a client or what they call a *vício*, a word that literally means "vice" or "addiction" and that refers to a male, often encountered on the street while they are working, with whom they have sex for free. Sometimes, if the vício is especially attractive, is known to have an especially large penis, or is known to be especially versatile in bed, the travesti will even pay *him*.

The Body in Context

At this point, having illustrated the way in which the body of a travesti is constructed, thought about, and used in a variety of contexts, I am ready to address the question of cultural intelligibility and personal desirability. Why do travestis want the kind of body they create for themselves? What is it about Brazilian culture that incites and sustains desire for a male body made feminine through hormones and silicone?

By phrasing that question primarily in terms of culture, I do not mean to deny that there are also social and economic considerations behind the production of travesti bodies and subjectivities. As I noted above, a body full of silicone translates into cash in the Brazilian sexual marketplace. It is important to understand, however – particularly because popular and academic discourses about prostitution tend to frame it so narrowly in terms of victimization, poverty, and exploitation – that males do not become travestis because they were sexually abused as children or just for economic gain. Only one of the approximately 40 travestis in my close circle of acquaintances was clearly the victim of childhood sexual abuse. And while the vast majority of travestis (like, one must realize, the vast majority of people in Brazil) come from working-class or poor backgrounds, it is far from impossible for poor, openly effeminate homosexual males to find employment, especially in the professions of hairdressers, cooks, and housecleaners, where they are quite heavily represented.

Another factor that makes it problematic to view travestis primarily in social or economic terms is the fact that the sexual marketplace does not require males who prostitute themselves to be travestis. Male prostitution (where the prostitutes, who are called *michês*, look and act like men) is widespread in Brazil and has been the topic of one published ethnographic study (Perlongher 1987). Also, even transgendered prostitution does not require the radical body modifications that travestis undertake. Before hormones and silicone became widely available (in the mid-1970s and mid-1980s, respectively) males dressed up as females, using wigs and foam-rubber padding *(pirelli)*, and worked successfully as prostitutes. Some males still do this today.

Finally, it should be appreciated that travestis do not need to actually have sex with their clients to earn money as prostitutes. A large percentage (in some cases, the bulk) of a travesti's income from clients is derived from robbing them. In order to rob a client, all that is required is that a travesti come into close physical proximity with him. Once a travesti is in a client's car or once she has begun caressing a passerby's penis, asking him seductively if he *"quer gozar"* (wants to cum), the rest, for most travestis, is easy. Either by pickpocketing the client, assaulting him, or if she does have sex with him, by threatening afterward to create a public scandal, the travesti will often walk away with all the client's money (Kulick 1996a). Thus it is entirely possible to derive a respectable income from prostitution and still not consume hormones and inject silicone into one's body.

In addition to all those considerations, I also phrase the question of travestis in terms of culture because, even if it were possible to claim that males who become travestis do so because of poverty, early sexual exploitation, or some enigmatic inner psychic orientation, the mystery of travestis as a sociocultural phenomenon would remain unsolved. What is it about the understandings, representations, and definitions of sexuality, gender, and sex in Brazilian society that makes travesti subjectivity imaginable and intelligible?

Let me begin answering that question by noting an aspect of travesti language that initially puzzled me. In their talk to one another, travestis frequently refer to biological males by using feminine pronouns and feminine adjectival endings. Thus the common utterance "*ela ficou doida*" (she was furious) can refer to a travesti, a woman, a gay male, or a heterosexual male who has allowed himself to be penetrated by another male. All of these different people are classified by travestis in the same manner. This classificatory system is quite subtle, complex, and context sensitive; travestis narrating their life stories frequently use masculine pronouns and adjectival endings when talking about themselves as children but switch to feminine forms when discussing their present-day lives. In a similar way, clients are often referred to as "she," but the same client will be referred to with different gendered pronouns depending on the actions he performs. When a travesti recounts that she struggled with a client over money or when she describes him paying, for example, his gender will often change from feminine to masculine. The important point here is that the gender of males is subject to fluctuation and change in travesti talk. Males are sometimes referred to as "she" and sometimes as "he." Males, in other words, can shift gender depending on the context and the actions they perform. The same is not true for females. Females, even the several extremely brawny and conspicuously unfeminine lesbians who associate with the travestis I know, are never referred to as "he" (Kulick 1996b). So whereas the gender of females remains fixed, the gender of males fluctuates and shifts continually.

Why can males be either male or female, but females can only be female? The answer, I believe, lies in the way that the gender system that the travestis draw on is constituted. Debates about transgendered individuals such as eighteenth-century mollies, Byzantine eunuchs, Indian *hijras*, Native American *berdaches*, US transsexuals, and others often suggest that those individuals constitute a third, or intermediate, gender, one that is neither male or female or one that combines both male and female.[10] Journalists and social commentators in Brazil sometimes take a similar line when they write about travestis, arguing that travestis transcend maleness and femaleness and constitute a kind of postmodern androgyny.

My contention is the opposite. Despite outward physical appearances and despite local claims to the contrary, there is no third or intermediate sex here; travestis only arise and are only culturally intelligible within a gender system based on a strict dichotomy. That gender system, however, is structured according to a dichotomy different from the one with which many of us are familiar, anchored in and arising from principles different from those that structure and give meaning to gender in northern Europe and North America.

The fundamental difference is that, whereas the northern Euro-American gender system is based on sex, the gender system that structures travestis' perceptions and actions is based on sexuality. The dominant idea in northern Euro-American societies is that one is a man or a woman because of the genitals one possesses. That biological difference is understood to accrete differences in behavior, language, sexuality, perception, emotion, and so on. As scholars such as Harold Garfinkel (1967), Suzanne Kessler and Wendy McKenna (1985 [1978]), and Janice Raymond (1979) have pointed out, it is within such a cultural system that a transsexual body can arise, because here biological males, for example, who do not feel or behave as men should, can make sense of that difference by reference to their genitals. They are not men; therefore they must be women, and to be a woman means to have the genitals of a female.

While the biological differences between men and women are certainly not ignored in Brazil, the possession of genitals is fundamentally conflated with what they can be used for, and in the particular configuration of sexuality, gender, and sex that has developed there, the determinative criterion in the identification of males and females is not so much the genitals as it is the role those genitals perform in sexual encounters. Here the locus of gender difference is the act of penetration. If one *only* penetrates, one is a man, but if one gets penetrated, one is not a man, which, in this case, means that one is either a *viado* (a faggot) or a *mulher* (a woman). Tina, a 27-year-old travesti, makes the parallels clear in a story about why she eventually left one of her ex-boyfriends:

1 *Tina*: For three years [my *marido*] was a man for me. A total man (*foi homíssimo*). Then I was the man, and he was the faggot (*viado*).
2 *Don*: What?
3 *Tina*: Do you see?
4 *Don*: Yes. . . . But no, how?
5 *Tina*: For three years he was a man for me, and after those three years he became a woman (*ele foi mulher*). I was the man, and he was the woman. The first three years I was together with him, do you see, he penetrated me (*ele me comia*) and I sucked [his penis]. I was his woman.
6 *Don*: Yeah . . .
7 *Tina*: And after those three years, I was his man. Do you understand now? Now you get it.
8 *Don*: But what happened? What, what made him . . .
9 *Tina*: Change?
10 *Don*: Change, yeah.
11 *Tina*: It changed with him touching my penis. . . . He began doing other kinds of sex things. "You don't have to cum [i.e., have orgasms] on the street [with clients]" [he told me], "I can jerk you off (*eu bato uma punhetinha pra você*). And later on we can do other new things." He gives me his ass, he gave me his ass, started to suck [my penis], and well, there you are.

Note how Tina explains that she was her boyfriend's woman, in that "he penetrated me and I sucked [his penis]" (line 5). Note also how Tina uses the words *viado* (faggot) and *mulher* (woman) interchangeably (lines 1 and 5) to express what her boyfriend became after he started expressing an interest in her penis and after he started "giving his ass" to her. This discursive conflation is similar to that used when travestis talk about their clients, the vast majority of whom are believed by travestis to desire to be anally penetrated by the travesti – a desire that, as I just explained, disqualifies them from being men and makes them into viados, like the travestis themselves. Hence they are commonly referred to in travestis' talk by the feminine pronoun *ela* (she).

Anal penetration figures prominently as an engendering device in another important dimension of travestis' lives, namely, their self-discovery as travestis.

When I asked travestis to tell me when they first began to understand that they were travestis, the most common response, as I noted earlier, was that they discovered this in connection with attraction to males. Sooner or later, this attraction always led to sexuality, which in practice means that the travesti began allowing herself to be penetrated anally. This act is always cited by travestis as crucial in their self-understanding as travestis.

A final example of the role that anal penetration plays as a determining factor in gender assignment is the particular way in which travestis talk about gay men. Travestis frequently dismiss and disparage gay men for "pretending to be men" (*[andar/passar] como se fosse homem*), a phrase that initially confounded me, especially when it was used by travestis in reference to me. One Sunday afternoon, for example, I was standing with two travesti friends eating candy in one of Salvador's main plazas. As two policemen walked by, one travesti began to giggle. "They see you standing here with us," she said to me, "and they probably think you're a man." Both travestis then collapsed in laughter at the sheer outrageousness of such a profound misunderstanding. It took me, however, a long time to figure out what was so funny.

I finally came to realize that as a gay man, a *viado*, I am assumed by travestis to *dar* (be penetrated by men). I am, therefore, the same as them. But I and all other gay men who do not dress as women and modify their bodies to be more feminine disguise this sameness. We hide, we deceive, we pretend to be men, when we really are not men at all. It is in this sense that travestis can perceive themselves to be more honest, and much more radical, than "butch" (*machuda*) homosexuals like myself. It is also in this sense that travestis simply do not understand the discrimination that they face throughout Brazil at the hands of gay men, many of whom feel that travestis compromise the public image of homosexuals and give gay men a bad name.

What all these examples point to is that for travestis, as reflected in their actions and in all their talk about themselves, clients, boyfriends, *vícios*, gay men, women, and sexuality, there are two genders; there is a binary system of opposites very firmly in place and in operation. But the salient difference in this system is not between men and women. It is, instead, between those who penetrate (*comer*, literally "to eat" in Brazilian Portuguese) and those who get penetrated (*dar*, literally "to give"), *in a system where the act of being penetrated has transformative force*. Thus those who only "eat" (and *never* "give") in this system are culturally designated as "men"; those who give (even if they *also* eat) are classified as being something else, a something that I will call, partly for want of a culturally elaborated label and partly to foreground my conviction that the gender system that makes it possible for travestis to emerge and make sense is one massively oriented towards, if not determined by, male subjectivity, male desire, and male pleasure, as those are culturally elaborated in Brazil: "not men." What this particular binarity implies is that females and males who enjoy being penetrated belong to the same classificatory category, they are on the same side of the gendered binary. They share, in other words, a gender.

This sharing is the reason why the overwhelming majority of travestis do not self-identify as women and have no desire to have an operation to become a woman even though they spend their lives dramatically modifying their bodies to make them look more feminine. Culturally speaking, travestis, because they enjoy being penetrated, are structurally equivalent to, even if they are not biologically identical to, women. Because they already share a gender with women, a sex-change operation would (again, culturally speaking) give a travesti nothing that she does not already have. All a sex-change operation would do is rob her of a significant source of pleasure and income.

It is important to stress that the claim I am making here is that travestis share a gender with women, not that they *are* women (or that women are travestis). Individual travestis will not always or necessarily share individual women's roles, goals, or social status. Just as the worldviews, self-images, social statuses, and possibilities of, say, a poor black mother, a single mulatto prostitute, and a rich white businesswoman in Brazil differ dramatically, even though all those individuals share a gender, so will the goals, perspectives, and possibilities of individual travestis differ from those of individual women, even though all those individuals share a gender. But inasmuch as travestis share the same gender as women, they are understood to share (and feel themselves to share) a whole spectrum of tastes, perceptions, behaviors, styles, feelings, and desires. And one of the most important of those desires is understood and felt to be the desire to attract and be attractive for persons of the opposite gender.[11] The desire to be attractive for persons of the opposite gender puts pressure on individuals to attempt to approximate cultural ideals of beauty, thereby drawing them into patriarchal and heterosexual imperatives that guide aesthetic values and that frame the direction and the content of the erotic gaze.[12] And although attractive male bodies get quite a lot of attention and exposure in Brazil, the pressure to conform to cultural ideals of beauty, in Brazil as in northern Euro-American societies, is much stronger on females than on males. In all these societies, the ones who are culturally incited to look (with all the subtexts of power and control that that action can imply) are males, and the ones who are exhorted to desire to be looked *at* are females.

In Brazil, the paragon of beauty, the body that is held forth, disseminated, and extolled as desirable – in the media, on television, in popular music, during Carnival, and in the day-to-day public practices of both individual men and women (comments and catcalls from groups of males at women passing by, microscopic string bikinis, known throughout the country as *fio dental* (dental floss), worn by women at the beach) – is a feminine body with smallish breasts, ample buttocks, and high, wide hips. Anyone wishing to be considered desirable to a man should do what she can to approximate that ideal. And this, of course, is precisely what travestis do. They appropriate and incorporate the ideals of beauty that their culture offers them in order to be attractive to men: both real men (i.e., boyfriends, some clients, and *vícios*), and males who publicly "pretend to be men" (clients and *vícios* who enjoy being penetrated).

Conclusion: Penetrating Gender

What exactly is gender and what is the relationship between sex and gender? Despite several decades of research, discussion, and intense debate, there is still no agreed-upon, widely accepted answer to those basic questions. Researchers who discuss gender tend to either not define it or, if they do define it, do so by placing it in a seemingly necessary relationship to sex. But one of the main reasons for the great success of Judith Butler's *Gender Trouble* (and in anthropology, Marilyn Strathern's *The Gender of the Gift*) is surely because those books called sharp critical attention to understandings of gender that see it as the cultural reading of a precultural, or prediscursive, sex. "And what is 'sex' anyway?" asks Butler in a key passage:

> Is it natural, anatomical, chromosomal, or hormonal, and how is a feminist critic to assess the scientific discourses which purport to establish such "facts" for us? Does sex have a history? Does each sex have a different history, or histories? Is there a history of how the duality of sex was established, a genealogy that might expose the binary options as variable construction? Are the ostensibly natural facts of sex discursively produced by various scientific discourses in the service of other political and social interests? If the immutable character of sex is contested, perhaps this construct called "sex" is as culturally constructed as gender; indeed, perhaps it was always already gender, with the consequence that the distinction between sex and gender turns out to be no distinction at all. (1990: 6–7)

It is only when one fully appreciates Butler's point and realizes that sex stands in no particularly privileged, or even necessary, relation to gender that one can begin to understand the various ways in which social groups can organize gender in different ways. My work among travestis has led me to define gender, more or less following Eve Sedgwick (1990: 27–8), as a social and symbolic arena of ongoing contestation over specific identities, behaviors, rights, obligations, and sexualities. These identities and so forth are bound up with and productive of male and female persons, in a hierarchically ordered cultural system in which the male/female dichotomy functions as a primary and perhaps a model binarism for a wide range of values, processes, relationships, and behaviors. Gender, in this rendering, does not have to be about "men" and "women." It can just as probably be about "men" and "not-men," a slight but extremely significant difference in social classification that opens up different social configurations and facilitates the production of different identities, understandings, relationships, and imaginings.

One of the main puzzles I have found myself having to solve about Brazilian travestis is why they exist at all. Turning to the rich and growing literature on homosexuality in Latin America was less helpful than I had hoped, because the arguments developed there cannot account for (1) the cultural forces at work that make it seem logical and reasonable for some males to permanently alter their bodies to make them look more like women, even though they do not consider themselves to be women and (2) the fact that travestis regularly (not to say daily) perform both the role of penetrator and penetrated in their various sexual interactions with clients, *vícios*, and boyfriends. In the first case the literature on homosexuality in Latin America indicates that it should not be necessary to go to the extremes that Brazilian travestis go to (they could simply live as effeminate, yet still clearly male, homosexuals), and in the second case, the literature leads one to expect that travestis would restrict their sexual roles, by and large, to that of being penetrated.[13] Wrong on both counts.

What is lacking in this literature, and what I hope this essay will help to provide, is a sharper understanding of the ways in which sexuality and gender configure with one another throughout Latin America. My main point is that for the travestis with whom I work in Salvador, gender identity is thought to be determined by one's sexual behavior.[14] My contention is that travestis did not just pull this understanding out of thin air; on the contrary, I believe that they have distilled and clarified a relationship between sexuality and gender that seems to be widespread throughout Latin America. Past research on homosexual roles in Latin America (and by extension, since that literature builds on it, past research on male and female roles in Latin America) has perceived the links to sexuality and gender to which I have drawn attention (see, for example, Parker 1986: 157; 1991: 43–53, 167), but it has been prevented from theorizing those links in the way I have done in this article because it has conflated sex and gender. Researchers have assumed that gender is a cultural reading of biological males and females and that there are, therefore, two genders: man and woman. Effeminate male homosexuals do not fit into this particular binary; they are clearly not women, but culturally speaking they are not men either. So what are they? Calling them "not quite men, not quite women," as Roger Lancaster (1992: 274) does in his analysis of Nicaraguan *cochones*, is hedging: a slippage into "third gender" language to describe a society in which gender, as Lancaster so carefully documents, is structured according to a powerful and coercive binary. It is also not hearing what *cochones*, travestis, and other effeminate Latin American homosexuals are saying. When travestis, *maricas*, or *cochones* call each other "she" or when they call men who have been anally penetrated "she," they are not just being campy and subcultural, as analyses of the language of homosexual males usually conclude; I suggest that they are perceptively and incisively reading off and enunciating core messages generated by their cultures' arrangements of sexuality, gender, and sex.

I realize that this interpretation of travestis and other effeminate male homosexuals as belonging to the same gender as women will seem counterintuitive for many Latin Americans and students of Latin America. Certainly in Brazil, people generally do not refer to travestis as "she," and many people, travestis will be the first to tell you, seem to enjoy going out of their way to offend travestis by addressing them loudly and mockingly as "o senhor" (sir or mister).[15] The very word *travesti* is grammatically masculine in Brazilian Portuguese (*o travesti*), which makes it not only easy but logical to address the word's referent using masculine forms.[16]

There are certainly many reasons why Brazilians generally contest and mock individual travestis' claims to femininity, not least among them being travestis' strong associations with homosexuality, prostitution, and AIDS – all highly stigmatized issues that tend to elicit harsh condemnation and censure from many people. Refusal to acknowledge travestis' gender is one readily available way of refusing to acknowledge travestis' right to exist at all. It is a way of putting travestis back in their (decently gendered) place, a way of denying and defending against the possibilities that exist within the gender system itself for males to shift from one category to the other.[17]

During the time I have spent in Brazil, I have also noted that the harshest scorn is reserved for unattractive travestis. Travestis such as Roberta Close and some of my own acquaintances in Salvador who closely approximate cultural ideals of feminine beauty are generally not publicly insulted and mocked and addressed as men. On the contrary, such travestis are often admired and regarded with a kind of awe. One conclusion I draw from this is that the commonplace denial of travestis' gender as not-men may not be so much a reaction against them as gender crossers as it is a reaction against unattractiveness in people (women and other not-men), whose job it is to make themselves attractive for men. Seen in this light, some of the hostility against (unattractive) travestis becomes intelligible as a reaction against them as failed women, not failed men, as more orthodox interpretations have usually argued.

Whether or not I am correct in claiming that the patterns I have discussed here have a more widespread existence throughout Latin America remains to be seen. Some of what I argue here may be specific to Brazil, and some of it will inevitably be class specific. In a large, extraordinarily divided, and complex area like Latin America, many different and competing discourses and understandings about sexuality and gender will be available in different ways to different individuals. Those differences need to be investigated and documented in detail. My purpose here is not to suggest a monolithic and immutable model of gender and sexuality for everyone in Latin America. I readily admit to having close firsthand understanding only of the travestis with whom I worked in Salvador, and the arguments presented in this essay have been developed in an ongoing attempt to make sense of their words, choices, actions, and relationships.

At the same time, though, I am struck by the close similarities in gender and sexual roles that I read in other anthropologists' reports about homosexuality and male–female relations in countries and places far away from Salvador, and I think that the points discussed here can be helpful in understanding a number of issues not explicitly analyzed, such as why males throughout Latin America so violently fear being anally penetrated, why men who have sex with or even live with effeminate homosexuals often consider themselves to be heterosexual, why societies like Brazil can grant star status to particularly fetching travestis (they are just like women in that they are not-men, and sometimes they are more beautiful than women), why women in a place like Brazil are generally not offended or outraged by the prominence in the popular imagination of travestis like Roberta Close (like women, travestis like Close are also not-men, and hence they share women's tastes, perceptions, feelings, and desires), why many males in Latin American countries appear to be able to relatively unproblematically enjoy sexual encounters with effeminate homosexuals and travestis (they are definitionally not-men, and hence sexual relations with them do not readily call into question one's self-identity as a man), and why such men even pay to be penetrated by these not-men (for some men being penetrated by a not-man is perhaps not as status- and identity-threatening as being penetrated by a man; for other men it is perhaps more threatening, and maybe, therefore, more exciting). If this essay makes any contribution to our understanding of gender and sexuality in Latin America, it will be in revitalizing exploration of the relationship between sexuality and gender and in providing a clearer framework within which we might be able to see connections that have not been visible before.

Notes

Acknowledgments. Research support for fieldwork in Brazil was generously provided by the Swedish Council for Research in the Humanities and Social Sciences (HSFR) and the Wenner-Gren Foundation for Anthropological Research. The essay has benefited immensely from the critical comments of Inês Alfano, Lars Fant, Mark Graham, Barbara Hobson, Kenneth Hyltenstam, Heather Levi, Jerry Lombardi, Thaïs Machado-Borges, Cecilia McCallum, Stephen Murray, Bambi Schieffelin, Michael Silverstein, Britt-Marie Thurén, David Valentine, Unni Wikan, and Margaret Willson. My biggest debt is to the travestis in Salvador with whom I work and, especially, to my teacher and coworker, Keila Simpsom, to whom I owe everything.

 1 Chauncey 1994; Crisp 1968; Jackson 1989; Nanda 1990; Trumbach 1989; Whitehead 1981; Wikan 1977.

 2 See, for example, Almaguer 1991; Carrier 1995; Fry 1986; Guttman 1996; Lancaster 1992; Leiner 1994; Murray 1987, 1995; Parker 1991; Prieur 1994; and Trevisan 1986.

 3 One of the few contexts in which ideas similar to Latin American ones are preserved in North American and northern European understandings of male sexuality is prisons. See, for example, Wooden and Parker 1982.

 4 This article is based on 11 months of anthropological fieldwork and archival research and more than 50 hours of recorded speech and interviews with travestis between the ages of 11 and 60 in Salvador, Brazil's third-largest city, with a population of over 2 million people. Details about the fieldwork and the transcriptions are in Kulick n.d.

 5 Travestis are also the subject of two short anthropological monographs in Portuguese: de Oliveira 1994 and Silva 1993. There is also an article in English on travestis in Salvador: Cornwall 1994. As far as I can see, however, all the ethnographic data on travestis in that article are drawn from de Oliveira's unpublished master's thesis, which later became her monograph, and from other published sources. Some of the information in the article, such as the author's claim that 90 percent of the travestis in Salvador are devotees of the Afro-Brazilian religion *candomblé*, is also hugely inaccurate.

 6 In the summer months leading up to Carnival, travestis from other Brazilian cities flock to Salvador to cash in on the fact that the many popular festivals preceding Carnival put men in festive moods and predispose them to spend their money on prostitutes.

 7 de Oliveira 1994; Kulick 1996a; Mott and Assunção 1987; Silva 1993.

 8 The literal translation of *se sentir mulher* is "to feel woman," and taken out of context, it could be read as meaning that travestis feel themselves to be women. In all instances in which it is used by travestis, however, the phrase means "to feel like a woman," "to feel as if one were a woman (even though one is not)." Its contrastive opposite is *ser mulher* (to be woman).

 9 In her study of female prostitutes in London, for example, Day explains that "a prostitute creates distinctions with her body so that work involves very little physical contact in contrast to private sexual contacts. Thus . . . at work . . . only certain types of sex are acceptable while sex outside work involves neither physical barriers nor forbidden zones" (1990: 98). The distinctions to which Day refers here are inverted in travesti sexual relationships.

10 Bornstein 1994; Elkins and King 1996; Herdt 1994.

11 One gendered, absolutely central, and culturally incited desire that is almost entirely absent from this picture is the desire for motherhood. Although some readers of this article have suggested to me that the absence of maternal desires negates my thesis that travestis share a gender with women, I am more inclined to see the absence of such desire as yet another reflex of the famous Madonna–Whore complex: travestis align themselves, exuberantly and literally, with the Whore avatar of Latin womanhood, not the Mother incarnation. Also, note again that my claim here is not that travestis *are* women. The claim is that the particular configurations of sex, gender, and sexuality in Brazil and other Latin American societies differ from the dominant configurations in northern Europe and North America, and generate different arrangements of gender, those that I am calling men and not-men. Motherhood is indisputably a crucial component of female roles and desires, in that a female may not be considered to have

achieved full womanhood without it (and in this sense, travestis (like female prostitutes?) can only ever remain incomplete, or failed, women). I contend, however, that motherhood is not *determinative* of gender in the way that I am claiming sexuality is.

12 I use the word *heterosexuality* purposely because travesti–boyfriend relationships are generally considered, by travestis and their boyfriends, to be *hetero*sexual. I once asked Edilson, a 35-year-old *marido* who has had two long-term relationships in his life, both of them with travestis, whether he considered himself to be heterosexual, bisexual, or homosexual. "I'm heterosexual; I'm a man," was his immediate reply. "I won't feel love for another heterosexual," he continued, significantly, demonstrating how very lightly the northern Euro-American classificatory system has been grafted onto more meaningful Brazilian ways of organizing erotic relationships: "[For two males to be able to feel love], one of the two has to be gay."

13 One important exception to this is the Norwegian sociologist Annick Prieur's (1994) sensitive work on Mexican *jotas*.

14 Note that this relationship between sexuality and gender is the *opposite* of what George Chauncey reports for early-twentieth-century New York. Whereas Chauncey argues that sexuality and gender in that place and time were organized so that "one's sexual behavior was necessarily thought to be determined by one's gender identity" (1994: 48), my argument is that for travestis in Salvador, and possibly for many people throughout Latin America, one's gender identity is necessarily thought to be determined by one's sexual behavior.

   One more point here. I wish to note that Unni Wikan, upon reading this paper as a reviewer for the *American Anthropologist*, pointed out that she made a similar claim to the one I argue for here in her 1977 article on the Omani xanith. Rereading that article, I discovered this to be true (see Wikan 1977: 309), and I acknowledge that here. A major difference between Wikan's argument and my own, however, is that it is never entirely clear whether Omanis (or Wikan) conceptualize(s) xaniths as men, women, or as a third gender. (For a summary of the xanith debate, see Murray 1997.)

15 The exceptions to this are boyfriends, who often – but, interestingly, not always – use feminine grammatical forms when speaking to and about their travesti girlfriends, and clients, who invariably use feminine forms when negotiating sex with travestis.

16 In their day-to-day language practices, travestis subvert these grammatical strictures by most often using the grammatically feminine words *mona* and *bicha* instead of *travesti*.

17 The possibility for males to shift gender – at least temporarily, in (hopefully) hidden, private encounters – seems to be one of the major attractions that travestis have for clients. From what many different travestis told me, it seems clear that the erotic pleasure that clients derive from being anally penetrated is frequently expressed in very specific, heavily gender-saturated, ways. I heard numerous stories of clients who not only wanted to be penetrated but also, as they were being penetrated, wanted the travesti to call them *gostosa* (delicious/sexy, using the feminine grammatical ending) and address them by female names. Stories of this kind are so common that I find it hard to escape the conclusion that a significant measure of the erotic delight that many clients derive from anal penetration is traceable to the fact that the sexual act is an engendering act that shifts their gender and transforms them from men into not-men.

References

Almaguer, Tomás 1991 Chicano Men: A Cartography of Homosexual Identity and Behavior. *Differences* 3: 75–100.

Bornstein, Kate 1994 *Gender Outlaw: On Men, Women and the Rest of Us.* London: Routledge.

Brandes, Stanley 1981 Like Wounded Stags: Male Sexual Ideology in an Andalusian Town. In *Sexual Meanings: The Cultural Construction of Gender and Sexuality.* S. B. Ortner and H. Whitehead (eds.) Pp. 216–39. Cambridge: Cambridge University Press.

Butler, Judith 1990 *Gender Trouble: Feminism and the Subversion of Identity.* London: Routledge.

Carrier, Joseph 1995 *De los Otros: Intimacy and Homosexuality among Mexican Men.* New York: Columbia University Press.

Chauncey, George 1994 *Gay New York: Gender, Urban Culture and the Making of the Gay Male World, 1890–1940.* New York: Basic Books.

Cornwall, Andrea 1994 Gendered Identities and Gender Ambiguity among Travestis in Salvador, Brazil. In *Dislocating Masculinity: Comparative Ethnographies.* A. Cornwall and N. Lindisfarne (eds.) Pp. 111–32. London: Routledge.

Crisp, Quentin 1968 *The Naked Civil Servant.* New York: New American Library.

Day, Sophie 1990 Prostitute Women and the Ideology of Work in London. In *Culture and AIDS.* D. A. Feldman (ed.) Pp. 93–109. New York: Praeger.

de Oliveira, Neuza Maria 1994 *Damas de paus: O jogo aberto dos travestis no espelho da mulher.* Salvador, Brazil: Centro Editorial e Didático da UFBA.

Dynes, Wayne 1987 Portugayese. In *Male Homosexuality in Central and South America.* S. O. Murray (ed.) Pp. 183–91. San Francisco: Instituto Obregón.

Elkins, Richard, and Dave King 1996 *Blending Genders: Social Aspects of Cross-dressing and Sex-changing.* London: Routledge.

Fry, Peter 1986 Male Homosexuality and Spirit Possession in Brazil. In *The Many Faces of Homosexuality: Anthropological Approaches to Homosexual Behavior.* E. Blackwood (ed.) Pp. 137–53. New York: Harrington Park Press.

Garfinkel, Harold 1967 *Studies in Ethnomethodology.* Englewood Cliffs, NJ: Prentice-Hall.

Guttman, Matthew C. 1996 *The Meanings of Macho: Being a Man in Mexico City.* Berkeley: University of California Press.

Herdt, Gilbert (ed.) 1994 *Third Sex, Third Gender: Beyond Sexual Dimorphism in Culture and History.* New York: Zone Books.

Jackson, Peter A. 1989 *Male Homosexuality in Thailand: An Interpretation of Contemporary Thai Sources.* New York: Global Academic Publishers.

Kessler, Suzanne J., and Wendy McKenna 1985 [1978] *Gender: An Ethnomethodological Approach.* Chicago: University of Chicago Press.

Kulick, Don 1996a Causing a Commotion: Public Scandals as Resistance among Brazilian Transgendered Prostitutes. *Anthropology Today* 12/6: 3–7.

—— 1996b Fe/male Trouble: The Unsettling Place of Lesbians in the Self-images of Male Transgendered Prostitutes in Salvador, Brazil. Paper presented at 95th annual meeting of the American Anthropological Association, San Francisco.

—— n.d. Practically Woman: The Lives, Loves and Work of Brazilian Travesti Prostitutes. Manuscript under review.

Lancaster, Roger N. 1992 *Life Is Hard: Machismo, Danger, and the Intimacy of Power in Nicaragua.* Berkeley: University of California Press.

Leiner, Marvin 1994 *Sexual Politics in Cuba: Machismo, Homosexuality and AIDS.* Boulder, CO: Westview Press.

Mott, Luis, and Aroldo Assunção 1987 Gilete na carne: Etnografia das automutilaçoes dos travestis da Bahia. *Revista do Instituto de Medicina Social de São Paulo* 4/1: 41–56.

Murray, Stephen O. 1997 The Sohari Khanith. In *Islamic Homosexualities: Culture, History, and Literature.* S. O. Murray and W. Roscoe. Pp. 244–55. New York: New York University Press.

Murray, Stephen O. (ed.) 1995 *Latin American Male Homosexualities.* Albuquerque: University of New Mexico Press.

—— 1987 *Male Homosexuality in Central and South America*. San Francisco: Instituto Obregón.

Murray, Stephen O., and Wayne Dynes 1987 Hispanic Homosexuals: Spanish Lexicon. In *Male Homosexuality in Central and South America*. S. O. Murray (ed.) Pp. 170–82. San Francisco: Instituto Obregón.

Nanda, Serena 1990 *Neither Man nor Woman: The Hijras of India*. Belmont, CA: Wadsworth Publishing.

Newton, Esther 1972 *Mother Camp: Female Impersonators in America*. Englewood Cliffs, NJ: Prentice-Hall.

Parker, Richard G. 1986 Masculinity, Femininity, and Homosexuality: On the Anthropological Interpretation of Sexual Meanings in Brazil. In *The Many Faces of Homosexuality: Anthropological Approaches to Homosexual Behavior*. E. Blackwood (ed.) Pp. 155–63. New York: Harrington Park Press.

—— 1991 *Bodies, Pleasures and Passions: Sexual Culture in Contemporary Brazil*. Boston: Beacon Press.

Perlongher, Nestor 1987 *O negócio do michê: Prostituição viril em São Paulo*. São Paulo: Editora Brasiliense.

Prieur, Annick 1994 *Iscensettelser av kjønn: Tranvestitter og machomenn i Mexico by*. Oslo: Pax Forlag.

Raymond, Janice 1979 *The Transsexual Empire*. London: Women's Press.

Sedgwick, Eve Kosofsky 1990 *Epistemology of the Closet*. Berkeley: University of California Press.

Silva, Hélio R. S. 1993 *Travesti: A invenção do feminino*. Rio de Janeiro: Relume-Dumará.

Strathern, Marilyn 1988 *The Gender of the Gift: Problems with Women and Problems with Society in Melanesia*. Berkeley: University of California Press.

Trevisan, João Silvério 1986 *Perverts in Paradise*. London: Gay Men's Press.

Trumbach, Randolph 1989 The Birth of the Queen: Sodomy and the Emergence of Gender Equality in Modern Culture, 1660–1750. In *Hidden from History: Reclaiming the Gay and Lesbian Past*. M. B. Duberman, M. Vicinus, and G. Chauncey Jr. (eds.) Pp. 129–40. New York: New American Library.

Whitehead, Harriet 1981 The Bow and the Burden Strap: A New Look at Institutionalized Homosexuality in Native North America. In *Sexual Meanings: The Cultural Construction of Gender and Sexuality*. S. B. Ortner and H. Whitehead (eds.) Pp. 80–115. Cambridge: Cambridge University Press.

Wikan, Unni 1977 Man Becomes Woman: Transsexualism in Oman as a Key to Gender Roles. *Man*, ns 12: 304–19.

Wooden, Wayne S., and Jay Parker 1982 *Men behind Bars: Sexual Exploitation in Prison*. New York: Da Capo Press.

Index